T0203026

Lecture Notes in Computer Science 14726

Founding Editors

Gerhard Goos
Juris Hartmanis

The series Lecture Notes in Computer Science (LNCS), including its subseries Lecture Notes in Artificial Intelligence (LNAI) and Lecture Notes in Bioinformatics (LNBI), has established itself as a medium for the publication of new developments in computer science and information technology research, teaching, and education.

LNCS enjoys close cooperation with the computer science R & D community, the series counts many renowned academics among its volume editors and paper authors, and collaborates with prestigious societies. Its mission is to serve this international community by providing an invaluable service, mainly focused on the publication of conference and workshop proceedings and postproceedings. LNCS commenced publication in 1973.

Qin Gao · Jia Zhou
Editors

Human Aspects of IT for the Aged Population

10th International Conference, ITAP 2024
Held as Part of the 26th HCI International Conference, HCII 2024
Washington, DC, USA, June 29 – July 4, 2024
Proceedings, Part II

 Springer

Editors
Qin Gao
Tsinghua University
Beijing, China

Jia Zhou
Chongqing University
Chongqing, China

ISSN 0302-9743　　　　　　ISSN 1611-3349　(electronic)
Lecture Notes in Computer Science
ISBN 978-3-031-61545-0　　　ISBN 978-3-031-61546-7　(eBook)
https://doi.org/10.1007/978-3-031-61546-7

This Springer imprint is published by the registered company Springer Nature Switzerland AG
The registered company address is: Gewerbestrasse 11, 6330 Cham, Switzerland

If disposing of this product, please recycle the paper.

Foreword

This year we celebrate 40 years since the establishment of the HCI International (HCII) Conference, which has been a hub for presenting groundbreaking research and novel ideas and collaboration for people from all over the world.

The HCII conference was founded in 1984 by Prof. Gavriel Salvendy (Purdue University, USA, Tsinghua University, P.R. China, and University of Central Florida, USA) and the first event of the series, "1st USA-Japan Conference on Human-Computer Interaction", was held in Honolulu, Hawaii, USA, 18–20 August. Since then, HCI International is held jointly with several Thematic Areas and Affiliated Conferences, with each one under the auspices of a distinguished international Program Board and under one management and one registration. Twenty-six HCI International Conferences have been organized so far (every two years until 2013, and annually thereafter).

Over the years, this conference has served as a platform for scholars, researchers, industry experts and students to exchange ideas, connect, and address challenges in the ever-evolving HCI field. Throughout these 40 years, the conference has evolved itself, adapting to new technologies and emerging trends, while staying committed to its core mission of advancing knowledge and driving change.

As we celebrate this milestone anniversary, we reflect on the contributions of its founding members and appreciate the commitment of its current and past Affiliated Conference Program Board Chairs and members. We are also thankful to all past conference attendees who have shaped this community into what it is today.

The 26th International Conference on Human-Computer Interaction, HCI International 2024 (HCII 2024), was held as a 'hybrid' event at the Washington Hilton Hotel, Washington, DC, USA, during 29 June – 4 July 2024. It incorporated the 21 thematic areas and affiliated conferences listed below.

A total of 5108 individuals from academia, research institutes, industry, and government agencies from 85 countries submitted contributions, and 1271 papers and 309 posters were included in the volumes of the proceedings that were published just before the start of the conference, these are listed below. The contributions thoroughly cover the entire field of human-computer interaction, addressing major advances in knowledge and effective use of computers in a variety of application areas. These papers provide academics, researchers, engineers, scientists, practitioners and students with state-of-the-art information on the most recent advances in HCI.

The HCI International (HCII) conference also offers the option of presenting 'Late Breaking Work', and this applies both for papers and posters, with corresponding volumes of proceedings that will be published after the conference. Full papers will be included in the 'HCII 2024 - Late Breaking Papers' volumes of the proceedings to be published in the Springer LNCS series, while 'Poster Extended Abstracts' will be included as short research papers in the 'HCII 2024 - Late Breaking Posters' volumes to be published in the Springer CCIS series.

I would like to thank the Program Board Chairs and the members of the Program Boards of all thematic areas and affiliated conferences for their contribution towards the high scientific quality and overall success of the HCI International 2024 conference. Their manifold support in terms of paper reviewing (single-blind review process, with a minimum of two reviews per submission), session organization and their willingness to act as goodwill ambassadors for the conference is most highly appreciated.

This conference would not have been possible without the continuous and unwavering support and advice of Gavriel Salvendy, founder, General Chair Emeritus, and Scientific Advisor. For his outstanding efforts, I would like to express my sincere appreciation to Abbas Moallem, Communications Chair and Editor of HCI International News.

July 2024   Constantine Stephanidis

HCI International 2024 Thematic Areas and Affiliated Conferences

- HCI: Human-Computer Interaction Thematic Area
- HIMI: Human Interface and the Management of Information Thematic Area
- EPCE: 21st International Conference on Engineering Psychology and Cognitive Ergonomics
- AC: 18th International Conference on Augmented Cognition
- UAHCI: 18th International Conference on Universal Access in Human-Computer Interaction
- CCD: 16th International Conference on Cross-Cultural Design
- SCSM: 16th International Conference on Social Computing and Social Media
- VAMR: 16th International Conference on Virtual, Augmented and Mixed Reality
- DHM: 15th International Conference on Digital Human Modeling & Applications in Health, Safety, Ergonomics & Risk Management
- DUXU: 13th International Conference on Design, User Experience and Usability
- C&C: 12th International Conference on Culture and Computing
- DAPI: 12th International Conference on Distributed, Ambient and Pervasive Interactions
- HCIBGO: 11th International Conference on HCI in Business, Government and Organizations
- LCT: 11th International Conference on Learning and Collaboration Technologies
- ITAP: 10th International Conference on Human Aspects of IT for the Aged Population
- AIS: 6th International Conference on Adaptive Instructional Systems
- HCI-CPT: 6th International Conference on HCI for Cybersecurity, Privacy and Trust
- HCI-Games: 6th International Conference on HCI in Games
- MobiTAS: 6th International Conference on HCI in Mobility, Transport and Automotive Systems
- AI-HCI: 5th International Conference on Artificial Intelligence in HCI
- MOBILE: 5th International Conference on Human-Centered Design, Operation and Evaluation of Mobile Communications

List of Conference Proceedings Volumes Appearing Before the Conference

1. LNCS 14684, Human-Computer Interaction: Part I, edited by Masaaki Kurosu and Ayako Hashizume
2. LNCS 14685, Human-Computer Interaction: Part II, edited by Masaaki Kurosu and Ayako Hashizume
3. LNCS 14686, Human-Computer Interaction: Part III, edited by Masaaki Kurosu and Ayako Hashizume
4. LNCS 14687, Human-Computer Interaction: Part IV, edited by Masaaki Kurosu and Ayako Hashizume
5. LNCS 14688, Human-Computer Interaction: Part V, edited by Masaaki Kurosu and Ayako Hashizume
6. LNCS 14689, Human Interface and the Management of Information: Part I, edited by Hirohiko Mori and Yumi Asahi
7. LNCS 14690, Human Interface and the Management of Information: Part II, edited by Hirohiko Mori and Yumi Asahi
8. LNCS 14691, Human Interface and the Management of Information: Part III, edited by Hirohiko Mori and Yumi Asahi
9. LNAI 14692, Engineering Psychology and Cognitive Ergonomics: Part I, edited by Don Harris and Wen-Chin Li
10. LNAI 14693, Engineering Psychology and Cognitive Ergonomics: Part II, edited by Don Harris and Wen-Chin Li
11. LNAI 14694, Augmented Cognition, Part I, edited by Dylan D. Schmorrow and Cali M. Fidopiastis
12. LNAI 14695, Augmented Cognition, Part II, edited by Dylan D. Schmorrow and Cali M. Fidopiastis
13. LNCS 14696, Universal Access in Human-Computer Interaction: Part I, edited by Margherita Antona and Constantine Stephanidis
14. LNCS 14697, Universal Access in Human-Computer Interaction: Part II, edited by Margherita Antona and Constantine Stephanidis
15. LNCS 14698, Universal Access in Human-Computer Interaction: Part III, edited by Margherita Antona and Constantine Stephanidis
16. LNCS 14699, Cross-Cultural Design: Part I, edited by Pei-Luen Patrick Rau
17. LNCS 14700, Cross-Cultural Design: Part II, edited by Pei-Luen Patrick Rau
18. LNCS 14701, Cross-Cultural Design: Part III, edited by Pei-Luen Patrick Rau
19. LNCS 14702, Cross-Cultural Design: Part IV, edited by Pei-Luen Patrick Rau
20. LNCS 14703, Social Computing and Social Media: Part I, edited by Adela Coman and Simona Vasilache
21. LNCS 14704, Social Computing and Social Media: Part II, edited by Adela Coman and Simona Vasilache
22. LNCS 14705, Social Computing and Social Media: Part III, edited by Adela Coman and Simona Vasilache

47. LNCS 14730, HCI in Games: Part I, edited by Xiaowen Fang
48. LNCS 14731, HCI in Games: Part II, edited by Xiaowen Fang
49. LNCS 14732, HCI in Mobility, Transport and Automotive Systems: Part I, edited by Heidi Krömker
50. LNCS 14733, HCI in Mobility, Transport and Automotive Systems: Part II, edited by Heidi Krömker
51. LNAI 14734, Artificial Intelligence in HCI: Part I, edited by Helmut Degen and Stavroula Ntoa
52. LNAI 14735, Artificial Intelligence in HCI: Part II, edited by Helmut Degen and Stavroula Ntoa
53. LNAI 14736, Artificial Intelligence in HCI: Part III, edited by Helmut Degen and Stavroula Ntoa
54. LNCS 14737, Design, Operation and Evaluation of Mobile Communications: Part I, edited by June Wei and George Margetis
55. LNCS 14738, Design, Operation and Evaluation of Mobile Communications: Part II, edited by June Wei and George Margetis
56. CCIS 2114, HCI International 2024 Posters - Part I, edited by Constantine Stephanidis, Margherita Antona, Stavroula Ntoa and Gavriel Salvendy
57. CCIS 2115, HCI International 2024 Posters - Part II, edited by Constantine Stephanidis, Margherita Antona, Stavroula Ntoa and Gavriel Salvendy
58. CCIS 2116, HCI International 2024 Posters - Part III, edited by Constantine Stephanidis, Margherita Antona, Stavroula Ntoa and Gavriel Salvendy
59. CCIS 2117, HCI International 2024 Posters - Part IV, edited by Constantine Stephanidis, Margherita Antona, Stavroula Ntoa and Gavriel Salvendy
60. CCIS 2118, HCI International 2024 Posters - Part V, edited by Constantine Stephanidis, Margherita Antona, Stavroula Ntoa and Gavriel Salvendy
61. CCIS 2119, HCI International 2024 Posters - Part VI, edited by Constantine Stephanidis, Margherita Antona, Stavroula Ntoa and Gavriel Salvendy
62. CCIS 2120, HCI International 2024 Posters - Part VII, edited by Constantine Stephanidis, Margherita Antona, Stavroula Ntoa and Gavriel Salvendy

https://2024.hci.international/proceedings

Preface

The 10th International Conference on Human Aspects of IT for the Aged Population (ITAP 2024) was part of HCI International 2024. The ITAP conference addresses the design, adaptation, and use of IT technologies targeted to older people in order to counterbalance ability changes due to age, support cognitive, physical, and social activities, and maintain independent living and quality of life.

This year's proceedings address a variety of topics. While understanding and addressing the needs and constraints of older individuals, along with designing technologies that support and empower them, remains a consistent theme, this year's discussions focus more on the challenge posed by rapidly emerging technologies. There is a notable increase in research focusing on innovative design approaches and methods aimed at integrating older adults into ongoing technological advancements. At the same time, researchers have explored more methods and strategies to help older people to acquire new digital skills in order to stay current with evolving technologies. Another emerging theme of this year is the re-examination of chatbots and AI, particularly in light of recent advancements in large language models, regarding their potential to benefit older people's quality of life and possible approaches to incorporate older adults' requirements into the design lifecycle of these technologies. These changes highlight the importance of design approaches adopting a dynamic view of the relationship between older people and digital technologies. Continuous innovation and adaptation are crucial to ensure that the needs of the aging population are integral to the ongoing evolution of technology.

Two volumes of the HCII 2024 proceedings are dedicated to this year's edition of the ITAP conference. The first focuses on topics related to Designing for Older Adults; Older Adults' User Experience; Older Adults' Digital Competences and User Behavior; and Aging and Social Media. The second focuses on topics related to Healthy Aging; Supporting Mobility and Leisure; and Aging, Chatbots and AI.

The papers of these volumes were accepted for publication after a minimum of two single-blind reviews from the members of the ITAP Program Board or, in some cases, from members of the Program Boards of other affiliated conferences. We would like to thank all of them for their invaluable contribution, support, and efforts.

July 2024

Qin Gao
Jia Zhou

10th International Conference on Human Aspects of IT for the Aged Population (ITAP 2024)

Program Board Chairs: **Qin Gao**, *Tsinghua University, P.R. China*, and **Jia Zhou**, *Chongqing University, P.R. China*

- Bessam Abdulrazak, *University of Sherbrooke, Canada*
- Ines Amaral, *University of Coimbra, Portugal*
- Maria Jose Brites, *Lusófona University, CICANT, Portugal*
- Alan Chan, *City University of Hong Kong, P.R. China*
- Yue Chen, *East China University of Science and Technology, P.R. China*
- Yong Gu Ji, *Yonsei University, Korea*
- Hai-Ning Liang, *Xi'an Jiaotong-Liverpool University, P.R. China*
- Eugene Loos, *Utrecht University, Netherlands*
- Yan Luximon, *The Hong Kong Polytechnic University, Hong Kong, P.R. China*
- Zhaoyi Ma, *Nanjing University of Science and Technology, P.R. China*
- Lourdes Moreno Lopez, *Universidad Carlos III de Madrid, Spain*
- Jinging Qiu, *University of Electronic Science and Technology of China, P.R. China*
- Alvaro Taveira, *University of Wisconsin-Whitewater, USA*
- Wang-Chin Tsai, *YunTech, Taiwan*
- Ana Isabel Veloso, *University of Aveiro, Portugal*
- Nadine Vigouroux, *Paul Sabatier University, France*
- Jiaoyun Yang, *Hefei University of Technology, P.R. China*

The full list with the Program Board Chairs and the members of the Program Boards of all thematic areas and affiliated conferences of HCII 2024 is available online at:

http://www.hci.international/board-members-2024.php

HCI International 2025 Conference

The 27th International Conference on Human-Computer Interaction, HCI International 2025, will be held jointly with the affiliated conferences at the Swedish Exhibition & Congress Centre and Gothia Towers Hotel, Gothenburg, Sweden, June 22–27, 2025. It will cover a broad spectrum of themes related to Human-Computer Interaction, including theoretical issues, methods, tools, processes, and case studies in HCI design, as well as novel interaction techniques, interfaces, and applications. The proceedings will be published by Springer. More information will become available on the conference website: https://2025.hci.international/.

General Chair
Prof. Constantine Stephanidis
University of Crete and ICS-FORTH
Heraklion, Crete, Greece
Email: general_chair@2025.hci.international

https://2025.hci.international/

Contents – Part II

Supporting Mobility and Leisure

Aging, Chatbots and AI

Contents – Part I

Older Adults' User Experience

Older Adults' Digital Competences and User Behavior

Aging and Social Media

Healthy Aging

Exploring User Preferences and Acceptance of Digital Art Therapy Among Older Chinese Adults with Mild Cognitive Impairment

Sihan An and Qingchuan Li[✉]

School of Humanities and Social Sciences, Harbin Institute of Technology, Shenzhen, China
ansihan1216@163.com, liqingchuan@hit.edu.cn

Abstract. Mild cognitive impairment (MCI) occurs between the stages of normal aging and dementia and has a high possibility of progressing to Alzheimer's disease. Early and effective intervention or treatment is essential to prevent the progression of MCI to Alzheimer's disease in older adults. Art therapy, as one of the non-pharmacological approaches to creative activities through the medium of art, improves mood, cognition, and performance. Simultaneously, the emergence of digital art therapy has expanded the potential of traditional art therapy by enabling remote participation and enhancing intense sensory stimulation. However, unaddressed questions need to be answered regarding how older adults perceive and adopt digital art therapy and how therapists and designers should develop digital art therapy to meet older adults' needs and preferences. To address these problems, a qualitative study was conducted among older adults over 65 years of age. The participants were asked to report their needs and preferences for digital art therapy. Compared with other participants, participants with MCI showed a lower willingness to use digital art therapy and were more sensitive to technological barriers. However, this study revealed a list of relevant factors that can influence the acceptance of digital art therapy among older Chinese adults with MCI, including control beliefs, attitudinal beliefs, and gerontechnology anxiety. By addressing potential influential factors, the results can help facilitate older adults' acceptance and adoption of digital art therapy and ultimately enhancing older Chinese adults' well-being and quality of life.

Keywords: Digital Art Therapy · Mild Cognitive Impairment · User Preference · Technology Acceptance · Older Adults

1 Introduction

With the deepening of global aging, the number of older adults with cognitive impairments is rapidly increasing. Inevitably, a decline in cognitive function has become an important factor influencing older adults' quality of life and overall well-being and has placed a lot of pressure on family caregivers and healthcare professionals. Mild cognitive impairment (MCI) is a transitional stage of cognitive impairment between normal aging and dementia, which indicates a mild decline in memory and other cognitive functions, such as visual and spatial perceptions, with basic daily functioning [1].

© The Author(s), under exclusive license to Springer Nature Switzerland AG 2024
Q. Gao and J. Zhou (Eds.): HCII 2024, LNCS 14726, pp. 3–21, 2024.
https://doi.org/10.1007/978-3-031-61546-7_1

As reported in a nationwide cross-sectional study, the prevalence of dementia has reached 6.04% among people aged 60 years or older in China, comprising 15.07 million patients [2]. Furthermore, the prevalence of MCI among Chinese people over 60 years old is 15.54%, with a total of 38.77 million patients [2]. It is important to note that there is a significantly higher risk of progressing to dementia for older adults with MCI compared to those with average cognitive ability [3]. As reported, the annual conversion rate from MCI to Alzheimer's disease is about 8–25%, which is 10 times higher than the incidence rate of Alzheimer's disease in the normal population [4–6]. Therefore, early and effective intervention or treatment is essential to prevent the progression of MCI to Alzheimer's disease in older adults [7].

Pharmacological and non-pharmacological therapies have been widely applied in the treatment of MCI and dementia. Although many attempts have been made in the medical field, the effectiveness of pharmacological interventions is quite limited in preventing behavioral and psychological symptoms associated with cognitive impairment, with the side effects becoming even more prominent [8, 9]. Instead, non-pharmacological treatments, such as psychotherapy, cognitive intervention, and exercise, have been leveraged as more natural, low-cost, low-risk, and easily accessible ways to prevent and slow the progression of MCI at an early stage [10].

In particular, art therapy is a form of non-pharmacological treatment involving creative artistic activities, such as painting, music, drama, and dancing. It can improve individuals' cognitive abilities, mental health, and social engagement by facilitating their self-expression, self-awareness, and self-growth through non-verbal expression [11]. Therefore, art therapy has been widely employed in the treatment of various physical diseases and psychological disorders, such as trauma, depression, psychosis, dementia, and cancer [11]. By enhancing cognitive abilities, alleviating negative emotions, and promoting social interaction, art therapy can improve the quality of life of older adults with MCI [12, 13].

With the emergence of digital technologies, an increasing number of novel creative forms and artistic media have been applied to art therapy [14]. In this vein, so-called digital art therapy, which can be implemented with digital screens, virtual reality (VR), augmented reality (AR), or artificial intelligence (AI), has expanded the potential of traditional art therapy by enabling remote participation and enhancing intense sensory stimulation [15]. On the one hand, the use of abundant digital media can provide more innovative and engaging interactive experiences through the implementation of personalized interventions [16]. On the other hand, digital technologies and intelligent systems are promising in facilitating remote assistance and administration, which is helpful in improving the convenience and flexibility of therapy activities, as well as reducing cost [17, 18].

Digital art therapy combines the advantages and strengths of digital technologies with creative and meaningful art activities [19], thus holding great promise in meeting the diversity of needs of older adults with MCI and further improving their cognitive and mental well-being [20]. However, considering that older adults tend to hesitate to accept novel technologies and present difficulties in technology operation [21], there is a need to explore how older adults perceive and adopt digital art therapy to inform future digital art therapy systems design for therapists and practitioners.

Therefore, this study aims to address the problems mentioned above by fulfilling three objectives: (a) to identify older adults' past experiences, preferences, feelings, and perceptions for art therapy activities, (b) to understand older adults' needs and expectations for digital art therapy, and (c) to investigate older adults' acceptance and adoption of digital art therapy and examine possible factors that influence the process.

2   Literature Review

2.1   Intervention Effects of Art Therapy

MCI is mainly characterized by impairments in memory, language, attention, executive function, and other mental functions, which include affective disorders, such as depression, anxiety, and irritability, but do not meet the full diagnostic criteria for dementia [22]. With the increased focus on non-pharmacological therapies, there has been increasing interest in the role that art therapy can play in MCI and dementia care. The intervention effects of art therapy in alleviating cognitive deterioration, reducing negative emotions, promoting social interaction, and improving quality of life have been gradually confirmed and have accumulated research results [23, 24]. Based on the above benefits, we focused on the participants' feelings regarding health ability, personal interest, emotional regulation, social behavior, and family relationships due to arts activities in our interviews.

A recent pilot study showed that expressive arts therapy (EAT) can improve cognitive functioning, mental health, and daily living skills in older adults with MCI. Preliminary findings of the study suggest improvements in the participants' cognitive and language functioning and social relationships, as well as anxiety and depression, after the EAT intervention [12]. Therefore, EAT, as an effective intervention, can be used to improve cognitive and mental health in older adults with MCI [12]. An 18-week study explored the health benefits of dance therapy for older women with MCI [25]. The study subjected the participants to moderate-intensity square dance exercises, which revealed their significant effect on cognitive function and quality of life [25]. A recent systematic review of randomized controlled trials showed that arts-based interventions can potentially improve cognitive functioning in older adults with MCI, with 10 out of the 13 included interventions reporting at least one significant outcome [26]. Art therapy is not only enjoyable with minimal side effects but is also scalable. However, there was heterogeneity in how cognitive was operationalized, the measures used, and the domains assessed across studies; thus, more rigorous research on arts-based interventions as a treatment modality for MCI is warranted [26]. Based on existing studies, we found that the intervention effects of art therapy on older adults with MCI are pluralistic and varied, which may be related to different sample data and experimental designs.

2.2   Development of Digital Art Therapy

As digital technology changes our daily lifestyles, digital art therapy is gradually stepping into people's views. In the age of intelligence, digital art therapy has a broad scope for development. Whether or not participants have an artistic foundation or ability, the support and assistance of technology can be used to reduce barriers to artistic creation and to further improve physical and mental health.

Blok et al. [16] explored the use of information and communication technologies (ICTs) by older individuals with cognitive impairments through qualitative semi-structured interviews. They found that most participants with cognitive impairments used ICTs because they could help compensate for their cognitive or physical decline and fulfill their social and emotional needs in terms of interpersonal interactions, hobbies, or daily activities. In addition, this study pointed out that ICT use is jointly determined by perceived usefulness (PU) and perceived ease of use (PEOU), with PU motivating individuals to increase their PEOU. This finding could serve as a reference for our study. A recent scoping review showed that technology is being used to enhance a range of creative arts activities for people with MCI or dementia, including music, storytelling, and visual arts [17]. A recent 75-year bibliometric analysis study discussed future trends in art therapy from the perspective of promoting health and well-being. The study mentioned that art therapy needs to utilize emerging technologies to make effective interventions in its processes. For example, VR technology has shown potential intervention value in assisted art therapy. However, the application of digital technology to assist art therapy has not been sufficiently researched and is still in its infancy [11].

Overall, digital art therapy can provide positive intervention effects and unique interactions for older adults with MCI, promoting emotional expression and lyricism in art creation. In the age of intelligence, digital art therapy has a broad scope for development.

2.3 Technology Acceptance Model

The technology acceptance model (TAM) was proposed by Davis in 1989 based on the theory of rational behavior, which explains the acceptance behavior of users of information technology [27]. The model identifies the core factors influencing user acceptance and usage of technology, such as PU and PEOU [28]. Since its emergence, the technology acceptance model has been expanded and widely used to study the acceptance of new technologies and things [29].

However, the model ignores biophysical factors, such as cognitive and physical decline, and psychosocial factors, such as social isolation and fear of illness [30]. This only partially applies to technology acceptance studies in older adults [31]. Therefore, Chen and Chan built a senior technology acceptance model (STAM) based on the TAM, which was developed to predict older adults' acceptance of general technology [32]. The STAM consisted of 11 factors measured by 38 items and has shown satisfactory psychometric properties [32, 33]. The STAM has been used in an increasing number of studies to examine older adults' acceptance of digital technology. For example, by adopting the STAM, a cross-sectional study investigated technology acceptance among older Korean adults with multiple chronic diseases. The accuracy and validity of this model were further assessed, and the results revealed that older adults have good acceptance of new technologies [34].

To reduce respondent burden and increase response rates, Chen and Lou developed a brief, reliable, and valid version of a scale to measure older adults' acceptance of technology by shortening the STAM questionnaire [35]. The STAM questionnaire's final 14-item brief version consisted of a 4-factor structure, including attitudinal beliefs, control beliefs, gerontechnology anxiety, and health [35]. This short STAM has been used to assess older users' acceptance and use of technology [36, 37]. Based on the above model, this study developed an interview framework to explore the factors influencing older adults' use of digital art therapy.

3   Methodology

To fulfill the research objectives, a face-to-face, semi-structured interview was conducted in a local senior center in Guangdong, China, in September and October 2023 (see Fig. 1).

Fig. 1. Interviewing Older Adults at the Elderly Center.

The interviews comprised three sections. First, the participants' demographic information, including their gender, age, educational level, marriage situation, living arrangement, elderly care approach, and income source, was collected. At the same time, the participants were asked to complete a rapid assessment for MCI screening, namely the Montreal cognitive assessment-basic Chinese version (MoCA-BC). We then invited the participants to talk about their experiences, perceptions, and preferences about the art therapy activities they had attended, as well as their needs and expectations for the digital art therapy activities. Furthermore, we employed the vignette technique to assess the participants' acceptance of digital art therapy. The Vignette technique is widely used to elicit users' perceptions, attitudes, and impressions toward novel technologies or products by describing a hypothetical situation using text, pictures, or videos and inviting users to image themselves in it [38, 39]. Thus, this technique is particularly suitable for understanding participants' acceptance of digital art therapy since it is still quite new for a majority of older Chinese adults. The STAM was utilized as the interview guide to examine the participants' acceptance behavior, with the participants' control beliefs, attitudinal beliefs, gerontechnology anxiety, and behavioral intentions evaluated.

The participants were told that participation was totally voluntary and that they were able to quit the interview at any time without penalty. With knowledge of all the possible benefits and risks of the current research, the participants were required to sign informed consent forms. The entire interview section lasted about 30 min for each participant. Each participant received a prize worth RMB 30 (US$4) as a reward for participation.

3.1 Participants

Older adults aged over 65 years old who had the ability to recognize Chinese characters and communicate without obvious expression deficits were recruited as participants. Ultimately, 36 older adults (12 males and 24 females) with an average age of 70.36 years (age range: 65–76 years, SD = 2.76) participated in this study. Table 1 shows the participants' demographic information.

Table 1. Demographic information of all the participants (N = 36).

Characteristics		Frequency	Percentage (%)
Gender	Male	12	33.3
	Female	24	66.7
Age	65–69	13	36.1
	70–74	19	52.8
	75–80	4	11.1
Education level	Primary school and below	2	5.6
	Secondary school	8	22.2
	High school	13	36.1
	Undergraduate and above	13	36.1
Marriage situation	Married	30	83.3
	Widowed	6	16.7
Living arrangement	With the partner only	16	44.4
	With the child only	9	25.0
	With the partner and child	6	16.7
	Alone	5	13.9
Elderly care approach	Living at home	36	100.0
Income source	Pension	34	94.4
	employment	1	2.8
	Child support	1	2.8

3.2 Interview Design

MCI Test. A Chinese translated version of the MoCA-BC was used to test the participants' cognitive capabilities after it was checked and modified by two usability experts

[40]. As a rapid assessment scale to screen for MCI, the MoCA-BC shows good validity and reliability in detecting MCI symptoms in older adults with less education. The MoCA-BC evaluates the severity of cognitive impairment, including verbal fluency, orientation, visual perception, immediate recall, and delayed recall [40]. Specifically, it comprises 10 questions to assess the following cognitive domains: executive function, language, orientation, calculation, conceptual thinking, memory, visual perception, attention, and concentration. The MoCA-BC test lasts approximately 15 min and has a total score of 30. The optimal cutoff scores for MCI detection were 19 for individuals with 6 or fewer years of education, 22 for those with 7–12 years of education, and 24 for those with more than 12 years of education [40]. In this study, 14 older adults with MCI and 22 older adults were cognitively normal were included, with detailed scores, as shown in Table 2. Because most older adults with normal cognitive ability had total scores at a critical level and their feedback could be used as a cross-reference to older adults with MCI, our interviews encompassed participants with normal cognitive ability.

Table 2. Results of cognitive tests.

Participants	Mean	Standard Deviation	Highest score	Lowest score
MCI	21.07	1.86	24	17
Normal	24.55	1.50	27	21

Interview Questions. First, the interview questions were designed to understand MCI older adults' experiences and preferences for participating in art therapy activities, their feelings and perceptions of art therapy activities, and their needs and expectations for digital art therapy. As shown in Table 3, five questions (Q1–Q5) were developed to address these issues, with several follow-up open questions extended to gain insights, such as the participants' perceived benefits of art therapy activities in cognitive capabilities, emotional regulation, social behavior, family relationships, and so on, as well as their preferred ways of attending art therapy activities, such as the way of participation and location.

Second, this study investigated MCI older adults' acceptance of digital art therapy. The vignette materials, consisting of four video clips with descriptive wordings, were used to help the participants familiarize themselves with a variety of types of digital art therapy. Four cases of digital art therapy were included in the videos. As shown in Fig. 2, the first video lasted for 27 s, showing an older adult using a brush to draw a water painting on a digital screen; the second video lasted about 32 s, presenting the scene of the butterfly flutter through AR motion device; the third video lasted about 20 s, displaying players engaging with a multi-sensory digital interactive wall; and the fourth video lasted about 22 s, viewing a girl paining using VR device. After totally understanding the concepts and formats of digital art therapy based on the videos and explanations from interviewees, the participants were invited to report their perceptions of digital art therapy in terms of whether they would like to try digital art therapy, whether they think digital art therapy is helpful, and whether they have any concerns or worries about digital art therapy (see Q6–Q9 in Table 3).

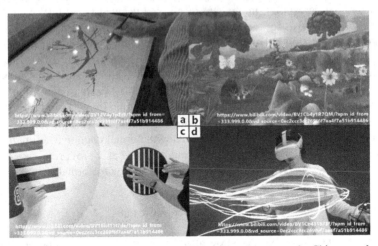

Fig. 2. Video screenshots of the four examples of digital art therapy: a: the Chinese-style painting table, b: scene of the butterfly flutter, c: the music interactive wall, and c: the VR drawing.

Table 3. Interview questions.

Categories	Questions	Examples of the follow-up questions
Experiences and Preferences for Art Therapy Activities	Q1- Do you have experience with art therapy activities? What is your favorite art form?	Please provide examples, which include the form of participation, length of time, space available for the activities, and the content of the activities
	Q2- Do you have an interest in participating in visual art therapy activities (e.g., drawing and calligraphy)?	
Feelings and Perceptions of Art Therapy Activities	Q3- How do you feel when you do art therapy activities?	Which aspects do you think you will benefit from after engaging in art activities? For example, how does it affect the development of your abilities, personal interests, emotional regulation, social behavior, and family relationships?
	Q4- Do you feel that being involved in the arts brings a sense of well-being and improves the quality of your life by enhancing your physical and mental health?	

(continued)

Table 3. (*continued*)

Categories	Questions	Examples of the follow-up questions
Needs and Expectations for Digital Art Therapy	Q5- Do you have any opinions or needs to be fulfilled about digital art therapy activities?	Which ways would you like to interact with art activities? For example, with peers in the community, or individually, alone in a home environment
STAM-Related Acceptance Behavior	Q6- If you have the opportunity, would you like to try your hand at digital art therapy?	Please choose your favorite of the four digital art therapy cases and explain why
	Q7- Do you think digital art therapy will help you in any way?	
	Q8- Do you have any concerns or worries about digital art therapy?	

3.3 Data Collection and Analysis

With the permission of the participants, all interviews were audio-recorded. The audio was then transcribed and analyzed using Atlas. Ti software. We coded the interview data in multiple rounds inductively and deductively. As shown in Table 4, the participants' responses were coded based on the eight initial categories developed by the interview questions. Then, 14 subcategories were finalized by inductively analyzing the transcripts.

Table 4. Code list for data analysis.

Categories	Subcategories
Experiences and Preferences for Art Therapy Activities	Practical experience
	Preference type
Feelings and Perceptions of Art Therapy Activities	Bodily function
	Mental health
	Social life
Needs and Expectations for Digital Art Therapy	Encouraging factors
	Discouraging factors

(*continued*)

Table 4. (*continued*)

Categories		Subcategories
STAM-Related Acceptance Behavior	Control Beliefs	Self-efficacy
		External factors
	Attitudinal Beliefs	Positive attitude
		Negative attitude
	Gerontechnology Anxiety	Perceived security
	Behavioral Intention to Use	Preference selection for four cases
		Overall willingness

4   Results

4.1   Experiences and Perceptions of Art Therapy Activities

Experiences and Preferences. Based on the interviews, various forms and types of art activities were reported by the participants, which can be further classified into three main categories based on the means of expression [41]: visual art therapy, music and drama therapy, and movement and multimodal therapy (e.g., horticultural therapy). Generally, older adults prefer music and drama therapy and movement therapy over visual art therapy. There were ten participants engaging with visual arts therapy activities, seventeen participants preferring music and drama therapy, and twenty-one participants enjoying movement and multimodal therapy activities, such as the Chinese square dance, opera, and tai chi exercises. Participants with MCI also preferred to engage in music and drama therapy, as well as movement and multimodal activities. However, it is notable that they expressed more anxiety and rejection about engaging in visual arts activities than the other participants.

The visual art therapy activities mentioned by the participants included Chinese calligraphy, traditional ink drawings, and craft activities. Twenty-one participants shared their interests in traditional ink drawings and Chinese calligraphy. They believed that such traditional Chinese visual arts could promote their health status by pacifying emotions and enabling a sense of achievement. Most of them indicated the experience of learning basic drawing skills in elderly centers and communities. One of the participants said, "I like painting because it makes me happy and brings fulfillment." However, a few older people expressed concerns about participating in visual art activities because they felt the threshold for attending visual art activities was relatively high, and they were too old to attend such activities. For example, one participant stated, "I'm interested in the visual art activities such as calligraphy, but I felt nervous and hesitated to learn because I didn't have a relevant foundation."

The music and drama therapy activities mentioned by the participants included singing, listening to music, and playing instruments. Five participants liked playing traditional instruments, such as the flute and erhu, and two indicated that they could not play the instruments well but enjoyed listening to them. Ten participants preferred choral singing, and they believed that it was a kind of community-based interactive activity that could promote immersion and integration. For instance, one participant expressed, "I used to like singing and playing erhu, but now I liked to sing. I have joined the choir and vocal classes organized by the community, which had a good atmosphere and allowed me to meet new friends."

Movement and multimodal therapy activities provide a variety of multi-sensory stimulations, such as visual, auditory, and movement stimuli, to promote older adults' interpersonal interaction, body movement, and emotional experience. Typical movement and multimodal activities mentioned by participants included dance and tai chi exercise, and Peking opera. First, we found that older adults were interested in movement and multimodal activities because they believed that the movement activities were good for improving their physical health status and that the multimodal stimulations brought more interesting and immersive experiences to engage them. A participant stated, "I participated in dancing to exercise and maintain a positive mental state. Time flies when you get involved." Notably, most participants over 70 years old expressed that heavy exercise and complex body movements had exhausted them, and they needed to explore some other hobbies, for example, "I used to enjoy square dancing, but now I can't do a lot of exercise with aging. I can only do some more simple activities around the home."

Feelings and Perceptions. When asked about their experiences with art activities, the participants described the beneficial effects of art activities on their physical health, emotional regulation, and social interaction. Twenty-eight participants shared that participating in art activities helped them relax and maintain a positive emotional state; for example, "Participating in art activities would allow me to gain more friendships and to forget unpleasant things." Twenty-seven participants mentioned that art activities could improve their physical health; for example, "I believed that dancing could improve my health status, such as maintaining normal blood pressure levels." Twenty participants felt that engaging in art activities could promote their social interaction, improve their quality of life, and bring happiness and fulfillment; for example, "I enjoyed increasing my social contacts while attending art activities." Some participants also mentioned that art activities positively impacted their family relationships. For example, one participant expressed, "My children supported me in the art activities and they were happy to see that I was healthy and active."

4.2 Needs and Expectations for Digital Art Therapy

The interviews revealed older adults' detailed needs and expectations for digital art therapy. Favorable features of digital art therapy, as well as potential difficulties and barriers, were identified and discussed by the participants.

Favorable Features. Six favorable features were summarized, including the needs for group interaction, fixed and well-organized activity location, flexible and reasonable schedule, professional and careful guidance, encouragement and affirmation, and novel and integrated traditional Chinese cultural characteristics. Remarkably, participants with MCI expressed more urgent demands for attentive guidance and practice demonstrations than others.

Seventeen participants indicated expectations for group interaction. They wanted to participate in art activities in community centers with their peers. For example, one participant expressed, "Completing activities with peers allowed us to have something in common to talk about and encouraged each other." As for the location of digital art therapy activities, five participants suggested that a fixed location in the community center or somewhere else would be better because staying at home made them easily influenced by trivial matters; thus, they could not remain focused for a long period. Nine participants proposed that the time schedule should be more flexible, with a time limit of 1–2 h. Five participants indicated that they would like to obtain additional guidance when learning new things. One participant said, "I was very nervous when I started to draw Chinese paintings. But later, under the teacher's patient guidance, I became more and more interested and Chinese painting gradually became my hobby." Encouragement and affirmation from others were also quite important for older adults. Four participants reported that encouragement and affirmations made them feel fulfilled and inspired. Furthermore, five participants mentioned that they preferred Chinese traditional art activities, for example, "I am very interested in traditional culture activities such as qin, chess, calligraphy and painting. I wanted the art activities to be more enriching."

Difficulties and Barriers. The participants also expressed concerns and worries about digital art therapy. We concluded some outstanding difficulties and barriers reported by the participants, which were divided into five aspects: physiological deterioration, psychological stress, cognitive impairment, lack of energy, and cost of participation. In particular, most participants with MCI were more concerned about the learning difficulties and barriers brought about by cognitive impairment, such as memory loss and slower reactions, when participating in digital art therapy activities. For instance, one of the participants said, "As aging, I am getting slower in reaction and cannot remember too many things. I'm not confident to participate in the digital art therapy." Another 12 participants mentioned that their health status, such as physical impairment, movement limitation, and sensory deterioration, would restrict their ability to perform complicated digital art therapy activities. One participant said, "What I want now is something more relaxed and enjoyable."

Mental stress was mentioned as another barrier influencing participants' perceptions of digital art therapy. Sixteen participants said that they felt great pressure when participating in the activities that they had attended. Five participants mentioned that they were resistant to accepting new things due to the influence of cognitive impairment or a lack of energy.

In addition, time conflicts and economic costs affect older adults' perceptions of digital art therapy. Five participants said that they usually participated in various activities and thus had no time to experience new activities. Three participants expressed hesitation about the cost of activities, such as buying musical instruments or painting tools; for example, "I liked Chinese calligraphy, but I was worried that it would be wasted to buy paper and ink if I did not write well."

4.3 Acceptance of Digital Art Therapy

Control Beliefs. Control beliefs refer to internal factors, proficiency with digital technology and self-efficacy, and external factors, support from environmental facilitation, that influence participants' acceptance and use of digital art therapy. Specifically, seven participants showed confidence in the use of digital art therapy. They felt that they were familiar with using electronic devices, such as smartphones, and thus would be interested in and willing to engage in digital art therapy under proper instruction and guidance. However, five participants indicated a lack of self-efficacy in using digital art therapy since they were afraid to use digital technologies. One such participant stated, "I do not even know how to use particular functions of my mobile phone, so I would be hesitant to use the digital art therapy."

Regarding external factors, fourteen participants claimed that they received help and guidance in using digital technologies from their families and friends. For example, their children taught them how to use the essential functions of smart devices, their friends shared the digital technology usage experiences together, and the community center held activities to teach them how to use digital technologies. All of these facilitating conditions provide convenience and essential support for them to conduct digital art therapy.

In particular, we found that PEOU was largely related to the participants' control beliefs regarding digital art therapy. Due to cognitive and physical impairments, older adults with MCI tend to spend more time engaging in digital art therapy activities. Therefore, digital art therapy should be simple and easy to implement for older adults with MCI, with patient guidance and help becoming essential in this process. Seventeen participants expressed worries about the learning burden and difficulty of participating in digital art therapy. However, with additional help and guidance, they are more likely to try.

Attitudinal Beliefs. Attitudinal beliefs were analyzed to investigate the participants' opinions about digital art therapy, which were divided into positive and negative attitudes in the current research. Twenty-seven participants indicated obvious positive attitudes toward digital art therapy. They felt that digital art therapy could enrich their lives. In contrast, nine participants showed negative attitudes, including five participants with MCI. One participant said, "I felt unfamiliar with digital art therapy, so I would not try it." Overall, participants with MCI had more pronounced and intense negative emotions than the others.

We found that PU was related to participants' attitudinal beliefs. PU included employing digital art therapy to improve older adults' cognitive abilities, facilitate social interaction, and benefit the quality of life. Six participants believed that digital art therapy was more innovative and interesting than traditional art activities; thus, it could be a new approach to exercising their cognitive skills. Three participants said that digital art therapy could help them expand their social circles and improve their social engagement. For instance, when attending digital art therapy, older adults believed that they could make some relevant short videos through TikTok (https://www.douyin.com/) and chat with their families and friends about the activities through instant messaging applications. Four participants expressed that attending digital art therapy would be a way to catch the pace of social development and that digital art therapy would be more convenient to benefit the quality of their lives.

Gerontechnology Anxiety. Gerontechnology anxiety is analyzed to evaluate participants' possible worries about using digital art therapy. Twelve participants clearly expressed their anxiety about digital technology. They were worried that declines in comprehension and memory could easily cause mistakes in operations. In spite of this, most of them were still willing to try digital art therapy systems. One participant expressed, "Digital technologies are helpful. If we rejected them, we would be far behind the society." Notably, participants with MCI showed more substantial technology anxiety and distrust. Three participants with MCI said that they were uncomfortable with the technological challenges in the digital era. Moreover, we found that older adults' anxiety was highly related to their perceived safety. For example, they feared that they would suffer from deception and insecurity due to their poor knowledge of digital technology. A participant stated, "Technologies were developed rapidly with many drawbacks, such as Internet fraud. Therefore, I intend to avoid these drawbacks by not using it."

Behavioral Intention to Use. The participants were asked about their preferences for the four types of digital art therapy presented as vignette materials. Most participants expressed interest in and curiosity about the digital art therapy activities of the Chinese-style painting table and the scene of butterfly flutter. Fifteen participants preferred the Chinese-style painting table because they thought the device looked simple and easy to use, with the advantages of saving paper and freedom of painting. Seven participants said that the drawing method using a VR device enabled a greater degree of drawing freedom. However, some participants felt that it could easily be dazzled and uncontrolled in the virtual environment. Simultaneously, they felt the type of scrawl in the AR space tended to be quite easy, which was more appropriate for collaborating with children to enable more intergenerational interactions.

Based on the initial understanding of digital art therapy, twenty-nine participants indicated behavioral intentions to use it. One such participant said, "Digital technology was distant from us. If we had the chance to try it out, we would closely follow the steps of the digital times." However, seven participants expressed an unwillingness to use digital art therapy, including all five older adults with MCI. Most were concerned that they would not be able to fully engage in the process of digital art therapy. They needed to make the decision after experiencing this type of activity. Overall, participants with MCI showed a lower willingness to use digital art therapy than the other participants.

5   Discussion and Conclusion

This study employed the approach of semi-structured interviews to investigate the preference for and acceptance of digital art therapy among older Chinese adults with MCI. The results revealed the possibility and feasibility of applying digital art therapy to older Chinese adults with MCI. This study observed that participants, including older adults with MCI, preferred multimodal art activities. Most of the MCI participants were worried about the high complexity required to attend multimodal art activities. Instead, they preferred to join some relaxing and easy art activities. In addition, a majority of the participants expressed a preference for Chinese traditional art activities, such as ink painting, calligraphy, Peking opera, and tai chi. By combining the elements of traditional Chinese culture, art therapy would be more acceptable for older adults and further lead to positive intervention effects, which is consistent with the results of previous studies [42, 43].

We found that most participants were willing to try digital art therapy. This is generally consistent with the findings of Engelbrecht et al. [44], who also demonstrated that digital technology could be an acceptable and effective art therapy intervention for older adults, helping to improve cognitive functioning in older adults with MCI [45]. However, older adults with MCI tend to indicate a more negative attitude and lower level of willingness to use digital art therapy.

In terms of acceptance of digital art therapy, the results are consistent with previous studies based on the STAM theoretical model [35]. We found that older adults' attitudinal beliefs were an important factor influencing their intentions to use digital art therapy. Positive attitudes might lead to a higher intention to use, whereas negative attitudes might lead to a lower intention to use. Therefore, we should consider how to change the negative perceptions of digital art therapy for older adults with MCI. At the same time, some studies have concluded that there are differences in users' opinions before and after using technology [46, 47]. Similarly, some participants in this study expressed that, despite their current negative attitudes, their improved health might attenuate negative attitudes when using digital art therapy. In addition, we found that social and external support in the control beliefs was more helpful in helping older adults use digital art therapy effectively, especially older adults with MCI. Because older adults with cognitive decline might be unable to use digital technology correctly without complete and adequate social support, external guidance and help, which could come from different groups, including peers, children or grandchildren, and community workers, were essential. Meanwhile, we found that self-efficacy in control beliefs and gerontechnology anxiety were significant barriers to the adoption of digital art therapy. This result was consistent with existing research, which showed that individuals with lower levels of self-efficacy and higher levels of gerontechnology anxiety had lower rates of technology acceptance [48].

In summary, the behavioral intention to use digital art therapy among older adults with MCI can be influenced by user characteristics and the social environment. Compared with other participants, participants with MCI showed a lower willingness to use digital art therapy and were more sensitive to technological barriers. Figure 3 summarizes the possible factors that influence the acceptance of digital art therapy among older adults with MCI. The main factors included control beliefs (i.e., self-efficacy, external environmental support, and PEOU), attitudinal beliefs (i.e., PU), and gerontechnology anxiety (i.e., perceived safety). The secondary factors included the user characteristics and health status of older adults with MCI (i.e., physical, psychological, and cognitive status), the environment of participation (the sustainability of space and time), the expected outcomes (i.e., cognitive, emotional, and behavioral improvements), the process of experience (instructive, fulfilling, fun, and interactive), and the form of participation (collective, diversified, and localized).

By revealing potential factors that may influence the acceptance of digital art therapy among older Chinese adults with MCI, this research can help designers, art therapists, and

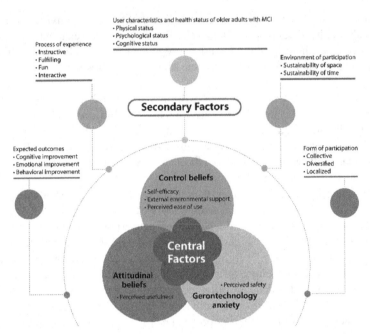

Fig. 3. Potential factors that influence the acceptance of digital art therapy among older adults with MCI

health practitioners develop more effective digital art therapy interventions to ultimately enhance older Chinese adults' well-being and quality of life.

There are some limitations to our study. First, the participants recruited in this research were from the first-tier city of China, which has a relatively high level of digital literacy. Thus, the results of the current study should be carefully applied to other populations with various cultural backgrounds and digital literacy. Second, we accessed the participants' perceptions and acceptance of digital art therapy through vignette materials, such as videos, pictures, and words, which needed further validation of empirical studies.

Acknowledgments. This study was funded by the MOE (Ministry of Education in China) Liberal Arts and Social Sciences Foundation (Grant number 21YJC760040), Featured Innovation Project in Higher Education of Guangdong (Grant number 2023WTSCX169) and General Program of Stable Support Plan for Universities in Shenzhen (Grant number GXWD20231129154726002).

Disclosure of Interests. The authors have no competing interests to declare that are relevant to the content of this article.

References

1. Petersen, R.C.: Mild cognitive impairment. CONTINUUM Lifelong Learn. Neurol. **22**(2 Dementia), 404 (2016)

2. Jia, L., Du, Y., Chu, L., et al.: Prevalence, risk factors, and management of dementia and mild cognitive impairment in adults aged 60 years or older in China: a cross-sectional study. Lancet Public Health **5**(12), e661–e671 (2020)
3. Petersen, R.C., Lopez, O., Armstrong, M.J., et al.: Practice guideline update summary: mild cognitive impairment: report of the guideline development, dissemination, and implementation subcommittee of the American Academy of Neurology. Neurology **90**(3), 126–135 (2018)
4. Ren, R., Qi, J., Lin, S., et al.: The China Alzheimer report 2022. General Psychiatry **35**(1), e100751 (2022)
5. Braus, M., Morton, B.: Art therapy in the time of COVID-19. Psychol. Trauma Theory Res. Pract. Policy **12**(S1), S267 (2020)
6. Du, X., An, P., Leung, J., et al.: DeepThInk: designing and probing human-AI co-creation in digital art therapy. Int. J. Hum Comput Stud. **181**, 103139 (2024)
7. Jia, L., Quan, M., Fu, Y., et al.: Dementia in China: epidemiology, clinical management, and research advances. Lancet Neurol. **19**(1), 81–92 (2020)
8. Popp, J., Arlt, S.: Pharmacological treatment of dementia and mild cognitive impairment due to Alzheimer's disease. Curr. Opin. Psychiatry **24**(6), 556–561 (2011)
9. Fink, H.A., Jutkowitz, E., McCarten, J.R., et al.: Pharmacologic interventions to prevent cognitive decline, mild cognitive impairment, and clinical Alzheimer-type dementia: a systematic review. Ann. Intern. Med. **168**(1), 39–51 (2018)
10. Kim, S., Schneider, C.E.: Protection of cognitive impairment in older adults through non-pharmacological interventions. J. Hum. Behav. Soc. Environ. **32**(5), 629–645 (2022)
11. Liu, Z., Yang, Z., Xiao, C., et al.: An investigation into art therapy aided health and well-being research: a 75-year bibliometric analysis. Int. J. Environ. Res. Public Health **19**(1), 232 (2021)
12. Yan, Y., Lin, R., Zhou, Y., et al.: Effects of expressive arts therapy in older adults with mild cognitive impairment: a pilot study. Geriatr. Nurs. **42**(1), 129–136 (2021)
13. Lin, R., Luo, Y., Yan, Y., et al.: Effects of an art-based intervention in older adults with mild cognitive impairment: a randomised controlled trial. Age Ageing **51**(7), afac144 (2022)
14. Orr, P.: Technology use in art therapy practice: 2004 and 2011 comparison. Arts Psychother. **39**(4), 234–238 (2012)
15. Leuty, V., Boger, J., Young, L., et al.: Engaging older adults with dementia in creative occupations using artificially intelligent assistive technology. Assist. Technol. **25**(2), 72–79 (2013)
16. Blok, M., van Ingen, E., de Boer, A.H., et al.: The use of information and communication technologies by older people with cognitive impairments: from barriers to benefits. Comput. Hum. Behav. **104**, 106173 (2020)
17. MacRitchie, J., Floridou, G.A., Christensen, J., et al.: The use of technology for arts-based activities in older adults living with mild cognitive impairment or dementia: a scoping review. Dementia **22**(1), 252–280 (2023)
18. Shu, S., Woo, B.K.: Use of technology and social media in dementia care: current and future directions. World J. Psychiatry **11**(4), 109 (2021)
19. Barber, B., Brandoff, R., Lombardi, R., et al.: Digital Art Therapy: Material, Methods, and Applications. Jessica Kingsley Publishers, London (2016)
20. Zubala, A., Kennell, N., Hackett, S.: Art therapy in the digital world: an integrative review of current practice and future directions. Front. Psychol. **12**, 595536 (2021)
21. Li, Q., Luximon, Y.: Understanding older adults' post-adoption usage behavior and perceptions of mobile technology. Int. J. Des. **12**(3), 93–110 (2018)
22. Lindbergh, C.A., Dishman, R.K., Miller, L.S.: Functional disability in mild cognitive impairment: a systematic review and meta-analysis. Neuropsychol. Rev. **26**, 129–159 (2016)
23. Galassi, F., Merizzi, A., D'Amen, B., et al.: Creativity and art therapies to promote healthy aging: a scoping review. Front. Psychol. **13**, 906191 (2022)

24. Masika, G.M., Yu, D.S.F., Li, P.W.C.: Visual art therapy as a treatment option for cognitive decline among older adults. A systematic review and meta-analysis. J. Adv. Nurs. **76**(8), 1892–1910 (2020)

25. Chang, J., Zhu, W., Zhang, J., et al.: The effect of Chinese square dance exercise on cognitive function in older women with mild cognitive impairment: the mediating effect of mood status and quality of life. Front. Psych. **12**, 711079 (2021)

26. Fong, Z.H., Tan, S.H., Mahendran, R., et al.: Arts-based interventions to improve cognition in older persons with mild cognitive impairment: a systematic review of randomized controlled trials. Aging Ment. Health **25**(9), 1605–1617 (2021)

27. Davis, F.D., Bagozzi, R.P., Warshaw, P.R.: User acceptance of computer technology: a comparison of two theoretical models. Manage. Sci. **35**(8), 982–1003 (1989)

28. Davis, F.D.: Perceived usefulness, perceived ease of use, and user acceptance of information technology. MIS Q. **13**(3), 319–340 (1989)

29. Lee, Y., Kozar, K.A., Larsen, K.R.T.: The technology acceptance model: past, present, and future. Commun. Assoc. Inf. Syst. **12**(1), 50 (2003)

30. Chen, K, Chan, A.H.S.: A review of technology acceptance by older adults. Gerontechnology **10**(1), 1–12 (2011)

31. Mitzner, T.L., Savla, J., Boot, W.R., et al.: Technology adoption by older adults: findings from the PRISM trial. Gerontologist **59**(1), 34–44 (2019)

32. Chen, K., Chan, A.H.S.: Gerontechnology acceptance by elderly Hong Kong Chinese: a senior technology acceptance model (STAM). Ergonomics **57**(5), 635–652 (2014)

33. Özungur, F., Hazer, O.: Analysis of the acceptance of communication technologies by technology acceptance model of the elderly: example of the Adana Province. Int. J. Eurasia Soc. Sci. **9**(31), 238–275 (2018)

34. Ha, J., Park, H.K.: Factors affecting the acceptability of technology in health care among older Korean adults with multiple chronic conditions: a cross-sectional study adopting the senior technology acceptance model. Clin. Interventions Aging **15**, 1873–1881 (2020)

35. Chen, K., Lou, V.W.Q.: Measuring senior technology acceptance: development of a brief, 14-item scale. Innov. Aging **4**(3), igaa016 (2020)

36. Tan, C.K.K., Lou, V.W.Q., Cheng, C.Y.M., et al.: Technology acceptance of a social robot (LOVOT) among single older adults in Hong Kong and Singapore: protocol for a multimethod study. JMIR Res. Protoc. **12**(1), e48618 (2023)

37. Park, H.K., Chung, J., Ha, J.: Acceptance of technology related to healthcare among older Korean adults in rural areas: a mixed-method study. Technol. Soc. **72**, 102182 (2023)

38. Lehmann, S., Ruf, E., Misoch, S.: Emotions and attitudes of older adults toward robots of different appearances and in different situations. In: Ziefle, M., Guldemond, N., Maciaszek, L.A. (eds.) ICT4AWE 2020. CCIS, vol. 1387, pp. 21–43. Springer, Cham (2021). https://doi.org/10.1007/978-3-030-70807-8_2

39. Chita-Tegmark, M., Ackerman, J.M., Scheutz, M.: Effects of assistive robot behavior on impressions of patient psychological attributes: Vignette-based human-robot interaction study. J. Med. Internet Res. **21**(6), e13729 (2019)

40. Chen, K.L., Xu, Y., Chu, A.Q., et al.: Validation of the Chinese version of Montreal cognitive assessment basic for screening mild cognitive impairment. J. Am. Geriatr. Soc. **64**(12), e285–e290 (2016)

41. Rong, L., Yuanjiao, Y., Yuting, L., Hong, L.: Research progress on the application of art therapy in the elderly with cognitive impairment. Chin. Nurs. Manage. **21**(8), 1240–1244 (2021)

42. Hsiao, C.C., Lin, C.C., Cheng, C.G., et al.: Self-reported beneficial effects of Chinese calligraphy handwriting training for individuals with mild cognitive impairment: an exploratory study. Int. J. Environ. Res. Public Health **20**(2), 1031 (2023)

43. Huang, M.X., Tang, W.W.W., Lo, K.W.K., et al.: MelodicBrush: a novel system for cross-modal digital art creation linking calligraphy and music. In: Proceedings of the Designing Interactive Systems Conference, pp. 418–427 (2012)
44. Engelbrecht, R., Shoemark, H.: The acceptability and efficacy of using iPads in music therapy to support wellbeing with older adults: a pilot study. Aust. J. Music. Ther. **26**, 52–73 (2015)
45. Luo, Y., Lin, R., Yan, Y., et al.: Effects of remote expressive arts program in older adults with mild cognitive impairment: a randomized controlled trial. J. Alzheimer's Dis. (Preprint) 1–17 (2023)
46. Merkel, S., Kucharski, A.: Participatory design in gerontechnology: a systematic literature review. Gerontologist **59**(1), e16–e25 (2019)
47. Sundgren, S., Stolt, M., Suhonen, R.: Ethical issues related to the use of gerontechnology in older people care: a scoping review. Nurs. Ethics **27**(1), 88–103 (2020)
48. Lee, D., Tak, S.H.: Barriers and facilitators of older adults' usage of mobility devices: a scoping review. Educ. Gerontol. **49**(2), 96–108 (2023)

An Exploration of Engagement and Collaboration Between Healthcare Professionals and Older Adults with Multimorbidity Using a Digital Health Platform

Julie Doyle[1]([envelope]) [ORCID], Patricia McAleer[1] [ORCID], Emma Murphy[2,3], Suzanne Smith[1] [ORCID], Mary Galvin[2,4], and John Dinsmore[2] [ORCID]

[1] NetwellCASALA, Dundalk Institute of Technology, Dundalk, Ireland
julie.doyle@dkit.ie
[2] Trinity Centre for Practice and Healthcare Innovation, Trinity College Dublin, Dublin, Ireland
[3] School of Computer Science, Technological University Dublin, Dublin, Ireland
[4] Department of Applied Social Studies, Munster Technological University, Cork, Ireland

Abstract. Multimorbidity, the occurrence of two or more chronic conditions in an individual, is a significant global health issue. It requires individuals to engage in complex self-management. It is understood that support from a care network, including healthcare professionals (HCPs), is crucial and can motivate adherence to self-management, act as an enabler to effective self-management and guide and reassure the person. However, people with multimorbidity (PwMs) often report challenges in their relationships with HCPs. Digital health technologies have potential to facilitate PwMs to share responsibility in their care by equipping them with the tools to better self-manage and to collaborate with their HCPs. This paper reports on findings from 60 PwM and 16 HCP participants who took part in the ProACT trial, whereby PwMs used the platform for a period of 12 months. Semi-structured interviews with participants resulted in four themes relating to engagement and collaboration in care, including HCP Scenarios of Engagement; The PwM Becoming a Collaborator in their Care; The Utility of Data; and Towards Integration of Care – Benefits and Challenges.

Keywords: Older adults · self-management · multimorbidity · healthcare professionals · digital health

1 Introduction

Multimorbidity, the occurrence of two or more chronic conditions in an individual, is a significant global health issue [1]. A recent systematic review estimates that the global prevalence rate of multimorbidity is 37.2%, with the highest prevalence in South America (45.7%), followed by North America (43.1%), Europe (39.2%) and Asia (35%) [2]. It is estimated that 50 million people in the European Union (EU) live with multimorbidity

© The Author(s), under exclusive license to Springer Nature Switzerland AG 2024
Q. Gao and J. Zhou (Eds.): HCII 2024, LNCS 14726, pp. 22–37, 2024.
https://doi.org/10.1007/978-3-031-61546-7_2

[3]. Further, more than half the global population of people aged 60 and over have multiple chronic conditions [3] and ageing populations are expected to worsen this scenario. However, multimorbidity is not solely an ageing problem with prevalence rates rising in younger populations across both high-income countries and low- and middle- income countries [1]. It is unsurprising therefore that countries globally face strong concerns over the sustainability of health services due to the increase in healthcare expenditure, as well as disparities in the number of practicing health professionals [4]. In the EU, 70–80% of healthcare costs are spent on chronic diseases, which corresponds to €700 billion [3].

There are significant challenges for people living with and managing multimorbidity. Multimorbidity is associated with high mortality rates, increased healthcare utilization and increased healthcare expenditure. Healthcare services are often repetitive (multiple appointments), inconvenient, inefficient (patients may see different clinicians who give conflicting advice), burdensome and potentially unsafe due to poorly integrated and coordinated care [5, 6]. In addition, people with multiple conditions may take many medications, which can be difficult to remember with some combinations potentially dangerous. These issues compound and significantly impact on reducing quality of life.

Many of these challenges occur because healthcare systems and clinical practice guidelines focus on a single disease model of care [7, 8], which are not appropriate to adequately manage the complexity of multimorbid care. People with multimorbidity therefore must navigate complex ecosystems of care, often seeing multiple different specialists and doctors for their different conditions. The lack of integration and communication amongst different providers results in fragmentation and disruption of care [9]. People with multimorbidity also often face challenges in their relationships with their healthcare professionals, which can negatively impact self-management efforts [10–12]. There is a need, therefore, to improve best practice around the provision of continued, well-coordinated, person-centred integrated care ecosystems for individuals with multimorbidity. Digital health solutions hold great potential to fulfill this need.

With this in mind, the ProACT Horizon2020 project[1] aimed to co-design, develop and evaluate the ProACT digital health platform with older PwMs and those who care for them. The platform was evaluated in a 12-month proof-of-concept trial in both Ireland and Belgium with 120 PwMs aged 65 or over and members of their care networks, including healthcare professionals (HCPs), informal and formal carers. This paper presents findings from 60 PwMs and 16 HCPs who took part in the Irish trial.

1.1 The ProACT Digital Health Platform

The platform supports PwMs in self-management of their multiple chronic conditions [13]. It was designed following an extensive requirements gathering and co-design process involving PwMs, informal carers (ICs), formal (paid) carers (FCs) and HCPs [14]. It has been initially designed to support those with diabetes, Chronic Obstructive Pulmonary Disease (COPD), Chronic Heart Disease (CHD) and Chronic Heart Failure (CHF), however the platform is flexible and new conditions can be easily integrated. From the PwM's point of view, the platform consists of sensing devices for measuring

---

[1] https://cordis.europa.eu/project/id/689996.

symptom and wellbeing parameters and a Health and Wellbeing application (Fig. 1). All PwMs received a tablet device with the application, a blood pressure monitor, weight scales and a watch to monitor activity and sleep. Those with diabetes received a blood glucometer and those with COPD received a pulse oximeter. Some symptoms (for example breathlessness, sputum) as well as wellbeing parameters (mood, social activity) were measured through self-reporting in the application. The PwM application had the following features:

Health and Wellbeing Monitoring. A dashboard with a quick-glance overview of current status (Fig. 1). Blue petals indicate that the data is within the person's personalised normal range (as set in collaboration with a nurse), a pink and slightly larger petal indicates that data is outside this normal range, while an orange petal highlights missing data (e.g. no data for a particular parameter received within the last five days). The logic behind the dashboard in terms of what is displayed ensures that if a condition is not being monitored, it is brought to the PwM's attention. This could be a prompt or alert to monitor symptoms relating to that condition and/or educational content being pushed to them. Simultaneously, highlighting the areas that need attention can reduce the complexity and the time burden of self-management [15]. The View Readings section of the app provided more detailed historical information on data trends over time for all parameters being monitored (Fig. 1(a)).

Education. Research has highlighted that lack of information is a significant barrier to both effective self-management and to motivation to engage in self-management actions [14]. Within the Health Tips section of the application there are two categories of content: 'Did you know?' contains educational content relevant to self-management of specific conditions and wellbeing; 'How do I?' contains custom-made video training content on how to use the devices and the application. Educational information for each disease was sourced from reputable sources known to PwMs. Where possible, content was delivered in three modalities, (video, audio and text) to cater for differences in learning styles and accessibility.

Personal Activity Goals. PwMs could set their own physical activity goals (e.g., steps/distance/time spent walking) and review progress. Messages and prompts were used to help PwMs in setting achievable and incremental goals. If a goal was not achieved, the user could provide context by choosing a reason from a pre-defined list (for example, they were unwell this week). As an alternative to setting their own goal, an analytic within the platform would recommend a realistic goal, based on the PwM's most recent activity data but within physical activity guidelines for older adults and adults with chronic conditions [16] to avoid giving major leaps in recommendations. The user could choose whether to accept the platform goal or determine their own.

Add a Care Network. PwMs could choose whom, within their care network, can support and contribute to their digital self-management. Within the application, the PwM could add someone to their network and choose what data to share with them.

Applications were also designed and built for care network stakeholders, including HCPs, informal and formal carers to enable them to view PwM data. The dashboards of these applications were slightly different to the PwM dashboard, showing a four-square two by two grid highlighting four key pieces of data. All stakeholders had access to the 'How Do I?' education on how to use the application.

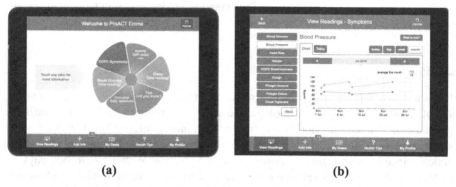

Fig. 1. (a) Application Dashboard showing current health and wellbeing status. Pink petals indicate a reading is outside a person's personalised range, orange indicates a reading hasn't been taken for a period of 5 days or more, while a blue petal indicates that all is ok (for symptoms) and acts as a quick link to another part of the platform; (b) Users can view historical readings by day, week or month in graph or table format. (Color figure online)

2   Methods

The study was a 12-month proof of concept (PoC) trial, which employed an action research design, to allow for continuous feedback from PwM participants and refinement of the platform throughout the trial. There were three action research cycles (ARCs) across the trial. Data collection from PwM participants was aligned with the end of each ARC, apart from ARC 1 where data was collected at the beginning of the ARC (T1 - which marked the start of the trial) and the end of the ARC (T2). T3 data collection took place at the end of ARC 2, while T4 data collection took place at the end of ARC 3. HCPs participated in an interview or focus group at T4. The study design incorporated a mixed methods approach across the ARCs. Ethical approval for the study was received from three research ethics committees, including two university committees and one health service committee. The full trial protocol has been published elsewhere [17].

2.1   Participant Recruitment

PwMs. In total, 60 PwMs consented to take part. Inclusion criteria were that the participant was 65 or over and had two or more of the chronic conditions of interest (see Sect. 1.1). Participants were recruited through several channels, including social groups for older adults (n = 11); diabetes and COPD support groups (n = 5); social media, radio and local newspaper advertising (n = 18); a formal care organisation (n = 17); HCPs and pharmacists (n = 8). One participant was also recruited following a referral from another trial participant. By the end of the trial, 8 participants had withdrawn, while 3 had passed away.

HCPs. HCP participants were nominated by PwM participants. Following nomination, the research team contacted the nominated HCP to go through the details in the participant information leaflet and consent form. If the nominated HCP expressed a wish to be involved in the trial, a consent form and information leaflet were sent to them either via email or post.

2.2 Procedures

PwMs who consented to participate were visited at their homes on two occasions at the start of the trial, to deploy the technology (see Sect. 1.1), provide training and conduct the first phase of T1 data collection. In addition to the training content within the application, participants were provided with a paper-based training manual. Throughout the trial, a clinical triage nursing team monitored the symptom data. Within one to two days of deployment, triage nurses called each participant to introduce themselves and further explain their role. Throughout the trial, the nursing team monitored for any alerts in the data, refined alert thresholds in collaboration with individual participants and scheduled a monthly check-in call. HCP participants who consented to take part were provided with login details to the application, typically via email or phone. Data was available to all participants in close to real-time (i.e. within one to two minutes) from time of entry by the PwM.

2.3 Data Collection and Analysis

For PwM participants there were four time points in the trial. Members of the research team conducted data collection, including questionnaires and semi-structured interviews at each time point, which coincided with the end of each ARC. All data collection took place at the participants' homes. HCP participants completed a demographic questionnaire on entry into the study and took part in a semi-structured interview or focus group at the end of the study period at their place of work.

All interviews and focus groups were audio recorded and transcribed verbatim. Transcripts were loaded in NVivo for qualitative analysis.

Engagement data was logged automatically through the platform. For PwM participants this included the date and time of symptom or wellbeing data being input (either through a digital device or through self-report) as well as how often participants engaged with different sections of the application. For HCP participants, the number of days a participant logged into their app was recorded.

Qualitative interview data underwent inductive Thematic Analysis (TA) to construct relevant themes [18]. Individual researchers coded transcripts according to an established analysis protocol. Pairs of researchers worked to collapse and categorise codes into themes. Discussions and re-coding workshops took place to ensure agreement on theme and sub-theme names were reached amongst the wider trial site teams. NVivo for Mac (Version 11) by QSR International was used to conduct the coding part of the analysis.

3 Findings

This section presents participant demographics, participants' objective engagement with the platform and findings from the thematic analysis. Four themes were constructed from the qualitative data and are presented below. Quotation attributions throughout the findings section are structured as (participant id, gender, age, condition profile, timepoint).

3.1 Participants

Sixty PwMs consented to take part in the trial. PwM participants ranged in age from 65 to 92 years (mean age 74.23 ± 6.4). Sixty percent (n = 36) were male. Ninety seven percent (n = 57) had two of the included chronic conditions, while three percent had three conditions.

Twenty PwM participants invited thirty-one HCPs to join their care network, of whom sixteen agreed to take part. The HCP average age was 48 years with females dominating by 70%. The average number of years of experience in their role was 16 years. There was a mix of professional backgrounds, including three General Practitioners (GPs), two diabetes clinical nurse specialists (CNS), one respiratory CNS, two respiratory consultants, two physiotherapists, three heart failure CNS's, one cardiologist consultant and two pharmacists. The environment of work was mainly acute hospital and GP practice. One HCP was working in the community in pharmacy and a physiotherapist was doing home visits to some patients. The duration of work experience with people with multimorbidity varied from substantial experience (89%) to some experience (11%).

3.2 Objective Engagement with the Platform

Detailed analysis of PwM engagement with the ProACT platform has been described elsewhere [13, 19]. In summary, the majority of PwM participants remained engaged with the trial, with three participants passing away and 8 withdrawing. PwMs took on average of 2 readings from the various sensing devices each day and there was an average of 40 participants taking daily readings throughout the trial.

Logged data from engagement with the HCP CareApp indicated that there were logins from HCPs on 24 days during the trial (out of a total of approximately 250 possible days due to HCPs being onboarded later than PwM participants). The next subsection indicates scenarios of engagement for HCPs.

3.3 Themes

HCP Scenarios of Engagement. HCPs reported a range of reasons for consenting to participate in the trial, including an interest in seeing how the technology could help people self-manage, how it could enhance care, and general curiosity about the research. Most HCPs reported that they only logged into the application at the start, to test their login details (which was evidenced in the logged engagement data from the platform). Their engagement with ProACT typically only occurred when a PwM participant brought their data with them to a clinical visit, which many PwM participants did proactively. In addition, this engagement was with the PwM's application, rather than the HCP's. In relation to reasons for non-usage of their personal CareApp, each HCP reported lack of time and resources as the reasons for not engaging, while some also mentioned the application being something 'new': *"it's just time again and resources, you know, and it's something new. I'm sorry but that's the reality"* (HCP016, F, HF CNS).

HCPs confirmed that they did, and in the future would, look at the application if one of their patients brought it to a visit. Some HCPs felt it would be ideal to be able to review their patient's data in between visits, but all felt that this would not be feasible with their current workloads: *"You're dealing with what you're dealing with on the day"* (HCP014, F, Respiratory physiotherapist); *"It's too much like pre-emptive work and there isn't capacity for that"* (HCP027, F, GP). The only scenario where data potentially would be reviewed pre-emptively, would be in advance of a scheduled clinic visit (e.g., a 6-monthly check-up appointment at one of the specialist clinics), whereby the data might be able to show that the person was stable and therefore didn't need to attend the appointment, and where a check-up phone call in relation to the data would be sufficient. However, during the trial this wasn't the case. A heart failure CNS reported that a participant called to report a slow heart rate, and rather than her checking the application to review the heart rate and other data, she brought the patient in for an ECG: *"a patient did ring us because his heart rate was a bit slow... and I suppose if I had time or if I had, if it was more familiar to me, I might have gone in (to the application) to see what they were talking about, slow, but we brought, we did bring him in and we did an ECG and we checked him out and it wasn't actually that slow at all. We were quite happy because we like heart rate slow, you know what I mean?"* (HCP016, F, heart failure CNS).

HCPs also spoke of conditions for future use, with all HCPs noting they would adopt the platform into practice under various conditions. The main condition cited was that it must benefit patients in terms of helping them self-manage, followed by it must be easy to use. Three HCPs noted that they would not need to see effectiveness data from a trial to adopt the application into their practice, as they are already requesting that their patients monitor this type of data as it's useful for them to have: *"I don't think we'd need to see a trial to show that it actually improves outcomes because I think we want to know this information anyway from our patients"* (HCP020, F, Cardiac Consultant). Another condition regularly cited was that using the application would have to be *"productive work"*, i.e., reduce or offset workload in some way, such as reducing the need for clinic visits, as outlined above. At the same time, some HCPs understood that patients are beginning to engage more with these types of technologies and that healthcare systems may need to adapt: *"even with our younger people... a lot of them are heading now towards wearing continuous glucose monitors and that information can be sent to their phone and things like that. So, we just have to – we have to keep up to date with it"* (HCP004, F, diabetes CNS).

The PwM Becoming an Active Collaborator in Their Care. Many PwM participants also reported that they brought their tablet device with their CareApp and data with them to doctor visits. For PwMs, their HCPs were not necessarily in their formal trial care network (i.e. were not participants of the ProACT trial). Furthermore, even those PwMs who did not formally invite a HCP to be part of their care network reported bringing their data to clinical visits. Several PwMs reported that the triage nurses would help them to prepare for clinical visits, encouraging them to bring their tablet with their data and helping them to form questions to ask their HCPs. PwMs reported mixed views and opinions of their HCPs of the trial and their data. Some HCPs looked favourably upon their participation in the trial: *"I used to bring that iPad with me* [to the heart efficiency clinic]. *They thought it was absolutely brilliant, the heart efficiency girls thought they were great because they could run back on it and look at my blood pressure and my weight going back for weeks and months, you know"* (P031, M, 70, CHF+CHD, T3). Other PwMs reported more negative feedback from HCPs: *"I did* [show my GP my readings], *yeah. And comments, words like 'daft' were used"* (P009, M, 71, COPD+CHD+diabetes, T3).

PwMs also spoke of how they discussed their readings with HCPs during clinical visits. Many reported a change in the conversations they were having with their HCPs, some querying about healthy ranges to aim for, and what they could do to achieve them: *"My doctor.. I asked him what should I be thinking about. I have no idea what a healthy sleep pattern is, if I sleep fifteen hours a day instead of eight or nine hours a day you know. Is that not good for me? I hadn't discussed the blood pressure with him at all* [before the trial]. *I just said you know... what sort of a range and he just threw it at me"* (P015, M, 82, diabetes+CHD, T3). For some, HCPs confirming that their readings were 'good' appeared to provide reassurance: *"But when I went for the annual check to the diabetic clinic, I took that* [app] *with me and the doctor that looked through, he said there was nothing to worry about. He said it was perfect. So, from that respect I think it's worth everything, you know"* (P023, M, 73, diabetes+CHD, T4).

For some PwMs, the nature of the visit and conversation changed due to them having more knowledge regarding their conditions and readings: *"Well, you know, maybe a bit more of where he's coming from when he speaks to you on where you are with different readings and that, whereas before this* [trial], *you wouldn't be aware of them and you didn't take it on board at all"* (P026, M, 75, COPD+CHD, T4). Others noted how using the platform made them more aware of additional supports they needed in relation to their health and prompted them to request these: *"Yes it has helped me question, because the supplies of* [oxygen] *I was put on. I went on this oxygen I think November' 17... And the settings from the supplier on this had me on a flow rate of five. But I knew, well I mean I'm on a flow rate of two litres at the minute. And I got very sick with pneumonia in August. And I was in intensive care. And I asked them* [consultants] *to please... Figure out what flow rate. So* [this trial] *helped me sort of tune into that. To be very much aware of it and to try and investigate the flow rates more"* (P043, F, 77, COPD+CHD, T3).

PwM participants also reported taking more responsibility for their care as a result of using the platform, due to increased confidence in how to self-manage and increased knowledge of their health and wellbeing as a result of monitoring. Some participants felt that their perception of the role of the GP had changed since using the platform as they now felt ownership of their health, and more confident in telling the GP what was wrong with them: *"In a sort of a way yes in the sense that it's becoming more your own personal responsibility to track the numbers. That you're not just leaving it entirely to the GP to do it"* (P033, M, 65, diabetes+CHD, T4). PwMs also spoke about becoming less reliant on the GP: *"because when I got an attack* [during the trial], *the COPD or whatever flared, I could recognise whether I needed an antibiotic or not and I didn't see the point in going to a doctor when I couldn't breathe right, but there was no sign of infection. Whereas before* [the trial] *as soon as my breathing sort of laboured I'd be at the doctor..."* (P045, F, 74, COPD and diabetes).

HCPs also spoke of discussing readings with PwMs and of being impressed at how they were using the technology to self-manage and how motivated they were: *"He actually did more of that* [showing graphs with data] *with me. He was actually, you know, showing me through the app. He was so motivated."* (HCP005, F, diabetes CNS); *"I've been surprised that the number of older people that are* [using the platform]*"* (HCP004, F, diabetes CNS). HCPs felt the data could help focus participants on a particular period in time in relation to the data, for example the time leading up to an out-of-range reading, which would then in turn prompt further discussion.

The Utility of Data. HCPs commented on the various data types within ProACT, whether they found them useful and how they would use the data. Each HCP specialty (e.g. COPD consultant, GP) had their own opinion on what symptom data they would find most useful for dealing with their patients. As one might expect, specialists were primarily interested in symptom data directly relevant to their specialty. Therefore, while one of the aims of the CareApp for HCPs was to provide a more holistic overview of the participant to the HCP on their dashboard (e.g. showing someone's COPD data, as well as their diabetes data), consultants and clinical nurse specialists wanted only the data of relevance to them on the dashboard of the app, stating they could dig deeper for other information if they wished: *"If we're looking at it* [the dashboard] *from a respiratory point of view, it's going to be different to what the diabetes people want to see. It's going to be different from what the heart failure people want to see"* (HCP012, M, respiratory consultant); *"It's a very busy - we are very a busy clinic and we are kind of trying to focus on the cardiac symptoms, whereas our heart failure nurses are excellent and they take a more holistic approach..."* (HCP020, F, cardiac consultant).

HCPs also discussed the wellbeing data available in the app. Activity data was deemed to be useful for all HCPs across all conditions. This was often related to knowing that the person was being active but was also deemed useful because of the links between activity and symptom data: *"We know that the more active someone is, the better it is for the heart health, for the blood sugar levels – you know for the blood pressure so it's of – definite benefit"* (HCP005, F, diabetes CNS). HCPs noted how the wellbeing data, for example low activity or mood, or poor sleep also highlights issues, which could prompt earlier intervention or the need to come in for a visit. During a typical visit HCPs can take vitals and get some insight into symptoms, albeit point-in-time. However, they noted that they don't typically ask about sleep, physical activity or mood, even though they think these parameters are important for the person's care. However, having access to them during a visit was deemed useful.

The mood data available in the app (self-reported by PwMs participants) generated a lot of discussion. In relation to mood, HCP004, a diabetes clinical nurse specialist said: *"It would* [be helpful] *– it is, but it wouldn't be something we'd, I suppose, it wouldn't be something we would be looking at on a regular basis"*. HCPs noted that if a patient reports they are experiencing low mood or anxiety they would be advised to go to their GP. However, it was generally agreed that having access to mood data would be beneficial for understanding certain readings (e.g. unstable blood sugars, low physical activity) or explaining lack of engagement in self-management. The specialist HCPs noted the importance of addressing mood and anxiety issues to facilitate self-management. HCPs felt that having access to mood data would be particularly useful for some people who may find it difficult to discuss issues they have around depression and anxiety. They felt the self-reported data on mood could help ease into a conversation on it. *"sometimes people come into a hospital setting or a primary care setting and they feel it's very clinical and they mightn't even discuss that aspect of their care so, you know, and it might be their first time to meet this, you, yourself as well so, it's bringing, you know, it might actually open up that conversation quicker."* (HCP005, F, diabetes CNS). However, mood was not deemed useful by any of the GP participants and not something they would typically ask about: *"Not unless they have a history of depression and anxiety and we are treating it and we want to see a response to treatment but if it is a new thing, no, I don't think so"* (HCP027, F, GP).

HCPs also spoke of how the data could help inform treatment, decision making and medication adjustments. As would be expected, HCPs all felt that having historical data from patients is more beneficial than point in time data on a particular day, in terms of providing a better picture of how the person has been in between visits. It was felt that having the trend of data could ultimately supporting more informed decisions around care: *"You have data over time, historical data, and that is very useful rather than just on the spot and things like blood pressure readings"* (HCP027, F, GP). Some HCPs recalled how they had made adjustments to a participant's medication having viewed data in the PwM's app that then led to further investigation. HCPs within the heart failure clinic felt that the data would be extremely useful for supporting them in titrating (adjusting to find the right dosage) their patients' medications, as the symptom data would show if the patient tolerated a medication change: *"We would definitely titrate them using this data... We could titrate up their medication much quicker and so that would all be of a huge benefit"* (HCP016, F, heart failure CNS). This in turn could negate the need for a clinic visit to assess this.

Towards Integration of Care – Benefits and Challenges. The care network feature in the CareApp (that allows a PwM to add people to their care network and choose which information to share with each individual) was discussed with PwMs and HCPs. PwM participants discussed their reasons for not involving a care network. For some participants, they did not think that their HCPs were interested in being involved in the trial or that they would have sufficient time to oversee their health readings: *"I mentioned it to* [clinic HCPs], *they didn't seem one bit interested. It didn't generate a conversation or anything"* (P005, M, 72, CHF+CHD, T2); *"And then again,* [doctors are] *pushed for time as well. They've enough paperwork and ticking boxes as it is, you know, so I'm with him 25 years. He's on board as well, but he expects me to do* [the trial] *independent of him"* (P034, M, 67, COPD+CHF, T2). Some participants expressed surprise that HCPs didn't want to be part of their care network when asked. However, most PwMs put this down to time pressures for HCPs: *"Actually told him that he could get me on the thing if he programmed into it and he'd be able to see it for himself, but I don't think he ever done it. I wouldn't run him down in any way. He's a brilliant doctor... but I know he's* *a very busy person, so he probably doesn't want to be going into my details when he knows I'm going into him"* (P047, M, 69, COPD+CHD, T4).

HCPs felt that a care network is very important for PwMs, and that data being available to those in their care network would be a selling point for them, and also provide reassurance. HCPs also said they would find it useful to know who is in their patient's care network, and they might not have this information otherwise: *"I suppose, at the moment we are trying to move heart failure care into the community with links to the hospital network so you could have multiple people looking after heart failure with all the same goals.. whoever is looking after the patient, the patient themselves, the heart failure nurse in the hospital, the consultant who's I suppose overseeing the heart failure clinic in the hospital, the GP and the heart failure nurse in the community. So, yes, I think that is very good, yes"* (HCP020, F, cardiac consultant). They highlighted, however, that integration of care could only be achieved if all relevant clinics and HCPs are linked into the care network. In addition, they noted that being able to communicate with other care network members would be necessary. In contrast, one GP felt that having too many people in the care network could cause problems: *"I think it shouldn't be a multiplicity of people, it should be just one or two specific care people or otherwise, yes, you would just have a talking shop and I think it would be – it wouldn't be very helpful if there are too many cooks in the kitchen"* (HCP028, M, GP).

While the benefits of a care network to support integrated care were acknowledged, several concerns were also raised. The primary concern raised was that there needed to be clarity, primarily for the PwM, on how regularly, if at all, their data was being checked or reviewed by HCPs. For example, in showing the care network feature within the app to one HCP, she noted how the PwM could see that she was in her network. However, she hadn't ever proactively logged in to review the participant's data: *"I suppose, now we're on that but to be honest I've never accessed it"* (HCP016, F, heart failure CNS). Thus, setting expectations was considered important. Another concern raised by some HCPs was that someone, whether it be a HCP, triage nurse or PwM, needs to be the 'go-to' person - the person who has responsibility for ensuring data is acted upon and that care network members are aware of it: *"So, unless it is integrated and then, you see, somebody has to be in control of it and make decisions, so it depends who is going to do that or who is going to kind of say if it was a hospital consultant – are they going to get in touch with us or how are they going to share that?... Because that is a level of responsibility that, you know, needs to be decided on so that somebody takes ownership of that and uses it and it depends how is that is worked"* (HCP027, F, GP).

Finally, GPs highlighted that informal carers would need training on understanding the data and thresholds, to ensure that having this data doesn't result in increased calls to the GP due to informal carers panicking over data. *"they are phoning us up and saying so and so's blood pressure is this, that and the other and you thinking yes but that could be just a temporary thing and unless, so, it depends what the network is used for and it depends who has responsibility for what"* (HCP027, F, GP).

4 Discussion

Digital health technologies have the potential to support individuals to become active collaborators in their health and wellbeing management, altering the power imbalance in traditional healthcare by empowering the person to share responsibility for their care with their HCPs [20]. While there is a substantial amount of research exploring collaborations and relationships between patients and their HCPs, including some involving people with multimorbidity [10, 11, 21] there is limited research on studies involving older adults with multimorbidity and their HCPs using such technology in practice. The ProACT trial involved 60 older PwMs in Ireland using the digital health platform ProACT to self-manage their health and wellbeing over a period of 12 months, with optional support from a care network. As indicated in our findings, older adults engaged with the platform regularly with low attrition rates observed. While HCPs did not engage with their own digital application, they did engage in discussion of the data with PwM participants who brought their data with them to appointments, with this sometimes impacting treatment, for example medications being altered.

Healthcare has traditionally been paternalistic, with HCPs responsible for directing and managing all aspects of a person's care [22]. However, with ageing populations expected to result in higher prevalence rates of chronic conditions, alongside the availability of digital self-management technologies, there is a shift towards more person-centred care, with individuals having shared responsibility for their health and wellbeing management [12]. Leveraging patient expertise and experience has been noted as important to empowering shared responsibility [22] and has the potential to increase adherence to self-management. It also has potential to create an "equalising effect" in the relationship between HCPs and their patients [20]. The findings from the ProACT trial, presented above and elsewhere [13, 19] indicate that PwM participants actively engaged in day-to-day self-management, becoming more aware of their health and wellbeing and more adept at self-management. As a result, PwMs reported feeling more responsible for their care and proactively brought their tablet devices with their data to clinical visits to engage their HCPs in discussions centred on the data. PwMs also reported being more confident to initiate discussions with their HCPs and having more knowledge to ask informed questions. This demonstrates both initiative and a sense of ownership of one's self-management. At the same time, HCPs reported being impressed with their patients' motivation to self-manage and technology proficiency. Thus, PwM engagement in digital self-management facilitated a more equal partnership with their HCPs. In designing such technologies for older people, HCI researchers should ensure appropriate education and training content is available to end users, to facilitate their learning and their path to becoming experts in their own health and wellbeing management.

While empowering individuals to self-manage their health and wellbeing through digital technology is one key factor in moving towards shared responsibility, it is also necessary for HCPs to engage with the data generated from such technologies. Only half of the HCPs invited by PwMs in this study decided to participate, and those HCPs that did participate were emphatic in not wanting to be responsible for reviewing and reacting to their patients' data outside of clinical visits, indicating that this was the patient's responsibility. This confirms prior research which highlights that HCPs are not willing to monitor patient data [23]. Furthermore, despite PwM participants having multiple conditions, the majority of HCPs reported only being interested in data pertaining to their own specialty within the ProACT platform. This highlights the need for digital solutions to support PwMs to be the coordinators of their own holistic care. Designers should therefore ensure digital health technologies support PwMs in effective and efficient communication of the most pertinent health and wellbeing data with their different HCPs during short clinical visits, understanding that different specialties may wish to have certain data prioritised. For example, designers could support customisation of dashboards for different HCPs whereby prior to or during a visit a PwM could generate a data report highlighting data most relevant to a particular condition with the ability to then dig into additional data further if desired. Alternatively, a 'Me in a Month' summary could highlight the most important trends and anomalies in the data [24]. This type of summary could also highlight relevant wellbeing data, such as mood, which on the surface HCPs might not consider useful, but which could provide context for particular readings or behaviours. Other research has noted that while anomalies were easily identified in co-interpretation of self-tracked activity data by people with Parkinson's and their HCPs, identifying trends was difficult (e.g., recognising lower activity levels at weekends) [20]. A data summary automatically generated by a digital health platform could support easier interpretation or explanation of such trends.

Some research has cautioned against individual interpretation of self-tracked data by a patient (e.g., at home) as they may incorrectly interpret data [25]. Indeed, this may be particularly challenging in the context of the complexity of multimorbidity management, for example where conflicting advice can lead to PwMs prioritizing one condition over others without seeking advice from their HCPs [10]. However, the ProACT platform addressed this through the use of the dashboard (Fig. 1) which prioritised those symptoms and other areas of self-management that were most important for the PwM to address at a particular point in time. Furthermore, the clinical triage service provided supplementary human support and was instrumental in helping PwMs to learn to self-manage [12]. During clinical visits, HCPs also contributed to the PwM's learning (for example confirming that the data readings look normal as was mentioned by HCP016 in relation to a PwM's heart rate). There were no reports of incorrect interpretation of data at any point during the study from either PwM or HCP participants. Therefore, it is likely that empowering the PwM with appropriate knowledge, through a combination of digital and human support, on how to self-manage is likely to help avoid incorrect interpretation of data. Despite this, it is important to consider that as an older person with multiple chronic conditions continues to age and potentially gets additional condition diagnoses, more frequent support may be required to help them to continue to self-manage effectively. Informal carers will have an important role to play. As such, digital health platforms should support adaptations to the care network over time and should ensure that informal carers also receive appropriate education and knowledge to support them in their caring role.

5   Conclusion

Individuals with multimorbidity must undertake often complex and burdensome self-management routines to effectively manage their conditions, and digital health technologies can support such efforts, minimizing the burden of care and supporting prioritisation of self-management behaviours. It is well understood that support from a care network, in particular from HCPs, can also motivate and support self-management behaviours. However, in practice, PwMs often report challenges in their relationships with their HCPs. Furthermore, there is a dearth of research exploring how PwMs and HCPs collaborate in practice using digital platforms. This paper has presented findings from 60 PwMs and 16 HCPs who participated in the 12-month ProACT trial whereby PwMs used the ProACT platform to self-manage multiple conditions with optional support from their HCPs. Findings highlight the various scenarios of engagement of HCPs with PwM self-tracked health and wellbeing data, how PwMs proactively initiated collaboration with their HCPs during visits, the perceived benefits of different types of data and the benefits of challenges of supporting integration of care through a digital platform.

The contribution of this work involves providing insight into how a digital health platform can mediate collaborative care and multimorbidity management between older adults and their HCPs as well as how HCI researchers might design digital solutions to support such collaboration. Embracing such digital solutions not only has the potential to increase quality of life for those with multimorbidity but may also future proof healthcare systems to more effectively de-centralize health and social care to the community.

Acknowledgments. This work was part-funded by the ProACT and SEURO projects and has received funding from the European Union's Horizon 2020 research and innovation programme under Grant Agreement numbers 689996 and 945449. We would like to extend our gratitude to all participants who dedicated time to participating in the research.

Disclosure of Interests. The authors have no competing interests to declare that are relevant to the content of this article.

References

1. Multimorbidity: a priority for global health research. Academy of Medical Sciences. (2018). https://acmedsci.ac.uk/file-download/82222577. Accessed 19 Dec 2023
2. Chowdhury, S., Chandra Das, D., Sunna, T., Beyenne, J., Hossain, A.: Global and regional prevalence of multimorbidity in the adult population in community settings: a systematic review and meta-analysis. EClinicalMedicine **57**, 101860 (2023)
3. Rijken, M., Struckmann, V., Dyakova, M., Melchiorre, M.G., et al.: ICARE4EU: improving care for people with multiple chronic conditions in Europe. Eurohealth **19**(3), 29–31 (2013)
4. Figueroa, C., Harrison, R., Chauhan, A., Meyer, L.: Priorities and challenges for health leadership and workforce management globally: a rapid review. BMC Health Serv. Res. **19**, 239 (2019)
5. Liddy, C., Blazkho, V., Mill, K.: Challenges of self-management when living with multiple chronic conditions: systematic review of the qualitative literature. Can. Fam. Physician **60**(12), 1123–1133 (2014)
6. Breckner, A., Roth, C., Glassen, K., Wensing, M.: Self-management perspectives of elderly patients with multimorbidity and practitioners – status, challenges and further support needed? BMC Family Pract. **22**(238) (2021)
7. Technical series on safer primary care: Multimorbidity. World Health Organization (2016). https://www.who.int/publications/i/item/9789241511650. Accessed 19 Dec 2023

8. Kernick, D., Graham, C.A., O'Flynn, N.: Multimorbidity: clinical assessment and management. NICE Institute for Health and Care Excellence (2016). https://www.nice.org.uk/guidance/ng56. Accessed 19 Dec 2023

9. Aramrat, C., et al.: Advancing multimorbidity management in primary care: a narrative review. Prim. Health Care Res. Dev. **23**, e36 (2022)

10. Berry, A.B.L., et al.: Supporting communication about values between people with multiple chronic conditions and their providers. In: CHI 2019 Proceedings of the CHI 2019 Conference on Human Factors in Computing Systems (2019)

11. Ongwere, T., Cantor, G.S., Clawson, J., Shih, P.C., Connolly, K.: Design and care for discordance chronic comorbidities: a comparison of healthcare providers' perspectives. In: Pervasive Health, Proceedings of the 14th EAI Conference on Pervasive Computing Technologies for Healthcare (2020)

12. Doyle, J., et al.: The role of phone-based triage nurses in supporting older adults with multimorbidity to digitally self-manage – findings from the ProACT proof-of-concept study. Digit. Health **8**, 205520762211311 (2022)

13. Doyle, J., Murphy, E., Gavin, S., et al.: ProACT – a digital platform to support self-management of multiple chronic conditions: findings in relation to engagement during a one-year proof-of-concept trial. J. Med. Internet Res. (JMIR) **23**(12), e22672 (2021)

14. Doyle, J., et al.: Managing multimorbidity: identifying design requirements for a digital self-management tool to support older adults with multiple chronic conditions. In: CHI 2019 Proceedings of the CHI 2019 Conference on Human Factors in Computing Systems (2019)

15. Eton, D.T., Ramalho de Oliviera, D., Egginton, J.S., Ridgeway, J.L., et al.: Building a measurement framework of burden of treatment in complex patients with chronic conditions: a qualitative study. Patient Relat. Outcome Meas. (3), 39–49 (2012)

16. Tudor-Locke, C., Crai, C.L., Aoyagi, Y., Bell, R.C., Karen, A., et al.: How many steps/day are enough? For older adults and special populations. Int. J. Behav. Nutr. Phys. Act. **8**, 80 (2011)

17. Dinsmore, J., et al.: Digital health platform for integrated and ProACTive patient centred care (ProACT): protocol for an action-research proof of concept trial. JMIR Res. Protoc. **10**(12), e22125 (2021)

18. Braun, V., Clarke, V.: Using thematic analysis in psychology. Qual. Res. Psychol. **3**(2), 77–101 (2006)

19. Sheng, Y., Doyle, J., Bond, R., Jaiswal, R., Gavin, S., Dinsmore, J.: Home-based digital health technologies for older adults to self-manage multiple chronic conditions: a data-informed analysis of user engagement from a longitudinal trial. Digit. Health **8**, 20552076221125957 (2022)

20. Mentis, H.M., et al.: Crafting a view of self-tracking data in the clinical visit. In: Proceedings of the CHI 2017 Conference on Human Factors in Computing System (2017)

21. Ongwere, T., Cantor, G., Martin, S.R., et al.: Design hotspots for care of discordant chronic condition: patients perspectives. In: Proceedings of the 10th Nordic Conference on Human Computer Interaction (NordiCHI) (2018)

22. Pichon, A., et al.: Divided we stand: the collaborative work of patients and providers in an enigmatic chronic disease. ACM Hum. Comput. Interact. **4**, No. CSCW3 (2020)

23. Morton, K., Dennison, L., May, C., et al.: Using digital interventions for self-management of chronic physical conditions: a meta-ethnography review of published studies. Patient Educ. Couns. **100**(4), 616–635 (2017)

24. Tighe, S., Doyle, J., Harvey, S.: Co-design of a data summary feature with older adults as part of a digital health platform to support multimorbidity self-management. In: Pervasive Health, 17th EAI International Conference on Pervasive Computing Technologies for Healthcare (2023)
25. Redelmeier, D.A., Tversky, A.: On the belief that arthritis pain is related to the weather. Proc. Natl. Acad. Sci. **93**(7), 2895–2896 (1996)

Research on Older Adults' Interaction with E-Health Interface Based on Explainable Artificial Intelligence

Xueting Huang[1(✉)], Zhibo Zhang[2], Fusen Guo[3], Xianghao Wang[4], Kun Chi[5], and Kexin Wu[6]

[1] Faculty of Art Design, Guangzhou College of Commerce, Guangzhou, China
milasnow0326@gmail.com
[2] School of Engineering and Information Technology, University of New South Wales, Canberra, Australia
z5456678@unsw.edu.au
[3] School of Science, Computing and Engineering Technologies, Swinburne University of Technology, Melbourne, Australia
[4] College of Engineering, Computing and Cybernetics, Australian National University, Canberra, Australia
xianghao.wang@anu.edu.au
[5] College of Professional Studies, Northeastern University, Jersey City, NJ, USA
[6] Department of Computer Science, Cornell University, New York, USA
kw634@cornell.edu

Abstract. This paper proposed a comprehensive mixed-methods framework with varied samples of older adults, including user experience, usability assessments, and in-depth interviews with the integration of Explainable Artificial Intelligence (XAI) methods. The experience of older adults' interaction with the E-health interface is collected through interviews and transformed into operatable databases whereas XAI methods are utilized to explain the collected interview results in this research work. The results show that XAI-infused e-health interfaces could play an important role in bridging the age-related digital divide by investigating elders' preferences when interacting with E-health interfaces. Furthermore, the study identifies important design factors, such as intuitive visualization and straightforward explanations, that are critical for creating efficient Human-Computer Interaction (HCI) tools among older users. Furthermore, this study emphasizes the revolutionary potential of XAI in e-health interfaces for older users, emphasizing the importance of transparency and understandability in HCI-driven healthcare solutions. This study's findings have far-reaching implications for the design and development of user-centric e-health technologies, intending to increase the overall well-being of older adults.

Keywords: E-Health interface · User Experience · Explainable Artificial Intelligence (XAI) · Human-Computer Interaction (HCI) · Older Adults

X. Huang and Z. Zhang—Contributed equally to this work and should be considered co-first authors.

1 Introduction

The rapid evolution of technology has profoundly impacted various aspects of society, and the realm of healthcare is no exception [1]. As the aging population in China continues to grow, coupled with the persistent challenges posed by the COVID-19 epidemic, there has been a discernible surge in the adoption of e-health solutions among older adults, as statistical evidence underscores a rise in the frequency and number of Chinese older adults engaging in e-health after the epidemic was detected [2, 3]. This phenomenon has sparked an urgent need to understand and enhance the interaction between older adults and e-health interfaces, a crucial step towards ensuring the overall well-being of this demographic.

Despite the growing adoption of e-health, older adults in China encounter substantial challenges in using these digital platforms [4]. A notable obstacle is the lack of digital literacy among this demographic, hindering their ability to recognize and effectively utilize e-health interfaces [5]. Additionally, concerns about limited accessibility and other potential usability issues further compound the difficulties faced by older adults in engaging with digital health solutions [6].

To unravel the intricacies of older adults' interaction with e-health interfaces, our research employs a comprehensive mixed-methods framework. Questionnaires will be used primarily to collect user data, specifically focusing on measuring labeling. This quantitative approach is complemented by in-depth, semi-structured interviews and observations, which are designed to capture keywords and understand the nuanced experiences, preferences, and challenges faced by older users. The real-time observations during these interviews contribute to identifying specific usability issues within the e-health interface. This multifaceted approach ensures a comprehensive exploration of older adults' engagement with e-health interfaces, combining quantitative measurements of labeling with qualitative insights derived from interviews and observations.

The collected data will all be converted into a natural language database to facilitate the application of machine learning algorithms as classifiers. The decisions made by older adults during interviews serve as the ground truth for subsequent analysis. Notably, XAI methods, such as Local Interpretable Model-agnostic Explanations (LIME) and SHapley Additive exPlanations (SHAP), are integrated to explain the decisions made by the trained classifiers. This comprehensive framework allows for a transparent analysis of the rationale behind older adults' decisions during e-health interactions.

In the culmination of this research, the outcomes will be modeled and evaluated based on the User Experience Honeycomb (except Value) framework [7]. This framework provides a structured approach to assess the holistic impact of e-health interfaces on older adults, considering factors crucial for their effective engagement and overall satisfaction.

In summary, the rise of e-health adoption among China's aging population, accelerated by the challenges of the COVID-19 epidemic, highlights the need to investigate and enhance the interaction between older adults and e-health interfaces. To alleviate dilemmas such as digital literacy and usability concerns, our research utilizes a mixed-methods approach, combining questionnaires, interviews, observations, and XAI, with outcomes assessed through the User Experience Honeycomb framework for a comprehensive understanding of older adults' engagement and satisfaction.

2   Literature Review

2.1   Older Adults and E-Health Digital Interface

The intersection of aging populations and e-health technologies is a burgeoning area of research, particularly in the context of a rapidly aging society. E-health platforms offer potential benefits in terms of accessibility and efficiency, but they also present unique challenges for older users, particularly in terms of usability and user experience [8].

The adoption of e-health services by older adults is influenced by a variety of factors. A significant challenge is the digital literacy gap. Older adults often exhibit lower levels of digital literacy compared to younger populations, which can hinder their ability to effectively use e-health services [9]. Moreover, age-related physical and cognitive declines can impact the ease with which older adults interact with digital interfaces, potentially leading to frustration and disengagement [10]. The design of e-health interfaces often fails to accommodate the specific needs of older users. Usability issues such as complex navigation, small font sizes, and inadequate instructions can exacerbate the challenges faced by this demographic [11]. Accessibility concerns, including the need for more intuitive and senior-friendly designs, are critical in ensuring that e-health technologies are equally beneficial to all age groups [12].

Traditional e-health interfaces often fall short in meeting the diverse needs of older adults, primarily due to a lack of human-computer interaction (HCI) design principles that cater to this demographic. Previous methods in HCI-based user experience surveys have typically utilized standard usability metrics, which may not fully capture the unique challenges faced by older users. These traditional methods often overlook the subtleties of how age-related factors, such as cognitive and physical impairments, affect the interaction with digital health interfaces [13]. Cham: Springer International Publishing. Moreover, conventional approaches lack a nuanced understanding of older adults' emotional responses and personal preferences when using e-health platforms, leading to a gap in truly personalized user experience design [14]. This oversight can result in interfaces that are technically sound but fail to resonate with or accommodate the practical realities of older users.

In summary, the limitations of the traditional approach to e-health interfaces and corresponding user experience surveys highlight the need for more sophisticated and resonant methods in HCI research. In response to these deficiencies, there is a need for advanced methods to explore the barriers and facilitators that influence older adults' use of e-health interfaces more accurately and transparently. We need a more inclusive, intuitive, and effective approach to user experience surveys. Such an approach would not only address the current deficiencies in the design of e-health interfaces but also inform the development of user-centered technologies that ultimately improve the well-being of the aging population.

2.2   Explainable Artificial Intelligence Background

The European Union's General Data Protection Regulation [15] has revealed the issue of insufficient explainability in Artificial Intelligence (AI). It emphasizes the need for understanding the rationale behind AI algorithmic decisions that adversely affect individuals. To ensure trust in the decisions made by AI systems, it is essential for AI methods to be both transparent and easily interpretable. To meet these requirements, a variety of approaches have been suggested to make the decisions of AI more comprehensible to people. These approaches, commonly referred to as "Explainable Artificial Intelligence", have been applied in numerous fields including healthcare, Natural Language Processing, and financial services [16].

Categorizations of XAI methods encompass a detailed classification of diverse techniques designed to enhance the transparency and interpretability of Artificial Intelligence, focusing on differentiating these methods based on their explanation stages, explanation scopes, and explanation output format [17]. Therefore, a more accurate and specific categorization of a single XAI technique can be achieved by viewing it from various categorization angles [18]. This approach allows for a deeper understanding and revelation of the method's features and information at multiple levels.

Whereas the main objective of HCI (Human-Computer Interaction) is to design interactions that consider and accommodate the desires and capabilities of the users [19], the utilization of XAI approaches in HCI areas could ensure that decision-makers such as developers and designers better understand the results, thereby helping users become more effective in making decisions [20]. Vicente et al. (2020) [21] conducted a study to address the scarcity of literature on how users perceive different aspects of artistic image recommendation systems, from the perspective of domain expertise, relevance, and explainability. This research explored various facets of user experience with an artistic photo recommender system from both algorithmic and HCI viewpoints. The study utilized three distinct recommender interfaces and two separate Visual Content-based Recommender (VCBR) algorithms. Zhang et al. (2023) [22] applied XAI techniques in combination with various machine learning algorithms to develop a robust explainable reputation model. This model was used for the classification of human emotion using brainwave signals. Notably, the key features influencing the assessment of emotions varied between the different XAI-based frameworks. Zhang et al. (2022) [23] employed a Convolutional Neural Network (CNN) model to categorize image spam, while post-hoc XAI methods were used to elucidate the decisions made by the black-box CNN models in detecting spam images. The findings demonstrated that the XAI-based framework achieved commendable detection effectiveness for decision-makers.

However, ensuring that E-health systems are comprehensible to their intended users remains a challenge in HCI. Adhering to user-centered design principles, it is vital to create E-health systems that are understandable and tailored to the users' specific needs and skill levels, particularly for older adults interacting with E-Health devices.

In response to these challenges, this study introduces an innovative mixed-methods approach that integrates user experience, usability evaluations, and explainable artificial intelligence (XAI) techniques. This novel approach is specifically designed to investigate how older adults interact with E-Health interfaces, addressing the unique needs of this demographic. By combining these diverse methodologies, the research aims to contribute significantly to the fields of HCI and E-Health, offering new insights into the development of more accessible and user-friendly digital health technologies.

3 Methodology

This paper examines the interaction of older adults with e-health interfaces, integrating principles from HCI, gerontology, and XAI. It focuses on how cognitive and physical challenges unique to the aging population affect these interactions and explores how XAI can enhance the transparency and usability of e-health systems surveys. Emphasizing user-centered design, this research aims to create accessible and intuitive e-health interfaces for older users.

The methodology of this paper adopts both quantitative and qualitative data collection approaches. Quantitative data, derived from structured questionnaires, capture a wide range of older adults' experiences with e-health interfaces, providing a substantial dataset for XAI analysis to identify trends and interaction patterns. Qualitative data, obtained from in-depth interviews and observations, offer insights into the personal and subjective experiences of older adults with these technologies. These combined methods aim to deliver a comprehensive understanding of older adults' engagement with e-health systems, informing the development of more effective and user-friendly digital health solutions.

3.1 Data Collection

Survey Subjects. From June to September 2023, this study targeted elderly residents in Guangzhou City, Guangdong Province. Employing a multi-stage sampling method, a diverse sample from two central urban and two suburban districts, encompassing 48 communities, was selected. Participants included permanent residents aged 55 and above for females, and 60 and above for males, who were in good mental health, had basic literacy skills, and consented to participate. Individuals with serious illnesses were excluded to ensure data reliability.

Survey Instrument. A comprehensive questionnaire, including multiple-choice and Likert scale questions, was used to assess the elderly's interaction with e-health interfaces. Likert-scale questionnaires. Open-ended questions provided insights into their personal experiences. Additionally, 40 elderly residents participated in semi-structured interviews, enriching the data with detailed accounts of their challenges and satisfaction with e-health technologies.

Development and Validation. The survey was tailored to the elderly lifestyle in Guangzhou, focusing on the popular WeChat Public Service app for e-health. The value of WeChat application in chronic diseases management in China. The questions, based on literature review and existing tools, were pilot-tested and refined with expert input in gerontology and HCI.

Content of the Survey. The questionnaire explored usage frequency, navigation ease, content readability, and overall satisfaction. Different metrics were included, aligned with the User Experience Honeycomb framework. Interview topics delved into personal barriers, difficulties encountered, and trust in digital health information.

Administration of the Survey and Ethical Considerations. The survey was conducted both online and in-person over a three-month period to suit the varying needs of the participants, adhering to methods suitable for diverse contexts. Clear instructions were provided to ensure understanding, with assistance readily available. Ethical standards were strictly maintained, with all participants informed about the study's purpose and their rights, including confidentiality and voluntariness. Informed consent was obtained prior to data collection, ensuring ethical integrity and adherence to research standards.

3.2 Explainable Artificial Intelligence Methods

As described in Sect. 1, the XAI methodology will provide insight and transparency into understanding older adults' interactions with the e-health interface, which will help to increase the efficiency of evaluating the user experience using the Experience Honeycomb (except Value) framework. Specifically, this work will use XAI techniques including Shapley Additive Explanation (SHAP), Local Interpretable Model-agnostic Explanations (LIME), and Anchors explainers to improve the user experience of the interaction process.

SHAP, introduced as a model-agnostic way of interpreting machine learning models, employs the concept of Shapley values. These values are derived by assessing a team's performance with and without each player, analogous to understanding each feature's impact in a machine learning model. This approach measures how the absence or presence of a feature affects the model's performance, thereby determining its influence. It helps to identify whether each feature positively or negatively influences the prediction. According to a source, SHAP values are considered a more effective method for explanation compared to traditional feature importance. Feature significance, in this context, refers to the process of assigning scores to each input attribute of a specific model, with the scores representing the importance of each feature. SHAP method conducts the explanations as the following equation:

$$g(z') = \phi_0 + \sum_{j=1}^{M} \phi_j z_j' \tag{1}$$

where g represents the model to be explained, $z' \in \{0, 1\}^M$ implies the coalition feature, M means the maximized coalition size, whereas $\phi_j \in R$ stands for the attribution of specified feature j.

The main objective of LIME explainer is to develop a model that is both interpretable and locally faithful to the original classifier, while also being comprehensible to human users. In this approach, for a complex classifier, an easier-to-understand model (like a linear program) is employed, incorporating interpretable features. This simpler model is designed to closely mimic the performance of the more complex model in a local context.

The explanation model in LIME is described as g, belonging to a set G of interpretable models that are visually presentable to users, like a linear model. The function $\pi_x(z)$ is used to measure the closeness between an instance z and x, establishing the local area around x. An objective function $\xi(x)$ is then defined. Within this function, the L-function in $\xi(x)$ acts as a measure of how well the interpretable model g approximates the complex model f, assessed through $\pi_x(z)$ in a local context. The goal is to minimize the L-function for an optimal solution of $\xi(x)$, ensuring that the complexity of the explanation model $\Omega(g)$ remains sufficiently low for human comprehension. And the L-function is minimized to obtain the optimal solution of the objective function when $\Omega(g)$ (the explanatory model complexity) is low enough to be understood by humans. The explanation function $\xi(x)$ formulated by the LIME algorithm is structured as:

$$\xi(x) = \arg \min_{g \in G} L(f, g, \pi_x(z)) + \Omega(g) \tag{2}$$

The method for determining the similarity degree $\pi_x(z)$ is described by the following formula:

$$\pi_x(z) = \exp\left(-\frac{D(x, z)^2}{\sigma^2}\right) \tag{3}$$

Based on the definition of the similarity degree $\pi_x(z)$ as given in Eq. 3, the initial objective function is reformulated in Eq. 4. In this equation, $f(z)$ represents the predicted outcome of the perturbed sample in the d-dimensional space (original features), considering this prediction as the response. Meanwhile, $g(z')$ signifies the predicted value in the d'-dimensional space (interpretable features). The similarity measure is then applied as a weighting feature, allowing the optimization of the aforementioned objective function through linear regression.

$$\xi(x) = \sum_{z,z' \in Z} \pi_x(z)\left(f(z) - g(z')\right)^2 \tag{4}$$

Anchor, a different method for interpreting classification models, was developed by Marco Tulio Ribeiro in 2018 [24]. Sharing LIME's philosophy, Anchor utilizes a perturbation-based approach to generate local explanations, capable of elucidating the specific predictions of any "black box" model. This method is characterized as being "Local", "Post hoc", and "Model agnostic". Notably, Anchor's interpretations are more aligned with human comprehension compared to other methods like LIME or SHAP, offering clear prediction rules that clarify how the model arrived at its results.

4   Research Process

In this section, the detailed research process of the proposed mixed-methods framework for investigating older adults' interaction with E-health interfaces is illustrated. Figure 1 describes the overall diagram of the proposed approach. Steps including Data Collection by Questionnaires, Interviews, and Observation, Data Preprocessing and Augmentation, Data Annotation by User Experience are conducted in the previous steps to collect and process data. The processed data would be annotated from different user experience evaluation perspectives, whereas user-based classifiers would be trained based on the annotations and processed data. A user-based explainer is developed for understanding the user requirements based on the user-based classifier whereas the user experience without the explainer is also evaluated for comparison. The interview results show that user satisfaction levels improved in different user experience evaluation metrics.

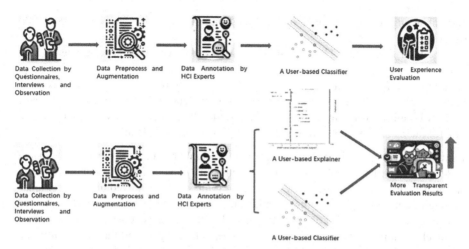

Fig. 1. The diagram of the proposed older adults' user experience evaluation framework.

The study conducted a comprehensive data collection exercise from June to September 2023 involving 480 elderly residents of Guangzhou City, Guangdong Province. The participant demographic comprised females aged 55 and above and males aged 60 and above, offering a representative sample for understanding the HCI and UX aspects of elderly interactions with E-health interfaces. The data showed that older users had varying levels of engagement with the e-health platform. It is notable that older users with more than a high school education were more likely to support health through e-health, which provided valuable insights into the usability and accessibility of the interface from an older user's perspective. Participants frequently cited issues such as navigation difficulty, small text size, and complex interface layouts. These findings underscore the need for an age-appropriate HCI design that accommodates the physical and cognitive changes associated with aging. Despite the challenges, a positive attitude towards the convenience and efficiency of E-health services was observed, highlighting the importance of these services in the daily lives of the elderly, especially during the pandemic.

To address potential dataset limitations and biases, and to ensure a comprehensive analysis relevant to HCI and UX research, data augmentation methods were employed. Therefore, four data augmentation methods for text data are utilized, each aimed at enhancing the diversity and volume of the collected dataset for user experience evaluation tasks. The first method, Synonym Replacement, substitutes a randomly selected word in a sentence with one of its synonyms, leveraging the WordNet lexical database for synonym-selection. The second method, Random Insertion, involves the duplication of a randomly chosen word by inserting it at another random position within the text, thereby increasing text length and introducing repetition. The third method, Random Swap, randomly interchanges the positions of two words within the text, subtly altering the sentence structure without significant impact on overall meaning. Lastly, the fourth method, Random Deletion, randomly removes words from the text with a predefined probability, simulating scenarios of missing or incomplete data. These methods collectively contribute to a more robust and varied dataset, which is crucial for training and enhancing the performance of Machine Learning classifiers and subsequent XAI explainers.

The User Experience Honeycomb framework is known for its comprehensive approach to user experience evaluation. We chose the concept of this framework (except value) to analyze the data because it is relevant to the study of user decision-making in human-computer interaction and helps to analyze in detail key areas of user experience such as Usability, Usefulness, Desirability, Findability, Accessibility, and Credibility. The following six concepts serve as a basis for analyzing the data:

Usability. Evaluates whether the system solves actual problems for the user. The paper collected data with the goal of finding out whether participants found the interface useful or not. The questionnaire asked the participant if the interface solved his/her problems. Through interviews, participants complemented the reasons why the interface solved and failed to solve their problems. In particular, the responsiveness of the interface, the level of fault tolerance, the support of multiple languages, and the availability of a specific interface channel for older adults could influence participants' decision to use or not use e-health. In addition, the layout, consistency, intuitiveness, accessibility, and availability of help channels influenced participants' decision to continue using or not using e-health.

Usefulness. Evaluates how easy the system is to use and how efficiently the user is able to complete the tasks. The data was based on the total time spent by the participants in completing the tasks using questionnaires. Additionally, during the interviews, the interviewer recorded the barriers or assistance that users encountered in interacting with the interface in order to understand which situations specifically affected the time it took for users to complete the tasks. Particularly, participants indicated that user knowledge and training had the greatest impact on the efficiency of using the e-health interface, with the role of the trainer typically being played by a junior member of the family, a peer, or a caregiver. Secondly, the performance of the device and the data also had a large impact on the efficiency of completing tasks.

Desirability. Evaluates whether the design of the interface evokes positive emotions and appreciation from the user. Data were collected using a questionnaire in which participants rated their satisfaction with each module of WeChat Public Service's e-health (including the seven modules of medical care, health insurance, COVID-19 prevention, off-site medical care, medical information, vaccinations, and emergency centers) in order to derive the user's overall satisfaction with the interface. Usage context-based interviews and observations were used to understand which specific modules of the interface led to user satisfaction or dissatisfaction and why.

Findability. Evaluates how easy it is for users to find information and navigate the system. Data was collected using questionnaires to understand how difficult it is for participants to find specific features. Interviews and observations were used to understand which specific interaction processes and levels of interaction contribute to finding barriers and finding easiness. Physiological barriers such as poor eyesight, poor hearing, unclear speech, and shaky hands are known to contribute to the participants' finding barriers, while non-physical factors such as the participants' native Cantonese (the system is predominantly in Mandarin), the low frequency of use of e-health, and the uncertainty and fear associated with being unfamiliar with the technology mainly affect the participants' finding easiness.

Accessibility. Evaluates whether the system is easily accessible to users of all abilities and disabilities. Data were collected using interviews and observations to determine which interface design factors hinder and facilitate access to the interface for participants with different abilities (including six factors: typography and readability, contrast and color, font and icon design, navigation and menu structure, consistency of interface design, and message input methods) based on a specific context to understand which specific situations lead to low accessibility or high accessibility.

Credibility. Evaluates whether the user trusts the information and the system. Data was collected using a questionnaire to understand how much the participants trusted the system. Participants were also interviewed and observed to determine which situations resulted in low or high credibility. In particular, less exposure to digital technology, being sensitive to privacy and security issues, questioning the accuracy of health information, frustration with AI robot services, and being surrounded by fewer peers who are using e-health are factors that heavily influence participants' credibility of the interface.

5   Results

Using the survey data collected based on the User Experience Honeycomb framework, a Random Forest classifier is trained and then explained using XAI methods including LIME and SHAP. The visualized XAI explanation results are illustrated and shown to the interviewed older adults to evaluate the improvement of user experience from different perspectives of the User Experience Honeycomb framework. Figures 2, 3, 4, 5 and 6 show some of the survey data's explanation results of LIME explainer, Word Cloud, and SHAP explainer, whereas the detailed discussion of these XAI results and how these would help to improve user experience is described as well.

From the sample XAI results from Figs. 2, 3, 4, 5 and 6, XAI explanation results could provide more transparent explanations for both designers and users. For instance, from Fig. 2, LIME Explanation of positive and negative sample results from the user experience evaluation perspective of usability and credibility, the visualized keywords that contribute to users' final decision of being satisfied or unsatisfied with usability and credibility are compared and evaluated. From this figure, it can be concluded that although keywords like "Guangdong", and "province" contribute a lot to the final decisions, older users tend to highlight their locations no matter whether they are satisfied or not. Apparently, when interacting with e-health, the feature that the participant's native language is Cantonese and the system's language is Mandarin received great attention, and therefore, whether the voice and text inputs support Cantonese or not became one of the determining factors of user satisfaction. On the other hand, "interface" and "platform" are keywords that affect older users negatively whereas "cultural" and "friendly" are keywords with positive feedback. We could conclude that much of the dissatisfaction with e-health among older participants was due to the lack of inclusive and elder-friendly interface design, and that they expected culturally appropriate and user-friendly e-health products. As a result, with the help of XAI, the understanding of the user experience of

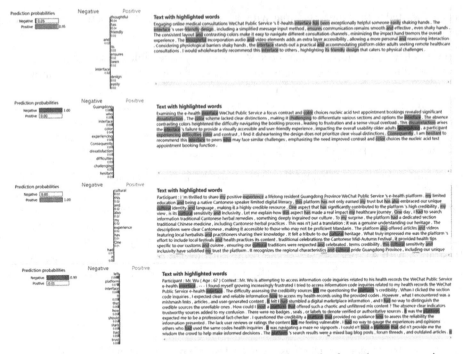

Fig. 2. LIME Explanation of positive and negative sample results from the user experience evaluation perspective of usability and credibility.

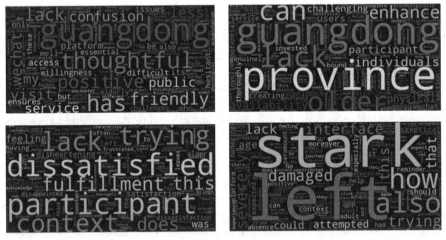

Fig. 3. Word Cloud Explanation results from the user experience evaluation perspective of desirability, findability, accessibility, and credibility.

older adults will improve, and both keywords related to the positive and those related to the negative will be highlighted.

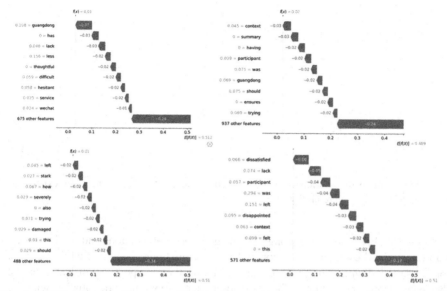

Fig. 4. SHAP keywords importance Explanation results from the user experience evaluation perspective of desirability, findability, accessibility, and credibility.

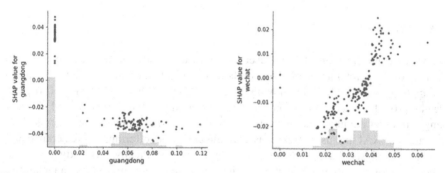

Fig. 5. SHAP value distribution of words "guangdong" and "wechat" from the user experience evaluation perspective of usability.

From Fig. 3, the Word Cloud Explanation results from the user experience evaluation perspective of desirability, findability, accessibility, and credibility, older users, especially those with visual impairment, could understand their needs from different requirement perspectives intuitively. As for Fig. 4, it provides a significant supplement for Fig. 4 that, although some keywords play important roles in older adults' classification, users' final decision on be satisfied or not is determined more by many other factors.

From Fig. 5, the SHAP value distribution of words "guangdong" and "wechat" from the user experience evaluation perspective of usability, provide other views of user experience. While most users are not satisfied with "Guangdong" from the usability perspective, not all older adult users are critical of "wechat" from the usability perspective.

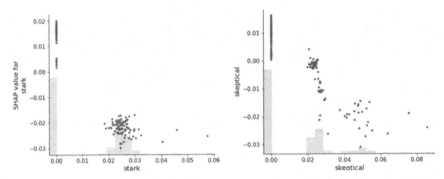

Fig. 6. SHAP value distribution of words "skeptical" and "stark" from the user experience evaluation perspective of credibility.

Although "wechat" and "guangdong" are the geographical locations and used software of all interviewed users, it can be concluded from this figure that older adult users are more dissatisfied with their geographical city rather than the popular software. On the other hand, from Fig. 6, almost all older adult users are strongly dissatisfied with the situation of "stark" from the view of credibility whereas many of them do not care about the "skeptical".

6 Conclusion

In advancing the field of HCI and user research, this study presents an approach to understanding the interaction of older adults with e-health interfaces, rooted in the practical application of XAI. By employing XAI techniques such as SHAP and LIME, this research provides a deeper, more nuanced understanding of how cognitive and physical changes in older adults impact their user experience with digital health platforms. This integration of XAI into user research is a significant stride, offering a more detailed and transparent analysis of user behavior and preferences. Specifically, this study highlights the necessity of language inclusivity, intuitive interface design, and cultural adaptability in e-health systems, thereby enhancing the overall user experience for older adults.

The study, however, is not without its limitations. The focus on a specific demographic in Guangzhou City may limit the generalizability of the findings to other cultural and regional contexts. Additionally, the research methodology, primarily reliant on self-reporting, could be expanded in future studies to include more objective data collection techniques such as real-time user interaction tracking. This would provide a more comprehensive understanding of the user experience and help to mitigate any potential response biases. Besides, the collected data contains many meaningless features that need to be pruned in future work.

The implications of this research are substantial for the future of e-health interface design and development. By incorporating XAI into the analysis of older adults' interactions with e-health platforms, this study not only enriches decision-makers understanding of user needs and preferences but also lays the groundwork for more user-centric, accessible, and empathetic digital health solutions. This approach emphasizes the importance of tailoring e-health technologies to meet the specific needs of older users, taking into account their unique challenges and preferences. Ultimately, this research contributes to a more inclusive and effective digital health environment, promising to enhance the quality of life for the aging population by offering more personalized, understandable, and user-friendly e-health experiences.

References

1. Biancone, P., Secinaro, S., Marseglia, R., Calandra, D.: E-health for the future. Managerial perspectives using a multiple case study approach. Technovation **120**, 102406 (2023). https://doi.org/10.1016/j.technovation.2021.102406
2. Tebeje, T.H., Klein, J.: Applications of e-Health to support person-centered health care at the time of COVID-19 pandemic. Telemed. E-Health **27**(2), 150–158 (2021). https://doi.org/10.1089/tmj.2020.0201
3. Wang, W., Sun, L., Liu, T., Lai, T.: The use of E-health during the COVID-19 pandemic: a case study in China's Hubei province. Health Sociol. Rev. **31**(3), 215–231 (2022). https://doi.org/10.1080/14461242.2021.1941184
4. Wilson, J., Heinsch, M., Betts, D., et al.: Barriers and facilitators to the use of e-health by older adults: a scoping review. BMC Public Health **21**, 1–12 (2021)
5. Shi, Y., Ma, D., Zhang, J., et al.: In the digital age: a systematic literature review of the e-health literacy and influencing factors among Chinese older adults. J. Public Health **31**(5), 679–687 (2023)
6. Ramdowar, H., Khedo, K.K., Chooramun, N.: A comprehensive review of mobile user interfaces in mHealth applications for elderly and the related ageing barriers. Univ. Access Inf. Soc. 1–17 (2023)
7. Morville, P.: Information architecture for the Web and beyond. https://cir.nii.ac.jp/crid/1130000794076236032. Accessed 25 Jan 2024
8. Ahmad, A., Mozelius, P.: Critical factors for human computer interaction of eHealth for older adults. In: Proceedings of the 5th International Conference on e-Society, e-Learning and e-Technologies, in ICSLT 2019, New York, NY, USA. Association for Computing Machinery, January 2019, pp. 58–62 (2019). https://doi.org/10.1145/3312714.3312730
9. Arcury, T.A., et al.: Older adult internet use and eHealth literacy. J. Appl. Gerontol. **39**(2), 141–150 (2020)
10. Pourrazavi, S., Kouzekanani, K., Asghari Jafarabadi, M., Bazargan-Hejazi, S., Hashemiparast, M., Allahverdipour, H.: Correlates of older adults' E-health information-seeking behaviors. Gerontology **68**(8), 935–942 (2022)
11. Fisk, A.D., Czaja, S.J., Rogers, W.A., Charness, N., Sharit, J.: Designing for Older Adults: Principles and Creative Human Factors Approaches. CRC Press, New York (2020)
12. Li, L., Chen, C., Pan, L., Zhang, J., Xiang, Y.: SigD: a cross-session dataset for PPG-based user authentication in different demographic groups. In: 2023 International Joint Conference on Neural Networks (IJCNN), pp. 1–8. IEEE, June 2023
13. Nogueira, M.R., et al.: Design and usability of an e-health mobile application. In: Marcus, A., Rosenzweig, E. (eds.) HCII 2020. LNCS, vol. 12202, pp. 314–328. Springer, Cham (2020). https://doi.org/10.1007/978-3-030-49757-6_22
14. Curtis, R.G., et al.: Improving user experience of virtual health assistants: scoping review. J. Med. Internet Res. **23**(12), e31737 (2021). https://doi.org/10.2196/31737
15. Goodman, B., Flaxman, S.: European Union Regulations on algorithmic decision-making and a 'right to explanation'. AI Mag. **38**(3), Article no. 3 (2017). https://doi.org/10.1609/aimag.v38i3.2741

16. Zhang, Z., Hamadi, H.A., Damiani, E., Yeun, C.Y., Taher, F.: Explainable artificial intelligence applications in cyber security: state-of-the-art in research. IEEE Access **10**, 93104–93139 (2022). https://doi.org/10.1109/ACCESS.2022.3204051

17. Barredo Arrieta, A., et al.: Explainable Artificial Intelligence (XAI): concepts, taxonomies, opportunities and challenges toward responsible AI. Inf. Fusion **58**, 82–115 (2020). https://doi.org/10.1016/j.inffus.2019.12.012

18. Zhang, Z., et al.: Explainable data poison attacks on human emotion evaluation systems based on EEG signals. arXiv (2023). https://doi.org/10.48550/arXiv.2301.06923

19. Li, Z., Lu, Z., Yin, M.: Towards better detection of biased language with scarce, noisy, and biased annotations. In: Proceedings of the 2022 AAAI/ACM Conference on AI, Ethics, and Society, pp. 411–423 (2022)

20. Nazar, M., Alam, M.M., Yafi, E., Su'ud, M.M.: A systematic review of human–computer interaction and explainable artificial intelligence in healthcare with artificial intelligence techniques. IEEE Access **9**, 153316–153348 (2021). https://doi.org/10.1109/ACCESS.2021.312 7881

21. Dominguez, V., Donoso-Guzmán, I., Messina, P., Parra, D.: Algorithmic and HCI aspects for explaining recommendations of artistic images. ACM Trans. Interact. Intell. Syst. **10**(4), 30:1–30:31 (2020). https://doi.org/10.1145/3369396

22. Zhang, Z., Li, P., Al Hammadi, A.Y., Guo, F., Damiani, E., Yeun, C.Y.: Reputation-based federated learning defense to mitigate threats in EEG signal classification. arXiv preprint arXiv:2401.01896 (2023)

23. Zhang, Z., Damiani, E., Hamadi, H.A., Yeun, C.Y., Taher, F.: Explainable artificial intelligence to detect image spam using convolutional neural network. In: 2022 International Conference on Cyber Resilience (ICCR), pp. 1–5, October 2022. https://doi.org/10.1109/ICCR56254. 2022.9995839

24. Ribeiro, M.T., Singh, S., Guestrin, C.: Anchors: high-precision model-agnostic explanations. Proc. AAAI Conf. Artif. Intell. **32**(1), Article no. 1 (2018). https://doi.org/10.1609/aaai.v32i1. 11491

Development of a Model for Estimating Cognitive Function in the Elderly Using EEG and Heart Rate Variability

Kentarou Kanai[✉], Yuri Nakagawa, and Midori Sugaya

Shibaura Institute of Technology, 3-7-5 Toyosu, Koto-ku, Tokyo 135-8548, Japan
{ma22036,nb23112,doly}@shibaura-it.ac.jp

Abstract. In recent years, the number of people with dementia has been increasing. Treatment of dementia is important. Dementia is a progressive disease that requires treatment and care according to the progress of the disease. As of now, the progress of the disease, such as cognitive decline, is generally diagnosed through various examinations. These methods are time-consuming and are not suitable for simple diagnosis in outpatient settings or welfare facilities. The purpose of this study is to estimate cognitive function using a simpler method. As a proposal for this purpose, a model was constructed using support vector machines (SVM) and logistic regression with data measured by a simple electroencephalograph (EEG) and a heart rate monitor as explanatory variables and neuropsychological examination, which are often used in examination for dementia, as objective variables. The results showed that SVM could estimate cognitive function with an accuracy of up to 71.6%.

Keywords: machine-learning · cognitive · dementia · EEG · heart rate

1 Introduction

1.1 Background

The number of dementia patients among the elderly (65 years and older) is increasing in Japan. According to the Cabinet Office, 18% of the elderly population had dementia in 2020, while this figure is expected to increase to 25% by 2040 [1]. Currently, there is no strict treatment for dementia. However, the onset of dementia not only causes memory impairment and wandering, which are disabilities for the patient, but also affects caregivers and family members by causing problems such as caregiver fatigue. Therefore, early detection of dementia and delaying its progression are important for the patient, family members, and caregivers [2, 3]. In large facilities such as hospitals today, many examinations are required to diagnose cognitive function in the elderly, including medical interviews, imaging examination using MRI (Magnetic Resonance Imaging), and neuropsychological examination such as MMSE (Mini Mental State Examination) [2, 3]. These diagnostic methods are used to accurately measure cognitive function. While these diagnostic methods can accurately measure them, they are burdensome for the elderly because they require a large number of examinations. In recent years, brain imaging methods such as Magnetic Resonance Imaging (fMRI) and Positron Emission Tomography (PET) have been offered at hospitals for early detection of cognitive impairment. These methods have the advantage of measuring cognitive function more accurately using brain information. On the other hand, there are issues such as the increased burden caused by the high cost of measurement equipment and the burden caused by the restraints such as the large amount of time required for the measurement. As the number of patients with dementia will inevitably increase in the future, there is a need for a simple method to measure brain information and to understand the cognitive function.

1.2 Related Research and Issues

A simple method has been proposed to determine the level of cognitive function of elderly people based on their cognitive function measurements [4, 5]. Electroencephalograph (EEG) is a useful measurement method for estimating cognitive function in the elderly because it directly reflects the neural function of the cerebral cortex [6]. Heart rate variability is an index that can be created from the heartbeat interval, and many of the indexes show a negative relationship with cognitive function, indicating that it is greatly related to cognitive function in the elderly and can be used to evaluate cognitive function [7]. Based on these facts, it is thought that EEG and heart rate variability can be used to measure the cognitive function in the elderly.

Je-Eon et al. used EEG and neuropsychological examination to understand cognitive function [4]. Specifically, they constructed a machine learning model to measure cognitive function in elderly people using EEG acquired from an electroencephalograph that can acquire data from one channel of the frontal lobe and the Verbal Fluency Test (VFT), one of neuropsychological examinations. The VFT is an examination that measures cognitive function based on the number of words in a specified category (e.g., animals, vehicles, etc.) uttered in 60 s, and is often used in the outpatient diagnosis of dementia [8]. They constructed a machine learning model to estimate the cognitive function of elderly people using an SVM (Support Vector Machine) with EEG as an explanatory variable and VFT results as an objective variable. As a result, the accuracy of the constructed model was about 65%. The method proposed in this study has the advantage that only one channel of EEG acquired from the frontal lobe can be easily measured. On the other hand, it is difficult to obtain information on the entire brain.

Eaman et al. constructed a machine learning model for estimating cognitive function by using heart rate variability from a wearable device [5]. As a result, the accuracy of the constructed machine learning model was about 82%. One of the issues in this research is that it is unclear whether heart rate variability alone can be used for advanced measurement, since cognitive function is closely related to the brain; dementia being a brain disease.

2 Purpose and Proposal

To consider improving the accuracy of a machine learning model for estimating the cognitive function of the elderly, it should be used for both of the brain wave and heat rate variability. However, there are fewer approaches to employ the model using both.

Therefore, the purpose of this study was to construct a machine learning model using EEG and heart rate variability indexes data for simple and objective estimation of cognitive function in the elderly.

To realize this objective, we firstly conducted the experiments for elderly subjects. EEG and heart rate were measured in the experiment, and then, we constructed the model with the following procedures. First, the features of EEG and heart rate variability were extracted from the measured data. Then, feature selection was performed from the extracted features. Mutual information content and Random Forest Variable Importance Classification and Regression were used as feature selection methods. Based on the results, we used SVM and logistic regression to construct a model for estimating the cognitive function of the elderly.

SVM is a pattern recognition model presented by Bernhand et al. in 1992 [9] and is a method that finds a hyperplane that divides each class. Logistic regression is a statistical regression model presented by David et al. in 1958 [10] and is a classification method that uses probability regression. The reason for employing these methods is that they have been used in many classification methods using biometric information and have produced certain results, so we adopted them in this study as well [11].

3   Experiment

In this study, an experiment was conducted to construct an estimation model of cognitive function of the elderly by obtaining the results of neuropsychological examination EEG and heart rate variability of the elderly under normal conditions. The subjects of the experiment were 26 elderly men and women residing in a nursing home.

3.1   Acquisition of Biological Indexes

In this experiment, an electroencephalograph (EEG) and a heart rate monitor were used to acquire EEG and heart rate variability. The EEG was measured using NeuroSky's MindWave mobile2, which can acquire EEG from a single channel near the left frontal lobe. This position corresponds to fp1 of the International 10–20 method of electrode placement for EEG. The sampling frequency of the sensor is 256 Hz.

Heart rate variability was measured using a Union Tool myBeat heart rate monitor. myBeat can measure heart rate variability by placing it under the heart, around the solar plexus. The sampling frequency of the sensor is 1000 Hz, and the heartbeat interval IBI is obtained from the obtained ECG.

3.2   Measurement of Cognitive Function

The Mini Mental State Examination (MMSE) was used as a neuropsychological examination to assess cognitive function.

The MMSE is a neuropsychological examination widely used in the diagnosis of dementia. This neuropsychological examination was chosen because it can measure cognitive function from various items such as memory, reading, and recitation, and it can measure cognitive function more accurately than a single item examination [12].

The examination was administered with a maximum score of 30 points, and the results were classified into three classes: 28 points or higher for without dementia, 24 points to 27 points for patients with mild dementia, and 23 points or lower for patients with dementia. Examples of questions in this examination include memory questions such as "What day is today?" and "What prefecture are we in now?" and "What prefecture are we in?". Behavioral questions included "Please read what is written on the paper and perform the action described" and "Please repeat what I have just said".

3.3 Experimental Procedures

The experimental procedure is as follows.

1. Explanation of the experiment.
2. Acquisition of EEG and heart rate variability during 5 min of resting with eyes closed (normal condition).
3. Perform MMSE.

   Figure 1 shows a scene from the experiment.

Fig. 1. Photo of the experiment in progress.

3.4 Results of Neuropsychological Examination

The distribution of each class is shown in Table 1 from the results of the neuropsychological examination conducted during the experiment.

Table 1. Distribution of subjects in each class.

Classification	Number of people
Dementia	14
Mild Dementia	7
Without Dementia	5

The following EEG indexes and heart rate variability indices were calculated from the EEG and heart rate variability data obtained for the construction of a machine learning model for estimating cognitive function in the elderly. The following 9 EEG indexes were calculated (Table 2).

Table 2. Calculated EEG indexes.

Index	Frequency Bandwidth	Interpretation
δ	1–3	Deep sleep, unconscious
θ	4–7	Intuitive, Creative, Dreaming
Low-α	8–9	Relaxed, Calm
High-α	10–12	Relaxed and focused
Low-β	13–17	Thinking, awareness of self and environment
High-β	18–30	Alert, agitation
Low-γ	31–40	Memory, higher mental activity
Mid-γ	41–50	Visual information processing
totalpower	1–50	Sum of each frequency band

In addition to the above, moving averages were performed for EEG indexes with window widths of 5, 10, 15, 20, 25, and 30. The moving averaged indices are hereinafter referred to as MAx (x = window width). The relative power of each frequency band divided by the total power was also calculated. Relative power is indicated by "relative" in front of the frequency band. A total of 119 EEG indexes were calculated.

Then, 16 types of EEG indexes were calculated from the acquired heart rate variability. The details are as follows (Table 3).

Table 3. Calculated Heart Rate Variability indexes.

Index	Calculation Method	Interpretation
IBI	Heartbeat interval, in ms	–
IBI_difference	Difference from one previous IBI	–
HR	Number of oscillations per minute	Tension/Calmness
pNNx (x = 10,20,30,40,50)	Percentage of adjacent IBIs whose absolute values exceed x ms	Pleasant/Discomfort, Parasympathetic
SDNN	Standard deviation of IBIs	Sympathetic, Parasympathetic
RMSSD	Root-mean-square of the difference between adjacent IBIs	Parasympathetic

(*continued*)

Table 3. (*continued*)

Index	Calculation Method	Interpretation
SDNN/RMSSD	SDNN/RMSSD	Sympathetic
CVNN	Coefficient of variation of IBI	Sympathetic, Parasympathetic
VLF	Power values at 0.01–0.04 Hz from frequency analysis of IBIs	–
LF	Power values from 0.04–0.15 Hz for frequency analysis of IBI	Sympathetic, Parasympathetic
HF	Power values from 0.15–0.40 Hz for frequency analysis of the IBI	Parasympathetic
LF/HF	LF divided by HF	Sympathetic

The number of calculated indices was 119 for EEG indexes and 16 for heart rate variability indexes, a difference of about 10 times in the number of indices. Therefore, we used the mutual information content to determine the optimal window width of the moving average. Specifically, feature selection was performed using all indicators, and the average value was calculated for each window width. As a result, the window width with the highest mean value was adopted for future analysis. The results are shown in Table 4.

Table 4. Average mutual information content of EEG indexes for each moving average value

	MA0	MA5	MA10	MA15	MA20	MA25	MA30
Δ	0.352	0.637	0.687	0.692	0.694	0.694	0.694
θ	0.011	0.044	0.041	0.099	0.108	0.139	0.170
Low-α	0.123	0.291	0.368	0.452	0.536	0.583	0.606
High-α	0.036	0.080	0.100	0.163	0.199	0.238	0.268
Low-β	0.024	0.034	0.055	0.044	0.089	0.061	0.091
High-β	0.004	0.062	0.136	0.189	0.255	0.245	0.266
Low-γ	0.157	0.415	0.520	0.584	0.611	0.612	0.632
Mid-γ	0.062	0.159	0.191	0.277	0.312	0.340	0.376
Average	**0.096**	**0.215**	**0.262**	**0.313**	**0.351**	**0.364**	**0.388**

Table 4 shows that window width 30 has the highest value of 0.388. Therefore, 17 EEG indexes were used in the future analysis, which were moving averaged values with a window width of 30.

4 Machine Learning Model Construction

4.1 Feature Selection

In building the machine learning model, feature selection was performed from the acquired feature data. Two feature selection methods, mutual information content and random forest variable importance, were used in the analysis to select features that are important for understanding the cognitive function of the elderly [13, 14]. These two methods were selected because they are used in feature selection with biological information such as EEG and heartbeat [11, 15].

In this study, feature selection was performed by regression and classification of these methods. Namely, classification and regression of mutual information content, classification and regression of the importance of random forest variables, and classification and regression of the importance of random forest variables.

The top 50% (16 indices) of the 33 calculated EEG indexes and heart rate variability indices and their values are shown.

The results of the classification of mutual informativeness and the regression of mutual informativeness are shown in Fig. 2. The importance of each index is shown in the blue color for EEG indexes and the orange color for heart rate variability indexes.

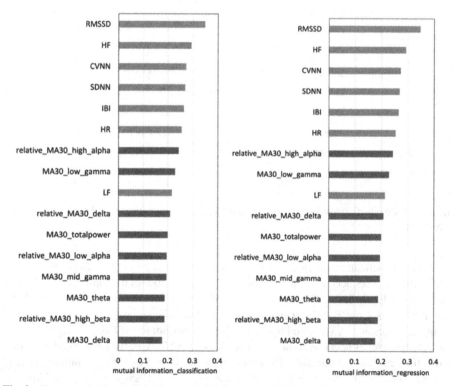

Fig. 2. Feature selection results for mutual information (left: classification, right: regression). (Color figure online)

From Fig. 2, the results of the feature selection for the top 50% were the same for classification and regression using the amount of the mutual information. In feature selection using mutual information content, the top 6 indicators were all heart rate variability indicators, indicating that heart rate variability indicators tend to rank high. In addition, RMSSD and HF ranked first and second, respectively, suggesting that parasympathetic indicators may easily rank high.

Next, the classification results of the variable importance in the random forest and the regression results of variable importance in the random forest are shown in Fig. 3.

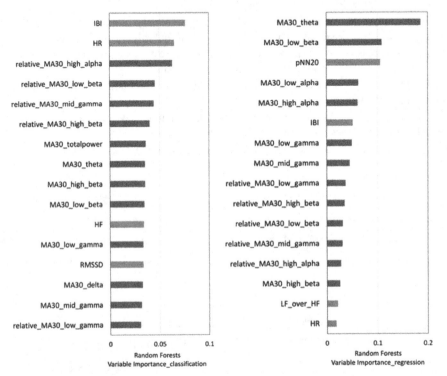

Fig. 3. Feature selection results for Random Forest Variable Importance (left: classification, right: regression)

In the classification of variable importance in the random forest from the left in Fig. 3, EEG indexes accounted for 12 out of 17, or about 70% of the top-ranked indexes. Among the EEG indexes, the relative power of EEG indexes related to concentration, such as High_α, Low_β, Mid_γ, and High_β, tended to be higher.

In the regression of variable importance for the random forest from the right side of Fig. 3, EEG indexes accounted for 12 out of 17, or about 70% of the top-ranked indexes, as was the case for classification. However, in the regression of variable importance for the random forest, the absolute power of θ, Low_β, Low_α, High_α, Low_γ, and Mid_γ was higher. This indicates that the absolute power of EEG indexes is important, unlike the classification of variable importance for random forests.

Thus, it was found that the results differed greatly depending on the feature selection method. However, it is unclear how the feature selection results affect the actual construction of the cognitive function estimation model for the elderly. Therefore, we conducted model construction using three feature selection results: mutual information content, classification of variable importance of random forests, and regression of variable importance of random forests.

4.2 Model Building

Based on the results of feature selection, SVM and logistic regression were used to construct a model for estimating cognitive function in the elderly.

In this study, 17 indicators that ranked high in feature selection were used as explanatory variables, and the MMSE scores were classified into three levels as objective variables.

Two types of the cross-validation were used to verify the accuracy of the model. k-stratified cross-validation (k = 10) was used as the first cross-validation method. In this cross-validation method, the data is divided into k parts. One of the k parts is the test data, and the rest are the training data; the test data is replaced k times.

The second cross-validation was the leave-one-subject-out (LOSO) cross-validation. In this cross-validation, the data of one collaborator was used as test data and the data of the remaining collaborators as training data, and the data of the collaborators who were to become test data were replaced until all collaborators became test data.

Table 5 shows the average accuracy of the models that were tested using stratified k-partition cross-validation (k = 10).

Table 5. Model building results using stratified k-partition cross-validation (k = 10).

	SVM (%)	Logistic regression (%)
Mutual Information	60.0	61.4
Random Forest Variable Importance (classification)	62.0	59.7
Random Forest Variable Importance (regression)	71.6	66.1

Table 5 shows that the model of SVM using the feature selection results of the regression of variable importance of random forests as explanatory variables showed the greatest accuracy at 71.6%. This accuracy is more than 5% higher than that of Je-Eon et al.'s model, which was constructed using only a single-channel electroencephalograph to estimate cognitive function. This indicates that the use of the heart rate variability indexes in addition to EEG improves the accuracy of the model for estimating cognitive function in the elderly.

Next, Table 6 shows the confusion matrix of the SVM with the feature selection results of the regression of random forest variable importance as explanatory variables.

In Table 6, the reproducibility is used to check the estimation level. Reproducibility is a value that indicates the degree to which a given correct value is correctly estimated. In

Table 6. Confusion matrix of SVM model with feature selection results of random forest variable importance (regression) as explanatory variables (stratified k-partition cross-validation (k = 10))

		prediction		
		Dementia	Mild Dementia	Without Dementia
actual	Dementia	3058	491	805
	Mild Dementia	1308	109	426
	Without Dementia	946	581	7

this case, for example, it shows the percentage of correctly predicted dementia out of the data of actual dementia. The results showed that the estimates were almost always incorrect for mild dementia and no dementia: 0.702 for dementia, 0.059 for mild dementia, and 0.005 for no dementia.

One of the reasons for this is that the amount of data for mild dementia and no dementia is relatively small compared to the amount of data for dementia.

Table 7 shows the average accuracy of the models that were tested for accuracy in the LOSO cross-validation.

Table 7. Model building results using LOSO cross-validation.

	SVM (%)	Logistic regression (%)
Mutual Information	43.9	46.7
Random Forest Variable Importance (classification)	44.2	44.5
Random Forest Variable Importance (regression)	39.3	44.7

Table 7 shows that the LOSO cross-validation resulted in an accuracy of about 40% for all methods.

The reason for the nearly 30% drop in accuracy for all methods compared to the stratified k-fold cross-validation is the large individual differences in biometric information for each collaborator. When looking at the accuracy of the test data for each collaborator, there were more than seven subjects with an accuracy of zero for all methods. On the other hand, there were also test data from collaborators with 100% accuracy. The fact that the accuracy varied greatly depending on the data used as the test data suggests that the accuracy may have decreased due to large individual differences.

5 Conclusion

In this study, we constructed a cognitive function estimation model for the elderly using the results of EEG, heart rate variability, and neuropsychological examination. Based on the results of the regression analysis of variable importance in random forests, the features important for model construction were used as explanatory variables, and the cognitive function estimation model constructed using SVM achieved an accuracy of 71.6%. This result was about 5% higher than that of the model constructed by the previous study from Jo-Eon et al. using the results of single-channel EEG and language examination. On the other hand, the confusion matrix tends to incorrectly classify mild dementia and no dementia, so we will examine methods to construct a model that can correctly classify mild dementia and no dementia. In addition, when looking at the results using LOSO cross-validation, the accuracy of all methods was almost 30% lower than when accuracy was verified using stratified k-partition cross-validation (k = 10).

Acknowledgment. The authors would like to thank the staff members of the "Care Home for the Elderly Sawayaka Kinu no Sato Shinshu Okaya" for their cooperation in this experiment, the subjects and their families, Mr. Yosuke Uchida and Mr. Eiji Otsuka of TPR Corporation for their support in conducting this experiment.

References

1. Cabinet Office. Health and Welfare of the Elderly. https://www8.cao.go.jp/kourei/whitepaper/w-2016/html/gaiyou/s1_2_3.html. See 14 Feb 2022
2. Overshott, R., Burns, A.: Treatment of dementia. J. Neurol. Neurosurg. Psychiatry **76**(suppl 5), P53–P59 (2005)
3. Petersen, R.C., et al.: Practice parameter: early detection of dementia: mild cognitive impairment (an evidence-based review). Neurology **56**, 1133–1142 (2001)
4. Lee, J.-E., Park, J., You, S.: Combining single-channel EEG measurement and verbal fluency test—a groundwork for ambulatory diagnosis of dementia. In: 14th International Conference on Ubiquitous Robots and Ambient Intelligence (URAI) (2017)
5. Alharbi, E., Alomainy, A.: Machine learning approach to predict cognitive performance using HRV. In: 2022 2nd International Conference on Computing and Information Technology (ICCIT), pp. 25–27 (2022)
6. Alacao, S.M., Fonseca, M.J.: Emotion recognition using EEG signals: a survey. IEEE Trans. Affect. Comput. 1–12 (2017)
7. Alharbi, E., Alomainy, A., Jones, J.M.: Detecting cognitive decline in early Alzheimer's patients using wearable technologies. In: IEEE International Conference on Healthcare Informatics (ICHI) (2020)
8. Lopes, M., et al.: Semantic verbal fluency test in dementia preliminary retrospective analysis. Dement. Neuropsychol. **3**, 315–320 (2009)
9. Vapnik, V., Lerner, A.: Pattern recognition using generalized portrait method. Autom. Remote Control **24** (1963)
10. Cox, D.R.: The regression analysis of binary sequences. J. R. Stat. Soc. Ser. B (Methodol.) **20**(2), 215–242 (1958)
11. Khosla, A., Khandnor, P., Chand, T.: A comparative analysis of signal processing and classification methods for different applications based on EEG signals. Biocybern. Biomed. Eng. **40**(2), 649–690 (2020)
12. Upton, J.: Mini-Mental State Examination. Encyclopedia of Behavioral Medicine, pp. 1248–1249 (1975)
13. Shannon, C.E.: A mathematical theory of communication. Bell Syst. Tech. J. **27**, 379–423, 623–656 (1948)
14. Breiman, L.: Random forests. Mach. Learn. **45**, 5–32 (2001)
15. Kei, S., Tipporn, L., Ryota, M., Midori, S.: Constructing an emotion estimation model based on EEG/HRV indexes using feature extraction and feature selection algorithms. Sensors **21**(9), 2910 (2021)

Attitudes and Use of Health Information and Communication Technology Among Older Adults' in Iceland - Changes from 2019 to 2022

Ágústa Pálsdóttir[(⊠)]

School of Social Sciences, Information Science, University of Iceland, Oddi v/Sæmundargötu, 101 Reykjavík, Iceland
agustap@hi.is

Abstract. The paper examined adoption of a national healthcare ICT system as well as experience of the possibilities to adopt ICT, among Icelanders' aged 56 years and older. Data gathered in 2019 and in 2022 were compared to reveal possible changes during this period. The following research questions were asked: (1) How motivated are people towards health information? (2) What opinions do people have about the usefulness of ICT for obtaining information about their own health? (3) How has the adoption of the national healthcare system to seek information in relation to people's own health, and about various other health issues, developed in the period 2019 to 2022? (4) How has peoples experience of adopting ICT, and receiving help at using it, developed in the period 2019 to 2022? Random samples were used, and data gathered by telephone surveys and internet surveys from 173 people in 2019 and 214 in 2022. For each year the datasets were merged. The total response rate was 39% in 2019 and 45% in 2022. The main findings are that there was a positive development in the use of the healthcare system for being in contact with health professionals and to gain information tailored to people's health. Although people were in general motivated towards health information, the use of the system for information about healthy living and other health issues remained extremely low in the period. In 2019 the options for adopting ICT were not considered satisfactory but an important change happened in the period as majority of participants considered their possibilities for it to be good in 2022. They, furthermore, believed that using ICT made it easier for them to get information related to their own health.

Keywords: adoption of ICT · Covid-19 · healthcare systems · older adults

1 Introduction

This paper examines information behaviour in relation to progress in the adoption of information and communication technology (ICT) for healthcare services in Iceland for people aged 56 years and older, as well as and how they perceive their possibilities to adopt ICT. Results from surveys conducted in 2019 and 2022 will be compared, thus the emphasis is on the development that has happened in this period. Furthermore,

Q. Gao and J. Zhou (Eds.): HCII 2024, LNCS 14726, pp. 64–77, 2024.
https://doi.org/10.1007/978-3-031-61546-7_5

differences by sex will be examined. The start of a retirement age is sometimes used to define "elderly" in Western countries [1]. Retirement age varies, however, between countries, it starts for example at 58 years in Lithuania, while in Iceland people can retire at the age of 65 [2, 3]. Thus, defining older age by retirement age is rather arbitrary. Considering that there is no clearly defined age when people become older adults it was decided to examine people who have reached the age of 56 years and older.

The options of producing, disseminating, and accessing health information have been rapidly changed by ICT, a development that can be expected to continue in the coming years. In recent decades, attention has increasingly focused on the use of ICT within healthcare and the potentials that it can bring.

It has been pointed out that it is possible to use ICT to bring the healthcare system closer to people. For example, poor accessibility because of geographical isolation, or other difficulties that make it problematic for people, or even hinders them, in using healthcare service on-site, can be countered using ICT. [4, 5]. Furthermore, it has been mentioned that individuals can be empowered to become more involved in their own healthcare through enhanced digital information and communication exchange between them and healthcare professionals, with information that is tailored to the needs of the individual [6]. Hence, for people to be able to actively manage their health and improve their health behaviour, it is imperative that they can access quality health information that satisfy their needs.

Previous studies have reported about favourable use of health ICT for communication and support by healthcare professionals. It has been noted that it holds several benefits for people, such as leading to better health knowledge and improvements in health behaviour [7], as well as having promoted participation in self-care by the individuals [7, 8]. In addition, a relationship which is based more on partnership and mutual decision making may become possible, which in turn can improve the quality of the healthcare service [6].

The importance of ICT for health information exchange between individuals and healthcare professionals was further revealed at the outbreak of COVID-19 in 2020 [9]. In response to the pandemic and, in order to limit the possible transmission of infection and the risk of COVID-19, people in various countries were recommended to use ICT for communication rather than visiting healthcare clinics [10–12].

Although studies have found that healthcare ICT can benefit older people in various ways it is known that it can also pose challenges [13]. It is important that they possess the informational and technological competence which is needed to take advantage of health ICT [14]. It is equally important that people are confident that they have the support which is necessary for taking technology into use [15]. This is particularly essential for older adults who may need to rely on assistance from relatives, even though they find it difficult to ask them for help and may have a certain reluctance to do so [16, 17]. Other factors that can have positive effects on people's willingness to engage in using healthcare ICT include the belief that it will satisfy their need for information, and that the use of it will be beneficial and valuable for them [18–20].

In addition, demographic factors, such as age [21–24], education [21, 24], and sex [23, 24], have been reported to be associated with the use of healthcare ICT. Studies have in general found that women, people with better education, and those who are younger use healthcare ICT more than men, less educated people, and older adults.

Better understanding of the growth in the use of healthcare ICT and the factors that can affect the adoption of it has been called for [25]. It is in particular important to promote knowledge about older adults.

Cconditions in Iceland for obtaining digital health information can be considered excellent because of a widespread access to the Internet [26]. It, nevertheless, needs to be kept in mind that access to the Internet does not necessarily translate into the use of digital health information [27], thus other aspects related to the use of health technology need also to be considered. Steps have been taken to improve access to health information in Iceland. In 2009, a new legal framework was set to ensure people the right to access to their health history through their health records, however many of the files are not yet in a digital form [28]. In addition, a national ICT system, which is a multipurpose tool, has been developed. Through the system's website, access to a wide range of information from health professionals about diseases, health issues and healthy lifestyle is being offered. Thus, the Website allows users the opportunity to seek, examine, and gain knowledge from reliable health sources. The system is also a communication system for health professionals and the users. This part of the system offers various functions that provide a possibility for people to get various health information tailored to their own needs. It allows people, for example, to book appointments with their physicians or other specialists, drug prescriptions can be examined and requests for renewal sent, history of vaccinations can be observed, and short questions or comments can be sent to physicians and answers from them received. During opening hours, a health professional is available for webchat. Some parts of people's health history are already being recorded into the system daily, while other types of access are still under development. This includes for example health records made during doctors' appointments, which are not accessible yet through the system [29].

1.1 Aim and Research Questions

The paper aims to examine the adoption of a national healthcare ICT system in Iceland, as well as the experience of the possibilities to adopt ICT, among Icelanders'. Who have reached the age of 56 years and older?

Data gathered in 2019 and in 2022 will be compared to reveal possible changes during this period. The following research questions were asked:

1. How motivated are people towards health information?
2. What opinions do people have about the usefulness of ICT for obtaining information about their own health?
3. How has the adoption of the national healthcare system to seek information in relation to people's own health, and about various other health issues, developed in the period 2019 to 2022?
4. How has peoples experience of adopting ICT, and receiving help at using it, developed in the period 2019 to 2022?

The purpose of addressing this is to understand better how people can benefit from development in health ICT and thereby enhance their abilities to become more engaged in their own healthcare. A better understanding of factors that relate to this can have implications for digital health care services and be used by health professionals and health authorities to work on improvements as needed.

2 Methods

Quantitative methods were chosen, and surveys conducted in 2019 and 2022.

2.1 Data Collection

For each survey, the data were gathered from two random samples from the National Register of Persons in Iceland, using internet and telephone surveys. The surveys were conducted in January 2019 and in July 2022. In 2019 the total sample size was 1.800 people, 18 years and older. For the telephone survey, a random sample of 300 people aged 60 years and older was used, while for the internet survey a random sample of 1.500 people at the age of 18 to 59 years was used. In 2022 the total sample consisted of 1.200 hundred people, 18 years and older. The telephone survey used a random sample of 300 people aged 60 years and older and for the internet survey a random sample of 900 people at the age of 18 to 59 years was used.

For the telephone surveys in both years, samples randomly selected from the National Register of Persons in Iceland were used. For the internet surveys, random samples from the Social Science Research Institute at the University of Iceland net panel, was used. The net panel is based on a random sample from the National Register of Persons in Iceland and consists of people aged 18 years or older from the whole country who has agreed to participate in online surveys organized by the organization. For the surveys each year, both datasets (internet and telephone surveys) were merged, allowing answers from all individuals belonging to each set of data. The total response rate was 39% in 2019 and in 2022 it was 45%.

The focus of the paper is only on people that are 56 years or older. In 2019 the number of participants in that age group was 173 and in 2022 it was 214.

2.2 Measurements and Data Analysis

In addition to the background variables, sex, age, education and residence, the measurements for the part of the surveys presented in the paper consisted of one question asked only in 2019 and one asked only in 2022, as well as four questions that were examined in 2019 and in 2022:

1. Motivation for receiving health information was examined by two questions in 019. A five-point response scale was used (Very interested/often – Very low interest/Seldom or never).
   a. How interested are you in information about health issues?
   b. How often do you discuss health issues with others?

2. Attitudes towards the usefulness of ICT for getting health information was measured by one question asked in 2022, in the form of a statement: ICT makes it easier for me to get knowledge about my health. A five-point response scale was used for both statements (Strongly agree – Strongly disagree):
3. The use of the healthcare ICT system was examined by two questions. A five-point response scale was used for both questions (Very often – Never):
   a. The participants use of the healthcare ICT system in relation to their own health was examined by the question: How often or seldom have you used Heilsuveru to communicate with health professionals or to get information about your own health (e.g. due to appointments, renew drug prescriptions, or send a message to your family physician)?
   b. The use of the system to seek information about various health issues was examined by the question: How often or rarely have you used Heilsuveru to get information about a healthy lifestyle, such as nutrition or exercise, or other health related issues?
4. The possibilities of taking new health ICT in use were examined by two questions which were in the form of statements. A five-point response scale was used for both statements (Strongly agree – Strongly disagree):
   a. I find it difficult to adopt new technologies.
   b. I can easily get help using ICT if needed.

Because of the response rate in the studies, the data for both years were weighted by sex (male, female), age in six categories, residence (within or outside the capital area) and education (primary, secondary, university) of participants so that it corresponds with the distribution in the population. Reference figures for age, sex and place of residence were obtained from the National Registry of Iceland and for level of education from Statistics Iceland. Ranking method was used, with 5 as upper limit and 0.2 as lower limit. Based on previous analyses of the data it was decided to use sex for the examination. The analysis of the data is descriptive, and all analyses are based on weighed data. Survey results from 2019 and 2022 will be compared.

3   Results

The section starts by introducing results from 2019 about the participants motivation towards health information, and results from 2022 about their opinion of the usefulness of ICT for health information related to their own health. After that, a comparison of the results from 2019 and 2022, about the development in the use of the national healthcare ICT system are presented, as well as the development in their possibilities to adopt health ICT.

Figure 1 shows that the participants are in general motivated towards getting health information. Majority of both men and women claimed to be interested in information. However, there was a difference by sex ($p < 0.010$), with women being more interested than men. In addition, majority of women and close to half of men discussed the topic often with others. Difference by sex was not significant ($p = .084$).

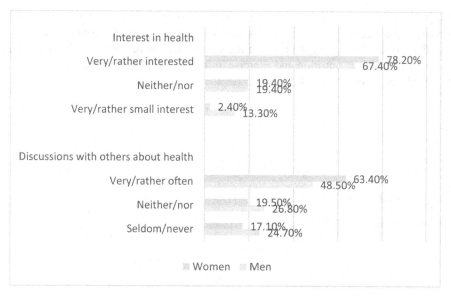

Fig. 1. Motivation towards health information

In 2022, the participants were asked to give their opinion about the statement: ICT makes it easier for me to get knowledge about my health.

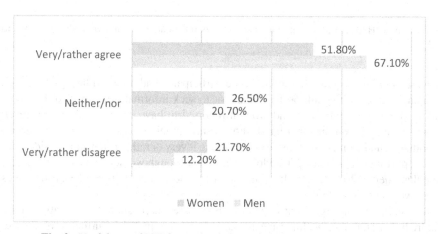

Fig. 2. Usefulness of ICT for getting information about people's own health

As can be seen in Fig. 2, the majority of the participants were of the opinion that ICT made it easier for them to get information about their own health. Although men were more in agreement with this than women, difference by sex was not significant (p = .111).

Two questions examined the participants use of the national health ICT system. One of the questions asked how often they had used it for activities such as to communicate with health professionals to get information in relation to their own health (e.g. booking appointments, renewing prescriptions, or sending messages to their physician). In addition, they were asked about their use of the system to seek information about various health issues, such as nutrition and exercise, or other health related issues. The results are introduced in Figs. 3 and 4.

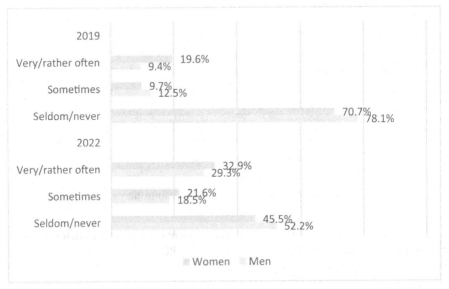

Fig. 3. Use of 'Heilsuvera' to communicate and seek information about own health in 2019 and 2022

Results in Fig. 3 show that in 2019, the participants had not used the system much to communicate with health professionals, or to seek information related to their own health. Majority of both men and women reported to have done so seldom or never. Results from 2022, on the other hand, show a substantial increase in use of the system, for both men and women, with more people using it very or rather often and considerably fewer reporting that they used it seldom or never. Although women had used the system more than men in 2019 (p = .108), and somewhat more in 2022 (p = .663), differences by sex were not significant.

As can be seen in Fig. 4, participants of both sexes rarely sought information about healthy living and other health issues through the system in 2019. Furthermore, the use of the system continued to be very low in 2022 and was almost identical to what it was as in 2019. No significant difference was found between men and women, neither in 2019 (p = .306) nor in 2022 (p = .495).

In addition, the participants were asked how difficult it had been for them to adopt new ICT, and about their possibilities of getting assistance at using technology. Results about the statement "I find it difficult to adopt new technologies" are presented in Fig. 5.

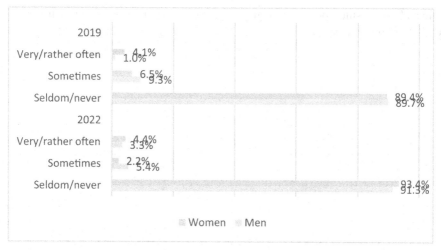

Fig. 4. Use of 'Heilsuvera' to seek information about health issues in 2019 and 2022

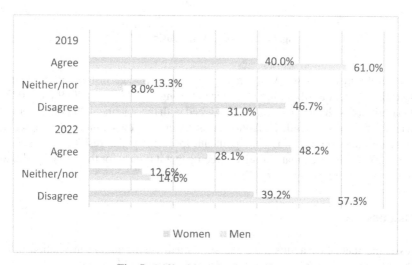

Fig. 5. Difficulties adopting new ICT

Figure 5 shows that there are substantial changes between 2019 and 2022 in how difficult participants found it to adopt health ICT. In 2019, there was a significant difference by sex (p < 0.010), with men in particularly agreed that this is difficult, while women were considerably less likely to do so. Results for women were though more mixed, with a similar rate of them agreeing that it is difficult as disagreeing to it. In 2022, however, the results for men are reversed, with majority of them disagreeing to this. The results for women, on the other hand, show that the rate of those who agree that it is difficult to adopt ICT has gone up and for those who disagree has gone down. Difference by sex was significant (p < 0.010).

In addition, results about the statement "I can easily get help at using ICT if needed" are introduced in Fig. 6.

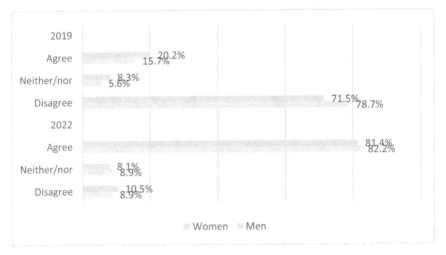

Fig. 6. Getting get help at using ICT

The results in Fig. 6 show that there was a huge change in how the participants assessed their potential of getting assistance at using ICT between 2019 and 2022. In 2019 majority of both men and women disagreed with the statement "It is easy for me to get help at using ICT if needed". Although men were somewhat more in disagreement than women the difference was not significant (p = .510). The results were, however, reverse in 2022, with the great majority agreeing that it is easy for them to get help, with no significant difference by sex (p = .930).

4 Discussion

It is essential that older adults have access to quality information in relation to their health and healthy lifestyle so that they can make informed health decisions. ICT can open possibilities for them to retrieve more information relevant to their needs, as well as offering new ways to communicate with health professionals.

Results from the study in 2019 show that the participants were in general motivated towards getting health information, particularly women who were significantly more interested in information than men. Despite of this, the great majority of both men and women had hardly ever used the healthcare system to seek information about healthy living and other health issues, neither in 2019 nor in 2022. It is essential that people seek and use health information from trustworthy sources. In particular because of the increase in disinformation and misinformation about various health issues [1]. It is therefore vital that health authorities focus on the promotion of this part of the system, so that people understand that it offers access to quality information from health experts.

Majority of the participants had rarely used the system for communicating with health professionals, or to get information tailored towards their own health, in 2019. There was, however, an important change in 2022, with a higher rate of both men and women reporting that they had often or very often used the system for this, and considerably lower rate of people claiming to have used it seldom or never.

The healthcare system had not been introduced much in 2019 and in most of the health clinics in Iceland it had been in use for a relatively short time. Considering this it is not particularly surprising that it was used so rarely. It needs to be kept in mind that when a new system is put into use it takes some time to, first introduce it to people, and secondly, engage people in adopting it. Furthermore, to encourage adoption people need to be helped to deal with various challenges that come with new technology. Among other things, they must be convinced that the use of it will provide them with valuable information tailored to their own needs, and that it will be beneficial for them to adopt it [13, 18]. When Covid-19 happened in 2020 more was done to promote the system and the pressure on people to use it increased. This is similar to what was done in various other countries, where people were encouraged to use ICT for health communication rather than visit healthcare clinics on-site [10–12]. The system was used to promote information about Covid-19, for example to book appointments for testing for Covid-19, for receiving test results, and to order certificates. And on the whole people were recommended to use it more, not only for information about Covid-19 but for information related to their health in general. Thus, the explanation for the increased use of the system can, at least partly, be the fact that people were advised to, if possible, to use it rather than visiting the health clinics.

In 2022, majority of the participants believed that using ICT made it easier for them to get information related to their own health. This is of relevance, it has been reported that if people believe that the use of ICT is likely to be beneficial for them and satisfy their need for information, it may have positive effects on how willing they are to engage in using it [18–20].

Other factors that can have a bearing on how ready people are to adopt ICT is their belief in being able to handle it [14], as well as their confidence at having the support which is necessary for taking technology into use [15–17]. The examination of participants experiences of adopting new ICT shows that it had changed considerably from 2019 to 2022. There was a significant difference by sex, with majority of men finding it challenging to start using new ICT in 2019, while women were much more confident about their abilities regarding it. This had, however, changed in 2022, when majority of men did not consider this difficult, while the rate of women who claimed that it was hard had gone up. It is unclear what caused this change. It is possible that men have gained more confident through increased use of the healthcare system, but then the same should have applied for women which does not seem to be the case.

Furthermore, there was a huge change in how people assessed their possibilities of getting assistance at using ICT. In 2019, majority of participants considered it difficult to get help at using ICT, but in 2022 they claimed that when they needed assistance at using technology, they could easily get it. Having an easy access to assistance at using technology is imperative and can make a difference in whether older people adopt technology and how much it is used [15–17]. Thus, something happened during those years that changed the picture in a very positive way, that helped people to adopt new health ICT.

5   Conclusion, Limitations and Policy Implications

To explore how people aged 56 years and older had adopted a national healthcare ICT system, as well as the experience of the possibilities to do so, the study asked four research questions. The relationship to sex was, furthermore, explored for all the questions. The purpose was to understand better how ICT can benefit people and enhance their abilities to become more engaged in their own healthcare. For policy implications, a better understanding of factors that relate to this can have implications for digital healthcare services and be used by health professionals and health authorities to work on improvements as needed.

The first research question of the study asked: How motivated are people towards health information? The results show that the participants were in general motivated towards getting health information, in particular women who were significantly more interested in health information than men. Secondly, the study asked: What opinions do people have about the usefulness of ICT for obtaining information about their own health? The study found that majority of the participants believed that using ICT made it easier for them to get information related to their own health. No significant difference was detected by sex.

The third research question asked: How has the adoption of the national healthcare system to seek information in relation to people's own health, and about various other health issues, developed in the period 2019 to 2022? The results revealed a positive development in the use of it for being in contact with health professionals and to gain information tailored to people's health. The increase in use of the system in 2022 was substantial for both men and women, a significant difference by sex was not detected. Furthermore, despite people being motivated towards health information, there was no increase in the use of the system for obtaining various high-quality information from health professionals regarding issues that were not directly connected to their health history. Both in 2019 and 2022 information about healthy living and other health issues were rarely sought, with no significant difference by sex. Because the system offers reliable information that can be used to make informed decisions about healthy living, it is essential that health authorities put an effort into introducing this part of the system better.

Finally, the study asked: How has people's experience of adopting ICT, and receiving help at using it, developed in the period 2019 to 2022? A significant difference was detected by sex. In 2022, majority of men did not consider it demanding to adopt ICT, which is the opposite of the results in 2019, while women were more likely to find this difficult in 2022 than in 2019. Furthermore, when asked about the possibility of getting assistance at using ICT there was a huge change with the great majority of both men and women claiming their possibilities to be good in 2022, which is opposite to the results in 2019. Thus, overall, the study found that an important change had happened in this period. This was particularly the case regarding the option of having access to help at adopting technologies, which can be regarded as an important factor.

The overall studies are limited by a total response rate of 39% in 2019 and 45% in 2022. To compensate for this and reduce the impact of non-response bias, the data were weighed by gender, age, place of residence and education, so that it corresponds with the distribution in the population. The findings may, therefore, offer valuable information about the changes in adoption of new ICT among older Icelanders'.

The outbreak of Covid-19 highlighted the importance of healthcare ICT for information exchange between individuals and healthcare professionals. The period during which Covid-19 was active began in the early year of 2020, that is, after the first data collection took place, and was still ongoing when data for the second survey was collected. It is not possible to assert that the conditions during Covid-19, when it became more important for people to use technology for health information, caused a positive change in older people's perception of their possibilities to adopt health ICT. Nevertheless, it can be assumed that the Covid-19 situation, together with the fact that people had had more time to become knowledgeable about the healthcare system, were among the influencing factors. Thus, the results of the study indicate that older people are likely to use health ICT when the situation requires it, and they receive the necessary support to do so.

Acknowledgments. The research project was supported by the University of Iceland Research Fund.

References

1. Thane, P.: History and the sociology of ageing. Soc. Hist. Med. **2**(1), 93–96 (1989)
2. Social Insurance Administration: 65 years+. https://www.tr.is/en/65-years
3. OECD: OECD Pensions at a Glance 2021: OECD and G20 Indicators. OECD Publishing, Paris (2021). https://doi.org/10.1787/ca401ebd-en
4. Alvarez, R.C.: The promise of e-Health: a Canadian perspective. EHealth Int. **1**(1), 4 (2002). https://ehealthinternational.biomedcentral.com/articles/https://doi.org/10.1186/1476-3591-1-4
5. Shao, M., Fan, J., Huang, Z., Chen, M.: The impact of information and communication technologies (ICTs) on health outcomes: a mediating effect analysis based on cross-national panel data. J. Environ. Public Health **2022**, 2225723 (2022). https://doi.org/10.1155/2022/2225723
6. Eysenbach, G.: What is e-health? J. Med. Internet Res. **3**(2) (2001). https://doi.org/10.2196/jmir.3.2
7. Tapuria, A., Porat, T., Kalra, D., Dsouza, G., Xiaohui, S., Curcin, V.: Impact of patient access to their electronic health record: systematic review. Inform. Health Soc. Care **46**(2), 194–206 (2021). https://doi.org/10.1080/17538157.2021.1879810
8. Lindberg, B., Nilsson, C., Zotterman, D., Söderberg, S., Skär, L.: Using information and communication technology in home care for communication between patients, family members, and healthcare professionals: a systematic review. Int. J. Telemed. Appl. **2013**, Article ID 461829 (2013). https://doi.org/10.1155/2013/461829
9. Budd, J., Miller, B.S., Manning, E.M., et al.: Digital technologies in the public-health response to COVID-19. Nat. Med. **26**, 1183–1192 (2020). https://doi.org/10.1038/s41591-020-1011-4
10. Ortegaa, G., et al.: Telemedicine, COVID-19, and disparities: policy implications. Health Policy Technol. **9**, 368–371 (2020). https://doi.org/10.3389/fpubh.2020.556720

11. Bhaskar, S., et al.: Telemedicine, Covid 19, and disparities: policy implications. Health Policy Technol. **16**(8), 556720 (2020). https://doi.org/10.3389/fpubh.2020.556720

12. Murphy, M., Scott, L.J., Salisbury, C., et al.: Implementation of remote consulting in UK primary care following the COVID-19 pandemic: a mixed-methods longitudinal study. Br. J. Gen. Pract. **71**(704), e167 (2021). https://doi.org/10.3399/BJGP.2020.0948

13. Arsad, F.S., et al.: The impact of eHealth applications in healthcare intervention: a systematic review. J. Health Res. **37**(3), 178–189 (2023)

14. Bol, N., van Weert, J.C., Loos, E.F., Romano Bergstrom, J.C., Bolle, S., Smets, E.M.: How are online health messages processed? Using eye tracking to predict recall of information in younger and older adults. J. Health Commun. **21**(4), 387–396 (2016). https://doi.org/10. 1080/10810730.2015.1080327

15. Anderson, M., Perrin, A.: Tech adoption climbs among older adults: roughly two-thirds of those ages 65 and older go online and a record share now own smartphones: although many seniors remain relatively divorced from digital life. Pew Research Centre (2017). https://www. pewinternet.org/2017/05/17/tech-adoption-climbs-among-older-adults/

16. Pálsdóttir, Á.: Elderly peoples' information behaviour: accepting support from relatives. Libri: Int. J. Libr. Inf. Serv. **62**(2), 135–144 (2012a)

17. Pálsdóttir, Á.: Relatives as supporters of elderly peoples' information behavior. Inf. Res. **17**(4), paper 546 (2012b). http://InformationR.net/ir/17-4/paper546.html

18. Gu, D., et al.: Assessing the adoption of e-Health technology in a developing country: an extension of the UTAUT model. SAGE Open **11**(3), 215824402110275 (2021). https://doi. org/10.1177/21582440211027565

19. Jimison, H., et al.: Barriers and Drivers of Health Information Technology Use for the Elderly, Chronically Ill, and Underserved. Evidence Report/Technology Assessment No. 175. AHRQ Publication No. 09-E004. Agency for Healthcare Research and Quality: Rockville, MD (2008)

20. Loos, E.: Senior citizens: digital immigrants in their own country? Observatorio **6**(1), 1–23 (2012)

21. Kontos, E., Blake, K.D., Chou, W.Y.S., Prestin, A.: Predictors of eHealth usage: insights on the digital divide from the health information national trends survey 2012. J. Med. Internet Res. **16**(7), e172 (2014). https://doi.org/10.2196/jmir.3117

22. Sun, R., Wu, L., Barnett, S., Deyo, P., Swartwout, E.: Socio-demographic predictors associated with capacity to engage in health care. Patient Experience J. **6**(2), 35–41 (2019). https://doi. org/10.35680/2372-0247.1355

23. Sana, S., Kollmann, J., Magnée, T., Merkelbach, I., Denktaş, S., Kocken, P.L.: The role of socio-demographic and health factors during COVID-19 in remote access to GP Care in low-income neighbourhoods: a cross-sectional survey of GP patients. BMC Primary Care **23**, 289 (2022). https://doi.org/10.1186/s12875-022-01887-5

24. Ali, M.A., Alama, K., Taylor, B.: Determinants of ICT usage for healthcare among people with disabilities: the moderating role of technological and behavioural constraints. J. Biomed. Inform. **108**, 103480 (2020). https://doi.org/10.1016/j.jbi.2020.103480

25. da Fonseca, M.H., Kovaleski, F., Picinin, C.T., Pedroso, B., Rubbo, P.: E-Health practices and technologies: a systematic review from 2014 to 2019. Healthcare (Basel) **9**(9), 1192 (2021). https://doi.org/10.3390/healthcare9091192.PMID:34574966;PMCID:PMC8470487

26. Statistics Iceland: Computer and Internet Usage in Iceland and Other European Countries 2013. Statistical Series: Tourism, Transport and IT 2014, 1 (2014). https://hagstofa.is/utgafur/ utgafa/visindi-og-taekni/tolvu-og-netnotkun-a-islandi-og-i-odrum-evropulondum-2013/

27. Ono, H., Zavodny, M.: Digital inequality: a five-country comparison using microdata. Soc. Sci. Res. **36**(3), 1135–1155 (2007)

28. Health Records Act nr. 55, 27 April 2009. https://www.government.is/media/velferdarradune yti-media/media/acrobat-enskar_sidur/Health-Records-Act-No-55-2009-as-amended-2016. pdf

29. Directory of Health: Heilsuvera: Mínar Heilbrigðisupplýsingar (2016). https://www.landla eknir.is/gaedi-og-eftirlit/heilbrigdisthjonusta/rafraen-sjukraskra/heilsuvera-minar-heilbrigd isupplysingar/
30. WHO. Fighting misinformation in the time of CoVID-19, one click at the time (2020). https://www.who.int/news-room/feature-stories/detail/fighting-misinformation-in-the-time-of-covid-19-one-click-at-a-time

Family Care Partner Perceptions of a Social Assistive Robot to Support Connectedness and Health Behaviors in Assisted Living

Shannon R. Power[1]([envelope]) [ID], Kasey N. Smith[2] [ID], Reuben Abedine[1], Lydia M. Burton[3], Anne E. Adams[2], and Jenay M. Beer[3] [ID]

[1] University of Georgia School of Social Work, 279 Williams Street, Athens, GA 30605, USA
shannonpower@uga.edu
[2] SimpleC LLC, 611 Campbell Hill Street, NW #105, Marietta, GA 30060, USA
research@simplec.com
[3] University of Georgia Institute of Gerontology, 102 Spear Road, Athens, GA 30602, USA

Abstract. Social assistive robots (SAR) have potential to offer social and cognitive engagement for older adults residing in assisted living facilities. There is a need for expanded socialization opportunities for residents with or at risk for dementia given the growing rate of dementia and limited professional caregiving workforce. This was an exploratory study investigating family care partners' first impressions and feedback on SAR (both physical and virtual robot) technology during development. The goal was to capture family care partner attitudes (positive, negative, mixed) and recommendations of SAR. Family care partners (n = 10) viewed videos of SAR interactions and participated in online semi-structured discussions. Qualitative content analysis identified predominately positive attitudes of SAR benefit ($f = 111$) over concerns ($f = 65$) or mixed opinions ($f = 39$). These attitudes and recommendations ($f = 256$) were analyzed using a codebook created from foundational technology acceptance models. Perceived usefulness/function was the leading theme across benefits, concerns, and recommendations, which is aligned with previous findings of it being a predictive factor for technology adoption. Future research should explore customization of SAR for persons with cognitive impairment, adapting usefulness/function for disease progression.

Keywords: Social Assistive Robot · Perceived Usefulness · Social Engagement · Dementia · Caregiving

1 Introduction

1.1 Literature Review

The world's population is getting older. In 2022 alone, 771 million people worldwide were 65 years and older, accounting for nearly 10% of the world's population [1]. This percentage is expected to grow to 16% by 2050, for an estimated 2.1 billion adults over the age of 60, and 24% by 2100 [1, 2]. Following global trends, older adults are the fastest growing population in the United States [1, 3].

Q. Gao and J. Zhou (Eds.): HCII 2024, LNCS 14726, pp. 78–97, 2024.
https://doi.org/10.1007/978-3-031-61546-7_6

As of 2011, over 10,000 people reach the age of 65 each day [4], and one out of every nine of those adults develops Alzheimer's disease [5]. An estimated 6.7 million Americans aged 65+ are living with Alzheimer's disease as of 2023, which is projected to more than double to 13.8 million by 2060 pending the development of treatments that prevent, cure, or hinder the progression of Alzheimer's disease or a related dementia [5].

Dementia is an umbrella term used to represent a variety of often progressive diseases that affect the brain, with Alzheimer's disease contributing to the majority (60–70%) of cases [6]. In 2019 alone, dementia cost the global economy 1.3 trillion US dollars, with approximately 50% of these costs being covered by informal care partners, such as family members and close friends [6].

Living with dementia is both physically and mentally demanding, often leading to isolation of both caregivers and persons living with dementia [7, 8]. Dementia-related behaviors are a major cause of social isolation for persons living with dementia with disease progression, leading to poor physical and mental health, and a reduced quality of life [7, 9–11]. Furthermore, more than half of all family care partners live with or develop a physical or mental disorder themselves, with over a quarter of family caregivers experiencing severe depression [5].

For many persons living with dementia and their care partners, one choice is to seek professional care in residential care units, such as assisted living facilities. In the United States, assisted living is one of the most rapidly growing housing options for older adults with or at risk for dementia [1, 3]. Roughly 81% of residents in smaller homes and 63% in larger, well-funded facilities are living with dementia [12]. Nearly 75% of persons living with dementia spend time in an assisted living facility or in a nursing home [13]. Assisted living facilities provide an abundant experience of socialization, necessary assistance, and relief for both care partners and persons living with dementia [14, 15].

Outside of assistance with tasks of daily living, assisted living facilities address an often-underserved need of persons living with dementia: social engagement. Social engagement is a core element of healthy aging and quality of life in older persons [14–16]. Assisted living facilities provide ample opportunity for social engagement such as group entertainment and dining, where many residents forge friendships with their peers in residential units [14, 15]. These relationships often lead to a reduction in symptoms of depression among older adults living in residential care settings [14].

Despite the benefits of assistive care, assisted living facilities are often stretched thin in terms of staffing manpower to meet resident needs [17]. In 2019, the United States Federal Government proposed new requirements on minimum nurse staffing and time spent per staff member per resident [17]. The proposed congressional bill stated that skilled nursing facilities are expected to spend 4.1 total hours per resident per day, but as of 2019, only 25% of skilled nursing facilities have met this proposed minimum [17]. To meet the federally proposed requirements, an estimated additional 35,804 registered nurses, 3,509 licensed practical nurses, and 116,929 certified nursing assistants would need to enter the assisted living facility workforce, costing an estimated $7.25 billion annually in salary costs [17]. With current staffing limitations, assisted living facilities and their employees may benefit from assistive technology that offers residents social and cognitive engagement opportunities autonomously.

Social assistive robots (SAR) have much potential to provide social and cognitive engagement for older adults with and at risk for dementia in assisted living facilities. SARs is a field of robotics that focuses on assisting users through social interaction [18]. Because of their wide range of abilities, SARs are a good candidate for placement in assisted living facilities by interacting with residents in both individual and group settings, providing dialogue and entertainment, promoting cognitive engagement such as games, and tailoring those experiences through artificial intelligence [19]. Thus, SARs have potential to supplement the engagement from staff members, allowing staff more effective time management. For example, a number of studies have investigated the use of SARs in dementia caregiving assistance [20–24] and for sensory, behavioral, and psychological therapeutic purposes [25–27].

Several systematic reviews have found that SARs have positive effects on older adult engagement, emotions, relationships, and reduced stress and loneliness [28, 29]. However, care for a person living with dementia is multifaceted and complex, involving the intersections of fatigued family care partners and understaffed professional healthcare providers. The implementation of SARs for older adult social and cognitive engagement should involve multiple stakeholders: the older adult, the family care partner(s), and the professional healthcare professionals. A plethora of Human-Robot Interaction (HRI) work has focused on attitudes and technology acceptance of SARs from an older adult perspective [30]; yet few studies have included other stakeholders such as care partners or assisted living staff [28, 31].

The data reported here are part of a series of studies working towards the goal of developing a SAR system to engage persons with mild cognitive impairment or dementia residing in assisted living facilities in a natural language conversation as psychosocial support. The system consists of a physical robot (SAR) and a virtual robot (SARv) as part of the SimpleC platform. This paper reports on data from family care partners.

This study specifically focused on gaining an in-depth understanding of robot acceptance by family care partners. Family care partners are an important stakeholder for two reasons: First, family care partners can often articulate the personal experiences and needs of their loved one with dementia, giving the research team deep insight to possible benefits and concerns of technology implementation. Second, family care partners often serve an important role in healthcare decision making, alongside the resident and professional care provider; thus, their buy-in for health-related social or cognitive technology support is crucial.

1.2 Goals of Research

This was an exploratory study to obtain family care partners' initial impressions and feedback of a SAR system during the development process. The following research questions led our study:

1. What are family care partners' attitudes toward a SAR system designed to provide social and cognitive interaction with persons with or at risk for dementia in assisted living (i.e., residents)?
2. What are family care partners' recommendations for improving the design, function, and/or implementation of a SAR system in assisted living?

2   Method

Family care partners participated in a semi-structured interview held via Zoom. A total of five sessions were completed, with each session containing one to three participants discussing six scenarios of a SAR System. Sterling Institutional Review Board (protocol number: 7645) reviewed and approved all study materials and study-related procedures prior to beginning the study. All participants issued verbal informed consent. Questions were answered to ensure all participants understood the study-related procedures, risks, benefits, incentives, and data privacy practices. The tenets of the Declaration of Helsinki were adhered to during this study.

2.1   Participants

The participants included adult family care partners (n = 10) of assisted living residents with or at risk for dementia. Participants either identified as non-Hispanic White (90%) or non-Hispanic Black (10%). There were 6 male and 4 female participants. The mean age was 61 years old (SD = 11). The participants predominately held college degrees (90%). They had no prior experience with robotics.

2.2   Social Assistive Robot (SAR) System

The SAR system consists of a physical SAR, a virtual SAR, and the SimpleC Platform. The SAR system was used for both personalized individual and group interactions.

Physical SAR. The intent of SAR is to act as an "Assistant Activity Director" in a community room setting. The SAR used was a Softbank Robotics Pepper robot, a 121 cm tall humanoid robot with a tablet on its chest (Fig. 1). The Pepper robot is equipped with 4 microphones, multiple cameras, touch sensors (i.e., hands, head), and 20 motors to allow for head, shoulder, elbow, wrist, hand, waist, and torso movement. The Pepper robot runs via NAOQi Robot Operating System (ROS). It is enhanced with high quality capabilities built-in functions, such as text-to-speech and computer vision, via integration with various cloud services. The programming for SAR was done in Python 2.7, using SoftBank's NAOQi Software Development Kit (SDK).

Virtual SAR (SARv). The intent of SARv is to enable residents to interact with an animated version of the SAR via a tablet in their personal residence. A Unity-based animated version of the physical Pepper SAR was custom created (Fig. 1). The SARv shared common appearance characteristics and social attributes in voice and movement. It was built from the ground-up for iOS and Android, utilizing Unity engine for animation and rendering, integrating with various cloud services. The programming for SARv was in Nativescript 6.0, a cross-platform development language, with a significant number of custom plugins using Java for Android and Swift for iOS.

SimpleC Platform. The SimpleC platform facilitates seamless communication, care, and connection through a customizable suite of mobile applications that can fit any environment and workflow. The resident-facing application *Companion* delivers non-pharmacological interventions for chronic care. Both SAR and SARv were incorporated in the SimpleC Platform.

Fig. 1. Physical SAR (Left) and Virtual SAR (SARv) (Right)

SAR and SARv Movements. The SAR and SARv movements and animations were created once and automatically generated for all platforms, ensuring a consistent experience. First, using Softbank's proprietary Choreograph development environment, animations were created for SAR, Softbank's Pepper robot, by specifying motor positions in 3D for each time interval. Then, using a custom-developed converter, each animation sequence was converted to a format used by SARv. Verbal utterances were customized for speech speed, voice gender, pitch, emotions, etc. The elements of an interaction were arranged in a timestamped sequence, using a proprietary JavaScript Object Notation (JSON) file format. A library of robot gestures was developed of 70+ robot animations (e.g., hand movements, body gestures to express excitement, surprise, and laughter) to pair with utterances.

SAR and SARv Social Interactions. The social interaction goals for the SAR and SARv are: Participate–Engage–Connect. To carefully construct these interactions, the team focused on the following interaction-design considerations: (1) content to best support cognitive engagement; (2) the interaction timeline; (3) custom SAR/SARv natural language utterances, paired with 70+ animations (e.g., body movements) to support HRI. A total of 82 question and answer interactions were designed for the trivia program.

2.3 SAR and SARv Video Demonstrations

Videos (ranging in length from 30 s to 3 min long) were created by the development teams for the purposes of this study. The videos portrayed SAR or SARv in introduction of self, trivia activity reminder/invitation, simulated trivia session with residents, and health reminder.

SAR Introduction and Invitation. In the first video, the physical SAR introduced itself, its purpose (a *"personal assistant"*), and highlighted a few of its interaction capabilities (e.g., *"I can play trivia, exercise, and dance."*). The physical SAR then shared that trivia is beginning in 30 min and inquired if the user would like to attend. The physical SAR moved its head slightly and gestured with its hands while speaking.

SARv Introduction and Reminder. In the second video, the virtual SAR introduced itself, its purpose (*"a personal assistant"*), and highlighted a few of its capabilities (e.g., *"I'm here to help you build healthy habits, schedule your day, and track your progress. I can play music, photo albums, videos, and voice messages."*) An off-camera voice then asked the virtual SAR, *"Hey Eliza, what's on the schedule for today?"* and Eliza responded, *"Here, let me show you,"* before the video clip ended. The virtual SAR gestured with its hands while speaking.

SARv Trivia Invitation. In the third video, the virtual SAR reminded the user in the resident room that trivia is starting in 30 min. The virtual SAR inquired if the user would like to join. An off-camera voice agreed, to which the virtual SAR responded, *"Ok, I will let the activity director know."* The virtual SAR gestured with its hands while speaking.

SAR Led Trivia. The fourth video depicted the physical SAR leading a session of classic TV trivia (Fig. 2). The trivia question appeared on the tablet on the SAR's chest. The SAR provided a hint, and an off-camera voice correctly guessed the answer. SAR responded with an interesting fact. This was repeated with other trivia questions, and two off-camera voices discussed whether they knew the answer and commented on the trivia topic. While leading trivia, the physical SAR moved its head, made encouraging gestures, and played musical tunes related to the trivia. The area around its eyes lit up with varying colors, and it looked around the room.

SARv Led Trivia. The fifth video depicted the virtual SAR reminding the user that trivia in the community room will start in 15 min (Fig. 2). The SAR asked whether the user would like to join. An off-camera voice declined the invitation. The virtual SAR encouraged the user to join, but the user declined a second time. At this point, the virtual SAR offered to lead trivia in the resident's room, which the user accepted. The virtual SAR began trivia in a similar fashion to the physical SAR, only on the resident's tablet. The virtual SAR moved its head slightly and made hand and arm gestures while speaking.

SARv Health Reminder. The sixth video depicted the virtual SAR completing a health prompt. The virtual SAR used a family member's name to encourage the user: *"Anne wants me to check on your health and record the status of your UTI."* The virtual SAR then asked the user how many glasses of water they have had today. The virtual SAR heard the user's response and recorded the number. The virtual SAR moved its head slightly and made hand and arm gestures while speaking.

2.4 Procedure

Participants were referred by staff at the assisted living facility and then pre-screened by the research team to ensure that they met inclusion criteria. Initial consent and demographics were obtained during the pre-screening process. Participants received the interview date, time, a link to an online Zoom session, and log-in instructions prior to the scheduled study date.

Each session was run by one moderator and one to two research assistants. The moderator and research assistants were well trained and practiced at systematically

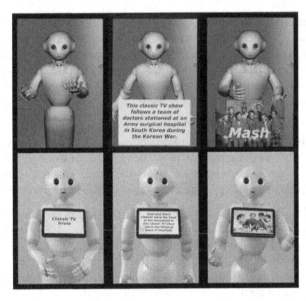

Fig. 2. Video screenshots of SARv (top row) and SAR (bottom row) leading trivia

interviewing and administering interview questions, per the methodological recommendations of Fisk and colleagues [32]. Upon arrival at the session, participants provided verbal consent to participate in the focus group/interview. Participants were informed that the discussion was to be digitally recorded and transcribed for analysis. The moderator ensured that the participants were in a private environment, with few distractions.

The moderator first outlined the study's goals and rules for the discussion. The interview script followed a specific structured outline, beginning with an icebreaker. Next, participants viewed videos of the physical and virtual SAR videos, in the order depicted in Fig. 3. Each video was followed by a series of open-ended questions to elicit discussion: *What are your first impressions? What did you like or dislike? What do you think would be benefits or concerns of using SAR/SARv to provide activity reminders? What other types of interactions would be helpful for SAR/SARv to provide? How useful do you think SAR/SARv would be in your community?*

At the conclusion of the semi-structured interview, participants were thanked, debriefed, and contact information was confirmed to mail their compensation. The average length of an interview session was 60 to 90 min. Participants were provided with a $10 Amazon or Target gift card as incentive.

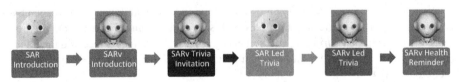

Fig. 3. Video and scenario presentation order

3 Results

3.1 Qualitative Content Analysis Strategy

The audio recordings were professionally transcribed verbatim, with speaker names dei-dentified. Transcriptions were uploaded into MaxQDA v.20 [33], a software program designed for qualitative data analysis. Next, transcripts were divided into segments of analysis. A segment was defined as a selection of text where a single participant responded to the moderator's question (i.e., typically a paragraph of analysis). Then, a content codebook was developed via qualitative conceptual content analysis. This analysis focused on the exact phrasing in the transcripts (explicit data) and the number of times certain themes exist (frequency) in each segment. The codebook was iteratively created including pre-derived language from technology acceptance models: Technology Acceptance Models [34–36], Unified Theory of Acceptance and Use of Technology (UTAUT) [37], Health Information Technology Acceptance Model (HITAM) [38], Senior Technology Acceptance Model (STAM) [39], and the ALMERE Model [40].

The codebook was applied by attitudinal sentiments (benefit, concern, mixed) and recommendations using the 11 technology-theory-driven themes: perceived usefulness/function, perceived ease of use, perceived engagement/entertainment/enjoyment, personalization/customization/adaptivity, social attributes/perceived sociability, appearance, health promotion/behavior/health belief, technology literacy/experience, long-term technology adoption, safety/privacy, and other (Table 1). To calculate inter-rater reliability, two researchers independently analyzed two (of the five) transcripts. One round of coding resulted in 87.5% agreement, calculated as the proportion of agreement judgement coding pairs between the 2 researchers. The researchers then reviewed the analysis, resolved conflicts, and adjusted the codebook as needed. The final codebook (Table 1) was then used to analyze the remaining transcripts.

Table 1. Final content analysis codebook

Theme	Definition	Citations
Perceived Usefulness/Function	Usefulness: The extent to which an individual believes that utilizing the system would improve their capacity within daily interactions and responsibilities Function: Characteristics related to performance, operation, action, or purpose	[34–40]
Perceived Ease of Use	The degree to which a person believes using a system would require no effort	[34]

(continued)

Table 1. (*continued*)

Theme	Definition	Citations
Perceived Engagement/Entertainment/Enjoyment	Engagement: Promotion of social connection and communication with others Entertainment: Potential to provide pleasure through sources of amusement, distraction, and alternative experiences	[36, 40]
Personalization/Customization/Adaptivity	Individualized user experience based on user needs or preference; the ability for the system to adapt to the needs of the user, especially over time	[40, 54]
Social Attributes/Perceived Sociability	Characteristics that promote social interaction and engagement of the user with the robot, others, and their environment	[40]
Appearance	Physical characteristics, presence, style, and aesthetics	[41, 42]
Health Promotion/Behavior/Belief	Potential to augment health behaviors/beliefs by engaging and encouraging the user to interact and complete cognitive, physical, and social reminders and activities	[38, 39]
Technology Literacy/Experience	Users' level of comfort, knowledge, experience, and ability to use technology	[36, 37]
Long-Term Technology Adoption	Concerns about continuance and interaction over time	[43, 44]
Safety/Privacy	Protection of the user, their sensitive information, and their sharing preferences	[45]
Other	Attitudes and recommendations unrelated to any of the above codes	

3.2 User Attitudes

Overall theme frequencies were first organized by affect: Perceived benefits, concerns, or mixed opinions (Fig. 4). Our analysis revealed predominantly positive perceptions of benefit (f = 111) from family care partners toward the SAR system, and when there were concerns (f = 65) or mixed responses (f = 39), recommendations (f = 256) often followed. A chi-square goodness of fit test confirmed a significantly different distribution of attitudes (X2 = 37.09, df = 2, p < .001), with benefits outweighing both concerns (X2 = 12.02, df = 1, p < .001) and mixed responses (X2 = 34.56, df = 1, p < .001). Significant overlap in top themes existed between benefits, concerns, and recommendations.

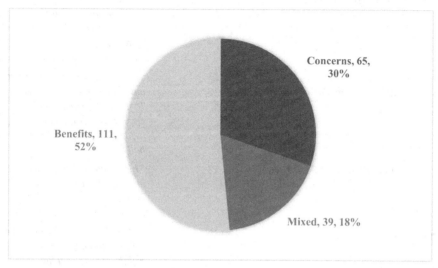

Fig. 4. Frequency of perceived benefits, concerns, and mixed opinions

3.3 Perceived Benefits

Family care partners' most frequently mentioned benefits of the SAR system include perceived usefulness/function ($f = 38$), perceived engagement/entertainment/enjoyment ($f = 23$), social attributes/perceived sociability ($f = 18$), and appearance ($f = 16$) (Table 2). When considering usefulness/function, family care partners assessed SAR with the capacity of their loved ones in mind. From their perspective, SAR usefulness was dependent upon its functioning for older people with potential memory impairment. Family care partners found SAR's reminder system important for users who may need multiple prompts over time to participate in an activity. SAR initiated and delivered engagement/entertainment opportunities seen as useful to family care partners. For example, the SARv could remind the user of trivia led by the physical SAR in the community room with other residents. This personal engagement by SARv to participate in entertainment by physical SAR was a benefit for family care partners desiring increased social opportunities for their loved ones. Family care partners' perceived SAR to have positive social attributes/sociability (e.g., pleasant voice, clear talking cadence, turn toward user, head tilt) and appearance (e.g., big eyes, cute, non-threatening, toy-like). These characteristics were important benefits to family care partners who felt approachable social attributes and appearance would enhance their loved ones' interest and continued use of the SAR.

Table 2. Top-rated perceived benefits

Theme	Frequency (f)	Quote
Perceived Usefulness/Function	$f = 38$	"I like the idea of providing health prompts to the residents like hydration, get up and stretch, move around, anything like that."
Perceived Engagement/Entertainment/Enjoyment	$f = 23$	"I'd like to see my mother get out of her room more often. To me, that [SAR] would encourage her to get up out of her chair and go down the hall."
Social Attributes/Perceived Sociability	$f = 18$	"I liked the way she tilted her head. And she was very patient, and gave [trivia] clues, if they needed them."
Appearance	$f = 16$	"I like the look and feel of the robot. It did a good job of relating to me as a human without wandering into the creepy, to the uncanny valley."

3.4 Perceived Concerns

Leading concerns had similar frequencies, with the top four themes being coded between 10 and 12 times (Table 3). Three of the four top concerns were also top benefits: perceived usefulness/function ($f = 12$), social attributes/perceived sociability ($f = 12$), and appearance ($f = 11$). Participants shared concerns about SAR that were specific to their loved ones with or at risk for dementia. While the activity and schedule reminders were seen as a useful function and overall benefit, family care partners also noted that they were concerned about the frequency and accuracy of these reminders. The health prompt of a hydration reminder was seen positively as a useful concept, but there were concerns about users responding to the reminder if a glass of water is not presented to them at the same time. There were similar drawbacks to trivia entertainment, where participants wondered if the SAR had the social attributes to maintain the interest of their loved ones. For example, family care partners felt the timing of SAR's responses to correct or incorrect trivia answers would impact how interactive the robot came across. In terms of appearance, while most participants had positive impressions, some felt it looked too robotic or technical. Unique to top concerns was the theme of ease of use ($f = 10$). Family care partners acknowledged that perceived ease of use was dependent upon prior technology experience of their loved ones and accessibility of the SAR.

Table 3. Top-rated concerns

Theme	Frequency (f)	Quote
Perceived Usefulness/Function	$f = 12$	*"No, because my mother…has dementia. It [SAR] would totally be useless for her. All of this would be, even if she was able to ask something, she wouldn't remember a few minutes later that she had asked."*
Social Attributes/Perceived Sociability	$f = 12$	*"I thought that was weird that the robot didn't acknowledge that he [the user] got the [trivia] answer right."*
Appearance	$f = 11$	*"I know my mom would be a little weary of it, just dealing with something like that. It looks robotic, it doesn't look human."*
Perceived Ease of Use	$f = 10$	*"Most of the residents are in wheelchairs. And I'm not sure that, given a four-foot-tall device with a screen that fits right there on its chest, I'm not sure if they could see the screen very well or necessarily hear what it was saying."*

3.5 Recommendations

Following benefits and concerns, family care partners made recommendations ($f = 256$) that connected to existing top themes: perceived usefulness/function ($f = 77$), perceived engagement/entertainment/enjoyment ($f = 46$), and social attributes/perceived sociability ($f = 39$) (Table 4). However, there was one new top theme that applied to many others: personalization/customization/adaptivity ($f = 37$). Family care partners frequently recommended ways to expand the personalization/customization of SAR to expand its usefulness, engagement, and social attributes. Participants felt that reminders and prompts designed specifically for the user would be more effective than general ones. Trivia entertainment malleable in difficulty and pacing would better hold the attention of users. Adjustable attributes like feminine or masculine voice could improve the social connection between the SAR and the user. Personalization/customization was a common thread throughout many of the recommendations, but there were others specific to design and function (e.g., greater mobility, privacy measures, accessibility features). Participants emphasized new entertainment content (e.g., bingo, solitaire, personal photos) and health prompts (e.g., hygiene, exercise) would keep users invested over the long-term. Ultimately, the recommendations made by family care partners had their expert knowledge of what mattered to their loved ones with or at risk for dementia and residing in assisted living.

Table 4. Top-rated recommendations

Theme	Frequency (f)	Quote
Perceived Usefulness/Function	$f = 38$	*"I think it'd be useful too as long as the tablet was sort of awaken in an active mode… I could picture my mother, you know, picking up a tablet and losing it on the side of her chair and then running out of battery…the technology becomes less useful at that point. But if it's sitting up like a picture frame on a table and it wakes up, 'Hey,' you know, 'time to hear about this.' I think that could be very useful."*
Perceived Engagement/Entertainment/Enjoyment	$f = 23$	*"I could see it having a role in augmenting activities. You know, maybe there's an art activity planned, and it could [offer], 'Hey, you know what? We're going to be doing this art activity here, let me show you some relevant pictures and teach you a little bit about it.'"*

(continued)

Table 4. (*continued*)

Theme	Frequency (f)	Quote
Social Attributes/Perceived Sociability	$f = 18$	*"If you had a combination of both the virtual tablet [SARv] and the physical robot, if... [they] didn't want to go to trivia. You could show, if it's possible, show a video of the robot, the robot's eye, of all the people who are participating, and then show that on the screen saying, 'Hey... you can see all your friends are participating. Don't you want to go, too?'"*
Personalization/Customization/Adaptivity	$f = 16$	*"It seems like all of our aging parents, or our aging relatives, are dealing with different, having different capabilities. So, the robot is going to need to interact with different people in different ways."*

4 Discussion

Assisted living facilities, healthcare providers, and families face many burdens prompted by the increased proportion of older adults at risk for and with dementia in the United States [5]. Much evidence supports the importance of social engagement for persons with dementia [14, 15], and SARs have great potential for facilitating unique and tailored social and cognitive engagement opportunities. However, little is known about the acceptance of SARs (within the context of technology acceptance models) in assisted living facilities, specifically designed for those with cognitive impairment. This study is a part of a much larger research program, investigating the implementation requirements and acceptance of SARs in assisted living. Our larger program involves not only family care partners, but also assisted living residents and staff [46–49]. This paper, however, specifically focused on reporting an in-depth understanding of robot acceptance by family care partners. The interviews were coded for participant attitudes toward SAR and SARv (hereafter referred to only as SAR): positive/benefit, negative/concern, mixed, and recommendations. Benefits, concerns, and recommendations will now be discussed in the context of social and cognitive engagement, as well as existing technology acceptance theories.

4.1 Benefits of SAR for Social and Cognitive Engagement

The top priority/benefit to family care partners was their perceptions of the SAR's usefulness and function, a finding which supports existing theories of technology adoption where usefulness is one of the most predictive variables for technology adoption [35]. In fact, perceived usefulness if one of the variables consistently present across nearly all technology acceptance models [34–40].

Family care partners' comments aligned with research on the benefits of SARs' autonomous, proactive, and reactive qualities [20, 26, 50, 51], specifically when considering the population with or at risk for dementia. These qualities describe why the activity/schedule reminders, health prompts, and trivia entertainment were perceived positively by participants, as they all offset traditional tasks of assisted living staff and family care partners.

In line with our previous studies (utilizing a different SAR and different set of tasks, such as stretching, music, and reminiscing) [48], the family care partners' perceptions of usefulness were heavily influenced by their discernments of the robot's social attributes and social engagement. In other words, the family care partners saw much benefit to the robot not only providing utilitarian cognitive support, such as reminders, but also assisting with tasks that require complex social interaction between the resident and the robot. They interpreted much of the SARs social behaviors (gaze, gestures, etc.) as holding much potential to keep their loved ones engaged and attentive.

It is important to note that family care partners did not indicate that the SAR should replace human interaction. Rather, family care partners felt it appropriate for SAR to augment and complement human social interaction, like SAR assisting the activity director at assisted living in leading trivia or making an announcement. They believed that the SAR has the potential to offer a greater number and variety of social engagement opportunities and ultimately enhance the assisted living experience.

4.2 Concerns of SAR for Social and Cognitive Engagement

Although our participants held significantly more positive attitudes toward the SAR than concerns, some concerns were still raised and are important to consider. User acceptance of technology is multifaceted and depends on weighing both the positive and negative aspects of the technology, as previously shown in older adult attitudes toward robotics [51–53].

Interestingly perceived usefulness/function, the most commonly discussed benefits, was also a note of concern. Family care partners were sensitive to mention concerns related to usefulness in effort to improve the technology for people impacted by dementia, above and beyond what was demonstrated to them in this study. For example, caregivers discussed the importance of useful dialogue, long battery life, and just-in-time reminders. Thus, their usefulness and functional concerns related to the logistics, timeliness, and flexibility of the task–rather than the task itself.

On a similar thread, social attributes/perceived sociability of the SAR were viewed as both a benefit and concern. Overall, the family care partners were enthusiastic about the social qualities of the SAR, but they held some reservations whether the social qualities would build a lasting connection, ideal for long-term technology adoption, after novelty wears off. They linked this concern with the appearance of the robot. While the care partners personally liked the SAR's appearance, they held some concern that it might feel intimidating to their loved ones and insisted that a cute and friendly appearance would aid in residents approaching and developing relationships with the SAR.

Lastly, family care partners found the SAR only as useful as it is easy to use, and this connection is supported by existing technology uptake theories [36]. In fact, many technologies are not designed with older adult capabilities and limitations in mind, a leading reason for the slower uptake of technology by older adults compared to younger adults [32]. When family care partners considered ease of use, they perceived its dependence upon their loved ones' prior technology experience and the accessibility of the technology. This finding is supported by the Senior Technology Acceptance Model, which emphasizes technology experience in geron-technology use [39].

4.3 Recommendations of SAR for Social and Cognitive Engagement

Family care partners had more recommendations than positive, negative, or mixed opinions combined. Recommendations were the thoroughfare for interview discussion, with all participants invested in improving the SAR for their loved ones' social and cognitive engagement benefit. The care partners were imaginative regarding what the SAR could do to help their loved ones. They particularly emphasized new entertainment content (e.g., bingo, solitaire, personal photos) and health prompts (e.g., hygiene, exercise). The reasoning for these recommendations was that the care partners felt that a variety of use cases would keep users invested over the long-term. The family care partners held expert knowledge of what mattered to their loved ones, and were very vocal about the need for meaningful, personalized uses.

Throughout the recommendations, there was a common theme of customization/personalization/adaptivity. One potential explanation for this emphasis is related to the progressive nature of dementia. The nature of the SAR's usefulness will inevitably change as the user with dementia progresses in their disease; therefore, the SAR must be designed with various levels of care in mind. Family care partners emphasized how customization could provide the user control (e.g., choosing when and how the SAR provides trivia); personalization, on the other hand can provide tailored experience (e.g., the trivia content matches the individual resident's interests) [54]. This focus on customization and personalization is common in HRI design recommendations [48, 52], because when technology is customized by the user, it may enhance how socially and cognitively engaging users perceive the SAR to be. The match between the technology capabilities and the user's capabilities, and the technology's ability to adapt, is critical for continued use, as supported by several technology acceptance models [37–40].

4.4 Methodological Strengths, Caveats, and Recommendations for Future Research

Our study identified important themes in attitudes toward SAR, with a lot of helpful information surrounding top themes of perceived usefulness/function, perceived engagement/entertainment/enjoyment, social attributes/perceived sociability, appearance, customization/personalization/adaptivity, and perceived ease of use. Our study utilized videos to demonstrate the SAR and SARv. While this is a useful methodology [51, 55], ideal for analyzing user attitudes, future research should utilize in-person human-robot interactions. Future research can further examine other themes that our research only began to address, like factors of long-term adoption and health outcomes. In fact, this study is part of a larger series of studies, and the study team is currently preparing a longer-term clinical trial in assisted living facilities. Given that our family care partners stressed the importance of long-term technology adoption and the needs for both customization and personalization, more research is needed to investigate trends in user acceptance of SARs in assisted living over time. This study provides qualitative data to an often quantitatively analyzed problem (i.e., health outcomes), and this can set the stage for larger clinical trial investigations in the future.

Our study is intended to explore family care partners' perceptions of SARs, a population often excluded from research. Generalization of our findings may be limited to the care partners demographically similar to our sample. Instead, we aimed to offer an in-depth examination of care partners' knowledgeable perspectives. Our sample was limited in its diversity of race/ethnicity, educational background, and geographic residence. Thus, to be able to generalize to more populations, future research should include larger sample sizes and a range of demographic and sociographic features.

5   Conclusion

In closing, family care partners in our study were generally positive toward the potential of the SAR to be implemented into assisted living facilities. This positive and open attitude was further supported by the participants' detailed perceived benefits of the technology. While the SAR can support health management through health prompts, the family care partners highlighted the specific benefit of the SAR in promoting social and cognitive engagement for people with or at risk for dementia. Future SAR development should focus on customization and personalization of the HRI experience and adapting support for persons with cognitive impairment as the disease progresses.

Acknowledgments. We thank the reviewers for their helpful comments.

Disclosure of Interests. Research reported was supported by the National Institute on Aging (NIA) of the National Institutes of Health (NIH) under award number R44AG058337, a partnership between the University of Georgia, Simple C LLC, and Advanced Medical Electronics. The content is solely the responsibility of the authors and does not necessarily represent the official views of the National Institutes of Health.

References

1. United Nations Department for Economic and Social Affairs, Population Division. World population prospects 2022: Summary of results. UN (2023). www.unpopulation.org
2. World Health Organization (WHO). Ageing and health. WHO (2022). https://www.who.int/news-room/fact-sheets/detail/ageing-and-health

3. High, K.P., Kritchevsky, S.: Translational research in the fastest-growing population: Older adults. In: Principles of Translational Science in Medicine, pp. 299–311. Academic Press (2015)
4. Pew Research Center: Baby Boomers approach 65—Glumly: Survey findings about America's largest generation (2010). https://www.pewresearch.org/social-trends/2010/12/20/baby-boomers-approach-65-glumly/
5. Alzheimer's Association. Alzheimer's disease facts and figures. Alzheimer's Dement. **19**, 1598–1695 (2023). https://doi.org/10.1002/alz.13016
6. World Health Organization (WHO). Dementia. WHO (2023). https://www.who.int/news-room/fact-sheets/detail/dementia
7. Azevedo, L.V.D.S., et al.: Impact of social isolation on people with dementia and their family caregivers. J. Alzheimer's Dis. **81**(2), 607–617 (2021)
8. Teri, L.: Behavior and caregiver burden: behavioral problems in patients with Alzheimer disease and its association with caregiver distress. Alzheimer Dis. Assoc. Disord. **11**, S35–S38 (1997)
9. Brodaty, H., Donkin, M.: Family caregivers of people with dementia. Dialogues Clin. Neurosci. **11**(2), 217–228 (2009)
10. Herrmann, L.K., et al.: A systematic review of dementia-related stigma research: can we move the stigma dial? Am. J. Geriatr. Psychiatry **26**(3), 316–331 (2018)
11. Kovaleva, M., Spangler, S., Clevenger, C., Hepburn, K.: Chronic stress, social isolation, and perceived loneliness in dementia caregivers. J. Psychosoc. Nurs. Ment. Health Serv. **56**(10), 36–43 (2018)
12. Han, K., Trinkoff, A.M., Storr, C.L., Lerner, N., Yang, B.K.: Variation across US assisted living facilities: admissions, resident care needs, and staffing. J. Nurs. Scholarsh. **49**(1), 24–32 (2017)
13. Sloane, P.D., Zimmerman, S., Williams, C.S., Reed, P.S., Gill, K.S., Preisser, J.S.: Evaluating the quality of life of long-term care residents with dementia. Gerontologist **45**(suppl_1), 37–49 (2005)
14. Jang, Y., Park, N.S., Dominguez, D.D., Molinari, V.: Social engagement in older residents of assisted living facilities. Aging Ment. Health **18**(5), 642–647 (2014)
15. Park, N.S., Zimmerman, S., Kinslow, K., Shin, H.J., Roff, L.L.: Social engagement in assisted living and implications for practice. J. Appl. Gerontol. **31**(2), 215–238 (2012)
16. Zimmerman, S., et al.: Social engagement and its relationship to service provision in residential care and assisted living. Soc. Work Res. **27**(1), 6–18 (2003)
17. Hawk, T., White, E.M., Bishnoi, C., Schwartz, L.B., Baier, R.R., Gifford, D.R.: Facility characteristics and costs associated with meeting proposed minimum staffing levels in skilled nursing facilities. J. Am. Geriatr. Soc. **70**(4), 1198–1207 (2022)
18. Feil-Seifer, D., Matarić, M.J.: Socially assistive robotics. IEEE Robot. Autom. Mag. **18**(1), 24–31 (2011)
19. Broadbent, E., Billinghurst, M., Boardman, S.G., Doraiswamy, P.M.: Enhancing social connectedness with companion robots using AI. Sci. Robot. **8**(80), eadi6347 (2023)
20. Chen, K., Lou, V.W., Tan, K.C., Wai, M., Chan, L.: Effects of a humanoid companion robot on dementia symptoms and caregiver distress for residents in long-term care. J. Am. Med. Dir. Assoc. **21**(11), 1724-1728.e3 (2020)
21. Chu, M.-T., Khosla, R., Khaksar, S.M.S., Nguyen, K.: Service innovation through social robot engagement to improve dementia care quality. Assist. Technol. **29**(1), 8–18 (2017)
22. Lin, X.Y., Saksono, H., Stowell, E., Lachman, M.E., Castaneda-Sceppa, C., Parker, A.G.: Go&Grow: an evaluation of a pervasive social exergame for caregivers of loved ones with dementia. Proc. ACM Hum.-Comput. Interact. **4**(CSCW2), 1–28 (2020)

23. Moharana, S., Panduro, A.E., Lee, H.R., Riek, L.D.: Robots for joy, robots for sorrow: community based robot design for dementia caregivers. In: 2019 14th ACM/IEEE International Conference on Human-Robot Interaction (HRI), pp. 458–467 (2019)

24. Pfadenhauer, M., Dukat, C.: Robot caregiver or robot-supported caregiving? Int. J. Soc. Robot. **7**(3), 393–406 (2015)

25. Chan, W.L., Šabanovic, S., Huber, L.: Use of seal-like robot PARO in sensory group therapy for older adults with dementia. In: 2013 8th ACM/IEEE International Conference on Human-Robot Interaction (HRI), pp. 101–102 (2013)

26. Marti, P., Bacigalupo, M., Giusti, L., Mennecozzi, C., Shibata, T.: Socially assistive robotics in the treatment of behavioural and psychological symptoms of dementia. In: The First IEEE/RAS-EMBS International Conference on Biomedical Robotics and Biomechatronics 2006. BioRob 2006, pp. 483–488 (2006)

27. Šabanović, S., Bennett, C.C., Chang, W., Huber, L.: PARO robot affects diverse interaction modalities in group sensory therapy for older adults with dementia. In: 2013 IEEE 13th International Conference on Rehabilitation Robotics (ICORR), pp. 1–6 (2013)

28. Kachouie, R., Sedighadeli, S., Khosla, R., Chu, M.-T.: Socially assistive robots in elderly care: a mixed-method systematic literature review. Int. J. Hum. Comput. Int. **30**, 369–393 (2014)

29. Pu, L., Moyle, W., Jones, C., Todorovic, M.: The effectiveness of social robots for older adults: a systematic review and meta-analysis of randomized controlled studies. Gerontologist **59**(1), e37–e51 (2019)

30. Vandemeulebroucke, T., de Casterlé, B.D., Gastmans, C.: How do older adults experience and perceive socially assistive robots in aged care: a systematic review of qualitative evidence. Aging Ment. Health **22**(2), 149–167 (2018)

31. Savela, N., Turja, T., Oksanen, A.: Social acceptance of robots in different occupational fields: a systematic literature review. Int. J. Soc. Robot. **10**(4), 493–502 (2018)

32. Fisk, A.D., Rogers, W.A., Charness, N., Czaja, S.J., Sharit, J.: Designing for Older Adults: Principles and Creative Human Factors Approaches, 2nd edn. CRC Press, Boca Raton (2009)

33. VERBI Software. MAXQDA 2022. Computer software (2021). https://www.maxqda.com/

34. Davis, F.D.: Perceived usefulness, perceived ease of use, and user acceptance of information technology. MIS Q. **13**(3), 319–340 (1989). https://doi.org/10.2307/249008

35. Venkatesh, V., Davis, F.D.: A theoretical extension of the technology acceptance model: four longitudinal field studies. Manage. Sci. **46**(2), 186–204 (2000)

36. Venkatesh, V., Bala, H.: Technology acceptance model 3 and a research agenda on interventions. Decis. Sci. **39**(2), 273–315 (2008)

37. Venkatesh, V., Morris, M.G., Davis, G.B., Davis, F.D.: User acceptance of information technology: toward a unified view. MIS Q. **27**, 425–478 (2003)

38. Kim, J., Park, H.-A.: Development of a health information technology acceptance model using consumers' health behavior intention. J. Med. Internet Res. **14**(5), e133 (2012)

39. Chen, K., Chan, A.H.S.: Gerontechnology acceptance by elderly Hong Kong Chinese: a senior technology acceptance model (STAM). Ergonomics **57**(5), 635–652 (2014). https://doi.org/10.1080/00140139.2014.895855

40. Heerink, M., Kröse, B., Evers, V., et al.: Assessing acceptance of assistive social agent technology by older adults: the Almere model. Int. J. Soc. Robot. **2**, 361–375 (2010)

41. Prakash, A., Rogers, W.A.: Why some humanoid faces are perceived more positively than others: effects of human-likeness and task. Int. J. Soc. Robot. **7**(2), 309–331 (2015)

42. Li, D., Rau, P.P., Li, Y.: A cross-cultural study: effect of robot appearance and task. Int. J. Soc. Robot. **2**, 175–186 (2010)

43. Czaja, S.J., et al.: Factors predicting the use of technology: findings from the Center for Research and Education on Aging and Technology Enhancement (CREATE). Psychol. Aging **21**(2), 333–352 (2006). https://doi.org/10.1037/0882-7974.21.2.333

44. Forquer, H.A., Christensen, J.L., Tan, A.S.L.: Predicting continuance—findings from a longitudinal study of older adults using an eHealth newsletter. Health Commun. **29**(9), 937–946 (2014). https://doi.org/10.1080/10410236.2013.833580

45. Yao, S., Xie, L., Chen, Y., Zhang, Y., Chen, Y., Gao, M.: Influence of perceived safety in the technology acceptance model. Transport. Res. F: Traffic Psychol. Behav. **99**, 36–51 (2023)

46. Adams, A.E., Beer, J.M., Wu, X., Komsky, J., Zamer, J.: Social activities in community settings: Impact of COVID-19 and technology solutions. Abstracts Gerontol. Soc. Am. Annu. Conf. **4**(1), 957 (2020)

47. Power, S., Smith, K., Abedine, R., Burton, L., Adams, A., Beer, J.M.: Assisted living with a social robot: benefits and concerns of family care partners. In: APHA 2023 Annual Meeting and Expo. APHA (2023)

48. Wu, X., et al.: Socially assistive robots for dementia care: exploring caregiver perceptions of use cases and acceptance. In: Proceedings of the Human Factors and Ergonomics Society Annual Meeting, vol. 65(1), pp. 6–10. Sage CA: Los Angeles, CA: SAGE Publications (2021)

49. Zamer, J., Adams, A.E., Beer, J.M., Wu, X., Komsky, J.: Social assistive robots for assisting activity professionals. Abstracts Gerontol. Soc. Am. Annu. Conf. **4**(1), 929 (2020)

50. Beer, J.M., Fisk, A.D., Rogers, W.A.: Toward a framework for levels of robot autonomy in human-robot interaction. J. Human-Robot Interact. **3**(2), 74 (2014)

51. Smarr, C.A., et al.: Domestic robots for older adults: attitudes, preferences, and potential. Int. J. Soc. Robot. **6**, 229–247 (2014)

52. Beer, J.M., et al.: The domesticated robot: design guidelines for assisting older adults to age in place. In: 7th ACM/IEEE International Conference on Human-Robot Interaction, Boston, MA, March 2012, pp. 335–342 (2012)

53. Broadbent, E., et al.: Attitudes towards health-care robots in a retirement village. Australas. J. Ageing **31**(2), 115–120 (2012)

54. Lacroix, D., Wullenkord, R., Eyssel, F.: Who's in charge? Using personalization vs. customization distinction to inform HRI research on adaptation to users. In: Companion of the 2023 ACM/IEEE International Conference on Human-Robot Interaction, pp. 580–586 (2023). https://doi.org/10.1145/3568294.3580152

55. Woods, S.N., Walters, M.L., Koay, K.L., Dautenhahn, K.: Methodological issues in HRI: a comparison of live and video-based methods in robot to human approach direction trials. In: ROMAN 2006-the 15th IEEE International Symposium on Robot and Human Interactive Communication, pp. 51–58. IEEE (2006)

Technology for Prolonged Independent Life – A Pilot Study

Marie Sjölinder[1]([⊠]), Yvonne Eriksson[2], and Christine Gustafsson[2,3]

[1] RISE, Box 1263, 164 29 Kista, Sweden
marie.sjolinder@ri.se
[2] Mälardalen University, Hamngatan 15, 632 17 Eskilstuna, Sweden
[3] Sophiahemmet University, Box 5605, 114 86 Stockholm, Sweden

Abstract. This paper takes a system approach to implementation of future health and welfare technology aiming at prolonging independent life. A study was conducted where different relevant stakeholders such as older adults, care staff, managers, and decision makers were interviewed about their visions and attitudes towards the use of technology in a future context. Further, the paper elaborates on how information design can contribute to the understanding of different needs and how it can be applied in the development of health and welfare technology that empowers future older adults and contribute to a prolonged independent life. Finally, communication and interaction design are discussed in relationship to the usage of future health and welfare technology.

Keywords: Older Adults · Technology Usage · Prolonged Independent Life

1 Introduction

Healthcare and social care (including elderly care) are facing a shift in which digitalization, such as health and welfare technology (HWT) use will play an increasingly important role in specific healthcare and care solutions but also in obtaining more effective patient- or client-focused services and processes and facilitating independent life. HWT is a broad term and covers for example assistive technology, digital technology, medical devices (used "outside" the hospital), telehealth and remote monitoring, ehealth, mhealth, erehabilitaion and different technological aids. Examples of HWT include security alarms, night cameras, remote monitoring, and various types of digital planning tools. HWT is expected to offer a range of benefits, such as improved patient outcomes, increased patient satisfaction, enhanced collaboration among healthcare providers, better use of staff competence and increased cost efficiency (Stoumpos, Kitsios, & Talias, 2023). HWT can deliver healthcare to rural and remote populations and improve the accessibility of healthcare among rural and remote populations (Alkhaldi, Sahama, Huxley, & Gajanayake, 2014), and thus provide the opportunity to reduce overall costs and stress on often overburdened welfare systems. HWT can mitigate this by providing out-of-hospital care and reduce the overuse of emergency care and the travel expenses accumulated by rural patients as well as provide regular check-ups using digital solutions (Alvarez, 2002).

Q. Gao and J. Zhou (Eds.): HCII 2024, LNCS 14726, pp. 98–111, 2024.
https://doi.org/10.1007/978-3-031-61546-7_7

In contemplating the future, one must grapple with its multifaceted nature, which varies depending on the context and timeframe considered. Merriam-Webster (2024) provides several definitions of the future, among which two are particularly relevant: the anticipation of what is to come and the expectation of advancement or progressive development. Undeniably, one aspect of the future that looms large is the demographic shift toward an increasingly aged population. However, the timeline for planning and addressing the consequences of this shift remains uncertain and under-discussed.

Understanding the future is inherently linked to our comprehension of the present. It is challenging to envisage scenarios we have not encountered or predict outcomes without grounding in current realities. In Sweden, for instance, there seems to be a pre-vailing belief among policymakers that increasing employment rates will alleviate the challenges posed by an aging population. However, this overlooks a fundamental issue: there simply will not be enough individuals available to fill those job vacancies (Swedish Association of Local Authorities and Regions (2022). Thus, it becomes imperative to seek solutions that adopt a more preventive stance. This proactive approach encompasses various facets, including lifestyle adjustments and leveraging technological innovations like HWT. Embracing preventive measures not only addresses immediate concerns but also fosters a more sustainable and resilient future. By integrating HWT that support aging in place (c.f.Yarker et al., 2024), individuals can maintain independence and qual-ity of life while alleviating strain on traditional care systems. Furthermore, promoting healthier lifestyles and community engagement can delay the onset of age-related health issues, reducing the burden on healthcare resources in the long run. In essence, navigat-ing the future requires a holistic understanding that acknowledges both the challenges and opportunities presented by demographic shifts. By adopting a proactive mindset and investing in preventative strategies, we can pave the way for a future that is not only accommodating of an aging population but also characterized by progress and sustainable development.

It is likely that we need to implement digital technology such HWT in various ways to support a prolonged independent living in the future. Therefore, Sweden has a focus on radical digitalization of society. Digitalization should be regarded as a manifold, socio-technical phenomenon, with processes of adopting and using these technologies taking place within broader individual, organizational, and societal contexts (Legener et al., 2017). Older adults are both very different from previous generations and there are large variations between individuals (Pericu, 2017). A large part of the older population also has experience with technology and are used to having access to technical devices and new services. However, there are great expectations and worries of the impact dig-italization will have on individuals both in work life and on daily life. This involves various sectors such as industry, service, healthcare, and social services. The challenge is that we meet different kinds of user needs, employees in companies and public sectors, caregivers and older adults in healthcare and social services, and users that are dependent on technology in daily life duties such as paying bills.

Today, technology sometimes plays a greater role in older adult's lives than when they previously were at work. Many people who have retired have been using technology both at home and at work for a long time and they have used a variety of services and different devices (Rogers, 2014). Much of the HCI research has been focusing on compensating for age-related decline in terms of different assistive technologies (Rogers et al, 2014). With the new generation of older adults, existing usability guidelines must be challenged when technology experienced older adults still would like to use the same functionalities as before but have started to suffer from both physical and cognitive limitations. A larger focus must be placed on possibilities and benefits with respect to design of new digital services and how the technology can fulfill other needs in life than compensating for age-related decline (Rogers et al, 2014). The use of digital services for prevention purposes will also demand a balance between moralization and to get people to use services supporting a healthy lifestyle.

This paper will take a system approach to implementation of future technologies (HWT) aiming at prolonging independent life. A study will be presented where different relevant stakeholders such as older adults, care staff, managers, and decision makers have been interviewed about their visions and attitudes towards the use of technology in a future context. Further, it will be elaborated how information design can contribute to the understanding of different needs and how it can be applied in the development of HWT that empowers future older adults and contribute to a prolonged independent life. We will also discuss what incentives are needed when it comes to communicating existing and forthcoming HWT.

2 Method

The study was a first exploratory pilot study with the aim to gain a first insight in the topic. Semi-structured focus group interviews with question areas were held with older adults, care staff, managers, and decision makers. Questions were asked about their vision and attitudes towards the use of HWT in a future context. One group interview was conducted with each group/stakeholder and the questions were modified to some extent to adapt to the different perspectives of each stakeholder perspective.

The number of participants varied between the different stakeholders from 5 to 2. Convenience sampling was used due to a short deadline, the authors network was used to recruit participants to focus group interviews with a set date and time for the interview. Before the focus group session started, the group was informed about the aim with the session and conditions for participating based on ethical principles. After that each participant gave their consent to record the session.

The groups were asked about experiences from current HWT devices used to support older people to be independent in their daily lives. What kind of HWT devices they were aware of, what they thought of them and what challenges or successes of using HWT they have experienced. The groups were also given questions about future HWT, what expectations they had and what functions or features they would like to see in HWT and services. Further, the groups discussed collaboration between different stakeholders in relation to the implementation and use of new HWT. Finally, the participants were asked about information (manuals) about how to use different HWT, and about how they perceived the interaction with different HWT.

The interviews were made online, on one occasion with each group, and lasted for 1 h/group. The interviews were recorded and transcribed. In addition, notes were taken during the interviews.

The study takes a qualitative approach, applying qualitative descriptive methodology (Sandelowski, 2000) in analyzing the interviews. Data extraction was conducted based on the aim, the interview questions, and the questions areas. After that a comprehensive summary of the question areas was created. This with the aim to summarize the perceptions, experiences, and expectations of HWT for independent life among seniors, elderly care staff, elderly care managers, and elderly care decision-makers when it comes to aging in place in a future context.

In terms of respecting participants' informed consent, the research was carried out in accordance with the Declaration of Helsinki. Throughout the study, the ethical principles of the Swedish Research Council (Swedish Research Council, 2017) and the principles of the Declaration of Helsinki Ethical Principles for Medical Research Involving Human Subjects (WMA, 2022) were followed. Information concerning the interviewees' participation and the right to withdraw at any time was provided to all the informants before the group interview. Consequently, all the included interviewees provided their oral informed consent and were informed about guaranteed confidentiality.

3   Results

Initially, the results section provides a comprehensive summary of the findings derived from the study of stakeholders such as older adults, care staff, managers, and decision-makers, exploring their visions and attitudes towards the use of technology in a future context. Additionally, it delves into stakeholders' experiences and perceptions of how information design can contribute to understanding different needs and how it can be applied in the development of HCI that empowers future older adults and contributes to prolonged independent living. This section encapsulates the key insights obtained through the exploration of various question areas, including the valuation of existing technological aids, expectations regarding prolonged independence, and information design and adaptation to user needs. The initial summary is followed by a presentation of the findings from each area of question; Evaluation of HWT, Visions and expectations on future HWT, Collaboration between stakeholders, Expectations on prolonged independence and Information design and adaptation to user needs.

3.1   Overarching Comprehensive Summary

The results show that there is a growing awareness of the importance of HWT in elderly care. These aids have the potential to enhance the independence and quality of life for older individuals when they choose to age in their own homes (aging in place). However, there are still challenges that must be overcome to realize this vision.

To meet future needs, a holistic approach to HWT for seniors is required, with collaboration among various stakeholders and customization to individual needs. It is also crucial that the technology remains stable and doesn't become outdated quickly, which necessitates a long-term strategy for technology development and implementation. From a developmental perspective, it is important to include advanced technologies such as AI and nanotechnology to meet the specific needs of older people. Collaboration and funding from various stakeholders are necessary to realize these visions.

Local authorities should be proactive and invest in preventive measures, such as GPS alarms and other HWT solutions, to promote the safety and health of the older adults. HWT can also contribute to efficiency and reduce the burden on resources in elderly care through digital supervision and replacing certain visits with virtual meetings.

Some individual older adults have concerns about using HWT, which may be due to stigma or fear of not being able to use them. To overcome these concerns, it is important for local authorities (or a national initiative) to take a more proactive approach in informing and showing the older adults what is available and how HWT can enhance their independence.

Both the staff and decision-makers play a central role in the implementation and use of HWT. Staff members need support and training to increase their technological competence and overcome their fears of making mistakes. Decision-makers must consider the entire system around individuals, including their families, and involve them in the planning and implementation of HWT. Collaboration and clear allocation of responsibilities among different stakeholders are crucial for the successful implementation of HWT for seniors in elderly care. It is also important to avoid technology falling solely into the hands of vendors, and it should be clarified what responsibilities the public sector has compared to what individuals acquire in the private market.

To meet expectations of extended independence, the public sector and care providers must collaborate to offer tailored technical support and coaching. This requires a strategic and individualized approach to support measures and responsibilities. Finally, it is important to focus on simple and understandable information design to facilitate the use of HWT for both seniors and staff. This will contribute to increased independence, safety and security for seniors when aging in place.

3.2 Evaluation of HWT

It is evident that there is a growing awareness of the need for HWT in general and in elderly care, but efforts are still required to increase their usage and awareness of these solutions, as well as to facilitate their implementation and use.

For seniors, there is a wide range of HWT available, but there is a lack of knowledge and awareness about these solutions. Display environments can play a crucial role in disseminating information about available technology.

Individual seniors need to become more engaged in planning for their future aging and living arrangements, facilitating aging in place. This includes increasing awareness of available technology and its benefits.

It is necessary to clearly demonstrate the value and benefits of HWT to seniors and how it can contribute to increased independence and happiness. It should be emphasized that simple technology often works better than complex technology solutions.

Some HWT, such as GPS alarms and medication robots, have proven to be effective and useful. However, there are obstacles such as cognitive issues and lack of competence that might hinder the individual from benefiting from available technology.

Among the staff, there is variation in interest and competence when it comes to using technological aids. Some solutions, like medication robots and safety sensors, have been accepted and used more frequently.

Managers in elderly care have introduced various HWT, including medication robots, digital supervision visits, and training programs like "Habbi." Some solutions have been successful, while others, like night supervision cameras, have not gained the same popularity.

Decision-makers face challenges when it comes to implementing HWT, including internal processes and fragmented structures within municipalities and regions. However, there is potential to use self-monitoring for chronically ill individuals and improve collaboration between different authorities (Fig. 1).

Seniors	Personnel	Managers	Decision makers
• Technology that is easy to use works well • Social alarms have limited range, GPS-alarms work work well • The public sector should greater responsibility for the development • Cognitive limitations in relationship to IT • Older adults do not use and benefit from existing technology	• Services that work well: medicine robot, safety sensors, visit at doctor digitally • Digital aids is available but are not used • personnel lacks competence • For people with dementia - mainly tools for activity • Few know how the shower robot works	• Application for physical activity - very much appreciated • The interest of the personnel sets the agenda • Digital purchases • Mobile apps	• There are well-working existing platforms • Toilet robot • Avoid the word "robot" • Robot vacuum cleaner • Medicine robots • Night supervision cameras • Digital locks • Aids for personal hygiene

Fig. 1. Question 1. Evaluation of existing HWT

3.3 Visions and Expectations on Future HWT

The future demands HWT for seniors with a holistic approach, collaboration among various stakeholders, and customization to individual needs to achieve the goal of increased independence and a better quality of life for individual seniors when aging in place. To realize the vision of future technology in elderly care, cooperation among different actors and a larger societal transformation are necessary. It is essential to differentiate and tailor technology solutions for seniors and ensure that the technology remains stable and does not age quickly.

Future HWT for seniors should encompass advanced technologies such as AI and nanotechnology. It is crucial to include technology solutions specifically targeted at older people to meet their needs. For example, it is important not to lose sight of technology for older adults on the AI journey, but rather to develop AI and nanotechnology with older users as the target audience. Achieving these visions requires collaboration and financing from various stakeholders. Municipalities should be proactive and invest in preventive measures such as GPS alarms and other HWT solutions to promote safety, security and health when aging in place.

HWT can contribute to efficiency and reduce the burden on resources in elderly care while simultaneously improving the quality of life for seniors. This includes digital supervision, replacing some visits with digital meetings, the ability to shop online, and other practical aids.

There is concern among some seniors about using HWT, which may be due to stigma or fear of not being able to use them. Municipalities should take a more proactive approach in informing and showing older adults what is available and how HWT can enhance their independence. It is important to change the perception of HWT from being intimidating and impersonal to being a tool that can help seniors be self-reliant and maintain or even improve their quality of life. There must also be an awareness that there is no homogeneous group of individual seniors, and HWT solutions should be simple and differentiated to meet individual needs.

Seniors	Personnel	Managers	Decision makers
• Welfare technology creates safety • Simple technological solutions: online shopping, video doorbell, night camera/monitoring, video supported care, remote control for the lightning • Active participation in the development of AI, nanotechnology, 5G and 6G • Self-driving vehicles	• Digital assistant - home hub for: ordering supplies, register vital parameters, social conversation • Automatic beds • Common that the personnel are afraid of doing something wrong regarding new technology	• Technology under-used in home care • No information about existing aids • Digital meeting places • Social alarm • Digital visits to doctor • Medicine robot • Safety visits – face to face conversations • Previously physical visits - night camera is perceived negatively • Digital aids and their benefits must be anchored among older adults and personnel	• Technology has a great potential but can also increase isolation • Older users are very different, and the technology needs to be personalized. • Often lack of future perspective when implementing new technology, when implemented it is often already old. • Need for stable technology, not constant upgrades • Large potential for technology companies - users and organizations should define and demand what is needed • Implementation of digital aids is slow in Sweden • We must find new ways of working • The perspective of the relatives must gain a greater focus

Fig. 2. Question 2. Vision and expectations on future HWT

Among the staff, adapting to and using new technology, such HWT is a challenge, and many are afraid of making mistakes. Therefore, there needs to be support and training to increase technological competence.

Decision-makers must consider the entire system around individual seniors, including their families, and involve them in the planning and implementation of HWT. It is important to reduce the anxiety and stress of family members and increase the opportunities for longer and more social visits by the staff (Fig. 2).

3.4 Collaboration Between Stakeholders

Collaboration and clear responsibility allocation are crucial factors for successfully implementing HWT for seniors in general and in elderly care.

For seniors, there is a need for a more cohesive and clear approach from society and local government when it comes to HWT. It is important to avoid letting HWT fall into the hands of salespeople and to clarify the responsibilities of the public sector compared to what individuals need to acquire in the private market. Collaboration between housing companies/property owners and the local government is crucial to facilitate seniors staying at home longer.

The staff need to improve their ability to avoid silos and collaborate effectively. There must be clear decision-makers across time and organizational boundaries, and follow-ups must be improved. Working in silos can be inefficient, and it is important to gain a holistic perspective from a healthcare standpoint. There is a need for increased awareness of the need for collaboration, and experts within the organization need to be involved. For example, some HWT solutions are not allowed to bring in the transition from an ordinary living to a nursing home. This indicates lack of continuity, organizational obstacles and competence managing the transition from ordinary homes to a nursing home.

Managers experience that there are many different roles that must collaborate to implement HWT. Resistance to change has decreased, but it is important to clarify the purpose and benefits for the older adults. Communication must be clear and tailored to the target audience. It is important to address skeptics and actively work on change management, involving "technology nurses" (individuals with specific roles/competencies in HWT in social services/elderly care) for a smooth implementation.

Decision-makers experience that implementation of HWT is a challenge, especially when it comes to communicating with staff who are not linguistically strong. Resistance to HWT is primarily among the staff, and it is important to respect their concerns and involve them in the process. Evaluation and follow-up must be improved to ensure that the technology functions effectively and that the benefits are evident. Lastly, collaboration between the regions (county councils) and the municipal government is necessary to create demand and succeed in the implementation of HWT (Fig. 3).

3.5 Expectations on Prolonged Independence

To meet the expectations of extended independence when aging in place, the public sector and professional caregivers need to collaborate to provide tailored technical support and coaching, promote HWT usage, and ensure that seniors have control over their own lives

Seniors	Personnel	Managers	Decision makers
• Real estate companies and municipalities needs to collaborate to implement technological solutions in the houses • Short video calls with care personnel	• We are working in downpipes, difficult to get an overview from a caregiving perspective • The care giving organization are the experts and must be involved	• Collaboration is important and all stakeholders must be involved, it is easy to not involve the home care personnel	• Region/county and municipality must start to collaborate

Fig. 3. Question 3. Collaboration between stakeholders

and feel needed and independent. This requires a strategic and individual perspective on support measures and responsibility distribution.

Seniors demand better coordination among different public entities and systems to achieve extended independence. A strategic holistic approach and clarity regarding the division of responsibilities between individuals and the public sector are required. They want the opportunity to lead a good life at home, manage practical matters themselves, and actively participate in society with HWT assistance and support. Increased knowledge about the efficient use of HWT is also desirable.

Staff emphasize the importance of giving seniors control over their lives and the feeling of being needed. By preserving life stories and offering personal life coaching, a sense of independence can be promoted. It is also important to collect data on what everyone finds meaningful and how they experience their independence supported by HWT.

Managers recognize the need to increase understanding among the older adults regarding how HWT can support their independence.

Decision-makers emphasize that independence must be problematized and not categorized to find solutions. It is important to tailor support and resources individually to promote extended independence when aging in place (Fig. 4).

Seniors	Personnel	Managers	Decision makers
• Learn to be safe in the usage of technology • Technical support • Increased knowledge about how the technology can be used in an effective way	• Perception of independence is individual • The user can become more independent by using technological solutions	• The older adults must get an understanding of how technological aids can support independence	• Independence must be problematized. • Older adults are often categorized when trying to find solutions supporting independence

Fig. 4. Question 4. Expectations on prolonged independence

3.6 Information Design and Adaptation to User Needs

Staff members need support and training to increase their technological competence and overcome their fears of making mistakes.

It is apparent that even relatively simple HWT solutions can be challenging to use due to complex instructions, convoluted language, and password management issues. This is particularly challenging for individuals who do not have Swedish as their native language.

To facilitate the use of HWT, it is important to offer simple and easily understandable technology and provide effective support and assistance.

To achieve the best results in information design and customization, it is important to focus on user-friendliness and creating consistency within the operation. This will facilitate the use of HWT and, in turn, increase independence, safety and security for seniors in general and elderly care. To meet the needs of seniors and staff in elderly care, it is of utmost importance to create simpler and more tailored information design:

For seniors, clear and understandable communication is crucial. It is important to discuss HWT in a way that highlights its positive benefits in terms of possibilities and security, while avoiding concerns about surveillance and privacy. The HWT must be user-friendly and communicated in a language that is understandable for seniors.

Staff must be able to provide individually tailored instructions, as different individuals have varying levels of technical competence. Superusers who can offer support and training are an asset, and customized training for seniors in various HWT solutions is desirable.

Managers have access to resources such as videos and technical support phone numbers, but it is important to work on improving instructions for the staff so they can assist seniors more effectively.

Decision-makers have realized that intuitive and straightforward use of HWT is necessary. Clear information efforts, integrated technology in residences, and easy access to user instructions are important. There is a strong need for consistent and clear instructions that are the same throughout the operation, rather than many different cheat sheets at different levels (Fig. 5).

Seniors	Personnel	Managers	Decision makers
• Information is needed • Showrooms with integrated technology in the apartment • Large need for simple user instructions	• Many different "short manuals" that has been produced at different levels, and they often get lost • From a care perspective, it takes long time to learn • Super users are better than producing manuals.	• Good to go through how something should be used • Offer telephone support	• There is an idea that there is a need for producing local versions since the official manuals often not can be trusted • Better with instructions that are clear and the same with the entire organization

Fig. 5. Question 5. Information design and adaptation to user needs

4 Discussion

First, various groups such as decision makers in the health and welfare sector and politicians do have different understanding or interpretation of what the future means. While managers and decision makers often talk about the future that embraces the next two to three decades, the politician plans for the next term of office, and plans for the next election. This is rarely communicated in the debate of the future and especially not in relation to the aging population. Long term perspective is not prioritized in our contemporary society, and it does not put too much pressure on the political parties to take care of these issues. Secondly, it is also obvious in our pilot study that there is a lack of communication between different parts of the sector that are responsible for social welfare and aging individuals.

Based on the discussions in the focus groups and the participants' views on possibilities with HWT in the future three main areas could be seen and highlighted. AI was, not surprisingly, mentioned in all groups. One thing that was pointed out in the group of seniors was the importance of not forgetting HWT in the fast forward moving area of AI. If this technology will have the expected impact on our future applications and usage, it has to include all groups within society. Another technology area that was mentioned in the focus groups was self-monitoring and the use of sensors. These HWT solutions could be used for prevention in various ways, for example supporting a healthy lifestyle or reducing the risk of falling. Sensors for gathering information about health status could be used for increasing the control of chronic diseases and for faster adjustment of drugs. A third expected important future HWT area that was discussed and worth to be mentioned was the development and usage of personal agents. A digital companion based on AI and that can be interacted with in different ways. One future vision was that these personal agents also will be used for social purposes and that the distinction between social interaction between human friends and digital companions will become more blurred.

From an information design perspective, the result of the pilot study elucidates several challenges that are related to how to handle different tools and have knowledge about what exists on the market that could be useful for personal needs. We also find that there is a discrepancy between the knowledge that exists regarding what is needed to meet future needs to take care of an aging population and how society acts. Much has to do with treatment, many old people are technology mature but do have cognitive limitations depending on age (Eriksson & Sjölinder, 2019). In the focus group with the seniors this was expressed as a need for less updates of existing HWT, where the added functionality often does not provide extra value but instead it causes trouble and demands the need to adapt to a new appearance of the interface. Another issue is when an older adult has the need to move to a caring home, they are not allowed to bring their HWT with them.

This might reflect an organizational challenge with different stakeholders involved in providing the HWT to the older adult. On the other hand, it might also to some extent reflect an underlying attitude that when we get that old and vulnerable, we are no longer capable of using the HWT.

Further, the increasing demand on social welfare resources, the ethical consideration related to avoiding stereotypes and intentions in empowering people to remain as independent, if possible, suggest larger efforts in including older adults in the development and usage of new HWT. Participatory design methods for involving different user groups have been applied for several years and there are methods to gain a better understanding of the users' context and to avoid stereotypes related to a specific target group (Östlund et al., 2020). The involvement of older adults in the co-creation process will also make use of their knowledge and contribute with knowledge about how digitals services can be implemented in a way that is perceived as meaningful for this target group.

In general, information design will play an important role in the future society due to digitalization. In relation to elderly care the challenge for creating meaningful infor-mation, that is information that reaches the target group with the intended aim, exists on several levels (Eriksson & Carlsson, 2022). Firstly, what is needed to communicate, secondly, how and lastly, how to get people engaged in the information or what is com-municated in order to change attitude. Therefore, how HWT is communicated will affect the reception of the same.

There has been a long tradition of negative attitudes to aids for disabilities such as hearing aids, white mobility sticks, walkers etc. This still influences how individ-ual seniors experience using HWT. To change the attitude regarding different kinds of HWT to overcome disabilities that come with age requires not only information to the target group as such, but also change related to aging. On the other hand, there exists a disbelief that older adults can handle technology, even HWT, themselves. It is also a self-perception that many seniors experience themself a contradiction between the acceptance to use different kinds of aid and still show a maturity when it comes to digital technology (Eriksson, 2016; Eriksson & Sjölinder, 2019). What is needed to communi-cate to older adults, is that it is possible to continue using digital technology and also to learn new things. But that of course requires instructions that are user friendly, and easy to follow and use (Eriksson & Sjölinder, 2019). The communication and information about existing HWT should address older adults, staff members, manager, and decision makers in order to create involvement and to be able to offer tailored support for both the older adults and caregivers (relatives and staff).

5 Conclusions

The study highlights the disparity in how different stakeholders perceive the future, with decision-makers focusing on shorter-term goals while managers and healthcare professionals consider longer-term implications. This discrepancy can lead to challenges in prioritizing and addressing issues related to aging in place and the use of HWT in eldercare.

Another key insight is the recognition of cognitive limitations among older adults, which can impact their ability to adopt and benefit from HWT solutions. While some older individuals may be technologically proficient, others may face challenges.

The study highlights a potential barrier to the use of HWT in eldercare, wherein older adults may lose access to their digital devices upon transitioning to caring homes. This raises questions about continuity of care and the integration of HWT within institutional settings.

To address the complex challenges identified in the study, there is a clear need for long-term planning and strategic investment in technology-enabled eldercare. This includes fostering collaboration among stakeholders, prioritizing user-friendly design, and addressing cognitive limitations through tailored solutions.

Integrating technology into care practices requires not only technological advancements but also changes in organizational culture and workflows. Training and support for healthcare staff are crucial to ensure effective implementation and utilization of HWT in eldercare settings.

A significant finding is the lack of communication and collaboration among various entities responsible for eldercare, including policymakers, healthcare professionals, and technology developers. This fragmentation impedes the development and implementation of effective solutions tailored to the needs of older adults.

The study underscores the importance of user-friendly information design in facilitating the adoption and use of HWT by older adults and healthcare staff. The complexity of technology and the diversity of user needs pose significant challenges that must be addressed through clear communication and tailored instructions.

In conclusion, the study underscores the importance of addressing the multifaceted challenges associated with aging in place and the use of HWT in general and in eldercare. By fostering collaboration, promoting user-friendly design, and adopting a holistic approach to care, stakeholders can work towards enhancing the independence and quality of life of older adults in the future.

Acknowledgments. The authors would like to than the participants in the focus group interviews.

Disclosure of Interests. The authors have no competing interests.

References

Alkhaldi, B., Sahama, T., Huxley, C., Gajanayake, R.: Barriers to implementing eHealth: a multidimensional perspective. Stud. Health Technol. Inform. **205**, 875–879 (2014)

Alvarez, R.C.: The promise of e-Health - a Canadian perspective. Ehealth Int. **1**(1), 4 (2002). https://doi.org/10.1186/1476-3591-1-4

Eriksson, Y.: Technologically Mature but with Limited Capabilties. In: 2nd International Conference of IT for the Aged Population, HCI 2016 International. Springer (2016)

Eriksson, Y., Carlsson, A.-L.: The challenge of designing meaningful information. In: Eriksson, Y. (ed.) Different Perspectives in Design Thinking, pp. 123–145. CRC Press (2022)

Eriksson, Y., Sjölinder. M.: The role of designers in the development and communication of new technology. In: Sayago, S., Sergio [ed.] Perspectives on Human-Computer Interaction Research with Older People. Springer (2019). https://doi.org/10.1007/978-3-030-06076-3

Legner, C., Eymann, T., Hess, T., et al.: Digitalization: opportunity and challenge for the business and information systems engineering community. Bus. Inf. Syst. Eng. **59**, 301–308 (2017)

Merriam-Webster (24/02/16) https://www.merriam-webster.com

Pericu, S.: Designing for an ageing society: products and services. Des. J. **20**(sup1), S2178–S2189 (2017). https://doi.org/10.1080/14606925.2017.1352734

Rogers, Y., Paay, J., Brereton, M., Vaisutis, K., Marsden, G. et al.: Never Too Old: Engaging Retired People Inventing the Future with MaKey MaKey. CHI 2014, April 26-May 1, 2014, Toronto, ON, Canada (2014). https://doi.org/10.1145/2556288.2557184

Sandelowski, M.: Whatever happened to qualitative description? Res. Nurs. Health **23**(4), 334–340 (2000). https://doi.org/10.1002/1098-240x(200008)23:4%3c334::aid-nur9%3e3.0.co;2-g

Stoumpos, A., Kitsios, F., Talias, M.: Digital transformation in healthcare: Technology acceptance and its applications. Int. J. Environ. Res. Public Health **15**(4) (2023). https://doi.org/10.3390/ijerph20043407

Swedish Association of Local Authorities and Regions. Welfare Sector Workforce Forecast 2021–2031 and How Welfare Can Address the Skills Challeng (In Swedish: Välfärdens kompetensförsörjning Personalprognos 2021–2031 och hur välfärden kan möta kompetensutmaningen) (2022). https://skr.se/skr/tjanster/rapporterochskrifter/publikationer/valfardenskompeten sforsorjning.68208.htm

Swedish Research Council (2017). Good research practice. https://www.vr.se/english/analysis/rep orts/our-reports/2017-08-31-goodresearch-practice.html

Yarker, S., Doran, P., Buffel, T.: Theorizing "Place" in Aging in Place: The Need for Territorial and Relational Perspectives, The Gerontologist, (64)2 (2024). https://doi-org.ep.bib.mdh.se/ https://doi.org/10.1093/geront/gnad002

WMA. Handbook of WMA policies (2022). https://www.wma.net/wpcontent/uploads/2022/11/HB-E-Version-2022-2-2.pdf

Östlund, B., et al.: Using academic work places to involve older people in the design of digital applications. In: Zhou, J., Gao, Q. (eds.) Human Aspects of IT for the Aged Population, Technologies, Design and User Experience, 6th International Conference, ITAP 2020, Held as Part of the 22nd HCI International Conference, HCII 2020, Copenhagen, July, 19–24. Proceedings, Part I, pp. 45–58. Springer (2020). https://doi.org/10.1007/978-3-030-50252-2_4

Exergames as Synchronous Collaborative Remote Training in Older Adults with Hypertension: A Mixed Methods Pilot Study

Susan Vorwerg-Gall⬤, Luis Perotti⬤, Rebecca Dahms⬤, and Oskar Stamm⁽⊠⁾⬤

Geriatrics Research Group, Charité - Universitätsmedizin Berlin, Reinickendorfer Str. 61, 13347 Berlin, Germany
oskar.stamm@charite.de

Abstract. Adhering to recommended training frequencies can be a challenge for older adults with hypertension. Remote training offers the opportunity to exercise independently, regardless of time and location. The pilot study aimed to test the feasibility of three different exergame prototypes for synchronous collaborative remote training of hypertensive older adults. A total of 12 participants diagnosed with hypertension were tested in two separate living labs using three exergame prototypes: "Workout Group" (WG), "Screen" and "HoloLens". Within WG, the participants were represented as gamified avatars on a screen. In the exergame Screen, the participants could see themselves and the trainer as a point cloud on a screen. In Hololens, the participants saw the trainer directly in front of them as a point cloud via a HoloLens 2 headset. No significant differences in heart rate were found between the three exergame sessions. However, there was a significant increase in heart rate in relation to the resting heart rate in all exergames (p < .001). The participants rated the usability on the system usability scale as good and had a high level of enjoyment in all physical activities. The most gamified exergame, WG, was favored by the older adults with hypertension (n = 9) and would be the most preferred by them in a future home setting (n = 6). The pilot study demonstrated the feasibility of different approaches for designing synchronous collaborative remote training in older adults with Hypertension and provided recommendations for future studies.

Keywords: Remote Exercising · HoloLens · Cardiac Rehabilitation · Real-Time · Physiotherapy · Workout

1 Introduction

Hypertension is one of the most common risk factors for cardiovascular disease. As the prevalence increases significantly with age, it is one of the most important determinants in the lives of older adults. According to a GEDA survey in Germany by the Robert Koch Institute, around two-thirds of people aged 65 and over suffer from hypertension. About 63.8% of women and 65.1% of men (23.967 participants were included in the study) say

© The Author(s), under exclusive license to Springer Nature Switzerland AG 2024
Q. Gao and J. Zhou (Eds.): HCII 2024, LNCS 14726, pp. 112–131, 2024.
https://doi.org/10.1007/978-3-031-61546-7_8

they are affected [1]. According to a NHANES survey, 70% of people over the age of 65 suffer from hypertension in the USA [2]. Globally, the treatment rate for hypertension is highest in those aged 65 and over [3]. In order to lower blood pressure, it is therefore recommended for the 65 s and older to do moderate-intensity endurance and strength exercises almost every day. The guidelines of the European Society of Cardiology and the European Society of Hypertension (ESC/ESH) recommend dynamic, aerobic exercise of moderate intensity (e.g. walking, jogging, or cycling) for at least 30 min on 5–7 days per week for hypertensive patients. This can be accompanied by strength training 2–3 days a week [4]. The WHO additionally recommends isometric resistance training consisting of 3 sessions per week over 8–10 weeks (e.g. 4 sets of 2 min and 1 min rest, at 30 to 40% of maximum voluntary contraction) as physical activity for hypertension in order to be able to bring about initial improvements. The recommendation also indicates that older adults have a higher training load than younger adults. It is therefore recommended to pay attention to the age-related framework conditions, such as the decline in muscle strength and performance as well as frequency, intensity, and duration, with the help of an experienced fitness trainer [5, 6]. Nevertheless, the continuity of the training frequency recommended in the guidelines can be a challenge for older adults [7]. In order to increase adherence and thus the continuity of physical activity in hypertension patients, group training programs are an effective method that has been investigated in several studies.

A study by Mehra et al. found that the study participants felt motivated in the presence of their peers and developed a good relationship with the group, in some cases forming friendships that lasted for years as a result of the sports courses [8]. A systematic review by Meredith et al. from 2023 also showed that physical activity in older adults (average: 79 years) promotes social interaction and enjoyment of exercise while reducing feelings of loneliness [9]. In the context of the COVID-19 pandemic, the need for online group exercise has become apparent due to the containment of the risk of infection. A literature review from 2022, which examined physical activity in older people during the pandemic with key exercises for hypertensive patients in virtual groups, identified benefits such as improved muscle strength, mood, quality of life, and social well-being [10]. Further studies have also shown that the satisfaction and acceptance of remote exercise programs among older adults during the COVID-19 pandemic is high [11, 12] and that the trainings support both deconditioning and the prevention of loss of autonomy [12]. In addition, the study by Granet et al. showed that online sports exercises improved physical health (BMI) and functional abilities (walking speed) [11].

To improve the continuity of online sports exercises in the case of physical health restrictions, such as in hypertension patients, telerehabilitation as remote exercising is an option that is independent of time and place. Several studies have already demonstrated the positive effects and potential of telerehabilitation. The systematic review and Fernandez et al. [13] showed significant improvements in isokinetic training exercises and subjective improvements in the perception of balance. In addition, a higher participation rate was achieved in the live video group compared to the face-to-face group [13]. Similar results were obtained in a study by Platz et al. [14]., in which 20 participants took part via video conference or as a health education group. The study emphasized the increase in adherence among the participants in the video conference and positive effects in the intervention group concerning endurance, leg strength, and balance [14].

A review by Shimbo et al. from 2023 shows the variance offered by cardiac telerehabilitation and the benefits of real-time telemonitoring and care, which increase patient safety and training effectiveness [15]. In most of the studies examined a mobile phone was used as the basic telemonitoring system, which, for example, ECG, heart rate, and heart failure were remotely monitored for objective data measurement.

Engaging in remote exergames can offer older adults significant advantages by encouraging physical activity and fostering social connections. Freed et al. [16] discovered that older individuals took pleasure in participating in exergames and viewed them as a potential solution to combat feelings of social isolation and loneliness, especially during times of social distancing. In the field of gaming, a distinction is made between different multiplayer games. The number of players in a game and how the players access the game defines a multiplayer game [17]. Online or networked multiplayer games connect players over a distance. Multiplayer games have three main categories of player interaction: competitive, cooperative, and collaborative. In competitive games, players or teams compete against each other. In cooperative games, players work together as a team to achieve a common goal. In collaborative games, players rely on each other to achieve a shared objective [17]. Moreover, the gameplay in multiplayer games can be designed as synchronous, where players compete against each other in real-time, while in asynchronous multiplayer games, players can compete against each other without having to play at the same time.

Exergames using AR or VR offer new opportunities e.g. collaborative and competitive play and are proving to be more effective in promoting movement than traditional training. A study by Wu et al. [18] examined traditional training compared to cooperative and competitive play within a 4-week intervention with 113 older adults. The results showed the importance of social presence in cooperative and competitive play as well as perceived behavioral control when older adults were supported during exercise. Furthermore, another VR exergame study during rehabilitation, in which collaborative gaming was compared with playing alone, showed that older people showed higher intrinsic motivation, physical exertion, and enjoyment in collaborative gaming than those who played alone [19].

New technologies offer the potential to engage older adults in physical activities in a novel and enjoyable way, but there has been no research on which technology and approach are assessed and preferred for remote training in older adults with chronic conditions such as hypertension.

The objective of this exploratory pilot study was to investigate the feasibility of multiplayer exergame as synchronous remote training in older adults with hypertension. The presented study is part of the joint project "BewARe - Sensor-supported movement training for senior citizens in an intelligent augmented reality system", which was funded by the German Federal Ministry of Education and Research. The following research questions will be determined:

Primary Research Questio

1. RQ1: What exercise intensities can be achieved in the applied exergames for remote training in older adults with hypertension?
2. RQ2: How do older adults with hypertension rate the usability of the exergames for remote training?

3. RQ3: How do older adults with hypertension rate the enjoyment of physical activity during remote training with exergames?

Secondary Research Questions

1. RQ4: What are the recommendations for future studies on the use of exergames for remote training in older adults with hypertension?

2 Methods

The intervention study aimed to test the feasibility of three demo exergames for remote training of older adults with hypertension. The study followed a mixed methods approach consisting of quantitative, qualitative, and task-based methods. Three exergames ("Workout Group", "Screen", "HoloLens") were applied at two separate training sites, each of which was equipped with a monitor, a Kinect v2 camera for skeletal tracking, a webcam, and HoloLens 2. In the course of remote training, these exercise stations represented separate living rooms. The participant tested the three exergames one after the other. In addition, the heart rate (HR) was measured via a smartwatch during the exercise game.

2.1 Procedure

Within the first exergame "Workout Group" (WG), the participants were represented as avatars on a screen together with another player (in the second living room). In the exergame WG, both had to perform one of the two physical exercises (arms circling or squats). The players had to agree on who would perform which exercise. The exercise time was 45 s. The exercises were repeated in three sets with a break of 45 s. During the whole time, the players could talk to each other via a headset and, for example, motivate/cheer each other on.

In the second movement game "Screen" the participants saw a recording of a trainer on a screen as well as themselves next to the trainer as a virtual point cloud. During the application, subjects received real-time instructions from a trainer, this Wizard-of-Oz method created the impression that they were performing a live workout. Point clouds were generated by the Kinect v2 and displayed on the screen. During the training, four physical exercises (arms circling, lateral lunge, lateral shuffle, and knee lift) were to be performed within approximately 5 min. The trainer demonstrated the exercises and guided the subjects accordingly. Communication took place via a headset.

In the third exergame "Hololens", the participants saw the trainer directly in front of them via HoloLens 2 headset. During the training, four physical exercises (arms circling, lateral lunge, forward lunge, and lateral shuffle) were also to be performed within 5 min. These were demonstrated by the trainer and the subjects were instructed accordingly. During the exergame, the participants' movements were recorded via a camera system and displayed to the trainer on a monitor. The trainer's exercise demonstration was recorded via the Kinect and streamed to the HoloLens in real-time. A headset was used for communication between the test persons and the trainer.

After each exergame, the participants were asked to complete the Physical Activity Enjoyment Scale (PACES) and the System Usability Scale (SUS). In addition, a short interview was conducted about the just-experienced exergame. All study participants gave informed consent to participate in the study.

2.2 Materials

Exergame 1: Workout Group. The first exergame was a web application prototype developed by ART + COM GmbH for the study (see Fig. 1). The game engine Unity3D was used to develop the web application. The exergame represented a collaborative remote workout, as if two people were playing a synchronous multiplayer exergame together in two spatially separated environments. Two participants were connected, each in a separate living lab. The living labs represented living rooms with a television.

Firstly, the participants received noise-cancelling headphones and were able to communicate with each other via these. A short tutorial video shown on the television explained the process to the two players. At the beginning, they could choose which exercise they wanted to perform. For this, they had to agree on who would take on which role. Options were arm circles or squats. The left character on the screen had to perform squats as quickly as possible and the right character had to perform arm circles as quickly as possible. Behind the left figure, a construction crane was moved to transport bricks by squatting. Behind the right character, a conveyor belt was moved by circling the arms. The aim was to move as many bricks as possible from the crane onto the conveyor belt and to get them to the end of the conveyor belt, where they would be automatically stacked to form a tower to build the highest possible tower in 45 s. There were three sets of 45 s each, starting with a countdown. After each set there were 45-s breaks during which participants could communicate with each other, E.G. for motivation, socializing, or small talk.

Before the exergame began, the participants were also instructed on how to conduct exercises by a physiotherapist. In the arm circles exercise, the person stands upright with their arms extended out to the side at shoulder height. Ensuring that the shoulders, elbows, and hands were in line was important. Next, the person begins to move their arms in small circles without raising their shoulders. During the squats, the arms should be stretched forward, and it should be ensured that the knees do not go beyond the tips of the toes if possible.

In the study, body tracking of the system was omitted for resource reasons, resulting in the application of a Wizard of OZ experiment approach. The participants interacted with the system and believed that the system autonomously monitored the exercise movements. In both rooms, the study staff pressed a key on the two controlling laptops at the start of each exercise repetition, whereupon an animation was played of the avatar performing the exercise. The study staff were positioned in such a way that they could not be heard or seen by the participants, but the staff had them in view. The communication was not implemented in the game due to development resources but was conducted via the Zoom platform in the background.

Fig. 1. Exergame UI of Workout Group.

Exergame 2: Screen. The second exergame "Screen" was also a prototype developed by ART + COM GmbH for the study. The exergame represented a screen-based remote workout with a holographic trainer (see Fig. 2). The scenario simulated a telerehabilitation approach in which an older adult is connected to a trainer/physiotherapist from their living room. On the screen in the living lab, the participants could see themselves and the trainer as a point cloud. The participant's bodies were transmitted on the screen in real-time using the Kinect v2. However, the trainer was recorded in advance to minimize the amount of data required for better transmission quality. The Wizard of Oz approach was used here as well. The participants thought that the trainer was performing the exercises from a different location at the same time. The trainer's audio output was activated via Zoom in the background so that the trainer could respond to questions and give feedback, creating the impression of a live training session. LiveScan3D [20], a free open-source system for live 3D data acquisition with the Kinect v2, was used to create a point cloud. The point cloud stream can be recorded or streamed to the Unity application. This was utilized by recording the trainer's exercises in advance and implementing them as animations in the Unity3D prototype. The participants, on the other hand, were recorded in the living lab with a Kinect v2 and the point cloud of their body was streamed in real-time to a position directly next to the trainer. At the beginning of the exergame, there was a brief camera ride to show the three-dimensionality of the room and the virtual people in it. The participants were then welcomed by the trainer and asked to move only in the circle that they saw on the floor in the virtual room. The first exercise was arm circling. As in the first game, the participants were asked to circle their arms, only this time with their left arm offset to the trainer so that they performed a circling movement around the trainer's arm. Lateral lunges were then performed alternately on both sides. The lunges were to be synchronized with the trainer. Afterward, lateral shuffles were to be performed in the third exercise. The participants should always perform the side shuffles opposite the trainer at the other end. The last exercise was knee lifts. Here the trainer indicated the height of the lift with an outstretched arm.

Fig. 2. Exergame Screen with the point cloud of participant and trainer.

Exergame 3: HoloLens. The third exergame "HoloLens" was a mixed reality (MR) prototype developed by ART + COM GmbH for the study. The exergame represented an MR-based remote workout with a holographic trainer (see Fig. 3). The scenario, like the second exergame, also simulated a telerehabilitation approach where an older adult is connected to a trainer/physiotherapist from their living room. However, the participant is wearing a HoloLens 2 and sees a trainer face-to-face in front of them. The LiveScan3D-Hololens [20] application was used in this exergame to stream the trainer's body as a point cloud to the Unity application in the HoloLens2. The application allows streaming of the reconstructed 3D point cloud to a remote location in real time. For this purpose, the trainer was recorded in a separate room with a Kinect v2 and transmitted live to the participant's Hololens2. As in the other exergames, the participants were given noise-canceling headphones through which they could communicate with the trainer via Zoom. The trainer was able to see the participants' movements live on a monitor connected to a camera in the living lab. During the practice time, the exercises were performed by the trainer live and she gave instructions and feedback on the execution. The following exercises were performed: arm circling, lateral lunge, forward lunge, and lateral shuffle. Except for the forward lunge, the exercises were already known from the previous games. In forward lunge, the participants had to step forward with one foot while keeping the other foot stationary. They should bend the knee of the leg that stepped forward while keeping the other leg straight. For the interaction with the trainer, they should high-five the trainer with both hands while stepping forward.

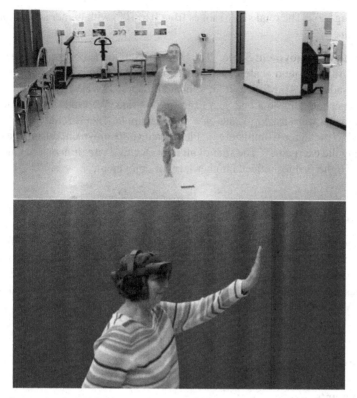

Fig. 3. Exergame HoloLens, above participant's view on the trainer's point cloud.

Polar M600. A Polar M600 smartwatch equipped with an optical pulse measurement system was placed on the participant's left wrist to measure their heart rate. The collected raw data were exported with Polar Flow and were processed as a CSV file. Previous research has demonstrated that the Polar M600 is a reliable tool for measuring heart rate [21, 22].

System Usability Scale. In our study, we assessed the usability of each exergame using the System Usability Scale (SUS), a validated questionnaire that has been widely used in various usability studies. Originally developed by John Brooke in 1986 [23], it enables the evaluation of a wide range of products and services, including hardware, software, mobile devices, websites, and applications. The SUS consists of 10 items, and responses are given on a five-point Likert scale ranging from 1 ("strongly disagree") to

5 ("strongly agree"). The total score ranges from 0 to 100, with higher scores indicating better usability.

Physical Activity Enjoyment Scale. The Physical Activity Enjoyment Scale (PACES) was originally an 18-item scale developed to assess the enjoyment of physical activity in young adults [24]. Mullen et al. validated a version with 8 items in a group of older adults participating in a one-year exercise program. We used this version here as well. Participants were asked to rate on a 7-point bipolar Likert scale (1 = "Disagree Completely"; 7 = "agree Completely") "Please rate your enjoyment during the physical activity using the exergame". The sum of all items forms a one-dimensional measure of enjoyment. Higher values reflect a higher level of enjoyment.

2.3 Data Analysis

The collected data were analyzed using SPSS 27 (IBM SPSS statistics version 27; IBM Corp., Armonk, NY, USA). The alpha level was set at 5%. The normal distribution of the sample's result values was examined using the Shapiro-Wilk test. If the sample's result values did not follow a normal distribution, the Wilcoxon signed-rank test and the Mann-Whitney U test were used to compare the samples. In the case of a normal distribution, a paired t-test was used.

3 Results

3.1 Participants

This study included 12 participants aged 74.42 ± 5.84 years diagnosed with hypertension. Three subjects were male and nine female. Half of the participants were active more than once a week. Whereas six participants only exercised 0 to 1 time per week. On average, the participants did sport 2.36 times a week (including strength training, gymnastics, Pilates, yoga, cycling, water aerobics, Nordic walking, balance training, and hiking).

3.2 Heartrate Polar M600

The heart rate was recorded using the Polar M600 at a sampling rate of 1 Hz for the entire duration of the remote training using the exergames. It became apparent that the average heart rate differed only slightly between the three exergames (see Fig. 4). Significant differences were not determined here (t-test; WG-screen $p = .179$; screen-hololens $p = .263$; WG-hololens $p = .162$). However, there was a significant increase in heart rate in relation to the resting heart rate in all exergames (t-test; $p < .001$).

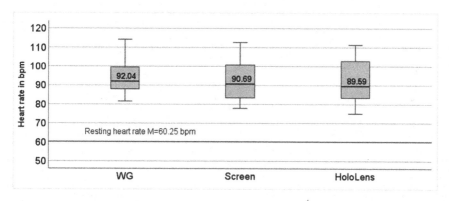

Fig. 4. Boxplots of the heart rate during the exergames (WG, Screen, HoloLens) compared to the resting heart rate.

3.3 SUS

The system usability wasassessed after each exergame. For the Workout Group, the mean SUS score was 84.79 ± 8.56 points, for the Screen exergame 75.42 ± 17.12 points, and for the exergame with the Hololens 79.79 ± 11.05 points (Fig. 5).

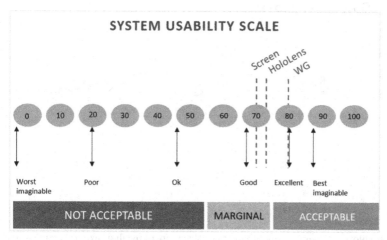

Fig. 5. Classification of the SUS score for the three exergames "Workout Group" (WG), "Screen", and "Hololens" in the interpretation scheme according to Bangor et al. [25].

Furthermore, we examined whether the three exergames differed significantly in terms of the usability rating (see Fig. 6). We found that there is no difference in usability for the "Screen" and "HoloLens" applications measured with the SUS ($t(11) = -1.3$, $p = .226$). However, significant differences were found between the "Workout Group" and the "Screen" application ($t(11) = 2.6$, $p = .025$).

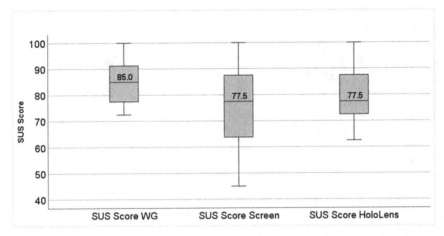

Fig. 6. Boxplots of SUS scores for the exergames with median, maximum, and minimum.

3.4 PACES

The results show that there was a very high level of enjoyment during the physical activity in all three exergames (see Fig. 7). Consequently, no significant differences were found between the three exergames (Wilcoxon test; WG-Screen p = .109; Screen-Hololens p = .612; WG-Hololens p = .513).

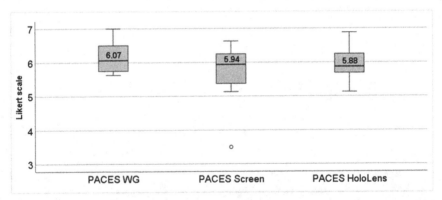

Fig. 7. Boxplots of the enjoyment of the physical activity of the three exergames measured using the PACES with median, maximum, minimum, and outliers.

3.5 Qualitative Results

Which Training Did you Enjoy the Most? Nine of the twelve participants liked the "Workout Group" exergame best. They considered the representations on the screen to be appealing and described them as pretty and cute (n = 3). However, one person described the depictions as too angular or too abstract and therefore in need of improvement. The physical exercises were perceived as challenging (n = 2). The logical structure of the game, the playful presentation ("The building blocks - that was very nice. Child's play, [...] so you feel transported back to childhood. You awaken your inner child.", P02, female, 62 years) and the cooperative nature of the exercises were positively emphasized. One person emphasized the collaborative aspect and found it beneficial that the players were dependent on each other during the exercises and therefore had to coordinate with their fellow players.

Two people reported that they enjoyed the exergame "Screen" the most and explained that this type of exercise was more physically challenging for the user. It was also perceived as particularly versatile (n = 1).

One participant favored the "WG" and "Hololens" at the same level. The exergame "Hololens" was described as interesting and stimulating (n = 1).

Which Technology gave you the Strongest Feeling that your Teammate or Trainer was Actually Present? With regard to the game WG, four people agreed that the other player appeared most real to them. One person had the feeling that the other player was physically present and was standing right behind the player. It was also mentioned that the aspect of social interaction (playing together with a partner) was an important aspect of the positive evaluation of the "workout group" (n = 2).

During the "Screen" exergame, two people stated that they perceived the instructor to be the most real. However, due to the representation shown on the television, one participant had the feeling that the trainer and the person doing the workout were standing inside each other or stepping on each other's feet, which was perceived as distracting. The digital representation of the trainer was therefore sometimes perceived as somewhat obstructive and confusing (n = 2).

Three participants perceived the trainer as being real in the "HoloLens" exercise game. However, it was mentioned here that it was difficult to evaluate the technology because the time of use during the workout was too short to fully get used to the technology (n = 1).

In addition, one person stated that the trainer/player seemed real in all three games, which was mainly due to the inclusion of their voices during exercise. According to two people, there was no difference between the exergames "Screen" and "HoloLens". One older adult commented that the depictions of the characters in these exergames were somewhat realistic, but not good enough to recognize the other player or the trainer. The pixel-like quality (the dots of the point clouds) as well as the proportions of the figures were criticized (n = 1).

Which Technology Would you be Most Likely to Use for Training at Home? Six of the older adults who took part in the study stated that they could best imagine playing the "workout group" exercise game at home. On the one hand, it was mentioned that the technical requirements for this game were considered to be low and the system would therefore be easier to set up and use therefore little technical knowledge was required when using the system (n = 2). One older adult stated that it was positive, that the system could be set up by oneself so that flexible training sessions would be possible.

In addition, the aspect of only having to concentrate on one task at a time was important to the participants in this exergame (n = 1).

Three older adults preferred the exercise game "Screen" for home use. One person noted that they would like to have these exercises available on CD/DVD at home and use them on the TV. This person preferred to use as little equipment and technical systems as possible when exercising. It was also highlighted as especially helpful during the "Screen" exergame that the trainer gave feedback on their performance during the exercises.

Three people mentioned exercises with the Hololens as their preferred technology for home use. This technology was perceived as the most innovative (n = 1). One person stated that they disliked screen-based activities due to their previous occupation, so they preferred the exercises using the glasses. It was also said to be an advantage to be able to see one's training partner during the workout (n = 1).

With Which Technology Did you have Safety Concerns? Only three of the older adults expressed safety concerns about the technologies and exercise techniques used. One person expressed concerns about using the HoloLens for physical activity. The concern was raised that the glasses could accidentally slip during exercises. Concerns about maintaining balance during exercise execution were also mentioned using the "Screen" exergame ("I was slightly off balance [...] but was able to catch myself.", P03, female, 66 years). A comment was also made on the subject of data protection. It was pointed out that the prevention of unauthorized access to the communication content (i.e. voice transmission) during the exercises should be taken into account.

Which Representation (Avatar, Virtual Person, Real Body) of Yourself Would you Prefer and Why? Five people preferred the representation of themselves as an avatar in the first ex-ergame. One person especially liked the representation of oneself and the partner as abstract characters and mentioned that the avatars still showed precisely how the exercises were to be carried out.

Four people stated that they preferred to be represented as a virtual person (i.e. as a point cloud in three-dimensional space) in the WG exergame. This was perceived as the most accurate way to determine whether and how to perform the exercises correctly (n = 1). It was also stated the trainer was able to react well to one's exercise performance.

Three people preferred the presentation in the Hololens, in which the integration of their own body was described as "real" (n = 2) and "natural" (n = 1). One person particularly liked the three-dimensionality, which was said to be most closely reflecting the real world.

Which Game Made you Feel the Most Supervised? Five people felt that the provided support was equally good for all three exergame variants and were unable to identify any differences. Four of the study participants felt that the supervision in the "HoloLens" exergame was the best. One of these older adults felt that the communication that took place during the exercises was like in real life and it was positively emphasized that good exercise correction was provided during the exercises, which prevented potential postural errors (n = 1). One person also highlighted the fact that the trainer and the person doing the exercises were facing each other during a workout in the "HoloLens" exergame.

Another person felt that the exercises using the "HoloLens" were more adaptable to individual preferences, as the speed of exercise performance was variable.

Two of the older adults experienced the support provided within the two exergames "Screen" and "HoloLens" to be equally good, while one person found the support provided during the exergame "Screen" to be the best.

How did you Feel About the Communication Between Yourself and Your Training Partner and Between Yourself and the Therapist. With regard to the evaluation of the communication with the training partner or trainer during the exergames, the comments by the older adults were predominantly positive. Seven of the participants felt that communication was good overall and attributed this to communication with both the trainer and the other player. According to one older adult, communication was very good despite wearing a hearing aid. Two people emphasized the importance of being able to communicate with each other during the exergames. The opportunity to communicate was perceived as supportive and encouraging (n = 1). In the future, using the exergame systems would make it possible to make appointments with a partner and do exercise together using the system (n = 1); this social aspect should be strengthened in the future, as the aspects of cooperation and support during exercises are important for older adults (n = 1).

However, two people did not realize initially that communication was possible during the exercises and only became aware of this when they were addressed by the trainer. In addition, two people noted that there were technical failures that impaired communication. One person perceived it as unusual to wear headphones during the exercises, while three others felt that communication during the exercises was not important overall. One person mentioned that the technical requirements for the use of all three systems were perceived as too high (n = 1), as a simple depiction of the exercises on the television would be sufficient (n = 1). That person also expressed the opinion, that for older adults traditional training with a real instructor would be more suitable. One study participant also said that there was no need to communicate during training and that they preferred to watch TV while exercising.

4 Discussion

Our pilot study revealed that all three exergames showed a minimal difference in heart rate compared to each other, but a significant increase compared to the resting heart rate. The WG achieved the highest SUS score with 84.79, followed by the Hololens exergame with 79.79 and the screen exergame with 75.42. Significant SUS score differences were observed between the WG and the Screen application. All exergames were highly enjoyable physical activities with no significant differences in enjoyment levels. Among the participants, the WG was the preferred exergame for nine out of twelve, two favored the Screen exergame, and one equally preferred the WG and Hololens.

Other studies that measured the heart rate during VR exergames with older participants found slightly higher average HR values compared to the results of our study, but the intervention period was significantly shorter in our case, which probably resulted in a lower load [26, 27]. The target HR zone 50–85% of the American Heart Association

[28] at the age of 65 is 78–132 bpm, where we are well positioned with our values, and thus a moderate training intensity is feasible with the exergames tested.

The results of the usability analysis measured with the SUS can be interpreted as "Good" according to Bangor [25]. Based on research findings, an SUS score below 68 is considered below average. All exergames were rated above average. The WG even had a mean SUS score of 84.79, which is very close to excellent usability. Significant differences were found between the exergames WG and Screen. The interviews revealed that orientation in the room was difficult in the Screen exergame, as they had to position themselves next to the trainer and in a circle, and the directions of movement were counter-intuitive for some. This could have resulted in a lower usability rating for the Screen exergame prototype. It was to be expected that there would be no differences in the enjoyment during the physical activity, as the exercises were all very similar to each other, partly identical, and also very similar in terms of load.

In the interviews, it became clear that the older adults were not primarily interested in the novelty of the technology, but in the enjoyment of the exergame. This was particularly high with the gamified exergame WG, which was very playful in design and also had the most collaborative character. Zhang et al. [29] found out that the positive effects of gameplay on older adults are highly dependent on the context of the game and the enjoyment of the relationship. The participants in our study commented that they liked the gamified presentation of the first game and it can be assumed that the gamified presentation of the training was a decisive factor in the high preference. Many studies show the influence of gamification of digitally supported physical exercises on the perception of older adults as a target group [30–33]. Furthermore, in all exergames, participants emphasized that the social and communicative aspect of remote training is important. The opportunity to communicate with teammates or trainers was positively emphasized. The motivational effect of collaborative activities when playing the exergames was mentioned by the study participants and is also stated in the study by Shah et al. [19]. In our study, older adults gave positive feedback on the potential social effects of using remote exergaming. The benefits of strengthening social ties with peers and reducing loneliness have been repeatedly documented in the literature and should be further investigated in long-term studies [34, 35].

An important component in the evaluation of the three exergame technologies was the accessibility factor. It was mentioned by the participants that the system should not be too technically complex to be used alone at home. It should not require extensive technological knowledge and should be easy to set up alone. Lee et al. [36] note that in terms of the usability of AR and VR technologies for older adults, insufficient attention is paid to the factor of accessibility. In an evaluation of augmented reality balance training for home use with the target group of older adults, a negative correlation between usability and the age of the participants was observed [37]. Problems with the calibration and comfort of AR headsets have been criticized by older adults in another study [38]. However, the perceived usefulness and personal benefits are decisive for the acceptance and use of AR and VR technologies by older adults [39].

According to a participant, the use of the "Hololens" for exercises was more adaptable to individual preferences due to the variable speed of exercise performance. A study by Schell et al. [40] showed how important adaptability in games is for older people. The performance of older adults in an eight-week Wii bowling tournament was influenced by physical factors such as visual impairment, balance, and strength.

Four people said that in the group where they had to work together, the other players seemed the most real to them, even though the avatars were the most abstract. When gamers play with other humans, they often experience a deeper sense of immersion [41]. According to Kothgassner et al. [42], elderly women are more likely to experience a VR interaction as more rewarding and realistic when it includes another person, whereas elderly men treat both computer-generated agents and human-controlled virtual entities the same. Females showed also higher levels of social presence and spatial presence in a VR conversation with a real human.

Three of the older adults expressed safety concerns about the technologies and exercise techniques used. According to a review by Skjæret et al. [43] of 60 studies, exergaming interventions might be safe for older adults as none of the studies reported any serious adverse events during exergaming. However, most studies were conducted in a laboratory, rehabilitation, or community center setting and applied extra safety measures such as supervision, walking frames, or gait belts.

4.1 Limitations

In our study, we investigated the feasibility of multiplayer exergame as synchronous remote training in older adults with hypertension. This study provides valuable insights into the acceptability of different technologies for the use of remote training for older adults and the use of these technologies in future studies. However, there are also several limitations of the pilot study presented that should be taken into account when interpreting the results.

Because of the exploratory nature of the pilot study, there was no predetermined sample size calculation. The statistical significance of the analysis is limited due to the small sample size, which increases the risk of a type II error. Furthermore, our study had an unbalanced gender distribution. Due to limited resources, the WG and Screen prototypes were not fully developed in terms of functionality and the Wizard of Oz approach was used. In a large-scale study, the prototypes should be developed to the point where they can be operated by older adults from home without technical support. This also leads to the next limitation, which is the laboratory environment. A laboratory setting may be sufficient for an efficacy study, but future studies should also be tested in the field and thus in the real environment of older people, e.g. in their homes. The training time should also be more realistic in terms of the duration prescribed by the guidelines for hypertensive patients. In our study, a session with an exergame lasted a maximum of 5 min. A further limitation is the comparability of the three exergame prototypes, which differ substantially from one another so that a variety of confounders can arise. For future studies, it is better to examine either three very similar exergames (e.g. 3 highly gamified exergames) with different display technologies (screen, HoloLens) or 3 different exergames (cartoonish vs. realistic representation of the persons) with only one display medium, e.g. HoloLens. Another limitation of the study is the lack of randomization. Although each participant had the same order of the exergame, this may still have influenced the perception of the games. For future studies, the technology affinity of older adults should be determined, as this can vary strongly and may influence the perception of the technology to be tested.

5 Conclusion

In conclusion, there were no significant differences in HR between the three exergames. The participants rated the usability as good and had a high level of enjoyment in all exergames. The least technically complex and most gamified exergame WG was preferred by the older adults with hypertension and was most conceivable to them in a future home setting.

Acknowledgments. The authors acknowledge the participants for their assistance during the study. We would also like to thank Kai Kruschel, Erik Freydank, Haruki Saito, and Jing He from ART+COM GmbH, who developed the exergame prototypes and provided them to us for the study.

References

1. Neuhauser, H., Kuhnert, R., Born, S.: 12-Monats-Prävalenz von Bluthochdruck in Deutschland. J. Health Monitoring **2**, 57–63 (2017)
2. Mozaffarian, D., Benjamin, E.J., Go, A.S., Arnett, D.K., Blaha, M.J.: Heart disease and stroke statistics–2015 update: a report from the American Heart Association. Circulation **131**, e29-322 (2015). https://doi.org/10.1161/CIR.0000000000000152
3. Zhou, B., Carrillo-Larco, R., Danaei, G., Paciorek, C., Stevens, G.: Worldwide trends in blood pressure from 1975 to 2015: a pooled analysis of 1479 population-based measurement studies with 19·1 million participants. Lancet **389**, 37–55 (2017). https://doi.org/10.1016/S0140-673 6(16)31919-5
4. Williams, B., Mancia, G., Spiering, W., Agabiti Rosei, E., Azizi, M.: 2018 ESC/ESH Guidelines for the management of arterial hypertension. Eur. Heart J. **39**, 3021–3104 (2018). https://doi.org/10.1093/eurheartj/ehy339
5. Wattanapisit, A., Ng, C.J., Angkurawaranon, C., Wattanapisit, S., Chaovalit, S., Stoutenberg, M.: Summary and application of the WHO 2020 physical activity guidelines for patients with essential hypertension in primary care. Heliyon. **8**, e11259 (2022). https://doi.org/10.1016/j.heliyon.2022.e11259
6. Finger, J.D., Mensink, G., Lange, C., Manz, K.: Health-enhancing physical activity during leisure time among adults in Germany (2017). https://doi.org/10.25646/2585
7. Luzak, A., et al.: KORA-Study Group: physical activity levels, duration pattern and adherence to WHO recommendations in German adults. PLoS ONE **12**, e0172503 (2017). https://doi.org/10.1371/journal.pone.0172503
8. Mehra, S., Dadema, T., Kröse, B.J.A., Visser, B., Engelbert, R.H.H., Van Den Helder, J., Weijs, P.J.M.: Attitudes of older adults in a group-based exercise program toward a blended intervention; a focus-group study. Front. Psychol. **7** (2016)
9. Meredith, S.J., et al.: Factors that influence older adults' participation in physical activity: a systematic review of qualitative studies. Age Ageing **52** (2023). https://doi.org/10.1093/ageing/afad145

10. Sari, N.L.P.D.Y., Prastikanala, I.K., Sari, F.N.: Physical exercise for older people with hypertension in COVID-19 pandemic: a literature review. Nursing Health Sci. J. (NHSJ) **2**, 244–253 (2022). https://doi.org/10.53713/nhs.v2i3.156
11. Granet, J., et al.: Online physical exercise intervention in older adults during lockdown: can we improve the recipe? Aging Clin. Exp. Res. **35**, 551–560 (2023). https://doi.org/10.1007/s40520-022-02329-z
12. Buckinx, F., et al.: Feasibility and acceptability of remote physical exercise programs to prevent mobility loss in pre-disabled older adults during isolation periods such as the COVID-19 pandemic. J. Nutr. Health Aging **25**, 1106–1111 (2021). https://doi.org/10.1007/s12603-021-1688-1
13. Fernandez, D., et al.: Physical Function effects of live video group exercise interventions for older adults: a systematic review and veteran's gerofit group case study. Telemed. e-Health. **29**, 829–840 (2023). https://doi.org/10.1089/tmj.2022.0175
14. Platz, K., et al.: Remote but together: live-video group exercise via zoom for heart failure patients has high adherence and satisfaction. J. Cardiac Fail. **26**, S90–S91 (2020). https://doi.org/10.1016/j.cardfail.2020.09.265
15. Mai, S., Eisuke, A., Komuro, I.: Telemonitoring during exercise training in cardiac telerehabilitation: a review. https://www.imrpress.com/journal/RCM/24/4/10.31083/j.rcm2404104/htm. Accessed 24 Jan 2024
16. Freed, S.A.,et al.: Feasibility and enjoyment of exercise video games in older adults. Front. Public Health **9** (2021)
17. Wendel, V., Konert, J.: Multiplayer serious games. In: Dörner, R., Göbel, S., Effelsberg, W., Wiemeyer, J. (eds.) Serious Games, pp. 211–241. Springer, Cham (2016). https://doi.org/10.1007/978-3-319-40612-1_8
18. Wu, Z., Li, J., Theng, Y.-L.: Examining the influencing factors of exercise intention among older adults: a controlled study between exergame and traditional exercise. Cyberpsychol. Behav. Soc. Netw. **18**, 521–527 (2015). https://doi.org/10.1089/cyber.2015.0065
19. Shah, S.H.H., Karlsen, A.S.T., Solberg, M., Hameed, I.A.: A social VR-based collaborative exergame for rehabilitation: codesign, development and user study. Virtual Reality **27**, 3403–3420 (2023). https://doi.org/10.1007/s10055-022-00721-8
20. Kowalski, M., Naruniec, J., Daniluk, M.: Livescan3D: a fast and inexpensive 3D data acquisition system for multiple kinect v2 sensors. In: 2015 International Conference on 3D Vision, pp. 318–325 (2015). https://doi.org/10.1109/3DV.2015.43
21. Horton, J.F., Stergiou, P., Fung, T.S., Katz, L.: Comparison of Polar M600 optical heart rate and ECG heart rate during exercise. Med. Sci. Sports Exerc. **49**, 2600–2607 (2017)
22. Zhang, Y., Weaver, R.G., Armstrong, B., Burkart, S., Zhang, S., Beets, M.W.: Validity of Wrist-Worn photoplethysmography devices to measure heart rate: a systematic review and meta-analysis. J. Sports Sci. **38**, 2021–2034 (2020)
23. Lewis, J.R., Sauro, J.: The factor structure of the system usability scale. In: Kurosu, M. (ed.) Human Centered Design, pp. 94–103. Springer, Heidelberg (2009). https://doi.org/10.1007/978-3-642-02806-9_12
24. Kendzierski, D., DeCarlo, K.J.: Physical activity enjoyment scale: two validation studies. J. Sport Exerc. Psychol. **13**, 50–64 (1991). https://doi.org/10.1123/jsep.13.1.50
25. Bangor, A., Kortum, P.T., Miller, J.T.: An empirical evaluation of the system usability scale. Int. J. Hum.-Comput. Interact. **24**, 574–594 (2008). https://doi.org/10.1080/10447310802205776
26. Vorwerg-Gall, S., Stamm, O., Haink, M.: Virtual reality exergame in older patients with hypertension: a preliminary study to determine load intensity and blood pressure. BMC Geriatr. **23**, 527 (2023). https://doi.org/10.1186/s12877-023-04245-x

27. Alves da Cruz, M.M., Ricci-Vitor, A.L., Bonini Borges, G.L., Fernanda da Silva, P., Ribeiro, F., Marques Vanderlei, L.C.: Acute hemodynamic effects of Virtual Reality–based therapy in patients of cardiovascular rehabilitation: a cluster randomized crossover trial. Arch. Phys. Med. Rehabil. **101**, 642–649 (2020)

28. Target Heart Rates Chart. https://www.heart.org/en/healthy-living/fitness/fitness-basics/tar get-heart-rates. Accessed 02 Feb 2024

29. Zhang, F., Kaufman, D.: The impacts of social interactions in MMORPGs on older adults' social capital. Comput. Hum. Behav. **51**, 495–503 (2015). https://doi.org/10.1016/j.chb.2015. 05.034

30. Schlomann, A., et al.: Augmented reality games for health promotion in old age. In: Geroimenko, V. (ed.) Augmented Reality Games II: The Gamification of Education, Medicine and Art, pp. 159–177. Springer, Cham (2019). https://doi.org/10.1007/978-3-030-15620-6_7

31. Molina, K.I., Ricci, N.A., de Moraes, S.A., Perracini, M.R.: Virtual reality using games for improving physical functioning in older adults: a systematic review. J. Neuroeng. Rehabil. **11**, 156 (2014). https://doi.org/10.1186/1743-0003-11-156

32. Rendon, A.A., Lohman, E.B., Thorpe, D., Johnson, E.G., Medina, E., Bradley, B.: The effect of virtual reality gaming on dynamic balance in older adults. Age Ageing **41**, 549–552 (2012). https://doi.org/10.1093/ageing/afs053

33. Miller, K.J., Adair, B.S., Pearce, A.J., Said, C.M., Ozanne, E., Morris, M.M.: Effectiveness and feasibility of virtual reality and gaming system use at home by older adults for enabling physical activity to improve health-related domains: a systematic review. Age Ageing **43**, 188–195 (2014). https://doi.org/10.1093/ageing/aft194

34. Hausknecht, S., Schell, R., Zhang, F., Kaufman, D.: Building seniors' social connections and reducing loneliness through a digital game: In: Proceedings of the 1st International Conference on Information and Communication Technologies for Ageing Well and e-Health, pp. 276–284. SCITEPRESS - Science and Technology Publications, Lisbon, Portugal (2015). https://doi.org/10.5220/0005526802760284

35. Li, J., Erdt, M., Chen, L., Cao, Y., Lee, S.-Q., Theng, Y.-L.: The social effects of exergames on older adults: systematic review and metric analysis. J. Med. Internet Res. **20**, e10486 (2018). https://doi.org/10.2196/10486

36. Lee, L.N., Kim, M.J., Hwang, W.J.: Potential of augmented reality and virtual reality technologies to promote wellbeing in older adults. Appl. Sci. **9**, 3556 (2019). https://doi.org/10. 3390/app9173556

37. Mostajeran, F., Steinicke, F., Ariza Nunez, O.J., Gatsios, D., Fotiadis, D.: Augmented reality for older adults: exploring acceptability of virtual coaches for home-based balance training in an aging population. In: Proceedings of the 2020 CHI Conference on Human Factors in Computing Systems, pp. 1–12. ACM, Honolulu HI USA (2020). https://doi.org/10.1145/331 3831.3376565

38. Blomqvist, S., Seipel, S., Engström, M.: Using augmented reality technology for balance training in the older adults: a feasibility pilot study. BMC Geriatr. **21**, 144 (2021). https://doi. org/10.1186/s12877-021-02061-9

39. Derby, J.L., Chaparro, B.S.: Use of augmented reality by older adults. In: Gao, Q., Zhou, J. (eds.) Human Aspects of IT for the Aged Population. Technologies, Design and User Experience, pp. 125–134. Springe, Cham (2020). https://doi.org/10.1007/978-3-030-50252-2_10

40. Schell, R., Hausknecht, S., Kaufman, D.: Barriers and adaptations of a digital game for older adults. In: Proceedings of the 1st International Conference on Information and Communication Technologies for Ageing Well and e-Health (CSEDU 2015) – AGEWELL, pp. 269–275 (2015). https://doi.org/10.5220/0005524002690275

41. Cairns, P., Cox, A.L., Day, M., Martin, H., Perryman, T.: Who but not where: the effect of social play on immersion in digital games. Int. J. Hum. Comput. Stud. **71**, 1069–1077 (2013). https://doi.org/10.1016/j.ijhcs.2013.08.015

42. Kothgassner, O.D., et al.: Agency and gender influence older adults' presence-related experiences in an interactive virtual environment. Cyberpsychol. Behav. Soc. Netw. **21**, 318–324 (2018). https://doi.org/10.1089/cyber.2017.0691

43. Skjæret, N., Nawaz, A., Morat, T., Schoene, D., Helbostad, J.L., Vereijken, B.: Exercise and rehabilitation delivered through exergames in older adults: an integrative review of technologies, safety and efficacy. Int. J. Med. Inform. **85**, 1–16 (2016). https://doi.org/10.1016/j.ijm edinf.2015.10.008

Iterative Co-design of an Activity-Planning Mobile App for People Living with Early-Stage Dementia

Michael Wilson[1]([⊠]) [iD], Dympna O'Sullivan[2] [iD], Jonathan Turner[2] [iD], and Julie Doyle[1] [iD]

[1] NetwellCASALA, Dundalk Institute of Technology, Dundalk, Ireland
{michael.wilson,julie.doyle}@dkit.ie
[2] ASCNet Research Group, Department of Computer Science, Technological University Dublin, Dublin, Ireland
{dympna.osullivan,jonathan.turner}@tudublin.ie

Abstract. Living well with dementia through delaying or preventing disability and enhancing quality of life has become a primary objective of public health policy across the world. This paper discusses a co-design approach applied to a project which aims to develop a digital toolkit to support someone living with mild-to-moderate dementia, together with their informal carer(s), to live independently for longer in their own homes through planning and monitoring personalised care goals, engaging in daily and meaningful activities, and encouraging and facilitating shared decision making. The paper will focus on the implementation of design recommendations arising out of the requirements gathering stage as well the co-design of the application involving both person living with dementia/informal carer dyads as well as health professionals.

Keywords: Co-design · dementia · self-management · digital health

1 Introduction

Dementia is a progressive and degenerative disease, characterized by cognitive limitations and degradation of everyday practical capabilities, which impact on the person living with dementia's (PLwD's) ability to access, process or remember information [1, 2]. There is growing awareness that those particularly in the early stages of dementia have many years in which they can live meaningful lives while managing their condition [3–5]. A key element of maintaining quality of life is the ability to engage in both independent activities of daily living (IADLs), as well as other meaningful activities that help promote health and mental well-being (e.g., social occupations, intellectual pursuits, recreational pastimes [6, 7].

In order to perform ADLs and IADLs, various functions are called upon, with cognitive (e.g., reasoning, planning), motor (e.g., balance, dexterity), and perceptual (e.g. dealing with sensory stimuli) abilities required. In addition, it is necessary to differentiate

Q. Gao and J. Zhou (Eds.): HCII 2024, LNCS 14726, pp. 132–148, 2024.
https://doi.org/10.1007/978-3-031-61546-7_9

between being able to complete a task due to physical ability, cognitive ability or a combination of both, and the capacity to realise or notice that a task needs to be completed in the first place, which is based on cognitive ability alone [8]. Up to mild-to-moderate cognitive impairment the ability to perform basic ADLs is generally maintained, with similar levels of independence in ADL functioning being found between individuals with MCI and individuals with no cognitive impairment [9]. Nevertheless, once cognitive impairment declines beyond the mild-to-moderate stage, an association is observed between ADL dependence and cognitive functioning [8]. Inability to successfully complete essential ADLs often results in poor QoL and has been shown to be significantly associated with severe cognitive fluctuations in PLwD [10]. As well as this, other factors such as medication side effects, social isolation and home environments can impact on a person's capacity to perform ADLs [11]. While disability has been shown to be reversible as ageing occurs [12], it is also the case that cognitive status is considered an accurate indicator of disability in older adults [13, 14]. With this in mind, it is imperative that strategies are developed to address cognitive decline in order to anticipate and delay the onset of disability and maintain ADL/IADL ability among older adults [15].

For PLwD, what makes an activity meaningful can depend on the degree to which it resonates with values and beliefs while also feeling relevant and familiar in terms of past interests, routines and roles [16]. More than solely experiencing a sense of enjoyment or leisure, benefits of engaging in meaningful activities are observed in other areas of overall wellbeing including social participation and cognitive stimulation as well as carer relationship. Feeling part of the family and being involved in the wider community allow for a sense of self to be retained, and these themes can be considered concrete indicators of quality of life [17]. Findings from Han et al.'s (2016) study also suggest that being connected is a crucial factor in maintaining quality of life for PLwD [18], which is consistent with Register and Herman's (2007) theory concerning six interrelated processes of being connected (metaphysically connected, spiritually connected, biologically connected, connected to others, environmentally connected, and connected to society) and their role in quality of life for older adults [19]. Indeed, a narrative review conducted by Nyman and Szymczynska (2016) found that the importance of maintaining meaningful activity among PLwD extends beyond merely allowing for moments of pleasure; rather, provision of such activity in fact addresses an individual's fundamental psychological needs [20].

It has been suggested that integration of a tablet into daily life by PLwD can limit attention on deficits and place more emphasis on intact abilities while also limiting stigmatisation in terms of incapacity to use technology in general [21]. Touchscreen technology has been used to provide support to people living with dementia in various activities of daily living in the form of calendars, diaries, video-calling services and location-tracking [22, 23]. However, a review on studies involving people with dementia and touchscreen technology noted that assessment delivery and test screening have been the primary function of applications built using such technology, highlighting the need for more emphasis to be placed on how mobile touchscreen technology could be used to provide support in the area of independent and meaningful activities [24]. Nonetheless, several positive factors were also reported across several studies in this review stemming from people living with dementia's independent use of touchscreen devices, such as relaxation and enjoyment [25], autonomy [23], engagement [26], motivation [27], and socialisation [28].

This paper presents an overview of the iterative process followed in the co-design of an activity planning mobile app for people living with early-stage dementia to support them in planning and engaging in daily and meaningful activities with support from their informal carers. An outline of work completed prior to the co-design stage is outlined below [29].

1.1 Requirements Gathering Phase

For the requirements gathering stage initial interviews and focus groups were conducted with three cohorts: PLwDs (n = 5), informal carers (n = 4), health professionals (n = 5). Semi-structured interviews were held with dyads in the participants' homes lasting approximately 60 min (PLwD1 was interviewed over Zoom due to Covid restrictions). The interviews were conducted between August 2021 and April 2022. Two separate semi–structured interviews were held in person with the dementia advisor, with each interview lasting approximately 90 min. Four OTs participated in two separate focus groups held over Zoom, each lasting approximately 90 min. The semi-structured interview with the dementia advisor and the focus groups with the OTs were held between September 2021 and December 2021.

Findings from thematic analysis of the qualitative data collected during the requirements gathering phase identified sense of purpose and identity as crucial to maintaining quality of life and that PLwDs should be encouraged to participate in activities to prevent skills being lost through lack of opportunity to practice [29]. Three design recommendations were outlined arising from this analysis: 1) educate PLwDs and carers on the benefits of maintaining engagement in activities for as long as is possible, with clear instructions on how to achieve this; 2) consider how technology can support collaborative care planning and engagement in meaningful activities, while balancing carer support with PLwD empowerment to engage; 3) prepare for the future - design systems that adapt with the progression of dementia [29].

2   Methods

2.1   Co-design

Following analysis of the data from the requirements gathering phase and the identification of design requirements, a series of co-design sessions were held with two cohorts, PLwD/informal carer dyads, and health professionals, to support the design and content creation of the mobile app.

Participants. A subset of the participants from the requirements gathering phase also participated in the co-design sessions (see Table 1).

Co-design with Dyads. Over the course of two weeks, two group-based co-design sessions were held with three PLwD/carer dyads, with each session lasting approximately 90 min (PlwD2/IC2, PLwD 4/IC4, PLwD5/IC5). Themes which were identified from the

Table 1. Participants

Participant ID	Age	Gender	Dementia Type	Relationship to IC	Profession
PLwD2	79	Male	Alzheimer's	IC2 (wife)	
PLwD4	79	Male	Alzheimer's	IC4 (wife)	
PLwD5	75	Male	Vascular	IC (wife)	
IC2	74	Female			
IC4	73	Female			
IC5	75	Female			
HP2	n/a	Female			Occupational Therapist
HP5	n/a	Female			Occupational Therapist

thematic analysis of the requirements gathering interviews and focus groups [29] were explored further during these sessions, in order to gain insight into user preferences regarding potential designs (see Table 2).

Table 2. Themes from requirements gathering analysis

Theme	Sub-theme
Maintaining sense of purpose and identity	*The impact of dementia on sense of self*
	Strategies for maintaining purpose
	Identifying future meaningful activities
Learned helplessness	*Fear and increased dependence*
	Harming when trying to help
Shared decision-making and collaboration	*Shared decision-making in care planning*
	Finding opportunities to share tasks
	Working together to try new things

Both sessions were held in a group format, with dyads working and speaking in pairs during tasks, followed by group discussions. Across both workshops a number of design and research tools developed by the MinD project [30] were used. These tools were developed to aid the research and design process and to include people living with dementia actively within it. Specifically, we used the Visual Cards and some of the activities contained in the Visual Diaries. The cards were designed to provide support both for a researcher and participant as prompts to facilitate discussion during an interview, with each showing the name of an IADL or meaningful activity, a brief description as well as an image showing the activity. The Visual Diaries comprise a range of activities which aim to collect information on two general topics; (1) personal information about goals, attitudes, experiences, motivation, capabilities, and social context; (2) information about areas of change and needs for preservation in one's life with respect to IADLs, leisure activities, social engagement and wellbeing. The Visual Diaries were designed such that certain activities can be selected and/or omitted to suit the participant, context and project aims. Specifically, we used the activities focusing on values, achievements and goals, and skills and abilities. These materials were also used to trigger discussion and inter-dyad conversations, and for ranking activities based on whether the participants living with dementia prefer to engage in certain activities alone or with others. Other materials were used including paper-based weekly planners, 'what if?' scenario cards, conversation starters to encourage self-reflection, and listing activities focusing on past achievements and interests as well future plans. Examples of questions used during tasks include:

- What do you feel are the three most important things that you've done in your life?
- What would you like to achieve in the future?
- What are the values most important to you? Why?
- Please tell us about any skills you are proud of.
- Try to think of and describe three experiences that had a major influence on your life.
- Please tell us what motivates you and gives you joy in life.
- What activities or daily tasks do you prefer to do on your own? Which ones are you happy for someone else to help with? Which ones are you happy for someone else to do for you?
- Please tell us about your favourite leisure activities. What do you like about them? Which ones do you prefer to do in company?

Using the paper-based weekly planners, participants were asked to plan out a typical week using the Visual Cards as prompts. Following this they were asked to plan out an 'ideal' week and encouraged to reflect on the differences between the two. Throughout the sessions all participants were encouraged to engage with others, ask follow-up questions, and expand on points whenever appropriate. Each workshop was audio recorded, hard copies of the participants' worksheets and activities were retained, and field notes were taken during observation. The resulting dataset was analysed to support design and development of app features in a timely manner. Audio files and field notes were reviewed, and a broad content analysis conducted focused specifically on content relating to design features [31].

Co-design with Health Professionals. Parallel to the dyad co-design sessions, co-design sessions were held with two occupational therapists (HP4, HP5) to develop and refine a comprehensive list of daily and meaningful activities for inclusion within the app, based on examples from existing scales and literature. The categorization and mapping during these co-design sessions was conducted in order to inform a computational model which would provide suggested replacement activities once a user has stopped engaging in a particular activity, either through declining ability or lack of interest. Using the model, the system will be able to suggest an alternative activity which closely matches the 'lost' activity in terms of the activity type, theme, the degree to which it supports or relates to a particular IADL, and the cognitive domains associated with the activity.

Fig. 1. Dyad co-design: activity preferences.

Fig. 2. Dyad co-design: discussing values.

Five separate sessions were held with the two occupational therapists. The first four were held remotely over Zoom, each lasting 40 min, while the final session was held in person and lasted two hours and 30 min. The Zoom sessions were recorded in both audio and video format and the final in-person session was audio recorded. In order to develop and refine a comprehensive list of activities, we drew upon the following sources: The Lawton Instrumental Activities of Daily Living (IADL) Scale [32], The Pleasant Events Schedule (PES-AD) [33], The National Health and Aging Trends Study (NHATS) [34], Phinney, Chaudhury and O'Connor's (2007) identification of activity types [5], work by Tuijt et al. (2020) into the development of the Meaningful and Enjoyable Activities Scale

(MEAS) [7], and the six cognitive domains as outlined in the Diagnostic and Statistical Manual of Mental Disorders (DSM-5) [35]. The reason for drawing from a selection of sources in this manner was to all allow for a varied and expansive list without limiting or restricting the options available to users based on the contents of one particular scale.

Each session followed on from the previous one and fed into the next, with the goal being to build consensus by progressively developing and refining the list of activities while also mapping each individual activity to various criteria (e.g. activity type, theme, cognitive domain). The structure and process involved was as follows:

Session 1. Familiarity with concept (sources etc.). For the first session, the researcher and the OTs discussed each source and decided together on a course of action for the next sessions. The decision was made to first refine the activity categories before mapping each activity.

Session 2 and 3. Refine types/domains into categories. With regard to activity type, Phinney, Chaudhury and O'Connor (2007) identified four types based on analysis of multiple interviews and observations of PLwD with mild-to-moderate impairment: (1) leisure and recreation (e.g. hobbies, going for walks, playing instruments, crossword puzzles), (2) household chores (e.g. making a bed, helping out with meal preparation, washing up, ironing clothes, vacuuming, as well as outside activities together with a family member such as running errands), (3) social involvements (e.g. continued contact with family members as well as interactions at support groups with other people living with dementia), (4) work-related activities (e.g. transferring work-related skills to everyday situations including offering guidance and advice) [5]. The NHATS used the following activity categories: self-care, productive activities, shopping, household activities, care of others, socializing, non-active leisure, active leisure, religious and organizational activities, other [35]. Finally, Tuijt et al.'s study resulted in the identification of six main life areas of meaningful activity which were then categorized into the following domains: (a) physical activity, (b) looking after my household, (c) enjoyable and leisure activities, (d) hobbies and personal interests, (e) staying mentally active and (f) social activities/community involvement [7]. The goal of Sessions 2 and 3 was to draw from these sources with the goal of categorizing activities by 'type' and 'theme' respectively. For the purposes of the application, activity 'type' was to be user-facing and 'theme' was to be used for the computational model.

Session 4. Refine list, remove duplicates, include others from requirements gathering interviews. The Lawton Instrumental Activities of Daily Living (IADL) Scale was developed in 1969 to assess and evaluate complex self-maintenance and independent living skills in older adults [32]. Eight domains of function are measured: ability to use a telephone, shop, food preparation, complete housework, laundering, utilize public transportation, administer medication, and handle financial responsibilities [36]. It allows for the identification of how an individual is functioning at that moment in time and provides insights into improvements or deterioration over a period of time. The PES-AD is a 53-item scale designed to assist professional and family care providers in identifying and monitoring activities that are enjoyable to individual patients. The PES-AD was adapted from previous scales to suit a dementia population: the PES [27], and the PES-Elderly [38], with the activities covering two primary domains, passive-active and social-nonsocial. Each activity from the PES-AD was discussed, with some removed or renamed based on the input from the OTs as to local context, relevance and overall appropriateness and usefulness for the purpose of planning activities. As well as this, activities discussed by the dyads during the requirements gathering interviews which did not appear in the PES-AD were added.

Session 5: The final session involved mapping each activity in the list to the categories agreed upon in the session (activity 'type' and activity 'theme'). As well as this, we discussed each individual activity in order to ascertain whether it could support an individual to engage in an IADL, and which cognitive domain(s) were involved while engaging in the activity (learning and memory, executive function, perceptual motor function, complex attention, language, an social cognition) so that this information could be included in the app as education for the PLwD and carer as to the benefits of engaging in such activity.

3 Results

3.1 Dyad Co-design – Preferences and Capabilities

The co-design sessions held with three PLwD/carer dyads further explored the themes identified from the interviews, and the resulting design recommendations aimed at encouraging participation of the PLwD in planning and executing daily and meaningful activities while balancing carer support. These sessions were held in a group format, with dyads working and speaking together simultaneously. However, for the purposes of this stage of the project, the sessions allowed for structured observation with regard to how the participants approached the tasks and activities and the degree to which the topics and concepts were understood and comprehended in general. The sessions confirmed a number of things with regard to how participants might engage with an activity-planning application both in terms of task/activity preferences concerning collaborative or independent engagement as well as content that may be personally relevant and useful.

Planning one's weekly schedule through the use of paper-based calendars was already something that all of the dyads engaged in regularly in their daily lives, and this concept did not pose any major difficulty or cause confusion. It was observed during an activity that involved participants completing a weekly planner and reflecting on a typical week for them that two of the people living with dementia (PLwD2 and PLwD5) viewed their daily lives as boring. For PlwD2, however, upon completing the 'ideal' weekly planner and reflecting on the differences, he felt that there were more interesting activities he could and should be engaging in during the week. This included using a computer, which was something he had stopped doing recently. PLwD5 struggled with this activity. His primary interest throughout his life was running, which he could no longer do having suffered a stroke. He explained that he had been finding it difficult to find any alternative activities that interested him. PLwD4 was comfortable with his weekly routine. When completing the 'ideal' weekly planner, he included more social activities, which he had stopped engaging in since Covid.

At the same time, the participants living with dementia were able to express clearly which daily activities they may require assistance with and which ones they generally would prefer to engage in alone. In general, they all wanted to remain independent wherever possible. The activities they would choose to do with someone present were either activities they already did together with their spouse (e.g. preparing meal together, watching TV, going shopping), or activities that could potentially lead to a fall (going for a walk, outdoor work). However, disagreement arose within dyads when selecting some activities to add to a weekly planner. In some instances, the informal carer in the dyad felt the need to intervene and explain that their partner had not engaged in this activity for a long time and would likely not be in a position to do so anymore. For one PLwD, this was due to his forgetting that he was no longer able to engage in this particular activity, while for PLwD5 it was due to a misunderstanding as to the task. PLwD5 was focusing on his favourite activity (running), despite being aware that he could no longer engage in this activity.

3.2   OT Co-design – Content Development

Development of the activity list first involved categorizing each activity according to type, which covered sessions 1–3. The following activity types were agreed upon, which went on to form part of the user interface: staying in touch, shopping and meals, household tasks, managing finances, family and friends, entertainment and hobbies, personal care, active leisure, and community and events. As well as this, for the purposes of the computational model, we categorized the activities according to theme as follows: physical activity/exercise/active leisure, household maintenance, enjoyable/hobbies/interests, mentally active/stimulating, social/community/religious and organizational activities, self-care/personal care, and care of others. Session 4 involved adapting and expanding the existing scales used to measure engagement in IADLs and meaningful activities [6, 7, 10]. This resulted in 87 activities overall, with some activities including follow-on questions to allow for more precision when planning. For example, selecting the activity 'pay bills', leads to the follow-on question 'how do you want to do this?'. The user can then select from 'in person, by phone, online'. Selecting 'in person', would then lead to another follow-on question: 'how do you want to get there?' with the user then selecting from 'drive, walk, organize/get a bus/train, organize/get a taxi, organize/get a lift'. This transport follow-on question was added to any activity where transport might be required (27 activities). Other examples of activities involving follow-on questions include 'watch TV' – 'what do you want to watch?' (current affairs, news, sports, soap opera, movie, documentary, quiz show, other), and 'go to an event' 'where would you like to go? (sporting event, arts including plays and concerts, cinema, bingo, other events). Providing granularity and detail in this manner allows for more insight into an individual's preferences as well as more refined and useful data in terms of the suggested replacement activities based on the computational model.

As mentioned previously, activities which were seen as relevant in a local context, along with others discussed during the requirements gathering interviews were also added to the list. Examples of these include 'go to Dementia Cafe,' Go to Men's Shed', 'View mass or church service online', 'Potter about the house'. Furthermore, where possible and appropriate, the IADLs were broken down into more detailed sub-tasks. An example of this was the activity type 'household tasks' (Lawton IADL Scale 'Complete Housework'), comprising 12 activities in total: 'clean floors, do the washing up, do laundry, make bed(s), clean bathroom, outside maintenance, handywork or DIY, potter about the house, put out bins or recycling, vehicle maintenance and repair, other household activities'.

All of the 87 activities and the follow-on options (total of 148 activity options) were also mapped to the six cognitive domains (learning and memory, executive function, perceptual motor function, complex attention, language, and social cognition) and the potential to support and maintain another IADLs. As discussed previously, this categorization was conducted in order to inform a computational model which would allow for suggested replacement activities in the event of a user no longer engaging in a particular activity, either through declining ability or lack of interest. The goal in this case is to encourage the user to explore a new activity which closely matches the lost activity regarding each of the categories, thereby limiting the potential loss of any skills or abilities associated with that activity (design recommendation 3).

3.3 Interface Design

To design the application the findings from the initial interviews, observations made during the dyad co-design sessions and the final activities list mapped to the types, themes and cognitive domains were triangulated. The goal was to arrive at a design that could address the design recommendations, allow for the elements confirmed by the dyads during the co-design sessions as usable and potentially useful (e.g. the weekly planner, option to select activity independence or collaboration) while also integrating the refined activities list from the OT co-design sessions. Following on from the co-design phase, an interface was designed incorporating the ability to set, track and achieve goals around IADLs and other activities considered meaningful or significant to the individual (see Fig. 3). Using the planner, dyads can plan out a week by selecting an activity using the activity type menu and scheduling the activity for morning, afternoon, or evening. Once an activity has been completed, this can also be added to the planner, which allows the user to track their progress (See Fig. 3: morning). The design also aims to allow for shared decision-making around care-planning, with users able to decide if an activity is to be completed alone or with the assistance and support of others (design recommendation 2) (see Fig. 4). As well as this, educational information was provided on each activity and the potential benefits of engagement, along with more general health and wellbeing education for both PLwDs and informal carers (design recommendation 1) (see Fig. 5).

Fig. 3. 'My Planner' Today view.

Fig. 4. Adding an activity to My Planner - Review

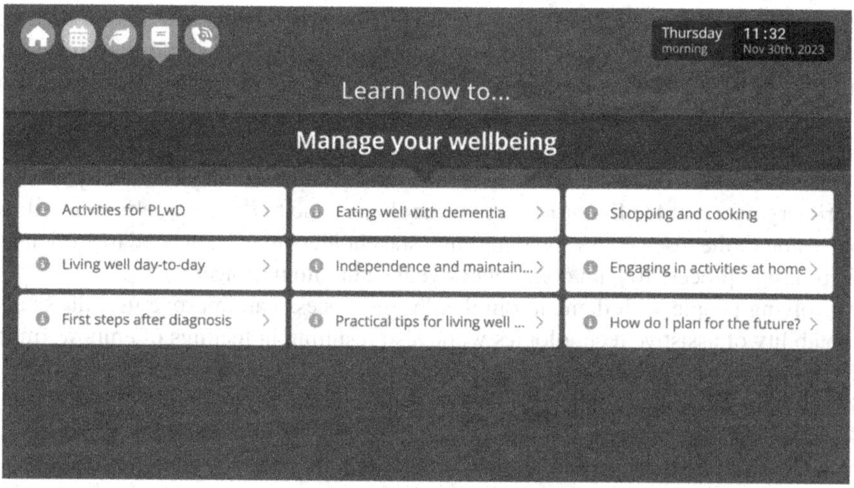

Fig. 5. Wellbeing Education

4 Discussion

In order to design technologies which focus on improving and maintaining the quality of life of people living with dementia, a deep understanding of symptoms, problems and user needs is required [39]. A key element of participatory co-design is the identification of appropriate stakeholders and the active involvement of the end user throughout the design process. As such, when considering technologies for PLwD, it is necessary to actively engage also with carers [40]. From the start of this project, every effort was made to include both PLwD and their informal carers in the process, both in terms of initial requirements gathering, as well as the early co-design workshops described in this paper. Further to this, we intend to include these dyads (and others) in the usability testing stage. The importance of ensuring both individuals in a dyad are involved was further underscored by the examples during the co-design sessions where the participants with dementia were selecting activities to engage in, which were no longer feasible for them due to physical or cognitive limitations. In these instances, such limitations were not necessarily clear or obvious to the researcher, and it required the input and intervention of the carer to make a correction and suggest possible alternatives. Examples such as this further demonstrate that collaborative usage of technologies involving both PLwDs and carers is likely. The challenge for designers, therefore, is to design systems that balance both support in the form of carer input and empowerment through independent usage.

Lindsay et al. (2012) suggest including carers in meetings to provide support during discussions where communication issues arise while also paying close attention to instances where the carer may speak on the care recipient's behalf [40]. In such instances, it may be necessary to ask the same question again but directed at the PLwD so as to confirm what was reported by the carer. It has also been pointed out that operating separate interviews and workshops for people living with dementia and for carers can allow participants to express themselves freely without either being spoken over (in the case of the person living with dementia) or feeling reluctant to discuss negative aspects of the caring process (in the case of carers) [22, 41]. However, in our experience the PLwD preferred having their informal carers with them during sessions and they felt more conformable when this was the case. The challenge for the researcher, therefore, is to strike the right balance between actively listening to the PLwD while also checking for confirmation from the carer in a manner that is both respectful and subtle. At the same time, it is important to consider that carers and family members may eventually become the primary user and facilitator of these technologies due to declining abilities and the progression of the disease. As such, multiple stakeholders may be needed to participate in a co-design process to gain comprehensive insight into user needs [16].

Involving people with dementia in the design process can improve usefulness and acceptability of assistive technologies while also resulting in feelings of empowerment [42]. Being given a voice in this manner has led to designs that improve social interaction [43] and help to maintain independence through support for activities of daily living [44]. This was also our aim for this project, with the focus throughout centering on exploring how a mobile app can provide support around planning activities and setting and tracking goals. Co-design also allows for the development of technologies that can be used for engaging in meaningful occupation rather than solely as a means of interrogation, resulting in an appropriate balance between support and empowerment [16]. Similarly, our aim is to strike such a balance by designing as system that provides value to both the person living with dementia and their carer in the form of education and information support as well as the facility to plan and set goals, while also empowering the person living with dementia to have genuine input into the decision-making process regarding their quality of life and how they spend their time.

Another factor that needs to be considered with regard to engagement in meaningful activity is the match between activity type and stage of dementia. While engaging in an activity may be beneficial at each dementia stage, differences exist across stages as to why this may be the case. Carers have described activities in mild stages as enhancing a sense self-worth and place in the world as well as positively affecting carer-recipient relationship; at moderate stages, carers saw benefits seen in terms of addressing progression of symptoms but noticed activities becoming more difficult once symptoms had progressed further [45]. Compensation strategies which address difficulties engaging in a favoured activity may be needed as dementia progresses. Where this is not possible, however, it is necessary to identify an alternative activity which can then act as a substitute provided it matches the value in the original activity sufficiently. In order to achieve this, it is vital that there is an understanding as to why the original activity was important to the individual in the first place [18]. Our goal with the workshops to categorise an activities list which could then inform a computational model of replacement activities was to provide a solution to this problem. Should engagement in a particular activity either decline significantly or cease entirely, replacement activities will be suggested to users wherever possible. It is hoped that any skills associated with the 'lost' activity will indeed be maintained through engaging in the new replacement activity as a result of the computational model finding and recommending the closet match in terms of activity type, theme, cognitive domain, and the potential to support IADLs.

A review by Jekel et al. (2015) looking at MCI and deficits in IADLs, which investigated how performance-based instruments detected differences in IADL functioning between healthy controls, individuals with MCI and PwD, revealed that all of the instruments showed MCI individuals needing less time to compete tasks than PwD but more time than healthy controls [46]. The results underscore the potential for an activity planning tool to assist individuals with MCI or early-stage dementia, highlighting the importance of providing timely interventions using co-designed digital tools. Overall, Jekel et al.'s review suggests that the likelihood of converting to dementia is higher for MCI individuals with IADL deficits than without. The aim with our project, therefore, is to provide supports to individuals with MCI or early-stage dementia in order to maintain existing IADL abilities, while also encouraging continued engagement in various meaningful activities. Perneczky et al. (2006) propose that IADL impairment occurs before the threshold of conventional dementia is in fact reached [47]. As such, it is vital that such functional impairments are detected early as failure to do so can in turn result in needs being neglected, a lack of appropriate training (e.g. occupational therapy) and inadequate community-based care services being accessed [46].

Following usability testing with dyads, the final version of the mobile application will be trialed with six PLwD/carer dyads in their homes for six months commencing in late 2023. The contributions of our work to date include a greater understanding of the importance of collaboration and shared decision making between PLwDs and their informal carers around daily and meaningful activities and the need to support carers in encouraging PLwD participation.

Acknowledgments. This material is based upon works supported by the Science Foundation Ireland under Grants No. 19/FFP/6917 and 22/NCF/OT/11241. We would like to thanks all of the participants who supported this research.

Disclosure of Interests. The authors have no competing interests to declare that are relevant to the content of this article.

References

1. Andersen, C.K., Wittrup-Jensen, K.U., Lolk, A., Anderson K., Kragh-Sorensen, P.: Ability to perform activities of daily living is the main factor affecting quality of life in patients with dementia. Health Quality Life Outcomes 2(1), 52 (2004)
2. Luttenberger, K., Schmiedeberg, A., Gräßel, E.: Activities of daily living in dementia: revalidation of the E-ADL test and suggestions for further development. In BMC Psychiatry 23(12), 208 (2012)
3. Gallagher-Thompson, D., et al.: Effectiveness of a psychoeducational skill training DVD program to reduce stress in Chinese American dementia caregivers: Results of a preliminary study. Aging and Mental Health 14(3) (2010)
4. Martin, F., Turner, A., Wallace, L.M., Stanley, D., Jesuthasan, J., Bradbury, N.: Qualitative evaluation of a self-management intervention for people in the early stage of dementia. Dementia 14(4), 418–435 (2015)
5. Phinney, A., Chaudhury, H., O'Connor, D.L.: Doing as much as I can do: the meaning of activity for people with dementia. Aging and Mental Health 11(4) (2007)
6. Logsdon, R.G., Teri, L.: The pleasant events schedule-AD: psychometric properties and relationship to depression and cognition in Alzheimer's disease patients. Gerontologist 37(1), 40–45 (1997)

7. Tuijt, R., Leung, P., Profyri, E., Orgeta, V.: Development and preliminary validation of the Meaningful and Enjoyable Activities Scale (MEAS) in mild dementia. Int. J. Geriatr. Psychiatry 35(8), 944–952 (2020). https://doi.org/10.1002/gps.5316. Epub 2020 Jun 8 PMID: 32363608

8. Mlinac, M.E., Feng, M.C.: Assessment of activities of daily living, self-care, and independence. Arch. Clin. Neuropsychol. 31(6), 506–516 (2016). https://doi.org/10.1093/arclin/acw049. Epub 2016 Jul 29 PMID: 27475282

9. Jefferson, A.L., Paul, R.H., Ozonoff, A., Cohen, R.A.: Evaluating elements of executive functioning as predictors of instrumental activities of daily living (IADLs). Arch. Clin. Neuropsychol. 21(4), 311–320 (2006). https://doi.org/10.1016/j.acn.2006.03.007.PMID:168 14980;PMCID:PMC2746400

10. Edemekong, P.F., Bomgaars, D.L., Sukumaran, S., et al.: Activities of Daily Living. [Updated 2023 Jun 26]. In: StatPearls [Internet]. Treasure Island (FL): StatPearls Publishing; 2024 January, https://www.ncbi.nlm.nih.gov/books/NBK470404/

11. Farias, S.T., Mungas, D., Reed, B.R., Harvey, D., Cahn-Weiner, D., Decarli, C.: MCI is associated with deficits in everyday functioning. Alzheimer Dis Assoc Disord. 20(4), 217–23 (2004). https://doi.org/10.1097/01.wad.0000213849.51495.d9. PMID: 17132965; PMCID: PMC2880610

12. Lin, S.F., Beck, A.N., Finch, B.K., Hummer, R.A., Masters, R.K. Trends in US older adult disability: exploring age, period, and cohort effects. Am. J. Public Health. 102(11), 2157–63 (2012). https://doi.org/10.2105/AJPH.2011.300602. Epub 2012 Sep 20. Erratum in: Am J Public Health. 2013 Jan; 103(1):e8. Master, Ryan K [corrected to Masters, Ryan K]. PMID: 22994192; PMCID: PMC3471673

13. Lee, Y., Kim, J.H., Lee, K.J., Han, G., Kim, J.L.: Association of cognitive status with functional limitation and disability in older adults. Aging Clin. Exp. Res. 17(1), 20–28 (2005). https://doi.org/10.1007/BF03337716. PMID: 15847118

14. Njegovan, V., Hing, M.M., Mitchell, S.L., Molnar, F.J.: The hierarchy of functional loss associated with cognitive decline in older persons. J. Gerontol. A Biol. Sci. Med. Sci. 56(10), M638–M643 (2001). https://doi.org/10.1093/gerona/56.10.m638. PMID: 11584037

15. Connolly, D., Garvey, J., McKee, G.: Factors associated with ADL/IADL disability in community dwelling older adults in the Irish longitudinal study on ageing (TILDA). Disabil. Rehabil. (2016). https://doi.org/10.3109/09638288.2016.1161848

16. Goodall, G., Taraldsen, K., Serrano, J.A.: The use of technology in creating individualized, meaningful activities for people living with dementia: a systematic review. Dementia 20(4), 1442–1469 (2021). https://doi.org/10.1177/1471301220928168

17. Phinney, A., Chaudhury, H., O'Connor, D.L.: Doing as much as I can do: the meaning of activity for people with dementia. Aging Ment. Health 11, 4 (2007)

18. Han, A., Radel, J., McDowd, J.M., Sabata, D.: Perspectives of people with dementia about meaningful activities: a synthesis. Am. J. Alzheimers Dis. Other Demen. 31(2), 115–123 (2016). https://doi.org/10.1177/1533317515598857. PMID: 26340962

19. Register, M., Herman, J.: A middle range theory for generative quality of life for the elderly. ANS Adv. Nurs. Sci. 29, 340–350 (2007). https://doi.org/10.1097/01.ANS.0000271100.555 05.d3

20. Nyman, S.R., Szymczynska, P.: Meaningful activities for improving the wellbeing of people with dementia: beyond mere pleasure to meeting fundamental psychological needs. Perspect. Public Health 136(2), 99–107 (2016). https://doi.org/10.1177/1757913915626193. PMID: 26933079

21. Smith, S.K., Mountain, G.A.: New forms of information and communication technology (ICT) and the potential to facilitate social and leisure activity for people living with dementia. J. Comput. Healthc (2012). 1

22. Meiland, F.J., et al.: Participation of end users in the design of assistive technology for people with mild to severe cognitive problems; the European Rosetta project. Int. Psychogeriatr. **26**(5), 769–779 (2014). https://doi.org/10.1017/S1041610214000088. Epub 2014 Feb 10 PMID: 24507571

23. Nijhof, N., Gemert-Pijnen, J., Burns, C., Seydel, E.: A personal assistant for dementia to stay at home safe at reduced cost. Gerontechnology **11**, 469–479 (2013). Doi:https://doi.org/10.4017/gt.2013.11.3.005.00

24. Joddrell, P., Astell, A.J.: Studies involving people with dementia and touchscreen technology: a literature review. JMIR Rehabil. Assist. Technol. **3**(2), e10 (2016). https://doi.org/10.2196/rehab.5788.PMID:28582254;PMCID:PMC5454556

25. Kerssens, C., et al.: Personalized technology to support older adults with and without cognitive impairment living at home. Am. J. Alzheimers Dis. Other Demen. **30**(1), 85–97 (2015). https://doi.org/10.1177/1533317514568338. Epub 2015 Jan 22. PMID: 25614507; PMCID: PMC4819239

26. Astell, A.J., Malone, B., Williams, G., Hwang, F., Ellis, M.P.: Leveraging everyday technology for people living with dementia: a case study. J. Assistive Technol. **8**(4), 164–176 (2014). https://doi.org/10.1108/JAT-01-2014-0004

27. Manera, V., et al.: Kitchen and cooking,' a serious game for mild cognitive impairment and Alzheimer's disease: a pilot study. Front Aging Neurosci **7**, 24 (2015). [FREE Full text]. https://doi.org/10.3389/fnagi.2015.00024 [Medline: 25852542]

28. Astell, A., Alm, N., Gowans, G., Ellis, M., Dye, R., Vaughan, P.: Involving older people with dementia and their carers in designing computer based support systems: some methodological considerations. Universal Access Inf. Soc. **8**(1), 49–58 (2008). https://doi.org/10.1007/s10209-008-0129-9

29. Wilson, M., Doyle, J., Turner, J., Nugent, C., O'Sullivan, D.: Designing technology to support greater participation of people living with dementia in daily and meaningful activities. Digit Health. **15**(10), 20552076231222428 (2024). https://doi.org/10.1177/20552076231222427. PMID:38235415;PMCID:PMC10793193

30. Mind: Designing for people with dementia (2020) Designing for Dementia. https://designingfordementia.eu. Accessed 30 Jan 2024

31. Bengtsson, M.: How to plan and perform a qualitative study using content analysis. Nursing Plus Open **2**, 8–14 (2016)

32. Lawton, M.P., Brody, E.M.: Assessment of older people: self-maintaining and instrumental activities of daily living. The Gerontologist **9**(3), 179–186 (1969)

33. Teri, L., Logsdon, R.G.: Identifying pleasant activities for Alzheimer's disease patients: the pleasant events schedule-AD. Gerontologist **31**(1), 124–127 (1991). https://doi.org/10.1093/geront/31.1.124. PMID: 2007468

34. Kasper, J.D., Freedman, V.A.: National Health and Aging Trends Study User Guide: Rounds 1–9 Final Release. Johns Hopkins University School of Public Health, Baltimore (2020)

35. American Psychiatric Association. Diagnostic and Statistical Manual of Mental Disorders. Fifth Edition. Arlington, VA: American Psychiatric Association (2013)

36. Farias, S.T., Harrell, E., Neumann, C., Houtz, A.: The relationship between neuropsychological performance and daily functioning in individuals with Alzheimer's disease: ecological validity of neuropsychological tests. Arch. Clin. Neuropsychol. **18**(6), 655–672 (2003)

37. Lewinsohn, P.M., Talkington, J.: Studies on the measurement of unpleasant events and relations with depression. Appl. Psychol. Meas. **3**, 83–101 (1979)

38. Teri, L., Lewinsohn, P.M.: Modification of the pleasant and unpleasant events schedules for use with the elderly. J. Consulting Clin. Psychol **50**, 444–445 (1982)

39. Mayer, J.M., Zach, J.: Lessons learned from participatory design with and for people with dementia. In: Proceedings of the 15th International Conference on Human-Computer Interaction with Mobile Devices and Services (MobileHCI 2013). Association for Computing Machinery, New York, pp. 540–545 (2013). https://doi.org/10.1145/2493190.2494436

40. Lindsay, S., Jackson, D., Schofield, G., Olivier, P.: Engaging older people using participatory design. In: Proceedings of the SIGCHI Conference on Human Factors in Computing Systems (CHI '12). Association for Computing Machinery, New York 1199–1208. https://doi.org/10.1145/2207676.2208570

41. Kerkhof, Y.J., Graff, M.J., Bergsma, A., de Vocht, H.H., Dröes, R.M.: Better self-management and meaningful activities thanks to tablets? Development of a person-centered program to support people with mild dementia and their carers through use of hand-held touch screen devices. Int. Psychogeriatr. **28**(11), 1917–1929 (2016). https://doi.org/10.1017/S104161021 6001071. Epub 2016 Jul 18 PMID: 27425002

42. Span, M., Hettinga, M., Vernooij-Dassen, M., Eefsting, J., Smits, C.: Involving people with dementia in the development of supportive IT applications: a systematic review. Ageing Res. Rev. **12**(2), 535–551 (2013). https://doi.org/10.1016/j.arr.2013.01.002. Epub 2013 Jan 11 PMID: 23318684

43. Dishman, E., Morris, M., Lundell, J.: Catalyzing social interaction with ubiquitous computing: a needs assessment of elders coping with cognitive decline. In: Proc. CHI' 2004 EA, (2004)

44. Hoey, J., Plotz, T., Jackson, D., Monk, A., Pham, C., Olivier, P.: Rapid specification and automated generation of prompting systems to assist people with dementia. Pervasive Mob. Comput. **7**(3), 299–318 (2010)

45. Roland, K.P., Chappell, N.L.: Meaningful activity for persons with dementia: family caregiver perspectives. Am. J. Alzheimers Dis. Other Demen. **30**(6), 559–568 (2015). https://doi.org/10.1177/1533317515576389. Epub 2015 Mar 18 PMID: 25788432

46. Jekel, K., et al.: Mild cognitive impairment and deficits in instrumental activities of daily living: a systematic review. Alzheimers Res Ther. **7**(1), 17 (2015). https://doi.org/10.1186/s13195-015-0099-0.PMID:25815063;PMCID:PMC4374414

47. Perneczky, R., et al.: Complex activities of daily living in mild cognitive impairment: conceptual and diagnostic issues. Age Ageing **35**, 240–245 (2006). https://doi.org/10.1109/ageing/afj054

Supporting Mobility and Leisure

Designing Autonomous Vehicle Interactions for a Super-Aged Society: A Formative Study

Jack Shen-Kuen Chang[1,2(✉)] ⓘ, Pin-Chun Chen[2], Hsin-Tzu Ma[2], Shang-En Li[3],
Wei-Ting Du[2], Ling-Hui Chang[4] ⓘ, Kuan-Yuan Wang[5], Chien-Ju Lin[2],
Hsiao-Feng Chieh[2], and Chen-Hsun Weng[2]

[1] Cross College Elite Program, National Cheng Kung University, Tainan City, Taiwan
JackSKChang@gmail.com
[2] Medical Device Innovation Center, National Cheng Kung University, Tainan City, Taiwan
[3] Institute of Creative Industries Design, National Cheng Kung University, Tainan City, Taiwan
[4] Department of Occupational Therapy, National Cheng Kung University, Tainan City, Taiwan
[5] Department of Geriatrics and Gerontology, National Cheng Kung University Hospital,
Tainan City, Taiwan

Abstract. Aging populations are increasing globally, impacting community mobility (CM), an important factor for older adults' (OA) quality of life. Taiwan, facing transportation challenges and complexity in its transition to a super-aged society (by 2025), highlights the importance of supporting OA's CM. While autonomous vehicles (AVs) promise potential benefits for OAs, current technologies often are not designed with OAs' needs and visions. We conducted contextual inquiry interviews with 18 participants (mostly OAs) to understand their current transportation challenges and their imaginations for an AV-enabled future. Thematic analysis identified five themes for current challenges, and five themes for future imaginations. Six design recommendations were proposed, underscoring: (1) social user research, (2) mixed-mode travels, (3) autonomous parking, (4) space customizability and shape transformability, (5) user experience for autonomous connectedness, and (6) regulatory improvements. This study, as one of the early works for studying AV in a super-aged society, offers region-specific insights that welcome commonalities and contrasts from the international research community.

Keywords: Autonomous Vehicles · Transportation · Community Mobility ·
Older Adults · Aging · Semi-Structured Interview · Design Recommendations

1 Introduction

With progress in healthcare, declining birth rates, and shifts in socioeconomic structures, there is a noticeable, if not significant increase in the older population across countries and regions. The percentage of senior citizens, often categorized as people aged 65 or older, is growing steadily or even rapidly. For example, the US recently (2023 May) had around 17% of seniors [1], and it was projected to reach around 25% by 2060 [2]. Also, by 2025 (in approximately just one year), such percentage in Taiwan is projected to surpass 20% [3], making it a "Super-Aged Society" [4].

While increased life expectancy is a positive indication of a society's development, living longer often is synonymous with emerging challenges and needs among each elderly, or the society as a whole. Because aging is a complex phenomenon, many factors contribute to achieving and sustaining healthy longevity: technology, healthcare, transportation, housing, finance, social connectiveness, recreation, etc.

We are particularly interested in transportation, the means for the older adults (OA) to travel between residences, neighborhoods, and beyond. Such ability and activity can also be characterized as "community mobility" (CM) [5, 6]. This is an important consideration for OAs to sustain an independent yet connected life (which was an even more vital topic during the COVID-19 pandemic's lockdown and shelter-in-place). CM is linked to the mental and physical wellbeing of older adults. Reduced access to healthcare, shopping, recreation, friends and family, can result in loneliness, depression, higher medical cost, poorer quality of life, etc.

However, many existing transportation systems were designed in the decades-long past, barely serving well for the OAs in the present, and unlikely to fulfill the needs for the future aging society. For example, for an older person living alone in a rural area, it may take a lot of effort and assistance (e.g., usage of multiple types of public transportation, help from family or caretakers) just for a regular hospital visit.

As envisioned by many countries and companies, autonomous vehicles (AVs) will be available and advanced in the near future to support and transform the transportation system. This promises benefits, innovation, and improvements for aging societies. While this future is likely to be realized, let's examine the present. The current transportation system, and its upcoming integration with AVs, lack careful and systematic considerations for the OAs, a growing part of the population with special needs (e.g., declined vision, hearing, and driving skills; changes in travelling behaviors and preferences; various level of acceptance and familiarly for new technologies). Therefore, we need to design for the future with the older adults in mind, now.

By employing research methodology in user-centered design and user experience (UX), we set out to understand stakeholders and transportation environments in Taiwan, particularly Tainan City. The selection of Tainan City is more than it being the town where the authors work. The city, due to many historical, cultural, and economic reasons, has complex transportation needs, various traffic challenges, and diverse age-related demographics. These supported our motivation to study and envision the future of AVs for the senior citizens.

The overall goal of this formative study was to inform the researchers about the current transportation needs, behaviors, pain points, and imaginations about AVs among the OAs in Tainan City. The formative study mainly consisted of semi-structured contextual inquiry interviews. We conducted 18 contextual inquiry interviews (12F/6M; average age: 67.72), with three kinds of roles: OA, Caretaker (mobility assistance provider), and Hybrid (participant who was both an OA and a Caretaker). Each interview was overall organized in these two parts: Understanding current mobility challenges; Imagining the opportunities and challenges that AVs could bring.

In this paper, we present the formative study's thematic analysis. We also share design implications, which potentially can inform the later design of autonomous vehicle interactions for Taiwan, a society on the verge of becoming "super-aged". Given this project is internationally supported, we also hope our findings, whether in the form of commonalities or contrasts, can "glocally" benefit other countries and regions.

2 Background

2.1 Aging and Transportation: A General View

As early as 1991, the United Nations released the Principles for Older Persons [7], advocating for global attention and preparedness for the aging trend. Decades have passed, aging has become a worldwide phenomenon. While this phenomenon demonstrates the improvements in aspects like nutrition, healthcare, social welfare, education, etc., longevity also brings emerging needs.

In 2002, WHO's "Active Ageing: A Policy Framework" defined active ageing as *"the process of optimizing opportunities for health, participation and security in order to enhance quality of life as people age"* [8]. To achieve a quality aging life, the report underscored the importance of participation, mobility, and access to social, economic, and cultural activities.

These international reports together provided the conceptual structure that aging is a global topic with opportunities and needs; and transportation is one of the means to meet the needs, as supporting OAs to get around places can maintain their wellbeing. And as aforementioned, CM has emerged as a term to support and operationalize relevant studies.

However, aging populations experience various kinds of transportation challenges. For example, in many countries, driving and the ability thereof, have been positively associated with the quality of life among senior citizens [9, 10]. Yet due to factors like cognitive or functional declines and impairments [11], "driving cessation" occurs and impacts the seniors' driving confidence and habits [11, 12]. On the other hand, public transportation supposedly provides a more affordable and social, less skill-demanding and assistance-relying means for senior citizens [13–15]. But in many societies, it has challenges like: the stops or stations are not well-located or have unclear signs, the hardware of the vehicles is not senior-friendly (e.g., buses lacking low floors, uncomfortable seating), or transportation policies being outdated [13, 16–19].

2.2 Transportation in a Super-Aged Society: Taiwan

Because of the low birth rate and the increasing aging population, Taiwan became an Aged Society in 2018, with more than 14% of the Taiwanese people aged 65 or above. Taiwan is expected to become a Super-Aged Society by 2025. Such society has around or more than 20% of population with age $\geq$ 65 years [20]. This fast and irreversible aging trend brings new challenges and needs, and has led to campaigns, actions, research, and policy reforms to foster and support "age-friendly" transportation systems in many Taiwanese cities [21–23]. Also, inspired by EU (European Union)'s AAI (Active Aging Index) [24], researchers in Taiwan constructed TAAI [25]. While AAI only has indirect indicators related to transportation (e.g., independent living, social connectedness), TAAI specifically and explicitly adds transportation-based indicators.

However, due to historical, cultural, and environmental reasons, transportation systems in Taiwan still need much improvement, particularly in regard to supporting OAs. Some challenges include: First, while Taiwan geographically is a relatively small island, it is topographically and environmentally diverse. This has led to infrastructural development differences between urban, suburban, and rural areas. Hence, traveling across, or even within cities often means changing types of transportation, getting on/off vehicles, navigating through complex stations. Second, unlike Western countries, scooters are a very popular choice of motorized vehicle in Taiwan, even among the seniors [26]. But the right of way, relevant regulations, and road systems, do not always support scooter riders in well-defined ways. Third, Taiwan is globally known for its strengths in ICT (Information and Communication Technology) and many ICT-supported Smart Transportation initiatives have been implemented as part of the Smart City Development [27, 28]. However, these smart ICT systems or products (e.g., rehabus reservation apps, smart bus stops, digital information displays in transportation hubs) are not always designed with consideration to meet the senior citizens' needs and habits.

2.3   Autonomous Vehicles for the Aging Population

Autonomous Vehicles (AV), or Driverless/Self-Driving vehicles, are designed to be partially or even fully free from human driving. SAE (Society of Automotive Engineers)'s J3016 [29] categorized AVs to have 6 levels of automation (Level 0 to 5). Per the categorization, some levels of AVs require mixed forms of driving (the collaboration between human driving and the car), while some levels of AVs can be fully capable of driving and navigating through the journey on their own.

Because AV's very premise is that it requires less or even no human operation, it promises many applications for OAs. For example, those who are functionally or cognitively declined due to aging can still maintain their community mobility without (much) driving skills. AVs can also work with flexible times and routes when the older travelers need to make transitions between transportation types. AVs are also part of the bigger Smart Transportation system that they can communicate with other AVs and traffic regulating devices.

While many of these applications potentially can support the aging population's needs in health, safety, and social connectedness, many design, technological, and legal aspects need to be carefully and systematically investigated before such potentials can fruit. We see a recent rise in AV-related studies with senior citizens as the stakeholders. For example: Rovira et al. [30] used multi-factor, mixed-model questionnaires to study how age differences contribute to aspects of trust in AVs; Coupled with the use of a driving simulator, Haghzare et al. [31] conducted a multi-condition experimental study to investigate FAV (Fully Automated Vehicle)'s acceptance factors among OAs; As a pilot study to design a cross-European research, McLoughlin et al. [32] conducted an interview study in Ireland to explore AV design for OAs' independent living; Faber and Lierop used posters of scenarios (types of automated vehicles) in focus groups in Netherland to explore OAs' mobility needs and AV imaginations [33].

3 Methods

3.1 Overview

We are motivated to study how AV and relevant traffic systems can be designed in Taiwan. Echoing with the Background section, the motivation is grounded in: (1) Taiwan is becoming a Super-Aged Society, hence many aspects of the transportation system need to be re-envisioned and re-designed to support the aging population's community mobility; (2) Taiwan's unique historical, social, environmental, and cultural transportation landscape require dedicated research to address existing challenges and to generate innovative plans; (3) While AVs promises many potentials, existing literature shows that AV-related studies (or, many transportation and mobility studies), are region-specific. We believe it is important to further our own knowledge about the society we live in, before we can examine whether and how the findings can be generalized for the international community.

As such, we employed user-centered design (UCD) for this formative study. More specifically, while the team's overall research vision is to generate insights and designs for a future AV-enabled society, we first set out to understand the stakeholders.

We designed and conducted contextual inquiry interviews with senior citizens and caretakers. "Contextual Inquiry" [34] is a research method that asks the participants to think, verbally share, or demonstrate (using the environments or objects) about a topic with a particular context. To build rapport and to obtain in-depth information, for each contextual inquiry interview we conducted, only one participant was involved, with two researchers: one as the primary interviewer, the other as the secondary interviewer. To maintain data collection consistency, one same researcher was in each interview, while other team members supported as the other interviewer per availability. Both were taking notes. Each interview was audio-recorded, with some photos taken.

This human subject study was approved by NCKU's IRB (HREC, Human Research Ethics Committee) with case number 111–683. Aspects related to participant recruitment, informed consent, data privacy, etc., followed what were approved.

3.2 Participant Recruitment

We recruited participants through word of mouth and snowballing. Interested community members got a web link to the sign-up questionnaire. The questionnaire asked for basic personal and contact information, such as age, gender, email address and/or phone number, etc. The interested person had to be at least 20 years old to sign up for the study.

The questionnaire also asked the interested person to choose a role: Older Adult, or Caretaker. In the questionnaire, we defined the OA role as someone over 50 years old. Many countries or systems defined this term in various ways. While utilizing 50 years old as a defining age was a less used number, we chose this age in hopes of broadening our participant sign-up number. (Note: In Results, we show that many of the participants who signed up as OA were over 60 and 65 years old, which does align more with more modern defining age of OAs.) Caretaker role refers to people who identify themselves as a transportation or mobility assistance providers in their households.

The questionnaire also asked about if they use assistive devices (hearing aid, walker, wheelchair, etc.) so we could accommodate to their needs for the interviews. The questionnaire asked level of education and current profession (or, retired) as optional questions.

To potentially conduct the interview in or closer to their mobility contexts, the questionnaire invited them to choose where they would like the interview to be held. They could choose one or several of: residence, community activity center, meeting space provided by the researchers, or other choices like cafes/restaurant near their residence.

Upon receiving their questionnaire responses, we called them to schedule the interview.

3.3 Interview Structure

We conducted semi-structured interviews for the participants. Each interview in general consisted of two parts: (A) Understanding current mobility challenges; (B) Imagining the opportunities and challenges that AVs could bring. This structure was designed to be for around one hour. More details are provided as follows below.

Part A: Understanding Current Mobility Challenges. After briefing the research, consent form signing, icebreaking, (A1) was basic demographics questions, particularly on the participant's relationship with the community, e.g., what district of the city do they reside in, how long have they lived in that district, do they live alone or with other people, their current jobs (or that before retirement) and hobbies, do they attend cultural, religious, or learning activities in the community, etc.

In (A2), we invited them to list two activities for each of these two categories: regular and non-regular travels. For each activity, we encouraged the participants to describe the trip's destination, purpose, frequency (daily, weekly, etc.), types of transportation used, what kind of information they need before and during the trip. (These are attributes inspired by studies using Travel Behavior Theory [35, 36].) We also asked about the challenges and the benefits for that activity, particularly on aspects relating to transportation, traffic, community mobility, vehicles, road systems, etc., and how they enjoyed those aspects, or what could be improved.

We encouraged them to demonstrate using the meeting space's objects, environment, gestures, and sketching. We prepared a pool of additional questions, e.g., if they mentioned the experience of taking buses, we further asked if they preferred a low-floor bus, or how they wait at a bus stop. Besides the pre-determined questions, we also asked spontaneous, on-the-spot, and free-flowing questions per the interview responses.

Part B: Imagining Future AV Opportunities and Challenges. After Part A, we quickly explored their existing knowledge or experiences with autonomous vehicles, e.g., how they thought AVs work, if they have seen, ridden, or driven one, when or where such experiences happened.

Then comes (B1). We played three online short videos we prepared: The first one, produced by Taiwan's MOTC (Ministry of Transportation and Communications), was a general introduction on AV, and the 6 SAE levels. The second one was a first-person view of a passenger sitting in the right back seat, in an Waymo AV driving on the street of a residential area in San Franciso. The third one was an external, slightly aerial view of a golf cart-like AV produced by Turing Drive (a Taiwanese company), running on a road near an industrial park.

The research team was not in any way affiliated with nor sponsored by those organizations (MOTC, Waymo, and Turing Drive). The videos were chosen merely because of their online availability, duration, and the content's general public-friendly nature (i.e., they did not cover technical details), and distinct viewing angles.

Each video was about 1 to 2 min long. The videos served as a triggering reference to evoke or elicit thoughts and comments in later discussion in the interview.

After watching the videos, we entered (B2). We asked them what they thought about the benefits, possibilities, and conveniences AV could provide. We also inquired what they imagined could be the challenges, dangers, and inconveniences from using AVs. (These envisioned opportunities and challenges needed not be based on the content in the videos). Then we invited the participants to choose two activities (preferably one regular, one non-regular from (A2) to imagine how AVs could support/improve, or hinder/complicate each of those activities.

Similar to Part A, for Part B's follow-up interview questions, we prepared predefined ones and asked spontaneous ones. We invited the participants to use objects, gestures, sketching to share their responses.

Finally, we invited the participants to share additional information or comments related to Part A and Part B. The interviews were concluded with appreciation and compensation (gift card worth $200 NTD).

4   Results

4.1   Participants and Interview Locations

A total of 18 interviews (12F/6M) were conducted. Their ages ranged from 48 to 83, with mean $= 67.72$, SD $= 10.09$. The interviews' duration ranged from around 40 min to 80 min.

For roles, 12 were OAs, 1 was Caretaker, and 5 were as "Hybrid" role. (The sign-up questionnaire only offered two main roles. We derived "Hybrid" role for people who identified as Caretaker but were also above 50 years of age, or, someone who signed up as an OA, and expressed their mobility assistance responsibilities during the interview. We believe this additional role can better convey and inform the composition of the participants.)

While we let the participants choose the interview location, most participants (15) chose to have the interview in the meeting room we provided in NCKU, the rest (3) allowed us to visit their residence to conduct the interview in their living rooms. We respected their preferences and planned for the interviews accordingly.

4.2   Thematic Analysis

With the notes taken during the interviews, and transcription from the audio recordings, we conducted qualitative thematic analysis [37] to inductively generate codes, then categories, and eventually themes. During the analysis, we also used affinity diagramming (also known as KJ method) to support our idea generation and organization. In total, three team members contributed to the data analysis.

Note: The interviews were conducted in Mandarin Chinese / Taiwanese Hokkien. As they were not in English, the reported analysis below will not list the original nor translated quotes from participants. We instead use summaries of their responses.

4.3   Themes from Part A (Understanding Current Mobility Challenges)

Summary of Travel Behavior. Overall, this group of participants have similar mobility characteristics. (More in Discussion.) They lived in parts of Tainan City that are not too far from NCKU and NCKUH campuses. Among the 18, 14 of them identified as retired or not currently employed (e.g., as a dedicated homemaker). As such, their more flexible schedules afforded their active participation in community activities designed for senior citizens.

For regular activities, 17 of the 18 shared the following transportation methods in lieu of, or in addition to driving. They mentioned walking, riding bicycles or scooters, and taking buses or taxis. These regular activities, on a weekly or daily basis, mainly included knowledge enrichment (e.g., book clubs, health seminars, computer techniques, foreign languages), volunteering, exercising, grocery shopping, etc.

For non-regular activities, while the purposes varied among the participants, most of them involved travelling to a farther part of the city, or to other cities. These travels were for: occasionally visiting family or friends, ceremonies (weddings, funerals, etc.), organized group trips to scenic spots, medical visits to hospitals. Such non-regular activities were mainly performed with multiple types (mixed-mode) of transportation. For example, P5 (age 64, OA) visits her professionally working son in Taipei by taking train, high-speed rail, bus in one journey; P10 (age 70, OA) visits scenic spots by riding bicycles to and from train stations, which also included hauling his bicycles inside trains.

Road Conditions. Participants expressed concerns about complex road conditions in Tainan City, or, generally in Taiwan. These included: narrow streets, constructions, road closures due to events, needs for improvements on people's "traffic literacy", traffic jams, confusing signs or signals, etc. Due to historical and developmental reasons, every city (or country) has its own transportation landscape and corresponding challenges. It is worth noting that in our study, the participants expressed concerns by combining road conditions with road users' behaviors.

For example, P11 (age 72, OA)'s recent cataract surgery made him more cautious about traffic lights and more worried about fast-moving cars. P17 (age 57, Hybrid) mentioned getting hit by a car when riding her scooter, due to a construction area's lane merge. P3 (age 73, OA) once missed his high-speed rail train due to a traffic jam when driving from home to the train station.

The Parking Conundrum. While the needs and issues for parking in general are part of infrastructure or even road conditions, we need to make it a separate theme because many participants (11 out of 18) brought up the topic of parking. Only one of them, P16, positively described parking as an easy task in a rural scenic spot, while the rest mentioned parking as a challenge.

In terms of regular activities, their parking challenges came from spatial constraints. For example, an older adult (like P9) may not want to drive to a community activity center located in a busy downtown area. Therefore, he has to deal with riding and parking his scooter near the center (which may take him a while because of lack of scooter parking space in downtown area), then walk to the designation. For non-regular activities, if it involved long-distance driving, the OAs particularly wanted to plan ahead for parking for periodical food or bathroom breaks, or for yet other types of mixed-mode transportation (e.g., driving to, parking at a location to meet other friends to board a tour bus).

Information Needs. The participants' needs for information can be categorized as: (1) planning for the trip, and (2) en route responses. While such categorization is common for travelers or commuters of many ages, these older participants from Tainan City and Taiwan had somewhat more unique, if not nuanced needs.

For (1), the participants needed to know information related to: progress of appointments in hospital or clinics, bus timetable, weather, choices for transfer, accessibility of public transportation (e.g., whether the bus has low floors, of if the taxi is wheelchair-friendly). Some participants also have special needs for planning. For example, P7 (age 52, Hybrid) lived in several cities and was also the caretaker for her parents. She compared the differences in rehabus booking apps among those cities.

For (2), they would like to know information like the updated location or timetable of buses (when they are not arriving on schedule), parking availability, traffic jam information, directions for transfers (e.g., when reading unclear signs in bigger train stations).

Safety and Comfort. Safey and comfort are primary mobility considerations among many ages. But these topics were frequently discussed among our participants. We see it as an indication that they, mostly older adults, were aware of and cautious about the effects of their physical declines on community mobility.

The participants cared about these safety factors: narrow bicycle lanes (or the lack thereof), uneven roads, conflicts or ambiguity for right of way between cars and scooters, driving with visual impairments, slower response to unexpected incidents, etc.

As for comfort, participants paid attention to cushioned seats for their lower back support when planning for long-distance travels. This echoed with their needs to rest on trains or in cars. They also preferred not to drive continuously for long journeys, unless there were sufficient rest stops. They preferred public buses with low floors (which can also be a safety consideration). When riding vans or buses with friends and family, they enjoyed it with socialization.

4.4 Themes from Part B (Imagining AV Opportunities and Challenges)

Trust. Resonating with related studies [32, 33], "trust" emerged as a significant theme in our study. This is because driving and riding AVs are human-robot interaction or human-AI interaction that involves advanced technologies, which in general older adults are less familiar with. Hence, such unfamiliarity leads to concerns or worries for them who put more emphasis on safety, response speed, comfort, and accessibility.

In our study, 13 participants voiced such worries on specific technological features, e.g., automatic navigation's reliability, battery's safety and endurance, detecting and responding to obstacles, sensing surrounding vehicles, understanding and responding to challenging conditions (rainy days, mountain roads), etc. These worries were heightened when we discussed higher SAE levels of driving automation (e.g., Level 4 and 5, in which human driving is not needed at all).

This connects to some interesting comments we heard from certain participants. Eight participants (P3, P5, P6, P8, P9, P11, P12, and P13), after watching the video with back seat passenger view, mentioned that they would feel nervous entering an AV (cars, taxis, buses) that did not have a human in the driver's seat. They further shared that even if the human in the driver's seat did not drive at all, they would still feel safer seeing a human occupancy in the driver's seat. Among them, P8 shared that he probably would not want to get into a Level 5 AV at all. Other participants shared similar worries when seeing a "human-less driving seat" if they were in another car or as a pedestrian.

Some participants who expressed concerns also doubted that autonomous technology could be fully ready for complex road conditions in the near future. Those participants felt safer if AVs ran on fixed routes (like the autonomous golf carts in golf courses), or in open rural areas.

Legal Considerations. As Part B of the study aimed to elicit ideas and evoke imagination, some participants brought up legal issues when a city or country is entering a more AV-enabled society. While not many participants made such comments, we believe such discussions were intriguing and important that they deserve a dedicated theme.

One participant (P13) was wondering if there should be validating or licensing mechanisms for an AV to pass before it can be allowed into real traffic. While such lab-based validation standards already exist (such as ISO-22737 [38]), P13 mentioned it from the concerns on how AVs can really function well in real and complex environments like Tainan City's.

P7 and P13 imagined a future scenario that it would be convenient for drunken drivers to call an AV to pick them up and take them home. But the discussions continued on issues like: If the AV causes an accident, is it considered DUI (Driving Under Influence) for the drunken person in the driver's seat (especially when the drunken driver hands over full control to an AV, not taking any operational responsibility)? And, when any AV-involved accidents happen, how do authorities decide who is at fault (the humans or the AVs)? How do insurance companies determine compensation?

P15 humanized AVs and wondered if they would start a strike if they had too much workload.

P8, after watching the video with the external view of an AV running on street, described her concerns for the AV as if it is a draught animal. More specifically, she was worried that if an AV runs without human drivers or passengers, it cannot protect itself when getting "bullied" on the streets, e.g., someone purposefully hits it or harasses it.

Smart and Autonomous Parking. Like Part A, parking was a topic that participants naturally brought up, not because of a pre-determined interview question. This reflects the need from OAs (in Tanan City and Taiwan) to have more convenient parking, and the anticipation that AVs may be a solution for the parking conundrum.

Eight participants (P1, P3, P5, P7, P8, P11, P12, and P13) had parking-related discussions with us. These included: imagining and anticipating how easy their lives would be if their cars can find parking fully on their own, or just with a little bit of instructions; what kinds of environment information can an AV detect to facilitate its autonomous parking task, and how to ask a parked AV to pick up the user.

Ownership. We noticed that for imagining scenarios or interactions using AVs, participants in our study often responded by assuming that they were the owner of vehicle, as opposed to AVs being a shared ride service (like Uber) or as a public transportation (e.g., autonomous buses). For example, P5 imagined owning her own AV would make journey planning much easier. P12 also shared a similar notion, and mentioned self-parking AV would make the mixed-mode trip less of a hassle. She also added that she would imagine AVs have sophisticated technologies that they require little maintenance from humans, but she would need a parking garage to keep it at home for easy access.

During the interviews, we did not dive into why participants started envisioning using AVs based on owning one. But we speculate it is related to topics discussed in Part A. For example, using an app to order a ride-sharing AV means another ICT hurdle, which may also increase the time and uncertainty for the vehicle's arrival due to the complex road conditions. Also, it may be because that OAs have more special mobility and physical needs (e.g., getting on or off a vehicle as a wheelchair or cane user), so their imagined, ideal future car would be one that is owned by them, near or in their living spaces.

An Autonomous Ecosystem. While participants expressed trust concerns on whether current or near-future AVs could accurately and responsively detect the surroundings, they also shared how they thought better future could be realized through more communications between AVs, pedestrians, bicycle/scooter riders, traffic signals, and other infrastructure.

Ten of the participants (P1, P2, P3, P4, P5, P12, P13, P15, P17, and P18) directly or implicitly shared, in the forms of hopes, visions, anticipations, on how a more connected autonomous system is a better system. For example, P3 mentioned his concern that AVs needed to be trained or updated with more high definition (HD) maps of mountain roads so he could feel safer in an AV. P5 and P12 discussed the possibility of AVs serving as smart shuttles or taxis that the AVs know when and where to pick up human passengers during their mixed-mode journeys. P2 imagined that there would be less traffic jams and accidents if AVs on the road could sense one another's speed and location to make real-time adjustments.

5 Discussion

5.1 Attitudinal Paradox

To provide a "demographic snapshot", overall, the participants can be described as a group of urban older adults who are in good socioeconomic status. Many of them received a good education. Many of their current or pre-retirement jobs are professionally at a higher level. Such descriptions can be supported by: They are physically active (with regular walking, bicycling, outdoor activities), pay attention to healthy regimen, enjoyed socialization, and used social gathering to support their senior learning. Since they live not too far from NCKU and NCKUH, they constantly pay attention to and signed up for research recruitments from the University. They mentioned doing so, to them was, both "giving back to the community" and knowledge enrichment.

However, these more educated and open-minded participants overall demonstrated a conservative, reserved, and even worried attitude toward introducing AVs into their lives. Only one among the 18 (P2, age 48, Caretaker) was very enthusiastic about AVs and imagined mostly the convenience and potentials AVs can provide, while the other participants shared mixed thoughts, with most of their thoughts as worries, concerns, and contemplation. (Note: P2 was also the youngest among the participants.)

We see this as an interesting attitudinal paradox among this group of (mainly) OAs. Further sampling with diverse and heterogeneous demographics is certainly needed to study such paradox. But in this formative study, we can already preliminarily deduce that such attitudinal paradox is based on the complex transportation landscape of Taiwan, and that OAs' motor or cognitive declines make them more reserved about AVs.

Such deduction echoes with the paradoxes mentioned by McLoughlin et al. [32] and Yang & Coughlin [38]. They described that the aging population will be the direct beneficiary of autonomous transportation, and they have more financial resources to purchase and own AVs. But OAs are often not the early adopters of new technologies, particulate that related to transportation.

5.2 Reflecting on Contextual Inquiry

Ideal contextual inquiries are conducted where and when the context happens. Per our design, it would have been ideal if we observed and interviewed all the participants at places like bus stops, train station, their residences, community activity centers, etc. However, we only got to conduct three interviews at the participants' homes, while the other 15 chose to be interviewed in the meeting space we provided on campus. Nevertheless, we believe this study is a good balance of collecting enough data for formative analysis, while respecting the participants preferences.

Studying community mobility can be intrusive, as it involves understanding someone's life across many locations, with mixed purposes. This conundrum escalates when studying OAs: their travels may involve personal or medical reasons, or, they need to deal with mobility challenges.

As such, the research team conducted another observation-only study, in which we visited transportation hubs (train and bus stations, busy street intersections). The study, also, approved by NCKU' IRB, was pure observation, and did not involve interactions with people. We are in the middle of analyzing the research. We hope the observation-based study can be used to triangulate with the findings in this paper.

6 Design Recommendations for Autonomous Transportation in a Super-Aged Society

We believe this paper is one of the very early research works to study community members' imagination and considerations on autonomous transportation for a upcoming super-aged society. Like many studies about older adults' community mobility, our research findings can be region-specific. But we hope to contribute to international research with our findings and design implications (as follows) so designers, researchers, manufactures, policy makers can in turn generate commonalities or contrasts.

6.1 Incorporate Social Interactions in User Research

User research using UCD methodology is important for understanding the OAs' considerations, opinions, and imagination for a future AV-enabled society. Because OAs' general needs and preferences for social connectedness, we believe such user research can benefit from group activities with more social interactions, such as focus groups, design workshops, etc. Such group activities can also include participants more than just senior citizens in the community, e.g., younger people, policy makers, or AV manufacturers to diversify and expand the discussion.

6.2 Support Mixed-Mode Travels

Older adults often travel within or outside their communities using multiple types of transportation. The choice of transportation may not only be based on vehicle preference or availability, but also due to physical or social needs. We recommend that autonomous transportation should be flexible and smart to accommodate to such mixed-mode travels. For example, there can be small-sized AVs running between bus stations, or indoor autonomous wheelchairs (running inside a big transportation hub building) to pick people up.

6.3 Autonomous Parking

Parking is related to both road conditions and mix-mode transportation. But per our research findings, we see the necessity of making it a dedicated consideration for OAs' community mobility. Currently, some AVs or non-autonomous cars are already equipped with a basic level of parking capability. We argue that in a super-aged society, autonomous parking probably is more important than a autonomous driving. We recommend parking should be emphasized more for OAs in autonomous transportation. There should be smarter, faster, diverse parking motor technologies to support OAs' mixed-mode travels in complex road conditions.

6.4 Space Customizability and Shape Transformability

Traveling in vehicles, OAs have special physical needs (e.g., they need to rest or use the bathroom more) and certain social preferences (e.g., they enjoy social interactions like chatting or singing karaoke). We recommend that the internal sitting space or even the external shape can be customized and transformed easily. Such customizability and transformability may seem unrelated to the notion of "driving" in self-driving", we believe this is valuable for designing future AVs. This is because AVs can relieve humans from (much) operation responsibility, both the drivers or passengers in privately-owned vehicles or public transportation can, and should, gain more positive experiences.

Some conceptual cars have such customizability or transformability available now. We believe these will be even more promising when the designs support the aging population's needs.

6.5   User Experience for an Ecosystem of Connectedness

Many ongoing autonomous technologies address V2V (vehicle-to-vehicle) communications. Other technologies innovate how vehicles communicate with traffic signals, infrastructures, etc. While we see this trend as positive and promising, we advocate that these technological endeavors should bear UCD in mind. User experience (UX) and usability are important topics for a super-aged society. ICTs that involve human interactions should be designed and developed for, or even with, transportation stakeholders.

6.6   Increase and Improve Regulations

Using AVs is essentially human-robot interaction and human-AI interaction. But unlike using robots in a simple and fixed space, or running AI programs on a computer, driving and riding with AVs lead to many legal considerations. They involve topics of safety and responsibilities for the human inside and outside vehicle, and even the vehicle itself. Our formative study yielded interesting and fruitful discussions on legal considerations. We recommend increasing and improving relevant regulations to prepare for an AV-enabled, super-aged society.

7   Conclusion

Globally there is a significant and rapid aging trend. Community mobility (CM) is important for physical, psychological, and social aspects of older adults' (OA) quality of life. As Taiwan is becoming a super-aged society, and it has many transportation challenges and complexity, supporting OAs' community mobility is an important topic in Taiwan. Autonomous vehicles (AV) promise transportation benefits for OAs. But currently, many of the AV designs and technologies do not consider the OAs' needs and visions. To address this gap, we conducted contextual inquiry interviews with 18 participants (12F/6M, age mean = 67.72, SD = 10.09) who were categorized into three roles: OA, Caretaker (of mobility), and Hybrid. The interviews mainly consisted of two parts: (A) Understanding current transportation challenges, and (B) Imagining a future with AVs.

We analyzed the data with thematic analysis and affinity diagramming. Five themes respectively for (A) and (B) were generated to summarize our findings. We also constructed 6 design recommendations: (1) Incorporate Social Interactions in User Research, (2) Support Mixed-Mode Travels, (3) Autonomous Parking, (4) Space Customizability & Shape Transformability, (5) User Experience for an Ecosystem of Connectedness, (6) Increase and Improve Regulations.

We believe this research contributes as one of the early works for studying autonomous transportation for an upcoming super-aged society. The findings, like most transportation research, may be region-specific. But we expect the study to provide commonalities and contrasts for the international community.

Acknowledgements. We thank for the support from "Healthy Longevity Global Grand Challenge (HLGC)", which was internationally initiated and organized by USA's NAM (National Academy of Medicine), with local funding provided and managed by Taiwan's Academia Sinica (grant number AS-HLGC-111-07). We also thank the participants for their time and the valuable input.

Disclosure of Interests. The authors have no competing interests to declare that are relevant to the content of this article.

References

1. United States Census Bureau: Older Americans Month: May 2023. https://www.census.gov/newsroom/stories/older-americans-month.html. Accessed 27 Oct 2023
2. United States Census Bureau: An Aging Nation: Projected Number of Children and Older Adults. https://www.census.gov/library/visualizations/2018/comm/historic-first.html. Accessed 28 Oct 2023
3. National Development Council of Taiwan: Population Aging. https://www.ndc.gov.tw/en/Content_List.aspx?n=85E9B2CDF4406753. Accessed 28 Oct 2023
4. OECD Library, World Health Organization: Health at a Glance: Asia/Pacific 2020: Measuring Progress Towards Universal Health Coverage: Ageing. OECD (2020). https://doi.org/10.1787/26b007cd-en
5. Patla, A.E., Shumway-Cook, A.: Dimensions of mobility: defining the complexity and difficulty associated with community mobility. J. Aging Phys. Act. 7, 7–19 (1999). https://doi.org/10.1123/japa.7.1.7
6. Zhu, L.: Measuring Community Mobility in Older Adults with Parkinson's Disease Using A Wearable GPS Sensor And Self-report Assessment Tools. Electronic Thesis and Dissertation Repository (2017)
7. United Nations Principles for Older Persons. https://www.ohchr.org/en/instruments-mechanisms/instruments/united-nations-principles-older-persons. Accessed 16 Feb 2024
8. Active Ageing: A Policy Framework. https://extranet.who.int/agefriendlyworld/active-ageing-a-policy-framework/. Accessed 16 Feb 2024
9. Kim, S., Ulfarsson, G.F.: Transportation in an aging society: linkage between transportation and quality of life. Transp. Res. Rec. 2357, 109–115 (2013). https://doi.org/10.3141/2357-13
10. Dickerson, A.E., et al.: Transportation and aging: an updated research agenda to advance safe mobility among older adults transitioning from driving to non-driving. Gerontologist 59, 215–221 (2019). https://doi.org/10.1093/geront/gnx120
11. Lyman, J.M., McGwin, G., Sims, R.V.: Factors related to driving difficulty and habits in older drivers. Accid. Anal. Prev. 33, 413–421 (2001). https://doi.org/10.1016/S0001-4575(00)00055-5
12. Yassuda, M.S., Wilson, J.J., von Mering, O.: Driving cessation: the perspective of senior drivers. Educ. Gerontol. 23, 525–538 (1997). https://doi.org/10.1080/0360127970230603
13. Lamanna, M., Klinger, C.A., Liu, A., Mirza, R.M.: The association between public transportation and social isolation in older adults: a scoping review of the literature. Canadian J. Aging/La Revue canadienne du vieillissement 39, 393–405 (2020). https://doi.org/10.1017/S0714980819000345
14. Nordbakke, S., Schwanen, T.: Well-being and mobility: a theoretical framework and literature review focusing on older people. Mobilities. 9, 104–129 (2014). https://doi.org/10.1080/17450101.2013.784542
15. Freudendal-Pedersen, M.: Mobility in Daily Life: Between Freedom and Unfreedom. Routledge, London (2016). https://doi.org/10.4324/9781315595764
16. Metz, D.: Transport policy for an ageing population. Transp. Rev. 23, 375–386 (2003). https://doi.org/10.1080/0144164032000048573
17. Banister, D., Bowling, A.: Quality of life for the elderly: the transport dimension. Transp. Policy 11, 105–115 (2004). https://doi.org/10.1016/S0967-070X(03)00052-0

18. Wong, R.C.P., Szeto, W.Y., Yang, L., Li, Y.C., Wong, S.C.: Elderly users' level of satisfaction with public transport services in a high-density and transit-oriented city. J. Transp. Health **7**, 209–217 (2017). https://doi.org/10.1016/j.jth.2017.10.004

19. Wong, R.C.P., Szeto, W.Y., Yang, L., Li, Y.C., Wong, S.C.: Public transport policy measures for improving elderly mobility. Transp. Policy **63**, 73–79 (2018). https://doi.org/10.1016/j.tranpol.2017.12.015

20. Council, N.D.: National Development Council. https://www.ndc.gov.tw/en/Content_List.aspx?n=85E9B2CDF4406753. Accessed 27 Oct 2023

21. Hsu, H.-C.: Associations of city-level active aging and age friendliness with well-being among older adults aged 55 and over in Taiwan. Int. J. Environ. Res. Public Health **17**, 4304 (2020). https://doi.org/10.3390/ijerph17124304

22. Chen, L.-K., et al.: Challenges of urban aging in Taiwan: Summary of urban aging forum. J. Clin. Gerontology Geriatrics **4**, 97–101 (2013). https://doi.org/10.1016/j.jcgg.2013.05.001

23. Shiau, T.-A., Huang, W.-K.: User perspective of age-friendly transportation: a case study of Taipei City. Transp. Policy **36**, 184–191 (2014). https://doi.org/10.1016/j.tranpol.2014.08.010

24. Active Ageing Index I UNECE. https://unece.org/population/active-ageing-index. Accessed 04 Feb 2024

25. Hsu, H.-C., Liang, J., Luh, D.-L., Chen, C.-F., Lin, L.-J.: Constructing Taiwan's active aging index and applications for international comparison. Soc. Indic. Res. **146**, 727–756 (2019). https://doi.org/10.1007/s11205-019-02128-6

26. 中華民國交通部 [Ministry of Transportation and Communications, Taiwan ROC]: 111 年民眾日常使用運具狀況調查摘要分析 [A Survey on Citizen's Daily Use of Vehicles, 2022]. https://www.motc.gov.tw/ch/app/data/view?module=survey&id=56&serno=202304280009. Accessed 16 Feb 2024

27. Ji, T., Chen, J.-H., Wei, H.-H., Su, Y.-C.: Towards people-centric smart city development: investigating the citizens' preferences and perceptions about smart-city services in Taiwan. Sustain. Cities Soc. **67**, 102691 (2021). https://doi.org/10.1016/j.scs.2020.102691

28. Leu, J.-H., Lin, B.-C., Liao, Y.-Y., Gan, D.-Y.: Smart city development in Taiwan. IET Smart Cities. **3**, 125–141 (2021). https://doi.org/10.1049/smc2.12008

29. J3016_202104: Taxonomy and Definitions for Terms Related to Driving Automation Systems for On-Road Motor Vehicles - SAE International. https://www.sae.org/standards/content/j3016_202104/. Accessed 06 Feb 2024

30. Rovira, E., McLaughlin, A.C., Pak, R., High, L.: Looking for Age Differences in Self-Driving Vehicles: Examining the Effects of Automation Reliability, Driving Risk, and Physical Impairment on Trust. Frontiers in Psychology. 10 (2019)

31. Haghzare, S., Campos, J.L., Bak, K., Mihailidis, A.: Older adults' acceptance of fully automated vehicles: Effects of exposure, driving style, age, and driving conditions. Accid. Anal. Prev. **150**, 105919 (2021). https://doi.org/10.1016/j.aap.2020.105919

32. McLoughlin, S., Prendergast, D., Donnellan, B.: Autonomous vehicles for independent living of older adults. In: Proceedings of the 7th International Conference on Smart Cities and Green ICT Systems, pp. 294–303. SCITEPRESS - Science and Technology Publications, Lda, Setubal, PRT (2018). https://doi.org/10.5220/0006777402940303

33. Faber, K., van Lierop, D.: How will older adults use automated vehicles? assessing the role of AVs in overcoming perceived mobility barriers. Transp. Res. Part A: Policy Practice **133**, 353–363 (2020). https://doi.org/10.1016/j.tra.2020.01.022

34. Beyer, H., Holtzblatt, K.: Contextual Design: Defining Customer-Centered Systems. Morgan Kaufmann Publishers Inc., San Francisco (1997)

35. Chen, Q., et al.: Impact of shared bus on campus travel and space optimization based on activity travel behavior. J. Adv. Transp. **2021**, e4928982 (2021). https://doi.org/10.1155/2021/4928982

36. Tak, S., Woo, S., Park, S., Kim, S.: The city-wide impacts of the interactions between shared autonomous vehicle-based mobility services and the public transportation system. Sustainability **13**, 6725 (2021). https://doi.org/10.3390/su13126725
37. Braun, V., Clarke, V.: Using thematic analysis in psychology. Qual. Res. Psychol. **3**, 77–101 (2006). https://doi.org/10.1191/1478088706qp063oa
38. Yang, J., Coughlin, J.F.: In-vehicle technology for self-driving cars: Advantages and challenges for aging drivers. The Korean Society of Automotive Engineers (2014)

An Exploration on Creative Approach of Animated Short Films Using Traditional Crafts as Media by Expert Analysis Method

Chia-Ling Chang[(✉)]

National Taitung University, 369, Sec. 2, University Rd., Taitung, Taiwan, Republic of China
idit007@gmail.com

Abstract. Traditional crafts are full of stories, coupled with the imagination and creativity of creators, which are quite suitable for animation media. This study conducted semi-structured interviews with six experts, to analyzed the timing and techniques, roles, camera moves, transitions, dubbing, incidental music, and other techniques used in the scripts of animation using traditional crafts. On narrative structure: 1. The introduction of traditional craft elements into the time point, the better time point is approximately one-fourth or one-eighth of the first act of the three-act play. 2. All experts have agreed that family affection is indeed easy to play in the theme of inheritance such as traditional crafts, but it is not limited to between parents and children, and grandparents and grandchildren across generations are also common elements. 3. There were different views on dubbing in the industry and academia. Industry experts encouraged the creators to feel the intimacy and sense of substitution. However, academic teachers hoped that students could learn to use plot and picture arrangement to tell the story. On formal techniques of animation: 1. In terms of camera moves, most of the traditional craft animation types have a gentle rhythm, and rarely uses dynamic camera moves. 2. In terms of transition, it is easier to use the transition mode of line deformation, or the transition with switches between shape, position, virtual and real, which can deepen the audience's impression of traditional crafts. 3. Unless the animation is related to the theme of traditional musical instruments, the incidental music does not necessarily need to use traditional musical instruments.

Keywords: Animation · Traditional Crafts · Expert Analysis Method

1 Research Background

Traditional craft is a manifestation of traditional folk life. The "present" is reflected in the life of the "past" [1]. Traditional craft carries the emotions and memories of a certain group of people and the previous generation, enriching people's imagination and yearning for the past. Therefore, we often use traditional craft to tell a story of affection, love, and memory [2]. Even though traditional craft does not flourish in modern society, it has also transformed its form and been applied in today's film and television works. How the tradition can become today's contemporary requires a little imagination and execution

Q. Gao and J. Zhou (Eds.): HCII 2024, LNCS 14726, pp. 168–178, 2024.
https://doi.org/10.1007/978-3-031-61546-7_11

[3]. Animation is one of the most common and important information and emotion communication media today, and its influence is enough to cross the gap between age, culture, and language. Animation making conveys content and emotion through narrative structure and formal techniques. Traditional crafts are full of stories, coupled with the imagination and creativity of creators, which are quite suitable for animation media. Therefore, this study explored the creative approaches used in animation by traditional crafts as media, and mainly discussed two issues as follows.

1. It discussed the emotional connection between traditional crafts and people, and the reason why they were suitable for animation narrative media.
2. It analyzed the timing and techniques, roles, camera moves, transitions, dubbing, incidental music, and other techniques used in the scripts of animation works.

2 Literature Review

2.1 Traditional Crafts and Animation Interpretation

The development of traditional crafts is closely related to the historical tradition, social situation, cultural context, economic system, life pattern, technology research and development and material supply of the society at that time. The development of folk traditional crafts is often linked to people's livelihood [1], traditional clothing, food, architecture, entertainment, festival rituals, life rituals, and religious beliefs. The relationship between people and various objects and even the surrounding environment forms a daily culture that emphasizes constancy, refinement, and stability [4]. Therefore, traditional crafts are the media that can best reflect and record our past lives and memories when the new and old societies are changed. With the rapid progress of science and technology, Taiwan's traditional culture seems to be gradually declining, but it always returns to our lives in different forms, which is still connected with our lives and emotions.

The development of technology is closely related to the social context, cultural context, user class, and life pattern of contemporary society, and crafts also carry the memories of us and our previous generations [3]. Animation is added with story richness and content thickness when cultural elements, such as folk beliefs, traditional skills, time phenomena and other elements are added in animation. It reflects that tradition has become the medium of expectation and transmission of film and television animation emotions [5].

Animation creation pays attention to the "non-verbal" form, and the audience can better perceive the emotions and feelings through the appropriate theme. Taiwan's animation does not lack hard strengths such as artistic design and technical ability, but soft appeal abilities such as how to tell stories with images, how to shape characters, how to arrange plots, and how to express to touch people's heart are the most lacking. This is also the soft strengths that Taiwan's animation creation lack [6]. Looking back on the development track of Taiwan's animation, it has overlapped the historical path of the overall social development of Taiwan. The embryonic stage of Taiwan's animation began around 1950s. In the 1970s, the output of Taiwan's animation reached as high as 170 animation works, when it was called the animation foundry kingdom. The story text of animation has been rooted in original stories sliced in different time and space, some are based on the theme of traditional crafts, some are from folklore, and some are derived from the director's life memory and experience. What these stories have in common is that they have obtained the audience's sense of empathy, sense of inclusion, and the memory of seeing themselves grow up in the story, forming emotional resonance.

As for the definition of animated short film, the internationally renowned Ottawa International Animation Festival has a clear specification for narrative animated short film: [Narration] is defined as having some kind of story happening. The length of the short film is recommended not to exceed 30 min https://reurl.cc/K4Kddn. The Academy award has defined animated short films as no more than 40 min in length. The history of film development shows that short film plots are not the condensed versions of feature-length films. The content of short films must be concise and to the point, in one go because of the short narrative time. Foreshadowing, sub-plots or multiple endings, which are commonly used in feature films, should be avoided in short films [7].

2.2 Narrative Structure and Formal Techniques of Animation

Animation works are rich in many techniques and elements that can be deeply analyzed, and there are many classification ways. Based on the related literature discussion on the appreciation and production process of animation in the past, this study divided the composition of animation into two categories of "narrative structure" and "formal techniques" [8, 9].

In the narrative structure of animation, the most common ones are the "script", "role", and "dubbing". Today, the most standard formula for the structure of an animated script is the three-act play [10], which is used to represent the timing of occurrence of a key object or an event. One of the ways animation captures the audience's attention is by relying on "role setting" [11, 12]. It is necessary to focus on role tasks and role conflicts before developing character style [13]. The dialogue tone and content of a character, namely dubbing, is a powerful tool to guide the audience to understand the character's personality and emotions. It can directly convey the content, psychological state, and emotional response of the character, and give subtle clues about the character's personality, and physiological state [14].

In addition to narrative structure, animation still needs to rely on "formal techniques" to strengthen visual expression. "Camera moves" are the communication media between the director and the audience. The rhythm of image narration can be created or the movement of characters can be simulated through moving the camera body. The use of different shots in film animation not only brings visual freshness to the work, but also plays a role in emotional presentation or prominence [15]. Lu et al. (2014) pointed out that it is always an important subject of animation works to accurately convey story concepts and characters' emotions by means of camera moves [16]. The "transition" effect of switching between images is also an important technique to convey emotional flow. Chen and Lee (2016) suggested that animation transition has unique skills and beauty, which is difficult to achieve in live action film and television [17]. In addition to the visual sense, auditory sense is also the understanding of the film's narration and the emotional elements of the characters, namely, the "incidental music". The function of incidental music is mainly divided into three levels as follows. It has pointed out on the physical level that the arrangement and design of the incidental music can clearly remind the audience about the region and year setting in the scene. In addition, the collocation of music and video is often used in the incidental music to strengthen each key action and turn, which is also a powerful and important technique [18].

3   Research Method

This study was intended to analyze the key creative techniques of "narrative structure" and "formal techniques" of animation. It belonged to exploratory study. Qualitative interview is one of the most widely used methods of collecting data in social science research. Investigators can obtain, understand, and explain the respondent's personal perception of the facts of the theme via dialogue with the respondents [19], focusing on the statement of the respondent's personal profession, life and experience. Therefore, this study conducted semi-structured interviews with experts in related fields, using a wider range of research questions as the basis for interviews. The advantage of semi-structured interviews is that they can provide a more realistic representation of respondents' cognitive feelings [20]. The framework of this study is shown in the Fig. 1 below.

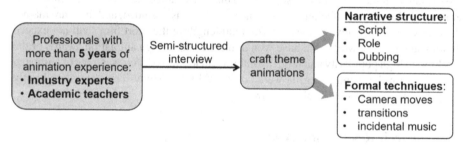

Fig. 1. Research framework

3.1   Screening Principles of Respondents

Experts should have a certain degree of professional knowledge and work experience in their field. The respondents invited in this study were professionals with more than five years of working experience in animation making, including industry animators and school animation teachers, so as to combine animation teaching and practical facets. The list of interviewed experts is shown in the Table 1. A total of 6 people are included, having 3 industry experts (IE) and 3 academic teachers (AT).

3.2   Animation Research Samples

It is better that the worldview of the animation work samples should be similar to the life experience of the respondents, so as to have cultural empathy resonance with the audience. Chinese culture has a long history, and traditional crafts contain cultural and inheritance emotions. On the selection of sample animation works in this study, animated short films with excellent crafts were first collected from two major Chinese animation

Table 1. List of interviewed experts

Category	Code	Seniority	Professional title
Industry expert	IE1	5	Animator
	IE2	5	Animator
	IE3	5	Animator
Academic teacher	AT1	26	Associate professor/ animation design, scene design
	AT2	9	Assistant professor/ puppet animation, character design
	AT3	17	Associate professor/ 2D animation, shot list and drawing

forums (Bahamut in Taiwan and Bilibili in China), referred to the length specifications of international animated short film, and considered the actual film length of watching the interview not too long. The sample screening principles formulated in this study are as follows. (1) The theme of animation has been Chinese crafts, and foreign themes are excluded in the scope of this study. (2) This study has focused on the discussion of emotional elements, so "technical teaching animation" is excluded, and there are mainly the crafts driven narrative works. (3) The total length of the short film shall not exceed 30 min, and (4) The works that have won domestic and foreign animation awards or the works with high popularity and high favorability are preferred. Four samples of animated short films on the theme of crafts were compiled by this study. The stories are briefly described as shown in the Table 2 below.

4 Research Results and Analysis

4.1 Narrative Structure: Script, Role, and Dubbing

Script. In terms of the discussion on the key object "traditional craft elements" should appear at what time point in the three-act play, and the appropriate time point of bringing traditional craft elements into the film, the first quarter of the short film should already have this entry point, which is better in this way (IE1). Memories Box used kendama as the key object of traditional craft, so the shot list or the main axis of the story would inadvertently bring this key object to show the protagonist's emotion between kendama and grandpa. The Enwinding Threads directly integrated the theme of traditional craft into its style (IE2). It is possible to introduce elements of traditional crafts at the beginning by using the problem-solving method, perhaps showing his studio in the background, or using tools, to give the audience a general understanding of the theme of the animation (IE3). The views of academic experts on the time point of bringing craft works into animation are as follows. There is usually such a "medium" at the beginning to start, with a hint first, and then most of the craft plot performance is in the middle section (AT1). If the film is divided into a traditional three-act play, there are elements at about half of the first quarter. They are not necessarily deliberate, which may be slightly mentioned (AT2). They are introduced with narrations according to the story plot (AT3). The views of the 6 experts on the time point of the introduction of the traditional crafts

Table 2. Description of animation samples in this study (compiled by this study)

Animation name	Crafts	Animation type	Length	Country	Video URL
Memories Box	Kendama	2D, puppet animation, freeze-frame	4′ 10″	Taiwan	https://reurl.cc/9O6znj
		The story of the founder of kendama in Tainan has been transformed into a short animation of affection between grandparent and grandchild. With the background of a grocery store, the paper-cut stop-motion animation with the painting style and the material of antique was adopted. The kendama was used throughout the whole story, bringing out the affection between grandparent and grandchild and the growth of the child. The grandpa hoped that his grandson would take the kendama away when his grandson left home, hoping that his grandson could have the achievements and happiness of playing kendama in the past. It also symbolized that he was accompanied by his grandson			
Hide In The Alley	Taylor	2D	3′ 20″	Taiwan	https://reurl.cc/Lp51Qe
		The traditional cloth has been interwoven with needles and threads, and the pin bag given to the granddaughter by the grandma symbolizes inheritance and continuation, bringing out the fantasy story of the prefectural city by metaphor. The granddaughter chased the cat through the streets. It was also with her running through the grandma's memory of the prefectural city. The cloth stores in alleys and daily street scenery have been the memories with families at a younger age of the grandma, which now are left to the cat to lead the granddaughter walk through, inheriting the good feelings			
Dragon of Lantern	Lantern	2D	5′ 12″	China	https://reurl.cc/3j4voV
		The process of lantern making and vivid lanterns were used to express the charm and wisdom of traditional crafts. The old man turned into a red lantern after burning, symbolizing that he devoted his life to the lantern making industry. The lanterns flying to the sky is to hope that the public can give respect and understanding to the creators of culture, art and traditional crafts			

(continued)

Table 2. *(continued)*

Animation name	Crafts	Animation type	Length	Country	Video URL
The Enwinding Threads	Embroidery	2D	7′ 04″	China	https://reurl.cc/e6y13R

<table>
<tr><td></td><td>The embroidery line is not only the outline of the soul of the picture, but also has the meaning of fate and connection, and even is the bridge connecting the family of grandparents and grandchildren. It has been narrated with emotions with embroidery line, which appears to have more temperature than the general approach, strengthening the sense of family connection. Therefore, the audience can enter the story atmosphere along the embroidery line</td></tr>
</table>

are summarized, and there is a consensus that the traditional craft elements appear in the 1/4 or 1/8 of the three-act play. Also, a "medium" can be used to solve the problem. For example, in the first 15 s of Memories Box, there was a scene of grandparent playing with a kendama. The opening of The Enwinding Threads was the transformation of the stitches into the construction of the scene, etc. All of them brought in the traditional craft elements without trace in the early stage of the three-act play, thus suggesting the audience the key craft elements of the animation.

Role. Because it is difficult to stack the details of getting along with people in a short time, family affection is often used as the key role in the short films. These four animations were mostly parent-child as the role subject. In my understanding, it has more "inheritance" meaning, namely, it is my turn to experience the same pain, and joy to experience the things done by my previous generation, having more feelings (IE1). The traditional craft has become a memory, which is possibly related to the experience of the family. The way to express parent-child affection (IE2) is even just an eye contact sometimes, or physical interaction between each other. Although these were not expressed by dubbing or dialogue, family affection was a familiar and easy to understand emotion (IE3). Because the introduction of the story of traditional crafts, namely, the so-called tradition, inheritance, and bringing into the parent-child relationship, just suits the traditional and warm theme (AT1). It takes time to get along with people, so that the audience can understand the emotions and conflicts of the roles. Therefore, the short films often use a specific "element" to guide the relationship, namely, the parent-child relationship must quickly connect the emotional links between the roles through some key objects, such as the kendama that grandpa gave to his grandson in Memories Box. The red embroidery thread of grandma and granddaughter in The Enwinding Threads could "kick back" with key object when the protagonist's mood turned, namely, the state of "returned to the original heart" (AT2). Crafts are often passed from one generation to the next, so parent-child roles are indeed more common in traditional craft themes. In the emotional portrayal of both sides, the emotional "stack and pull" in the first half and the final "balance" bridge were arranged in a potent way, and the emotions between parents and children were more profound (AT3). A "metaphorical" approach was used to bring in or repeatedly "stack" certain "elements" to make it run through the story. For example, The Enwinding Threads compared a part of the threads to the difficulties encountered in life, tying hands. Another part of the threads was also compared to the tie and bond between grandma and granddaughter. In the Memories Box, kendama repeatedly appeared in the relationship between grandpa and grandson, which became the emotional support throughout the story. It was worth noting that none of the six experts mentioned the appearance design of the character in particular. This might show the style design for the appearance of the character was relatively secondary, and the emphasis should be placed on the emotional depiction of the character.

Dubbing. Experts had different views. Among them, industry experts believe that students can try a variety of dubbing possibilities, with different spoken language and accent to have more interaction with the audience (IE1). Short animation must be very fast to attract the audience to stay, so as to arouse resonance. Thus, dubbing and voiceover need to have an emotional stack like listening to a story in order to help the audience understand the plot (IE2). However, most academic experts think that it should focus on the expression of pictures in the early stage of learning animation, and try not to use voiceover or dialogue as a way to promote the story (AT1). The key point of dubbing is that fund, time, and technology can be a great burden for students to achieve high quality dubbing of short animation (AT2).

4.2 Animation Narrative Structure: Camera Moves, Transitions, and Incidental Music

Camera Move. Camera move is one of the methods used to enrich the picture in the production of animation. These four craft theme animations are just static themes, so the shots are a little slower, or even zoom in, zoom out (IE1). Although these are static photography, they also have many different ways to present in the angle of the picture. In fact, the shot list can be caught out separately, it can be matched with a faster camera moves according to the continuity and transition parts of the story, so that the camera moves of the whole film cannot be too flat (IE3). The pace of craft animation is a little slower, having more gentleness, using "subjective perspective" to gaze, or having the most commonly used "two shot". I think they are quite in line with this kind of animation whether it is panorama, two people, or close-up hands that they use two shot (AT1). I personally feel that it is redundant to do the camera moves when they are unnecessary, and camera moves are not required when the story can be told well without them (AT2). A good camera move is the one that people actually cannot feel it. Therefore, there is not necessarily any time to use camera moves. Instead, they should be adopted when using shots to express can make the audience have more feelings (AT3).

Transition. Transition is a production technique that can leave a deep impression on people in animation. The interviewed experts mentioned that if the transition design could be combined with the theme elements of animation through the switches between the real and virtual, and the picture and the line, and the integration of the picture with reasonable elements, this could form a transition impressed the audience. Experts believe The

Enwinding Threads performed best in transitions. In The Enwinding Threads, through the transition of the line, the scenery could be seen, or the flowers, birds and so on of the scenery were moving forward with the change of time, and the feeling of time flow could be viewed. I think it is a very interesting way of presentation (IE2). The image style of The Enwinding Threads was not so close to the realistic world, it was illustrative, and the transformation was smoother (AT2). If a traditional craft is talked about and then shot list is required through the transitions, using that craft can also strengthen the impression of the traditional craft, so it is reasonable. However, there is no need to be too deliberate for transition, otherwise our emotions are easy to be out from the axis (AT3).

Incidental Music. On incidental music, the six experts agreed that the creation of animation atmosphere was more than the theme elements, emotion was the main axis of the incidental music. The traditional Chinese music, orchestral music, violin and other string instruments are not necessarily required. In fact, they can also be used, because they are also soft tunes (IE1). It does not have to be a whole piece with traditional instruments. It can be a twist, a tone change, or a stylistic shift (IE2). If the animation is not an introduction to traditional crafts, but is only used to make elements, it does not seem to have to be a traditional musical instrument (AT1).

Unless it is an animation related to the theme of traditional musical instruments, such as glove puppetry, Taiwan opera has an established and clear musical facet, and other craft themes are not necessarily directly related to traditional music (AT2), and emotion is the main axis of the incidental music (AT3).

5 Conclusions

This study focused on how traditional crafts were used as media in the production of animated short films. After literature discussion and interviews with six experts, the production methods are summarized as follows.

5.1 On Animation Narrative Structure:

1. As for the introduction of traditional craft elements into the time point, industry and academic experts have agreed that the "problem-solving method" can be used to bring traditional craft elements into the early stage of the scripts. The more exact time point is approximately one-fourth or one-eighth of the first act of the three-act play. Craft objects are used as the "media" at the beginning of the story, so that the audience can have "resonance" in the animation. Most people's past similar experiences are taken as the narration of the story, and then traditional craft elements are repeatedly stacked, or bringing into the plot in a metaphorical way, and then the elements are throughout the story.
2. In terms of role setting, experts have agreed that family affection is indeed easy to play in the theme of inheritance such as traditional crafts, but it is not limited to between parents and children, and grandparents and grandchildren across generations are also common elements. Moreover, all the experts did not mention the appearance design of the role, but focused on the expression of the interaction, the dialogue of the role,

or only the eyes and body contact. The key elements brought in act as the passenger of the role relationship, quickly conveying the emotions of the role, pulling the emotions of the audience, and achieving the resonance between the role.

3. There were different views on dubbing in the industry and academia. Industry experts encouraged the audience to feel the intimacy and sense of substitution in Formosan, provincial languages, and other languages, and accent in the traditional themes. However, academic experts did not encourage students to use voiceover to promote the story in the animation learning stage, and they hoped that students could learn to use plot and picture arrangement to tell the story.

5.2   On Formal Techniques of Animation:

1. In terms of camera moves, most of the traditional craft animation types have a gentle rhythm. This kind of animation often uses static images to present the picture with static shots from different angles, and rarely uses dynamic camera moves. The main scene can be introduced with vistas and panoramas. One shot, and two shot can be used when focusing on the character. The subjective perspective allows the audience to enter the character's vision in the first person. Close shot is suitable for hand action, tool operation, and work details.

2. In terms of transition, it is easier to use the transition mode of line deformation in 2D animation, or the transition with switches between shape, position, today and tomorrow, virtual and real. Therefore, when bringing in the craft theme, it can use its element for transition, which can deepen the audience's impression of traditional crafts and animation.

3. Unless the animation is related to the theme of traditional musical instruments, the incidental music does not necessarily need to use traditional musical instruments or music, orchestral music, violins and other soft string instruments, which are also helpful to the creation of the animation atmosphere.

Taiwan's animation has talents in art design and technology, but how to find the content IP that resonates is the most important. Traditional crafts constituted a tool of life in the old times, reflecting the social environment and cultural context at that time. The key to the application of traditional crafts as the media in animation lies in "resonance". The traditional craft elements are brought into the animation through the same experience. The characters' emotions are depicted and the incidental music is used to make the audience go deeper into the animation plot. This study also expects to give future creators who want to make traditional craft themes a preliminary creative direction, and compare and modify them in the process, so as to complete more splendid and moving animation works.

Acknowledgments. This study received partly financial support from the National Science and Technology Council (NSTC 111-2813-C-143-012-H). At the same time, this research would like to thank the students Chiao-Hsuan Wu, Ting-Chen Hsieh, and Ning-Xuan Zhang for participating in the discussion, and the interviewed experts for their valuable suggestions.

References

1. Kita, T.: Give Design Soul. Electronic Industry Press, Beijing (2012)
2. Lin, Y.D.: The status and research of china tradition craft art delivery. J. Nat. Taipei Teach. Coll. **13**, 519, 521–543 (2000)
3. Du, L.C.: Both traditional and contemporary: NCAF National Foundation for Culture and the Arts (2022). https://reurl.cc/E4WZX1
4. Wu, et al.: My Era of Craftsmanship: The Touching Journey of Twenty Organizational People. Labor Affair Bureau of Taichung City Government. Vista Publishing, Taichung (2018)
5. Hsiao, Y.H.: Creative Description of Animation Short "The Most Horrible One" Based on the Study of the Relationship between the Creators' Cultural Background and the Context of their Animation Shorts. [Unpublished master's dissertation]. National Yunlin University of Science and Technology (2017)
6. Lee, H.K., Lee, L.C.: Toward an effective narration in animated short film - structure and focalization design. Int. J. Digital Media Des. **9**(2), 23–41 (2017)
7. Lin, Z.Y.: The investigation and creations of the critical touching factors of short animation-A case study of short animation film "Choice of Dream". [Unpublished master's dissertation]. National Taichung University of Education (2015)
8. Lin, G.T., Chamg, Y.S., Hsu, T.I.: A narrative study via story structure, lens design, animation language and story intensity - take the animated short film "la maison en petits cubes" as example. Int. J. Digital Media Des. **12**(1), 13–31 (2020)
9. Yusa, I.M.M., Ardhana, I.K., Putra, I.N.D., Pujaastawa, I.B.G.: Reality in animation: a cultural studies point of view. Eduvest – J. Univ. Stud. **3**(1), 96–109 (2023)
10. Cantor, J., Valencia, P.: Inspired 3D Short Film Production. Gotop information Inc., Taipei (2006)
11. Ma, J.Y., Chen, C.C.: Examination the relationship between emotional change and functional animation. J. Design **24**(1), 1–16 (2019)
12. Weng, Y.S., Wang, N.T.: Creative methods of animation story. J. Des. Res. **5**, 55–68 (2012)
13. Wu, P.F.: A study on ideation mode of animation story design [Unpublished Doctor dissertation]. National Yunlin University of Science and Technology (2010)
14. Yang, P.S.: The influence of Chinese dubbing Japanese animation in different genres on the audience. [Unpublished master's dissertation]. National Yang Ming Chiao Tung University (2018)
15. Wyatt, A.: The Complete Manual of Digital Animation Design. New era Publisher, Taipei (2011)
16. Lu, S.Y., Hsieh, W.H., Lo, C.C., Chang, W.C.: The context analysis of the utilization of 3D camera shots through Pixar short films. Arts Rev. **26**, 71–111 (2014)
17. Chen, C.L., Lee, H.L.: The study of visual metamorphosis-using an animation titled "3× 7=28" as an example. J. Perform. Vis. Arts Stud. **9**(2), 99–129 (2016)
18. Wu, S.W.: A Study on the Application of Chinese Elements in Animated Film Scores and Sound Effects Design-Using the World of Warcraft: Mists of Pandaria Animation Remake Work as the Example [Unpublished master's dissertation]. Fu Jen Catholic University (2022)
19. Minichiello, V., Aroni, R., Timewell, E., Alexander, L.: In-depth Interviewing, 2nd edn. Longman, South Melbourne (1995)
20. Chang, F.F.: The five steps of qualitative data analysis: climbing up a ladder of abstraction. J. Elementary Educ. **35**, 87–120 (2010)

A Study on the Contemporary Arts and Crafts Design in Taiwan Based on the Aesthetics Perspectives of the Book of Changes

Tien-Li Chen and Yun-Chi Lee[✉]

Department of Industrial Design, College of Design, National Taipei University of Technology, Taipei, Taiwan
yunchilee0604@gmail.com

Abstract. The Book of Changes (Yijing) captures the philosophical thinking of the Eastern world, encapsulating the beliefs, spirituality, and mindset of the people of the Eastern world, which has profoundly influenced their culture and has even served as the basis for the thinking behind the design of art and crafts. The purpose of this study is to explore the contemporary craft design style in Taiwan through the aesthetic thinking of the Book of Changes, and selecting a government-sponsored National Craft Branding Program, the Yii Project," as a case study. This study was conducted based on several research methods, including in-depth interviews and content analysis, to analyze the aesthetic qualities of the artwork from the program from the aesthetic perspective of the Book of Changes. The results of the study demonstrate that the aesthetic principles of the Book of Changes, namely "Yin, Yang and Tai Chi," "Chi and the Changes of Times," "Enacting Emblematic Symbols," "State of Satisfaction," and "Metaphysicality". These principles may effectively analyze the aesthetics of the works of art produced from the Yii Project and show that the aesthetics principles of the Book of Changes can serve as the basis of the study of contemporary art and craft design style.

Keywords: The Book of Changes · Arts and Crafts Design · The Yii Arts and Crafts Fashion Project

1 Introduction

The philosophical thinking of a nation implies beliefs, spirituality, and attitudes towards the world, and reveals the social psychology, values, cultural characteristics, and lifestyle of a nation. Traditional Chinese philosophical thought emphasizes the changes and growth of all things in heaven and earth and considers how humans can co-exist in harmony and unity among all things. Several literary works of Chinese traditional philosophy such as the Book of Changes, the Book of Documents, the Book of Poetry, the Book of Rites, and the Spring and Autumn Annals, which the Book of Changes feature a philosophical view of nature and humanity, which have been repeatedly explored by many scholars throughout the ages. Not until Confucius wrote the great commentary, the Ten Wings Commentaries, on the Book of Changes did it finally take shape and become

Q. Gao and J. Zhou (Eds.): HCII 2024, LNCS 14726, pp. 179–192, 2024.
https://doi.org/10.1007/978-3-031-61546-7_12

a Confucian classic, which no longer focuses on fortunetelling, but emphasizes philosophical thinking [1, 2]. Such philosophical ideas have profoundly influenced various fields, such as astronomy and geography, politics, economics, military arts, management, education, arts and crafts, etc., in which the principles of operation can be realized, and have influenced Chinese culture until today. The aesthetics of craftsmanship in the Book of Changes emphasizes returning to nature and following the great principles. As the Book of Changes stated that "within the view they exhibited (in them) the way of heaven, calling (the lines) yin and yang; the way of earth, calling (them) the weak (or soft) and the strong (or hard); and the way of men, under the names of benevolence and righteousness". In other words, it suggested that we humans should explore the harmony between the yin and yang of heaven and earth, the movement of the four seasons, and discover the harmony and interaction between the advance and retreat, the opening and closing, the big and small, the move and still, the strength and the flexibility. Then, it mentions the principles of kindness, justice, discipline, and morality that one should possess in dealing with the world, and further develops the aesthetic philosophy of "respect for life and harmony of rules".

In 2007, NTCRDI cooperated with the Taiwan Creative Design Center to promote the "Craft New Look Cross-Disciplinary Creative Application Project - Art and Craft Fashion" [3, 4]. With the strategy of collaborative cross-disciplinary research and design and the participation of designers and craftworkers, NTCRDI attempted to combine traditional craft techniques with contemporary design thinking to highlight the impression of Taiwan's craft aesthetics. In 2008, NTCRDI created "Yii" as the name of Taiwan's craft and fashion brand for this extension project. The pronunciation of "Yii" in Chinese is the same as "Yi" (Chinese character spelling as "易", which connotes the meaning of change) and also the same as "Yi"(Chinese character "藝," which means art) which also describes the spirit of Taiwan's craft aesthetics [4] and connotes the philosophical ideas of "the Book of Changes," which respects nature, heaven, and earth, yin and yang [5]. In 2008, NTCRDI participated in the Paris Furniture Fair in France under the brand "Yii". The "Yii Craft Fashion Design Brand Project" (hereinafter referred to as the Yii Project) has been implemented for six years with a total of five periods [4]. It emphasizes the idea of highlighting the aesthetics of Taiwan's craftsmanship, the cross-disciplinary integration of contemporary design with traditional craftsmanship and local material technology, and collaborative design as a strategy to emphasize the spirituality and distinctiveness of Taiwan's craft aesthetics. The project involved 29 craftsmen and 31 designers between 2007 and 2012, producing a total of 120 works [4]. Later, based on the experience of the "Yii Project", NTCRDI developed several projects for cross-discipline cooperation in development and legacy transmission education, which have had a great impact on the development of Taiwan's craft industry and education in recent years. Therefore, since the artistic design of the Yii project is based on the aesthetics concepts of the Book of Changes, this study has chosen the Yii project as a research sample to investigate how the aesthetics of the Book of Changes is expressed in the contemporary Taiwanese arts and crafts design products.

2 Literature Review

This study chose to analyze the design strategies of the Yii Project's crafts based on the aesthetic viewpoints of crafts from the Book of Changes. The aesthetic viewpoints of crafts discussed in the Book of Changes were investigated and organized, and we learned that the important viewpoint of the aesthetic consciousness of the Book of Changes is the philosophical idea of pursuing the goal of reverence for nature and the unity of heaven and man. Various craft aesthetic perspectives from the Book of Changes, respectively, are perspectives that pursue this goal and can be broadly classified into the following five types.

2.1 The Craft Aesthetics of the Book of Changes

The Chinese philosophical thought is derived from the observation of the universe, nature, and all things, and the contemplation of the origin of all things and the reason for their existence. It is mentioned in The Great Treatise I, the Book of Changes, "in (the system of) the Yi there is the grand terminus, which produced the two elementary forms and those two Forms produced the Four emblematic Symbols, which again produced the eight Trigrams. The eight trigrams served to determine the good and evil (issues of events), and from this determination was produced the (successful prosecution of the) great business (of life)" [6]. This is a description of the origin of all things in the universe, the seasons, and even the description of natural phenomena, advising people to follow the rules of nature, the so-called "Tao". This idea is also mentioned in Laozi's "Tao Te Ching" chapter 42 that "the Tao produced one; one produced two; two produced three; three produced all things" [7]. We can regard Chinese philosophy as the philosophy of life, the philosophy of experiencing life through life and returning to nature through life. The attitude should also follow the principles, of being in harmony with heaven and earth, and integrating oneself with the laws of nature to achieve the harmonious development of the so-called " Unity of Nature and Humanity".

This study chose to analyze the design strategies of the Yii Project's crafts based on the aesthetic viewpoints of crafts from the Book of Changes. The aesthetic viewpoints of crafts discussed in the Book of Changes were investigated and organized, and we learned that the important viewpoint of the aesthetic consciousness of the Book of Changes is the philosophical idea of pursuing the goal of reverence for nature and the unity of heaven and man. Various craft aesthetic perspectives from the Book of Changes, respectively, are perspectives that pursue this goal and can be broadly classified into the following five types.

2.1.1 The Aesthetic View of "Harmonization of Yin and Yang" in Craftsmanship

The concept of "yin and yang" is derived from the observation of natural phenomena, as Tao Te Ching chapter 42 stated that "all things leave behind them the Obscurity (out of which they have come), and go forward to embrace the Brightness (into which they have emerged), while they are harmonized by the Breath of Vacancy." The idea is that everything must have a so-called yin and yang and that the interplay of yin and yang will eventually lead to a harmonious state. According to "The Book of Changes", the most important combination of the two trigrams "Qian" and "Kun" forms the other 62 trigrams. In the Book of Changes, says "Qian (symbolizes Heaven, which) directs the great beginnings of things; Kun (symbolizes Earth, which) gives to them their completion." What refers to "Qian" as the sky and the sun, and "Kun" as the earth, is that the two are indispensable for the creation of all things, just as the harmony of yin and yang. From the point of view of craft aesthetics, they are specifically expressed as follows: virtual and real, light and dark, large and small, strong and weak, dynamic and static, male and female, rigid and soft, which have conflicting, contradictory and contrasting characteristics, but are also mutually dependent and interdependent [8–10]. Similarly, in Chinese color theory, the idea of yin and yang can be elaborated as ink is the yang and paper is the yin, and ink is divided into five colors [11], which are combined with paper into one, with infinite variations.

2.1.2   The Aesthetic View of "Chi and the Changes of Times" in Craftsmanship

The interpretation of "Chi" can be found in "The Great Treatise II, The Book of Changes," which says that "the strong and the weak push themselves each into the place of the other, and hence the changes take place". This means that the process of growing is the intermingling of yin and yang and "Chi" is formed during that process. "Chi" has the connotation of the origin of life. Since "Chi" describes the process of mingling and meeting, it has the characteristics of "time" and "change". In other words, "change of times" describes the continuous growth, development, creation, and innovation of all things, yet with " unchanging" principles in it. The relationship between the laws of "change" and " non-change" is known as "Tao" in Lao Tzu's philosophy, and it is stated in Lao Tzu's Tao Te Ching in chapter 25 that "there was something undefined and complete, coming into existence before heaven and earth. How still it was and formless, standing alone, and undergoing no change, reaching everywhere and in no danger! It may be regarded as the Mother of all things. I do not know its name, and I give it the designation of the Tao [12]. It is also mentioned in "the Book of Changes, Jien" that "advancing will conduct to (greater) difficulties while remaining stationary will afford ground for praise:' - the proper course is to wait". It is said that we should be in tune with the time and act according to the laws of nature. Generally speaking, craftsmen should respect and understand the changes between heaven and earth, and follow the appropriate time, materials and techniques to respond to the harmonious relationship between heaven, earth, and human beings in their crafts. On top of that, they should also continue to create innovative works according to different times and opportunities to achieve innovative acts. However, the so-called innovative works do not mean the practice of pursuing novelty, but the innovative design to solve contemporary social problems due to the changing needs of society. Therefore, as the environment and social needs change, the creators need to face the changes in the external environment and solve the problems that they face.

2.1.3 The Aesthetic View of "Enacting Emblematic Symbols, Conveying Ideas" in Craftsmanship

In "The Great Treaties I, The Book of Changes" the Master said: "the written characters are not the full exponent of speech, and speech is not the full expression of ideas and sages made their emblematic symbols to set forth fully their ideas; appointed (all) the diagrams to show fully the truth and falsehood (of things); appended their explanations to give the full expression of their words". This refers to the relationship of imagery and intention and through "enacting emblematic symbols" to "convey ideas," which is the use of objective symbols as a medium for the transmission of the subjective perception of ideas. In other words, this similar to the craftsmanship aesthetics of "perceiving things, capturing the imagery" that formulates the subject-object relationship between "images and ideas" [6]. The "Book of Changes, The Great Treatise II" says, "looking up, he contemplated the brilliant forms exhibited in the sky, and looking down he surveyed the patterns shown on the earth. He contemplated the ornamental appearances of birds and beasts and the (different) suitabilities of the soil. Near at hand, in his person, he found things for consideration, and the same at a distance, in things in general". By observing all things that exist in heaven and earth and obtaining auspicious animals and plants as symbols and images, as well as social order, the symbols and images were used to bring order to what was said and to produce social order and civilization [10]. In terms of craft aesthetics, the artist should consider the suitability of humanistic and social conventions and attach an objective symbol with connotation to the craft, so that it can carry the function of ideas, and the user and the viewer can form a connection between the craft and the artist through the craft.

2.1.4 The Aesthetic View of "State of Satisfaction" in Craftsmanship

Modesty and self-restraint are the qualities of traditional Chinese philosophical thinking. It is particularly emphasized that individuals should seek a higher level of cultivation by pursuing self-discipline, waiting for opportunities, and acting within their capability. The concept of "a mountain, and above it that for water, form Jian. The superior man, in accordance with this, turns round (and examines) himself, and cultivates his virtue" as stated in "the Book of Changes, the Jien chapter" advises people to be content with what they have, and not to be deluded by glamor, profit, or material possessions that cause them to desire more than they deserve. The same idea is found in the Book of Changes, "Lu", "undivided, shows its subject treading the path that is level and easy - a quiet and solitary man, to whom, if he is firm and correct, there will be good fortune". Also in the Book of Changes, "The Great Treatise I," it mentioned that "It is by the ease with which it proceeds that Qian directs (as it does), and by its unhesitating response that Kun exhibits such ability. He who attains to this ease of Heaven will be easily understood, and he who attains to this freedom from laborious effort of the Earth will be easily followed". It can also be seen in Lao Tzu's "Tao Te Ching" chapter 44 that who is content needs fear no shame. Who knows to stop incurs no blame. From danger free long live shall he". "Contentment", in the aesthetic view of craftsmanship, means that the creator should not pursue flashy appearance, excessive decoration, and packaging, or over-exploitation of materials from nature and cost, which will turn into a design style to please the public.

It is important for the creator to respect the materials and create with a simple approach, using the idea that "less is more" [13, 14] without unnecessary decoration, so as to show the pure beauty of the material texture, the pure beauty of the shape, and the pure beauty of the idea in the craft.

2.1.5   The Aesthetic View of "Metaphysicality" in Craftsmanship

Transforming "form" into "spirit" is an important Chinese aesthetic concept, it goes beyond the level of symbols to convey messages, enabling people to comprehend meanings beyond words, sounds beyond strings, and visions beyond images. The such aesthetic mentality of craftsmanship constitutes the "spiritual essence" as an aesthetic discourse of philosophy, spirituality, faith, and life perception. The aesthetic expression of the craft emphasizes the mental aspect of the intention, which the artist or the viewer must appreciate through spirituality [8], and the aesthetic expression of the craft emphasizes the exploration of the relationship between "nihility and reality coexists" and "seeking the vacancy within reality". The ancient Chinese philosopher Kong Yingda (AD 574–648), in his book Zhou Yi Zheng Yi (The Commentary of Zhou Yi), stated that "the great extreme means that before heaven and earth were divided, the vital energy was mixed and was one, that is, the primordial and Oneness". The "Tao produced One" mentioned in Lao Tzu's "Tao Te Ching chapter 42" is a discussion surrounding "nothingness," which is the origin of all things that must be comprehended through spirituality.

3   Methodology

3.1   Confirmation on the Definition of the Aesthetic Perspectives of the Book of Changes

To confirm that the aesthetic perspective of the Book of Changes can be effectively applied to analyzing the aesthetic perspective of craft design products, this study invited three university professors with backgrounds in the field of the study Book of Changes, and two professors with backgrounds in the field of arts and crafts product designs for a total of five university professors to confirm the aforementioned five aesthetic perspectives of the Book of Changes based on the connotations of the Book of Changes and the literature. An expert meeting was held to discuss conceptual definitions of each aesthetic point of view that can be used to analyze process design products:

1. "Harmonization of Yin and Yang" can be defined as an aesthetic expression that uses two or more materials, shapes, colors, conditions, ideas, and techniques to create a work of art that appears to be contradictory, yet can be harmonized with each other.
2. "Chi and the Changes of Times" is defined as the reflection of the time, variability, and innovation of the work in the creation of the craft. In terms of time, for example, we choose the natural materials that grow at the moment of creation, consider the characteristics of user participation, and use materials that may vary over time; in terms of versatility and innovation, we create innovative and experimental acts in response to the needs of the times and society.

3. "Enacting Emblematic Symbols, Conveying Ideas" can be defined as a craft creation in which the creator expects to convey a social message to the user or viewer through the symbols of the shape, color, and decoration of the work, which may be a symbol of regional culture or a symbol of a common social constraint.

4. "State of Satisfaction" can be defined as: in the use of media, craft creators should design with the attitude of minimizing the exploitation of natural resources, be environmentally friendly, and respecting all things in nature as well as being able to think in terms of green design and sustainable design. As for expression and thought, the craft creator should simplify the decoration and create works with a simple, pure, pure, and natural style.

5. "Metaphysicality" can be defined as the emphasis on the spirit of the creator, such as the care for society and the disadvantaged, respect for nature, and the pursuit of sustainability. In this way, a higher level of faith and philosophy is conveyed in the craft, and the user and viewer are thus able to gain a spiritual understanding.

4 Analyzing the Crafts of the Yii Project from the Aesthetic Perspective of the Book of Changes

4.1 Harmonization of Yin and Yang

In the "Book of Changes, The Great Treatise I," it is mentioned that "the successive movement of the inactive and active operations constitutes what is called the course (of things). That which ensues as the result (of their movement) is goodness; that which shows it in its completeness is the natures (of men and things)." In traditional Chinese philosophy, it is believed that everything is generated by yin and yang, based on the two trigrams of qian and kun, with the application of yin and yang changes, and the resulting changes in the aesthetic expression of rigid and soft, dynamic and static, front and back, yin and yang, top and bottom, etc., is in conflict and contrast to find a state of integration and harmony. Of the 78 works that resulted from the Yii Project, a total of 52 works were considered to have the idea of "harmonization of yin and yang" in them, accounting for 66.7% of the total number of works. The specific aesthetic expression can be observed in the works in Figs. 1, 2 and 3. The shape of "Vase Blossom Kingdom" (Fig. 1) is a fusion of two traditional oriental porcelain vase shapes, and at the same time, the representation of the vase is made by the interplay of solid and void forms, which makes the work (solid) and space (void) interact, creating a feeling of interplay between the real and the figurative [14]. The material chosen for "Flower Scene" (Fig. 2) is a combination of bamboo and pottery, with the pottery itself being the soil and the bamboo being the growth on the soil, which is a combination of different materials but echoes the natural pattern of interdependence of all things in nature. On the form, the pottery below is expressed in a smooth, rounded shape, like the warmth of the earth, giving nourishment to all things. The bamboo weave above shows regularity and penetration, but by extending upward, it expresses the design concept of unending life. Such concept is mentioned in the previous sections, in "The Book of Changes, Li" that "Li means being attached to" the sun and moon have their place in the sky. All the grains, grass, and trees have their place on the earth. The double brightness (of the two trigrams) adheres to what is correct, and the result is the transforming and perfecting all under the sky. The weak (second line) occupies the middle and correct position, and gives the indication of 'a free and successful course;' and, moreover, 'nourishing (docility like that of) the cow' will lead to good fortune. "Lacquerware Washstand" (Fig. 3) is a combination of natural and rough rocks and delicate lacquer, creating a sense of conflict in the material. This piece is a water bowl for the garden to grow small aquatic plants. With the act of people participating in the use, the transparency, and ripples of the water in the rock soften the psychological feeling of the hardness of the rock. The ripples on the water surface and the rocks also create an interactive relationship between rigidity and flexibility, movement and stillness. In addition, through the refraction of the water ripples, visitors can see the painted images expressed in lacquer, which seem to be moving yet still as well as having a fleeting movement, giving the work much room for imagination.

4.2   Chi and the Changes of Times

Among the 78 works of the Yii Project, a total of 69 works were considered to have the idea of "Chi and the changes of times" in them, accounting for 88.4% of the total number of works. It is suggested that such an aesthetic viewpoint should be a common design viewpoint and approach used by the designers and craftspeople participating in the Yii Project, and to a certain extent reflects the aesthetic expression vocabulary that contemporary Taiwanese designers and craftspeople specialize in. The specific aesthetic expression can be observed in the works in Figs. 4, 5 and 6. Work "Three Generation Together" (Fig. 4) refers to the so-called three-generation cohabitation refers to the family structure in Taiwan from around 1950s to 2000s, that is, the family members include grandparents, parents, and children living together for three generations, which is the change of social patterns during the take-off stage of Taiwan's economic development from the earlier extended family form [17]. Since the year 2000, the overall socio-economic structure of Taiwan has changed and the concept of family in Taiwan has changed. Most of the families have become small, with parents living with their children, and more and more couples are not having children as a way of life. The work "Three Generations Together" is based on the wooden structured bamboo and rattan cushioned chairs and stools commonly found in 1950s homes, evoking the emotions of the users with the symbols of the times. In terms of structure, the six chairs and stools can be overlapped and combined into a single entity, which significantly reduces storage space and expresses the importance that traditional families in Taiwan attach to the idea of togetherness. This work clearly shows that the designers and craftsmen not only made good use of the symbolic language of the times when creating this work, but also designed the concept of storage and space utilization in response to the needs of modern living style [5]. The design of "Bamboo Lunchbox" (Fig. 5) makes use of the bamboo charcoal material developed in Taiwan in recent years combined with ceramic technology to produce the "Bamboo Charcoal Black Ceramic Lunchbox". The characteristics of the bamboo charcoal black pottery will produce far-infrared heat [18], has a high-quality thermal insulation function, in addition to highlighting Taiwan's special material technology, but also to meet the needs of modern working people's life, the outer layer of the bamboo protective cover, you can put environmentally friendly tableware, but also has a heat insulation and thermal insulation function。 (Fig. 6) In Taiwan, red brick and red tile were the main materials used for construction before the prosperity of concrete and steel buildings, and local brick-making began in Taiwan during the Dutch period (1624–1662), while red brick construction gradually flourished during Taiwan's Qing Dynasty (1683–1985), when brick kilns flourished due to the construction techniques introduced by the large number of people who came to Taiwan from Tangshan. Later, during the Japanese rule period (1895–1945), the Japanese government introduced construction techniques, making Taiwan's brick-making technology gradually mature and stable. Therefore, most of the existing ancient monuments and temples in Taiwan can be found in the red brick building style [19]. The "Brickwork" is a series of three works that use red bricks as the main material for flower vessels, and use a smooth, rounded form as the expression, in order to echo the cultural development of Taiwan's island. In addition, Taiwan has undergone many historical cycles of regime and administration, and people have become like rocks that keep on rolling, and eventually they have become an inwardly-constrained and well-rounded personality. The curved and rounded shape of this work not only gives the public the impression that red bricks should be square, but also emphasizes the maturity of Taiwan's bricklaying technology and material development. During the process of washing and grinding, the craftsman must finely adjust the ratio of cement, lime, and yellow sand to make them have the same hardness as the red bricks, so that the washing and grinding can become a curved shape, and the technique of gluing the red bricks can be firmly established, showing the brand impression of Taiwan's superior technology.

4.3 Enacting Emblematic Symbols, Conveying Ideas

In the "Book of Changes, The Great Treatise II" says "The appellations and names (of the diagrams and lines) are but small matters, but the classes of things comprehended under them are large. The meaning is distant, the words are written, the words are curved but neutral, and the events are unrestrained but hidden." The figurative symbols can be used to simulate or symbolize profound meanings and facts, that is, to convey intangible subjective messages through tangible and objective symbolic images. Here the concept of beauty is pursued as a conceptual, conscious activity, and the so-called message consciousness can be indicative of the normative meaning or the spiritual feeling of the mind. Among the 78 works of the "Yii Project", a total of 66 works are considered to have the idea of "enacting emblematic symbols, conveying ideas," accounting for 84.6% of the total number of works. This shows that designers and craftsmen often make use of symbolic images and shapes in their creation methods to convey a certain sense of message [8]. The specific aesthetic expression can be observed in the works in Figs. 7, 8 and 9. ⟨Life⟩ (Fig. 7) is a 3-m-long silk cloth that can be hung on the wall to serve as a ruler for parents to record their children's growth. This work employs advanced gradient botanical dyeing techniques, using different natural plant pigments on the same piece of silk fabric as the raw material for dyeing. Different colors are used to correspond to the life cycle of the growing children. The original color of silk fabric symbolizes the purity and innocence of a newborn baby. With growth, life begins to render colorful and diverse colors, symbolizing the colorful and infinite beauty of life's exploration of the world. Work "First Appearance" (Fig. 8) is a lantern with a wood-carved totem as its base. The designers and craftsmen chose wood-carved motifs, such as peonies, lotus flowers, and orchids, which are often used as symbols of nobility and good fortune in architecture and temples. The overall shape is a combination of exquisite carving and modern lighting methods, taking a blessing incense burner as a model, the designer chose to use a soft low-light source to show the inner change of light and shadow, just like the subtle character of Oriental people. "Random" (Fig. 9) is inspired by the impression of farmers carrying bamboo during the agricultural period in Taiwan, and transformed its shape into a laptop backpack for contemporary knowledge workers. The backpack is decorated with the patterns of the "Hakka people", one of the most important ethnic groups in Taiwan, which implies the attitude of the Hakka people, such as frugality, hard work and effort.

4.4 State of Satisfaction

The Tao Te Ching of Laozi (Chapter 44) says, "cautions or fame or life, Which do you hold more dear? or life or wealth, to which would you adhere? keep life and lose those other things; keep them and lose your life: - which brings sorrow and pain more near? Thus we may see, Who cleaves to fame Rejects what is more great." It expresses the traditional Chinese philosophical thinking and wisdom of the world, advising people to "understand normality", that is, to observe and analyze the laws of nature. "To stop" means that one should not take from nature out of greed, but in moderation. "To be satisfied" means that one must not let one's desires detach one from a harmonious relationship with nature, and to seek a harmonious development of "harmony between heaven and man" [12, 14]. Meanwhile, as mentioned earlier in the Book of Changes, "the superior man (emblemed here) by the yellow and correct (color), is possessed of comprehension and discrimination. he occupies the correct position (of supremacy), but (that emblem) is on (the lower part of) his person. His excellence is in the centre (of his being), but it diffuses a complacency over his four limbs, and is manifested in his (conduct of) affairs: this is the perfection of excellence." This also express about the same principle. Thinking from an aesthetic point of view illustrates the need to understand and analyze the characteristics of materials, to make good use of and respect the materials taken from nature, and not to waste or over-exploit them. The aesthetic spirit of pure transmission of ideas without excessive decoration should be emphasized in the modeling performance. Among the 78 works that resulted from the Yii Project, a total of 38 works were considered to have the idea of "state of satisfaction" in them, accounting for 48.7% of the total number of works. Compared to other aesthetic concepts, there are relatively few works that use the aesthetic concept of "contentment" as a form of expression. The specific aesthetic expression can be observed in the works in Figs. 10, 11 and 12. First of all, the analysis and study of the characteristics of the materials are fully expressed in the two works "Bamboo Sheet Rack" (Fig. 10) and "Bent Bamboo Triangle Stool" (Fig. 11). "Bamboo Sheet Rack" (Fig. 10) is an indoor cloak rack made of bamboo pieces. The simple design and the minimal amount of materials used in its production show the care and respect for the use of materials. The designers and craftsmen chose to use the toughness and flexibility of natural bamboo and the characteristics of plant growth to express the natural style of curves, which can be used to decorate the elegant feeling of the interior. "Bent Bamboo Triangle Stool" (Fig. 11) The chairs and stools made of bamboo are also selected, and the technology of using the material is actively developed so that they can be mass-produced with the technology of bending the bamboo pieces,

The extreme characteristics of the material are brought into play to achieve the benefits of environmental protection. In terms of modeling, this work is based on the "three-legged tripod", a common traditional Chinese vessel, to symbolize the cultural connotation of stability, blessing, peace and prosperity. In the design of "Bubble Sofa" (Fig. 12), the designers and craftsmen chose to use the purest form units to form a functional whole. The designer chose the bamboo ball, the most common child's play in early Taiwanese rural life, as the basic element. Taking advantage of the elasticity and lightness of the bamboo ball, the designer has combined it into a sofa form commonly seen in modern life. Overall, this work is a work of minimalist thinking, but at the same time functional, cultural and fun.

5   Conclusion

Studies in the past regarding the connotation and philosophical ideas of the Book of Changes have contained a discussion of the aesthetic viewpoints of the Book of Changes. However, these studies and literature omitted practical perspectives on the utilization of design, especially on the conceptual definition of aesthetic perspectives. As a matter of fact, design education in Taiwan often incorporates philosophical perspectives of Eastern art, which allows students to develop their own cultural identity, not to mention the expectation of infusing Eastern design ideas into their design works, but there has been a substantial shortage of such perspectives in the research field. In this study, we sought a rigorous process by inviting five experts in related fields of study to conduct a theoretical conceptualization of the aesthetic perspective of the Book of Changes by means of a meeting and then invited three different experts to conduct content analyses of samples of the craft design products. The results of this study showed relatively high levels of reliability, indicating that the five aspects of the Book of Changes aesthetic concepts can be used for analyzing the products of the craft design.

Based on such conviction, the study analyzed the craft aesthetic qualities of the works produced by the Yii Project from the five types of aesthetic perspectives of the Book of Changes. The content analysis conducted by the three university professors invited for the study shows that among the five aesthetic perspectives, namely " Harmonization of Yin and Yang," " Chi and the Changes of Times," "Enacting Emblematic Symbols," " State of Satisfaction," and "Metaphysicality," the aesthetic perspective of "Chi and the Changes of Times" made up 88.4% of the total number of works, which is the higher proportion among the five aesthetic perspectives. The second highest percentage was 84.6%, followed by the " Enacting Emblematic Symbols". It demonstrates the design thinking that contemporary Taiwanese designers and craftsmen utilize in the development of their crafts. This result shall provide a reference not only for future researchers but also for the practice of design.* This experiment was approved to be conducted without the permission of the ethical committee by "Department of Industrial Design, College of Design, National Taipei University of Technology, Taiwan" (Figs. 13, 14 and 15).

Fig. 1. Title: Vase Blossom Kingdom

Fig. 2. Title: Flower Scene

Fig. 3. Title: Lacquerware Washstand

Fig. 4. Title: Three Generation Together

Fig. 5. Title: Bamboo Lunch Box

Fig. 6. Title: Brickwork

Fig. 7. Title: Life

Fig. 8. Title: First Appearance

Fig. 9. Title: Random

Fig. 10. Title: Bamboo Sheet

Fig. 11. Title: Bent Bamboo Triangle Stool

Fig. 12. Title: Bubble Sofa

Fig. 13. Title: Traces of the Past

Fig. 14. Title: Harvest

Fig. 15. Title: Float

References

1. Legge, J.: The Sacred books of China: the texts of Confucianism. Motilal Banarsidass, Delhi (1966)
2. McClatchie, C.: Translation of the Confucian, or the "Classic of Change." American Presdyterian Mission Press, Shanghai (1876)

3. About NTCRI, NTCRI, Home Page. https://www.ntcri.gov.tw/en/content_91.html. Accessed 25 July 2023
4. Yii, Home Page. https://yii.ntcri.gov.tw/home/zh-tw. Accessed 11 July 2023
5. Hwang, S.H., Kao, Y.F., Miyazaki, K., Mitsuhashi, T.: Historical changing of bamboo craft industries in JhuShan town, Taiwan. Bull. Jpn. Soc. Sci. Des. **58**(2), 95–104 (2010)
6. Huang, A.: The complete I Ching: the definitive translation. Inner Traditions, Rochester (2004)
7. Laozi, Hansen, C.: Tao te ching: on the art of harmony: the new illustrated edition of the Chinese philosophical masterpiece. Duncan Baird Publishers, London (2009)
8. Hsieh, M.H., Guan S.S.: Investigating artistic commodity design through the shift between art and design. Bull. Jpn. Soc. Sci. Des. **61**(1), 77–86 (2014)
9. Heufler, G.: Design Basics from Ideas to Products. Ram Publications & Distribution Inc., Michigan (2004)
10. Karcher, S.: The Elements of I Ching. Shaftesbury, Dorset; Boston, Mass.: Element (1996)
11. Songkhai, K.: Implicit Meaning of Chinese vocabulary on colors in five elements elucidating socio-cultural context. Int. J. Linguist. **11**(5), 222 (2019)
12. Li, S.S.K.: The Ageless Wisdom: (According to Lao tzu). Marian Y.M. Li, San Francisco (1984)
13. van der Rohe, M., Beitin, A., Eiermann, W., Franzen, B., and Beitin, A.: Mies Van Der Rohe: Montage. Collage. Walther Konig (2017)
14. Peng, A.S., Chen, C.H., Yen, J.: Research on application of subtraction thinking into design (2013)
15. Kassarjian, H.H.: Content analysis in customer research. J. Consum. Res. **4**(1), 8–18 (1977)
16. Kassarjian, H.H., Kassarjian, W.M.: The impact of regulation on advertising: a content analysis. J. Consum. Policy **11**(3), 269–285 (1988). https://doi.org/10.1007/BF00411951
17. Family Group, National Academy for Educational Research (NAER), Home Page. https://terms.naer.edu.tw/detail/1301785/. Accessed 20 July 2023
18. Lin, C.A., An, T.C., Hsu, Y.H.: Study on the far infrared ray emission property and adsorption performance of bamboo charcoal/polyvinyl alcohol fiber. Polym.-Plast. Technol. Eng. **46**(11), 1073–1078 (2007)
19. Cultural Features, Ministry of Culture (MOC), Taiwan, Home Page. https://www.moc.gov.tw/en/features.html. Accessed 27 July 2023

A Case of Designing a Game to Support Older Adults in a Community Setting: Implications for Supporting Active Togetherness

Swaroop John, Szu-Yu Yang, and Aqueasha Martin-Hammond^(✉) ⓘ

Luddy School of Informatics, Computing, and Engineering, Indianapolis, IN, USA
aqumarti@iu.edu

Abstract. Community senior centers often play a significant role in fostering physical activity and social interactions among seniors in the communities they serve. Oftentimes, games are one way that centers engage seniors and provide recreational and social support. In recent years the growing emphasis on digital games for supporting seniors has led to new understanding of how to improve senior's wellness. However, much of the work in this area has examined games for improving physical activity with less emphasis on social interaction and design for community settings. In this paper, we partnered with a local senior center, to better understand the role of the center and the gaming sessions they provide in encouraging physical activity and social interactions among seniors. From initial observations and interviews, we identified implications for designing games for active togetherness, or supporting feeling of togetherness while engaging in short bursts of physical activity. We designed a hybrid game based on these implications and examined the perceived impact of our design had on seniors' social engagement and physical activity. Based on our findings, we contribute implications for game design that supports active togetherness in a senior community environment.

Keywords: Older adults · games · Social wellness · Physical wellness · Design · Community settings

1 Introduction

As the aging population increases, senior and community centers will continue to serve as an essential gateway for resources for over one million older adults 55 years of age or older [55]. Senior community centers often support community-dwelling older adults by offering a wide variety of recreational, nutritional, health, and social service programs [1, 17, 38, 55]. For older adults, the benefits of participating in community center activities can relate to their desire to socialize with other individuals of similar ages and remain active in later life through participation in group events and activities [1, 17, 38, 55]. One of the major activities that senior community centers in the United States often provide is opportunities for seniors to participate in games [37, 52].

© The Author(s), under exclusive license to Springer Nature Switzerland AG 2024
Q. Gao and J. Zhou (Eds.): HCII 2024, LNCS 14726, pp. 193–212, 2024.
https://doi.org/10.1007/978-3-031-61546-7_13

Games are well-recognized for providing different types of support to seniors inside and outside community centers [37, 52]. Although older adults may have varied preferences for games [5, 10, 13], many view games as one tool to improve older adults' physical and mental health and support social wellness. Therefore, over the years, researchers have examined the effect of existing and novel digital games on different aspects of senior wellness [27, 33, 42, 49, 50]. Yet, despite the known benefits of gaming, according to some researchers, the focus on social aspects of gaming among seniors is often much less studied than that of physical in game design [18, 32]. Further, in community settings, research often focuses on examining existing games [21, 22, 49], withstanding the center's existing community dynamics and environment. In this paper, we extend prior work to explore opportunities to design games that support social and physical activity among groups of seniors within a community setting.

We present results from a case study where we partnered with a local community senior center to conduct observations, interviews, and to prototype and test a game with older adults who regularly participated in weekly game sessions at the center. Our study aimed to identify opportunities and design implications for games that support *active togetherness* (i.e., supporting feelings of togetherness while being active). We conducted an observation of an existing gaming session followed by interviews with 11 participants, including both staff members and seniors. We asked participants about their current experiences, including the benefits and challenges of engaging in physical activity and socialization at the center.

We found that participants were socially active at home and at the center, although they also discussed challenges. Through the center, they had come to expand their network for social support and often came together to collectively advocate to keep activities at the center going. Yet, some seniors would only socialize regularly with people they already know. While participants played various games at the center, the most popular was Bingo. However, the game did not require much socialization and the seniors were also often sedentary throughout the gameplay process sitting for sometimes several hours at a time. Based on findings from observations and interviews, we developed a hybrid game to improve social and physical activity, with emphasis on designing for *active togetherness*, or improving connectedness among the community of seniors during game play while also encouraging moments of physical activity. We tested it with seven seniors and one staff member to understand how they believed the game might improve physical and social interactions in the center. We found that our design approach which emphasized capitalizing on existing interests and considering community members' diverse physical abilities, technical skills, and resources led to initial acceptance of the game.

Our work contributes to a better understanding of the experiences of older adults that engage in social and physical activities in a community center setting and how those activities are associated with seniors' social and physical wellness needs. We also contribute implications for designing games for active togetherness in senior community settings. Finally, we reflect on our design process and how our partnership, knowledge of existing community norms and dynamics, and the physical environment helped to design a game that reflected the values of the seniors who were members of the community at the center.

2   Related Work

We discuss the role of community centers for supporting seniors, and the use of games for increasing social and physical activities for seniors.

2.1   The Role of Community Centers for Supporting Seniors

Seniors often benefit from participating in community centers activities and these centers often play an integral role in supporting the social support system for seniors' health and wellness [1, 17, 38, 55]. Studies suggest that the majority of seniors feel that being a part of a community center makes them feel like a part of a group thereby improving their quality of life, and overall physical health [1, 35]. Community-based senior centers are also known to help reduce the long-term costs aging by keeping seniors healthier and presenting them with opportunities to socialize with other seniors every day [36]. Therefore, senior centers often are an integral part of the social support system of those seniors that participate.

One of the activities offered typically at community senior centers to support social interactions are games [37, 52]. While community centers are continually becoming more progressive and creative in their programming, gaming has been a mainstay [8]. Games are used in senior centers not just for enjoyment but also for rehabilitation [21, 22, 49] and health [4, 34]. For example, the 'Silver fit soft kinetic rehabilitation' is a gaming software used in senior centers for rehabilitation to improve seniors' physical health [53]. There have also been studies of other commercial games such as Nintendo Wii for use in group activities to support senior's health [7, 21, 27, 42]. For example, Glännfjord and colleagues found that participation in group Wii Fit activities improved seniors' quality-of-life and that as seniors played their overall well-being was improved [21]. Increasingly, however, researchers have been interested in the ways novel digital games can be designed and used to support seniors both inside and outside the centers [22, 32, 44].

2.2   Games for Improving Seniors' Social and Physical Activity

There has been significant research studying the role of games in the lives of seniors. Game preferences among senior can vary widely based on factors such as personality or demographics [5, 10, 13]. However, much of the recent focus of games with seniors has been on creating digital game interventions [3, 7, 32]. Games are known to be used by seniors for relaxation, entertainment, fun, and socialization [7, 25, 32]. Gamification can drive users' motivation, engagement, and enjoyment [15] therefore often games can be used to motivate people to participate in activities that they may find otherwise difficult or boring. Physical activity is among the routines that can become challenging for some seniors as they age due to declining interest, health, or due to disability. Sedentary behaviors can be a cause for concern for seniors as it often leads to declines in overall health [47]. Therefore, there is a continuously growing body of literature that studies games, in particular digital games, as tools to improve and maintain physical activity among older adults [21, 27, 42–44].

Physical activity game interventions sometime categorized as serious games, digital health games, or exergames include basic gaming concepts such as competition and reward, but have the goal of improving a user's overall physical activity or to rehabilitate [2, 4, 27, 33, 49]. For older adults, several physical activity interventions have been found to not only improve physical health but also cognitive abilities, and overall wellness [27]. Some physical activity games for older adults aim to improve a specific health outcome for example, balance or physical function [36, 45]. Other physical activity games for older adults are classified as exergames but focus on improving other aspects of health [40, 50]. For example, Rosenberg and colleagues developed an exergame to combat depression in seniors [40]. Some exergame studies have also studied social interactions [42] although studies emphasizing the social aspect of games for older adults are far less common than those studying physical improvement. Seah and colleagues argue that the vast number of game interventions for older adults have focused on improving physical activity opposed to social interaction [43]. However, research in this area is growing. Several studies have examined the use of digital games to understand social gameplay among older adults [30, 32]. For example, Kaufman and colleagues conducted a study on the impact of digital games for connecting seniors online [30–32]. Yet, there is an open need to better understand social needs in digital games that involve multiple players such as among a group or community of people [18]. Our study examines implications for designing a game that supports both physical and social activity within the game in a community senior center. Our aim is to better understand the influence of the community and its setting on game design for seniors.

3   Overview of Study Methods and Partner Site

Our study aimed to understand seniors' current experiences participating in social and physical activities at home and in the community, the role of games in their daily routine, and the impact of the community center and its gaming session on supporting seniors' physical and social needs. To do so, we partnered with a local community center in Indianapolis, Indiana throughout the design process. The community center supports local seniors 60 years of age or older and offers senior programming and an organized schedule of activities including games, art projects, and special field trip events each week. Seniors who sign up for the program live in the local community and can participate in activities at their leisure. Our main contact person throughout the study was the senior center coordinator who helped us to schedule time with seniors to observe one of their game sessions, interview them, and conduct a test play session with our proposed design. Over 6 months, we conducted a three-phase study including observations, interviews, and a test-play of the designed game. Our goal was to design a digital game that would increase both physical and social activity of seniors while at the center.

4   Observations and Interviews

Our main aim was to identify the benefits, limitations, and opportunities gaming could provide to help seniors meet their social and physical activity goals while at the center. To investigate current experiences and guide the design of the game, we first conducted interviews and observations with older adults and staff at a local community center. Our study was reviewed and approved by our institution's Institutional Review Board (IRB) before any data collection occurred. The following research questions guided the observations and interviews: (1) What are seniors' existing physical and social interactions at home and the center? (2) What are seniors' current gaming experiences and what is the role of the community center gaming sessions for promoting physical activity and socialization? (3) What factors related to the existing community and environment are critical considerations for designing games that support both physical activity and socialization in a community setting?

4.1 Observation Procedures

To begin our study, we first conducted an observation session of the current weekly game sessions at the center. The senior coordinator informed us of the best days to do observations. We learned that many seniors came to the center for Bingo, and we purposefully planned the observation on a day where we could observe the Bingo session.

The goal of the observation was to learn about the existing types of games seniors played while at the center, their social interactions during games, and how they engaged in play during the game sessions. On the day of the observation, we arrived at the community center early to prepare before the Bingo session started and to observe some of the other games the seniors played while at the center. We observed six seniors participating in Bingo with one senior serving as the facilitator. One researcher conducted the observation however, they took notes and photos which were shared with the research team for discussion. The observation session lasted approximately 3–4 h.

4.2 Interview Procedures

After the observation session, we returned to the center to conduct interviews with seniors and staff members who participated in the gaming sessions each week. We recruited participants for the interview with the help of the senior center coordinator who allowed us to talk about the interview study after we completed the observation session in the first phase, and during follow-up visits to the center for game sessions to solicit participation. We collected contact information from seniors who were willing to participate and contacted them later by phone to schedule the interview at the center.

We conducted interviews to develop a deeper understanding of the older adults' social and physical activities inside and outside the center and their prior gaming experiences. Nine seniors and two staff participated. Table 1 includes the demographics of the older adults that participated. Two staff members who assisted seniors with the gaming sessions also provided interviews. Because some seniors traveled to the center together and relied on each other for transport, we conducted a combination of group and individual interviews. Five interviews were conducted individually and two were conducted in pairs. The two staff were interviewed as a pair due to their time constraints. Each interview session lasted approximately 45 min and all interviews were conducted at the community center.

Before beginning the interviews, we summarized information about the study and provided a written copy of the study information sheet approved by our IRB office.

Table 1. Demographics of Older Adult Participants.

No.	Age	Gender	Visits to Center per Week
1	Not Shared	F	3–4 days a week
2	79	F	5 days a week
3	69	F	5 days a week
4	Not Shared	F	5 days a week
5	89	F	5 days a week
6	64	F	3–4 days a week
7	72	F	3–4 days a week
8	73	F	5 days a week
9	65	F	3–4 days a week

Afterward, we asked participants to sign a consent form informing them they could withdraw from the study at any time. If they agreed to continue, we asked their permission to audio record the session for later reflection. During the study, we asked participants about their social and physical activities at home and in the center, the role of games in their daily regimen, the kinds of games they play regularly, and the challenges they face engaging in social and physical activity inside and outside the center. For staff, we ask them to comment on their experiences working with the seniors and their perceptions of their physical and social interactions while at the center. We provided each participant with a $10 Walmart gift card for their interview.

4.3 Data Analysis

Observational data including notes and photographs were combined with interview data for analysis. Audio recordings of the interviews were transcribed and combined with researcher notes and accounts. For observational data, researchers met to review notes and photos to discuss and outline the interactions that occurred during the game play sessions. From those discussions we generate codes that relate to our understanding of what was happening during game play sessions.

For interview data, we used Atlas.ti to support the analysis process. We used thematic analysis [15] to identify an initial set of codes from the data using an open coding method. The research team conducted the first round of coding on a subset of the transcripts and met iteratively to discuss and compare codes. From these meetings we developed a list of codes which was applied to all interview transcripts to organize and categorize participants' quotes that corresponded to the codes and themes.

5 Observations and Interview Findings

We found that participants engaged in physical and social activities outside of the center, yet the center was important to the weekly social participation activities. We share findings related to their current engagement in physical and social activities, and the center's role in fostering social support including through the gaming session.

5.1 Current Engagement in Physical and Social Activities

Most participants were involved in physical and social activities outside of the senior center such as walking, however, the activities and their frequency varied. For example, P1 shared that she regularly had walk dates with her husband a couple of times a week. She stated, "Usually *on Tuesdays and Thursdays, we [my husband and I] like to go to Washington Square mall because it's not very busy and just walk around the mall sometimes. Sometimes he doesn't want, to go to the health spa buthe'll walk.*" Other participants however mentioned that they did not participate in physical exercise due to a health condition. P9, when asked about physical activity, stated, " *I have a really bad back and I had to retire early because of it. I have a pinched nerve in my leg. So, when I start doing things it flares up. My daughter lives with me and until last month, my mother was living with me and then she passed away. We were taking care of her... I do just a little, just a little bit of cooking [but] I can't stand very long cooking.*" Several other participants mentioned ongoing health conditions such as going through pulmonary rehab or chronic pain as reasons for not being physically active. One participant shared that she knew the importance of physical activity and used to be more active, but she was temporarily not as active due to a recent accident. Participant 7 stated, "*I was in an accident. I rolled my car twice, and it was upside down... Needed to bring me back over to get me out. So, I had a cracked rib, and my arm was lacerated. That's healed... So, I'm not real active right now, but I lead exercise downstairs a couple of times a week.*"

Most participants also had active social lives outside the center. For example, P7 shared that she participated in activities in her local apartment complex led by other residents. She shared, "*Well, like last night, one of the guys there brings a movie to show downstairs...They had the Lion King, it's really good. I'd seen it not too long ago. But I went down to see it... My neighbors are fun. There are about 53 apartments there and we have things going on, but I don't participate all the time. Like one girl leads Bible study once a week and so I go to that and when we have something called community Bingo at the apartments, then I go down for that.*" Other participants shared they also would connect to others by talking on the phone. P2 stated, "*So one of my friends, she had a hip replacement. So, we talk every day at least twice, three times a day... Spend about two hours [talking]. I stay on the phone. And then I talk to my daughter, but I talk to her on my cell phone. Then I talk to my grandkids.*" Some participants however shared that although they were currently more social, it has been a struggle for them over the years. P9 shared, "*I was always since I grew up so very quiet and shy. I really didn't develop that social skill of communicating with others...And so then when I would try to talk with people, it was like my mind would race on ahead, maybe a bit thinking [about] what I was going to say... so I would stumble over my words... So, I generally kept quiet, but in the last year and a half, two years, I've started socializing more.*" She later shared that her journey to becoming more social started at the center. She stated, *"It started here [at the center]. But I don't know whether that's helped make the change or not."*

5.2 The Center's Role in Fostering Social Support

Participants agreed that the senior center played an important role in supporting their physical and social activities. Some participants used the center's gym to walk and participate in other physical activities. Many participants also shared that they viewed the center as their main source of face-to-face socialization weekly. Therefore, in addition to opportunities for social engagement, participants also described ways that the center provided them with different types of social support including emotional, informational, and tangible that they received as part of being a member at the center [16].

Providing Opportunities for Physical and Social Activity. We learned that the center provided some organized opportunities for physical and social activity. The center provided exercise classes occasionally in the attached gym and some participants shared that they would sometimes participate. However, one staff member we interviewed shared that although the seniors used the gym and did some physical activities, they mostly played games and socialized when at the center, *"They enjoy the games. These are games they like to play. So, for the most part, honestly, they're just playing games. They're just back there. They're doing something. They're socializing. They're watching TV. They're playing games they are out enjoying while they can get out."* P2 explained that her main source of social interaction outside of calls to her family and friends was at the center, *"If I don't get out, I feel like there's nothing going on. So, it [visiting the center] helps me to socialize, it helps me to feel better about myself, in general, to get out and move around to things."* Other participants tried to socialize with people in their neighborhood but discussed that it could sometimes be challenging. P8 shared, *"I don't know the neighbors...I [used to] live like in a half-circle and everybody knew everybody. When we first moved in, you know, you want to do things to your house, neighbors would just come over help you paint and whatever, but over in my neighborhood now nobody gets out nobody sits out."* Therefore, the senior center played a significant role in supporting their continued social engagement. Another staff member shared, *" They [the seniors] do everything together. They go to the Salvation Army [together] weekly and they will go get something to eat [together]. Or like [Senior 1] and [Senior 2] they hopped on the red line and just rode that all the way north and then just turns around and came back."*

Games for Encouraging Socialization at the Center. All participants were active gamers at home and at the center. Most participants preferred group games that helped them socialize but one preferred individual games that could be played on her phone (Table 2). The types of games that participants played varied as well as their reason for playing. All participants participated in Bingo at the center. However, some only visited the center for Bingo while others played other games at the center such as dominoes or card games (e.g., Solitaire and Five Crown). For this study, we considered dominoes as a board game, and it was frequently played at the center.

The most popular game at the center was Bingo and it is offered three days a week. Both participants and staff noted that some seniors only come to play Bingo and it is a common activity that is frequented by the larger group of seniors that do not visit the

Table 2. Older Adult Participants' Gaming Preferences.

No.	Games Played	Preferred Games	Preferred Play
1	Mobile, Board, Card, Computer	Board, Mobile	Group
2	Mobile, Board, Casino, Video, Card	Mobile	Group
3	Puzzles, Trivia, Card, Board, Computer	Board	Group
4	Trivia, Casino, Computer, Board	Trivia	Group
5	Word, Card, Board	Board	Group
6	Computer, Board, Puzzles	Board	Group
7	Board	Board	Group
8	Card, Computer, Mobile	Card, Mobile	Group
9	Board, Mobile	Mobile	Individual

center every day. Either a senior or the senior coordinator would facilitate the games (Fig. 1). The gaming session usually lasted 2–3 h. To make the game more competitive, the seniors would add one dollar to a "pot", or a collective cup of money, and a winner would get a portion when they called Bingo (Fig. 1).

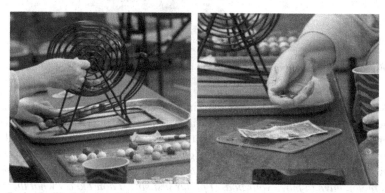

Fig. 1. Senior facilitating one of the Bingo sessions by rolling and selecting a numbered ball from the Gashapon machine. The facilitator distributes winnings from the collective "pot".

We observed that during Bingo, seniors would also play different versions of Bingo such as four corners and "X" and seniors played with more than one Bingo card (Fig. 2). When asked seniors shared that they liked to play different versions of Bingo and use different cards to increase their chances of winning. P6 explained in interviews, "*They play a different game on each game. They don't always play just straight Bingo. They play one game of straight bingo and then they play, each game is different and then the winner gets to choose. You get to choose the game that you'd like to play. So, it's all in different configurations and you have to think about it more and also gives you more of a chance to win because it's in a different pattern.*" We learned later in interviews, that the seniors also placed limits on the amount of time a person could win the game to allow everyone a chance at winning. For example, P6 shared that one senior who was very good at Bingo won three times, but *"she couldn't count it cause you can only win 2 times."* Seniors in the observation sessions shared that they would mostly use their winnings to buy lunch after the game finished at the deli located at the front of the center. These findings suggest that in addition to the inherent socialization built into the gaming session, the seniors also attempted to enhance the social atmosphere by developing "rules" to promote fairness and community. For example, limiting the number of wins and using winnings for a shared lunch.

Fig. 2. Seniors using multiple cards and layouts to increase chances of winning.

However, we also observed during the Bingo sessions that seniors would sit through the game sessions for hours with little physical activity. From interviews, we learned that some seniors preferred games that required little activity. For example, when asked about her preferences, P5 explained, *"I don't like games where you get up and down. I don't like those kinds of games... I can't think of one right offhand, but there are games like that where you have to move your body. I prefer just sit... I don't know what the reason is, but I'm much more comfortable and just the way Bingo is. I mean, you get up if you win and that's fine."* We also observed that even though the game promoted socialization in many ways, many of the seniors did not interact with each other apart from people at their table during the game. Several participants discussed the limited social activity in interviews as well. Participant 2 shared that they usually socialize during games, but not during Bingo, she stated, *"We typically socialize while playing games, but in Bingo we don't like to talk."* P6 and P7 noted that they believed that everyone was friendly, but there could be certain groups of people who talked more often, they shared, *"Well, it seems like to me there are cliques. I mean, everybody will talk to each other somewhat, but there's little pockets of people are rather than like big groups. It's little pockets of people."* Participant 9 agreed that seniors had places that they preferred to sit during games, *"They generally sit at the same table. You know, they have places that they like to sit. But I don't think there's much socializing during the Bingo at all, because you're too busy playing the game."* Therefore, while the lack of socialization was noticed, some participants considered it as part of the game play.

6 Game and Piloting: Supporting Active Togetherness

Based on findings from the interviews and observations, we designed a hybrid Bingo game [51] as a prototype that incorporated both physical and technical game elements. We knew that being active together is one way to improve social wellness and overall health [54], therefore our initial aim focused on improving social and physical activity. Yet we found aligned with other research that participation in a group activity alone does not necessarily automatically lead to connectedness and instead the design focus should be placed on fostering feelings of social support within the group [39]. Therefore, our goal for our design was to support *active togetherness* or ways we could emphasize social connectedness (togetherness) while also being active by including elements of game play that depend on both. We also initially planned to design a fully digital game, but after learning about the types of games participants enjoyed and the resources available at the center, we decided to create a hybrid game that makes use of different types of gaming elements (e.g., digital and physical) to accommodate different types of gameplay [28]. Hybrid games are often used to increase the diversity of players and interactions involved in the game [26, 45]. Because participants enjoyed Bingo, instead of creating an entirely new game, we chose to leverage existing interests and design around Bingo. Therefore, the game incorporated the basic concepts of Bingo in which participants must mark different numbers on a board in a specific pattern (i.e., diagonally, horizontally) that are randomly selected by a facilitator to win.

We learned from interviews that participants had different technical skills and the center also had limited technical resources, so we opted to use the resources available at the center including an LCD TV and existing Bingo game pieces in the game design. The game was facilitated by the host using a computer instead of a traditional Gashapon machine to draw numbers randomly (Fig. 3). The hybrid game was designed to allow participants to engage in their typical game play with the goal of increasing socialization and physical activity. Unlike traditional Bingo, where participants manage individual Bingo cards and have individual wins, the seniors were required to work in teams and cooperate with each other to win. When participants landed on the icons that replaced numbers on the Bingo cards participants were asked to complete small physical and social activity challenges to encourage them to interact more (Fig. 4). Therefore, unlike their typical Bingo sessions, seniors did not sit during the entire session and at times were required to socialize in order to complete the tasks (Fig. 4). Another goal of the game was to introduce seniors who felt they had limited technical skills to technology with the inclusion of the digital Gashapon machine that selected numbers. The game could be facilitated by a staff or senior who was more familiar with technology, but it allowed seniors with less technical skills to also interact in short periods with the computer when completing tasks that appeared during the gameplay sessions.

Fig. 3. A staff member facilitating the test play session using a laptop. The television displays the Gashapon machine that selects the numbers and the activity cards.

Fig. 4. Staff and participants interacting during the Bingo session. The seniors performed both cognitive and physical tasks and some tasks required teamwork to solve problems.

6.1 Test Play and Initial Feedback

To understand seniors' perceptions about the game and its roles in supporting active togetherness, we conducted a test play session to pilot and evaluate a game concept. We tested the game with seven seniors and one staff who originally participated in observation and interview sessions. The players were divided into two teams (e.g., Red and Blue) and played one round of the game which lasted approximately one hour. During the test play, we observed participants' interactions during the game, and after the game session ended, we conducted group interviews with each team and individual interviews with the staff to better understand the participants' experiences. Each participant received a $10 Walmart gift card for playing.

Participants also provided feedback about the gameplay including a suggestion to shorten the play time to 45 min and to modify some of the activity explanations to make them easier to understand. However, we found that overall, the seniors shared that they enjoyed the game and appreciated the inclusion of both physical and social activities during the game. For example, a participant from the Red team shared that she really enjoyed the game because "*I liked the variety of it. Just all the different things to do.*" A participant on the Blue team noted that she liked the game because they felt it was a new way of playing Bingo. She stated, "*This is original I have never heard of it like this. I enjoyed it.*" Therefore, participants seemed to like that the game provided a variety of tasks and ways of interacting with others throughout the game. Participants also discussed that they liked that the game required more physical activity compared to regular Bingo. A participant from the Blue team explained, "*Yes [I like it] because you have to get up out of your chair.*" Other participants agreed that they enjoyed the physical activities, even though they were initially hesitant that the game might require something too strenuous. A participant from the Red team explained, "*I thought it was good because it was doable. I said Well am I going to have to get up there and do deep knee bends because I have been having trouble with my knees? But, no it was very doable.*" However, another participant from the Blue team discussed that she would want more flexibility in activities because she felt that some of the tasks may be too hard. She stated, "*I thought the one where she had to put that thing on her knee would be hard for some people… I would want to hold on to something because I don't have good balance.*"

Participants also enjoyed that the game encouraged more socialization. Participants mentioned that they appreciated that the game allowed them to interact with others throughout the game even though most participants knew each other well. For example, a participant from the Blue team when asked whether they felt the game might improve socialization stated, "*Yes, I mean we are used to being around all of them, but yes.*" When asked what they liked about the game, a participant on the Blue team stated, "*Cause you have to interact with both teams.*" Several participants on the red team also shared that they enjoyed the interactions on and between teams. One participant shared that compared to the original Bingo, "*[It is] more interactive… Yeah I think so like the game of charades, we were all interactive in that.*" Another participant shared, "*I think helping each other to get all four cards, so you can holler 'Bingo'. Everybody, so you can do it together.*" One participant who initially hesitated to join the test session after participating in observations, shared, "*What really like about this is that has brought us together instead of fighting [arguing] all the time. Cause in the regular Bingo games they fight [argue]. I've been to several Bingo games and all they do is fight [argue] over who wins the game, and who wins the money. I like this kind of game here where it involves everybody and makes everybody happy.*" Therefore, all those who participated in the test play believed that the Hybrid Bingo game would be a good addition to the centers' list of games. However, they also emphasized that it should not replace regular Bingo but become an additional option. A participant on the Blue team explained, "*I'd play it again, I wouldn't want to play it all the time. I like the other Bingo too. But I would like if we could choose… Cause we like to win the money.*" Others on the team noted that they could adapt the game to involve incentives as well.

7 Implications for Designing for Active Togetherness in Community Settings

Our findings contribute to understanding older adults' experiences engaging in social and physical activities in a community center setting and the impact of participation on their social and physical wellness needs. In addition, our findings highlight the potential for hybrid games to support *active togetherness* by enhancing social interaction and physical activities among older adults in a community setting. We found that participation in activities, namely games, at the senior center provided participants with socialization opportunities outside of their families and friends. However, some were not physically active due to health or other reasons. Therefore, much of the time spent at the center involved games such as Bingo that required little movement or activity and while seniors interacted through game play, they did not socialize much. Based on interviews and observation, we designed and tested a prototype Hybrid Bingo game that required more social and physical activities and that participants felt increased opportunities for social and physical activity while at the center.

Being active together is one way to improve social wellness and overall health [54], yet as we found in our study, participation in group activity may not necessarily lead to socialization. This aligns with prior work suggesting the participation in group activity alone does not necessarily automatically lead to feelings of being included, rather often, connectedness is tied to broader feelings of social support [39]. Therefore, our goal for our design was to support active togetherness or ways to emphasize social connectedness (togetherness) while being active. Based on our findings, we discuss implications for designing for *active togetherness* in community settings. We also share our experiences designing a hybrid game to improve seniors social and physical activity in a community setting. We center our discussion around lessons learned from our design process and situate these reflections in broader work on designing for and with communities.

7.1 Leveraging Common Interests

There has been significant prior work that has examined how novel digital game inventions can benefit senior's health and wellness [4, 30]. There has also been emerging work on the potential of hybrid game formats to improve diversity of players [26, 28]. For instance, researchers have examined opportunities for hybrid games to support civic or urban engagement, such as design for neighborhoods [45]. Similarly, we found that the hybrid game format allowed us to consider the unique needs of seniors at the center while also considering design for the community environment. When designing our game, it was necessary to *leverage the existing and common gaming interests* of the members who frequented the senior center, in particular their fondness of Bingo and its importance to the existing community for fostering social interactions within.

Ijsselsteijn suggests that when we design games for seniors, we should actively look for ways to offer engaging content and pleasurable experiences [25]. While most participants played other types of games, Bingo was a staple in the center that was enjoyed by the majority of those who visit. While other studies have used Bingo as inspiration for designing games for seniors [41, 43], our inspiration for hybrid bingo was formed from understanding the seniors, and the community they had built at the center around the game sessions. For example, other studies have found that games such as Bingo can improve social interactions among groups of people [41, 43], yet we found that during Bingo sessions participants were less social than in other games. While there was concern among some in the center about the sedentary nature of playing games, participants viewed Bingo as an opportunity to interact with the larger community of seniors that visit the center and it was the most popular game activity. Therefore, it was important for us not only to incorporate existing and common interest, but also *look at ways to improve the existing game while integrating small changes to move toward common community goals.*

7.2 Designing for Inclusion

For our study, we found that it was important to *consider physical activities that align with diverse abilities within the community*. Several seniors mentioned that they were not able to engage in much physical activity due to health conditions or disabilities. When designing the physical activity cards for the games, we *considered game elements and tasks that might exclude seniors that would like to play and incorporated opportunities for seniors to help one another*. Although one of the goals of the study was to better understand ways to increase physical activity, we found that one of the core community values was to be welcoming to all (e.g., inclusive). Regardless of whether members socialized in smaller groups or not, they wanted the senior center to be a welcoming place. Therefore, in design, we prioritized that the game be inclusive to any senior that wanted to play regardless of ability even if it did not align with formal requirements for daily activity or benchmarks (e.g., 10,000 steps per day).

To overcome the limited social interactions, we designed the game to *include physical co-located teams and include elements of game play that required these teams to work together*. This deviated from traditional Bingo but allowed members to support each other which aligned with the values that they had built into their community. For example, in the test play when one participant felt they could not do one of the activities, another volunteered in their place to help. Therefore, seniors that were managing health conditions that limited their activity felt included and could benefit from the social interactions of the game while increasing their activity at a level they were comfortable. Other studies have noted that certain physical activity games can exclude some older adults as often they are not suitable for those with health conditions or disability [4, 19, 20]. While, our intention was not to provide rehabilitation or medical consultation, but only to improve sedentary behaviors, taking into consideration the existing physical abilities of the seniors was key to our design process. Therefore, our findings extend prior work [4, 19, 20] and encourages designer for senior communities to be aware and responsive to those with different abilities in the design.

7.3 Hybrid for Supporting Diverse Technical Skills and Access

Digital games have the potential to improve health and wellness among older adults [3, 25, 41], however our participants had varied experiences with technology, and while many enjoyed digital games, some did not use a computer regularly, or have access to a computer. Among those that did have access to a computer, they discussed that they only used it for certain things. Therefore, it was important for us to also *consider alternatives to fully digital games*. There are somewhat mixed reviews of whether or not older adults prefer digital games [5, 10, 13], however gameplay among older adults may have psycho-social context [14]. For example, De Schutter and Abeele found that older adults in their study enjoyed both individual and group game experiences, and enjoyed different aspects of the game when connecting, cultivating relationships, and contributing to learning for example, for their grandkids [14]. Our participants tended to prefer the option of having physical game elements and including those elements encouraged some to participate that may not have if the game were fully digital.

It is well-known that participatory approaches can be beneficial for designing with communities and for democratizing the design process [45]. Stokes and colleagues have argued that participatory approaches can also be useful for designing hybrid games that support neighborhoods since there is an inherent need to mix digital and physical elements (e.g., payphones, art) [29]. We also found when considering games for senior communities, *using more participatory approaches can be beneficial for identifying existing community values* thereby improving overall chances of acceptance by the community. Further, through this process we were able to also learn about the built environment and its potential impact on sustainability of the proposed game. The center had limited technical resources available for seniors to use and therefore we also needed to *consider how the introduction of digital games might impact the existing social environment and community norms*. The center itself served as a place for social interactions and the Bingo game was an integral part of the seniors' weekly activities and their community building. By using a hybrid approach, we were able to provide additional opportunity for seniors to meaningfully connect with others while also motivating moments of physical activity during gaming sessions. Therefore, while initially we considered a digital game, we opted for a hybrid game design that could take advantage of the resources that the center could provide to seniors on a daily basis. We felt this was particularly important given the chance that the game could be abandoned if the technology can no longer be sustained by the participants or organization [29]. Our game design therefore took into consideration the resources that may be available to participants in the future.

8 Limitations and Conclusion

As with most qualitative studies, our findings are not meant to be generalized [12]. However, we believe our findings may translate to similar situations and contexts to provide insights on approaching community-focused game design for seniors. Our findings are limited by our participant demographics, while we found recurring themes, our findings may not apply to other community organizations where the senior population has different demographics, technical skill, or resources available. We also acknowledge that communities and organizations are diverse and have different needs and values. Therefore, our findings may not transfer to communities and organizations whose needs and values do not align with those of our participants and their community.

In this study, we conducted an observation of a gaming session and conducted interviews with 11 seniors and staff to understand and identify ways for a game to improve physical and social interactions at the center. We found that participants were socially active and were involved in their communities. The community senior center played a significant role in expanding the seniors social support network and for helping them meet other people in the community. However, we found that the most popular activity at the center, Bingo that was played three times per week, did not provide much social interaction or physical movement for seniors during game play. Therefore, we developed a game to capitalize on seniors' interest in Bingo to improve active togetherness through social and physical interactions that were designed to capitalize on the existing social support values seniors build into their community. We contribute a better understanding of the influence of community centers on senior's physical activity and social interactions. We additionally contribute design implications for games that support seniors in community settings by serving members with diverse physical abilities, technical skills, and availability of technical resources.

Acknowledgments. We would like to thank our participants and partnering organization for sharing their experiences and feedback with us.

Disclosure of Interests. The authors have no competing interests to declare that are relevant to the content of this article.

References

1. Aday, R.H., Wallace, B., Krabill, J.J.: Linkages between the senior center as a public place and successful aging. Act. Adapt. Aging **43**, 211–231 (2019). https://doi.org/10.1080/01924788. 2018.1507584
2. Agmon, M., Perry, C.K., Phelan, E., Demiris, G., Nguyen, H.Q.: A pilot study of wii fit exergames to improve balance in older adults. J. Geriatr. Phys. Ther. **34**,161–167 (2011). https://doi.org/10.1519/JPT.0b013e3182191d98
3. Allaire, J.C., McLaughlin, A.C., Trujillo, A., Whitlock, L.A., LaPorte, L., Gandy, M.: Successful aging through digital games: socioemotional differences between older adult gamers and non-gamers. Comput. Human Behav. **29**, 1302–1306 (2013). https://doi.org/10.1016/j. chb.2013.01.014
4. Bleakley, C.M., Charles, D., Porter-Armstrong, A., McNeill, M.D.J., McDonough, S.M., McCormack, B.: Gaming for health: a systematic review of the physical and cognitive effects of interactive computer games in older adults. J. Appl. Gerontol. **34**, NP166–189 (2015). https://doi.org/10.1177/0733464812470747
5. Blocker, K.A., Wright, T.J., Boot, W.R.: Gaming preferences of aging generations. Gerontechnology **12**, 174–184 (2014)
6. Brown, J.A.: Let's play: understanding the role and meaning of digital games in the lives of older adults. In: Proceedings of the International Conference on the Foundations of Digital Games. Association for Computing Machinery, Raleigh, North Carolina, pp. 273–275 (2012)
7. Cannon, M.: Challenges, Experiences, and Future Directions of Senior Centers Serving the Portland Metropolitan Area. Dissertations and Theses (2015). https://doi.org/10.15760/etd. 2314
8. Carroll, J.M., Rosson, M.B.: Participatory design in community informatics. Des. Stud. **28**, 243–261 (2007). https://doi.org/10.1016/j.destud.2007.02.007

9. Carroll, J.M., Rosson, M.B.: Wild at home: the neighborhood as a living laboratory for HCI. ACM Trans. Comput-Hum. Interact **20**, 1–28 (2013). https://doi.org/10.1145/2491500.249 1504

10. Chesham, A., Wyss, P., Müri, R.M., Mosimann, U.P., Nef, T.: What older people like to play: genre preferences and acceptance of casual games. JMIR Serious Games **5**, e8 (2017). https://doi.org/10.2196/games.7025

11. Corbin, J., Strauss, A.L., Strauss, A.: Basics of Qualitative Research. SAGE, Newcastle upon Tyne (2015)

12. Creswell, J.W., Poth, C.N.: Qualitative Inquiry and Research Design: Choosing Among Five Approaches. SAGE Publications, Thousand Oaks (2016)

13. De Schutter, B.: Never too old to play: the appeal of digital games to an older audience. Games Culture **6**, 155–170 (2011). https://doi.org/10.1177/1555412010364978

14. De Schutter, B., Vanden Abeele, V.: Designing meaningful play within the psycho-social context of older adults. In: Proceedings of the 3rd International Conference on Fun and Games. Association for Computing Machinery, Leuven, Belgium, pp. 84–93 (2010)

15. Domínguez, A., Saenz-de-Navarrete, J., de-Marcos, L., Fernández-Sanz, L., Pagés, C., Martínez-Herráiz, J.-J.: Gamifying learning experiences: Practical implications and outcomes. Comput. Educ. **63**, 380–392 (2013). https://doi.org/10.1016/j.compedu.2012.12.020

16. Drageset, J.: Social Support. Springer (2021)

17. Felix, H.C., et al.: Barriers and facilitators to senior centers participating in translational research. Res. Aging **36**, 22–39 (2014). https://doi.org/10.1177/0164027512466874

18. Gajadhar, B.J., de Kort, Y.A.W., IJsselsteijn, W.A.: Shared fun is doubled fun: player enjoyment as a function of social setting. In: Markopoulos, P., de Ruyter, B., IJsselsteijn, W., Rowland, D. (eds.) Fun and Games. Fun and Games 2008, LNCS, vol. 5294, pp. 106–117. Springer, Berlin (2008). https://doi.org/10.1007/978-3-540-88322-7_11

19. Gerling, K.M., Masuch, M.: When gaming is not suitable for everyone: playtesting wii games with frail elderly. In: GAXID 2011 (2011)

20. Gerling. K.M., Schulte. F.P., Masuch, M.: Designing and evaluating digital games for frail elderly persons. In: Proceedings of the 8th International Conference on Advances in Computer Entertainment Technology. Association for Computing Machinery, New York, NY, USA, pp. 1–8 (2011)

21. Glännfjord, F., Hemmingsson, H., Larsson Ranada, Å.: Elderly people's perceptions of using Wii sports bowling - a qualitative study. Scand. J. Occup. Ther. **24**, 329–338 (2017). https://doi.org/10.1080/11038128.2016.1267259

22. Hall, A.K., Chavarria, E., Maneeratana, V., Chaney, B.H., Bernhardt, J.M.: Health benefits of digital videogames for older adults: a systematic review of the literature. Games Health J. **1**, 402–410 (2012). https://doi.org/10.1089/g4h.2012.0046

23. Harrington, C., Erete, S., Piper, A.M.: Deconstructing community-based collaborative design: towards more equitable participatory design engagements. Proc ACM Hum-Comput. Interact **3**, 216:1–216:25 (2019). https://doi.org/10.1145/3359318

24. Hayes, G.R.: The relationship of action research to human-computer interaction. ACM Trans. Comput-Hum Interact **18**, 15:1–15:20 (2011). https://doi.org/10.1145/1993060.1993065

25. Ijsselsteijn, W., Nap, H.H., Poels, K., De Kort, Y.: Digital game design for elderly users (2007)

26. Javanshir, R., Carroll, B., Millard, D.: Classifying multiplayer hybrid games to identify diverse player participation. In: Zagalo, N., Veloso, A., Costa, L., Mealha, Ó. (eds.) Videogame Sciences and Arts. VJ 2019. Communications in Computer and Information Science, vol. 1164, pp. 248–260. Springer, Cham (2019). https://doi.org/10.1007/978-3-030-37983-4_19

27. Jung, Y., Li, K.J., Janissa, N.S., Gladys, W.L.C., Lee, K.M.: Games for a better life: effects of playing Wii games on the well-being of seniors in a long-term care facility. In: Proceedings of the Sixth Australasian Conference on Interactive Entertainment. Association for Computing Machinery, Sydney, Australia, pp. 1–6 (2009)

28. Kankainen, V., Arjoranta, J., Nummenmaa, T.: Games as blends: understanding hybrid games. J. Virt. Real. Broadcasting **14** (2017). https://doi.org/10.20385/1860-2037/14.2017.4

29. Karkera, Y., Tandukar, B., Chandra, S., Martin-Hammond, A.: Building community capacity: exploring voice assistants to support older adults in an independent living community. In: Proceedings of the 2023 CHI Conference on Human Factors in Computing Systems. Association for Computing Machinery, New York, NY, USA, pp 1–17 (2023)

30. Kaufman, D., Sauve, L.: Digital gaming by older adults: can it enhance social connectedness?. In: Zhou, J., Salvendy, G. (eds.) Human Aspects of IT for the Aged Population. Social Media, Games and Assistive Environments. HCII 2019, LNCS, vol. 11593, pp. 167–176. Springer, Cham (2019). https://doi.org/10.1007/978-3-030-22015-0_13

31. Kaufman, D., Sauvé, L., Renaud, L., Sixsmith, A., Mortenson, B.: Older adults' digital gameplay: patterns, benefits, and challenges. Simul. Gaming **47**, 465–489 (2016). https://doi.org/10.1177/1046878116645736

32. Kaufman1, D., Ma2, M., Sauvé3, L., Renaud4, L., Dupláa5, E.: Benefits of digital gameplay for older adults: does game type make a difference? 1 2 (2019). https://doi.org/10.28933/ijoar-2019-07-2805

33. Loos, E.: Exergaming: meaningful play for older adults?. In: Zhou, J., Salvendy, G. (eds.) Human Aspects of IT for the Aged Population. Applications, Services and Contexts, ITAP 2017, LNCS, vol. 10298, pp. 254–265. Springer, Cham (2017). https://doi.org/10.1007/978-3-319-58536-9_21

34. Marston, H.R.: Digital gaming perspectives of older adults: content vs. interaction. Educ. Gerontol. **39**, 194–208 (2013). https://doi.org/10.1080/03601277.2012.700817

35. Miltiades, H.B., Sara, A.G., Cynthia, K.D.: Understanding the impact of senior community center participation on elders' health and well-being. Harrisburg, Pennsylvania: Commonwealth of Pennsylvania Department of Aging (2004)

36. Mutchler, J., Somerville, C., Khaniyan, M., Yang, M., Evans, M.: The Future of Aging in the Town of Brewster: Brewster Council on Aging Needs Assessment Study. Center for Social and Demographic Research on Aging Publications (2016)

37. O'Hanlon, J., Thomas, E.: The role of senior centers in promoting intergenerational play (2017)

38. Pardasani, M.: Senior centers: if you build will they come? Educ. Gerontol. **45**, 120–133 (2019). https://doi.org/10.1080/03601277.2019.1583407

39. Pels, F., Kleinert, J.: Loneliness and physical activity: a systematic review. Int. Rev. Sport Exerc. Psychol. **9**, 231–260 (2016). https://doi.org/10.1080/1750984X.2016.1177849

40. Rosenberg, D., et al.: Exergames for subsyndromal depression in older adults: a pilot study of a novel intervention. Am. J. Geriatr. Psychiatry **18**, 221–226 (2010). https://doi.org/10.1097/JGP.0b013e3181c534b5

41. Sauvé, L., Renaud, L., Kaufman, D., Duplàa, E.: Can digital games help seniors improve their quality of life? In: CSEDU (2016)

42. Schell, R., Hausknecht, S., Zhang, F., Kaufman, D.: Social benefits of playing wii bowling for older adults. Games Culture **11**, 81–103 (2016). https://doi.org/10.1177/1555412015607313

43. Seah, E., Kaufman, D., Sauvé, L., Zhang, F.: Play, Learn, connect: older adults' experience with a multiplayer, educational, digital bingo game. J. Educ. Comput. Res. **56**, 073563311772232 (2017). https://doi.org/10.1177/0735633117722329

44. Shim, N., Baecker, R., Birnholtz, J., Moffatt, K.: TableTalk poker: an online social gaming environment for seniors. In: Proceedings of the International Academic Conference on the Future of Game Design and Technology. Association for Computing Machinery, Vancouver, British Columbia, Canada, pp. 98–104 (2010)

45. Stokes, B., Baumann, K., Bar, F.: Hybrid games for stronger neighborhoods: connecting residents and urban objects to deepen the sense of place. In: Proceedings of the 14th Participatory Design Conference: Short Papers, Interactive Exhibitions, Workshops – vol. 2. Association for Computing Machinery, Aarhus, Denmark, pp. 105–106 (2016)

46. Tandukar, B., Vazirani, P.: Advocacy through design: partnering to improve online communications and connections in a life plan community. In: Systems Conference 2021 (2021)

47. Taylor, M.E., et al.: The role of cognitive function and physical activity in physical decline in older adults across the cognitive spectrum. Aging Ment. Health **23**, 863–871 (2019). https://doi.org/10.1080/13607863.2018.1474446

48. Wagner, I., Jacucci, G., Kensing, F., Blomberg, J.: Participatory Design and Action Research: Identical Twins or Synergetic Pair? In: Jacucci, G., Kensing, F., Blomberg, J. (eds.) Wagner I, pp. 93–96. Computer Professionals for Social Responsibility, Canada (2006)

49. Wiemeyer, J., Kliem, A.: Serious games in prevention and rehabilitation—a new panacea for elderly people? Eur. Rev. Aging Phys. Act **9**, 41–50 (2012). https://doi.org/10.1007/s11556-011-0093-x

50. Wollersheim, D., et al.: Physical and psychosocial effects of wii video game use among older women. Int. J. Emerg. Technol. Soc. **8**, 85–98 (2010)

51. Yang, S.-Y., John, S.: Team bingo: a game that increases physical activity and social interaction for seniors in a community setting. In: Extended Abstracts of the 2020 CHI Conference on Human Factors in Computing Systems. Association for Computing Machinery, New York, NY, USA, pp. 1–6 (2020)

52. Zhang, F., Hausknecht, S., Schell, R., Kaufman, D.: Factors affecting the gaming experience of older adults in community and senior centres. In: Costagliola, G., Uhomoibhi, J., Zvacek, S., McLaren, B. (eds.) Computers Supported Education, CSEDU 2016, CCIS, vol. 739, pp. 464–475. Springer, Cham (2017). https://doi.org/10.1007/978-3-319-63184-4_24

53. SilverFit: improving elderly care. In: SilverFit (2015). https://silverfit.com/en/. Accessed 7 May 2020

54. Social wellness toolkit — More resources. In: National Institutes of Health (NIH) (2017). https://www.nih.gov/health-information/social-wellness-toolkit-more-resources. Accessed 1 Feb 2024

55. Fact sheet: senior centers. In: The National Council on Aging. https://www.ncoa.org/article/get-the-facts-on-senior-centers. Accessed 15 Jan 2024

Leveraging Curiosity to Care for an Aging Population

Cassini Nazir[1]([⊠]) [iD], Kuo Wei Lee[2] [iD], and Mike Courtney[3]

[1] University of North Texas, Denton, TX, USA
cassini.nazir@unt.edu
[2] Georgia Institute of Technology, Atlanta, GA, USA
klee934@gatech.edu
[3] Aperio Insights, Dallas, TX, USA
mike@aperionsights.com

Abstract. The United States is experiencing a silver tsunami: an aging nation with baby boomers becoming the largest elderly population in the country's history. This demographic shift poses challenges for maintaining mobility and independence among older individuals. This paper will demonstrate an ongoing research project conducted for a major automotive maker that explores how an early research-and-development initiative might lengthen the driving years for older drivers. The paper will introduce the project, its scope, and constraints. It introduces the Inviting Curiosity framework, used to elicit moments of curiosity in interactive experiences. It shows how the Inviting Curiosity framework was used in a research-through-design approach to create mobile and tablet prototypes tested with automotive consumers. The paper provides a detailed account of each research phase, highlighting key findings and the evolution of the project, ultimately demonstrating how technology and innovative approaches can contribute to enhancing the driving experience for an aging population.

Keywords: curiosity · aging population · mobility · automotive

1 Introduction: The Silver Tsunami

There is an irony to aging. "The idea of living a long life appeals to everyone, but the idea of getting old doesn't appeal to anyone," radio and television writer Andy Rooney once noted. The United States, like many other nations, is currently seeing a *silver tsunami*, characterized by a significant increase in the number of elderly individuals in a population and increased life expectancy [1]. This demographic shift holds far-reaching implications across various sectors, such as increased demand for healthcare services, changes in labor dynamics and needs, and adjustments to the social support systems that help meet the needs of the elderly population.

Joseph Coughlin of MIT's AgeLab notes that people desire a longer life and want to live it with purpose, delight, and respect [2]. An underlying question in a longer life is the fundamental challenge of mobility: how will individuals independently navigate

Q. Gao and J. Zhou (Eds.): HCII 2024, LNCS 14726, pp. 213–226, 2024.
https://doi.org/10.1007/978-3-031-61546-7_14

to their activities, both inside and outside of the home? Igor Stravinsky's depiction of aging as "the ever-shrinking perimeter of pleasure" [3] conveys that getting older often means losing freedom, independence, and mobility. If we conceptualize our interactions with the world as a circle, this circle shrinks with each passing year.

Preserving the capacity for aging individuals to drive is an important aspect of the larger movement to help seniors safely maintain independence. However, with age comes a decline, particularly in functions needed for driving. Older drivers face a 3–20 times higher risk of fatal crash involvement compared to non-older drivers [4]. Studies reveal that older drivers have slower reaction times, an increased rate of collisions, reduced driving speed, and are less able to maintain a constant distance behind a paced vehicle than their younger counterparts [5]. Even those who are not yet seniors can empathize with the concepts of freedom and independence.

Paul Irving notes that private and public sectors have opportunities to innovate to support the needs and wants of older adults [6]. One such innovation is automakers' shift from motors to mobility [7]. This shift is enabling a wave of initiatives such as Mobility-as-a-Service (MaaS), Connected and Autonomous Vehicles (CAVs), and Autonomous Personal Aerial Vehicles (PAV) [8]. These new mobility vehicles will likely work in concert with other vehicles, such as in a vehicle-to-vehicle (V2V) setting, or with other internet-connected devices, such as in vehicle-to-everything (V2X) [9]. President and CEO of Ford Motors Jim Hackett explained the factors driving this shift in the automotive market: *rapidly advancing technology* and a *deep need for a smarter transportation system* [10]. McKinsey estimates that a connected car processes up to 25 gigabytes of data every hour [11]. This data set presents opportunities for vehicle makers to monetize vehicle data, driver patterns, and mobility services just as social media and internet giants have monetized online user data. As these innovations and smarter transportation systems intersect with an aging population, they enable better futures.

While these developments hold promising futures, problems persist for the present-day aging population who still need mobility solutions. This paper discusses an early research project conducted for a major automotive maker that explored the possibility of lengthening the driving years for older drivers. It will present ways that developed prototypes employed a curiosity model to invite behaviors.

2   Research: A Four-Phase Approach to Understanding Driving

A major automotive maker approached Aperio Insights [12], a Dallas-based research and strategic foresight agency, to research the potential for a solution that might increase the driving years for older drivers. At the project's outset, the team was convinced that such a solution would necessitate a driver assessment. This idea changed and shifted as the project went forward. Table 1 outlines four distinct phases of the project and the primary outputs from each phase.

Table 1. Four Phases of the Project

Phase 1	**Initial Research: Towards a Driving Assessment** Outlined potential approaches to conduct driving assessments Yielded foundational principles, an assessment framework, and basic information architecture of a mobile app
Phase 2	**Quantitative Research** Explored consumer awareness about their current vehicle's safety features. Yielded an understanding of what consumers might expect of a safety checkup
Phase 3	**Initial App Prototypes** Explored how to translate a safety assessment into a digital experience Yielded initial low- and medium-fidelity prototypes
Phase 4	**App Refinements** Explored how to attract consumers and change minds and behaviors Yielded high-fidelity prototypes that can be further tested and refined

This paper will now discuss the research approach and learnings from each phase.

2.1   Phase 1. Initial Research: Driving Assessment

The initial research phase laid a strong foundation for subsequent phases. This first phase involved (1) outlining potential approaches for conducting driving assessments, (2) identifying process flows and specific functions for each step, and (3) creating a rudimentary assessment process involving scenarios that measure the driver's ability to react and make safe driving decisions based on various situations.

The team reviewed academic and industry publications related to health and wellness and reviewed driving assessment tools. Two sets of interviews were conducted: one with the target audience (individuals 45 years or older) and another with subject matter experts. Fifteen in-depth interviews (IDIs) were conducted via Zoom with drivers 45 years or older who desire to drive as long as possible. These 15 interviews, sectioned into three groups (adults 45–55, seniors aged 65 and older, and adults with chronic health conditions), aimed to:

- Identify beliefs, desires, and behaviors regarding health improvement and retention of driving ability.
- Uncover core beliefs connecting health and driving competency.
- Explore what circumstances might make individuals voluntarily relinquish driving privileges.
- Explore actions they would want the vehicle to take under specific health or driving conditions.

The team also conducted eight interviews with subject-matter experts (SME) with experience in medical complications associated with late-adult or geriatric care, including primary care providers and insurance experts. The SME interviews aimed to:

- Identify notable signs and indicators suggesting a driver's health may impact their driving ability.
- Explore beliefs about proactive steps that might extend driving years.

- Identify additional health and wellness factors that might extend safe driving.

Both sets of interviews introduced a product concept narrative. These 23 interviews surfaced key findings, three of which are presented below.

1. Individuals often continue driving regardless of caution from an application or the danger they present to other drivers on the road.
2. Medical professionals viewed the concept as a powerful diagnostic tool that indicated markers of change over time and appreciated the idea of a patient-generated report.
3. The potential consequence of a negative assessment needs to be carefully considered. One participant expressed concern about the assessment, "Am I going to have to give up my keys because I'm not scoring as well on the reaction time part of this assessment?"

These insights led the team to develop foundational principles that would help in future product development. This included emphasizing prevention over intervention, recognizing the power of accomplishment in motivating individuals, and acknowledging that various complex factors contribute to driving ability. The principles were in mind as the team developed a basic information architecture for an app. Through a series of workshops, the design team shifted the idea from a "driving exam" to a "driving safety checkup." The proposed driving safety checkup would address four key questions, three focusing on the driver and the fourth on the vehicle itself: (1) Does the driver possess the *knowledge* to drive safely? (2) Does the driver possess the *ability* to drive safely? (3) Does the driver have the *mindset* to drive safely? (4) Is the *vehicle capable* of keeping the driver and passengers safe? This transition from exam to safety checkup facilitated the development of more comprehensive stimuli that could be validated in the next phase, a quantitative study.

2.2   Phase 2. Quantitative Study

The project's second phase investigated the education of existing safety features among consumers. A quantitative study involving 141 participants was conducted through the online platform Remesh, with more than 90% of respondents above age 55. This study aimed to:

- Understand consumer awareness regarding their vehicle's safety features.
- Validate consumer interest in learning how vehicle features, particularly safety features, operate.
- Explore the preferred methods consumers would like to employ to learn more about their vehicle's safety features.

Two-thirds of participants expressed a lack of knowledge about the majority of safety features in their vehicle. Participants also expressed a desire to learn more about these features and were receptive to receiving personalized, proactive recommendations from the vehicle.

2.3   Phase 3. Initial Prototypes

During the third phase of the project, three prototypes were developed:

- A non-branded white-label mobile prototype that could be used for later testing
- A branded mobile prototype developed for the client
- A non-branded white-label prototype for a stand-alone kiosk

The development of these prototypes was heavily shaped by insights from four behavior models: BJ Fogg's motivation model [13], Nir Eyal's hooked model [14], Mihaly Csikszentmihalyi's concept of flow [15], and Cassini Nazir's Inviting Curiosity framework [16]. All three prototypes were developed using Figma and featured mock-ups incorporating three assessments: wellness, driving, and brain training. Subsequent sections will delve into the planning and development that went into this pivotal project phase.

2.4 Phase 4. Kiosk Study and App Refinement

This fourth and final phase of the project focused on gaining a deeper understanding of two key aspects related to a stand-alone kiosk. First, what are strategies to attract consumers to engage in a health and driving checkup at a kiosk? Second, in what ways might the kiosk experience with its health and driving checkups change their minds about driving safety? Intercepts were conducted with a mock kiosk placed strategically at three Dallas-area car dealerships to gather insights. This allowed the research team to observe visitors, understand what drew them to the kiosk, and disclose their thoughts, feelings, and beliefs about the concept. The prototypes developed during the project's third phase were further refined during this phase.

This paper will now delve into various ways that the mobile app prototypes were designed to invite curiosity and foster engagement and participation.

3 Prototype and Design

User experiences for commercial products often emphasize efficiency. Joshua Porter's diagram (Fig. 1) underscores the critical distinction that designing a product to be efficient—i.e., easy to use by minimizing usability errors or reducing cognitive load—does not automatically translate into a willingness for users to engage with it (motivation). Understanding how extrinsic motivators (positive rewards or negative consequences) might evolve into intrinsic motivators (curiosity, satisfaction, or a sense of accomplishment) was a driving force. Because curiosity is an intrinsic motivation to explore, the design team used the invitation-response-reward model in the Inviting Curiosity framework [16] to stimulate user interaction and cultivate curiosity. The subsequent sections of this paper will demonstrate how the Inviting Curiosity framework was instrumental in crafting moments of interaction with users and fostering a sense of curiosity.

3.1 Invitations

As mentioned earlier, the initial project phase surfaced questions on four topics that might comprise a driver assessment: the driver's knowledge, ability, and mindset and the vehicle's capabilities of keeping passengers safe. These four topics, derived from a driver

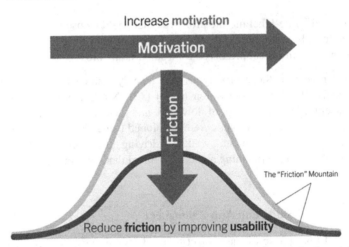

Fig. 1. Contrasting design approaches: reducing friction vs increasing motivation. Adapted from Joshua Porter.

assessment, were invitations woven into the mobile application. In the Inviting Curiosity framework, an invitation is an intentionally formulated approach that seeks to provoke a moment of curiosity in an individual. The design team's approach explored how key information might be couched in a series of invitations around these topics (Table 2). Because trust is a fundamental emotion necessary to create and sustain curiosity [17, 18], an overarching inquiry supporting each question was: How might the vehicle build trust with the driver?

Table 2. Key invitations from which subsequent app prototype screens were developed

Driver Knowledge	What are ways the vehicle assisted the driver? How well does the driver adhere to road safety procedures?
Driver Ability	What are ways the driver improved over time? What are ways the vehicle might help with driving mechanics? What are ways the driver might extend their abilities through healthier behaviors?
Driver Mindset	What are ways to engage driver's curiosity?
Vehicle Capabilities	What are ways the vehicle might inform the driver about useful or relevant features?

What are ways the vehicle might build trust with the driver?

3.2 Knowledge Invitation: How Has the Vehicle Assisted the Driver?

A set of screens were designed to invite curiosity regarding situations where the vehicle assisted the driver. Many safety systems in modern vehicles operate automatically, some without the driver's explicit awareness or knowledge. Vehicle sensors collect data that can be utilized in a feedforward system, anticipating potential problems and adjusting accordingly. Such systems often engage during routine driving activities. For example, Lane Departure Warning (LDW) provides visible or audible notifications to the driver when veering out of a lane. At the same time, Lane Keep Assist (LKA) helps drivers maintain a proper position on the road. Automatic High Beams (AHB) improve road visibility at night by toggling the vehicle's headlights between high and low beams based on the surrounding conditions. Lane Departure Warnings, Lane Keep Assist, and Automatic High Beams are a part of an extensive suite of vehicle safety features commonly known as Advanced Driver Assistance System (ADAS). ADAS systems may warn drivers of current behaviors to avoid (speeding), assist drivers in situations (guide them back into a lane), or entirely take over control of the vehicle (brake when a pedestrian is crossing). The mobile app sought to render these moments of assistance more visible to the driver.

Figure 2 is a prototype screen developed during the third phase of the project showing how the vehicle's sensor data can be used to demonstrate potentially prevented accidents. In this case, three rear-end crashes, one pedestrian accident, and a side-swipe collision. Because these events occurred at night and on the highway, it prompts the driver to take appropriate actions that might improve their driving experience, such as cleaning the windshield and lamp covers or turning on automatic high beams. Rendering the use of these systems more visible to the driver improves the driver's familiarity and awareness of them. It can elicit greater curiosity about how these systems are used in the vehicle.

Fig. 2. An app prototype screen that shows how the vehicle has assisted the driver.

3.3 Ability Invitation: How Has the Driver Improved over Time?

Another benefit of tracking how the vehicle has assisted the driver over time is the accumulation of longitudinal information, allowing drivers to see patterns over time. This might reveal improvement, decline, or maintaining driving abilities. In Fig. 3 (left), the app prototype screens show that 35 potential accidents have been prevented since 2019: 24 rear-end (presumably due to abrupt braking), six side-swipe collisions, and five pedestrian accidents. Presenting this information in a way that does not provoke, frustrate, or infuriate the driver is a delicate balance. Interviews conducted in phase one revealed serious concerns about who gets to view driver data, whether this data might include false positives and the consequences of poor driving. It is important to note an opposing viewpoint presented by one interviewee: In a situation where family members falsely perceive the older family member's driving to be unsafe, such data can provide proof of a driver's record of safety.

Fig. 3. App prototype screen showing a driver's longitudinal data (left) and driver's current and predicted trends (right).

Predictive analytics can project present behavior patterns forward, showing near-future possibilities. Figure 3 (right) shows a possible situation where a driver has an overall reduction of not using the turn signal but an increase in abrupt braking. In the case of not using the turn signal, the driver has shown dramatic improvement over time. The app screen reinforces this positive behavior. The system also predicts a continued increase in abrupt braking and recommends appropriate actions informing the driver about braking and helpful add-ons. One of them is a hypothetical product called the brake-helper, a heads-up display that might provide visual assistance of a proper braking distance on the windshield.

Such longitudinal data need not be limited to individual drivers. Over time, data about neighborhoods, districts, highways, cities, or regions could be derived. Figure 4 below shows screens where this longitudinal data compares drivers of similar age as well as drivers in the same city. These screens show positive improvements, but the screens can be adapted to balance declines (where drivers score low) with specific ways that the driver might improve.

Fig. 4. App prototype screen showing how a driver's behavior pattern compares to others

Other situations or systems where the vehicle might inform the driver of assistance include:

- Parking Assistance: How have the vehicle's automatic parking features or 360-degree cameras assisted drivers in parking by providing visual and sometimes automatic steering guidance?
- Traffic Sign Recognition: How has the vehicle used cameras to recognize and display traffic signs and help drivers stay informed about speed limits, no-entry signs, and other road regulations?
- Driver Monitoring Systems: How has the vehicle used cockpit sensors and cameras to monitor the driver's behavior to provide alerts when signs of drowsiness or distraction are detected?
- Automatic High Beams: How have Automatic High Beam systems automatically switched between high and low beams to improve visibility at night?
- Cross Traffic Alert: How has the vehicle alerted drivers of approaching traffic when backing out of parking spaces?
- Voice Recognition and Infotainment Systems: How might voice-activated controls and infotainment systems allow drivers to operate various functions hands-free?

In many of these situations identified, reinforcing to the drivers the number of times of usage can increase curiosity about usage and trust in-vehicle systems.

3.4   Capability Invitation: How Can the Vehicle Display Relevant Features?

Understanding vehicle safety features is particularly important when driving a vehicle for the first time. Cooper notes that most users are neither beginners nor experts but perpetual intermediates with little inclination to gain additional knowledge [19]. Drivers may be less inclined to use vehicle safety systems unfamiliar to them or familiar safety systems that operate differently from their mental models. Research conducted in the project's second phase revealed that two-thirds of participants (n = 141) expressed a lack of knowledge about the safety features of their vehicles.

An additional complication is the increasing use of a software-first approach to vehicle operating systems. Unlike in the past, where vehicle systems were primarily mechanical (and thus static), many vehicle system improvements are deployed through over-the-air updates. These upgrades often include bug fixes to current features and, like mobile phones and laptops, may include entirely new vehicle features. These new features may go unnoticed or unused by drivers. Depending on their implementation, features may confuse drivers, causing them to turn them off or ignore them altogether. Curiosity is a fragile emotion and can easily disintegrate into frustration.

Figure 5 shows two app prototype screens that demonstrate a driver's behavior of tailgating and lane hugging. While not always dangerous, lane hugging, when compounded with other factors such as driver fatigue or distraction, may cause an accident. In this case, the app nudges drivers to explore how the Lane Departure Warning system can help and appeals to the short amount of time it would take to set up or adjust this feature.

Some systems may need to be altogether reimagined, particularly for aging drivers. It is important to distinguish between a feedback system, where the vehicle may provide the current status of a component, versus feedforward systems, where the vehicle helps avoid an unfortunate situation. Tire pressure monitoring systems (TPMS), for example, are a type of feedback system that provides real-time information about tire inflation and warns the driver when pressure falls below requisite levels. Rendering TPMS as a feedforward system might also require tracking weather data for the vehicle's location. When the weather transitions between warm and cold, it might notify drivers that they should proactively inflate their tires. A robust feedforward system would automatically inflate tires to the safe pressure levels.

3.5   Responses and Rewards

In the Inviting Curiosity framework, the designer's invitation is met by a user's response, followed by a meaningful reward. In a previous paper, the authors outlined ten approaches to inviting curiosity. This section will discuss how challenges, one of the ten approaches, were used as an approach and the rewards that the app prototype demonstrated.

Fig. 5. App prototype screens showing tailgating and lane hugging with prompts to enable appropriate functions

Designing a series of appropriate challenges is essential to gameplay and is often used in app design. This can create curiosity around the user's ability to meet that challenge. The app prototype developed in phases three and four crafted challenges for the user and presented clear progress toward a goal, offering rewards (Fig. 6). This included time-based challenges, which can be accomplished in a convenient amount of time. In Fig. 6, challenges can be completed in a short amount of time (4 or 6 min for physical or mental challenges) or a longer amount of time (20 min of driving). The driving challenge can be done passively (the driver just needs to initiate this challenge). In contrast, the other two physical and mental challenges are active and require both attention and effort. The rewards here might be combined with personalized promotions or discounts to participating vendors.

Figure 7 shows an overall driving score, here 81 out of 100. A safety score at the bottom left indicates that the user also has improvement. The app indicates this user has had 25 tailgates, following too closely behind another vehicle. Because reaction time slows as we age, this is an important factor in changing behavior.

Fig. 6. Prototype of rewards system. Fixed challenges. Time-based challenges.

Fig. 7. Overall driving score.

4 Discussion and Conclusion

This paper focused on the development of a mobile application and its relationship to curiosity. It introduced a four-phase project that explored ways to enable older drivers to make small changes that allow them to continue driving as they age. It demonstrated a series of invitations, posed as key questions, used to create mobile app prototype screens that encourage curiosity around driving behavior patterns and vehicle features.

These initial prototypes required further testing and iteration to improve flaws in the concept, find and correct usability errors, and increase the likelihood of users becoming curious about their ability to drive. A mobile application is one of a variety of mediums the vehicle can use to invite curiosity in the driver and change behavior. Further research should explore how the vehicle might provide timely information and cues through additional mediums or devices, such as voice commands or the vehicle's central console. Many of the systems described in this paper enable drivers who need minor adjustments to their driving behaviors to continue to drive. More substantial changes to the vehicle are likely needed with drivers with more persistent health or mobility challenges.

The application will need to consider its role in insurance. Insurance companies currently leverage some of the data described in this paper from their policyholders. Usage-based insurance collects data through a mobile app or an onboard diagnostic scanner and calculates premiums explicitly based on driver behavior patterns. For some drivers, this may represent cost savings. However, as driver age and reaction times slow, these behavior-based calculations of insurance premiums are unlikely to help older drivers. Additionally, the mobile applications developed by insurance companies are more concerned with reporting driver behavior, not improving it.

As mentioned earlier, study participants voiced legitimate concerns about privacy. These concerns must be addressed and clarified in the application's future form. For example, what should happen if the system detects a driver is a grave danger to other drivers? Legal issues around liability and responsibility will need to be clarified long before deployment. Further collaborations with medical and health professionals, such as kinesiologists, would explore which behaviors, such as proper stretching or specific types of exercise, might improve driving.

Betty Friedan's *Fountain of Age* cites studies conveying that the physical and cognitive decline associated with aging is not inevitable [20]. Proactive steps can be taken to reduce the deterioration. Perhaps Andy Rooney was right: we have a choice in how we age.

References

1. Henderson, L., Maniam, B., Leavell, H.: The silver tsunami: evaluating the impact of population aging in the US. J. Bus. Account. **10**(1), 153–1690 (2017)
2. Coughlin, J.F.: The Longevity Economy Unlocking the World's Fastest-Growing, Most Misunderstood Market.Most Misunderstood Mark. PublicAffairs, New York, NY (2017)
3. Scarry, E.: The Body in Pain: The Making and Unmaking of the World. Oxford University Press, New York (2006)
4. Pitta, L.S., et al.: Older drivers are at increased risk of fatal crash involvement: results of a systematic review and meta-analysis. Arch. Gerontol. Geriatr. **95**, 104414 (2021)

5. Doroudgar, S., Chuang, H.M., Perry, P.J., Thomas, K., Bohnert, K., Canedo, J.: Driving performance comparing older versus younger drivers. Traffic Inj. Prev. **18**, 41–46 (2016)

6. Irving, P.: The Upside of Aging: How Long Life is Changing the World of Health, Work, Innovation, Policy and Purpose. Wiley, Hoboken (2014)

7. Bell, D.L., Gluesing, J.C.: The vision for the future of mobility. J. Bus. Anthropol. **9**, 225–250 (2020)

8. Nikitas, A., Michalakopoulou, K., Njoya, E.T., Karampatzakis, D.: Artificial intelligence, transport and the smart city: definitions and dimensions of a new mobility era. Sustainability **12**, 2789 (2020)

9. Zhou, H., Xu, W., Chen, J., Wang, W.: Evolutionary V2X technologies toward the internet of vehicles: challenges and opportunities. Proc. IEEE **108**, 308–323 (2020)

10. Ford Motors 2018 Annual Report. https://s201.q4cdn.com/771113172/files/doc_financials/2018/ar/2018-Annual-Report.pdf. Accessed 15 Jan 2024

11. What's driving the Connected Car. https://www.mckinsey.com/industries/automotive-and-assembly/our-insights/whats-driving-the-connected-car. Accessed 15 Jan 2024

12. Aperio Insights. https://www.aperioinsights.com. Accessed 15 Jan 2024

13. Fogg, B.: A behavior model for persuasive design. In: Proceedings of the 4th International Conference on Persuasive Technology, pp. 1–7 (2009)

14. Eyal, N., Hoover, R.: Hooked: How To Build Habit-Forming Products. Penguin Business, New York, NY (2019)

15. Csikszentmihalyi, M.: Flow: The Psychology of Optimal Experience. Harper and Row, New York, NY (2009)

16. Nazir, C.: Designing curiosity: A Beginner's Guide - User Experience Magazine. https://uxpamagazine.org/designing-curiosity-a-beginners-guide/. Accessed 15 Jan 2024

17. Voss, H.-G., Keller, H.: Curiosity and Exploration: Theories and Results. Academic Press, New York, NY (1983)

18. Plutchik, R.: The nature of emotions. Am. Sci. **89**, 344 (2001)

19. Cooper, A., Reimann, R., Cronin, D., Cooper, A.: About Face: The Essentials of Interaction Design. Wiley, Indianapolis (2014)

20. Friedan, B.: The Fountain of Age. Simon & Schuster, New York, NY (2006)

Towards a New (Old) Generation of Cyclotourists: Implementing an Improved Concept of Jizo Brand

Cláudia Pedro Ortet(✉) 📷, Ana Isabel Veloso📷, and Liliana Vale Costa📷

DigiMedia, Department of Communication and Art, University of Aveiro, Aveiro, Portugal
{claudiaortet,aiv,lilianavale}@ua.pt

Abstract. Modern civilization is being impacted by the digital revolution, which is evolving at an astounding rate. ICT are rapidly developing, widely adopted, and used by people worldwide for social networking, travel, and physical exercise. Gamified cyclotourism, which combines the concepts of ICT, tourism, and exercise, may be a technological solution that encourages the senior public to participate in the activity. It offers many advantages, including low-impact physical activity, sustainability, social and cultural interaction, and health and wellbeing. The purpose of this study is to report the development and evaluation of Gen from Jizo, an improved concept of a senior cyclotourism app entitled Jizo, following a development research methodology. Twelve senior citizens and five ICT informed individuals were involved, at different moments, in the testing and evaluation of the app and website hi-fi prototypes. Despite suggesting some changes, the results generally imply that participants thought the interfaces were easy to use, straightforward, and compliant with design and interaction standards. It is claimed that these solutions fight against social isolation, encourage consistent physical exercise, and provide enriching experiences that encourage social contact among users.

Keywords: Gen from Jizo · Gamification · Application · Website · Cyclotourism · Active and Healthy Ageing

1 Introduction

The world demographic pyramid, which is inverted, depicts the exponential rise in the ageing population at the biological (increasing susceptibility to disease and aging), social (societal roles and expectations), and psychological (choices, proximity to death, contribution to future generations) levels (Paúl, 2017). In fact, it is predicted that 1 in 6 persons on the planet will be 60 years of age or older in 2030, and that percentage of the global population that is over 60 will tend to rise from 12% to 22% between 2015 and 2050 (WHO, 2021). Additionally, the info-communicational period in which we live is defined by networks, interconnections, and fluxes (Castells, 2010), which emphasizes the digital inclusion or exclusion in the social appropriation of Information and communication technologies (ICT).

© The Author(s), under exclusive license to Springer Nature Switzerland AG 2024
Q. Gao and J. Zhou (Eds.): HCII 2024, LNCS 14726, pp. 227–242, 2024.
https://doi.org/10.1007/978-3-031-61546-7_15

The digital revolution is affecting modern society and developing at a remarkable rate (Bucci et al., 2019). ICT—which include apps for smartphones and smartwatches—are evolving quickly, becoming extensively embraced, and being utilized by people everywhere for social media, travel, and physical activity (Quamar et al., 2020). Senior citizens represent a demographic that is frequently left out of this scenario, despite the recent advancements in ICT and its potential (Mubarak & Suomi, 2022). People are more likely to experience social isolation, inactivity, and a decline in quality of life as they get older (Taylor et al., 2016), thus, this exclusion can be caused by a variety of factors, including a lack of digital literacy and accessibility. The older population is noticeably double excluded from both access and appropriation in the technology society. Due to their lack of prior access to ICT in their everyday lives, senior citizens now have more challenges while utilizing ICT, creating a divide between younger and older generations (Zheng et al., 2013). Thus, the usage of digital platforms and the phenomena of active and healthy ageing in the information and communication era have drawn the attention of the scientific field of gerontechnology (i.e., study, idealization, and design of new technologies targeted at enhancing senior citizens' quality of life and overall wellbeing).

Given that modern civilization is undergoing a longevity revolution, which is characterized by a rise in the average life expectancy and demographic age worldwide, it is especially worrisome in this regard (WHO, 2020). Global ageing of the population is a phenomena that has brought forth many issues for society, including political and financial strains on social security, welfare, and public health systems (UN, 2019). In that vein, research suggests that engaging in regular physical activity helps preventing chronic and debilitating age-related disorders from starting and spreading (Mcleod et al., 2019). Similarly, Hu and colleagues (2023) describe tourism as an additional activity that can support senior citizens in enhancing their functional capacities for day-to-day tasks and preserving their quality of life. Additionally, the use of ICT has demonstrated effective in raising tourism-related awareness (Gössling, 2021) and enhancing senior citizens' wellbeing (Sen et al., 2022).

Aligned with the combination of ICT, tourism and exercise concepts, gamified cyclotourism may be a technological solution that fosters the encouragement of the senior public to engage in the activity, which has numerous benefits such as health and wellbeing, sustainability, social and cultural interaction, in addition to being a low-impact physical activity (Deenihan & Caulfield, 2015; Gazzola, 2018; Pucher & Buehler, 2021). On the one hand, gamification for active and healthy ageing may be categorized as an improved ageing technology and is likely to have a significant impact on behavior modifications and motivation for prolonged usage. On the other hand, cyclotourism can be viewed as a positive activity that fosters socialization, and both mental and physical wellbeing. Notwithstanding the advantages of this endeavor, there exist certain obstacles linked to its advocacy and involvement among the elderly population. Lack of interest and drive, ignorance of safe and suitable routes for their needs, and absence of social connection during activities are some of the primary issues.

To get past these challenges a suggestion for refining the Jizo concept (a gamified registered app for senior cyclotourism developed by Ortet and colleagues (2019)) is Gen from Jizo with a multidevice approach. In order to promote senior cyclotourism through gamification, this renewed brand relies upon the development of an Android mobile application, a website, layout design, interaction flow description, and interactive smartwatch prototypes. Gen from Jizo aims to create an enjoyable, stimulating, and socially engaging atmosphere with game elements such as challenges, incentives, friendly competitions, and sharing of accomplishments. Moreover, in-depth information on safe routes, attractions, support services, and events pertaining to senior cyclotourism is another goal of this technological solution. The website and app will also have monitoring capabilities that let users create objectives, keep tabs on their progress, and engage in online communities.

The purpose of this study is to restructure and further implement the concept of Jizo, rebranding and redefining the multidevice approach for the practice of senior cyclotourism, aiming at improving senior citizens' experience through the adaptation and inclusion of different devices. To accomplish such goal, the methodology followed was based on development research, as it was intention to assess the usability and accessibility of Gen from Jizo's app and website through two different tests in different moments: (i) with potential users (i.e., senior citizens) and (ii) with a group of experts with relevant knowledge and experience in the field. A total of 12 senior citizens aged between 65 and 77 years old tested and evaluated the high fidelity prototype through a script with usage scenarios for the app and website and data was collected by field notes and questionnaires. Also, a heuristic evaluation was conducted with 5 experts in developing ICT for this target audience.

This paper is structured as follows: Sect. 1 is introductory and presents the problematic and background research; Sect. 2 is devoted to the development of Gen from Jizo, focusing on the visual identity, the selected devices (i.e., app, website and smartwatch), the prototyping from wireframes to hi-fi, and the implementation; Sect. 3 presents the methodology, focusing on the potential users evaluation and feedback from heuristic evaluation with experts in ICT for active and healthy ageing; Sect. 4 discusses the main results; and Sect. 5 ends with some considerations, limitations and future work.

2   Gen from Jizo: A Senior-Centric Gamified Cyclotourism App

Gen from Jizo's was conducted within the context of IC Senior X (Impact of Information and Communication on Senior's eXperience in miOne[1] Online Community), being also part of a bachelor's degree final project. Its mission is to use technology as a tool capable of helping to encourage the senior community to practice cyclotourism, thus encouraging active and healthy ageing. Project Based on this principle, it is intended to apply gamification strategies to captivate and motivate users to change sustainable behaviors.

Gen from Jizo is a secondary brand of the mother brand Jizo (Fig. 1), which is registered with the Portuguese National Institute of Industrial Property[2] (INPI) with numbers 691688 and 691689. The Jizo brand proposed a solution combined with gamification for senior cyclotourism and aims to motivate senior citizens to the activity. It had already

---

[1] https://mione.altice.pt/ [Accessed January 2024].

[2] https://servicosonline.inpi.pt/pesquisas/main/marcas.jsp?lang=pt search for the name of the bran "Jizo". [Accessed January 2024].

a prototype of an application that was previously studied and had its functionalities validated by the target audience.

The senior public's needs and preferences were taken into consideration throughout the creation of Gen from Jizo, given the research problematic and background discussed previously. Thus, the four primary areas of design, communication, technology, and the relationship with the mother brand were used to define the project goals and products (Fig. 2): (i) app; (ii) website; and (iii) smartwatch.

Fig. 1. Screenshot of Jizo app interface (Ortet et al., 2019).

Gen from Jizo comes from the combination of objectives established in the development of Jizo (i.e., gamification to motivate behaviors through progress monitoring, route suggestions, competition and challenges, feedback, rewards) and the current demographic and technological situation. This brand symbolizes a new generation that is not X or Z, but the Jizo Generation. Gen because it was made for people of a generation, the generation of cyclotourists, the Generation from Jizo!

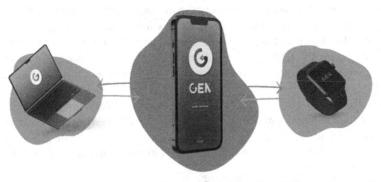

Fig. 2. Multidevice approach of Gen from Jizo.

In short, a set of functional (e.g., register in the app, tutorial, save route, edit profile, follow a friend) and non-functional (e.g., safety, performance, scalability, usability, geolocation) requirements was integrated, defining the specific functionalities that devices must offer, in order to ensure that all functionalities meet users' needs and are understood from the beginning of the development process.

Moreover, a benchmarking on similar apps was done and a study of chromatic adequation crossed with the psychology of colors (Scott-Kemmis, 2009) enabled the establishment of the chromatic palette (Fig. 3), and the primary and secondary logos (Fig. 4) for the visual identity.

#EE7301   #183249   #2F7F89

Fig. 3. Gen from Jizo brand color palette.

According to Scott-Kemmis (2009): (i) the color orange gives a sensation of movement, excitement, enthusiasm and desire for action. This color combines the physical with the emotional, it is pleasantly stimulating and reactive, while also suggesting stability; (ii) the color blue provides a feeling of calm, serenity and tranquility. This color produces few stimuli, which means it has the power to increase productivity, and it is common to use it in corporate environments as it represents professionalism, stability and security, having also the ability to help lower heart pressure; and (iii) green enables a sensation of balance, nature, peace and health. This color represents stability and possibility, has a calming effect and the ability to help relieve stress.

a)   b)

Fig. 4. a) Gen from Jizo primary logo and b) secondary logo (used when it is not possible to apply the primary logo, namely for reasons of space and visualization).

With the color palette already defined, the visual concepts that would be addressed in the brand were studied. After some attempts, an agreement was reached on the capital and sans-serif typography Arial regular and Arial Rounded MT Bold to ensure legibility, also making accessibility for the senior public clear. In this way, the letters "G", "E" and "N" were drawn with rounded ends in Illustrator and graphic elements were used that induce and lead to the idea of "path" or "route".

When creating the logo design, some fundamental shapes were implemented for the brand's context. The arrow at the end of the "G" represents the route, location, navigation, directions to explore our project's routes. And the point parallel to the "N" represents the sun, a "north" (i.e., direction), whereas the half in the "N" was designed to represent the intersection of the possible paths in senior cyclotourism.

2.1 Prototyping the App, Website and Smartwatch Interfaces

Given the definition of the brand concept and visual identity, the prototyping of Gen from Jizo solutions used an iterative design thinking and user-centered approach with direct end-user involvement. It was an approach that tried to consider the possible user's physical, cognitive, and social characteristics while being aware of their needs and preferences.

During the process of designing and developing of the interfaces for the website and application, 3 phases were defined: (i) development of a lo-fi prototype (wireframes); (ii) development of a mid-fi prototype; and (iii) production of the hi-fi interface.

In addition to specifying the pages that would be developed, wireframes (Fig. 5) were created to consider the organization of the interfaces and the visual conveyance of the fundamental functionality. The previous layouts, which was a reformulation of the Jizo interface, served as a basic and low-fidelity prototype for the application interface since they outlined the essential components of the interface.

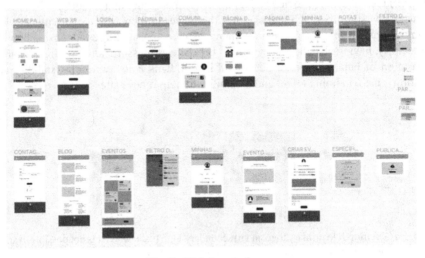

Fig. 5. Website wireframes

The second stage of development was crucial since its development was based on iterative tests with experts and potential users. To test the foundational capabilities, a medium fidelity prototype (Fig. 6) needed to be created during this phase, which required a lot of attention. Then, these prior layouts were modified for the hi-fi interface production based on input gathered from testing, and enhancements were applied.

The aforementioned devices were prioritized due to senior citizens' preferences and the researchers' availability. Thus, the smartwatch interface was developed considering de feedback from the other devices and represent a hi-fi prototype with several game elements such as health monitoring, tracking effort, and encouraging messages (Fig. 7).

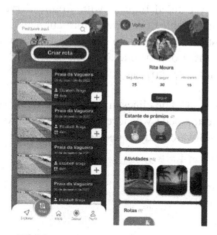

Fig. 6. App mid-fi prototype interface

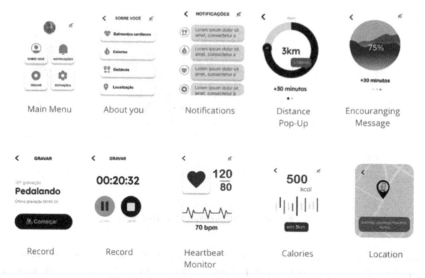

Fig. 7. Smartwatch hi-fi prototype interface

2.2 Implementation

Considering the requirements of ensuring scalability, performance and ease of maintenance of the infrastructure that supports Gen from Jizo, the development team opted for a structure based on microservices (Fig. 8) instead of a monolithic architecture (i.e., instead of building it all in one piece, it was divided into smaller services). To achieve this, the software developers used several already established technologies and protocols such as AMQP (Advanced Message Queuing Protocol), GraphQL, Docker, and Git and CI/CD pipelines (GitLabCI).

By using a technology entitled Express with Apollo Server in the Backend For Frontend (BFF), the team was able to organize information and send messages between different parts of the systems. Moreover, to guarantee that everything works properly, two types of test were carried out: (i) one to check each part by itself (i.e., unit tests with Mocha); and (ii) other to see how they all work together (i.e., integration tests with Postman API).

These protocols (e.g., CI/CD pipelines in the GitLabCI) enabled the system to automatically test and update the code whenever changes were/are made, having always the latest version of the software ready to test and making bug fixing and error logging simpler and more efficient.

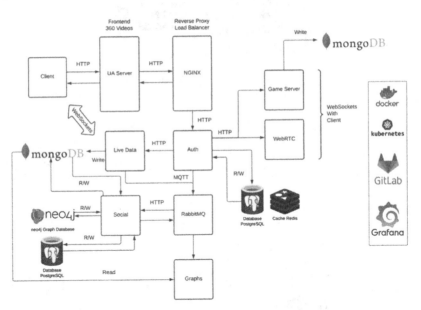

Fig. 8. Gen from Jizo system architecture

Regarding user interaction with the system, a separable and scalable service is presented through BFF that helps handle requests and send back information, enabling that different parts and microservices are running smoothly (i.e., GraphQL service that publishes messages to the appropriate channel in the RabbitMQ). The information is then processed and sent back to the user. In this way, this point of scalability is solidified, making microservices independent and streamlining their communication without creating direct dependencies (Ćatović et al., 2022).

The Authentication system is based on JSON Web Tokens, in which the validation system keeps user data safe by implementing protection against malicious code injection.

For instance, it communicates with the PostGreSQL database, whereas the Social service is what controls everything on the social network, working in the Neo4J graph database to create nodes and their relationships (Nikam et al., 2020).

3 Concept Evaluation and User Study

As already mentioned, this study was carried out in students' final bachelor project under the framework of the miOne online community, a senior community created by and for senior citizens with an emphasis on knowledge and experience exchange in the virtual space. It is designed to (i) evaluate the effects of employing ICT and (ii) provide iterative guidance for a collaborative design of the online community through the usage of "miOne".

A collaboration with the Ageing Lab (Laboratório do Envelhecimento) in Aveiro, Portugal, made it feasible to test the app's and website's mid-fidelity prototypes. In short, regarding the tests with the target audience, the convenience sample consisted of 12 senior citizens with an average age of 73.5 years old (min = 65; max = 78; SD = 3.47), where 34% were male (n = 4), and 66% female (n = 8).

Moreover, heuristic usability tests with 5 experts in technologies for senior citizens were also conducted at the Department of Communication of Art, University of Aveiro.

3.1 Procedures

Considering the senior target audience, the researchers sought to develop an inclusive design in the creation of devices in order to meet the needs and capabilities of this specific audience, focusing on issues of usability and accessibility.

The evaluation consisted of developing scenarios and tasks that reflected the main functionalities of the application and website (Fig. 9) that were dictated to the participants (i.e., script). While participants performed the tests, they were observed, and field notes were taken. They later filled out two questionnaires (Table 1), one for the app and the other for the website, based on heuristic statements evaluated with a Likert scale where 1 (one) means that they do not totally agree, and 5 (five) means they totally agree; and with open questions on the difficulty in using the solution, and the main strengths and weaknesses.

First, the objectives of the app and the topics of cyclotourism, gamification and active and healthy ageing were initially presented to the participants with the aim of contextualizing them on the project theme. There were two groups of tests (app and website), separated into two moments, where there was an average of one observer for every two participants. After testing, participants answered the questionnaire.

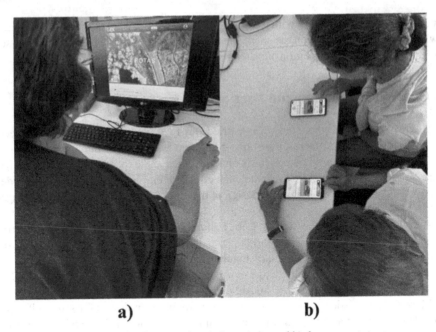

Fig. 9. Target audience testing a) the website and b) the app prototype

Table 1. Questions from the questionnaires based on the heuristics used with experts

Q1. I understand the purpose of the Gen from Jizo app/website
Q2. I can understand the language used in the Gen from Jizo app
Q3. I feel like it was easy to use the Gen from Jizo app/website
Q4. I feel like I do not need to worry about whether different words/terms/icons have the same meaning
Q5. I feel like the design of the Gen from Jizo app/website validated my actions, (e.g., animations or color changes when saving routes or joining events)
Q6. I need guidance to perform the tasks proposed in the Gen from Jizo app/website
Q7. I can use Gen from Jizo even though I do not have experience/knowledge of the app/website
Q8. I feel like the design reflects the cyclotourism theme
Q9. I feel like the support/help information is easy to access (e.g., the contact page and FAQ)
Q10. I feel that the Gen from Jizo app/website presents information in a clear and organized way

Regarding the Nielsen's 10 usability heuristic evaluation with experts[3], the test was similar to the one with the target audience, however their questionnaire was only based on the Nielsen's heuristics (1994) and contained the following open questions: (i) how easy or difficult is the app/website utilization; (ii) what you like and dislike about the app/website; and (iii) what are the main strengths and weaknesses?.

3.2 Ethical Considerations

This study, which is part of the IC Senior X research project, was created under the guidance of a doctorate candidate whose thesis has been authorized by the University of Aveiro's Council of Ethics and Deontology. It protects: (a) the participants' informed permission if they are 50 years of age or over; (b) their voluntary participation; (c) the research team's engagement in the process; and (d) the idea that the hazards of taking part in the study do not outweigh the dangers that participants face in their everyday lives.

4 Results and Discussion

The participants from the Ageing Lab evaluated both the app and website hi-fi proto-types. These participants did not typically use these devices or solutions in relation to cyclotourism, demonstrating difficulties when dealing with ICT. However, as partici-pant testing becomes feasible, validation becomes more thorough and in-depth. At this point, the prototype was modified based on the findings to better meet the requirements and challenges of today's senior citizens, thereby enabling greater use for tomorrow's seniors, who may have more interaction with technology and develop into users with higher levels of digital literacy.

Overall, the participants showed that they were able to understand the topic of gam-ified cyclotourism presented on the platforms and were able to carry out the proposed tasks. Nevertheless, when asked if they can use Gen from Jizo even if they do not have experience/knowledge (Q1), 58% of the participants believed most senior users would not (n = 7), and 16% (n = 2) also that they have difficulties in understand words/terms/icons (Q4). Furthermore, mostly, participants demonstrated comprehen-sion about the language used (Q2), and that the design reflect the topic of cyclotourism (Q8), however, the website usage seemed to be more complicated when comparing to the app.

---

[3] The heuristics were: H1. Keeps the user up to date with the issues, use and purpose of Gen from Jizo.; H2. The language used in Gen from Jizo is understandable even to those who are not experts in the topic.; H3. The Gen from Jizo guides the users, but also allows them to use it freely.; H4. The user does not need to worry whether different words/terms/icons have the same meaning.; H5. The design of the Gen from Jizo carefully avoids possible errors or usage problems.; H6. There is a minimization of the user's memory resource by providing instructions.; H7. Gen from Jizo can be used by an experienced or inexperienced user.; H8. The aesthetic design and information available in Gen from Jizo do not interfere with the information provided.; H9. Help and solutions are offered to resolve possible usage errors.; H10. Gen from Jizo provides information in a concise way, without getting in the way of carrying out the task.

As for the main difficulties felt when dealing with Gen from Jizo, the following participants' quotes sustain the above statements:

"If I had concentrated more or had more practice, I'm sure I could do this the first time." – P1

"I enjoyed using the app. However I have lack of experience when dealing with the computer, especially the mouse, so the tasks were difficult." – P2

"It wasn't easy to get there without help." – P10

Nevertheless, the main strengths identified on the app were: (i) the theme of cyclotourism; (ii) the routes; and (iii) the colors used; the pros of the website were: (i) the size of icons and text; (ii) the illustration; (iii) practicality; and (iv) routes. As for weaknesses, participants pointed out that the website should provide more routes in different terrains and locations for the cyclotourism practice.

After user testing, five experts with know-how and experience in the development of ICT for senior citizens were recruited to test and provide an in-depth analysis of the prototypes. Similar to the previous testing session, they were invited to test and evaluate the app using the heuristics and open answer questions, and then do the same for the website. Table 2 illustrates the overall results between heuristic in both app and website contexts, demonstrating mostly positive usability aspects.

Table 2. Overall results from the heuristic evaluation with experts.

	App	Website
H1	3.8	3.8
H2	4.4	3.8
H3	4.6	4.2
H4	4.2	3.4
H5	3.6	4
H6	4.2	4.2
H7	3.8	4.2
H8	4.4	3.8
H9	3.6	3.8
H10	4.2	4.6
Total	4.5	4

The following quotes of the experts are worth mentioning to support the results and highlight possible improvements to implement:

"Along with the website, using the application is simple and intuitive. Follows interaction design standards and complies with standard iconography. However, I found the application to be simpler to use compared to the website." – E1

"I really like the UI design, but I think the UX design could be improved in some points that I have already pointed out throughout the test – namely, the routes in the profile (saved and mine), and the end of recording the route. (...) I found [using the website] quite easy, but I think some button behaviors could be more explicit – as well as the repetition of these throughout the interface should only occur when they mean the same behavior." – E3

Moreover, experts also mentioned the following strengths for the app: (i) simple and concise design, (ii) motivation to the practice of cyclotourism through gamification; and (iii) ease of use; and for the website: (i) reduced effort by suggest routes; (ii) promotion of social interaction; (ii) text legibility; (iii) provision of relevant and interesting content; and (iv) the concept of creating and sharing routes.

Still, some weaknesses were identified for both platforms, namely: (i) double meaning of icons; (ii) terms used in English other than Portuguese; and (iii) lack of contextual aid.

Therefore, usability and accessibility problems were found during the testing and fixed given the participants and experts' feedback. Aspects such as typography, font size, colors, and contrasts of the elements complied with the demands of our target audience, not requiring improvements.

Additionally, it was feasible to spot elements that the general public would find challenging, including the usage of highly technical terms or certain generic English terms like "Login" (which is equivalent to "Entrar" in Portuguese).

The usage of various buttons' icons, such the "+" icon on the website for adding events or the "hamburger" icon (menu) in the application, was another problem. These icons were occasionally not very obvious. Thus, the change made was to add a description of the functionality of these buttons. One of these buttons was to save an event, which consisted of a "+" icon and was replaced by "save event", with the addition of the "save" icon in order to unify this icon both in the application and on the website (Fig. 10).

Fig. 10. From left to right, save button before as "+" icon and later with description.

The onboarding display, which lacked a title or any other description, was one of the issues with the website's initial design. All that was visible to participants was the logo and a start button; they did not click on anything else and ultimately were left wondering what they were supposed to do. The solution relied on establishing the onboarding starting with the title "Tutorial".

The size of the first pictures or gifs that begin each page with a title was another issue that was noted. Due to the massive size of these initial images/gifs, which took up the full screen when a participant entered a page, occasionally they did not realize they needed to "scroll" in order to explore the page and remained still, unsure of what to do. Consequently, the solution was to make these opening graphics smaller in size and add an arrow with a caption alerting the user to "scroll down" the page to view further material. It also included a change to the description to direct the user to the correct page.

On the app smaller changes were applied. One difficulty observed was identifying the hamburger menu, which users did not understand what it was and did not know how to find it. Thus, a fixed menu was added to all pages to facilitate navigation, as previously it was only found on the home page. Lastly, other difficulty experienced by senior participants in understanding the icon that represented saving the route was also analyzed. Therefore, the solution was based on having written support for the icon, using icon and text together.

5   Conclusion

It is apparent from the context of technological goods targeted at cyclotourism that Gen from Jizo solutions contribute significantly to enhancing the experience of cyclotourists. With the help of Gen from Jizo, senior citizens can now explore customized itineraries, find interesting sites along their route, and share their experiences with other enthusiasts, opening up social interactions and even new business opportunities. These kinds of solutions may lessen the effects brought on by age-related issues and digitally mediated society. Furthermore, tourism sites may benefit from Gen technology, as it can assist in promoting and turning public bicycle routes, destinations, nearby sites of interest, and services associated with cyclotourism. This has the potential to strengthen the local economy, promote environmentally friendly travel, and encourage the construction and improvement of infrastructure (e.g., bicycle lanes, bike parking, and rest places).

Nonetheless, some limitations should be considered for this study and results should be interpret with caution. Firstly, a small convenience sample of both the target audience and experts was recruited, thus more iterations are needed to acknowledge the improvements made in both prototypes. Secondly, the fact that this work relies on a redefinition of Jizo brand and its previous results, demonstrates fragility and little assertiveness in results, thus, requiring iterative approaches with a variety of senior public profiles (e.g., with and without digital literacy; cyclotourist or not). Finally, the smartwatch prototype was never tested, not guaranteeing good design and usability for both the target audience and context of cyclotourism.

Given the aforementioned limitations, there are several promising areas that can be explored to further deepen knowledge and contribute to the advancement of the field. Future research plans include researching and thoroughly testing gamification techniques to promote and enhance cyclotourism activities. This work will be done with the goal of creating a ranking system, challenges, and rewards to make the experience even more competitive. In addition, there is a desire to enhance the pleasure and safety of cyclotourists by investing in the growth of real-time monitoring and feedback systems. Although the Gen application for smartwatches could not be realized completely, it is necessary to support the multidevice idea further in the future and implement it.

In terms of technology, several choices were taken in order to support the project's or product's scalability. Even though TypeScript (Runtime NodeJS) has been used to create the majority of microservices, alternative technologies may be investigated in the future to increase performance. One of the issues with technologies like NodeJS, PHP, or even Python is that they are single-threaded programming languages. Parallel processing is essential in a production setting when you want to maximize the use of hardware and computing power. When compared to computer languages that offer multithreading, these languages have additional overhead since they do not allow you to run several instances or even utilize a Process Scheduler and separate processes.

However, as asynchronous messages are the foundation of the system's operation, these microservices can eventually be replaced with others that are built using different technologies (e.g., GoLang). To lower request latency in this type of architecture, it is also critical to research distributed caching concepts.

Artificial intelligence and machine learning might also potentially be used to create a virtual assistant for the mobile application as well as the website. Alternatively, using internal strategies, training a bot with data from the website as well as the context of cycle tourism and necessary safety measures; using machine learning frameworks like PyTorch or TensorFlow and applying any of the most well-known machine learning models for NLP (natural language processing), like RNN (recurrent neural networks) or even GPT (generative pre-trained transformer), with each model's pros and cons having to be considered.

Finally, not all edge situations have been examined in the absence of a QA (Quality Assurance) staff, therefore faults could occur. Before deploying to production, more pipeline optimization work as well as unit and integration testing should be done.

Acknowldegments. The study reported in this publication was supported by FCT– Foundation for Science and Technology (Fundação para a Ciência e Tecnologia) nr. 2020.04815.BD, by IC Senior X – Impact of Information and Communication on Senior's eXperience in "miOne." online community, under the project GIP3_2022 and DigiMedia Research Center, under the project UIDB/05460/2020. The authors wish to thank the commitment and contribution of students Giovanna Silva, Gonçalo Marques, Marina Biancardine and Rodrigo Coelho for the development of the prototype in the scope of their bachelor's final project. Additionally, acknowledge to the participants of the Ageing Lab (Laboratório do Envelhecimento) who made the testing with potential users possible.

References

Bucci, S., Schwannauer, M., Berry, N.: The digital revolution and its impact on mental health care. Psychol. Psychother. Theor. Res. Pract. **92**(2) 277–297 (2019). https://doi.org/10.1111/papt.12222

Castells, M.: The Information Age: Economy, Society and Culture (2nd edn. with a new preface [rev.]). Wiley-Blackwell, Chichester, West Sussex (2010)

Ćatović, A., Buzađija, N., Lemeš, S.: Microservice development using RabbitMQ message broker. Sci. Eng. Technol. **2**(1), 30–37 (2022). https://doi.org/10.54327/set2022/v2.i1.19

Deenihan, G., Caulfield, B.: Do tourists value different levels of cycling infrastructure? Tour. Manage. **46**, 92–101 (2015). https://doi.org/10.1016/j.touman.2014.06.012

Gazzola, P., Pavione, E., Grechi, D., Ossola, P.: Cycle tourism as a driver for the sustainable development of little-known or remote territories: the experience of the Apennine regions of Northern Italy. Sustainability **10**(6), 1863 (2018). https://doi.org/10.3390/su10061863

Gössling, S.: Tourism, technology and ICT: a critical review of affordances and concessions. J. Sustain. Tour. **29**(5), 733–750 (2021). https://doi.org/10.1080/09669582.2021.1873353

Hu, F., Wen, J., Phau, I., Ying, T., Aston, J., Wang, W.: The role of tourism in healthy aging: an interdisciplinary literature review and conceptual model. J. Hospit. Tour. Manage. **56**, 356–366 (2023). https://doi.org/10.1016/j.jhtm.2023.07.013

Mcleod, J.C., Stokes, T., Phillips, S.M.: Resistance exercise training as a primary countermeasure to age-related chronic disease. Front. Physiol. **10**, 441213 (2019). https://doi.org/10.3389/fphys.2019.00645

Mubarak, F., Suomi, R.: Elderly forgotten? Digital exclusion in the information age and the rising grey digital divide. INQUIRY (United States) **59**, 469580221096272 (2022). https://doi.org/10.1177/00469580221096272

Nielsen, J.: Heuristic evaluation. In: Nielsen, J., Mack, R.L. (eds.) Usability Inspection Methods, pp. 25–64. Wiley, New York (1994)

Nikam, P., Bhoite, S., Shenoy, A.: Neo4j graph database implementation for LinkedIn. Int. J. Sci. Res. Comput. Sci. Eng. Inf. Technol. **6**(6), 339–342 (2020). https://doi.org/10.32628/CSEIT206665

Ortet, C.P., Costa, L.V., Veloso, A.I.: Jizo: a gamified digital app for senior cyclo-tourism in the miOne community. In: Zagalo, N., Veloso, A., Costa, L., Mealha, Ó. (eds.) Videogame Sciences and Arts, VJ 2019. CCIS, vol. 1164, pp. 195–207. Springer, Cham (2019). https://doi.org/10.1007/978-3-030-37983-4_15

Paúl, C.: Envelhecimento Activo e Redes De Suporte Social. Sociologia: Revista Da Faculdade De Letras Da Universidade Do Porto, 15 (2017). https://ojs.letras.up.pt/index.php/Sociologia/article/view/2392. Accessed Jan 2024

Pucher, J., Buehler, R.: Introduction: cycling to sustainability. In: Buehler, R., Pucher, J. (ed.) Cycling for Sustainable Cities. The MIT Press, Cambridge, Massachusetts (2021)

Quamar, A.H., Schmeler, M.R., Collins, D.M., Schein, R.M.: Information communication technology-enabled instrumental activities of daily living: a paradigm shift in functional assessment. Disabil. Rehabil. Assistive Technol. **15**(7), 746–753 (2020). https://doi.org/10.1080/17483107.2019.1650298

Scott-Kemmis, J.: Empowered By Color (2009). https://www.empower-yourself-with-color-psychology.com/. Accessed Jan 2024

Sen, K., Prybutok, G., Prybutok, V.: The use of digital technology for social wellbeing reduces social isolation in older adults: a systematic review. SSM – Popul. Health **17**, 101020 (2022). https://doi.org/10.1016/j.ssmph.2021.101020

Taylor, H.O., Taylor, R.J., Nguyen, A.W., Chatters, L.: Social isolation, depression, and psychological distress among older adults. J. Aging Health **30**(2), 229–246 (2016). https://doi.org/10.1177/0898264316673511

UN – United Nation: 2019 Revision of World Population Prospects. United Nations, Department of Economic and Social Affairs, Population Division (2019). https://population.un.org/wpp/. Accessed January 2022

World Health Organization: Advice for the Public: Coronavirus Disease (COVID-19). Geneva: World Health Organization (2021)

World Health Organization: Decade of healthy ageing: baseline report. World Health Organization, Geneva (2020)

Zheng, R.Z., Hill, R.D., Gardner, M.K.: Engaging Older Adults with Modern Technology: Internet Use and Information Access Needs. Information Science Reference, Hershey, Pa (2013)

Poptoys: Playing and Tradition to Promote Intergenerational Experiences Through a Digital App

Viviane Peçaibes[1]([✉]) [iD], Andreia Pinto de Sousa[1,2,3] [iD], and Rute Mata João[1] [iD]

[1] Faculty of Fine Arts, University of Porto, Porto, Portugal
vivianepecaibes@gmail.com
[2] Centro Universitário do Porto, Lusófona University, Lisbon, Portugal
[3] HEI-Lab: Digital Human-Environment Interaction Labs, Lusófona University, Lisbon, Portugal

Abstract. Intergenerational contact bridges the generation gap. It is a collaborative process where all generations generate ideas, share knowledge, and interactively improve skills, attitudes, and values, fostering equality, tolerance, and mutual respect. On the other hand, popular Portuguese toys have a historical and anthropological significance, preserving the local knowledge, traditions, and customs of the population, particularly those related to agricultural culture and nature. We created POPToys to promote intergenerational contact with popular Portuguese toys through virtual environments in this context. This application was developed using the human-centred design methodology: we conducted user research and created personas, context scenarios, functional, information, context, user, and experience requirements. Wireflows were developed to define the interaction, navigation, and information architecture. Finally, a high-fidelity prototype was designed, and the prototype's usability was evaluated through a moderated test. The tests were carried out with two groups of participants: five children aged between 6 and 10 and five older adults over 65 with an average level of digital literacy. We can identify some navigation errors, information architecture and visual design inconsistencies, and some aspects to improve the user experience; it also revealed that both children and older adults found the experience fun and exciting. We realise that this digital play intervention brought the children closer to the over-65s as technology-enabled intergenerational relationships.

Keywords: Intergenerational digital experiences · Popular Portuguese Toys · Preservation of Cultural Heritage · Human Centred Design

1 Playing and Tradition to Promote Intergenerational Experiences

At the beginning of the 19th century, the emergence of theories about people as a cultural collective and the notion of popular culture meant a significant advance, incorporating ethnographic and anthropological elements that shaped national identity. According to Leal [1], popular culture has become intrinsic to a nation, constituting an essential aspect

Q. Gao and J. Zhou (Eds.): HCII 2024, LNCS 14726, pp. 243–260, 2024.
https://doi.org/10.1007/978-3-031-61546-7_16

of its being. Since then, there has been a substantial body of literature, characterised by continuous reinterpretations, progressions, and occasional setbacks, dedicated to identifying and safeguarding the legacy of popular culture in Portugal and across Europe. Popular toys, here considered cultural heritage, are related to their local context, closely linked to the rural way of life and agricultural practices, with records of them existing all over the world and considered a collective memory of humanity [1–3].

Amado [2] characterises these artefacts as "a gateway to the world" for generations of children who have made them over the centuries, participating in countless games and hobbies. The author emphasises that these were not mere toys but avenues for exploration and sharing; they went beyond imitation of adult activities to embody a realm of magic, mystery, spontaneity, and limitless freedom, where childhood reigned supreme.

The creation of popular Toys was a personal undertaking, using materials from nature or everyday objects, with or without adult assistance. Although perishable, they preserved acquired skills and knowledge transmitted from generation to generation. It is essential to differentiate them from handmade toys, which are equally valuable and culturally significant, created by artisans using manual processes and subsequently sold [2, 4].

When playing with popular toys, children assumed roles as tightrope walkers, painters, botanists, hunters, sculptors and researchers, among others, as outlined by Amado [2]. These activities, normally learned in "street school", allowed children to absorb the cultural legacy of their community perfectly, nurturing different skills in an integrated way.

These popular toys incorporate a historical and anthropological heritage, reflecting the Portuguese population's local knowledge, traditions and customs, a cultural heritage that must be preserved for future generations. Heritage has become a synonym for social bonding, especially given the material and immaterial aspects that are assumed and inseparable, which, on numerous occasions, will be determining factors in local development [5].

Leal [1] points out that popular cultures have been reformatted based on ideas such as hybridity and creativity. In this sense, design can mediate the possibilities of articulating cultural heritage and technology.

Safeguarding this heritage could pave the way for a more balanced future regarding human interactions and environmental sustainability, with design acting as a facilitator to improve our engagement with virtual environments and enrich our experiences.

2 Bridging Generational Gaps Through Educational Intergenerational Digital Experiences

In today's society, characterised by increased longevity and the simultaneous coexistence of multiple generations, there is a notable lack of interaction between age groups. Intergenerational learning can be defined as the process during which people from different generations come together for meaningful activities and interactions, thereby increasing the level of understanding between people from different generations [6]. Negative stereotypes and different perspectives create a separation that prevents the mutual construction of generational knowledge and understanding. Intergenerational contact and solidarity are crucial to breaking this cycle through a collaborative process in which all generations come together to generate, promote and use ideas, knowledge, skills, attitudes and values interactively, promoting personal improvement and community development, fostering equality, tolerance and mutual respect. This approach emphasises sharing feelings, emotions, interpretations and experiences, promoting common ground and recognising differences [7].

Contemporary literature reinforces that contact between generations can lead to intergenerational learning for participants [8, 9].

However, the critical issue of generational separation extends beyond children, youth, and older adults to encompass all age groups [10]. Particularly in Portuguese families, maintaining frequent contact with older relatives proves challenging, jeopardising the essential social support for older adults [7]. To build more fruitful relationships and diminish intergenerational conflicts in ageing societies, transforming negative perceptions becomes imperative.

By creating spaces for empathetic dialogue based on shared sentiments, intergenerational education can enhance a more positive perception among generations of the understanding and appreciation of individuals across various age groups and cultures in contemporary social contexts [9]. To achieve this, fostering curiosity, interest, and a relaxed atmosphere - potentially using local community materials - becomes essential, facilitating the identification of a common identity among generations.

Therefore, so intergenerational education takes place, there is a need to create means that promote this interaction and are attractive and engaging for both generations. Digital technologies can provide experiences that bring people of different ages closer together to reduce the gap. Often, the adoption of technology by older people can be perceived as a challenge due to ageism, in which stereotypes, prejudices, and discriminatory assumptions about older age could impact design decisions [11].

On the other hand, digital experiences, such as games on mobile phones, are increasingly becoming a means of entertainment for older people, with a growing following worldwide. It is known that these experiences with digital activities provide cognitive, physical, and socio-emotional benefits [12].

In this sense, it can be seen that there is greater involvement of old people with technology and that to mitigate any tension or resistance on the part of this group of users Mannheim [11] points out that even design experiences highlight the importance of a true "partnership" with older individuals throughout the iterative design process. This participatory approach contributes to successful outcomes, fostering designs that meet their needs and reducing intergenerational tensions. However, older individuals have diverse perspectives and increasingly embrace digital technologies positively. Their interactions with technology, influenced by personal motivations and needs, shape the perceived image of older persons concerning digital advancements.

Digital technologies and popular toys are points of intergenerational dialogue, bringing people together and inviting them to a more remarkable coexistence. At the same time, knowledge is transmitted to preserve cultural heritage. In this sense, this article presents the development process of the POPToys app as a way to preserve cultural heritage and promote problem-solving skills, creativity, and imagination. Using the app, children can learn about older adults' historical and tacit knowledge about these toys while encouraging interaction between different generations.

The POPToys application seeks to promote intergenerational experiences through virtual environments, as it teaches children aged 6 to 10 how to build popular Portuguese toys, such as the chickpea doll, the walnut shell boat, the chestnut animal, the wire and cork car [2].These toys have a historical and anthropological significance, preserving the Portuguese people's local knowledge, traditions and customs, particularly those related to agricultural culture and nature [4, 13]. In addition, POPToys brings children closer to elders to foster empathetic dialogue between the generations, sharing stories to bridge generational gaps through intergenerational educational digital experiences bringing two generations to build toys together.

3   Methodology

POPToys was developed following the principles of Human-Centred Design (HCD) [14], and utilising the Participatory Design approach [15]. This methodology serves as a guiding framework to ensure that the design process is focused on meeting the needs and preferences of users.

The development process began with an analysis phase, through fifteen interviews, one workshop, and one cultural probe, seeking to understand the users' needs, preferences, pain points, behaviours, motivations, and context of use. The output of this analysis phase was the creation of three personas that represent different user archetypes, interaction scenarios to envision how our users would interact with the app in different contexts, and a list of requirements outlining the key features and functionalities that the POPToys app should encompass.

With the personas, interaction scenarios, and requirements defined, the prototyping phase ensued. Wireflows and low-fidelity prototypes were initially created to visualise the user flow, interface structure, functionalities, and user interactions. Finally, a high-fidelity prototype was developed to be assessed by the users.

The testing was conducted with one group of 5 children aged 6–10 and one group of 5 older people to evaluate the usability and effectiveness of the product and collect their feedback and observations to ensure that it effectively addressed the needs and preferences of the users.

3.1   Analysis and Specification Phase

The user research we conducted comprises different methods to obtain information about the habits, behaviours, and perceptions of children aged 6–10 and their adult guardians. We realised it was essential to understand what this audience experienced the most significant difficulties related to play and imagination and what strategies to mitigate them. Therefore, qualitative data was collected through a co-creation workshop, cultural probes with children, and interviewing specialists and guardians. Questions such as where they play, when, and what activities they engage in, including their interaction with nature, were central to our investigation. Our aim was to deepen their experiences, recognising the importance of understanding the main challenges related to play and imagination for this audience.

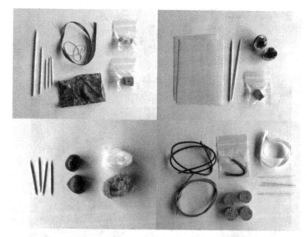

Fig. 1. From top left to bottom right: Materials from the chickpea doll kit; walnut shell boat; chestnut animal; and wire and cork car.

Co-creation Workshop. The workshop [17] was conducted on the 23rd of November 2022 with 26 elementary school children between 6 and 10 years old, with two educators and a moderator[1]. Four kits were drawn to build different toys: a chickpea doll, a walnut shell boat, a chestnut animal, and a wire and cork car. The kits (see Fig. 1) contained all the materials needed to build the toy and a sheet with instructions.

During the workshop, the children, among themselves or through the motivation of the two educators who attended the session and the moderator, were invited to travel back in time through the toys they were going to build. Some followed the brief instructions on the sheet, others abandoned the instructions and gave free rein to their imagination, creativity, and will, exploring ways to achieve the challenge. (see Fig. 2 and 3).

At the end of the workshop, some questions were asked to the children to understand the immediate impact on them and their level of satisfaction performing the task. They could identify which moments they liked most, with the majority (15 in 26) mentioning the moment of building the toy. The moment in which they felt the most difficulty was related to manual skills related to fine motor skills, such as (i) tying knots - a skill necessary for building the chickpea doll; (ii) sticking a toothpick in a chestnut - a skill necessary for building the animal. Every participant mentioned they would like to build these types of toys again.

Cultural Probe. The day after the workshop (24th November 22), in the same group of children, individual sheets were distributed as a way of collecting more information about the children's interests, which would allow us to map their context in the universe of toys and playing moments and an invitation to write a story and made an illustration about the toy built [16]. Of the 26 forms distributed, only 16 were filled out.

---

[1] Five groups of children of varying ages were created to experience the spirit of sharing and mutual help, which, according to Amado [2], is closely linked to how popular toys are constructed.

Fig. 2. Children building the toys during the workshop.

Fig. 3. Popular toys built by children during the workshop.

The favourite games mentioned were board games, card games, and football (on the computer and the street). Among their favourite toys, the vast majority indicated soft toys. The favourite colours of this group are pink, yellow, green, and blue. In the stories and drawings created by the participants, it was possible to verify that the majority invoked a differentiating character to the toy they built, defining it as magical and unique (see Fig. 4).

Specialists Interviews. The interviews [18] with the specialists in education and psychology for early childhood revealed that children in this age group have difficulty solving problems creatively, poor development of their fine motor skills, and a lack

Fig. 4. Examples of the story and illustration created through the Cultural Probe.

of opportunities to experience the body, the outdoors and nature. Two interviews were conducted with early childhood educators and two with child psychologists between November 23rd and 29th, 2022.

The identified challenges encompassed difficulty managing frustration, creative problem-solving challenges, reliance on adult presence for play, and a lack of free creation and exploration moments. Issues such as laterality problems, quick boredom, an overabundance of toys limiting exploration, and limited participation in decision-making were also noted. The need to express emotions and justify decisions, along with few outdoor and imaginative play opportunities, emerged as critical challenges. Excessive digital media exposure, underdeveloped fine motor skills, emotional control challenges, and empathy difficulties were also observed.

Furthermore, limited senses of time and space and insufficient moments for self-discovery were highlighted as areas of concern. Regarding stimulating imagination, children preferred to play "make-believe", preferably when accompanied and engaged in activities like music, drawing, and crafts, often within a school context.

When exploring parental and grandparental involvement, it was found that engaging parents depended on their level of interest and awareness. Informed and motivated parents were seen as more likely to participate actively. However, reaching grandparents, mainly through simple applications like a tablet, was considered more accessible. Grandparents were viewed as having more time, greater adaptability, and a willingness to participate actively in the child's activities.

While parents might assist grandparents in adapting to applications, there's a potential risk of parents being overly involved, hindering the child's autonomy and learning experiences. The importance of informed parents understanding the child's immediate and long-term benefits was emphasised.

Grandparents were recognised as essential contributors, offering valuable time, a slower pace, and a willingness to let children explore freely. The emotional and genetic connection with grandparents was highlighted, underscoring the importance of proximity for a child's emotional well-being.

Acknowledging the importance of children's interaction with nature raised concerns about controlling material collection from natural environments. Some educators suggested a potential reliance on domestic resources to replace natural elements.

In summary, insights from specialists provide a comprehensive understanding of the challenges and opportunities in children's development, emphasising the crucial roles of parents, grandparents, and nature in shaping a child's holistic growth.

Guardians Interviews. Eleven tutors aged 35 to 57 were interviewed between November 25th and December 4th, 2022. Of these, 7 were parents, 3 were uncles, and 1 was a grandmother. The tutors also mention their children's difficulty being quiet and entertained, emphasising that they get upset quickly. As for their biggest fears, the guardians fear that they will hurt themselves or that something will affect their well-being. It was also interesting to note that, although all the guardians mentioned the difficulty of having quality time with the children, the happiest moments they remember are those spent in the family and outdoors.

When asked about the involvement of parents over 65 with a digital application, participants provided diverse responses. Some said grandparents, especially grandfathers, would be more comfortable with technology. In contrast, others highlighted the potential for grandmothers to enjoy reminiscing about traditional toys and building them with their grandchildren, sharing stories. The consensus was that grandparents, when engaged, contribute positively to various activities, from playing games to watching videos. However, concerns were raised about the comfort level of some grandparents with technology, with variations based on individual experiences and the perceived simplicity of the application. Despite potential challenges, it was also consensual that with adequate explanation and a simple, coherent interface, most grandparents could become involved, provided they understood the benefits for their grandchildren. It was acknowledged that simplicity and patience would be crucial for successful engagement with older generations.

Affinity Maps. To analyse the qualitative data gathered from the interviews, we developed an Affinity Map [16] that comprehensively explored the challenges children and their guardians encounter (see Fig. 5). This approach allowed us to delve into the characteristics of playtime moments within the family context, including interactions with grandparents. Furthermore, we identified how children engage with their imagination and explore their relationship with nature. This method provided a structured framework to map various app construction possibilities.

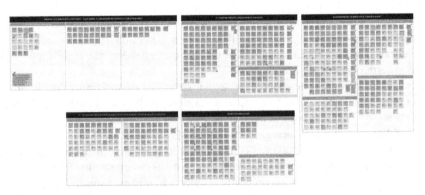

Fig. 5. Affinity Map

Table 1. Summary of the developed personas.

Persona 1: Beatriz Simões, 7 years old, the explorer

This spirited 7-year-old is an adept cat cuddler and a second-grade student in Porto. During the week, she resides with her mother and spends alternating weekends with her father. Beatriz's adventurous nature shines through her favourite pastime: chasing chickens when visiting her grandparents' house.

Beatriz's love for cats extends to her favourite activity of mimicking dances from TikTok and YouTube, especially on lively Sunday afternoons with her extended family. Despite her proficiency in subjects like History, Geography, and Natural Sciences, she encounters challenges in Portuguese due to her dislike for writing compositions.

A lively and assertive personality, Beatriz questions incorrect answers in school, advocating for the validity of all options. Her father's weekend outings to the park bring immense joy, allowing her to conquer climbing challenges. Beatriz wishes for more family time and opportunities to explore nature.

Weekends become memorable when she visits her paternal grandparents, engaging in activities like wearing boots, playing with dirt, and chasing chickens. Curiously, she dislikes playing with clay but enjoys the virtual world of Fashion Shop Tycoon on her tablet, showcasing different doll outfits to her school friends.

Beatriz's distinct characteristics include an extroverted, curious, and adventurous nature. While she faces limited free playtime and moderate difficulty in concentration and fine motor tasks, her unwavering interest in technology and family interactions defines her vibrant personality.

Persona 2: Joana Costa, 35 years old, the fun-loving.

Originally from Brazil, the fun-loving Joana has called Porto home since she was 8. Her zest for life is evident in her love for socialising and having a good time with family and friends. Currently immersed in remote work, Joana finds the experience fantastic, granting her extra leisure time to indulge in reading, cinema outings, city strolls, or simply relaxing at home with her favourite series.

Joana enjoys orchestrating family moments, like a recent outing to the Paiva Walkways. Regrettably, the plan didn't unfold smoothly as she overlooked activities for the little ones, resulting in boredom after just an hour. Witnessing their impatience saddened Joana, leading to an early return home without completing the intended route.

She supports her sister and brother-in-law weekly by looking after her nieces and nephew twice a week post-school, providing the couple with much-needed time for household tasks. Juggling everything simultaneously proves challenging for them, and exhaustion is a frequent companion.

Joana's primary concern is the excessive amount of screen time her young relatives spend on their phones. Despite attempts to redirect their focus to alternative activities like colouring or enjoying nostalgic cartoons, they resist, deeming them too slow. Eventually, Joana allows them tablet play while she tackles other tasks, but the children quickly demand her attention, potentially leading to tantrums.

(*continued*)

Table 1. (*continued*)

Secondary Persona: Manuel Silva, 68 years old, the garden tinkerer
Manuel Silva epitomises family joy and cherished moments. Originally from Beja, he settled in the north after military service, nurturing a nearly 50-year marriage with Emília. In retirement's first year, Manuel indulged in beloved hobbies, especially tending his garden, which he now enjoys leisurely. Committed to staying tech-savvy, Manuel and Emília took a New Technologies course pre-retirement, reflecting his resolve to stay connected and assist their children. Handling family tax returns online for three years underscores his adaptability and learning eagerness. A natural storyteller, Manuel shares army tales from Porto and childhood adventures in Alentejo, valuing memories as cherished treasures and preserving traditions. Playing with grandchildren brings immense joy, shared through family Facebook pictures despite the distance. Rainy days invite card games or dominos, with Manuel often letting youngsters win. The kitchen buzzes with laughter, new recipes from YouTube, and flour-covered aprons. Known for growing the sweetest apples in Mira Cambra, Manuel modestly attributes it to love for his trees. Manuel's personality blends introverted and extroverted traits fueled by curiosity and organisational tendencies. He has a keen interest in popular toys and commendable digital literacy. Despite facing time constraints for play, occasional concentration issues, and motor skill challenges, imaginative pursuits come effortlessly to him.

Personas. Building on the insights gained from the Affinity Map, we developed two primary personas [19] corresponding to the child and the guardian: the explorer Beatriz Simões (7 yo.) and the fun-loving Joana Costa (35 yo.) and one secondary persona representing the older adult: Manuel Silva (68 yo.), the garden tinkerer (see Table 1). This decision was based on recognising that older adults may have specific accessibility needs when using digital products.

Scenarios. By crafting the primary and secondary personas, we delineated various usage contexts [20], encompassing scenarios for parents/tutors and individuals over 65 and children. For the former, these scenarios involve the need to engage the child while tending to other tasks, family moments with inclusive interaction, purposeful outings to parks or nature, outdoor and indoor play, breaks from homework, and imparting knowledge to preserve memory and cultural heritage. The children's context scenarios include moments of difficulty in self-entertainment or with non-participative adult presence, instances of frustration, playful episodes, motor skills and spatial awareness development, and the stimulation of imagination and problem-solving abilities. Those insights give us rich information to create two context scenarios for each persona into situations where the app would find utility (see Table 2).

Table 2. Example of scenarios for the persona Beatriz Simões and Manuel Simões.

Persona	Scenarios
Beatriz Simões	Scenario 1: *Last week, Beatriz used the app to build a toy and received stamps; now, she wants to see how many she has. Now that she remembers how many stamps she received, she is very curious and eager to know this week's challenge. This week's challenge is to build the "Chickpea Doll", and she'll need to know what is needed to build this toy and collect all the materials with the help of her family*
	Scenario 2: *Beatriz was having difficulty understanding how to prepare the chickpeas for building the toy because she still struggles with reading, but she consulted the help provided in the app and managed to prepare all the materials. Now everything is ready to start the fun! Beatriz follows all the steps indicated until the challenge is completed. Ultimately, she may receive a reward for her effort - a new stamp for her ability to tie knots and bows*
Manuel Silva	Scenario 1: *Manuel is overjoyed! Today, he'll have his granddaughter Mariana at home all afternoon. As it was raining, they planned to build a popular toy with the help of the POPToys app. Manuel wants to confirm how many stamps Mariana has received to understand his granddaughter's fine motor skills*
	Scenario 2: *Mariana has arrived home from school, and both are curious to know what the challenge of the week proposed by the POPToys app will be - a Doll with Chickpeas. After identifying all the necessary materials, it's time to roll up their sleeves and prepare everything. Even Grandma Alice helped with the chickpeas that were already soaked for dinner. Now that everything is ready, they must let their imaginations soar and start building the toy*

Requirements. The scenarios outlined, and the insights gathered from the user research phase played a crucial role in shaping the requirements for the functional, information, context, user, and experience aspects [19].

The app should avoid predefined models, allowing children to explore and create freely, fostering creativity and imagination. It should also include a hint system to help children overcome challenges and frustration, creating a supportive learning environment. The app must provide an audio option for children still learning to read for accessibility and independent exploration. A task calendar spanning 15 to 30 days also motivates parents to engage regularly, promoting consistency and progress.

Tutors should be able to receive detailed skill development tracking information, encouraging continued involvement. Music integration enhances concentration, while storytelling provides context and guidance, enriching understanding, and enjoyment.

The app should minimise the time commitment required from parents, ensuring support for their child's learning journey without feeling overwhelmed. It encourages experimentation and embraces mistakes, promoting a growth mindset. To encourage exploration and creativity, the app could feature random material exploration through a shuffle option, fostering curiosity and discovery.

Additionally, the app features an appealing interface, an achievement system, and sharing capabilities to promote social interaction and collaboration between different generations. It also features tutorial videos to support parents in guiding their children effectively. The app aims to boost children's self-confidence and prioritise their emotional well-being, providing a positive and empowering learning experience. Overall, it offers a holistic and enriching environment for children to explore, create, and grow.

3.2   Prototyping

After this, we were able to synthesise insights more effectively and formulate a problem statement for our design process, laying a solid foundation for the subsequent phase. Wireflows [21] were developed to help define the interaction, navigation, and information architecture (see Fig. 6).

Fig. 6. Wireflows

We defined attributes for the app's identity and personality because it should be:

- Fun without infantilising;
- Good humoured and charismatic;
- Respectful but informal - She calls people "you", thanks them, says "please" and admits mistakes;
- Friendly and guiding without being rigid - Doesn't show arrogance or superiority;
- Confident, not dominant - Always promotes autonomy and the ability to solve problems;
- Dynamic but not hyperactive - Patient.

All these attributes have been translated into the aesthetics of the product (see Fig. 7). Ultimately, the high-fidelity prototype was designed and developed to show the user the complete experience of interacting with the app. We applied vibrant, fun, solid colours to aid and drive the experience - the traffic light system is adapted to the colours that users identify with to make it easier to recognise mistakes and successes when navigating the app. We implemented high-contrast resources, as this is a fundamental tool for guaranteeing accessibility for users, taking into account their needs but, above all, favouring use when they interact outdoors. The typography is intended to reflect the fun and inclusive spirit of POPToys, ensuring that all the information is comfortable to

Fig. 7. High-fidelity prototype

read. The typeface is composed of a single typeface, always with the use of contrast in black and white colours only.

In the hi-fi prototype, we have created a complete flow of interactions:

- At the app's start, users are invited to take on the weekly toy-building challenge;
- The introduction of the challenge includes a countdown;
- Users are given a list of materials needed for the specific toy, with detailed information and accessible tips for each material. Users then follow the steps to build the toy, with the option of listening to music and audio to assist in reading information;
- Upon completion, users can repeat or continue, receiving a stamp for their achievement;
- Afterwards, users can exit the application, greeted by an animated illustration that suggests a "See you soon" message.

To boost user involvement and support interaction, we've created POPCronies, who are friendly characters. They were all inspired by Portuguese popular culture. They give tips, suggest music, and help users get everything organised for tasks together.

With the first version of the hi-fi prototype concluded, we proceeded to the usability tests with the target audiences to realise whether POPToys meets intergenerational needs and provides a relevant and satisfactory experience.

3.3 Usability Test

The usability tests aim to perceive users' behaviours and attitudes towards the application, evaluating its usability and performance. The POPToys tests aim to assess various aspects in both children and individuals over the age of 65. For children, the focus is on:

- understanding whether children can effectively build a toy using the app;
- satisfaction with the experience, the presentation and the appeal of the theme;
- understanding how often children would use the app.

For individuals over 65, the usability test examines:

- the readability and comprehensibility of the information presented (taking into account the size and contrast of the fonts);
- motivation/intention to help a child use the application;
- the identification of the visual elements with the theme of popular toys;

- how often they would use the app with children.

To do this, we conducted tests with two different groups of users. The first group consisted of 5 children aged between 6 and 10 who were attending primary school or the last year of preschool. The second group consisted of 5 individuals over 65 with a moderate level of digital literacy.

Participants in both groups engaged in a series of 6 tasks aligned with illustrative scenarios. They were instructed to give feedback on their interaction with the application using the Think-aloud Protocol [16]. In addition, participants were invited to express their opinions through questionnaires administered during and after each test session. The behaviour of each participant in each task was observed and recorded in video and audio for after analysis.

The tests were conducted in person with a moderator's participation, who presented specific task scenarios to all the participants. In the tests with the over-65 group, the moderator played an immersive role, using role-play, assuming a child's perspective assisted by the tutor while building the proposed toy.

Some Results. Through the tests, we identified some navigation errors, inconsistencies in the information architecture and visual design and some aspects to improve the user experience, especially for the group of people over 65, which will be corrected in the future.

However, none of the participants successfully completed all task scenarios (see Fig. 8). The closest participant completed 94% of the set of steps/scenario, completing 23 steps unassisted out of a total of 24. This participant belongs to group 1, children. In group 2, participants over 65, the participant with the most steps completed reached 74%, completing 18 steps unassisted out of a total of 24. It is also noticeable that Group 2 (G2) faced significant challenges in accomplishing tasks from scenarios four, five, and six, whereas G1 completed 19 to 24 steps.

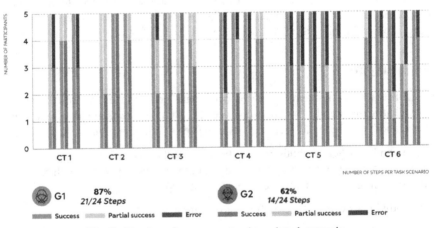

Fig. 8. Number of errors per step in each task scenario.

Analysing the usability tests, we realised that the main interaction errors are due to differences arising from intergenerationally (Table 3) since younger people have greater digital literacy than older people. However, some older people find it easier to read and understand than younger people.

Table 3. Highlights of each group's main errors and our mitigation strategies:

Group	Error	Mitigate Strategy
G2	Initial difficulties in perceiving use because of the group's low digital literacy	Creation of an explanatory video to be shown to the user before their first use (Onboarding Video)
	Difficult to understand the actions needed to carry out the tasks	
	Identify buttons	Apply labels to the buttons and make them bigger
	Return to "Home Menu"	Redesign the button
G1 and G2	Difficulties reading and generally understanding some tasks	Include more detailed audio options in each task and the elements that allow interaction will be enlarged and highlighted

Although the participants found it challenging to complete the tasks fully, they all said they liked the way the information was presented to them by the app (Fig. 9). However, the experience with the application showed that both children and older adults found the experience relevant, fun and exciting.

As for interest in continued use, the children were willing to use the app, mainly because there is the "Challenge of the Week", which seemed interesting and curious to them. The over-65 group indicated interest and availability of time to use the app as long as the child wanted to use it with them. Also, 5/5 participants would recommend the app to friends and family because they find it safe, interesting, and fun.

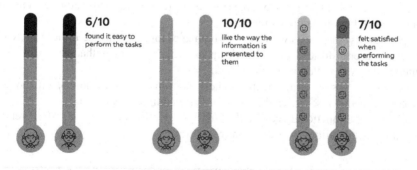

6/10 found it easy to perform the tasks

10/10 like the way the information is presented to them

7/10 felt satisfied when performing the tasks

Fig. 9. Satisfaction Level during the usability tests.

We believe that user satisfaction with the app's playful-pedagogical approach signals that we have a digital product that provides a relevant experience and that by implementing mitigation strategies, we can have a more coherent prototype that leads users to more accurate and satisfying interactions.

4   Final Considerations and Next Steps

In this article we present the design and development of a playful-pedagogical digital artefact that assists the construction of Portuguese popular toys to promote intergenerational proximity between children and older people. The aim is to promote inclusive playful interaction between these different generations and between them with nature. Through the exploration of the materials needed to create them in nature or with available household materials, the aim is for this exploration, supported by POPToys, to interact with an older person, who is presumed to be the holder of this cultural heritage and know-how.

Following the HCD methodology, POPToys aimed to create an experience that truly resonates with its users, providing them with a pleasant experience that bridges the gap between these generations. The participation of users during the design process was relevant to realising that this digital product can indeed serve as a means for joint learning and that popular toys are a subject of intergenerational interest, being something attractive that promotes the satisfaction of users of both ages.

The usability evaluation allowed us to realise that this type of digital play intervention brought children closer to people over 65 since technology facilitated intergenerational relations. The popular toy was perceived as a point of convergence between these different generations to promote the inclusion and valorisation of people over 65, as it allows the sharing of knowledge and human values that stimulate children [22] and reinforces learning through informal education.

As next steps for this project, we would like to highlight the following in general:

- Implementing the mitigation strategies mentioned above in this article - such as creating the onboarding video, applying audio to help identify activities, creating labels on all buttons, among others;
- Apply new usability tests with users of both ages together - to see if these strategies meet the users' difficulties and pick up on other challenges that may arise from interactions with children and the elders;
- Make the necessary adjustments to these new interactions - iterate on the hi-fi prototype so that it serves as the basis for the final implementation;
- Implement the functional version of POPToys - develop the app in its MVP version for future availability on different online platforms.

Acknowledgments. This article is funded by ID+ Research Institute for Design, Media and Culture (https://idmais.org/). This app was developed within the Specialisation Course in Interaction Design, Web and Games (https://ix.fba.up.pt/) and under HEI-Lab R&D Unit (UIDB/05380/2020, https://doi.org/https://doi.org/10.54499/UIDB/05380/2020).

References

1. Leal, J.: Da arte popular às culturas populares híbridas. Etnográfica **13**(2), 472–476 (2009). https://doi.org/10.4000/etnografica.1318
2. Amado, J.: Universo dos brinquedos populares, 2a. Quarteto Ed (2007)
3. Teixeira, M.B., Barroco, C.: O Brinquedo Português. Bertrand Editora (1987)
4. Benjamin, W.: Reflexões Sobre a Criança, o Brinquedo, a Educação, 1a. Editora 34 Ltda (2002)
5. Blank, D.M.P.: Cultura, Identidade e Memória: Repensando o Patrimônio (Cultural). Prisma Jurídico **13**(1), 37–70 (2014). https://doi.org/10.5585/prismaj.v13n1.4564
6. Schuller, T.: Age, generation und social capital. In: Bildung der Generationen, pp. 161–170. VS Verlag für Sozialwissenschaften, Wiesbaden (2011). https://doi.org/10.1007/978-3-531-92837-1_13
7. Villas-Boas, S., Ramos, N., Amado, J., Oliveira, A., Montero, I.: A redução de estereótipos e atitudes negativas entre gerações. Laplace Em Revista **3**(3), 206–220 (2017). https://doi.org/10.24115/S2446-6220201733365p.206-220
8. Mannion, G.: Intergenerational education: the significance of reciprocity and place. J. Intergenerational Relatsh. **10**(4), 386–399 (2012). https://doi.org/10.1080/15350770.2012.726601
9. Trujillo-Torres, J.M., Aznar-Díaz, I., Cáceres-Reche, M.P., Mentado-Labao, T., Barrera-Corominas, A.: Intergenerational learning and its impact on the improvement of educational processes. Educ. Sci. **13**(10), 1019 (2023). https://doi.org/10.3390/educsci13101019
10. Usmani, S., Asif, M.H., Mahmood, M.Z., Khan, M.Y., Burhan, M.: Generation X and Y: impact of work attitudes and work values on employee performance. J. Manag. Res. **6**(2), 51–84 (2019). https://doi.org/10.29145/jmr/62/060203
11. Mannheim, I., Weiss, D., van Zaalen, Y., Wouters, E.J.M.: An 'ultimate partnership': older persons' perspectives on age-stereotypes and intergenerational interaction in co-designing digital technologies. Arch. Gerontol. Geriatr. **113**, 105050 (2023). https://doi.org/10.1016/j.archger.2023.105050
12. Lee, A.R.: Breaking through digital barriers: exploring EFL students' views of zoom breakout room experiences. Korean J. Engl. Lang. Linguist. **21**, 510–524 (2021). http://journal.kasell.or.kr/xml/29542/29542.pdf. Accessed 16 Feb 2024
13. de Faria Oliveira, M.V., Costa, T., dos Santos Maia, L.F., Gomes, V.L.A., C.C.d.A., Campos, de Lima, P.J.D.: Brinquedos e brincadeira potiguares: identidade e memória. Editora do CEFET-RN (2007)
14. Conrad, J., Koehler, C., Wallach, D., Luedeke, T.: Design theory and methodology in HCI: applying CPM/PDD to UCD, pp. 27–39 (2018). https://doi.org/10.1007/978-3-319-91797-9_3
15. Simonsen, J., Robertson, T.: Routledge International Handbook of Participatory Design. Routledge (2012). https://doi.org/10.4324/9780203108543
16. Martin, B., Hanington, B.M.: Universal Methods of Design: 100 Ways to Research Complex Problems, Develop Innovative Ideas, and Design Effective Solutions. Rockport Publishers, Beverly, Mass (2012)
17. McKercher, K.A.: Beyond Sticky Notes. Cammeraygal Country. Inscope Books, Australia (2020)
18. DiCicco-Bloom, B., Crabtree, B.F.: The qualitative research interview. Med. Educ. **40**(4), 314–21 (2006). https://doi.org/10.1111/j.1365-2929.2006.02418.x
19. Goodwin, K.: Designing for the Digital Age: How to Create Human-Centered Products and Services. Wiley, Hoboken (2009)

20. Cooper, C., Reimann, R., Cronin, D., Noessel, C.: About Face: The Essentials of Interaction Design, 4th edn. Wiley, Hoboken (2014)
21. Szabo, P.W.: User Experience Mapping. Packt Publishing, UK (2017)
22. OECD: OECD Future of Education and Skills 2030, OECD Learning Compass 2030 - A Series of Concept Notes (2019)

Navigating Paris Digitally: An Exploratory Research of 360º Immersive Videos with Portuguese Participants

Francisco Regalado📵, Cláudia Pedro Ortet📵, Tânia Ribeiro📵, and Ana Isabel Veloso(✉)📵

DigiMedia, University of Aveiro, Aveiro, Portugal
{fsfregalado,claudiaortet,ribeirotania,aiv}@ua.pt

Abstract. Digital tourism does not replace the real experience, yet it can be a resource that democratizes tourism, especially in critical situations such as pandemics or when the tourist is impaired. This research involved an experiential activity enabling participants to virtually visit the Eiffel Tower and cycle through Parisian suburbs through 360º videos displayed in a VR headset. The experiment aimed to (i) assess the user experience, (ii) examine user adoption and motivation, (iii) evaluate social impact, (iv) analyze the feasibility of digital tourism, and (v) identify potential therapeutic benefits. This experiment involved two distinct groups, institutionalized adults and active ones, both from Portugal, totaling 114 participants. Results indicate that digital travel significantly contributes to active and healthy aging, and can possibly trigger positive social behaviors. The findings include the emergence of include strategic gaming approaches for navigating the virtual environment and the absence of motion sickness in the institutionalized group. This research underscores the potential of digital tourism as a viable and beneficial alternative, offering insights into its multifaceted impacts on user experiences, health, and social dynamics.

Keywords: Digital Travel · 360º video · Virtual Reality · Tourism

1 Introduction

In today's ever-evolving world, the unique needs and preferences of older adults in the context of tourism have gained increasing attention, although little focus is given to research in the aging field [1]. Moreover, Meiners and Seeberger [2] state that this older age cohort represents an important market opportunity that can stimulate the tourism industry. Nonetheless, as individuals age, factors such as limited mobility [3], health concerns [4], and the desire for meaningful social engagement [5] become significant considerations whenever considering the development of new value propositions.

One of the critical aspects affecting older adults' tourism experiences is the limitation imposed by physical constraints, which can often restrict their ability to travel and explore new destinations. Moreover, as recently witnessed, public health problems such as the COVID-19 pandemic can introduce challenges in commuting older people [6], as some

Q. Gao and J. Zhou (Eds.): HCII 2024, LNCS 14726, pp. 261–278, 2024.
https://doi.org/10.1007/978-3-031-61546-7_17

of the implemented measures included social distancing and isolation to contain the spread of the virus.

Social isolation is the general lack of social contact or communication and participation in social activities [7], and it leads to emotional loneliness – a personal experience of lack of meaningful social connections, which gives rise to negative feelings (e.g., disinterest, boredom, fatigue, apathy). The consequences of social isolation and emotional loneliness increase older adults' vulnerability to depression and expose them to a greater risk of death [8].

Therefore, to limit the negative impact of social isolation and allow universal access to tourism activities, there is a need to reinvent strategies and technologies to allow safe touristic solutions [9]. Even if digital tourism is not yet recognized as a new type of tourism, it is currently a reality, offering some facilities and privileged access to a more substantial number of tourist experiences. Digital tourism does not replace the real experience. However, it can be a resource that democratizes tourism, especially in critical situations (e.g., pandemics and impaired individuals) [9].

Technologies that are presented as solutions to digital traveling (e.g., virtual words) allow exploring and experiencing tourist products from a pre-visit information perspective [10] or even carrying out virtual tours without the need for physical travel [11].

Milgram and colleagues [12] first introduced the scale between reality and virtuality in a synthesized world, where the experiences between the extremes of virtual and real are called mixed reality (M.R.) experiences. Two aspects are important within the M.R. specter: (i) Presence, which can be defined as one's sense of being in the virtual world. This phenomenon is an illusion created by the perceptual system where a synthesized word is perceived as real, as the objects and the brain-body system automatically react to the changes in the artificial environment as if they were in the real world [13]; and (ii) immersion that stands for the objective level of sensory fidelity provided by a M.R. system, being the user's engagement with a synthesized word system that results in a flow state [14].

With such, immersive environments provided by virtual reality (VR) and augmented reality (A.R.) technologies that combine sensory and psychological elements enable greater involvement in the experience. VR, virtual environment, and 3D models break the traditional way of image viewing, expand 2D view to panoramic view, which brings audiences a sense of Presence, and provide a new viewing experience that breaks [13].

In the same vein, the 360° trend in technology is one recent development [15]. Users can look in every direction as they would in real-life scenarios thanks to the 360° camera's ability to record the surroundings. Furthermore, it is inexpensive and simple to use for those without specialized technical knowledge [16]. Moreover, users can view the entire panorama using immersive 360° technology and a head-mounted displays (H.M.D.) VR headset, giving them a strong sensation of presence and immersion that makes them feel as though they are actually inside the scene [17].

Since an experience where the user experience captions of the real world in a virtual environment can be defined as VR, this exploratory study aims to answer the following research question "What is the experience of institutionalized adults and active ones to 360° Immersive videos?". In particular, the research question can be divided into the following particular goals: (i) assess the user experience – assess the ease of use, comfort, and enjoyment of virtual reality technology in a tourism context; (ii) examine user adoption and motivation – explore the factors that drive older adults to adopt VR technology, considering influences from social circles, caregivers, and/or personal motivation; (iii) evaluate social impact – assess the social implications of VR experiences, such as the potential for socialization, sharing experiences with friends and family, and its role in combating social isolation; (iv) analyze feasibility for tourism – observe the effectiveness of VR as a tool for promoting tourism, assessing its appeal and feasibility as a means to virtually experience different places; and (v) identify potential therapeutic benefits – explore the perceived therapeutic benefits of VR technology, specifically in terms of relaxation, mental well-being, and its potential as a safe exercise medium.

In detail, the researchers recruited a sample of institutionalized older adults to experience 360° videos of the Eiffel Tower and Paris suburbs through a virtual reality setup to understand its feasibility in digital travel. Besides, the same experience was performed with a comparison group of non-institutionalized adults to sustain the results.

2 Immersive Technologies for All: The Virtual Tourism Perspective

Considering the aim of this research, a set of studies on immersive technologies for an overall audience (i.e., adults and older adults) and the use of virtual reality in tourism had to be analyzed, which are covered in the next two subsections.

Technology that distorts the line between the real world and the virtual one and gives users a sensation of immersion is known as immersive technology [18]. According to Suh and Prophet [19], immersive technologies have been shown to improve learning experiences, encourage collaboration, and boost creativity and engagement in a range of sectors (e.g., education, health, tourism, gaming, and marketing).

Nevertheless, there is an importance in developing and applying immersive technologies that are inclusive, taking into account gender, age, race, culture, ethnicity, and physical and mental disabilities [20, 21]. Crabb and colleagues [22] state that the components of inclusion that should be addressed in immersive settings are (i) visual, (ii) cognitive, and (iii) communication access. In detail (Crabb et al., 2019): (i) users who have vision problems, as well as users who need temporary or situational vision accessibility, are both concerned with visual access; (ii) cognitive access has to do with how people process information and comprehend it, which might involve memory, fluid intelligence, attention, and emotional concerns; and (iii) communication access is concerned with how individuals interact with their environment through speech, hearing, and language.

According to the literature, user reactions to and personal experiences with immersive technology are influenced by individual characteristics [19]. For instance, female users (when compared to male users) are more likely to experience negative cognitive effects (e.g., motion sickness) when using immersive technology [23]. Moreover, younger users are more likely to be engaged with immersive environments than older users [24]. However, other studies [e.g., 25] revealed no variation in engagement levels across age groups, supporting the theory of individual differences' impact in user reaction to these technologies. Additionally, users with a low tendency to seek sensations in an immersive environment report a better sense of Presence than users with a high tendency to sensation-seeking (i.e., personality characteristic that describes people who actively seeks out new, intense, and thrilling events to satiate their craving for sensation), regardless of age [26].

In 1995, Williams and Hobson [27] predicted that VR would be able to recreate illusions and mimic human senses such as smell and taste. Fast-forwarding to now, digital technologies are playing a highly transformative role in the virtual tourism environment [28]. Thus, coupled with sustainability, technology is a strategic pillar for the further development of virtual tourism [29, 30].

The potential transformation of tourism experiences is imminent with the integration of cutting-edge technology, leveraging market intelligence, fostering innovative business models, and enabling the co-creation of value [29]. In fact, mobile devices have been playing a pivotal role in enriching the tourist experiences by driving the tourism ecosystems [28], thus facilitating the exchange of information and increasing the tourist's competences [31].

Moreover, interactions with e-commerce [32] and online communities [33] have also shown their importance in the interaction between tourists, reinforcing that the digitalization of tourism depends on compatibility, convenience, and perceived risk [34]. Following this line of thought, the electronic word of mouth emerges, emphasizing the important role that digital technologies play in enhancing the sharing of service quality, satisfaction, and social identity [35].

With more recent developments in the field of information and communication technologies, new, more immersive, personalized, and smart ways of developing virtual tourism are starting to be explored. Big data analytics and data mining empower the application of social media analytics, encompassing spatial and semantic analysis. By leveraging user data, location information, and engagement patterns with the external environment, smart urban tourism can be significantly enhanced [28, 36]. Moreover, in the study conducted by Buhalis and colleagues [37], various technological disruptions such as virtual/augmented reality, robots, drones, AI-enabled devices, and location-based services were explored as means to revolutionize the tourism ecosystem. It was also highlighted the significance of real-time co-creation and the immediacy of services in shaping customer-oriented experiences [38].

In fact, VR-based technologies enable access to tourism while considering physical, age-related, or financial limitations [39], having a great potential to replace conventional tourism with telepresence facilitated by wearable gadgets and immersive technology that stimulates sensory experiences [40].

Additionally, VR platforms have significant implications for the perception of authenticity and the transformation of tourist experiences. These platforms can potentially alter visitors' understanding and perception of actual tourism destinations [41]. They offer unique ways to showcase destinations, influencing tourists' perceptions of authenticity in the tourism context [42]. Furthermore, it has been suggested that VR tourism should highlight the best seasonal specials and present previously inaccessible attractions. This approach enhances the overall VR tourism experience by providing visitors with exclusive and captivating offerings [42].

The integration of VR technology in nature-based tourism has opened up exciting educational opportunities for both tourists and operators. VR enables the provision of immersive and informative experiences that showcase remote and isolated destinations, which may be unfamiliar to many tourists [43]. Lastly, the successful implementation of VR in marketing campaigns, as demonstrated in the case of the Lake District National Park, has proven effective in attracting new tourists and promoting destinations [44].

3 Method and Materials

The experimental approach was contextual and occurred in a laboratory setting under the publicized activity "Virtual Reality Meeting: A Trip to Paris", conducted from 20th October to 17th November 2021 in the Department of Communication and Art at the University of Aveiro, Portugal. The researchers planned and developed a VR Parisienne travel to fulfill the request of senior institutions to provide a realistic and fun experience to older adults addressing the research question and goals pointed in the introductory section.

With this in mind, participants were split into two groups participants: (i) the institutionalized group (I.G.) of portuguese retired older adults institutionalized at nursing homes; and (ii) the active group (A.G.) of non-institutionalized portuguese adults from all walks of life in their working years. For the A.G., the inclusion criteria included (i) being aged 50 or over, (ii) institutionalized, (iii) not having any form of blindness, (iv) knowing how to read and write, and (v) voluntary participation. As for the I.G., the inclusion criteria included (i) being aged 18 or over, (ii) not being institutionalized, (iii) knowing how to read and write, and (iv) voluntary participation. In both groups, failing to do the activity or complete the questionnaire resulted in the exclusion of the data related to the participant.

The activity was programmed to enable an adaptation of VR technology and to exceed expectations with an adventure and physical exercise – please refer to Table 1 for a detailed overview of the experiment. In detail, Part 1 was the Eiffel Tower visit through 360° videos[1], aiming at the adaptation to the H.M.D.; Part 2 was centered on a semi-structured group conversation to check the mood of the participants; Part 3 focused on a Paris Suburbs Cycling tour through 360° videos[2]; and Part 4 ended with some experience evaluation and feedback. Moreover, throughout the experience, Parisian music[3] was played in the background to set the mood. The activity was programmed to correspond to the expectations following the parts systematized at Table 1.

Moreover, the experience setting contained: (i) a Virtual reality headset: H.T.C. Vive[4]; (ii) a computer connected to the headset; (iii) a 58-inch L.E.D. Ultra H.D. (4K) Smart T.V. with HDMI connection to the computer; (iv) two cameras; (v) chairs for the observing participants; (vi) an armchair for the testing participant; (vii) a stationary bicycle; and (viii) a fan.

---

[1] Available at: https://youtu.be/HNApxhvK1Hg (Access date: 15-12-2023).

[2] Available at: https://youtu.be/tI3bKRRMAKA (Access date: 15-12-2023).

[3] Available at: https://youtu.be/tkjIYxUf4-M (Access date: 15-12-2023).

[4] Available at: https://vr-compare.com/headset/htcvive (Access date: 15-12-2023).

Table 1. Description of Experiment's Parts.

	Activity	Main Materials	Purpose
Part 1	Eiffel Tower Visit	Armchair, H.M.D.	Adaptation to H.M.D. and virtual reality
Part 2	Semi-structure group conversation	Observation	Check the mood of the participants
Part 3	Paris Suburbs Cycling Tour	Stationary bicycle, H.M.D.	Experience with a sense of movement
Part 4	Overall Feedback	Questionnaire	Evaluation of the overall experience

A questionnaire was developed based on the previously defined research goals, and on a Technology Acceptance Model of Barsasella and colleagues [45] to evaluate the experience – Part 4. It was divided into sample demography, whether participants visited Paris, and satisfaction of use related to the 360° VR experience, with thirteen questions answered using a 5-point Likert scale ranging from strongly disagree to strongly agree (Table 2). From the thirteen questions developed by the aforementioned authors [45], seven (Q2–Q8) were kept although slightly adapted for participants' understanding. The remaining six questions (Q1, Q9–Q13) delved into the significance of evaluating the ease of experiencing content through the H.M.D. compared to viewing it on a Smart T.V. They also explored whether these activities could encourage social interactions and assessed the relevance of all cyclotourism-related data when merging VR technology with this specific subject and target audience.

Table 2. Questionnaire overview on data collection and analysis

Data Collection	Data Analysis	Research Goals
Q1. The experience was easy to see	What are the main factors of virtual reality that influence participants' engagement?	(i) Assess the user experience
Q2. The experience was comfortable (e.g., no sickness)		
Q3. I enjoyed using virtual reality technology	Is virtual reality a useful tool for immersive entertainment for this target audience?	
Q4. I had fun using virtual reality technology		
Q5. My family and friends influenced me to use virtual reality	Are participants influenced by people close to them?	(ii) examine user adoption and motivation
Q6. My caregivers encouraged me to use virtual reality		

(continued)

Table 2. (*continued*)

Data Collection	Data Analysis	Research Goals
Q7. Virtual reality can be a technology capable of improving my state of mind	Is virtual reality a useful tool for improving well-being?	(v) Identify potential therapeutic benefits
Q8. In the future, I would like to use virtual reality to relax my mind		
Q9. The virtual reality experience is good to do tourism	Which are the key features that a virtual reality experience should have to be similar to real tourism?	(iv) Analyze the feasibility of tourism
Q10. The experience of virtual reality, combined with cyclotourism, is an effective way to get to know places in a safe way	What main factors of using virtual reality in cyclotourism contribute to tourism and active and healthy aging?	
Q11. The virtual reality experience on the bike is an effective way to exercise in a safe way		(v) Identify potential therapeutic benefits
Q12. The experience of virtual reality with a bicycle was an enjoyable time for socializing	Can virtual reality enhance sociability behaviors?	(iii) Evaluate social impact
Q13. The virtual reality experience makes me want to share it with my friends and family		

The main purpose of the questionnaire was to answer the research question and the predefined goals regarding the participants' experience, and assess their motivations for adoption, its feasibility for tourism, and identify potential therapeutic benefits. Moreover, as aforementioned, Q6 was unsuitable for the A.G.; thus, it was not considered for their questionnaire.

The qualitative findings, derived from participant feedback during the experience, underwent analysis focusing on key testimonies. Additionally, quantitative data underwent coding and analysis in SPSS. This involved employing descriptive statistics for identified groups, calculating means and standard deviations for each question, and resorting to Spearman's correlation to examine the relationship between age and questions results.

4 Results

The research involved a total of $N = 117$ participants, of whom $N = 114$ were deemed eligible for subsequent analyses. Three participants failed to complete the questionnaire on A.G. – thus not meeting the inclusion criteria. The following sections give a detailed overview of the outcomes of the two groups (i.e., I.G. and A.G.). For further details regarding the data collected, please refer to the published database [46]. The presentation of results and subsequent analysis and discussion are based on this reference.

4.1 Institutionalized Group's Outcomes

Following the application of inclusion criteria, I.G. comprises a total of $N = 57$ participants, with an average age of 77 years, an average age of 79 years, and a standard deviation (S.D.) of 9 years. The age range within this cohort spans from a minimum of 56 years to a maximum of 97 years (Table 3).

Table 3. I.G. demographic characterisation ($n = 57$)

Variable	Example	Frequencies and percentages
I.G. Age group	55–59	$N = 2$ (3.5%)
	60–64	$N = 3$ (5.3%)
	65–69	$N = 6$ (10.5%)
	70–74	$N = 10$ (17.5%)
	75–79	$N = 10$ (17.5%)
	80–84	$N = 8$ (14.0%)
	85–90	$N = 14$ (24.6%)
	90–94	$N = 3$ (5.3%)
	95–99	$N = 1$ (1.8%)
I.G. Gender	Female	$N = 43$ (75.4%)
	Male	$N = 14$ (24.6%)
I.G. Paris prior visit	Yes	$N = 42$ (73.7%)
	No	$N = 15$ (26.3%)

Regarding the questionnaire output, applied at the end of the experiment, it gives an overview regarding the overall enjoyment felt in the previous parts. The mean result for each question is always near 5 points, i.e., participants' agreement with the questions' statements is near the strongly agree (Fig. 1). Nonetheless, it is important to highlight questions number 3, 4, 9, 11, 12 and 13, which had a score of exactly 5 points. Therefore, the sense of enjoyment and fun (Q3 and 4) were particularly important for the participants. Moreover, the perception of using VR for tourism is very good (Q9), being also a good way to exercise safely when combined with a bicycle (Q11). It should also be emphasized that the social aspect has a very important role for older adults, as they found this experience an enjoyable time for socializing (Q12), and they expressed a desire to share it with their friends and family (Q13).

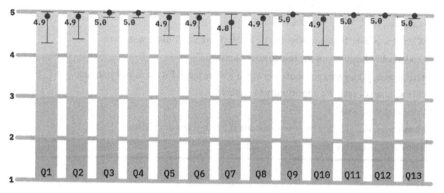

Fig. 1. I.G., Part 4 outcomes: mean and standard deviation.

Additionally, the results of the Spearman's correlation coefficient revealed that there was no significant correlation between age and the posed questions, except for Q5 – which presented a correlation coefficient value of 0.5 [47].

Simultaneously, and as previously mentioned, observations were also collected throughout all parts of the experiment. Thus, it was possible to observe that, at the beginning of the experience, I.G. showed an initial reluctance towards the technology, which appeared to be associated with a limited understanding of the presented setting. In certain groups, the caregiver's proactive involvement played a pivotal role in overcoming this initial resistance. After the visual presentation featuring the Eiffel Tower, the group promptly expressed an eagerness to engage in the activity. Following the experiment, participants in the I.G. reported a sense of surprise and novelty, describing the experience as if they were genuinely present at the presented location. Some participants even initiated conversations with wax figures resembling Gustave Eiffel and Thomas Edison, appearing at some point in the video. Furthermore, certain groups spontaneously began constructing narratives around individual participants' remarks, and in instances where participants had familial ties to France, they recounted life memories associated with their lives.

No motion sickness was observed during the experiment. Moving on to the experiment's Part 3, the participants who took the initiative in performing this activity were the ones with no signs of physical impairments. Besides, these same participants influenced the others to further engage in the experiment. Some of the replies are systematized on Table 4.

Lastly, a noteworthy case involved a female participant with mobility impairments who initially declined to participate due to her inability to walk. Encouraged by her peers, she eventually overcame her reluctance and actively participated in the cycling experience.

Table 4. Feedback of I.G.

I.G. Group
"It's even hard to go back to the real world. It's really cool."
"Worth it (...) I really felt like I was there."
"Is all this Paris? We are so lucky!"
"When it was over I was surprised to be in the room, it felt like I was there."
"I had already heard about the tower, now I know it!"
"That's exactly how you see the tower when you're there. I want to go back there."
"Oh cool... and I take the opportunity to exercise."
"I'm going at speed!"
"I don't even like riding a bike, but this one is much more interesting."
"Being able to do this is very good for self-esteem."

Moreover, it was also observed that the participants were enthusiastic about creating narratives around the bicycling tour, saying things like, "You got a ticket. Our institution is not going to pay", or inventing that someday they will pull over the cycle and go shopping in Paris. This gamification of the experiment naturally emerged as a prevalent practice within the group dynamics (Fig. 2).

Fig. 2. A Experiment Part 3: Paris Suburbs Cycling Tour: Experience with a sense of movement using a stationary bicycle, H.M.D.

4.2   Active Group Outcomes

Regarding A.G., it comprises a total of N = 57 participants with an average age of 44 years, and a standard deviation (S.D.) of 15 years. The A.G. youngest participant was 20 years old, and the oldest one was 77 years old (Table 5).

Table 5. A.G. demographic characterisation (n = 57)

Variable	Example	Frequencies and percentages
A.G. Age group	20–24	N = 7 (12.3%)
	25–29	N = 7 (12.3%)
	30–34	N = 5 (8.8%)
	35–39	N = 2 (3.5%)
	40–44	N = 3 (5.3%)
	45–49	N = 8 (14.0%)
	50–54	N = 10 (17.5%)
	55–59	N = 9 (15.8%)
	65–69	N = 1 (1.8%)
	70–74	N = 3 (5.3%)
	75–79	N = 2 (3.5%)
A.G. Gender	Female	N = 43 (75.4%)
	Male	N = 14 (26.6%)
A.G. Paris prior visit	Yes	N = 25 (43.9%)
	No	N = 32 (56.1%)

Regarding the questionnaire feedback, overall, the participants felt the experience was positive (Fig. 3). Nonetheless, it is important to highlight that some of the results are not as uniform as the ones presented in the previous section. Thus, Q5, regarding the influence of family and friends on using virtual reality, shows that there is a tendency for the value to be closer to 3, i.e., neutral. However, when paying close attention to its standard deviation, it is possible to observe that there are very divergent results. The remaining questions have all a mean above 4, with special emphasis on questions Q1 – related to the ease of seeing the experience through the H.M.D.; Q3 – focused on the enjoyment felt; and Q4 – regarding the fun experienced throughout the contact with virtual reality.

Additionally, the Spearman's correlation coefficient results revealed no significant correlation between age and the posed questions, thus suggesting that the results are independent of participants' age.

Similarly, to the previous group, observations were also collected throughout all parts of the experiment. Thus, it was observed that the participants were very curious about the technology, often asking technical questions regarding the design of the experiment – e.g., if there is a computer supporting the visualization, how the 360° videos are recorded,

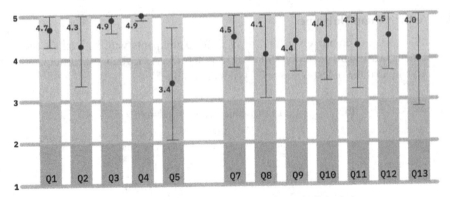

Fig. 3. A.G., Part 4 outcomes: mean and standard deviation.

or if the bicycle pedals control the speed of the video. Additionally, some participants reported motion sickness in the first moments of the experiments, but none gave up on the first part of experiment.

Regarding Part 3, the experiment with the bicycle, some participants expressed confusion and frustration due to the system's inability to turn right and left (reports systematized in Table 6). The creation of narratives around the traveling moment with the bicycle was also a verified within this group.

Table 6. Feedback of A.G.

A.G. Group
"But it's already over? Could last longer..."
"It would be so nice to have scents associated, like the iron of the Eiffel Tower."
"How I missed these buildings."
"What a pity the sound is not immersive."
"It really seems like I'm the one who influences the bike's movement."
"I want to turn and break, but I can't."
"It is an opportunity to discover new places if you have vertigo and fear of flying."
"Great way to exercise while getting to know new places."
"It's even hard to go back to the real world."
"This is the future!"

Overall, both groups shared positive feedback regarding the use of 360° VR to perform digital traveling. The following section discusses the experience's main findings, emphasizing the intersection of the results obtained and the available literature, and answering the research goals.

5 Discussion

This paper has presented a tourism-based 360° VR experience while aiming to answer the research question – i.e., "What is the experience of institutionalized adults and active ones to 360° Immersive videos?" –, and the five pre-defined goals presented on the introductory chapter – i.e., (i) assess the user experience: (ii) examine user adoption and motivation; (iii) evaluate social impact; (iv) analyze feasibility for tourism; and (v) identify potential therapeutic benefits. Once the various goals have been addressed, the research question is naturally fulfilled – please refer to Table 2, as it crosses the questions posed during data collection and the research goals.

Regarding the first goal, multiple previous research have shown that VR can provide a positive user experience – whether with older adults [48, 49], or in the tourism context [50, 51]. Corroborating these results, the observed data from both groups shows that the user experience was extremely positive, highlighting the positive feedback on ease of seeing (Q1), enjoyment (Q3), and fun (Q4). In fact, technological advances have played a key role in these results, guaranteeing greater immersion and Presence [41, 52, 53]. Nonetheless, Q2 on A.G. has a slightly lower score, with higher standard-deviation, since during part 1 of the experiment, some participants reported motion sickness in the first moments. These results were unexpected, since there was a preconceived idea that older adults would experience it more. However, it is important to emphasize that the experiment settings may have influenced the occurrence of motion sickness – as highlighted by Potter and colleagues [43], sitting in the direction of movement may help to maintain a stable body position and reduce the occurrence of nausea.

Proceeding to the second goal, it's worth mentioning that the A.G. did not answer one question as it didn't align with their reality. It seems evident that the I.G. has a strong influence from their peers when it comes to using VR technology. From the researchers' experience of extensive contact with older people, these results were to be expected since institutions define the daily routine and activities of their patients. From the perspective of integrating this VR technology into virtual tourism while targeting wider audiences, it is important to emphasize the need for a moment of encouragement between peers and sharing of experiences.

Turning to social impact assessment with the third goal, the aim was to understand whether VR can motivate social behaviors. Throughout the two groups – I.G. and A.G., spontaneous rules and forms of play were created. For example, during the cyclotourism experience, participants often created rules for engaging in the virtual world – e.g., following the traffic rules to navigate the Paris streets, as well as penalties in case of broken rules –; and stories. These results reinforce what was previously verified by Salen and Zimmerman [54]: arbitrary signs may gain value through a common convention shared among players, amplifying the possibility of creating group gameplay strategies and mechanics. In addition to these moments of co-creation, there was a visible sharing of the experience with peers in the I.G. group, also encouraging experimentation. These results corroborate the findings of other research studies [55–57], in which peer support influences the use of I.C.T.

Analyzing the fourth goal – related to the feasibility of VR for tourism – the results corroborate what was found in other studies [41, 52, 53] – i.e., the use of immersive virtual experiences can be a potentially effective strategy for promoting tourism and getting to know new places safely. Setting up the experiment in a way that everyone could try it proved crucial to achieving these results.

Lastly, the fifth goal, related to the identification of potential therapeutic benefits, both physical and psychological, was confirmed in both groups. The I.G. revealed a fairly high score on the questions related to it, ensuring a perceived ability to improve mental state, willingness to use it to relax the mind, and consider it a good way to exercise. These results corroborate what has already been verified [57–60], emphasizing that digital technology and VR can help older populations in the abovementioned fields.

Overall, this research's findings shed a light on innovative pathways to digitize tourism, fostering experiences that not only enrich but also enhance the active and healthy ageing journey. The exploration of virtual reality technology within the context of tourism revealed promising avenues for facilitating engagement, social interaction, and potentially therapeutic benefits among older adults. These insights underline the transformative potential of VR in redefining travel experiences, especially for those facing physical constraints or seeking novel ways to explore and connect with the world.

6 Conclusion

This research experiment further extended current knowledge on 360° VR tourism. Through results collected from the four-part experiment – i.e., (i) visiting the Eiffel Tower, (ii) semi-structured group conversation, (iii) city suburbs cycling tour, and (iv) evaluating the experience and collecting feedback – it was revealed that VR can impact positively digital travel. Therefore, it may be a safe alternative for the tourism industry and aged populations.

Returning to the research question, i.e., "What is the experience of institutionalized adults and active ones to 360° Immersive videos?", it was possible to conclude that the experience proved fruitful on several levels, including high levels of satisfaction and recognition of this technology as an important benefit in tourism. In particular, this form of digital travel can effectively contribute to active and healthy aging, and enhance social behaviors. Additionally, unexpected results were observed, such as creating game strategies to navigate the virtual world and the absence of motion sickness in I.G.

However, some limitations may be considered for this study: (i) a convenience sample was used, which results in group disparities, and the attempt to generalize these outcomes is not ensured; (ii) there may be some participants' bias since there were members from the same social and institutional group; (iii) due to the deep social isolation in which many of the I.G. participants had been for nearly two years – imposed by the pandemic –, their perception of the experience may have been affected when compared to a normal setting; and (iv) the design of the questionnaire tended to lean towards positively framed questions, potentially introducing a bias towards more affirmative responses – thus, future iterations of the questionnaire should incorporate reverse or negatively framed questions.

In future work, experiment improvements may be applied in sample recruitment and destination choice and addons of game elements and destinations' relatable smells and sounds to make it more immersive. Additionally, the extension of the experiment would provide more reliable longitudinal results, which is also something to consider.

Acknowledgments. The authors wish to thank not only the participants of this study but also DigiMedia, the Department of Communication and Art at the University of Aveiro, namely Dr. Ana Cristina Silva, for managing the participants, providing the Virtual Reality room and gadgets to carry out the experience. The study reported in this publication was supported by F.C.T. – Foundation for Science and Technology (Fundação para a Ciência e Tecnologia), I.P. nr. SFRH/BD/143863/2019, nr. 2020.04815. B.D., nr. 2021.06465. B.D., and, DigiMedia Research Center, under the project UIDB/05460/2020, and the project SEDUCE 2.0 - Use of Communication and Information in the miOne online community by senior citizens, funded by F.C.T. – Fundação para a Ciência e a Tecnologia, I.P., COMPETE 2020, Portugal 2020 and European Union, under the European Regional Development Fund, POCI-01-0145-FEDER-031696 SEDUCE 2.0.

Disclosure of Interests. The authors declare no conflict of interest. Informed consent was obtained from all participants involved in the study. Ethical concerns followed Ethics and Deontology Council of the University of Aveiro Ethical Approval for the SEDUCE 2.0 research project POCI-01-0145-FEDER-031696.

References

1. Patterson, I., Balderas, A.: Continuing and emerging trends of senior tourism: a review of the literature. J. Popul. Ageing **13**(3), 385–399 (2018). https://doi.org/10.1007/S12062-018-9228-4

2. Meiners, N.H., Seeberger, B.: Marketing to senior citizens: challenges and opportunities. J. Soc. Polit. Econ. Stud. **35** (2010)

3. Brahms, C.M., Hortobágyi, T., Kressig, R.W., Granacher, U.: The interaction between mobility status and exercise specificity in older adults. Exerc. Sport Sci. Rev. **49**, 15–22 (2021). https://doi.org/10.1249/JES.0000000000000237

4. Rattan, S.I.S.: Healthy ageing, but what is health? Biogerontology **14**, 673–677 (2013). https://doi.org/10.1007/S10522-013-9442-7

5. Taylor, H.O., Taylor, R.J., Nguyen, A.W., Chatters, L.: Social isolation, depression, and psychological distress among older adults. J. Aging Health **30**, 229–246 (2018). https://doi.org/10.1177/0898264316673511

6. WHO: The impact of the COVID-19 pandemic on noncommunicable disease resources and services: results of a rapid assessment, Geneva (2020)

7. Smith, B., Lim, M.: How the COVID-19 pandemic is focusing attention on loneliness and social isolation. Public Health Res. Pract. **30** (2020). https://doi.org/10.17061/phrp3022008

8. Beller, J., Wagner, A.: Loneliness, social isolation, their synergistic interaction, and mortality. Health Psychol. **37**, 808–813 (2018). https://doi.org/10.1037/hea0000605

9. Škare, M., Soriano, D.R., Porada-Rochoń, M.: Impact of COVID-19 on the travel and tourism industry. Technol. Forecast. Soc. Change **163**, 120469 (2021). https://doi.org/10.1016/J.TECHFORE.2020.120469

10. Huang, Y.C., Backman, K.F., Backman, S.J., Chang, L.L.: Exploring the implications of virtual reality technology in tourism marketing: an integrated research framework. Int. J. Tour. Res. **18**, 116–128 (2016). https://doi.org/10.1002/JTR.2038

11. Yung, R., Khoo-Lattimore, C.: New realities: a systematic literature review on virtual reality and augmented reality in tourism research. Curr. Issue Tour. **22**, 2056–2081 (2019). https://doi.org/10.1080/13683500.2017.1417359

12. Milgram, P., Drascic, D., Grodski, J., Restogi, A., Zhai, S., Zhou, C.: Merging real and virtual worlds. In: Proceedings of IMAGINA 1995, Monte Carlo (1995)

13. Floridi, L.: The philosophy of presence: from epistemic failure to successful observation. Presence Teleoper. Virtual Environ. **14**, 656–667 (2005). https://doi.org/10.1162/105474605 775196553

14. Slater, M., Wilbur, S.: A framework for immersive virtual environments (FIVE): speculations on the role of presence in virtual environments. Presence Teleoper. Virtual Environ. **6**, 603–616 (1997). https://doi.org/10.1162/PRES.1997.6.6.603

15. Huang, J., Chen, Z., Ceylan, D., Jin, H.: 6-DOF VR videos with a single 360-camera. In: 2017 IEEE Virtual Reality (VR), pp. 37–44. IEEE (2017). https://doi.org/10.1109/VR.2017. 7892229

16. Serino, S., et al.: Picture interpretation test (PIT) 360°: an innovative measure of executive functions. Sci. Rep. **7**, 16000 (2017). https://doi.org/10.1038/s41598-017-16121-x

17. Ventura, S., Brivio, E., Riva, G., Baños, R.M.: Immersive versus non-immersive experience: exploring the feasibility of memory assessment through 360° technology. Front. Psychol. **10** (2019). https://doi.org/10.3389/fpsyg.2019.02509

18. Lee, Y.-C.N., Shan, L.-T., Chen, C.-H.: System development of immersive technology theatre in museum. Presented at the (2013). https://doi.org/10.1007/978-3-642-39420-1_42.

19. Suh, A., Prophet, J.: The state of immersive technology research: a literature analysis. Comput. Hum. Behav. **86**, 77–90 (2018). https://doi.org/10.1016/j.chb.2018.04.019

20. Creed, C., Al-Kalbani, M., Theil, A., Sarcar, S., Williams, I.: Inclusive AR/VR: accessibility barriers for immersive technologies. Univers. Access Inf. Soc. (2023). https://doi.org/10.1007/s10209-023-00969-0

21. Peck, T.C., McMullen, K.A., Quarles, J.: DiVRsify: break the cycle and develop VR for everyone. IEEE Comput. Graph. Appl. **41**, 133–142 (2021). https://doi.org/10.1109/MCG. 2021.3113455

22. Crabb, M., Clarke, D., Alwaer, H., Heron, M., Laing, R.: Inclusive design for immersive spaces. Des. J. **22**, 2105–2118 (2019). https://doi.org/10.1080/14606925.2019.1594934

23. Munafo, J., Diedrick, M., Stoffregen, T.A.: The virtual reality head-mounted display Oculus Rift induces motion sickness and is sexist in its effects. Exp. Brain Res. **235**, 889–901 (2017). https://doi.org/10.1007/s00221-016-4846-7

24. Coxon, M., Kelly, N., Page, S.: Individual differences in virtual reality: are spatial presence and spatial ability linked? Virtual Real. **20**, 203–212 (2016). https://doi.org/10.1007/s10055-016-0292-x

25. Alelis, G., Bobrowicz, A., Ang, C.S.: Comparison of engagement and emotional responses of older and younger adults interacting with 3D cultural heritage artefacts on personal devices. Behav. Inf. Technol. **34**, 1064–1078 (2015). https://doi.org/10.1080/0144929X.2015.1056548

26. Lin, J.-H.T.: Fear in virtual reality (VR): fear elements, coping reactions, immediate and next-day fright responses toward a survival horror zombie virtual reality game. Comput. Hum. Behav. **72**, 350–361 (2017). https://doi.org/10.1016/j.chb.2017.02.057

27. Williams, P., Hobson, J.P.: Virtual reality and tourism: fact or fantasy? Tour. Manag. **16**, 423–427 (1995). https://doi.org/10.1016/0261-5177(95)00050-X

28. Verma, S., Warrier, L., Bolia, B., Mehta, S.: Past, present, and future of virtual tourism-a literature review. Int. J. Inf. Manag. Data Insights **2**, 100085 (2022). https://doi.org/10.1016/j.jjimei.2022.100085

29. Sigala, M.: New technologies in tourism: from multi-disciplinary to anti-disciplinary advances and trajectories. Tour. Manag. Perspect. **25**, 151–155 (2018). https://doi.org/10.1016/j.tmp. 2017.12.003

30. Tussyadiah, I.P., Wang, D., Jung, T.H., tom Dieck, M.C.: Virtual reality, presence, and attitude change: empirical evidence from tourism. Tour. Manag. **66**, 140–154 (2018). https://doi.org/ 10.1016/j.tourman.2017.12.003

31. Dickinson, J.E., Ghali, K., Cherrett, T., Speed, C., Davies, N., Norgate, S.: Tourism and the smartphone app: capabilities, emerging practice and scope in the travel domain. Curr. Issue Tour. **17**, 84–101 (2014). https://doi.org/10.1080/13683500.2012.718323
32. Oliveira, T., Martins, M.F.: Information technology adoption models at firm level: review of literature. In: 4th European Conference on Information Management and Evaluation, ECIME 2010, pp. 312–322 (2010)
33. Wang, Y., Fesenmaier, D.R.: Towards understanding members' general participation in and active contribution to an online travel community. Tour. Manag. **25**, 709–722 (2004). https://doi.org/10.1016/j.tourman.2003.09.011
34. Amaro, S., Duarte, P.: An integrative model of consumers' intentions to purchase travel online. Tour. Manag. **46**, 64–79 (2015). https://doi.org/10.1016/j.tourman.2014.06.006
35. Serra Cantallops, A., Salvi, F.: New consumer behavior: a review of research on eWOM and hotels. Int. J. Hosp. Manag. **36**, 41–51 (2014). https://doi.org/10.1016/J.IJHM.2013.08.007
36. Brandt, T., Bendler, J., Neumann, D.: Social media analytics and value creation in urban smart tourism ecosystems. Inf. Manag. **54**, 703–713 (2017). https://doi.org/10.1016/J.IM.2017.01.004
37. Buhalis, D., Harwood, T., Bogicevic, V., Viglia, G., Beldona, S., Hofacker, C.: Technological disruptions in services: lessons from tourism and hospitality. J. Serv. Manag. **30**, 484–506 (2019). https://doi.org/10.1108/JOSM-12-2018-0398/FULL/XML
38. Buhalis, D., Sinarta, Y.: Real-time co-creation and nowness service: lessons from tourism and hospitality **36**, 563–582 (2019). https://doi.org/10.1080/10548408.2019.1592059
39. Guttentag, D.A.: Virtual reality: applications and implications for tourism. Tour. Manag. **31**, 637–651 (2010). https://doi.org/10.1016/J.TOURMAN.2009.07.003
40. Martins, J., Gonçalves, R., Branco, F., Barbosa, L., Melo, M., Bessa, M.: A multisensory virtual experience model for thematic tourism: a Port wine tourism application proposal. J. Destin. Mark. Manag. **6**, 103–109 (2017). https://doi.org/10.1016/J.JDMM.2017.02.002
41. Jung, T., Dieck, M.C.T., Moorhouse, N., Dieck, D.T.: Tourists' experience of virtual reality applications. In: 2017 IEEE International Conference on Consumer Electronics, ICCE 2017, pp. 208–210 (2017). https://doi.org/10.1109/ICCE.2017.7889287
42. Gao, B.W., Zhu, C., Song, H., Dempsey, I.M.B.: Interpreting the perceptions of authenticity in virtual reality tourism through postmodernist approach. Inf. Technol. Tour. **24**, 31–55 (2022). https://doi.org/10.1007/S40558-022-00221-0
43. Potter, L.E., Carter, L., Coghlan, A.: Virtual reality and nature based tourism: an opportunity for operators and visitors. In: Proceedings of the 28th Australian Conference on Computer-Human Interaction, pp. 652–654. Association for Computing Machinery, New York (2016). https://doi.org/10.1145/3010915.3011854
44. Dieck, D., Dieck, M.C., Jung, T., Moorhouse, N.: Tourists' virtual reality adoption: an exploratory study from Lake District National Park **37**, 371–383 (2018). https://doi.org/10.1080/02614367.2018.1466905
45. Barsasella, D., et al.: Opinions regarding virtual reality among older people in Taiwan. In: Proceedings of the 6th International Conference on Information and Communication Technologies for Ageing Well and e-Health, pp. 165–171. SCITEPRESS - Science and Technology Publications (2020). https://doi.org/10.5220/0009425801650171
46. Ribeiro, T., Regalado, F., Ortet, C., Veloso, A.I.: Navigating paris digitally: an exploratory research of 360° immersive videos (2024). https://doi.org/10.7910/DVN/PHGK7C
47. Zar, J.H.: Spearman rank correlation. In: Encyclopedia of Biostatistics. Wiley, Hoboken (2005). https://doi.org/10.1002/0470011815.b2a15150
48. Kim, M.J., Kang, Y.: Older adults' user experience of virtual tourism: exploring presence and experiential value with respect to age difference. Virtual Real. (2023). https://doi.org/10.1007/S10055-023-00849-1

49. Park, S., Lee, H., Kwon, M., Jung, H., Jung, H.: Understanding experiences of older adults in virtual reality environments with a subway fire disaster scenario. Univers. Access Inf. Soc. **22**, 771–783 (2023). https://doi.org/10.1007/S10209-022-00878-8

50. Li, J., Wider, W., Ochiai, Y., Fauzi, M.A.: A bibliometric analysis of immersive technology in museum exhibitions: exploring user experience. Front. Virtual Real. **4** (2023). https://doi.org/10.3389/FRVIR.2023.1240562

51. Baker, J., Nam, K., Dutt, C.S.: A user experience perspective on heritage tourism in the metaverse: empirical evidence and design dilemmas for VR. Inf. Technol. Tour. **25**, 265–306 (2023). https://doi.org/10.1007/S40558-023-00256-X

52. Potter, L.E., Carter, L., Coghlan, A.: Virtual reality and nature based tourism. In: Proceedings of the 28th Australian Conference on Computer-Human Interaction - OzCHI 2016, pp. 652–654. ACM Press, New York (2016). https://doi.org/10.1145/3010915.3011854

53. Schiopu, A.F., Hornoiu, R.I., Padurean, M.A., Nica, A.-M.: Virus tinged? Exploring the facets of virtual reality use in tourism as a result of the COVID-19 pandemic. Telemat. Inform. **60**, 101575 (2021). https://doi.org/10.1016/j.tele.2021.101575

54. Salen, K., Zimmerman, E.: Rules of play: game design fundamentals. Int. J. Artif. Intell. Tools **9** (2004)

55. Kim, S., Gajos, K.Z., Muller, M., Grosz, B.J.: Acceptance of mobile technology by older adults: a preliminary study. In: Proceedings of the 18th International Conference on Human-Computer Interaction with Mobile Devices and Services, MobileHCI 2016, pp. 147–157 (2016). https://doi.org/10.1145/2935334.2935380

56. Wang, L., Rau, P.L.P., Salvendy, G.: Older adults' acceptance of information technology. Educ. Gerontol. **37**, 1081–1099 (2011). https://doi.org/10.1080/03601277.2010.500588

57. Høeg, E.R., et al.: Buddy biking: a user study on social collaboration in a virtual reality exergame for rehabilitation. Virtual Real. (2023). https://doi.org/10.1007/S10055-021-005 44-Z

58. Kim, J., Lee, J., Kim, Y., Nuseibeh, B., Han, S.: The effects of a nature-based virtual reality program on emotional health and quality of life among older adults with dementia. Am. J. Health Behav. **47**, 3–12 (2023). https://doi.org/10.5993/AJHB.47.1.1

59. Restout, J., et al.: Fully immersive virtual reality using 360° videos to manage well-being in older adults: a scoping review. J. Am. Med. Dir. Assoc. **24**, 564–572 (2023). https://doi.org/10.1016/J.JAMDA.2022.12.026

60. Kim, H., Kim, G., Kim, Y., Ha, J.: The effects of ICT-based interventions on physical mobility of older adults: a systematic literature review and meta-analysis. Int. J. Clin. Pract. **2023**, 1–23 (2023). https://doi.org/10.1155/2023/5779711

Research on Adaptive Interface Warning Information Design for Situational Awareness

Dapeng Wei[1], Shijun Ge[1(✉)], Chi Zhang[1], Yuxuan Wang[1], Long Lin[1], and Yi Zhou[2]

[1] Beijing Institute of Technology, Beijing 100081, China
3120215892@bit.edu.cn
[2] Applied Technology College of Soochow University, Suzhou 215325, China

Abstract. This research concentrates on the elderly user group, proposing an innovative dynamic adaptive visualization mechanism within the realm of in-vehicle human-machine interface (HMI). The essence of this mechanism is the real-time analysis of users' cognitive states, utilizing advanced adaptive algorithms for the intelligent encoding and dynamic adjustment of interface information. This design allows for the flexible variation of interface elements based on the users' cognitive load and specific task requirements, while also providing real-time feedback on user operations, effectively enhancing the situational awareness (SA) of elderly users. The study not only delves into the technical aspects of this adaptive interface design but also empirically examines its effectiveness in enhancing the situational awareness of the elderly user demographic. The findings indicate that this mechanism significantly improves attention distribution, information processing, and decision-making response capabilities among elderly users during in-vehicle HMI interactions, thereby enhancing their overall driving safety.

Keywords: Human-Machine Interaction · Adaptive Interface · Aging-Friendly Design · Situational Awareness

1 Introduction

The continuous growth of the elderly population has become a global trend. Particularly in the realm of transportation, the number of older adults relying on private vehicles is expected to increase. However, with advancing age, there is a general decline in cognitive abilities, vision, reaction time, and attention, especially in perception, comprehension, and prediction skills, which directly impact the situational awareness and driving safety of older adults. In complex traffic environments, elderly drivers may find it challenging to effectively perceive and process surrounding information, especially in emergency situations.

In comparative studies, researchers like McFee employed the Wechsler Memory Scale to examine the response times of older adults (average age 64) versus younger adults (average age 22.6) in retrieving and downloading 14 types of road warning signs in an online environment. Findings indicate that the average response time for the elderly group was 1750 ms [1], significantly slower compared to the 1125 ms of the younger

© The Author(s), under exclusive license to Springer Nature Switzerland AG 2024
Q. Gao and J. Zhou (Eds.): HCII 2024, LNCS 14726, pp. 279–296, 2024.
https://doi.org/10.1007/978-3-031-61546-7_18

group. Under time pressure, older participants exhibited notable difficulties in making accurate judgments and struggled with handling multiple task simultaneously [2]. Additionally, another study compared the responses of university students (average age 20.1) and older drivers (average age 46.4) to various emergency situations in hazardous road scenarios. The experiment set up two types of emergencies: one involving a pair of circular red objects simulating brake lights in the middle of the road, and the other featuring random appearances of red humanoid figures at the roadside. This experiment involved two types of distractions: participants had to perform specific actions and answer questions of varying difficulty while engaging in simulated driving. The results showed a decline in the ability of older adults to handle complex situations and in their reaction times under distraction as they age [3]. Concurrently, studies across developed countries in Europe, Asia, and North America affirm that elderly drivers do not pose excessive risk or threat to other road users. They are more likely to harm themselves rather than putting others at risk [4]. Therefore, enhancing their situational awareness could improve their road safety and benefit the entire transportation network.

According to existing research, in-vehicle human-machine interaction (HMI) assistive interfaces can address the functional decline and avoidable behaviors of elderly drivers, assisting them in driving activities and enhancing road safety. Musselwhite and Haddad note that elderly individuals are quite receptive to in-vehicle interaction methods that aid in driving [5], showing a slight preference for technologies that provide feedback rather than those that reduce workload. This underscores that the evolution of in-vehicle interaction design offers new avenues for enhancing the driving capabilities of older drivers. By designing more intuitive and easy-to-understand interfaces, elderly drivers can be effectively assisted in better understanding vehicle status and the surrounding environment, thereby improving their situational awareness. For example, simplified interface designs and larger font displays can help older individuals recognize important information more quickly [6].

Furthermore, with the emergence of novel interaction technologies, adaptive interaction design mechanisms demonstrate great potential in the automotive HMI field. Such designs not only cater to specific user needs but can also dynamically adjust according to different driving environments and scenarios, thus offering more personalized support for elderly drivers.

This study focuses on exploring warning information as an example to investigate its application in adaptive design, particularly in how to encode this information to enhance the situational awareness of the elderly. By analyzing the characteristics of elderly drivers' situational awareness in different road traffic environments, this paper aims to provide important references for future research in adaptive vehicle-human interaction design. By combining theoretical research and practical testing, we hope to provide a safer and more intuitive driving experience for elderly drivers and to offer new insights into the field of adaptive human-machine interaction design.

2 Related Work

2.1 Adaptive Mechanisms in Human-Machine Interaction Interfaces

Research on the value of information and guidance of user attention in adaptive interfaces is scarcely reported in the literature. Adaptive interface design involves collecting personalized user data and real-time task characteristics (input layer), employing established information organization strategies (strategy layer), and constructing specific user interfaces in real-time during human-machine interaction phases (output layer) [7]. This approach emphasizes individual user differences and the task-specific characteristics of interface information. Reflecting on adaptive mechanisms, scholars have proposed the 'Taxonomy of Adaptations', which includes modification of function allocation, modification of task scheduling, modification of interaction, and modification of content. This demonstrates the immense potential of adaptive mechanisms to optimize visualization outcomes from a structural standpoint [8] (Fig. 1).

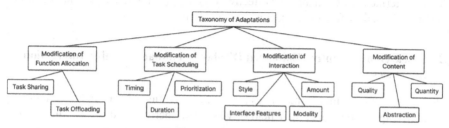

Fig. 1. Taxonomy of Adaptations

The objective of adaptive interfaces is to dynamically adjust interaction interfaces to optimize user experience and information processing efficiency through real-time analysis and response to user behavior, preferences, and environmental changes. The essence of this mechanism is to comprehensively utilize user interaction data, such as eye-tracking, operational habits, and reaction times, to identify user needs and preferences. This data is collected in real-time through the input layer, then processed in the strategy layer using preset rules or learning algorithms, forming effective information organization strategies. Based on these strategies, the system can construct and adjust user interfaces in real-time on the output layer, such as changing the layout and modifying the presentation of information, to meet current user needs. The design of adaptive interfaces encompasses not only the physical display of information but also a deep understanding of users' psychological cognitive states and task characteristics, ensuring effective information transmission and rational guidance of user attention. In complex monitoring environments, such as rail transport control or aerospace systems, adaptive mechanisms enhance the speed and accuracy of information acquisition and reduce cognitive load by precisely analyzing users' attention behavior and task progress characteristics, thereby improving the overall efficiency and safety of the system.

Current adaptive interface decision models are often based on deep learning algorithms of user habit data or recognition of interface characteristics, such as intelligent menu displays, smartphone app recommendations, recent usage inductions, and regional intelligent cursors. These models, designed for traditional display interaction environments, fail to adequately track user monitoring behavior and the progression of tasks in monitoring missions, potentially disrupting real-time psychological expectations and causing loss of attention and confusion in information understanding [9]. A reasonable decision model needs to analyze user attention decision behavior and synchronize task progression characteristics, predicting and guiding user attention behavior. This requires building a comprehensive attention prediction and decision model based on cognitive theory and information theory. Such research will provide theoretical support for the enhancement of human-machine interfaces in elderly driving scenarios and offer effective techniques and tools for the analysis of user attention behavior and situational awareness.

Employing adaptive interface theory in the construction of human-machine interaction interfaces can better reflect the habits and characteristics of elderly driving, identify task progress, signal system risks, and reflect task characteristics. Therefore, researching enhanced display in human-machine interaction interfaces for elderly driving using adaptive interface design theory can effectively address the bottleneck of low situational awareness caused by functional decline in the elderly.

2.2 Research on Adaptive Enhanced Display in Human-Machine Interaction Interfaces

Elderly drivers face primary challenges in cognitive abilities, vision, and reaction speed during driving. As they age, their field of vision may narrow, and their ability to concentrate and process information can slow down, affecting their situational awareness (SA) in complex traffic environments. Situational awareness refers to the driver's ability to perceive, understand, and predict the surrounding environment, which is crucial for ensuring driving safety. In light of this, our study employs an adaptive mechanism oriented towards visualization presentation (Fig. 2). This mechanism requires a thorough consideration of human factors and task status in its final visual display [10].

In this context, using adaptive mechanisms to display warning information on in-vehicle human-machine interaction screens can optimize for the specific needs of elderly drivers. For instance, the adaptive system could adjust the size, contrast, and color of warning messages according to the visual capabilities and cognitive load of elderly drivers, making them easier to recognize and understand. Additionally, the system can dynamically adjust the urgency and presentation of warning messages based on the driving environment and behavior patterns of elderly drivers, such as using more prominent and intuitive visual signals in complex traffic conditions.

Adaptive display of warning information not only enhances the visibility and readability of information but also helps elderly drivers focus more effectively by reducing unnecessary distractions and information overload. This personalized and context-relevant presentation of information is conducive to enhancing the situational awareness of elderly drivers, enabling them to perceive their surroundings more quickly and accurately, and make more appropriate driving decisions. By improving the situational awareness of elderly drivers, adaptive interaction design plays a key role in enhancing road safety and reducing the risk of accidents.

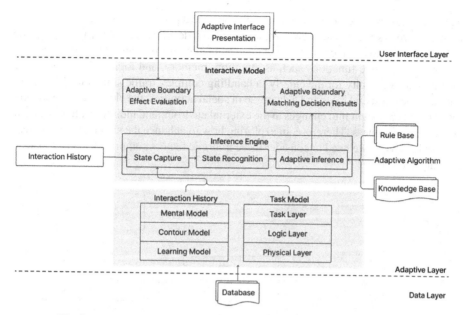

Fig. 2. Adaptive Mechanism Oriented Towards Visualization Presentation

2.3 Situational Awareness

Situational awareness refers to the process through which individuals perceive and understand information and predict subsequent possibilities [11]. Situational information encompasses not only past and present states but also predictions of future trends and the interrelationships between various elements. With increasing age, an individual's situational awareness tends to decline (Fig. 3). This decline is not caused by a single factor but is the result of a combination of physiological, psychological, and social factors. Physiologically, the nervous system and sensory organs of the elderly gradually deteriorate, leading to a weakened ability to receive and process environmental information. Psychologically, cognitive functions such as attention, memory, and thinking ability are affected, reducing their perception and understanding of situations. Additionally, changes in social roles and reduced social activities may make the elderly less sensitive to changes in the external environment. As they age, the challenges faced by elderly drivers in the driving process become increasingly prominent, primarily focused on the gradual decline in cognitive abilities, visual function, and reaction speed. Specifically, in the aging process, an individual's field of vision may narrow, directly affecting the driver's comprehensive observation of the surroundings. Concurrently, a decline in concentration and information processing efficiency may make it difficult to make rapid and accurate judgments in constantly changing traffic conditions. These changes collectively affect the situational awareness of the elderly - the ability to perceive, deeply understand, and accurately predict elements in the driving environment, which is a crucial factor for ensuring driving safety.

A deeper analysis of this trend reveals that the decline in situational awareness is not caused by a single factor, but rather is the result of the interplay of complex physiological, psychological, and social factors. From a physiological perspective, as age increases, the human nervous system and sensory organs inevitably degenerate, directly weakening the elderly's ability to receive and interpret environmental information. Psychologically, the decline in cognitive functions such as attention, memory, and logical thinking further increases the difficulty for the elderly in handling complex traffic situations. Moreover, with changes in social roles and a decrease in social activities, the elderly may gradually lose their keen insight into changes in the external environment, indirectly affecting their situational awareness. Therefore, in exploring how to enhance the situational awareness of elderly drivers, we need to consider these multiple factors comprehensively and seek holistic solutions.

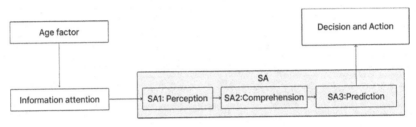

Fig. 3. Flowchart of the Impact of Age on Situational Awareness

3 Method

This study employed a comprehensive subjective assessment approach for the participants, utilizing two commonly used subjective measurement methods: NASA-TLX and 3D-SART12.

3.1 NASA-TLX Scale

In the fields of human-machine interaction, psychology, and ergonomics, the NASA-TLX scale has become an authoritative tool for measuring individual subjective workload during task execution due to its multidimensional and comprehensive assessment approach. Originating from in-depth research by the National Aeronautics and Space Administration (NASA), the scale aims to quantitatively assess the cognitive and physical burden experienced by operators while performing a variety of tasks.

The core structure of NASA-TLX consists of six dimensions: mental demand, physical demand, temporal demand, effort, performance, and frustration level. These dimensions collectively establish a comprehensive and detailed framework for workload assessment. Mental demand reflects the challenge a task poses to an individual's attention and information processing capabilities; physical demand indicates the physical movement and muscular strain required by the task; temporal demand reveals the control over speed and rhythm imposed by the task; effort represents the degree of engagement an individual invests in task execution; performance directly relates to the quality and efficiency of task completion; and frustration level captures the difficulties and setbacks encountered during task execution.

The advantage of this multidimensional assessment method lies in its ability to reveal the true nature of workload in complex tasks more accurately. Traditional single workload indicators, such as task difficulty or time pressure, often provide limited perspectives. In contrast, NASA-TLX integrates multiple dimensions, offering researchers a more comprehensive and in-depth insight into workload.

Besides its multidimensionality, NASA-TLX is also renowned for its flexibility. The dimensions of the scale are not fixed but can be adjusted or reweighted according to specific research contexts and requirements. This flexibility enables NASA-TLX to cater to research needs across various fields, whether in aerospace, automotive driving, medical diagnostics, or human-machine interaction.

A key step in applying NASA-TLX is to require participants to complete it immediately after task completion. This immediacy ensures that the assessment accurately reflects the workload experienced during the task. By comparing NASA-TLX scores across different tasks or conditions, researchers can precisely identify which factors significantly impact workload, thereby providing robust data support for task design and system optimization.

In summary, as a multidimensional, comprehensive, and flexible assessment tool, the NASA-TLX scale plays an irreplaceable role in workload assessment, task analysis, and human-machine interaction design. Its ability to provide deep insights into workload offers a solid theoretical foundation and practical guidance for enhancing system efficiency, optimizing task design, and improving user experience.

Overall, NASA-TLX, as a mature and effective subjective assessment tool, holds broad application prospects in workload assessment, task analysis, and human-machine interaction design. Utilizing NASA-TLX enables researchers to gain a deeper understanding of operators' real feelings and needs during task execution, thus offering robust support for enhancing system efficiency and user experience.

3.2 3D-SART Scale

The 3D-SART (3-Dimensional Situational Awareness Rating Technique) is a convenient and effective measurement tool. In the realm of situational awareness (SA) research, the 3D-SART stands out with its unique three core assessment indicators: Demand (attention resource demand), Supply (attention resource supply), and Understand (degree of situational understanding) [13]. This scale not only provides researchers with a comprehensive and detailed assessment framework but also reveals the psychological state of subjects during task performance through its ingenious scoring method, which is the sum of Supply and Understand minus Demand. Notably, in this study, the 3D-SART scale employs a seven-level grading system, where higher levels correspond to greater situational awareness, providing a solid foundation for quantitative analysis.

The superiority of the 3D-SART scale lies not only in its theoretical framework but also in its practical applicability and effectiveness. The scale is user-friendly and swiftly gathers crucial data from subjects, with its measurement validity rigorously verified to ensure reliability and accuracy of research results.

Moreover, this study innovatively introduces the concept of 'Attention Resource Surplus' (ARS), assessing the surplus of attention resources by calculating the difference between Supply and Demand. This indicator reflects the subject's subjective assessment of the amount of attention resources available beyond task completion, offering researchers a more comprehensive perspective to explore cognitive states during task performance.

Another significant advantage of the 3D-SART scale in measuring situational awareness is its simulation of real three-dimensional environments. Traditional SA assessment tools are often limited to two-dimensional planes or simplified task scenarios, failing to fully capture the cognitive processing of subjects in actual tasks. In contrast, the 3D-SART scale, by incorporating more realistic three-dimensional spatial stimuli, immerses subjects deeper into tasks, allowing for more accurate assessment of their SA. This design not only enhances the ecological validity of the assessment but also makes the research findings more practically applicable.

In addition to realistically simulating three-dimensional environments, the 3D-SART scale also employs a multidimensional assessment approach. It delves into various aspects of the cognitive process, such as attention allocation, information search, and pattern recognition, beyond merely focusing on performance outcomes in spatial tasks. This multidimensional approach more comprehensively reveals subjects' situational awareness capabilities, aiding researchers in identifying potential issues and directions for improvement.

In the application of the 3D-SART scale, its immediacy and accuracy requirements are fully met. Subjects typically complete the scale immediately after task completion, ensuring that the assessment accurately reflects the situational awareness experienced during the task. By comparing assessment results across different tasks or conditions, researchers can precisely identify which factors significantly influence situational awareness, providing strong support for subsequent research and applications.

In summary, the 3D-SART scale, with its realistic simulation of three-dimensional environments, multidimensional assessment method, high flexibility, and expandability, as well as immediate and accurate assessment outcomes, demonstrates exceptional superiority in measuring situational awareness capabilities. It not only offers researchers a comprehensive and profound tool to delve into the psychological state of subjects during task execution but also provides robust support for optimizing task design, enhancing task efficiency, and improving safety.

3.3 Automated Monitoring Tasks

With the continuous advancement of automation technology, the division of labor between humans and machines exhibits diverse characteristics across different levels of automation (Table 1). Particularly in monitoring tasks [14], which represent a critical application domain, the human-machine collaboration model is essential for ensuring system safety, stability, and efficient operation. Especially in monitoring environments with a medium-to-high level of automation, the value of adaptability becomes increasingly prominent, emerging as a core element for optimizing human-machine division of labor and enhancing monitoring quality.

At this level of automation, although monitoring systems are capable of processing a large amount of routine data and information, human wisdom and judgment are still required when facing complex, variable, or unknown monitoring scenarios. Scholars have researched cognitive load mechanisms in adaptive interfaces, highlighting their relationship with the automation process [15]. In this context, effective collaboration and reasonable division of labor between humans and machines become key. The system provides basic monitoring results through real-time data collection and preliminary analysis, while humans validate, adjust, or intervene in the system outputs based on their rich experience and intuitive judgment. This complementary collaboration model helps to enhance the comprehensiveness and accuracy of monitoring.

The introduction of adaptability further strengthens the advantages of human-machine collaboration. Adaptability refers to the system's ability to automatically adjust its behavior in response to changes in the external environment and internal states, adapting to new situations. In monitoring tasks, adaptability manifests as the system's capability to sense changes in the monitoring environment in real time, such as changes in lighting, noise, or target movement, and accordingly automatically adjust monitoring strategies, optimize data processing workflows, and even predict future trends. This dynamic adjustment enhances the system's ability to handle complex scenarios, reducing false alarms and missed alerts, thereby improving monitoring efficiency and safety.

For elderly individuals, the importance of adaptability is even more pronounced [16]. As they age, elderly people may experience declines in cognitive, visual, and auditory abilities, presenting additional challenges in handling monitoring tasks. Therefore, a monitoring system with adaptability can cater to the changing operational habits and capabilities of elderly users, providing personalized interface displays, auditory cues, and decision-making support to reduce their cognitive load and enhance the convenience and accuracy of operations. Simultaneously, the rich life experience and intuitive judgment of elderly individuals can provide valuable supplementary input to the system, creating a mutually beneficial human-machine collaboration.

In conclusion, adaptability plays a pivotal role in the division of labor in monitoring tasks involving human-machine interaction. By optimizing the human-machine collaboration model, enhancing the system's capacity to handle complex scenarios, and meeting the specific needs of elderly users, adaptability contributes to achieving more efficient, safe, and user-friendly monitoring goals.

Table 1. Human-Machine Division of Labor Across Different Levels of Automation

	Grade	Automation Level	Monitor	Mimetic Chronicle	Decision	Execute
unmanned	10	Fully automated	Machine	Machine	Machine	Machine
	9	Supervisory control	Human/Machine	Machine	Machine	Machine
Human main task: monitoring	8	Automatic decision-making	Human/Machine	Human/Machine	Machine	Machine
	7	Rigid System	Human/Machine	Human/Machine	Human	Machine
	6	Mixed decision-making	Human/Machine	Human/Machine	Human/Machine	Machine
Human main tasks: operation+monitoring	5	Assistant Decision	Human/Machine	Human/Machine	Human	Machine
	4	Shared control	Human/Machine	Human/Machine	Human	Human/Machine
	3	Collaborative assistance	Human/Machine	Human	Human	Machine
Human main task: operation	2	Action support	Human/Machine	Human	Human	Human/Machine
	1	Manual	Human	Human	Human	Human

4 Experimental Design

This study is dedicated to exploring the potential utility of adaptive alarm signals in vehicular human-machine interaction interfaces for enhancing the situational awareness of elderly drivers. The research focuses on assessing the impact of three key visual attributes of alarm signals—color, value, and position—on the responses of elderly drivers. These attributes are considered crucial factors affecting information recognition efficiency and driving safety.

4.1 Participant Recruitment

The experimental subjects were 15 elderly drivers aged 55 and above, all of whom held valid driving licenses and had regular driving experience. The selection of this group was to ensure the specificity and applicability of the research results.

4.2 Dependent Variable : Color

In this study, the color of the alarm signals was selected as one of the key dependent variables to investigate its impact on the situational awareness of elderly drivers. We carefully chose five different colors as experimental conditions: FF0000 (pure red), FFF500 (off-white with a yellow tint), 05FF00 (emerald green), 0029FF (deep blue), and 8F00FF (reddish-purple). The distinct visual differences of these colors aid in comprehensively assessing their potential impact on the situational awareness of elderly drivers.

We hypothesize that different colors of alarm signals may produce varying effects in different situational awareness states. For instance, a bright color like pure red might be more effective in attracting the attention of elderly drivers in situations requiring high alertness, thereby enhancing their situational awareness. Conversely, in more relaxed driving environments, softer colors like emerald green or deep blue might be more appropriate, as they would not overly stimulate the driver's visual system.

To test these hypotheses, we will systematically manipulate the color of the alarm signals during the experiment and observe the responses of elderly drivers under different situational awareness states. We will record their reaction times, accuracy, and cognitive load levels measured through the NASA-TLX scale. Additionally, we will collect subjective evaluations from elderly drivers on each color of the alarm signal to understand their preferences and acceptance of different color signals.

By analyzing this data comprehensively, we aim to reveal which color of alarm signal most effectively enhances the situational awareness of elderly drivers. This finding will provide valuable guidance for the design of alarm systems, potentially improving the driving safety and comfort of elderly drivers.

4.3 Dependent Variable:Value

In the experimental design of this study, the value level of the alarm signals was identified as another core independent variable. To systematically investigate the impact of value on the situational awareness of elderly drivers, we divided the value of the alarm signals into five levels: 100%, 80%, 60%, 40%, and 20%. This division aims to cover a wide range from the highest value to lower value levels, thereby simulating various lighting conditions that may be encountered in actual driving environments.

Within our theoretical framework, we hypothesize that the display value of alarm signals directly affects the visual attention and information processing capabilities of elderly drivers. Specifically, higher value levels might quickly attract the driver's attention in the short term, but prolonged exposure to high value could lead to visual fatigue and distraction. Conversely, lower value levels might be more suitable for situations requiring sustained monitoring, as they reduce the risk of visual fatigue but may compromise the ability to immediately capture attention in some urgent situations.

To validate these hypotheses, we will precisely control the value of the alarm signals in a simulated driving environment and record the responses of elderly drivers under different value conditions. Using the NASA-TLX scale and other related indicators, we will assess the specific impact of different value levels on drivers' cognitive load and situational awareness. Additionally, we will collect subjective feedback on value comfort and visibility to more comprehensively understand the acceptance and preferences of elderly drivers towards alarm signals at different value levels.

Through a comprehensive analysis of this data, we aim to reveal the complex relationship between the display value of alarm signals and the situational awareness of elderly drivers. This research will not only enhance our understanding of the visual information processing mechanisms of elderly drivers but also provide important insights for the optimization of alarm systems, aiming to improve driving safety and user experience.

4.4 Dependent Variable : Postion

When investigating the impact of alarm signals on the situational awareness of elderly drivers, the location of the alarm signal on the vehicular interface was identified as a key variable. To comprehensively assess the potential impact of different positions on situational awareness, we categorized the alarm signal locations into five configurations: center, left, right, top, and bottom of the screen.

The center of the screen is generally considered the focal area for attention concentration. Thus, placing the alarm signal here may aid in rapidly capturing the attention of elderly drivers. The left and right positions might show varying degrees of attention dispersion or shift compared to the center. The top and bottom positions might be influenced by visual search strategies and interface layout, requiring further exploration through experimentation.

In the experiment, we will systematically vary the position of the alarm signals and observe the responses of elderly drivers under different positional conditions. By recording reaction times, eye-tracking data, and cognitive load levels measured through the NASA-TLX scale, we aim to reveal the specific impacts of different positions on the situational awareness of elderly drivers. Additionally, we will collect subjective feedback on interface layout and alarm signal positions to more comprehensively understand the acceptance and preferences of elderly drivers towards alarm signals in different locations.

Through a comprehensive analysis of this data, we hope to determine which alarm signal position most effectively enhances the situational awareness of elderly drivers. This finding will provide valuable guidance for the design of vehicular interfaces and the layout of alarm systems, aiming to improve the driving safety and user experience of elderly drivers. Moreover, this will lay a foundation for future research to further explore optimization strategies for interface layouts and alarm signal positions in different driving scenarios and user groups (Fig. 4).

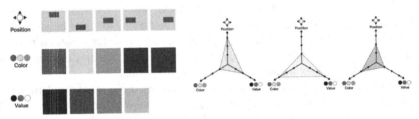

Fig. 4. Adaptive design coding potential solutions

4.5 3D-SART

This study utilized the 3-item version of the Situational Awareness Rating Technique (SART), commonly known as 3D SART. This measurement standard includes the following dimensions: Demand – the need for attentional resources; Supply – the provision of attentional resources; and Understanding – comprehension of the situation. Each question is rated on a scale from 1 to 11. The wording of the items and the endpoints of the scale are indicated in brackets as follows: the situation is (very stable, simple and straightforward, few variables changing - unstable, sudden changes, many interconnected components, many variables changing); attention, my effort is (low vigilance, focused on one aspect, surplus - high vigilance, focused on multiple aspects, no surplus); my understanding of the situation is (fully informed and comprehensively understood, very familiar situation - very limited information/understanding, very novel situation).

4.6 Experimental Procedure

During the preparatory phase of this experiment, we conducted a comprehensive pre-experiment briefing for participants to ensure the accuracy and effectiveness of the experiment. This phase involved explaining the purpose of the experiment, detailing the experimental procedure, and instructing on the use of the NASA Task Load Index (NASA-TLX) scale. This scale was used to assess the cognitive load of participants during the experiment. To simulate different driving scenarios, the experimental conditions were carefully designed, including various versions of alarm signals that differ in color, size, or position. This diversity in design aims to better mimic the range of situations encountered in real driving, ensuring the practical applicability of the experimental results (Fig. 5).

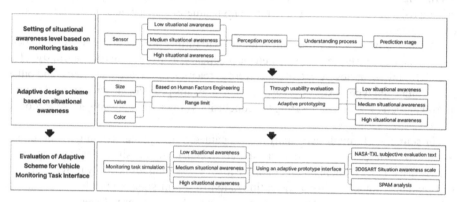

Fig. 5. Experiment Program Based on Adaptive Visualization

During the simulated driving test phase, participants experienced these different versions of alarm signals in a controlled simulated environment. This method allowed us to more effectively evaluate the practical effectiveness of each signal in actual driving situations. Additionally, to comprehensively assess the utility of each alarm signal, the NASA-TLX scale was utilized in the latter part of the experiment to evaluate the cognitive load of participants after experiencing each type of alarm signal. Participants' subjective feedback on the clarity, recognizability, and impact on situational awareness of each signal was also collected. These comprehensive assessments help us to deeply understand the potential utility of different alarm signals in enhancing the situational awareness of elderly drivers and reducing their cognitive load, providing essential baseline data for subsequent data analysis and optimization of alarm signals.

4.7 Data Processing and Analysis

After completing the simulated driving test phase, we conducted an in-depth analysis of the collected data, aiming to evaluate the effectiveness of different versions of alarm signals in enhancing the situational awareness of elderly drivers and reducing their cognitive load.

Firstly, we performed statistical analysis on the results of the NASA-TLX scale. This scale quantitatively assesses participants' cognitive load during the experiment across multiple dimensions, such as mental demand, physical demand, and temporal demand. By comparing the scores obtained by participants after experiencing different alarm signals, we observed that certain versions of alarm signals showed significant advantages in reducing cognitive load. These signals typically had higher contrast and recognizability in terms of color, size, or position, enabling elderly drivers to notice and understand them more quickly.

Secondly, we conducted content analysis on the subjective feedback provided by participants. This feedback pertained to aspects such as the clarity, recognizability, and impact on situational awareness of the alarm signals. Through analyzing this feedback, we found that elderly drivers generally preferred intuitive, straightforward, and non-distracting alarm signals. These signals not only helped them to quickly identify potential driving risks but also aided in maintaining high situational awareness in complex traffic environments.

Additionally, we applied statistical methods to further process and analyze the experimental data. For instance, we evaluated the practical effectiveness of each alarm signal in actual driving scenarios by calculating average reaction times, accuracy rates, and other metrics for each type of signal. These analytical results provided us with more objective and quantified evidence, supporting the conclusions drawn from our subjective feedback analysis.

In summary, through data analysis, we gained a deep understanding of the effectiveness of different versions of alarm signals in enhancing the situational awareness of elderly drivers and reducing their cognitive load. These findings not only provide important guidance for the subsequent optimization of alarm signals but also offer strong support for improving the driving experience and safety of elderly drivers.

5   Conclusion

5.1   Analysis of 3D-SART Scale Results

The 3D-SART scale was used to subjectively evaluate the Situational Awareness (SA) of the participants. The scale assesses SA from three aspects: Demand (attention resource demand), Supply (attention resource supply), and Understanding (comprehension of the situation). Additionally, the Attention Resource Surplus (ARS) was used to reflect the surplus of attention resources available to participants during the task. The descriptive statistical results of the 3D-SART scale scores, including sub dimensions, are presented in Table 2.

In this study, we delved into the relationship between attention resource supply and demand and the role of situational comprehension within this context. Through calculations and analysis of a series of data, we obtained important insights regarding attention resource demand (D), attention resource supply (S), understanding of the situation (U), attention resource surplus (ARS), and the overall situational attention resource state (SA).

Regarding color, 'FF0000' and '8F00FF' showed high SA values, with the highest levels of attention resource surplus. This may be due to both colors being in the warm spectrum, suggesting that warm-colored alarm signals are more likely to capture the attention of elderly users and enhance their situational awareness. However, we also found that yellow and green tones are not suitable as alarm signal colors for elderly drivers, possibly due to age-related decline in their ability to distinguish these colors.

In terms of Value, we obtained results that were quite different from our initial predictions. While we anticipated that a 100% Value would receive the highest weighting, the results indicated otherwise. It appears that an 80% Value in alarm signal brightness enhances the situational awareness of elderly drivers. This could be because a 100% Value might be overly stimulating for elderly users, requiring them to expend more attentional resources for analysis, thereby producing a negative effect.

Regarding the position of the alarm signals, we were surprised to find that when positioned on the left, users' situational awareness was the highest, which contrasts with our prediction of the center position being optimal. This may be due to the display interfaces being located on the right side of drivers, and the eye movement of elderly individuals is not as flexible as younger people, so displaying information in the closest position to their field of vision can help them achieve optimal situational awareness performance (Tables 3, 4 and 5).

Table 2. 3D-SART Weightings for Color Encoding

	FF0000	FFF500	05FF00	0029FF	8F00FF
D	2.34	2.46	2.46	3.0	3.2
	0.9361	0.6308	0.6308	0.1581	0.0707
S	3.38	3.38	3.18	3.12	4.18
	0.8650	0.6977	0.5459	0.3512	0.8222
U	0.94	2.84	1.42	3.8	1.47
	0.4427	0.3493	0.2683	0.4899	0.6285
ARS	1.04	0.92	0.2	0.14	0.98
	1.1972	0.5745	0.9774	0.4387	0.8346
SA	1.96	3.7	2.14	3.94	2.44
	1.2806	0.4583	0.7746	0.5374	0.9165

Note: D = Demand for attention resources; S = Supply of attention resources; U = Degree of situational understanding; ARS = S − D = Attention Resource Surplus; SA = S − D + U; For all measured indicators, Mean (M) is presented above, and Standard Deviation (SD) is presented below

5.2 Analysis Based on the NASA-TLX Scale

In the aforementioned study, we identified the indicators with the highest individual weights. However, in a real interface, multiple elements need to be recombined for a holistic display. Therefore, we combined the top three weighted elements from each category (resulting in 27 different interface combinations) and used the NASA-TLX scale to subjectively evaluate the cognitive load of participants. This approach was adopted to explore the correctness of the preliminary research and to analyze the presentation mechanisms in the design of adaptive interfaces. According to the experimental analysis results, the top three adaptive interface combinations with the highest NASA scale

Table 3. 3D-SART Weightings for Value

	100%	80%	60%	40%	20%
D	2.06	1.7	1.48	1.72	1.7
	0.6285	0.2121	0.2939	0.5767	0.5671
S	3.0	2.8	2.6	2.4	2.36
	0.7906	0.4427	0.3742	0.3742	0.4919
U	2.22	3.42	2.88	2.28	1.94
	0.9747	1.1662	1.0382	0.8974	0.4714
ARS	1.06	1.1	1.12	0.7	0.66
	0.2879	0.4359	0.2939	0.2828	0.3857
SA	3.16	4.52	4.0	2.94	2.6
	0.6285	1.2042	0.9798	0.6992	0.4658

Table 4. 3D-SART Weightings for Position

	center	Left	Right	Top	Bottom
D	2.98	1.86	1.18	1.6	1.18
	0.4060	0.5339	0.0837	0.2828	0.0837
S	4.2	2.4	2.38	2.28	4.18
	0.7958	0.1118	0.2263	0.1643	0.7739
U	1.5	2.82	1.82	1.94	2.58
	0.6225	1.1662	0.3033	0.4447	0.3493
ARS	1.22	0.54	1.2	0.7	3.0
	0.7446	0.6304	0.2236	0.2915	0.7280
SA	2.7	3.36	3.02	2.62	5.58
	0.9798	1.3772	0.3195	0.6443	1.0120

Table 5. Workload Weightings for adaptive interfaces

	Interface 1	Interface 2	Interface 3
workload	10.805	10.864	12.137
	3.141	3.187	3.698

Note: For all measured indicators, Mean (M) is presented above, and Standard Deviation (SD) is presented below

weights are as follows: Interface 1 combines color FF0000, Value 80%, positioned on the left side of the interface; Interface 2 combines FF0000, Value 80%, positioned at the bottom of the interface; and Interface 3 combines FF0000, Value 80%, positioned at the center of the interface.

Based on the results, it is evident that in actual interface design, combining elements with higher adaptive weights can enable users to achieve higher situational awareness and lower workloads, or perceived workloads. This also corroborates the results of the 3D-SART analysis.

6 Conclusion

This study focuses on elderly users, proposing a dynamic adaptive visualization mechanism within vehicular human-machine interaction interfaces. By deeply analyzing users' real-time cognitive states and employing advanced adaptive algorithms for intelligent encoding and dynamic presentation of interface information, the study aims to optimize situational awareness (SA) and task execution efficiency for elderly users.

In our data analysis, we employed the 3D-SART scale for subjective evaluation of participants' SA, assessing from the perspectives of attention resource demand, supply, and comprehension of the situation. The results indicated that certain combinations of colors and positions significantly enhance the SA of elderly users. Particularly, warm colors performed exceptionally well in attracting the attention of elderly users and enhancing situational awareness, while yellow and green hues were found to be less suitable for alarm signal colors. Moreover, a Value of 80% was considered most appropriate for elderly drivers' alarm signal colors, striking a balance between information prominence and cognitive load. Regarding the position of alarm signals, the highest situational awareness was observed when they were placed on the left side of the interface, possibly related to the reduced flexibility in eye movements of elderly users.

To further validate these findings, we combined the top three weighted elements from each category and conducted subjective evaluations of cognitive load using the NASA-TLX scale. The results show that by combining elements with higher adaptive weights, users can achieve higher situational awareness and lower workload. This further confirms the results of the 3D-SART analysis, suggesting that the adaptive interface design mechanism proposed in this study has potential applicability in vehicular human-machine interaction interfaces for elderly users.

In summary, through in-depth data analysis and experimental validation, this study reveals the importance of the relationship between attention resource supply and demand, and the degree of situational understanding in the design of adaptive interfaces for vehicles. Moving forward, these findings can guide further optimization of adaptive algorithms and interface design mechanisms to enhance the safety, comfort, and efficiency of elderly users when interacting with vehicular human-machine interfaces. Moreover, this study provides valuable insights and implications for adaptive interface design tailored to other user groups and application scenarios.

References

1. McPhee, L.C., Scialfa, C.T., Dennis, W.M., Ho, G., Caird, J.K.: Age differences in visual search for traffic signs during a simulated conversation. Hum. Factors **46**(4), 674–685 (2004)
2. Brouwer, W.H., Waterink, W., Van Wolffelaar, P.C., Rothengatter, T.: Divided attention in experienced young and older drivers: lane tracking and visual analysis in a dynamic driving simulator. Hum. Factors **33**(5), 573–582 (1991)
3. Justin, M.O., Richard, L.: The effects of age and distraction on reaction time in a driving simulator. J. Vis. **2**(7), 632a (2002)
4. Maycock, G.: The safety of older car-drivers in the European Union (1997)
5. Musselwhite, C., Haddad, H.: Prolonging the safe driving of older people through technology. Centre Transp. Soc. **155** (2007)
6. Guo, A.W., Brake, J.F., Edwards, S.J., Blythe, P.T., Fairchild, R.G.: The application of in-vehicle systems for elderly drivers. Eur. Transp. Res. Rev. **2**, 165–174 (2010)
7. Norcio, A.F., Stanley, J.: Adaptive human-computer interfaces: a literature survey and perspective. IEEE Trans. Syst. Man Cybern. **19**(2), 399–408 (1989)
8. Feigh, K.M., Dorneich, M.C., Hayes, C.C.: Toward a characterization of adaptive systems a framework for researchers and system designers. Hum. Factors J. Hum. Factors Ergon. Soc. **54**(6), 1008–1024 (2012)
9. Cockburn, A., Gutwin, C., Greenberg, S.: A predictive model of menu performance. In: Proceedings of the SIGCHI Conference on Human Factors in Computing Systems, pp. 627–636 (2007)
10. Langley, P.: User modeling in adaptive interface. In: UM99 User Modeling: Proceedings of the Seventh International Conference, pp. 357–370. Vienna: Springer Vienna (1999). https://doi.org/10.1007/978-3-7091-2490-1_48
11. Endsley, M.R., Garland, D.J.: Theoretical underpinnings of situation awareness: a critical review. Situation Awareness Analy. Measur. **1**(1), 3–21 (2000)
12. Taylor, R.M.: Situational awareness rating technique (SART): the development of a tool for aircrew systems design. In: Situational awareness, pp. 111–128. Routledge (2017)
13. Jeannot, E.: Situation Awareness Synthesis and Literature Search (EEC Note No. 16/00). Eurocontrol Experimental Centre, France (2000)
14. Ponsa Asensio, P., Vilanova, R., Amante García, B.: Human intervention and interface design in automation systems. Int. J. Comput. Commun. Control **6**(1), 166–174 (2011)
15. Hancock, P.A., Chignell, M.H.: Mental workload dynamics in adaptive interface design. IEEE Trans. Syst. Man Cybern. **18**(4), 647–658 (1988)
16. Gonçalves, V.P., et al.: Providing adaptive smartphone interfaces targeted at elderly people: an approach that takes into account diversity among the elderly. Univ. Access Inf. Soc. **16**, 129–149 (2017)

Take Pleasure in One's Old Age-User-Friendly Interface and Functional Design to Meet the Needs of Elderly Tourism

Tingting Xiong[1], Xuyi Li[1], Ruirong Ren[1]([⊠]), and Nanyi Wang[2]

[1] School of Architecture and Design, Nanchang University, Nanchang, China
renruirong77@outlook.com
[2] School of Design and Art, Beijing Institute of Technology, Beijing, China

Abstract. Population aging is an important trend in social development as well as a common global reality. In a digital society, difficulties in applying technology and barriers to accessing information limit elders' travel experience. Although many digital products, including mobile, have been age-adapted under the call of the government and society, many problems still lead to the inability to truly meet the needs of the elderly. In order to narrow this gap, this paper proposes to combine the mental model with the concept of service design and apply it to the elderly-oriented interactive interface of tourism, which can help the elderly plan and participate in tourism activities more pleasantly. First of all, we deeply entered the living field of the elderly as volunteers to conduct observations, interviews, and questionnaires on the elderly group and collate specific data. Afterward, based on the collated data, we constructed the mental model of elderly-oriented tourism interaction design. Finally, combined with the concept of service design, we constructed the modeling frameworks, such as user profile, service system, and user journey, in order to better understand the needs, pain points, and opportunity points in the service process, and then formed a specific plan of interaction design. The results show that this study can realize the elderly orientation and the group intelligence innovation of tourism interaction and also provide reference and inspiration for the fuzzy front-end development of the human-computer interaction interface.

Keywords: Elderly Users · Mental Model · Service Design · Interface Design · Tourism Needs

1 Introduction

Population aging is an important trend of social development, a common status quo faced by the whole world, and an essential feature of the international community for a long period of time in the future. In the information age, since the elderly population has attenuated abilities in vision, hearing, and movement, their speed of acceptance and understanding of new technologies is far less than that of the younger population, so how to provide services to meet the needs of the elderly through well-designed user interfaces and functions will have a far-reaching impact on the aging industry. However, there are many problems with current elderly-oriented interaction apps, such as poor user experience, lack of personalized services, bottlenecks in service content, and lack of technology acceptance. In order to narrow these gaps, many scholars have started to explore the elderly orientation of personalized interaction technologies. For example, Paiva [1] et al. developed some mobile apps focusing on geriatric healthcare and made some suggestions for solutions for elderly health.

Yuan [2] et al. investigated elders' preferences for gamification features in health apps and summarized the functional attributes and the attribute levels of gamification design. The Carnot model was used to determine the elderly-oriented attributes and the attribute levels, and a conjoint analysis was used to obtain the importance of all the attributes and the utility value of the attribute levels. Bastos [3] et al. created a physical activity monitoring system for smart cities to motivate elderly people to achieve a more active lifestyle, which was monitored and adapted by healthcare professionals for optimal results. In past research on elderly-oriented interaction design, more attention was focused on the physical and mental health of the elderly population, which resulted in the birth of numerous health care, medical treatment, and monitoring strategies. With the liberalization of COVID-19, daily travel has also become a pressing need for the elderly population. Kwakye [5] et al. assessed the challenges faced by paratransit services for the elderly population. An interactive Android mobile application was developed to alleviate and significantly encourage vulnerable road users, especially the elderly and disabled, to use paratransit services and improve their travel experience. Lu [6] et al. refined a set of design recommendations for digital accessibility improvement in order to improve the user experience of mobile smart terminals for the elderly, thus increasing the usability and inclusiveness of assistive tools in different contexts and reducing the psychological pressure caused by unfamiliar interfaces, which led to the realization of an accessible design of mobile terminals for the elderly.

Compared with the elderly-oriented travel interaction, the development of elderly-oriented interaction for the elderly population travel is more concerned about the enjoyment and experience of the elderly population. As the elderly begin to shift to a higher level of spiritual needs and have higher expectations for the quality of their lives, traveling has become one of the most important ways to enrich their retirement life, maintain their health, and expand their social circles. The elderly-oriented travel interaction is more focused on helping the elderly plan their trips, book accommodations, find attractions, etc., and there is still a lack of development for such interaction strategies. In this study, we understood the physical and mental needs of the elderly from an interdisciplinary perspective and entered the living field of the elderly as volunteers to conduct observations, interviews, and questionnaires on the elderly group and collate specific data. Afterward, we constructed the mind space of the whole travel process based on the information data and filled in the gaps of the mind space at each stage. In the process of interaction interface design, we combined the concept of service design and drew the user profile, service system map, and user journey map to better understand the needs, pain points, and opportunity points in the service process, and then formed the design scheme. The contributions of this paper are as follows.

In the development of elderly-oriented interaction design, we integrated the mental model and the framework process of service design, such as user profile, user journey map, and service system, to accurately capture the real needs of the elderly group.

We developed an interaction system for the elderly group, which was evaluated and verified to be in line with the elderly-oriented imagery and satisfy the users' emotions.

We proposed a design closure loop of user feedback, design iteration, and reevaluation to ensure that the design solution could better meet the needs and expectations of the elderly so as to provide reference and inspiration for the fuzzy front-end development of the human-computer interaction interface.

2 Research Methodology

2.1 Application of Mental Model in Interaction Design

Kenneth Craik, a British psychologist, first proposed the theory of mental modeling. He considered that the mental model shows a person's thinking process about how something works, such as human perception and understanding of the real world. Through this model, people can make analogies between their observations and impressions of the external world, which can be transformed into relevant knowledge in the human brain so that people can recognize and interpret the world more quickly and efficiently. When people are in unknown or complex environments, based on their experience of past things or even intuition, mental models can be the psychological basis for people to prepare their behavioral activities and influence their approaches to solving problems [7]. Due to the continuity of people's cognitive activities in the outside world, mental models are solidified and updated in this process, showing the characteristics of dynamic development [8].

Donald A. Norman introduced the concept of the mental model into the field of interaction design, and he believed that the internal mental models formed during the interaction between human beings and their environment, technological products, etc., can provide predictive and explanatory capabilities for people to understand interaction, and can accurately reveal the mental activities of users, which is one of the important methods to explore user needs [9]. In his theories of conceptual model and user model, it is pointed out that designers can extract the user's mental model, i.e., analyzing the target user's past experience, behavioral habits, and usage needs, and then transform the acquired mental information through design methods to design an easy-to-understand system interface or system model. Therefore, more and more designers and developers take the acquisition of the target user's mental model as an important basis for user research and guidance of product design and recognize that the closer the system model presented by the product is to the user's mental model, which means that the usability of the product's interactive interface will be higher. Walden, Justin, et al. (2015) [10] interviewed 45 elders about their expectations of human-computer interaction and anticipated need for robots, and the study showed that elders' mental models of robots were shaped by their recent experiences with advanced communication technologies and mediated representations of robots in popular culture. Revell, K. M, et al. (2018) [11] matched 20 pairs of participants by age, gender, and home heating experience to confirm that the design of a home heating interface could positively influence the achievement of home heating goals if it was specifically designed to express how a system of user mental model works.

The rapid speed of the innovation of electronic information technology makes many elders who lack experience in using the internet feel unfamiliar with the system model and the interface of modern electronic products, so they are unable to form a level of mind matching the use of digital products. Therefore, this paper starts with the theory and construction method of the mental model. By understanding the mental model of the elderly group, we analyze the past experiences, behavioral habits, and needs of the elderly when they use digital products such as travel apps so as to achieve an interactive interface design that meets the needs of the elderly group when they travel in a real sense.

2.2 Service Design Thinking in Interaction Design

The study of service design theory originated from the American marketing scientist G. Lynn Shostack (1982) [12], who proposed the concept of service design in management and marketing. According to the concept, he considered that even though services and products are different, there exists a close symbiotic connection between them. In the study of management, according to Theodore Levitt (1981) [13], "services" are classified as "intangible products", and Christian Gronroos (1984) [14] considered that services solve one or more of the behaviors that occur between the customer and the service provider, the tangible product or the service system in an intangible way. In the study of design, the intangible "service design" is required to meet the reasonable and expected needs of customers and to create services that are economical and practical by utilizing existing resources. According to Bill Hollins (1991) [15] in Total Design, the concept of "service design" is articulated based on the subject of design, which explains how to plan and design the intangible product, "Service". Through the specific research of service design theory, people can quickly and effectively carry out continuous design planning and research in various fields, such as information technology, medical services, the internet of Things, entertainment media, etc. "User experience" is the key core of service design. The utilization of user experience constitutes the service system of service design, which can carry out the interactive behavior of value transfer and service transfer through the docking of people and people, people and things. Compared with traditional design, service design requires targeted analysis of users through information technology while collecting relevant data and materials for multi-interested cooperation in order to improve the user service experience.

Dan Saffer (2007) [16] considered interaction design to be the art of facilitating interaction between people through products and services. Service design contains a variety of design analysis methods, such as Personas, in which designers establish a virtual object of data through user profile research and utilize the user characteristics formed by the creation of the virtual object to establish the interaction product, and thus produce an interaction design product with a sense of service. Therefore, service design thinking has received wide attention in the interaction field. Yuan L(2015) [17] proposed the possibility and advantages of combining the scene-based interface with the elderly mobile phones in the service design thinking and summarized the design method to provide new ideas for the future development of the interface design. Long L et al. (2010) [18] proposed the general principle of interaction design for elderly products and constructed the design process of interactive products for the elderly as well as the model of elderly users' participation in product design. A sample study of elderly mobile phone users was carried out by questionnaire survey in service design, and the feedback information on the appearance and function of mobile phones was analyzed to obtain the design model of mobile phones for elderly users. Jeung Jihong et al. (2023) [19] believed that interaction design should fully consider the sensory state of the elderly, as well as adopt simple and friendly interfaces and multimodal interaction. In terms of humanistic care, it is important to focus on the elderly's acceptance of technology and the emotional experience while using it. Reeder, Blaine (2011) [20], by observing the characteristics of the elderly, the resulting personas, design recommendations, and methods of persona construction could be a useful tool for information specialists and system designers. In a word, due to the development of science and technology, most of the apps have neglected the experience of elderly users. The interaction application under service design thinking should be based on Personas, user experience maps, user expectation analysis, service scenarios, service principles, service system maps, service blueprints, and other data to build design strategies in order to help the elderly enjoy the convenience brought by digital, and accelerate the development of the travel app from the current stage of the elderly "don't use" or "usable" to "good to use" and "love to use."

3 Research Process

3.1 Collection of Mental Information of the Elderly Tourism

In the construction of the mental model, first of all, it is necessary to fully obtain the mental information of the target users in the process of using the product, so this paper conducted a preliminary questionnaire survey on the use of travel apps for the elderly over 60 years old, with a total of 14 questions (see in Table 1). A total of 53 valid data were collected in this survey, including 20 males and 33 females. Regarding the education level of the participants, 16 of them were educated at the level of junior high school or below, 25 were educated at the level of senior high school, technical secondary school, and technical school, 8 were educated at the level of junior college, and 4 were educated at the level of undergraduate college or above. In this questionnaire survey, the majority of the participants could operate their smartphones to a simple degree or above, and only 4 of them showed unfamiliarity with the operation of smartphones. However, when they encountered operational difficulties in the process of using smartphones, 42 of them would ask for help from their friends and relatives, and 11 of them would choose to inquire on their own. Regarding the use of travel apps, 22 of them have actually used this type of travel app, 26 of them have not used it, 2 of them have not heard of it, and 3 of them said that they could not operate this type of app. Finally, everyone gave their expectations and suggestions, such as improving information recognition, reducing advertisements, and keeping information safe (see in Fig. 1).

Based on the survey results collected from the questionnaire survey, this paper organized and transformed them into textual data, extracted the high-frequency keywords appearing in the answers, coded them, and refined a total of 25 keyword texts. According-ing to the basic process of product operation, i.e., the download and login process, the

Table 1. Two sets of questions were asked in the survey on the use of travel by the elderly

Personal issues	Travel app related issues
Your gender	How do you usually plan your trip
Your age	Familiarity with smartphone use
Your level of education	How do you solve the problem of smartphone use
Your physical condition	Smartphone use is a common activity
Your job before retirement	Use of travel apps
Your main source of income now	Problems with using travel apps or smartphones
Your travel frequency	Expectations and suggestions for travel app

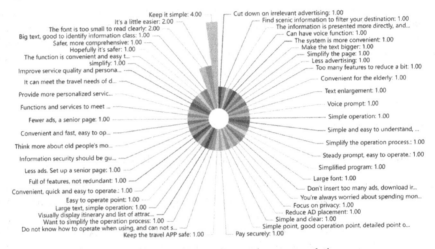

Fig. 1. Travel app expectations and recommendations

operation process, and the tourism process, the semantically similar keywords were summarized and sorted, and the nodes of users' cognition, behavior, and decision-making at different stages while using the travel app were also obtained. Finally, the keyword texts extracted from the survey, regarded as key nodes, correspond to the time sequence of the appearance of the mind nodes in the three stages according to the users' order when operating the product, and thus obtain the three mindsets based on the temporal relationship of A, B, and C (see in Table 2).

In the behavioral analysis of the users, the text data collected from this questionnaire was disassembled by using the disassembly method in causal analysis in order to extract the common and more frequently occurring reasons [21]. For example, the factors for users being unable to find information about attractions (b5) include that the interface has too much irrelevant information (b1), the text is too small, resulting in not being able to recognize the information (b3), the interface is complex (b10), and the process is complicated to operate (b11). In this way, the mutual indexing between nodes was

Table 2. Data encoding and node linking table

Serial number	ID	Data	Node	Link node
1	A1	I'm not familiar with the operation of smartphones	inoperable	A3
2	A2	I didn't know there was a travel app	Will not download the app because of the lack of information channels	A4
3	A3	I only know how to use WeChat and Douyin	Not very familiar with the operation of mobile phone use	A1
4	A4	I don't know how to download	Won't download apps	A2
5	A5	I can't read the login information	Login information not recognized	A6, A7
6	A6	I don't have an account. The kids help	Will not register an account	A5, A7
7	A7	Can't see what I can fill in	Difficulty identifying information	A5, A6, B3
8	A8	It's not safe to fill in that much information	Lack of trust	B9, B12
9	B1	The interface inside is so complicated	Too much irrelevant information	B4, B5
10	B2	I can't operate the interface	Operating difficulty	A3, C5
11	B3	The text is too small	Unidentifiable information	A7
12	B4	Always downloading irrelevant stuff	over-advertising	B9
13	B5	No attractions found	The information is not clear enough for an accurate search	B1, B3, B10, B11
14	B6	A wrong click will not return	The operation is difficult, and it is easy to point wrong	A1, B2, B7
15	B7	I'm afraid I'll break my phone	Difficult operation, lack of confidence	A1
16	B8	I'm afraid that the binding of the bank card will deduct my money	Worry about overcharges	A8, B9, B12

(continued)

Table 2. (*continued*)

Serial number	ID	Data	Node	Link node
17	B9	There are so many advertisements that I'm afraid of being cheated	Lack of trust, too much advertising	A8, B8, B12
18	B10	Information is cluttered	Complex interface	A1, B11, B11
19	B11	The process is too tedious	Too much irrelevant information is confusing	A1, B1, B10
20	B12	I'm afraid I'll be charged if I make a mistake	Lack of trust	A9, B12
21	C1	Children are afraid of getting lost	Children check their parents' location	C7
22	C2	I just wanted to change my plan	Difficult operation Lack of flexibility in operation	C3, C4, C6
23	C3	Don't know how to use orders	Operation difficulties Order operation difficulties	A1, B10, B11
24	C4	I don't know about changing the order	Fear of wrong order information cumbersome fear of wrong	C2, C3, C4
25	C5	The order destination cannot be found	One-click map function	C1

established to obtain the relationship between nodes in different sets of minds, which was expressed as 37 associated connecting lines. The mutual indexing between nodes completed the diagram of the users' mind flow links (see in Fig. 2). The use of the link diagram allows the exploration of the logical relationships and process links of the users' minds and thus completes the structural relationships between different semantic elements.

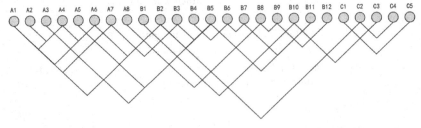

Fig. 2. Link diagram of mental flow in the process of elderly people using the travel app

3.2 Construction of Mental Model for the Elderly Tourism

In this paper, we applied the method of affinity diagram used by Indi Young in the stage of constructing a mental model [22]. The different "tasks" summarized according to the user's mental activities when using the product are clustered into "task towers" according to their mutual affinity, and then the "task towers" are clustered again to form a mental space, which completely represents all the mental cognition formed by the users when using the product. The user's travel behavior was divided into different task towers (a, b, and c) according to the three stages, including downloading the app and information binding, the operation process of the app, and the travel process, as the typical tasks to be accomplished by the user during the travel process. Meanwhile, each task tower of the mind space was filled based on the clustering results of the mind nodes obtained in the previous mind information collection stage (see in Fig. 3).

The application of the mental model in product design usually includes four strategies: filling, combining, splitting, and mutating. In the process of using affinity diagrams to establish the mental space for the elderly tourism, based on the mental level of the elderly group, the method of filling and combining the mental space was used to compensate for the deficiencies in the design of the current product, in order to deal with the shortcomings of the elderly in terms of their existing mental experience and ability, as well as to simplify the interaction process and improve the usability of the product. For example, at the stage of downloading the app and binding the information, the elderly have problems such as " being unable to recognize the login information (a5)" and " being unable to register the account (a6)", etc. Therefore, the solution to fill the gap in the design of this product is to simplify the process of registering and logging in as well as to simplify the text information to strengthen the visual perception in order to eliminate the difficulties caused by the lack of mental ability. In the operation process of the app, in order to solve the problem of the elderly "not being able to accurately search for attraction information (b5)", it proposes the function of intelligent planning for tourist attractions so as to save searching time and satisfy the needs for the elderly to travel in different situations. In the travel process, for the problem of "children wanting to check the location of their parents (c1)", the function of sharing the travel schedule is provided to ensure the safety of the elderly on the trip. Combining mind space is mainly reflected in the rational combination of duplicated mind content in the same task tower or different task towers in order to simplify the complicated tasks that the user needs to complete and improve the user experience. For example, the three mental nodes of " difficulties in operation, resulting in mistakes (b6)", "lack of confidence in operation (b7)" and "lack of trust towards the app (b8)" in the task tower of the app's operation process are combined to propose the function of assistance and guidance for misoperation to avoid elders' panic and distrust towards the app due to operation errors. Similarly, other similar mental nodes in the task tower are combined to simplify the process of using the travel app and generate the appropriate product strategy to help the elderly complete the tasks successfully and efficiently.

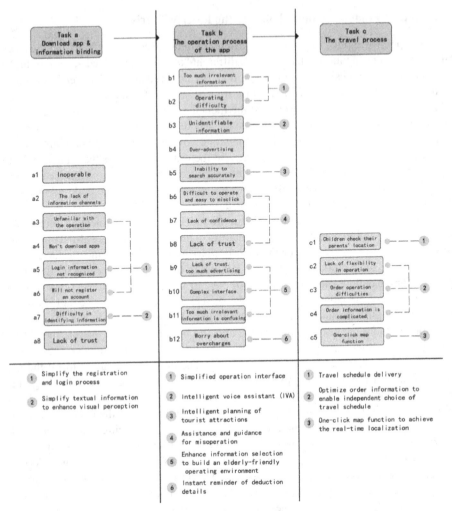

Fig. 3. Mental space in the process of elderly people using the travel app

3.3 Construction of the Service Process

Services for elderly observers are complex social systems, and thus, they can only adapt to complexity by recognizing themselves as systems and gaining experience, with the whole experience being designed as a unity. A good system design regards the whole process as a humanized and socialized system. In order to better define the processes and needs of the user interface interaction design for elderly tourism, we used a service system diagram to analyze it. The system process coordinates different stakeholders while considering the mutual flow of service information, service content, service recipients, capital, and government. The UI system is used to achieve information delivery to the elderly population and optimize the user experience. We optimize the interactive interface of the travel app through the survey of the elderly population and promote the age-appropriate travel app, thus constructing a system of production and guarantee services (see in Fig. 4). For elderly observers, services are provided to the elderly in the app platform, and the elderly give feedback to the platform for evaluation. Elderly tourists put forward their personal needs to the customer service, and the customer service answers relevant questions from the elderly tourists. Service providers offer technology development for the platform. Government departments provide financial support for the app platform. Third-party suppliers provide business cooperation and advertising promotion for the platform. Travel companies provide travel packages for the platform. The app platform selects travel packages and puts them on the shelves. Designers provide customized solutions for the platform. Social platforms provide services for the app platform. The platform provides feedback and support services to service providers and social platforms.

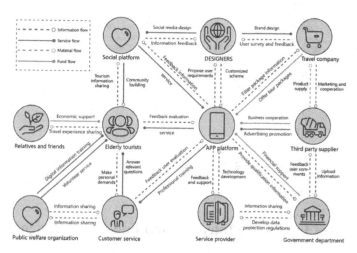

Fig. 4. Service system diagram

Service touchpoint is an important part of the service design process. In the research and analysis stage, simulating the user perspective to draw the user. The experience map can fully explore the potential demand, sort out the specific use process, and show the relationship between the elements in the service system [23]. In the user journey map, the user's perspective is used to experience the whole service process, which presents the emotional changes and demand points in the use process and transforms them into opportunity points for design (see in Fig. 5). The user journey map shows the three stages of pre-service, in-service, and post-service. In the pre-service, users are in the stage of downloading and registering, understanding the operation, and personalized privacy settings. We can find that during this period in the user experience, there will be anticipation and curiosity about the app, as well as a variety of operational difficulties, so we need to pay attention to the simplification of the design process and provide a clear guide and well-defined privacy settings, etc. During the service, users' goals are to find travel services, safely complete bookings, and not miss travel arrangements. In this stage, there will be an emotional experience of satisfaction, reassurance, and anticipation, but also a certain degree of dissatisfaction, such as encountering incomprehensible travel information, reading difficulties, etc. In the post-service, users will engage in behaviors such as social sharing and feedback evaluation. Through the analysis of the emotional fallout points, we are able to find that this stage needs to pay attention to responding positively to user feedback, adding the mechanism of appreciation and rewards to promote the motivation of users to help improve the functions and services, and thus get a positive cycle.

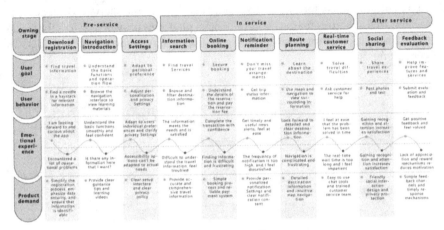

Fig. 5. User journey diagram

4 Practice of Interactive Interface and Functional Design

The content of the homepage of the travel app for elderly users is mainly divided as follows: the interface design of pre-service, in-service, and post-service (see in Fig. 6). In the pre-service, the app platform presents a simple and clear interface of setting board through personalized interface design. Firstly, the setting of the emergency contact for the elderly users, in order to ensure the safety of the elderly users when traveling, can quickly call the user's family members through the button at any time while identifying the location of the user through rapid localization, so that the elderly users and their families can use it at ease. Secondly, some elders, due to the decline of eyesight, can improve their cognition of the interface by adjusting the font size of their mobile phones. Thirdly, considering the cultural level of some elders, they cannot accurately input the travel information. In order to ensure that elderly users can successfully obtain important information from the travel app, the voice language settings can be targeted to recognize the voices of elderly users. Fourthly, the elderly are prone to be afraid to click on the non-confirmation elements when they encounter unclear icons in a new app. Setting the icon explanation module can help elderly users understand how to use the app more conveniently so that elderly users will use it easily. Fifthly, the login method of the interface is set to the switchable mode of mobile phone number and Email account so that the user can switch the login at any time by using the verification code of the mobile phone or the email account.

In the service, the type of travel on the homepage of the app platform is mainly divided into private customization and group customization. When elderly users need to travel on their own, they need to use private customization primarily. The private customization uses air tickets, high-speed train tickets, bus tickets, and hotels as the booking method. When elderly users need a time-saving and effortless method, they can choose group customization, i.e., travel packages launched by travel companies, which is the main method. The function of the travel schedule in the service can record the date of the user's ticket, travel schedule, and round trip time in detail so that elderly users can quickly search for the current day's travel plan. Regarding the app platform for elderly users in the post-service, the emergency contact and customer service are set on the homepage, which is convenient for elderly users to find their family members or friends easily. Meanwhile, customer service can further help elderly users to deal with order problems. By reducing the operation level and highlighting the service points, it can avoid the wrong operation of the travel app by elderly users as much as possible and reduce the fear of the elderly to the app platform.

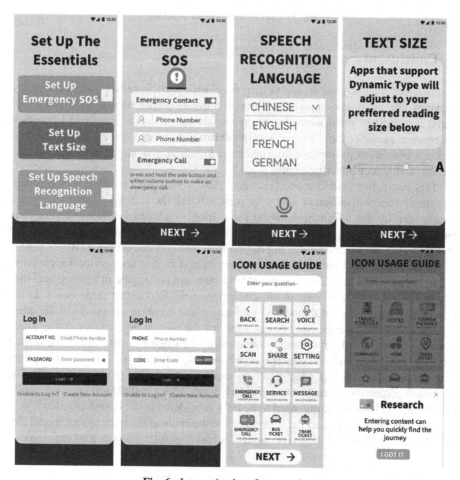

Fig. 6. Interactive interface practice

Fig. 7. Interactive interface practice

5 Conclusion

In this paper, we designed an app to help the elderly participate in travel planning and activities efficiently and enjoyably. Through a questionnaire survey of 53 elders, we found that most of them were able to operate the smart device simply and proposed their own expectations and suggestions respectively in the end, among which the most frequent ones were to improve information recognition, pay attention to security and privacy, and reduce advertisements.

This interactive interface and functional design were able to adapt to the visual-perceptual habits of different elders by personalizing the settings so that they could clearly identify the information on the page. It also included functions such as page guidance, privacy settings, and voice customer service so that the user group could feel at ease during the process of use and inspire trust that they could operate it.

In this study, we demonstrate that applying mental models and service design thinking to interaction design can help the elderly plan and participate in tourism activities efficiently and enjoyably. And in this design, we need to consider three issues. In the first place, using the mental model to summarize and organize the results of the questionnaire survey can effectively compensate for the mental deficiencies in the whole process. Afterward, the information obtained in the stage of constructing the mental model is combined with the concept of service design to construct the service system map and user journey map, which can fully explore the potential needs of users. Finally, the visual-perceptual characteristics of elderly users, which include text cognition, color cognition, and layout reading, need to be fully considered in the design practice.

In conclusion, our research results show that the application of the mental model theory targeted analyzes all the users' psychological cognition, such as past experiences, behavioral habits, and usage needs, in the process of using the product, which provides a corresponding basis for guiding the product design in the paper. Meanwhile, the integration of service design theory comprehensively provides new ideas and referable practical methods for the application in the field of elderly-oriented design for digital products.

Disclosure of Interests. It is now necessary to declare any competing interests or to specifically state that the authors have no competing interests.

References

1. Paiva, J.O., et al.: Mobile applications for elderly healthcare: a systematic map. Plos One **15**(7), e0236091 (2020)
2. Yuan, T., Guo, Y.: Gamification design of health apps for the elderly based on the kano model and conjoint analysis method. In: International Conference on Human-Computer Interaction. Cham, Springer International Publishing(2021). https://doi.org/10.1007/978-3-030-78111-8_12
3. Bastos, D., et al.: Smartwalk mobile–a context-aware m-health app for promoting physical activity among the elderly. In: New Knowledge in Information Systems and Technologies: Volume 2. Springer International Publishing (2019). https://doi.org/10.1007/978-3-030-16184-2_79
4. Niu, X., Li, H., Zhang, C.: A study on the design strategy of walking health APP for the elderly from the behavioral theory perspective. In: International Conference on Human-Computer Interaction. Cham: Springer Nature Switzerland (2023)
5. Kwakye, K., Seong, Y., Yi, S.: An Android-based mobile paratransit application for vulnerable road users. In: Proceedings of the 24th Symposium on International Database Engineering & Applications (2020)
6. Lu, J., et al.: An emotional-aware mobile terminal accessibility-assisted recommendation system for the elderly based on haptic recognition. Int. J. Hum. Comput. Interact. (2023)
7. Weinschenk, S.: 100 Things Every Designer Needs to Know About People. Pearson Education (2011)
8. van Ments, L., Treur, J.: Reflections on dynamics, adaptation and control: a cognitive architecture for mental models. Cogn. Syst. Res. **70**, 1–9 (2021)
9. Norman, D.: The Design of Everyday Things: Revised and Expanded Edition. Basic Books (2013)
10. Walden, J., et al.: Mental models of robots among senior citizens: an interview study of interaction expectations and design implications. Interact. Stud. **16**(1), 68–88 (2015)
11. Revell, K.M.A., Stanton, N.A.: Mental model interface design: putting users in control of home heating. Build. Res. Inf. **46**(3), 251–271 (2018)
12. Shostack, G.L.: Designing Services That Deliver. Harvard Business Review 41.1 (1984)
13. Levitt, T.: Marketing Intangible Products and Product Intangibles. Cornell Hotel and Restaurant Administration Quarterly (1981)
14. Grönroos, C.A.: Service Quality Model and Its Marketing Implications (1984)
15. Hollins, G., Hollins, B.: Total Design: Managing the Design Process in the Service Sector. Pitman (1991)
16. Dan, S.: Designing for Interaction. New Riders, pp. 521–530 (2007)
17. Liu, Y., et al.: Smart Phone Scene-based Interface Design for the Elderly. Packaging Engineering (2015)
18. Liu, L., Yu, Y., Sun, T.: Design of products for elder based on human machine interaction. Ind. Eng. J. **13**(5), 89–94 (2010)

19. Zhang, W., Diao, Y., Jiang, J., Jeung, J.: Research on the experience design of products for the elderly in the age of intelligence. Sci. Technol. Rev. **41**(8), 94–103 (2023)
20. Reeder, B., Zaslavksy, O., Wilamowska, K.M., Demiris, G., Thompson, H.J.: Modeling the oldest old: personas to design technology-based solutions for older adults. In: AMIA Annual Symposium Proceedings, p. 1166. American Medical Informatics Association (2011)
21. Gabriela, et al.: Inspiring design ideas with texts. Design Studies (2011)
22. Young, I.: Mental Models: Aligning Design Strategy with Human Behavior. Rosenfield Press, USA (2008)
23. Norman, D.A.: Living with Complexity. MIT Press (2016)

Knowledge Service Optimization Based on Human Factors Engineering - Focusing on the Elderly Reader Group in Libraries

Yujia Zhai[1](✉) and Shijun Ge[2]

[1] China University of Political Science and Law, Beijing 100088, China
yujiazhai@cupl.edu.cn
[2] Beijing Institute of Technology, Beijing 100081, China
3120215892@bit.edu.cn

Abstract. In the era of digital intelligence, the elderly population aged 60 and above faces considerable challenges in acquiring and utilizing knowledge. This article takes library elderly readers as the target group, uses the theoretical methods of human factors engineering, and conducts in-depth research on the knowledge needs of the elderly population. It proposes an optimized knowledge service strategy for the elderly population, providing theoretical and practical guidance for the aging design of knowledge services. For the elderly population, the key to knowledge service lies in presenting knowledge in a form that fits their cognitive characteristics and understanding methods, helping them to acquire and utilize knowledge more efficiently. To this end, this article has designed a library aging-friendly knowledge service platform, promoting the structural reform of the knowledge service supply side by optimizing the presentation channels of knowledge content, structure, application, and evaluation. This not only promotes the deep integration and development of resources but also realizes the rapid implementation of service innovation concepts, ultimately building a high-quality knowledge service ecosystem.

Keywords: knowledge Service · Aging-friendly · Human Factors Engineering · Library · Visualization

1 Introduction

With the rapid development of information technology, digital knowledge has become an indispensable part of people's learning, work, and daily life. However, for the elderly population aged 60 and above, this transformation has brought significant challenges. They have an urgent need to access information and improve their quality of life, but are often limited by the "digital divide." This dilemma not only affects their quality of life but also weakens their social participation. In 2021, the Ministry of Industry and Information Technology in China issued the "General Design Specification for Age-friendly Internet Websites" and the "General Design Specification for Age-friendly Mobile Internet Applications (APPs)" [1], marking the policy's emphasis on elderly people's equal access to information services and barrier-free knowledge services, and also indicating that addressing the issue of age-friendly knowledge services has become an essential part of achieving comprehensive social informatization and building a learning society.

Scholars in the library field have recognized that elderly readers are gradually integrating into the trend of smart reading, and libraries have a responsibility to promote the popularization and optimization of smart reading among the elderly population [2]. However, existing literature shows that, in addition to barrier-free space design [3], mobile social [4, 5], digital divide governance [6], and reading services [7], research on age-friendly knowledge services is relatively lacking and needs further exploration.

This article, based on the theoretical methods of human factors engineering, analyzes the knowledge needs of elderly readers in libraries and discusses the knowledge service strategies for the elderly population. This will help provide theoretical support and practical guidance for the design of age-friendly knowledge services, enabling the elderly to enjoy a richer and higher-quality spiritual life in the information age and achieve the mission of fair, just, and convenient knowledge services.

2 Current Situation of Library Knowledge Service for Elderly Readers in the Digital Age

Elderly readers are an essential target group for library knowledge services. They not only have the right to access, process, exchange, and share knowledge, but the depth and quality of this knowledge should also be fully guaranteed. The knowledge environment of libraries is undergoing unprecedented changes, with digitalization, networking, and intelligence becoming new markers of library services. However, this change in knowledge acquisition and dissemination has formed multiple dilemmas for the elderly reader group.

2.1 Survey of Elderly Reader Group

The sample source of this article includes two parts. The first part is the feedback from readers on library services and their demands received by some public libraries and university libraries (985/211) in the Beijing area since January 1, 2021. These feedback channels include face-to-face communication, messages, and complaints, etc., from which 27 opinions from elderly readers aged 60 and above were extracted, accounting for 12.1% of the total number of opinions.

The second part involves interviewing 30 representative elderly readers during visits to the above libraries, asking about the problems they encounter when using library resources and services. These readers have a balanced gender distribution (15 males and 15 females), with an age range of 60–75 years (18 people aged 60–65, 11 people aged 66–70, and 1 person aged 71–75), and a higher level of education (4 high school graduates, 11 junior college graduates, and 15 bachelor's degree holders or above). These readers have a higher interaction with the library, with 9 people saying they come "whenever they have time," 11 people coming "once or twice a week," 8 people coming "once or twice a month," and 2 people coming "occasionally, but often read the library's e-books."

Table 1. Feedback on Problems of Elderly Reader Group

Sequence Number	Problem/Demand	Source	Number of People	Reason	Scenario
1	Finding books in the system, there are many similar books displayed, and it's more difficult to find the desired ones. After finally finding the needed book, it's hard to find it in reality	Public Libraries& University Libraries	32	The book presentation is not clear enough, some books are borrowed, and the system shows zero available copies, but the elderly may not notice. Sometimes, the book is actually on the shelf, but the elderly are not familiar with the arrangement rules, and their vision is not good, making it difficult to find	Book Borrowing
2	The self-service borrowing and returning machine is not easy to use, the buttons are not clear, and there is no response when pressing borrow book/return book/put the book on the counter	Public Libraries& University Libraries	24	Some function buttons have small names, the interface color and layout contrast are low, and the touch screen and borrowing counter response is not sensitive	Space Equipment
3	Searching for information is too troublesome, and a lot of irrelevant information comes up when inputting a keyword	Public Libraries& University Libraries	10	The resource revelation path planning is unreasonable	Information Retrieval

(*continued*)

Table 1. (*continued*)

Sequence Number	Problem/Demand	Source	Number of People	Reason	Scenario
4	Don't know where to find *** magazine	University Libraries	9	The magazine arrangement is complex, and the system display is not clear	Book Borrowing
5	Want to find *** information but don't know which platform to use	University Libraries	7	The library has purchased many databases, lacking integration and summary	Information Retrieval
6	Hope to have a book exhibition for elderly readers	Public Libraries	6	Reading promotion activities are not refined	Book Borrowing
7	The mobile library APP is not easy to use, and only a few pages of the book can be seen	University Libraries	5	Some books have not been purchased in full, and there are various reading channels. These designs are not friendly enough to the elderly	Mobile Services
8	Expect to receive book expiration/overdue notices	University Libraries	5	The reader card binding requirements are not clear, and the elderly readers mistakenly think that subscribing to the public account is enough	Mobile Services
9	The lighting is too bright/dark when reading at the seat	Public Libraries& University Libraries	3	The facilities are not suitable	Space Equipment

(*continued*)

Table 1. (*continued*)

Sequence Number	Problem/Demand	Source	Number of People	Reason	Scenario
10	The library table is too short	Public Libraries	1	The facilities are not suitable	Space Equipment
11	Want to recommend books to the library but don't know how to operate	University Libraries	1	The book recommendation process is complex, and there is no notification channel after the book arrives	Book Borrowing

Among these 30 readers, they can basically use the library's self-service equipment, websites, systems, APPs, and other information facilities.

Finally, the two parts of data (27 opinions and 30 interview results) were summarized and organized (see Table 1).

The above table reveals the following issues:

Firstly, the sensory abilities of elderly readers decline, especially in terms of visual acuity, focusing ability, and color discrimination. To meet the special needs of elderly readers during the reading process, some libraries are equipped with facilities for elderly readers, such as magnifying glasses and hearing aids. At the same time, some signs have also been designed to be age-friendly for easy identification by elderly readers. However, most libraries have not made corresponding adjustments to the interfaces of equipment, platforms, apps, etc., lacking elderly-friendly visual elements such as large font sizes, wide spacing, and high contrast, as well as necessary auditory and tactile feedback.

Secondly, the logical reasoning, memory, and learning abilities of the elderly decline. They often exhibit inertial thinking when solving problems. Coupled with the limitations of knowledge and experience brought about by their age, they may have difficulty establishing new connections unrelated to past experiences, thus reducing their agility and flexibility. In the digital environment, reading and learning methods present characteristics such as diversification, fragmentation, and socialization, all of which pose challenges to the cognitive habits of elderly readers. However, most library systems do not provide integrated special features for elderly readers, let alone planning according to their usage needs and frequency. As a result, they often forget how to use the systems again after learning to use them for the first time.

Thirdly, the knowledge needs of elderly readers are diverse and well-structured. They usually have rich life experiences and a wide range of interests and hobbies, which gives them a broad exploration and personalized demand for knowledge acquisition. This difference in scope and ability often leads to many unsuitable aspects in universal knowledge services, making it difficult to help them effectively establish knowledge connections in the digital environment.

2.2 Challenges of Age-Friendly Design for Knowledge Services

Knowledge service is a comprehensive and integrated service [8]. From the feedback of the elderly mentioned above, the issues they reflect include various scenarios such as book borrowing, information retrieval, mobile services, and the use of space and equipment. To meet the specific needs of the elderly reader group and help them adapt to the knowledge acquisition mode in the digital intelligent environment, libraries must optimize the design of these scenarios and form a more humanized knowledge service plan based on their cognitive characteristics and habits. To this end, a user journey map of elderly reader knowledge services can be drawn (see Fig. 1). From the user journey map, it can be seen that libraries need to address the following aspects.

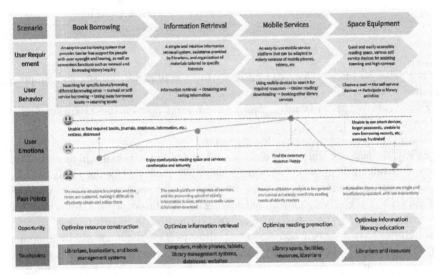

Fig. 1. User Journey Map of Elderly Reader Knowledge Service

1. Challenges of Resource Construction: Balancing Integration and Utilization

   The foundation of knowledge service lies in resources, and its value does not solely depend on the quantity of resources, but also on the effectiveness of assisting users in mastering these resources. Libraries have a wealth of database resources and unique electronic collections, but the feedback from elderly readers reveals that the potential of these resources has not been fully tapped. One reason is the diverse types of resources (including books, journals, audio, video, and images) and various sources (such as purchase, open access, interlibrary loan, document delivery, and alliance sharing), which are challenges faced by many libraries. However, while most libraries enhance platform performance to increase resource storage, they seldom consider the presentation format and standards of resources. This oversight creates obstacles for elderly readers in utilizing resources at the initial stage of knowledge service.

2. Challenges of Information Retrieval: Knowledge Filtering and Information Overload

   Library knowledge services differ significantly from internet information retrieval, with the core goal of classifying and displaying the right knowledge information according to certain conditions, thus saving users the tedious process of identifying the authenticity of information. This is where the value of knowledge service lies. However, with the continuous accumulation of massive, multi-source, and heterogeneous data, the information flow that users can access per unit of time greatly increases, making it more difficult for elderly readers to objectively identify required information and form knowledge. Libraries usually collect and organize resources before presenting them in a searchable format. However, in the digital environment, information is dense and knowledge is diverse, but the resource revelation function has not kept pace with resource development. Search platforms typically integrate all services, but the characteristics of elderly thinking are slow information processing speed and difficulty in filtering irrelevant information. This design approach greatly reduces the perceived relevance of elderly users interacting with the system. Under the existing navigation system, the complex relationships between different knowledge elements and the potential value of knowledge have not been fully presented, and the distributed heterogeneous data and its weak association revelation make it difficult for elderly readers to locate the required information, leading to cognitive overload and disorientation.

3. Challenges of Reading Promotion: Conflict between Extensive Services and Precision Mining

   In the digital intelligence environment, libraries often analyze readers' information behavior through big data to improve the level of reading promotion services. However, these analyses rarely focus solely on elderly readers, and the results of resource utilization are too general to accurately match the reading needs of elderly readers. In terms of screening, investigating, and distributing the required literature for elderly readers, libraries lack sufficient effort, promotion activities lack interaction and guidance, and knowledge sharing and communication channels have not been fully developed, resulting in the reading needs of elderly readers not being fully met and deeply explored.

4. (Challenges of Information Literacy Education: Urgency of Meeting Diverse Needs and Enhancing Interaction Efficiency

   Currently, some libraries offer single and outdated learning resources in information literacy education, with low interaction, which keeps educational consulting services at a surface level without going in-depth. For elderly readers, they depend more on established knowledge systems and habits to understand new information. However, existing inefficient interaction methods do not stimulate their interest and motivation to use library resources for in-depth learning.

3 Dimensions for Enhancing Elderly Reader Knowledge Service Efficiency Through Human Factors Engineering

To better address the challenges of aging-friendly design in knowledge services, libraries can introduce human factors engineering design methods to optimize various aspects of knowledge service work and address the unique needs and issues of the elderly.

3.1 Basic Principles and Methods of Human Factors Engineering

Human factors engineering is a discipline that studies the role and behavior of people in systems, with the goal of finding the best fit between humans, machines, and the environment to achieve optimal overall performance [9]. Following the principles of human factors engineering, service design should place human factors at the core, involving a deep understanding of human physiological characteristics, cognitive patterns, behavioral habits, and specific needs [9], and integrating these elements into technical design.

For the special user group of the elderly, delicate consideration and precise planning should be given to their human factors in knowledge services to achieve efficient communication of information and make complex content easier to understand and accept [9]. To this end, knowledge services should adhere to principles such as simplicity, consistency, contrast, and guidance in aging-friendly design. Simplicity helps older people quickly focus on key information by simplifying visual elements and removing unnecessary decorations; consistency enhances the recognizability and understandability of information by unifying elements such as color, font, and graphics; contrast improves the readability and attractiveness of information by highlighting key information; and guidance helps older people understand information more easily by guiding their sight and thinking through the layout and organization of visual elements. Under this framework, the service design process can be divided into three main steps (see Fig. 2).

First, summarize audience needs. Identify the target audience (i.e., elderly readers), analyze their characteristics, and collect, organize, classify, and summarize their needs. Elderly people usually face limitations in information processing capabilities, diverse knowledge needs, information overload, and coarse services. Libraries need to optimize these issues accordingly.

Second, prototype design. Choose appropriate visual elements, such as color, line, shape, and layout, for preliminary display and testing based on needs. Proper graphic analysis methods can convey suitable emotions and meanings, enhance the readability and attractiveness of information [10], and help elderly readers quickly extract knowledge elements from data, deconstruct and transmit complex information, and build a usable knowledge network.

Third, experience evaluation. Adjust and optimize according to the feedback from elderly readers, ensuring that the final design solution meets the knowledge needs of the elderly while reflecting respect and care for them.

3.2 Human Factors Engineering Strategies for Optimizing Knowledge Services

Based on the human factors design process and the characteristics of the elderly reader group, a complete set of knowledge service optimization strategies is proposed (see Fig. 3). To further improve the implementation of services and ensure the rigorous connection between the displayed knowledge logic and the cognitive habits and needs of the elderly group, comprehensive and meticulous considerations need to be made in the key aspects of knowledge production, mining, dissemination, and transformation.

1. Planning for Knowledge Production: Optimization of Resource Construction
     Libraries not only need to enrich resources that reflect the needs of the elderly but also manage and plan the presentation of these resources. The focus of a world-class

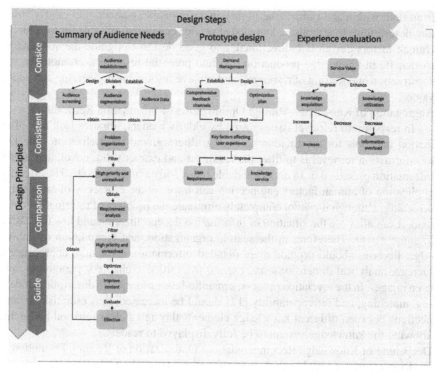

Fig. 2. Aging-friendly Knowledge Service Human Factors Design Process

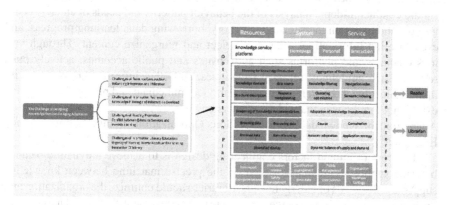

Fig. 3. Knowledge Service Optimization Plan

information resource service system is on knowledge presentation [11], and libraries are gradually transforming traditional collection, editing, and cataloging workflows into the organization and management of knowledge elements and data elements. Therefore, libraries need to organize digital books, ancient literature, papers, journals, newspapers, multimedia, microfilm, documents, and encyclopedia resources from both within and outside the library in a reasonable manner, and clearly structure descriptions to establish a knowledge service ecosystem suitable for the elderly. Human factors design is bidirectional, and good design can guide the audience to participate in knowledge production, tap into potential resources, promote the co-construction and sharing of resources, and achieve resource reengineering and added value.

2. Aggregation of Knowledge Mining: Optimization of Information Retrieval

In response to retrieval issues raised by elderly readers, libraries lack not information but tools for information screening, filtering, and internalization. The key to information retrieval is to filter the result set and extract valid, novel, and useful information presented in an understandable index and navigation mode. The effective application of human factors engineering can improve the efficiency of knowledge screening, although it cannot completely eliminate the problem of information overload, it can alleviate the situation of information decentralization and low utilization to some extent. Therefore, in the search, organization, and compilation of knowledge, libraries should provide more detailed information revelation, appropriately increase analytical dimensions, and expand from titles to chapters, paragraphs, and even images. In the revelation process, semantic-level information description, indexing, matching, and interoperability [12] should be increased, thus establishing connections between different knowledge elements through a clear retrieval hierarchy, allowing the knowledge system to be fully displayed to readers.

3. Deepening of Knowledge Recommendation: Optimization of Reading Promotion

Rich resources provide the content foundation for library knowledge services, which needs to be effectively communicated and promoted. Diverse content presentation and scientifically reasonable layout forms can help break new ground. Libraries should conduct in-depth analysis of the behavior patterns and needs of elderly reader groups, and based on their browsing history, borrowing data, learning progress, and even location information, accurately select and reorganize content. Through various channels and platforms such as websites and public accounts, actively push related usage guidelines, retrieval techniques, and other information, interact with them, collect feedback in real-time, and provide immediate and personalized service experiences in the way that elderly readers enjoy.

4. Adaptation of Knowledge Transformation: Optimization of Information Literacy Education

The core of human factors engineering design is to achieve a dynamic balance between supply and demand. Based on the precise matching between knowledge supply and the needs of elderly readers, libraries should optimize the organization and presentation of teaching resources and create more convenient channels. This can help elderly readers accurately find the path to solve knowledge in massive information and achieve effective application, thus better digesting and absorbing knowledge. In the information literacy education process, libraries should adopt a series of highly adaptable knowledge transformation strategies to promote deep understanding and widespread application of knowledge. Only in this way, can the knowledge gap be truly bridged, a comprehensive knowledge service system be constructed, and the activity of elderly readers be enhanced.

4 Aging-Friendly Knowledge Service Platform Designed for Human Factors

For the elderly population, the key to knowledge service lies in presenting knowledge in a way that fits their cognitive characteristics and understanding, helping them to acquire and utilize knowledge more efficiently. Based on the above optimization scheme, libraries can design an aging-friendly knowledge service platform by optimizing the presentation of knowledge content, structure, application, and evaluation to enhance the effectiveness and practicality of the service (see Fig. 4).

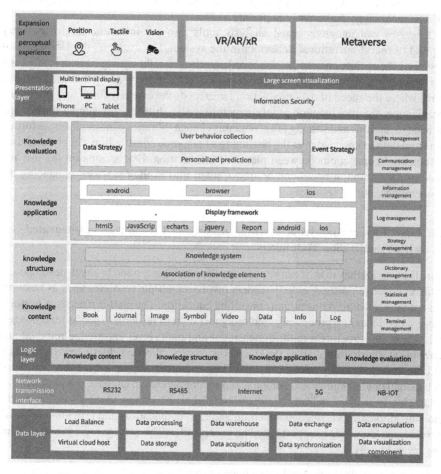

Fig. 4. Framework of the aging-friendly knowledge service platform

4.1 Data Layer: Infrastructure Based on Big Data Technology

In today's increasingly mature cloud computing technology, cloud-based knowledge acquisition has become a norm. The continuous development of server and application software virtualization technology makes the construction of cloud-based knowledge sharing platforms extremely convenient. Currently, the storage and display of library digital resources rely on these advanced infrastructures. These facilities not only need to provide high-speed and secure storage and computing services but also increasingly focus on supporting distributed collaboration and data analysis to meet users' needs in metadata development, reorganization, and application. In knowledge service, the power of data is key to in-depth analysis and presentation, making the infrastructure based on big data technology particularly important.

Libraries can integrate visual analysis tools into the infrastructure to precisely respond to users' operational behaviors in the system. For example, the University of Virginia Library has created an enhanced interface for the storage system, allowing users to preview interactively through 3D models before downloading the data [13]. In a world where the speed of data production far exceeds the capacity for management and organization, the core function of infrastructure is also shifting from simple storage and retrieval to analysis and sharing [14]. With this change, libraries can start the transformation from data to knowledge at the beginning of resource construction, deeply revealing the potential connections between pieces of information. By focusing on the use and reuse of data, implicit needs can be transformed into explicit services, enhancing the regenerative value of resources.

4.2 Logic Layer: Knowledge Reorganization and Customization Integrated with Visualization Technology

From the user journey map, it can be seen that the precise grasp and in-depth development of the knowledge needs of elderly readers involves multiple scenarios such as resource construction, reading services, and consulting education. The platform needs to perform fine-grained indexing, processing, and reorganization of resources such as text, images, and videos, constructing a multi-dimensional and multi-level knowledge retrieval and browsing system to fully display the knowledge system, allowing elderly readers to easily find the knowledge they need in the abundant resources. At the same time, combined with visualization engines and personalized recommendation engines, the platform can group elderly readers and manage them with labels according to their specific needs, realizing automated knowledge matching and recommendation, and providing in-depth personalized knowledge support based on user profiles. This service logic can be divided into several levels.

1. Visualization abstraction of knowledge content

By abstracting, summarizing, and refining knowledge content, it is transformed into visual elements that are easy to understand and remember, such as graphics, symbols, and animations. At the same time, using visual elements such as color and font to strengthen the key information of knowledge content, improving the transmission efficiency and application value of knowledge.

2. Visualization organization of knowledge structure

Through logical analysis of knowledge structure, it is transformed into a knowledge organization framework that is easy to understand and master. For example, tree diagrams and flowcharts show the relationship and hierarchy between knowledge, helping readers to better understand and master the content of knowledge.

3. Visualization display of knowledge application

The platform needs to simulate the application scenarios of knowledge and transform them into intuitive and vivid visual experiences, which are displayed through carriers such as browsers, APPs, and mini-programs. Virtual reality, augmented reality, and other technologies can be integrated to immerse users in the effects and values of knowledge in real life, improving user stickiness.

4. Visualization feedback of knowledge evaluation

By evaluating and feedback the learning effects of knowledge, it is transformed into actionable visual results. In addition to the faceted revelation of the result set, data mining and intelligent algorithms can be used to realize personalized predictions of knowledge needs, proactively pushing information and resources that elderly readers may need, and transforming passive services into active services [15].

4.3 Presentation Layer: Knowledge Experience Expansion Integrating User-Friendly Interaction and Personalized Services

In the presentation layer, the comprehensive application of technology plays a core role, integrating the functions of the data layer and the logic layer to meet the knowledge needs of elderly readers in a way that conforms to practical applications. The knowledge transmission in this layer not only includes the mining of knowledge supply and the retrieval of the receiving end but also involves the knowledge construction of librarians and the actual application of elderly readers. To ensure the clarity and depth of knowledge transmission, the platform needs to optimize key functions such as user interface, content reading, operation prompts, and voice assistance, and enhance the intuitiveness and immediacy of guidance through diverse interaction methods such as smart voice interaction, vibration feedback, and visual effects.

With the development of technologies such as artificial intelligence, visual recognition, language processing, and natural interaction, "omnidirectional smart knowledge service" [16] has become a new trend in library services. Since the concept of "meta-universe library" [17] was proposed, creating a highly interactive reading world, building a virtual space integrating auditory, visual, tactile, olfactory, and gustatory multisensory systems, and "experiential knowledge service" [18] have become the dream of the library community. This goal may seem remote, but there is actually a specific technology roadmap. By combining information from the real and virtual worlds, using technologies such as 3D modeling, multi-sensor fusion, real-time tracking, and scene integration, libraries can achieve instant switching of knowledge application scenarios, upgrade reading experiences from two-dimensional to three-dimensional, expand from single sensory to multi-sensory, and advance knowledge services to a deeper level of perception. Immersion and extensibility are marking the direction of the evolution of knowledge services towards the future [19].

For elderly readers, these seemingly "youthful" technologies also have significant importance. As people age, they may face various physical and cognitive challenges such as declining vision, hand flexibility, and memory. An intuitive and multi-level knowledge experience is especially critical for them. Once applied to knowledge services, the all-around sensory connection virtual environment built by meta-universe technology will provide a safe and comfortable learning and exploration space for elderly readers. The rich feelings brought by the multi-sensory experience can enhance memory and understanding, and the comprehensive and immersive knowledge service will help elderly people remain actively engaged in learning and knowledge acquisition despite physical and cognitive limitations.

5   Conclusions

In the era of digital intelligence, library knowledge services are facing both challenges and opportunities. How to extract and disseminate knowledge from massive and diverse resources has become a key issue that must be deeply considered in the process of library intelligence transformation. Among them, knowledge services for elderly readers are an issue worth special attention. Human-centered design provides a series of principles that offer guidance for libraries in caring for and satisfying the knowledge service needs of the elderly. When facing the contradiction between technological rationality and humanistic care, the knowledge presentation strategy of human-centered design can promote the structural reform of the knowledge service supply side, drive the deep integration and development of resources, and realize the rapid implementation of service innovation concepts. Building a high-quality knowledge service ecosystem is a necessary path for libraries to adapt to the construction of an aging society.

References

1. China Government Network, Ministry of Industry and Information Technology Releases General Design Specifications for APPs Suitable for the Elderly. https://www.gov.cn/xinwen/2021-04/13/content_5599223.htm. Accessed 17 Nov 2023
2. Chen, D., Yue, X., Zhang, L.: Research review of library services for the elderly in the context of intelligent technology. Libr. Work Res. 11, 113–120 (2022)
3. Zhengde, Z., Hu, Y.: Digital infrastructure suitable for the elderly in the context of spatial justice: local progress and limitations. Learn. Pract. 10, 32–41 (2023)
4. Yang, H.-L., Lin, S.-L.: The reasons why elderly mobile users adopt ubiquitous mobile social service. Comput. Hum. Behav. 93, 62–75 (2019)
5. Jin, Y., Liu, Z., Bi, C.: Research on APP ageing transformation in the context of information accessibility. Mod. Inf. 42(08), 96–106 (2022)
6. Rao, Q., Christian, M., Leitner, G., et al.: Bridging the digital divide and promoting digital inclusion: the new mission of libraries in the information society. Libr. J. 40(02), 4–19 (2021)
7. Li, Y., Zhu, T.: Research on AI-powered public library reading services for the elderly - a case study of Hangzhou. New Century Libr. 01, 23–27 (2022)

8. Wang, S., Xu, K., Cui, W., Zhou, H.: Research on the evolution of the ubiquitous library knowledge ecosystem in the context of lifelong learning. Libr. Inf. Work **56**(11), 23–27 (2012)

9. Guo, F., Shengsan, Q.: Human Factors Engineering. 2nd Edition, p.1–30, 166. Mechanical Industry Press, Beijing (2021)

10. Chengqi, X., et al.: Human Factors in Human-Machine Interface System Design, p. 52. National Defense Industry Press, Beijing (2022)

11. Xuefang, Z., Wang, G., Qi, B.: Research on the intelligent service of digital information resources in the 5G era. Inf. Sci. Pract. **43**(11), 16–21 (2020)

12. Lancheng, W., Qiong, Z.: Research on ontology-based knowledge retrieval model and presentation technology. Libr. Inf. Work **53**(5), 98–102 (2009)

13. CLIR, 3D/VR in the academic library: emerging practices and trends. https://www.clir.org/wp-content/uploads/sites/6/2019/02/Pub-176.pdf. Accessed 17 Nov 2023

14. Zhang, X.: A visual monitoring platform for library business data based on data warehouse technology - a case study of xiamen library. Modern Inf. **33**(04), 150–153, 158 (2013)

15. Li, Y.: Analysis of user participation in library knowledge services. Libr. Sci. Res. **17**, 82–89 (2021)

16. Xiong, L., Lian, S., Zhang, C.: Research on the construction of big data knowledge service system based on "5G + artificial intelligence". Libr. Theory Pract. (03), 58–63, 85 (2022)

17. Xinya, Y., Guofu, Q., et al.: Is the metaverse the future of libraries? Libr. Forum **41**(12), 35–44 (2021)

18. Wu, A.: Exploring the innovation of knowledge service model in university libraries in the post-pandemic era - a case study of peking university library. Modern Inf. **42**(05), 132–140 (2022)

19. Zhang, Q.L., Su, Y.: Library and metaverse: relationship, function, and future. Libr. Inf. **06**, 75–80 (2021)

Aging, Chatbots and AI

Design of an Emotion Care System
for the Elderly Based on Precisely Detecting
Emotion States

Wan Dai[1], Hao Chen[1], Lei Zhu[1], YunFei Chen[1], Mo Chen[2], and Yan Zhang[1(✉)]

[1] School of Mechanical Engineering, Southeast University, Nanjing 211189,
People's Republic of China
{220214980,zhangyaner}@seu.edu.cn
[2] College of Art and Design, Nanjing Tech University, Nanjing 210096,
People's Republic of China

Abstract. With the global fertility rate in decline, the issue of an aging population grows ever more pressing, especially in developing nations where many elderly live alone, often deprived of familial emotional support and timely care. Addressing this, our study centers on emotional well-being and introduces a system capable of detecting and regulating the emotions of the elderly promptly. Utilizing sensors to capture facial imagery and vocal information, we employ a multimodal emotion recognition model for real-time analysis, enabling multi-channel emotional regulation. We validate the necessity for an elderly-specific dataset and confirm the reliability of our model's emotional recognition accuracy. Additionally, we demonstrate the effectiveness of our regulation strategies through empirical research. This study aims to enhance the quality of life for the elderly in their twilight years.

Keywords: emotion recognition · the elderly · emotion regulation · Multimodal recognition

1 Introduction

With the rapid advancement of medical technology and the continuous decline in the fertility rate, the international population is undergoing a gradual and noticeable shift towards aging. According to the United Nations statistics, the number of people aged 60 and above reached 140 million in 2019, accounting for 11% of the total global population. This proportion is projected to rise to 22% by 2050. The increasing elderly population poses several challenges to an aging society [1], and one significant issue is the rise in emotional problems. Many older individuals experience emotional distress, such as loneliness, anxiety, and depression, which profoundly impact their quality of life and may exacerbate physical and mental health issues, creating a detrimental cycle. Thus, it is crucial to prioritize the emotional health of the elderly and to recognize their emotion in a timely and accurate manner.

© The Author(s), under exclusive license to Springer Nature Switzerland AG 2024
Q. Gao and J. Zhou (Eds.): HCII 2024, LNCS 14726, pp. 331–346, 2024.
https://doi.org/10.1007/978-3-031-61546-7_21

The elderly is more prone to being influenced by external stimuli both psychologically and physiologically, and their emotional changes are also more pronounced and frequent [2]. Currently, emotion recognition methods mainly include Visual Emotion Recognition (VER), Speech Emotion Recognition (SER), and Physiological Emotion Recognition (PER). Compared to the previous two non-invasive methods, PER requires the collection of biological signals from older adults to analyze, which is not suitable for daily emotion recognition [3]. Additionally, Albert Mehrabian proposed that 55% of people's emotion transmission in daily life communication is through vision and 38% through speech [4]. Therefore, current research mainly focuses on VER and SER.

Contemporary investigations into emotion recognition are commonly centered around deep learning methods. Compared to traditional machine learning, deep learning possesses a stronger capability for feature extraction and more powerful emotion prediction. The flexibility and richness of deep learning network structures make them highly suitable for various tasks. In the realm of VER, Andrea Caroppo et al. [5] proposed an elderly facial expression recognition method based on deep neural networks combined with stacked denoising autoencoders. As for SER, an emotion recognition method integrating speech features and embedding attention mechanisms for the elderly was proposed by Jian et al. [6], which effectively improves the accuracy of speech emotion recognition for the elderly.

However, unimodal emotion recognition, such as VER and SER, often has great limitations, as it is susceptible to various forms of noise and may struggle to fully capture the complexity of emotional states [7]. So, more and more research is considering the fusion of multiple modalities, which allows for the integration of multiple modalities to establish emotion computing models with better recognition performance [8]. The fusion of speech and image modalities involves two main techniques: feature layer fusion and decision layer fusion. In feature layer fusion, the feature information from both modalities is concatenated into a new feature vector, which is then utilized in the subsequent step of emotion recognition [9]. For instance, De Silva et al. [10] independently extracted emotion features from audio and video, fused the two modalities' features, and fed them into a classifier for emotion recognition, resulting in improved recognition results compared to any single modality. The decision layer fusion is to extract features for both modalities separately, send them to their respective classifiers, and then fuse the results of each classifier based on some principle to obtain the final result. This is easier to do than feature-level fusion and takes into account the differences in modal features. Alepis et al. [11] showed that facial expressions and emotional language are complementary, and the fusion of these two modalities at the decision layer enables a more accurate differentiation of emotional states.

Additionally, flexible emotion regulation strategies are crucial for mental health and daily life [11]. After detecting emotions in the elderly, timely feedback and adjustment are required. This can be achieved by considering the influence of sensory channels such as visual, auditory, olfactory, and tactile on emotion regulation. By selecting appropriate sensory channels and interaction methods, the task of emotion regulation can be completed, allowing the elderly's emotions to return to a state of moderate arousal and positive valence.

Current research related to emotion regulation of the elderly is mainly based on the smart home aspect. Philips Lighting has introduced the Hue series of smart lamps, which can adjust color, brightness, and modes based on the elderly's mood, enabling emotion regulation based on the visual channel. Meanwhile, companies like Xiaomi and HomeKit utilize intelligent voice products like Classmate AI to achieve auditory regulation, providing users with a comfortable home experience [12]. Additionally, some works have proved that aromatherapy can effectively improve the quality of life for the elderly and alleviate fatigue, depression, and other adverse emotions through olfactory perception [13]. Regarding tactile regulation, several studies suggested that maintaining the right temperature and humidity in the home could bring a pleasant mood to the elderly [14].

Apart from the perspective of sensory access, the impact of family attributes on the emotional well-being of older adults has also been studied abroad [15]. Furthermore, some studies have suggested the future adoption of robots to fulfill the role of human-machine communication for the elderly [16]. Researchers like X Yu, CT Salmon et al. have investigated artificial companion robots, which play a constructive role in providing emotional companionship to the elderly [17].

These studies provide compelling evidence that the study of emotional recognition and regulation in elderly individuals is of significant importance in improving their quality of life in later years. They demonstrate that emotion technology assists in elderly care by providing emotional support and companionship. Therefore, the objective of this paper is to focus on elderly individuals and delve into emotion design. By utilizing emotion recognition technology and corresponding regulation strategies, a speech and expression-based multimodal emotion care system for the elderly has been developed. This system is capable of real-time detection of emotional states and provides timely intervention and regulation. The research team has named this system "EmotionCare." Additionally, this study emphasizes the practical application of emotion recognition and regulation technology in the system, conducts usability testing on the proposed emotion recognition model, and verifies the feasibility of the system through emotion regulation experiments.

2 System Architecture

The EmotionCare Multimodal Elderly Emotion Nursing System is designed with a user-centric approach and comprises 4 components: facial image acquisition, voice acquisition, cloud processor, and emotion regulation, as depicted in Fig. 1. Firstly, it collects face expression image data and voice data through visual and auditory channels, and transmits the collected data to the cloud server, the core module of the system. Then, the data is processed in the cloud server to recognize the emotional states. When emotions are recognized, the emotion regulation module is activated, which acts directly on the elderly and uses multiple emotion interaction methods to positively regulate their emotions. After the elderly' emotions are regulated, the monitoring and identification continue, and the user's emotional data will be detected by the audio-visual channel again, forming a closed loop. This ensures continuous care and support for the elderly users, promoting their emotional well-being and overall quality of life.

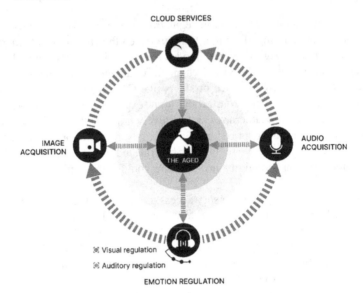

Fig. 1. System framework diagram.

2.1 Data Acquisition

Data acquisition serves as the fundamental pillar of the entire system, primarily achieved through the uses of sensors to capture the user's facial expression data and voice data. This data provides support for the emotion regulation system, and the quality of the collected data directly impacts the system's recognition capabilities. Compared to the collection of ECG, RSP, and other physiological indicators, facial expression and voice data are more intuitive and easier to obtain. They can provide a more accurate representation of the emotional state of the human body and are better suited for monitoring the emotional well-being of elderly individuals during their regular activities. As a result, this paper adopts a non-invasive approach, utilizing cameras and microphones to collect user data. This method is more realistic and allows for seamless integration into the daily lives of the elderly users, ensuring a more practical and user-friendly emotional care system.

2.2 Cloud ServerSide

The primary functions of the cloud server include data preprocessing, emotion recognition, model and data storage. Upon receiving uploaded raw data, the cloud server takes charge of preprocessing the data before feeding it into the emotion recognition algorithm for accurate emotion analysis. Simultaneously, the server stores relevant information and transmits the classification results to both the cell phone client and computer client. Clients can conveniently interact with the various modules on the cloud server through diverse transmission networks like WIFI, GPRS, CDMA, 4G, and 5G.

2.3 Emotion Regulation

The emotion regulation module consists of two parts: hardware interaction and software interaction, providing regulation strategies for various sensory channels, including visual, auditory, olfactory, and tactile, to help users improve emotions. In the visual aspect, it mainly involves adjusting the color and intensity of the light and displaying emoticons on the escort robot for real-time interaction with the user. For the auditory aspect, the module automatically plays appropriate music based on the user's preferences to soothe emotions and also facilitates effective improvement through voice chats with the escort robot. Meanwhile, it supports the elderly in a state of persistent depression in a timely manner with their children to improve the mood of the video call; In the olfactory aspect, the module utilizes aroma adjustments to enhance emotional experiences, while in the tactile aspect, it includes interactive and feedback elements related to the touch and other actions of the escort robot, providing a soft and comfortable tactile experience, allowing the user to relax during the process.

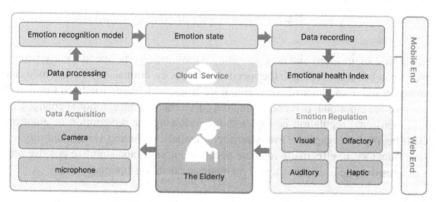

Fig. 2. System architecture flowchart.

The EmotionCare system proposed in this paper, with its specific architecture flow as illustrated in Fig. 2, is primarily designed for home environments, as depicted in Fig. 3, but is also applicable to nursing homes and similar settings. By accessing the cloud server to do the technical support behind, so as to start the whole system, the specific process: first of all, through the camera and microphone to the elderly for the collection of raw images and voice, after the collection of video into the streaming media server to realize the transmission of images and audio. Then the emotion detection n module in the cloud service will store and process the data, recognize and record the emotions through the multimodal emotion recognition model that integrates voice and image, and finally carry out emotion regulation. The system is equipped with an application for real-time monitoring and management of the emotional state of the elderly, including the elderly client and the children's client, and supports both mobile and PC. Emotion query, emotion warning, emotion statistics. Users can query their own emotional state through the software, and their children can also query the emotional state of their concerned family members at any time. Emotional alerts include early warning information,

Fig. 3. System Scenario Diagram.

early warning suggestions and corresponding measures, and the specific early warning measures can be set according to the specific situation; emotional statistics include emotional health index and historical emotional statistics, which are visualized through the bar chart of the emotional percentage and the curve chart of the emotional changes, etc. Multi-dimensional regulation is implemented following the recognition of emotional states. It begins by engaging various sensory channels, including visual, auditory, tactile, and olfactory, to effectively regulate negative emotions and stabilize positive ones. This ensures that the user consistently maintains a positive emotional state.

3 Emotion Recognition

The definition and categorization of emotions is a prerequisite for emotion recognition, and this study adopts the discrete emotion model proposed by Paul Ekman [18], which quantitatively categorizes emotions into seven basic categories, i.e., anger, disgust, fear, happiness, sadness, surprise, and neutral emotions. This EmotionCare system uses deep learning technology, and the technical framework of the emotion recognition model is shown in Fig. 4, which consists of two parts, the facial expression recognition model and the speech emotion recognition model, fused at the decision layer.

3.1 Datasets

Deep learning techniques typically require large datasets for training. Unfortunately, there is a notable scarcity of publicly available datasets specifically catering to older adults. Notably, research has demonstrated that the aging process introduces distinct alterations in facial expression dynamics and vocal characteristics [19]. Additionally, findings from cross-dataset generalization experiments underscore the challenges of

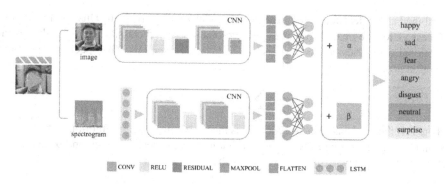

Fig. 4. Framework diagram of emotion recognition model.

transferring models trained on one age group to another [20]. Hence, the imperative of cultivating a dataset tailored to the elderly demographic becomes evident. In this experiment, we adopt two ways to establish the dataset, one is based on the existing expression dataset to filter out the elderly part to form a small elderly expression dataset AGED, and the other is to select the TV series featuring the elderly as the main characters as the material library to establish the elderly multimodal dataset AGEDS.

3.2   Emotion Recognition Network Model

The facial expression recognition module employs the Xception model [21] with depth-wise separable convolutions for processing image data. Initially, the collected raw images are cropped to a uniform size. Subsequently, multiple convolutions are applied using 3 × 3 convolutional kernels, followed by batch normalization of the output feature maps. Max-pooling operations with 3 × 3 pooling windows are performed, and the Residual Linkage utilizes a 1 × 1 convolutional kernel to perform convolutional operations on the previous output feature maps, resulting in new residual feature maps. Finally, a softmax activation function is applied for classification, yielding a probability matrix for classification.

Speech emotion recognition uses MFCC to convert speech signals into images, and then utilizes Long Short-Term Memory (LSTM) [22] and Convolutional Neural Networks (CNN) to understand speech emotions. The specific process of converting into images involves preprocessing the speech signal, including framing and windowing. Then, Fast Fourier Transform (FFT) is applied, followed by Mel filter banks. The output of the Mel filter banks undergoes Discrete Cosine Transform (DCT) to obtain Mel-frequency cepstral coefficients (MFCC). Finally, normalization and visualization of MFCC lead to successful conversion. The LSTM model can effectively capture temporal information, while the CNN model, through a combination of convolutional layers and pooling layers, can effectively capture relevant emotional features and thus recognize emotions. The emotion recognition models leverage pre-trained deep learning computer vision and speech models within the TensorFlow framework. These models are employed to generate intermediate representations stored as h5 files for both speech and image modalities. Subsequently, the recognition outcomes from distinct channels are combined at the decision layer, incorporating a weighting criterion. This amalgamation process yields the final output, presenting probabilities and classifications for the seven emotional categories across various emotional classifications. The specific weighting criterion is delineated by the following equation:

$$E = max \sum_{i=1}^{n} \alpha \times P_p + \beta \times P_v \qquad (1)$$

where E is the final emotion category, P_p is the probability of each emotion on the image channel, P_v is the probability of each emotion on the speech channel, and α and β are the weights on the two channels, respectively.

4 Experiments

This subsection is to verify the relevance of the production of data sets for the elderly by testing and validating the same model using both the elderly data set and the public data set, respectively,; and also to test the multimodal emotion recognition model proposed in this study on the multimodal dataset to validate the effectiveness of the model by comparing the unimodal with the multimodal experiments.

4.1 Experimental Environment and Data Sets

This experiment is realized on Python 3.8 based on tensorflow framework, the hardware platform is AMD Ryzen 7 4800H with Radeon Graphics CPU, and GPU is NVIDA GeForce GTX 1650 Ti(8 GB).

The self-constructed elderly facial expression dataset for this experiment was created by integrating selected data from the RAF-DB and MMI datasets, resulting in a dataset named AGED, comprising 1560 images. For comparative purposes, the publicly available RaFD dataset was chosen, which includes 8 facial expressions captured from 5 different camera angles. To better control variables, only frontal-facing shots of 7 emotion categories, totaling 1407 images, were selected from the RaFD. From the AGED dataset, a substantial number of image data was extracted, denoted as AGED1, while the remaining 153 images were designated as the test set, known as AGED2. For the elderly multimodal dataset AGED, materials were sourced from the movie "The Happy Home." This dataset included 10 participants (5 males and 5 females) aged 60 and above. Editing software was used to ensure each video segment lasted for 3–5 s. From a total of 186 captured segments, 84 segments that met the required criteria were annotated. These segments were further manually assessed and labeled with seven emotional categories.

4.2 Elderly Dataset vs. Publicly Available Dataset

Data augmentation was applied separately to both the RaFD and AGED1 datasets, involving rotation, width shift, height shift, horizontal flipping, shearing, and zooming. Through ablation experiments, it was demonstrated that each data augmentation strategy indeed contributed to performance improvement. The experimental results are presented in Table 1.

Table 1. Results of data-enhanced ablation experiments.

Data Augmentation	RaFD_val acc	AGED1_val acc
none	54.00%	55.32%
+ rotation range = 5	56.12%	57.66%
+ width shift range = 0.01	58.42%	58.63%
+ height shift range = 0.01	60.09%	61.03%
+ horizontal flip = True	61.92%	62.26%
+ shear range = 0.1	64.45%	65.34%
+ zoom range = 0.1	65.42%	65.93%

In order to verify the significance of establishing the elderly dataset, the extracted elderly dataset AGED1 and the public dataset RaFD were trained in different backbone network modeling frameworks, and then both were tested with the test dataset AGED2, and the experimental results are as follows:

Table 2. Experimental test results of training each model on different datasets.

Method	RaFD_tes acc	AGED1_tes acc
simple CNN	60.42%	60.63%
big Xception	61.83%	63.93%
mini Xception	57.04%	57.68%
tiny Xception	51.70%	52.44%

The model trained using the elderly dataset AGED1 is better in actually recognizing the expressions of the elderly, as shown by the experimental findings in Table 2. The test accuracy in different models is improved with a maximum improvement of about 2.1%, thus proving the necessity of establishing an elderly dataset.

4.3 Unimodal vs. Multimodal Comparison

In order to verify whether multimodality is better than unimodality for emotion recognition, the big Xception model and the speech emotion recognition model with the best results are selected and fused at the decision-making level, the first time taking the value of 0.5 for both α and β, and the second time α taking the value of 0.6, and β taking the value of 0.4 for experiments respectively. The RAVDESS dataset [23] and the collected elderly emotion database AGEDS were used to test respectively.

As can be seen in Fig. 5, the unimodal facial expression recognition model is prone to identifying the "happy" emotion, with a maximum recognition rate of about 60%.

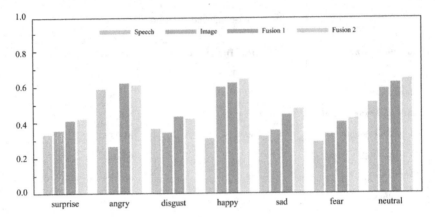

Fig. 5. Uni-bi-modal recognition results.

However, its recognition performance for other emotions is much poorer, which may result in biased recognition results. And the unimodal speech emotion recognition model has a relatively high recognition rate for the "anger" emotion, with a maximum of around 58%, but it also suffers from bias issues. The fusion model effectively mitigates the biases of both models and significantly improves the recognition accuracy of the seven types of expressions. The best results are achieved when α is set to 0.6 and β is set to 0.4. Simultaneously, the performance of the fusion model is also demonstrated through testing with our self-constructed dataset AGEDS. However, it should be noted that the relatively small size of the dataset and potential issues with data quality can impact the overall accuracy of emotion testing. As a result, the test results are not presented in this study. Nonetheless, these findings verify the superiority of multimodal information fusion for emotion recognition over unimodal approaches. Therefore, it is crucial to include more modal data in future research on emotion recognition among the elderly, in order to further improve the accuracy and reliability of the models.

5   Emotion Regulation Experiment

The purpose of this subsection is to verify the feasibility of the EmotionCare system emotion regulation program. The effectiveness of the emotion regulation strategy based on music was assessed using a trained emotion recognition model, and the general flow of the experimental design is shown in Fig. 6.

5.1   Experimental Design

1. Experimental content: assess the subjects' emotional state and regulation effect. Verify the feasibility of the proposed emotion system for the elderly, and help to verify whether the regulation strategy carries out effective regulation by recognizing emotions in real time through the emotion calculation model.
2. Experimental hypotheses: H0: Music conditioning has no effect on the mood of older adults; H1: Music conditioning has effects on the mood of older adults.

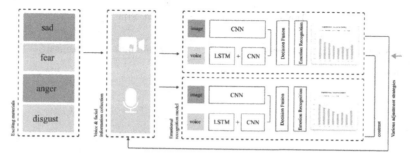

Fig. 6. Schematic diagram of the emotion regulation experiment.

3. Subjects: 30 elderly people aged 60–89 years old, 15 males and 15 females, with normal vision and hearing, and no history of mental disorders or brain injuries.
4. Experimental materials: video was chosen as the evoked stimulus because of its combination of audition and low requirements for environmental equipment and the evoked video material is shown in Table 3. Emotional clips were collected from popular movies, including four negative emotions: sadness, fear, anger, and disgust, and two 2.5-min induction videos were used for each emotion; and pure music with a light rhythm was selected as the modulation material.
5. Test equipment. Video player, emotion recognition system operation terminal (computer), Bluetooth headset
6. Experimental process.

- The experimental paper materials were distributed and the subjects were asked to sign the experimental informed consent form and the registration form for basic personal information. Afterwards, the subjects were introduced to the experimental procedure and practiced once with the practice material to familiarize themselves with the experiment more quickly, followed by a 2-min break.
- Two groups of experiments were completed under the guidance of the experimenter: Group A (control group): After playing video 1 to induce sadness, the subjects were asked to reproduce the above emotion clips and make an evaluation timed for 1 min, while using the Emotion Recognition System to record the whole emotional state.Group B (experimental group): After playing video 2 to induce sadness, the subjects were asked to reproduce the above emotional segments and make evaluations for 1 min while playing the music for regulation, and at the same time, the mood recogni-tion system was used to record the whole emotional state.
- Repeat the above steps to complete the other three emotional state regulation tasks, and the whole process of real-time voice and image information acquisition for recognition, as shown in Figure 7.
- Conduct statistical analysis of the experimental data, analyze the emotional changes of the subjects during the experimental process, verify the accuracy and usability of the emotion recognition algorithm, and explore the influence of different emotion regulation methods on the emotion and the degree of influence.

Table 3. Video evoked emotion material.

Target emotion	Material content	Duration/min	Segment
sadness	Tangshan Earthquake	2.5	2
fear	Anaconda	2.5	2
anger	the Nanjing Massacre	2.5	2
disgust	Harry Potter	2.5	2

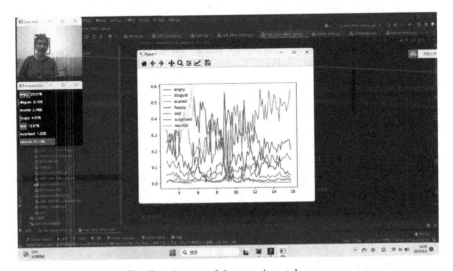

Fig. 7. Diagram of the experimental scene.

5.2 Analysis of Experimental Results

The experimental data processing of this experiment has the following two main parts:

1. Based on the emotional score data recognized in real-time by the emotion recognition model, drawing the curve graph of emotions before and after regulation, and initially determining whether music has a regulating effect on emotions.
2. To further determine whether music has an effect on mood, the statistical data were analyzed by ANOVA using SPSS software. The paired t-test was used to further determine the degree of influence of the experimental factor effects on the experimental results. The paired t-test is often used to compare the degree of difference between the means in a small sample, to infer the probability of difference, and to determine whether there is a significant difference between the two sets of means.

$$Z = \frac{\overline{x} - \mu}{s/\sqrt{n}} \tag{2}$$

where the first set of sample mean $\overline{x}$, another set of sample mean μ, the sample standard deviation s (this standard deviation s refers to the standard deviation of the mean $\overline{x}$)

and the sample size n (the number of samples with sample mean $\bar{x}$). The corresponding probability density function, or Z -distributio is:

$$f(Z) = \frac{T((v+1)/2)}{\sqrt{v\pi}\ T(v/2)}\left(1 + t^2/v\right)^{-(v+1)/2} \tag{3}$$

where $v = n - 1$. is called the degrees of freedom and T is the gamma function. $f(Z)$ is close to the standard normal distribution.

$$p = 1 - \Phi(z) \tag{4}$$

where z is the value of the statistic Z and Φ is the distribution function of the standard normal distribution. Professionally, the p-value is a decreasing indicator of the degree of reliability of the result, the larger the p-value, the more it cannot be considered the variable association in the sample as a reliable indicator for the variables association as a whole. p-values of 0.05 are generally considered to be the borderline level of acceptable error [24].

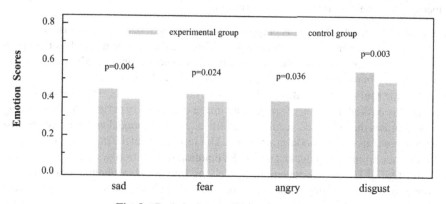

Fig. 8. Statistical analysis of emotion scores.

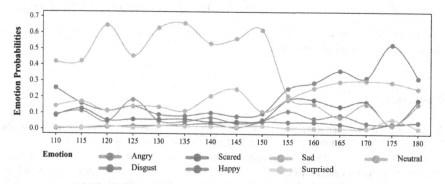

Fig. 9. Probability of real-time recognition of emotions.

As can be seen in Fig. 8, the test results between the experimental group and the control group for the four types of negative emotions are p = 0.004, p = 0.024, p =

0.036, p = 0.003, the p-value of the four groups is less than 0.05, which indicates that there is a significant difference between the mean values of the data of the two groups A and B. Therefore, the assumption that H1 is valid, verifies that the regulation of music for emotions is effective. At the same time, according to Fig. 9, the probability of real-time emotion recognition graph shows that after 150s, adding music regulation, the negative emotions decreased significantly, and the positive emotions represented by "happy" increased. This further proves the usability of the emotion recognition model and the effectiveness of emotion regulation.

6 Summary

Within the context of today's aging society and the prevailing mental health concerns among the elderly population, this study strategically centers its focus on emotions. A comprehensive multimodal emotion recognition and regulation system was meticulously crafted, tailored specifically to address the unique needs of the elderly demographic. This paper underscores the following key contributions:

- Creation of Elderly Dataset: A purposeful effort was undertaken to establish a specialized dataset catering to the elderly cohort. Empirical evidence derived from experiments affirms that models trained using this elderly-specific dataset exhibit heightened proficiency in recognizing facial expressions of the elderly.
- Real-time Multimodal Analysis: The study further achieved real-time analysis of user emotions through a fusion of speech and image data. This experimentation distinctly corroborates the enhanced accuracy and efficacy of multimodal emotion recognition compared to its single-modal counterpart. The superiority of the multimodal approach stands out prominently against unimodal emotion recognition systems.
- Validation of Emotion Regulation: By delving into auditory channel music regulation as a practical example, the study methodically substantiates the effectiveness of the emotion regulation strategy through controlled experiments. This comprehensive validation encompasses the entire trajectory from emotion recognition to regulation, encapsulating the multimodal emotion regulation system tailored for the elderly.

Disclosure of Interests. The authors have no competing interests to declare that are relevant to the content of this article.

References

1. Zhu, Y., Wu, W., Zhang, H., Qu, B.: Research on the relationship between the mental health and social support of the elderly. Chin. J. Health Stat. **05**, 699–701+706 (2022)
2. Khanal, S., Reis, A., Barroso, J., Filipe, V.: Using emotion recognition in intelligent interface design for elderly care. In: Rocha, Á., Adeli, H., Reis, L.P., Costanzo, S. (eds.) WorldCIST'18 2018. AISC, vol. 746, pp. 240–247. Springer, Cham (2018). https://doi.org/10.1007/978-3-319-77712-2_23
3. Picard, R.W., Vyzas, E., Healey, J.: Toward machine emotional intelligence: analysis of affective physiological state. IEEE Trans. Pattern Anal. Mach. Intell. **23**(10), 1175–1191 (2001)

4. Jiang, Y., Lu, D., Dang, L., Yang, Y., Shi, J.: Research progress on facial expression recognition. Intell. Comput. Appl. **06**, 43–50 (2021)
5. Caroppo, A., Leone, A., Siciliano, P.: Facial expression recognition in older adults using deep machine learning. In: AI* AAL@ AI* IA, pp. 30–43 (2017)
6. Jian, Q., Xiang, M., Huang, W.: A speech emotion recognition method for the elderly based on feature fusion and attention mechanism. In: Third International Conference on Electronics and Communication; Network and Computer Technology (ECNCT 2021), vol. 12167, pp. 398–403. SPIE (2022)
7. He, J., Liu, Y., He, Z.: Research progress on multimodal emotion recognition. Comput. Appl. Res. **35**(11), 3201–3205 (2018)
8. Song, X.: Research on Multimodal Emotion Recognition Based on Text, Speech and Video (Doctoral dissertation, Shan Dong University) (2019)
9. Metallinou, A., Lee, S., Narayanan, S.: Audio-visual emotion recognition using gaussian mixture models for face and voice. In: 2008 Tenth IEEE International Symposium on Multimedia, pp. 250–257. IEEE (2008)
10. De Silva, L.C., Miyasato, T., Nakatsu, R.: Facial emotion recognition using multi-modal information. In: Proceedings of ICICS, 1997 International Conference on Information, Communications and Signal Processing. Theme: Trends in Information Systems Engineering and Wireless Multimedia Communications (Cat. vol. 1, pp. 397–401. IEEE (1997)
11. Stathopoulou, I.O., Alepis, E., Tsihrintzis, G.A., Virvou, M.: On assisting a visual-facial affect recognition system with keyboard-stroke pattern information. Knowl.-Based Syst. **23**(4), 350–356 (2010)
12. Gai, S., Lu, Y., Zhang, Y., Zhou, L., Wang, X.: Research on proactive interaction design for intelligent home systems. J. Comput. Aid. Des. Graph. **02**, 230–237 (2023)
13. Farahani, M.A., et al.: Effect of aromatherapy on cancer complications: a systematic review. Complement. Ther. Med. **47**, 102169 (2019)
14. Schieweck, A., et al.: Smart homes and the control of indoor air quality. Renew. Sustain. Energy Rev. **94**, 705–718 (2018)
15. Teerawichitchainan, B., Pothisiri, W., Long, G.T.: How do living arrangements and intergenerational support matter for psychological health of elderly parents? evidence from Myanmar, Vietnam, and Thailand. Soc Sci Med **136**, 106–116 (2015)
16. Jenkins, S., Draper, H.: Care, monitoring, and companionship: views on care robots from older people and their carers. Int. J. Soc. Robot. **7**, 673–683 (2015)
17. Yu, X.: Emotional Interaction between Artificial Companion Agents and the Elderly. arXiv preprint arXiv:1601.05561 (2016)
18. Ekman, P., Friesen, W.V.: Constants across cultures in the face and emotion. J. Pers. Soc. Psychol. **17**(2), 124 (1971)
19. Ma, K., Wang, X., Yang, X., Zhang, M., Girard, J.M., Morency, L.P.: ElderReact: a multimodal dataset for recognizing emotional response in aging adults. In: 2019 International Conference on Multimodal Interaction, pp. 349–357 (2019)
20. Lozano-Monasor, E., López, M.T., Vigo-Bustos, F., Fernández-Caballero, A.: Facial expression recognition in ageing adults: from lab to ambient assisted living. J. Ambient. Intell. Humaniz. Comput. **8**(4), 567–578 (2017)
21. Chollet, F.: Xception: deep learning with depthwise separable convolutions. In: Proceedings of the IEEE Conference on Computer Vision and Pattern Recognition, pp. 1251–1258 (2017)
22. Hochreiter, S., Schmidhuber, J.: Long short-term memory. Neural Comput. **9**(8), 1735–1780 (1997)

23. Livingstone, S.R., Russo, F.A.: The ryerson audio-visual database of emotional speech and song (ravdess): a dynamic, multimodal set of facial and vocal expressions in North American English. PLoS ONE **13**(5), e0196391 (2018)
24. Hung, H.J., O'Neill, R.T., Bauer, P., Kohne, K.: The behavior of the p-value when the alternative hypothesis is true. Biometrics, 11–22 (1997)

The Co-design Process in the Creation of Conversational Agents for People with Dementia

Safia Dawood[1,2(✉)], Rakan Alsarhan[3], Abdulaziz Albesher[3], Fahad Alsedais[3], Abdullah Aldakheel[3], Sara Alangari[3], and Nora Almoammar[3]

[1] Software Engineering Department, Alfaisal University, Riyadh, Saudi Arabia
sdawood@alfaisal.edu
[2] AgeLab, AI Research Center, Alfaisal University, Riyadh, Saudi Arabia
[3] Human-Computer Interaction (HCI) Lab, Alfaisal University, Riyadh, Saudi Arabia
awabil@alfaisal.edu

Abstract. Many studies have been carried out to establish the effectiveness of conversational agents on the behavior of older people with dementia with positive findings. In recent years, studies have shown that conversational agents have potential in addressing behavioral and communication challenges for people with dementia and their caregivers. These technologies have been shown to provide cognitive stimulation, encourage social interaction, provide personal assistance and much more that will be mentioned throughout the paper.

In this study, we describe and report on the co-design process that was utilized for developing voice-based conversational agents. We describe the insights and recommendations that emerged from observing the three focus groups that included individuals with dementia and their caregivers. In this work, we explore the effectiveness of using co-design activities in the creation of voice-based conversational agents for people with dementia. We do this by addressing three key research questions: 1) What type of challenges and barriers affect the implementation of the co-design process for people with dementia and their caregivers? 2) How can we co-design technologies with participants who are directly involved in the provision of care for people with dementia? and 3) In what way does the resulting assistive technology support the provision of care for people with dementia and their caregivers. At the end of the study a number of challenges and insights are mentioned. The paper is organized into section introduction, literature review, results, discussions and conclusions.

Keywords: Spoken Dialogue Systems (SDS) · co-design · dementia · assistive technology · human computer interaction · voice conversational agent · Geotechnology across cultures and disciplines · involving older adults in HCI methodology · IT support for caregivers · IT use and leisure time activities of older adults · Natural language interfaces for older adults · Technology for cognitive well-being

© The Author(s), under exclusive license to Springer Nature Switzerland AG 2024
Q. Gao and J. Zhou (Eds.): HCII 2024, LNCS 14726, pp. 347–357, 2024.
https://doi.org/10.1007/978-3-031-61546-7_22

1 Introduction

In our study, we aimed to develop a mockup illustrating the process of connecting individuals with dementia with their physicians and caregivers through a smart watch connected application. The model suggested is based on the utilization of conversational agents to deliver reassuring conversational messages to individuals with dementia in different danger exposing situations.

In the study experiment, the conversational agent is set to communicate with the individuals with dementia in two specific scenarios, first scenario: when the individual's location is found to be out of the areas that are set on the application as safe zones, for example their own home or a caregiver home. In this case the application is supposed to use the conversational agent to narrate reassuring messages through the individual's wearable smart watch to calm them down and keep repeating to them to stay where they are until the assigned caregiver comes to pick them up. The second scenario involves detecting abnormalities in the individuals' vital signs indicating a state of confusion for the individuals, in this scenario the application will start the conversational agent with a different conversation that aims to calm the individual until a caregiver gets to them.

The novelty of the suggested mockup solution is in the nature of both narrations. The narrations are in Arabic language and more specifically in Saudi Arabian dialect using the voice of someone familiar and close to the individual to try and get the attention of the individual as much as possible. In addition to the uniqueness of the conversational agent, the application is supposed to notify physicians and caregivers in both scenarios.

1.1 Literature Review

Co-designing with and for people with disabilities has been explored across a range of domains with the ultimate goal of reaching a valuable meaningful outcome that is tailored to the needs of the targeted audience [1]. Co-design methods were used to develop mobile applications for carers [2, 3] interventions [4, 5] and reflections [6, 7]. Research has also demonstrated that co-designing technology with stakeholders is valued for creating meaningful technology solutions as well as for enriching and empowering the public in their own wellbeing [8]. Many researchers are now actively seeking to involve subject matter experts (SMEs) in the design of new technologies (e.g. [9, 10]). However, little research has explored inclusive co-design involving carers of people with dementia. Yet, this is particularly important when aiming to support aging populations so that the context is more authentically understood [11, 12].

The term Co-Design has its roots going back to design approaches developed in Scandinavia in the 1970s. Co-design gives importance to identifying and actively involving stakeholders of the project in the life cycle if producing the product to ensure maximum alignment between design and development processes and stakeholders satisfaction, which in return will increase usability [13] (Fig. 1).

In healthcare settings, the co-design approach must ensure alignment between patients, physicians, developers, healthcare providers, caregivers, family members, and the health-related service designers and developers [15]. Individualized solutions when it comes to healthcare is inherently personalized, and collaborative planning allows for tailored solutions to the individual needs, preferences and circumstances of individuals

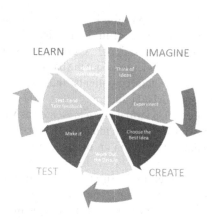

Fig. 1. MIT D-Lab's Co-Design Process Framework [14].

with dementia and caregivers is the right. This personalized approach is particularly important in the management of complex chronic conditions such as dementia, where patient needs can vary greatly [16].

Increased usability and acceptance of products or services developed through co-design tend to be user-friendly and meet practical needs of end-users, as it has led to increased utilization and adoption rates in health care treatment programs [17]. Collaborative thinking empowers individuals with dementia and caregivers by providing a voice for solutions that impact their lives. This involvement can lead to greater satisfaction, a sense of ownership of the healthcare solution, and improved health outcomes [18].

In healthcare domains involving healthcare specialists, care health providers, patients, and their family is of great importance. Knowledge and experience of healthcare professionals bring a wealth of knowledge about clinical aspects, treatment protocols, and the intricate dynamics of the healthcare system. Their involvement ensures that the proposed solution is clinically relevant and feasible within the existing healthcare system [19].

Access to caregivers often develops a deep understanding of the patient's daily challenges, wants, and needs. In dementia care, where individuals with dementia may find it difficult to communicate their needs, caregiver insight is invaluable in finding solutions that are practical and realistic to patients' life circumstances [20].

Including seniors, especially those with conditions such as dementia, provides a direct way to understand the lived experience. Their input helps shape a solution that is not only practical and user-friendly but also respectful and empowering to its users [21].

Collaboration in health care is not simply an option; It is a commitment to building truly user-centered, functional and effective solutions. By involving healthcare professionals, careers and older people in the process, we ensure that the solutions developed are not only based on clinical and practical facts but are empirically as they are also filled with the wisdom of life. As the healthcare industry continues to evolve, a collaborative design approach plays a critical role in ensuring that innovation is not only technologically advanced, but is also humane and considerate in a way that meets the real needs of individuals with dementia and their caregivers.

Conversational agents hold great promise in the healthcare domains. In this section, a brief description of the state of this tool in the medical domain is presented. Some utilization examples of Voice Conversational Agents (VCAs) in the medical domain include teaching individuals with dementia about the basic medical information in regard to their condition and treatment, retaining patients' interest and engagement with their physicians and caregivers, and decision making.

In the study by Bickmore et al. a virtual nurse presented as VCAs managed to engage in effective educational sessions with individuals with dementia about the importance of colorectal cancer screening resulting in an increase in the rate of performing these screening tests [22].

Another example was explored by Z Su et al., when they reflected on the role of VCAs during the pandemic by supporting telehealth, making it more accessible and allowing for remote guidance conversations and at the same time maintaining the social distancing restriction [23].

In the study by Laranjo et al., it was found that VCAs helped reduce the effort by physicians and healthcare providers in addition to other clinic employees when it comes to administrative work, for example, organizing and scheduling patients' appointments, processing bills and claims, and other tasks in the clinic which improved the overall workflow of the clinic [24].

A study by L Laranjo et al., explored the utilization of VCAs in healthcare and the contribution they can provide in data collection and clinical note generation. The VCAs can chat with individuals with dementia and collect information about their medical history, symptoms, and family history, VCAs can also participate in medical summaries and medical notes generation. This contribution was reported as useful for improving Electronic Health Records (EHRs) [24].

Dementia care presents unique challenges due to the progression and debilitating nature of the disease. This section examines the complexities of dementia care, considering the specific needs of individuals with dementia and their caregivers. Signs and symptoms of dementia include a decline in concentration, memory loss, and changes in behavior and personality. Caring for individuals with dementia can be emotionally and physically demanding. Caregivers often face challenges such as dealing with challenging behaviors, dealing with safety concerns, and dealing with communication difficulties. Disease progression is unpredictable, requiring continuous modification of care strategies [25].

Person-centered design is significant in individuals with dementia care providing. Every individual has specific needs, capabilities, preferences, and medical and family history, which makes it very essential to provide care plans that are tailored to every individual's specific needs and circumstances.

The study by Brooker and Sur, highlights the importance of person-centered care in the social development of individuals with dementia. It also brings forward the fact that the caregivers of individuals with dementia face significant stress and burden. Caring for family members or close individuals often causes elevated anxiety levels, stress, emotional burden, and burden that can lead to social isolation [26].

In a study by Gitlin et al., caregiver support programs that included education, counseling, and skills development, significantly reduced caregiver burden and improved the well-being of caregivers and individuals with dementia [27]. Additionally, the Alzheimer's Association (2019) reports that caregivers of individuals with dementia face financial challenges, and need to provide financial assistance and respite care services to ease some of the burden of care. Partnerships hold great promise for transforming health care by improving individual engagement, education, and productivity [28]. However, challenges such as data privacy concerns and the need for appropriate solutions need to be addressed. At the same time, dementia care presents unique challenges due to the complexity of the illness, emphasizing the need for person-centered care and comprehensive support for caregivers.

While co-design approaches have gained recognition and demonstrated their potential in various technology development contexts, a notable gap exists in the literature regarding their application to dementia care. Dementia is a complex and progressive condition with unique challenges that require tailored solutions. Despite the increasing prevalence of dementia and the growing demand for innovative care approaches, there is a scarcity of research focusing on co-design methodologies specific to dementia care technology.

Dementia care comes with challenges that are different in nature than other diseases which can be characterized by behavioral and communication issues and complex care settings. These challenges require the development of technological solutions that are sensitive to the needs and capabilities of individuals with dementia, their caregivers and health professionals.

Collaborative thinking in dementia care technologies can address this gap by engaging individuals with dementia, their caregivers and appropriate healthcare professionals in designing and developing innovative solutions Collaborative technologies as they incorporate the views of those directly affected by trauma using a person-centered approach carefully tailored to the specific needs, preferences and constraints of the community In addition, collaborative design in dementia care technology can enhance caregiver support, improve the quality of life for individuals with dementia, and contribute to more efficient and effective care Research in this area Feasibility, impact, and scalability of co-design approaches explore and ultimately advance dementia care.

2   Methodology

Our work is aligned with co-design methodologies for assistive technologies in the applied domain of intelligent cognitive assistants and speech-based interfaces.

This section includes a description of the methodology used in the co-design approach of the voice based conversational agents (VCAs) application designed to assist individuals with dementia and to help their caregivers in providing better care for them. The method is based on three focus groups with participants including individuals with dementia diagnosis and their caregivers.

Focus Group Selection and Composition. The focus groups need to conform to the following criteria:

Care givers: They are caregivers responsible for individuals with dementia support and assistance. This focus group included family members, friends, or neighbors. Those members' main role was to share their perspectives and personal experiences dealing with individuals with dementia, as well as their expectations and concerns about using VCAs as assistive tools.

Older individuals with professional diagnosis of dementia: They were individuals who were aged 65 or above and they have cognitive impairment. They were recruited from local senior centers and community platforms. Members of this group represent potential users of VCAs who might benefit from the main service of providing guidance when being in a state of confusion.

Participants diagnosed with dementia who live with a caregiver will be participating in this study through the introduction of their caregivers.

Caregivers of individuals with dementia will report on the different interaction the divisas with dementia have with different social applications and then build formative evaluations that provide the opportunity to improve the Dementia AI application design.

The recruitment process ensured diversity in terms of age, gender, education, and background. Each group included 2 to 4 members, and each session lasted up to 40 min. Sessions were conducted in person or through video conferencing platforms.

Co-design Framework. The co-design process consists of four main stages: exploration, ideation, prototyping, and evaluation. The framework involves various tasks and activities to engage participants in the design process as follows:

Exploration: In this study researchers aimed to explore context and identify the problem of using VCAs for focus groups. During this phase interviews and surveys sessions were conducted to collect demographic information, current practices, needs, preferences, and challenges of the focus group participants. Also, scenarios were used to extract clear reactions and opinions on many suggested situations and interactions involving VCAs [29].

Formative evaluation, and design consideration of other communication applications, like Facebook and WhatsApp were will be conducted. This evaluation process focused on the feedback given by the caregiver that reelected preferences of individuals of dementia under their care which includes elements of usability, usefulness, and relevance of the app. The purpose of this step is to capture as much as possible user experience to give insight to the design process that is used in software development.

Ideation: This stage focused on selecting the ideas, features and functions of the VCAs. This stage includes activities such as brainstorming and voting. Brainstorming sessions were used to extract and encourage individuals with dementia alongside their caregiver to engage and generate as many ideas as possible, without any judgment or influence. Voting sessions used to create a priority among ideas and select ideas based on feasibility and accuracy and possibility of further development.

Prototyping: This stage aimed to create a mockup prototype of the VCAs. The prototyping phase included visualizations of the appearance and interface of the VCAs, g, storyboarding used to illustrate the user journey and interaction flow of the VCAs, and role-playing used to simulate and evaluate the user experience and feedback of the VCAs [30].

Evaluation: This phase activity is focused on assessing and improving the effectiveness of the co-design process and the resulting mockups. This stage deploys assessment tools such as interviews and focus groups to measure the participants' satisfaction, engagement, and perceived usefulness of the co-design process and the VCAs visualizations. Also, the assessment is intended to collect the participants' feedback and suggestions for improvements [31].

Usability testing, user satisfaction, and user acceptance methods were used in the evaluation framework described in the next subsection. Each used test helped to assess different criteria of the proposed prototype. The evaluation process was conducted on both the final visual of process flows and the co-design process application to measure the efficiency and effectiveness of the framework in such a healthcare application scenario, summarized in Table 1.

Table 1. Testing methods and measures

Evaluation Session	Measures	Methods
Usability testing (Mockup, process flow)	effectiveness efficiency learnability	Interviews
user satisfaction	intention and willingness of usage	interviews

3   Results

This section will report on the findings of VCAs application co-design experiment involving individuals with dementia and their caregivers. This section is organized into two subsections: challenges and barriers, and co-design insights.

Challenges and Barriers. This section will reveal the challenges and barriers that need to be addressed when deploying co-design methodology as an innovation framework for dementia care applications. Interoperability and workflow integration: Health applications gather information from their users either by direct interactions or through continuous monitoring. Concerns arise when trying to incorporate these applications as a component that supplies and consumes data to the healthcare ecosystem. This incorporation process is considered challenging since healthcare ecosystems include a number of interconnect subsystems for example Electronic Health Records, medical data marts, and other healthcare applications like Tawakkalna and Sehaty. The co-design methodology should ensure seamless compatibility and integration with the existing healthcare ecosystem infrastructure. Also, it is important for the co-design approaches to take into consideration standards and protocols for data exchange enabling interoperability between different components of this ecosystem. It is also very important to address how complicated the healthcare workflow is and to keep the interruption caused by adopting the co-design approaches as minimal as possible to ensure smooth integration.

Regulatory compliance: The healthcare ecosystem is one of the highly regulated systems due to the important issues of maintaining patients' safety, and data privacy and security. If health application developer is to follow the co-design approaches, there must be way to ensure these approaches adherence to relevant regulations and healthcare laws introduced by local and global regulatory bodies like the Saudi Healthcare Development

Holding Company (HDH), the Ministry of Health (MOH), and HIPPA association and gain approval from these bodies.

Scalability and sustainability: In order for the co-design approach to be adopted in the healthcare ecosystem, it needs to prove its ability to be scaled accommodating for the ever-growing healthcare system on all dimensions, number of patients, technologies and clinical practices, and the new findings and discoveries in the healthcare domain. Scalability and sustainability should take into consideration long term support and maintenance in providing upgrades and update packages.

Stakeholder engagement: The stakeholders pool in the healthcare ecosystem is vast and diverse encompassing patients, caregiver, regulators, and healthcare specialists. Each of these stakeholders has their own set of priorities and interests. If the co-design approaches were to be adopted in the healthcare ecosystem, the need for feasible and effective communication and engagement mechanisms that align with the nature, needs and preferences of each stakeholder. This should take into consideration building consensus and addressing diverse perspectives.

Data privacy and security: Data safety and security is a very important and sensitive issue. Co-designed approaches need to showcase suitable safeguards for the healthcare ecosystem to encourage and promote the usage of its tools in such a domain. The safeguards should provide protection in cases such as unauthorized access, breaches, and misuse.

Co-design Insights. The co-design process implementation in this study, generated several insights and recommendations that enriched the co-design process and outcomes of dementia care in a healthcare setting. These insights and recommendations can be summarized in four themes: efficiency, safety and information quality, user experience, and clinical health outcomes.

Efficiency: the study suggested various features and functionalities to be integrated within the co-design process, such as providing information, advice, support, documentation, and reporting. Scenarios and situations should be included in the co-design activities, such as patients' scenarios at home or hospital.

Safety and information quality: The study stressed the need for ensuring the safety, quality and privacy measures during co-design process, such as complying with Health Insurance Portability and Accountability Act (HIPAA) and respecting the user's consent. The process should provide trustworthy and evidence-based data. The study also proposed enhancing safety and information quality measures, such as using encryption, authentication, and verification due to the sensitivity nature of the medical settings.

User experience: The experiment indicated that the co-design process should focus on the expectations and preferences of the user experience during the co-design process, such as their usability, acceptability, and satisfaction. The study proposed providing interactive experience for the co-design implementation process, such as using empathetic language and adapting to the user's needs and preferences and offering options and guidance.

Clinical and health outcomes: The study anticipated the potential impact and benefits of the co-design process outcome in healthcare context, such as improving patients' health and well-being, enhancing the quality and efficiency of healthcare changes, and influencing the new healthcare innovations adherence. The study proposed recommendations to measure and evaluate the clinical and health outcomes of the co-design process, such as quality of care indicators, and medical change techniques.

4 Discussion

The study provided a number of challenges that may arise when utilizing the co-design approach in healthcare domains.

And in this section, we discuss some of the considerations that need to be taken to make the co-design more suitable and effective in healthcare domains.

Adopting a unique visual of verbal or both communication techniques to accommodate individuals with cognitive impairments, in our case individuals with dementia.

Visual or verbal aids will allow for more effective co-design approach implementation since it facilitates ability to provide input, express preferences, or fully comprehend the design. These aids need careful design involving caregivers who have a better understanding of the needs of individuals with dementia to ensure availability and accessibility.

Most of the time, caregivers for individuals with cognitive impairments like dementia have time constraints and emotional stress that limits their active participation, an element that is the base for a successful co-design approach implementation. Co-design sessions need to be scheduled in a way that considers their availability and provides suitable alternatives such as online participation options and fixable sessions' schedules that take into consideration caregivers burnout and burdens.

The co-design approach should ensure that healthcare developed assistive technologies are tailored to fit the specific needs, preferences of those it is supposed to assist. In general, identifying the needs and preferences of individuals with dementia and their caregivers by conducting thorough research in the domain to be able to utilize the co-design approach in an effective way. This includes addressing the approach interviews, observations and focus groups.

5 Conclusion

This research aimed to co-design communication agents for dementia care, including three focus groups: one with healthcare professionals, one with careers, and one for people with dementia. The research followed a user-centered and participatory approach, consisting of four phases: research, ideation, prototyping, and evaluation. The research revealed a number of challenges and barriers as well as insights and recommendations for designing and implementing conversational agents in dementia care. Research also discussed the potential impact of co-designed conversational agents on functionality, safety and information quality, user experience, and users' clinical and health outcomes. The research contributes to the field of communication agents and dementia care, by providing a comprehensive and systematic framework for co-designing conversational agents with users and stakeholders, as well as conversational agents to support dementia care in different domains. By demonstrating the possibility and willingness to use agents.

Scenarios and situations. The research provides valuable insights and implications for future research and practice, focusing on the continuous improvement of co-design processes and technology development for dementia care.

Acknowledgments. The authors would like to thank the Solveathon program at Alfaisal University, the College of Engineering, and the AUEP enrichment programs at Alfaisal University for partially supporting this project.

References

1. Sarmiento-Pelayo, M.P.: Co-design: a central approach to the inclusion of people with disabilities. Rev. de la Facultad de Medicina **63**, 149–154 (2015)
2. Rathnayake, S., et al.: Co-design of an mHealth application for family caregivers of people with dementia to address functional disability care needs. Inform. Health Soc. Care **46**(1), 1–17 (2021)
3. Davies, N., et al.: A co-design process developing heuristics for practitioners providing end of life care for people with dementia. BMC Palliat. Care **15**(1), 1–11 (2016)
4. Yadav, U.N., et al.: Using a co-design process to develop an integrated model of care for delivering self-management intervention to multi-morbid COPD people in rural Nepal. Health Res. Policy Syst. **19**(1), 1–12 (2021)
5. Goeman, D.P., et al.: Partnering with people with dementia and their care partners, aged care service experts, policymakers and academics: a co-design process. Australas. J. Ageing **38**, 53–58 (2019)
6. Tong, C., et al.: Lessons and reflections from an extended co-design process developing an mHealth app with and for older adults: multiphase, mixed methods study. JMIR Aging **5**(4), e39189 (2022)
7. Moll, S., et al.: Are you really doing 'codesign'? critical reflections when working with vulnerable populations. BMJ Open **10**(11), e038339 (2020)
8. Sharpe, D., et al.: It's my diabetes: Co-production in practice with young people in delivering a 'perfect' care pathway for diabetes. Research for All (2018)
9. Threatt, A.L., et al.: The design, prototyping, and formative evaluation of an assistive robotic table (art) for stroke patients. HERD: Health Environ. Res. Des. J. **10**(3), 152–169 (2017)
10. Wray, T.B., et al.: User-centered, interaction design research approaches to inform the development of health risk behavior intervention technologies. Internet Interv. **15**, 1–9 (2019)
11. Niedderer, K., et al.: Designing with and for people with dementia: developing a mindful interdisciplinary co-design methodology (2020)
12. Wolters, M.K., Kelly, F., Kilgour, J.: Designing a spoken dialogue interface to an intelligent cognitive assistant for people with dementia. Health Inform. J. **22**(4), 854–866 (2016)
13. Donetto, S., et al.: Experience-based co-design and healthcare improvement: realizing participatory design in the public sector. Des. J. **18**(2), 227–248 (2015)
14. Light, T.: Designing usable impact frameworks to support youth entrepreneurship in Kenya. https://d-lab.mit.edu/news-blog/blog/designing-usable-impact-frameworks-support-youth-entrepreneurship-kenya. Accessed 03 Oct 2019
15. Sanders, E.B.-N., Stappers, P.J.: Co-creation and the new landscapes of design. Co-design **4**(1), 5–18 (2008)
16. Robert, G.: Participatory action research: using experience-based co-design to improve the quality of healthcare services. Understanding Using Health Experiences–Improving Patient Care, 138–150 (2013)

17. Bate, P., Robert, G.: Experience-based design: from redesigning the system around the patient to co-designing services with the patient. Qual. Saf. Health Care **15**(5), 307 (2006)
18. Palmer, V.J., et al.: The Participatory Zeitgeist: an explanatory theoretical model of change in an era of coproduction and codesign in healthcare improvement. Med. Humanit. (2018)
19. Steinert, Y., O'Sullivan, P.S., Irby, D.M.: Strengthening teachers' professional identities through faculty development. Acad. Med. **94**(7), 963–968 (2019)
20. Meiland, F., et al.: Technologies to support community-dwelling persons with dementia: a position paper on issues regarding development, usability, effectiveness and cost-effectiveness, deployment, and ethics. JMIR Rehabil. Assistive Technol. **4**(1), e6376 (2017)
21. Lindsay, S., et al.: Engaging older people using participatory design. In: Proceedings of the SIGCHI Conference on Human Factors in Computing Systems (2012)
22. Bickmore, T.W., Pfeifer, L.M., Jack, B.W.: Taking the time to care: empowering low health literacy hospital patients with virtual nurse agents. In: Proceedings of the SIGCHI Conference on Human Factors in Computing Systems (2009)
23. Su, Z., Schneider, J.A., Young, S.D.: The role of conversational agents for substance use disorder in social distancing contexts. Subst. Use Misuse **56**(11), 1732–1735 (2021)
24. Laranjo, L., et al.: Conversational agents in healthcare: a systematic review. J. Am. Med. Inform. Assoc. **25**(9), 1248–1258 (2018)
25. Yates, J., et al.: Challenges in disclosing and receiving a diagnosis of dementia: a systematic review of practice from the perspectives of people with dementia, carers, and healthcare professionals. Int. Psychogeriatr. **33**(11), 1161–1192 (2021)
26. Brooker, D., Surr, C.: Dementia Care Mapping: Principles and Practice. University of Bradford, Bradford Dementia Group (2005)
27. Gitlin, L.N., et al.: Effect of multicomponent interventions on caregiver burden and depression: the REACH multisite initiative at 6-month follow-up. Psychol. Aging **18**(3), 361 (2003)
28. Association, A.S.: Alzheimer's disease facts and figures. Alzheimer's Dementia **15**(3), 321–387 (2019)
29. Sadek, M., Calvo, R.A., Mougenot, C.: Co-designing conversational agents: a comprehensive review and recommendations for best practices. Des. Stud. **89**, 101230 (2023)
30. Heuer, M., et al.: Towards effective conversational agents: a prototype-based approach for facilitating their evaluation and improvement. In: International Conference on Human-Computer Interaction. Springer (2023). https://doi.org/10.1007/978-3-031-35708-4_23
31. Ding, H., et al.: Evaluation framework for conversational agents with artificial intelligence in health interventions: a systematic scoping review. J. Am. Med. Inform. Assoc. p. ocad222 (2023)

SafeSpace, the Smart Caretaker: An AI-Driven Safe and Comfortable Environment for the Well-Being of Alzheimer's and Dementia Patients

Kenneth King III[1]([✉])[ID] and Mohamed Azab[2][ID]

[1] Virginia Tech, Blacksburg, VA 24060, USA
{kking935,mazab}@vt.edu
[2] Virginia Military Institute, Lexington, VA 24450, USA
azabmm@vmi.edu

Abstract. In spite of the obstacles they face, many people living with dementia aspire to continue living independently for as long as possible. While technology cannot address all their needs, smart home systems have shown benefits for both patients and their caregivers. However, little research has explored how the recent improvements in Generative AI can re-imagine such systems. In this paper, we present SafeSpace, a smart home system designed to augment the dementia care process. By emphasizing privacy, security, personalization, accessibility, and augmentation, SafeSpace is a holistic solution with real-world feasibility. To showcase the system's design and potential, we implement an initial prototype and provide a qualitative evaluation of its flexibility and latency. We conclude by summarizing the main takeaways of SafeSpace and the key areas for future work.

Keywords: Human-Computer Interaction (HCI) · Generative AI · Internet of Things (IoT)

1 Introduction

Dementia profoundly impacts individuals and their families, turning daily life into a constant struggle. As the disease progresses, it diminishes memory and cognitive abilities, making everyday tasks increasingly hazardous. The risk of developing dementia grows with age, exacerbating the challenges faced by the elderly. Despite this, there is hope for maintaining a meaningful quality of life, highlighting the need for strategies that support independence for as long as possible [1,10]. In the face of dementia's advancement, the emphasis on maintaining some level of autonomy is crucial. Innovative care strategies, assistive technologies (ATs), and therapeutic interventions can help individuals engage meaningfully with their environment and maintain connections with their loved ones [7,13,14]. Supporting the individual's dignity and independence, along with providing resources and education for families and caregivers, forms the corner-stone of effective dementia care. Thus, amidst the challenges, a focus on person-alized care and the enhancement of well-being for both those with dementia and their caregivers is essential. It's about navigating dementia with dignity, under-scoring the importance of fostering independence and a high quality of life for as long as achievable. The responsibilities borne by the families and caregivers of dementia patients are immense and multifaceted, encompassing a wide range of duties that extend far beyond basic care. They find themselves in a perpetual state of vigilance, monitoring the patient's daily activities to ensure safety and prevent accidents, which becomes increasingly challenging as the patient's con-dition deteriorates. This monitoring includes managing medications, ensuring the patient eats and drinks properly, and preventing wandering—a common and dangerous issue among those with dementia.

Moreover, caregivers must also attend to the emotional and psychological needs of the patient, striving to maintain a sense of comfort and normalcy in their lives. This involves engaging the patient in activities that can help slow the progression of cognitive decline, providing emotional support, and managing episodes of confusion, aggression, or agitation, which are common as demen-tia progresses. The effort to balance these responsibilities while maintaining a nurturing environment is a source of significant stress and emotional labor for caregivers [12].

The impact on caregivers goes beyond the physical tasks of care; it encom-passes an emotional toll as they watch their loved ones decline and their per-sonalities change. The stress of caregiving can lead to burnout, depression, and health problems for caregivers themselves, highlighting the need for adequate support systems. In essence, the role of caregivers and families in managing the daily lives and comfort of dementia patients is a testament to their resilience and dedication. However, it also underscores the critical need for comprehensive support structures that address both the tangible and intangible challenges faced by those who care for individuals with dementia. Caregivers play a vital role in this mission, but it is clear they need more support. While 95% of elderly people with dementia rely on caregivers, the majority of these caregivers are unpaid and typically family of the patient. At the same time, the majority of US seniors with dementia live in poverty and one in three live on their own [3]. Both patients and caregivers have unmet needs, and they are in need of improved resources and solutions to live their best lives possible [1,2,12].

The integration of Artificial Intelligence (AI) and Large Language Models (LLMs) into healthcare, particularly in the context of dementia care, holds promising prospects for enhancing patient comfort and caregiver efficiency. The potential of these technologies to transform care delivery is significant, offer-ing innovative solutions that can be tailored to the unique needs of individuals with cognitive decline. This section elaborates on the applications of AI and LLMs in healthcare, the challenges of current care models, and the necessity of holistic approaches that combine technology with human-centered care. Recent advancements in AI and LLMs have demonstrated their applicability in healthcare settings, offering tools for diagnosis, personalized care, and patient engagement [5,15]. In dementia care, these technologies can be leveraged to monitor patient health indicators, track daily activities, and provide interactive engagement through conversational agents. LLMs, with their ability to process and generate natural language, can facilitate communication between patients and caregivers, offering reminders, information, and companionship, thereby reducing feelings of isolation. Despite the promising applications, the deployment of AI and smart monitoring devices in care settings is not without its challenges. Some significant hurdles include: the need for continuous monitoring by caregivers, the lack of comprehensive situation awareness, the limited understanding of the AI limitations by the users, and the lack of patient-centric and scalable solutions. Researchers have emphasized the importance of creating a serene and comfortable environment for individuals with dementia, noting the beneficial impact of familiar comfort objects, faces, and voices [9]. These elements can serve as effective distractions and provide a sense of security, underscoring the fact that technology alone cannot fulfill all the needs of dementia patients. While smart systems offer valuable tools for monitoring and interaction, they must be integrated into a broader care strategy that includes physical comfort, emotional support, and the promotion of a familiar, reassuring environment. To address these challenges, this paper presents a blend of the strengths of AI and LLMs with the nuanced understanding and compassion that human caregivers provide. The goal is to create a pathway to more AI-driven responsive and personalized care strategies. However, the success of these technologies depends on their integration into a holistic care model that values human touch as much as technological innovation. By augmenting the capabilities of AI with the irreplaceable presence of caregivers, it is possible to create a more supportive and comforting environment for individuals with dementia. This paper introduces SafeSpace, an innovative smart environment equipped with an AI-driven digital caregiver designed to assist elderly individuals with cognitive impairments. SafeSpace utilizes a network of smart sensors and appliances to enhance user safety and convenience through real-time monitoring, customized interactions, and proactive safety measures. The system is programmed to adhere to safety protocols set by caregivers, family, or medical professionals, ensuring patients remain within safe boundaries by monitoring their location, medication intake, and daily routines, and steering them clear of potential hazards.

In Sect. 2, we discuss previous work that has explored the benefits and challenges of technology in supporting people with dementia. In Sect. 3, we present the system requirements and corresponding design. We discuss the current implementation in Sect. 4 and evaluate its real-world feasibility in Sect. 5. Finally, we conclude the paper in Sect. 6 by discussing the main takeaways of SafeSpace and the key areas for future work.

2   Related Work

When exploring how the latest advancements in AI and LLMs can improve dementia care, it is critical to understand how technology is already being utilized in dementia care and what challenges exist. Dixon et al. [4] provide valuable insight into this question. They conducted a user study to explore in what ways mobile phones support people living with mild to moderate dementia, and their findings highlight five key domains:

- **Communication**: Participants used their phones to call/text their caregivers, doctors, and other members of their care team.
- **Entertainment**: Participants reported that they enjoyed using their phones for personal entertainment, such as social media, shopping, and the news.
- **Memory**: Participants reported that functions such as setting daily reminders, scheduling upcoming events, and taking notes helped counteract their declining memory.
- **Safety**: Some participants relied on their phones for safety features such as the ability to track their location if they get lost or contact emergency services if they are in danger.
- **Monitoring**: Certain participants reported that they connected their phones to medical devices to monitor their health.

While this study focused specifically on mobile phones, for many people living with dementia this represents the greatest extent of their technology use. Therefore, these findings demonstrate some of the main ways technology is already supporting people living with dementia and indicate where some of the greatest benefits may be found. However, the user study also uncovered critical challenges that remain unsolved. First, participants report that they still struggle to navigate their mobile devices due to small, complex, unintuitive and/or updated interfaces. Participants said that oftentimes they knew what action they wanted to take, but forgot how to so do. Similarly, participants also reported that at times they made mistakes when completing tasks on their phone, such as accidentally scheduling medical appointments for the wrong date. Finally, participants desired more intelligent systems that could interact with them through extended modalities such as voice and provide proactive assistance to reduce the effort and cognitive load on their end. Participants had personal examples of where they wanted greater automation, such as the ability for their phone to passively listen to their conversation with their doctor and automatically schedule events or ask questions based on the conversation. Notably, participants expressed that they wanted to be in control of the system for now, but wanted the system to take on greater control and autonomy once their mental condition worsens during the later stages of dementia.

Health-centered smart home systems have the potential to address these challenges and extend the potential benefits. Such systems are capable of integrating Internet-of-Things (IoT) devices such as smartwatches, motion sensors, and microphones to provide greater sensory input that the system can monitor and act on. IoT devices like speakers and smart TVs can also provide a way for the system to interact with the patient. Prior works [6,8,11] have shown promise for such systems, but these systems fail to holistically address the needs for personalization, accessibility, security, and privacy. Most of all, they are not well designed for the new era of AI and the requirements, challenges, and possibilities it brings.

3 System Design

3.1 System Requirements

To provide the best care possible, we identified several key requirements the system must follow:

1. **Privacy** - Since the system will process protected health information (PHI) about the patient, the system should follow strong privacy measures.
2. **Security** - The system must be secure against cyberattacks, tampering, and any other scenario where someone attempts to disturb the system or report fraudulent data.
3. **Personalization** - Each patient and caregiver has their own unique needs and preferences, and therefore the system must be highly customizable to support personalized care at each stage of dementia.
4. **Accessibility** - Patients and caregivers are limited in their resources, so the system should minimize hardware requirements while also maximizing support for any devices they do have.
5. **Augmentation** - The system should be well designed for machine-in-the-loop tasks, making automatic intelligent actions on the patient's behalf and augmenting the caregiver's job where feasible.

To address these system requirements, we propose a modular framework that abstracts various system components in a simple, scalable manner. There are six core modules that, in combination, provide a powerful framework for building an advanced smart home system for dementia care. The modules are as follows:

3.2 System Modules

The system allows for any models to be added and used interchangeably following a common interface based on the model's task. This provides support for more advanced AI use cases, such as fine-tuned LLMs and custom risk prediction models.

3.3 Sensing: System Inputs

Inputs introduce new data into the system. We identify two main types of inputs, physical IoT devices internal to the system and web APIs external to the system. Physical IoT devices such as smartwatches provide real-time sensory data related to the patient, caregiver, and their environment. In contrast, external APIs provide other relevant data such as the current weather, upcoming medical appointments, unread emails, and other information that is recorded from outside the system. Any data entering the system should be validated to ensure it is authentic and trustworthy before acting on it.

The collected data is then passed to the State Manager, a central component of the system responsible for managing and storing this information securely.

3.4   Actuation System Outputs

Outputs allow the system to interact with the outside world. Examples of outputs include text/email notification services, speakers to play audio, and smart TVs to play video.

3.5   Actions

Actions carry out specific tasks for the patient and caregiver. As part of their tasks, actions can access all other modules in the system (models, inputs, outputs, schedules, and state). This provides the tasks with full control to interact with the patient and caregiver, as well as interact with the system in ways like scheduling new tasks, adding new state watchers, and modifying metadata about the patient like whether they have exercised today.

For example, a custom action could use an LLM to hold context-aware conversations with the primary objective of keeping the patient focused on comforting topics and positive reminders. By incorporating additional IoT input devices such as a biometric smartwatch, the system can monitor the patient's mental and physical health at all times. While actions will not administer physical care, they can play a critical role in providing the patient with important reminders such as to take their daily medicines, not to use the stove, and so on.

3.6   States

State Managers are central components of the system responsible for managing and storing all input data and other system state information securely.

State Watchers monitor the inflow of data and trigger actions based on certain state scenarios. They can be easily configured to watch for standard risks such as high heart rate, low blood pressure, etc., but can also trigger actions based on more sophisticated scenarios and model predictions.

3.7   Activities Scheduler

The scheduler can be configured to trigger actions at specific times, dates, or intervals. For example, the scheduler could be used to automatically trigger the alarm clock at the same time each morning, remind the patient of an upcoming medical appointment on a specific date, or play a soothing song at the top of every hour.

With just these six modules, the system can be customized for virtually any task or scenario. Figure 1 demonstrates the flow of the system. The sensors write data to the state manager. When data is updated, the state watcher analyzes the state and triggers certain actions depending on certain scenarios / predicted risks. Actions can also be triggered by the scheduler, and are able to interact with the user by making function calls to the outputs module.

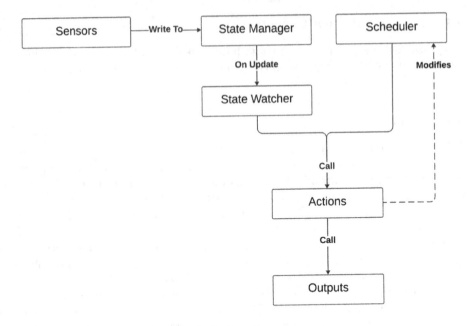

Fig. 1. System Overview.

4 System Prototype

To demonstrate the system design, we created an implementation of this modular framework running locally on a Macbook Pro M3 using Python 3 and various AI models. Each input runs on its own thread and the state manager uses locks to ensure thread safety. Similarly, each output also employs its own locks to ensure they only process one request at a time. This helps to prevent possible scenarios like two actions trying to play a message on a speaker at the same time. The specific details of the AI models, inputs, and outputs modules are as follows:

4.1 Models Implementation

We chose to support the three following tasks- speech recognition, speech synthesis, and text generation. For speech generation, we created a custom integration to run OpenAI's Whisper-v3 model locally.

Transcription. As a testament to SafeSpace's ability to support advanced AI integrations, our Whisper-v3 integration uses the whisper.cpp library with Core ML support to provide the fastest possible transcription speeds for our specific device. We also created simple integrations for API-based transcription services such as Hugging Face, Deepgram, AssemblyAI.

Speech Synthesis. For speech synthesis we created an integration for Eleven-Labs' commercial speech generation API, specifically selecting their multilingual-v2-turbo model for faster response times.

Text Generation. Finally, we created an integration for OpenAI's gpt-4-turbo model to use in text generation tasks.

4.2 Simulated and Collected Inputs

We implemented three example inputs- a microphone, a smartwatch, and a proximity sensor. The microphone input demonstrates an example of how simple it is to create device-specific integrations with advanced logic like voice activation and custom stop words. As the microphone input records audio, it uses the Whisper-v3 integration to transcribe the audio and record what the user said in the state. In contrast, the smartwatch and proximity sensor inputs demonstrate how the system can use simulated sensors. This is invaluable during development and testing to simulate specific scenarios. For example, our smartwatch simulates the functionality of a wearable health monitoring device and generates mock data related to the patient's vital signs, including heart rate, blood pressure, temperature, and oxygen levels.

4.3 Simulated Actions

We implemented three outputs- a smart speaker, a smart TV, and a notification system. The smart speaker output integrates with the built-in system speakers for the local device. For simplicity, the smart TV and notification system are both simulated and serve as high-level representations of real smart TVs like Samsung and notification services like Amazon SNS.

4.4 Implemented Actions

We implemented four actions- simple reminder, meditation, exercise, and conversation. The simple reminder action uses the ElevenLabs integration to generate an audio reminder and play the message over the speaker. The meditation action uses the speaker to play a short soothing song designed to help the patient relax. The exercise action uses the smart TV to play a short training video. Finally, the conversation action uses the GPT-4 and ElevenLabs integrations to generate audio in specific voices, then interacts with the patient by playing this audio over the speaker.

4.5 State Watchers

We created four rudimentary examples of state watchers. The first example monitors the patient's steps to predict whether they have exercised, updating their exercised state to true when they exceed their daily steps goal. Conversely, the second example tracks the steps and heart rate to predict anxiety, setting their anxious state to true and notifying the caregiver if the system observes that the patient has taken few steps today yet has an elevated heart rate. The third example monitors the proximity sensor to determine if the person is near an off-limits area of the house. If the proximity value is below a certain threshold, the system uses the simple reminder action to warn the patient that they are in an off-limits area and notify the caregiver. In the fourth and most advanced example, the watcher monitors the transcription state to see if the patient has said anything, and triggers the conversation action when the patient says something new.

4.6 The Main Task Scheduler

We configured the scheduler to automatically run the meditation action at a specific time each morning. We also created an example of a patient medical calendar to demonstrate how the scheduler can trigger reminders of these events at specific dates and times using the simple reminder action.

5 Qualitative Evaluation

Reflecting on this prototype, we feel that it adequately addresses each of the system requirements and therefore provides a strong system foundation that can be extended to many different care scenarios. As shown through our example implementations, the system is simple yet highly customizable to support many different AI models, inputs and outputs, actions, and monitoring tasks. For computationally expensive actions such as holding a natural conversation with the patient, slow response times significantly hind the feasibility of such actions and by extension the overall system. We addressed this in our implementation by choosing specific models that balance quality with speed and found that we can achieve response times within approximately 10 s. We believe this latency is within a feasible range for the common user, but it is unclear how slow response times could impact the mental state of dementia patients. It is possible that this short pause could confuse or distract users, and this is a key area of focus for our future work.

6 Ethical Considerations of Emerging Human-AI Interactions

SafeSpace's generative AI features open up new possibilities for novel human-AI interactions, but in many cases pose serious ethical questions. Perhaps most notably, as speech and video generation models continue to improve, it is becoming easier to automatically generate deepfake content of people with high levels of realism. Studies have demonstrated that people with dementia exhibit a more positive response to the familiar voices and faces of loved ones [9]. Therefore, one of the best ways for the system to engage with the patient could be through dynamically generated deepfake content of a friend or family member. The system could play this content on output devices like smart TVs and speakers. However, even if all parties consented to this and it showed significant health outcomes, it is still unclear if this would be ethical given the vulnerable mental state of the patient. Especially as they progress into the later stages of dementia, showing patients such deepfake content could confuse them, blur their sense of reality, and harm their cognitive health over time. In this regard, we hope SafeSpace will help start the conversation surrounding the ethical boundaries that should be applied to emerging use cases of AI to ensure the long-term well-being of patients, their caregivers, and others.

7   Conclusions and Future Work

In this work, we present a comprehensive smart environment driven by a smart digital caregiver designed to serve elderly people with limited cognitive abilities. The presented framework, SafeSpace, manages and controls various smart sensors and appliances to ensure safety and convenience for the user. The framework offers real-time monitoring and patient-aware customized conversations and actions. Guided by a customized strategy provided by the caregiver, family, or doctors, SafeSpace ensures that the patient always remains within the allowed safety boundaries. It checks geolocations both indoors and outdoors, medication usage, and daily habits, and gently enforces avoidance of hazards such as fireplaces and stoves.

At this stage of the project, SafeSpace is taking its first steps towards our ultimate goal of patient safety. In our subsequent evolution, SafeSpace will focus on convenience, which is crucial for elderly people with limited cognitive abilities. Given consent, in the sequel phase, SafeSpace will use speech cloning models to initiate conversations in the voices of the patient's loved ones. Using smart projection tools like TVs and photo frames, SafeSpace will ensure that images of those loved ones, along with convenient pictures from good memories, are always displayed and changing. The agent will be programmed to open conversations related to such images and will use deepfake technology to support these conversations with familiar faces and places of loved ones.

Acknowledgments. This study is sponsored in part by the Commonwealth Cyber Initiative, an investment in the advancement of cyber R&D, innovation, and workforce development. For more information about CCI, visit: www.cyberinitiative.org.

References

1. Alnes, R.E., Malmedal, W., Nordtug, B., Steinsheim, G., Blindheim, K.: Improving everyday life of people with dementia living at home: health care professionals' experiences. J. Nurs. Manag. **30**(7), 3628–3636 (2022). https://doi.org/10.1111/jonm.13819, https://onlinelibrary.wiley.com/doi/abs/10.1111/jonm.13819
2. Black, B.S., Johnston, D., Rabins, P.V., Morrison, A., Lyketsos, C., Samus, Q.M.: Unmet needs of community-residing persons with dementia and their informal caregivers: findings from the maximizing independence at home study. J. Am. Geriatr. Soc. **61**(12), 2087–2095 (2013). https://doi.org/10.1111/jgs.12549
3. Chi, W., et al.: Older Adults with Dementia and Their Caregivers: Key Indicators from the National Health and Aging Trends Study. The Office of the Assistant Secretary for Planning and Evaluation, Washington, DC (2019)
4. Dixon, E., et al.: Mobile phone use by people with mild to moderate dementia: uncovering challenges and identifying opportunities: mobile phone use by people with mild to moderate dementia. In: Proceedings of the 24th International ACM SIGACCESS Conference on Computers and Accessibility. ASSETS 2022, Association for Computing Machinery, New York, NY, USA (2022). https://doi.org/10.1145/3517428.3544809
5. Jo, E., Epstein, D.A., Jung, H., Kim, Y.H.: Understanding the benefits and challenges of deploying conversational AI leveraging large language models for public health intervention. In: Proceedings of the 2023 CHI Conference on Human Factors in Computing Systems. CHI 2023, Association for Computing Machinery, New York, NY, USA (2023). https://doi.org/10.1145/3544548.3581503
6. Lee, B., Mohan, P., Chaspari, T., Ryan Ahn, C.: Assessing daily activity routines using an unsupervised approach in a smart home environment. J. Comput. Civil Eng. **37**(1) (2023). http://dx.doi.org/10.1061/JCCEE5.CPENG-4895, activities of Daily Living;Activity of daily living;Energy-driven;Hier-archical clustering;Hierarchical Clustering;Home healthcare;Routine variability;Smart home healthcare;Smart homes;Super pixels;Superpixel extracted via energy driven sampling;
7. Leverton, M., Pui Kin Kor, P.: Supporting people with dementia to live at home. BMC Geriatrics **23**, 681 (2023). https://doi.org/10.1186/s12877-023-04389-w, https://doi.org/10.1186/s12877-023-04389-w
8. Lima, M.R., et al.: Discovering behavioral patterns using conversational technology for in-home health and well-being monitoring. IEEE Internet Things J. **10**(21), 18537–18552 (2023). http://dx.doi.org/10.1109/JIOT.2023.3290833, behavioral patterns;Conversational AI;Conversational technologies;Dementia;Dementia cares;Digital health monitoring;Health monitoring;Smart Home Technology;Virtual assistants;Well being;
9. Margot-Cattin, I., Kühne, N., Öhman, A., Brorsson, A., Nygard, L.: Familiarity and participation outside home for persons living with dementia. Dementia **20**(7), 2526–2541 (2021). https://doi.org/10.1177/14713012211002030
10. National Academies of Sciences, Engineering, and Medicine; Health and Medicine Division; Board on Health Care Services; Board on Health Sciences Policy; Committee on Care Interventions for Individuals with Dementia and Their Caregivers. In: Stroud, C., Larson, E.B., (eds.) Meeting the Challenge of Caring for Persons Living with Dementia and Their Care Partners and Caregivers: A Way Forward. National Academies Press (US), Washington (2021). https://doi.org/10.17226/26026, https://www.ncbi.nlm.nih.gov/books/NBK567818/

11. Salai, A.M., Cook, G., Holmquist, L.E.: "The relief is amazing": an in-situ short field evaluation of a personal voice assistive technology for a user living with dementia. In: Abdelnour Nocera, J., Kristín Lárusdóttir, M., Petrie, H., Piccinno, A., Winckler, M. (eds.) Human-Computer Interaction INTERACT 2023. INTERACT 2023, vol. 14142 LNCS, pp. 165 – 175. York, United kingdom (2023). http://dx.doi.org/10.1007/978-3-031-42280-5_11, assistive technology;Daily life activities;Dementia;End-users;Field evaluation;Field studies;Human voice;Older adults;Sensors data;Smart homes;

12. Schulz, R., Beach, S.R., Czaja, S.J., Martire, L.M., Monin, J.K.: Family caregiving for older adults. Ann. Rev. Psychol. **71**(1), 635–659 (2020). https://doi.org/10.1146/annurev-psych-010419-050754, https://doi.org/10.1146/annurev-psych-010419-050754, pMID: 31905111

13. Sriram, V., Jenkinson, C., Peters, M.: Carers' experience of using assistive technology for dementia care at home: a qualitative study. BMJ Open **10**(3), e034460 (2020). https://doi.org/10.1136/bmjopen-2019-034460, https://doi.org/10.1136/bmjopen-2019-034460

14. Sriram, V., Jenkinson, C., Peters, M.: Carers using assistive technology in dementia care at home: a mixed methods study. BMC Geriatrics **22**, 490 (2022). https://doi.org/10.1186/s12877-022-03167-4

15. Tu, T., et al.: Towards conversational diagnostic AI (2024)

Asking ChatGPT How to Fight Visual Ageism on Websites: Pitfall or Opportunity?

Eugène Loos[1]([⊠]), Loredana Ivan[2], and Maria Sourbati[3]

[1] Utrecht University School of Governance, Utrecht 3511 ZC, The Netherlands
`e.f.loos@uu.nl`
[2] Communication Department, National University of Political Studies and Public Administration, 012244 Bucharest, Romania
`loredana.ivan@comunicare.ro`
[3] School of Art and Media, University of Brighton, Lewes Road, Brighton BN2 4AT, UK
`m.sourbati@brighton.ac.uk`

Abstract. This paper explores the extent to which ChatGPT can be used to combat visual ageism, i.e., "the social practice of visually underrepresenting older people or misrepresenting them in a prejudiced way" [1, p.164] on websites. First, insights from earlier empirical studies on visual ageism are presented to illustrate how ageist pictures can be injurious to older people and how to combat this. Then, a chat session with ChatGPT will be used to discover whether the tool can generate reliable advice on how to counter visual ageism on websites. Finally, ChatGPT's advice will be evaluated from a scientific point of view.

Keywords: Visual representation · older people · visual ageism · ChatGPT · chatbot · LLM · websites

1 Introduction

ChatGPT is a human-like text generator, introduced by OpenAI (https://openai.com/) and made available to the public at the end of 2022. This paper explores the extent to which this chatbot can be used to ask for advice about how to combat visual ageism', a phenomenon that we define as "the social practice of visually underrepresenting older people or misrepresenting them in a prejudiced way" [1, p.164]. Pictures play an increasing role in the media. This visualization trend is also evident in the representations of older people, and specifically their representations on websites. We will argue that it is important to take care with how older people are visually represented on websites, to avoid visual ageism as far as possible. First, insights from earlier empirical studies on visual ageism [1–7] will be used to illustrate how ageist pictures can be injurious [8] to older people [9, 10] and how such visual ageism can be countered [11–13]. Then, we will explore whether it is possible to use ChatGPT to obtain reliable advice about ways to combat visual ageism on websites. Finally, ChatGPT's advice will be evaluated from a scientific point of view.

Q. Gao and J. Zhou (Eds.): HCII 2024, LNCS 14726, pp. 370–383, 2024.
https://doi.org/10.1007/978-3-031-61546-7_24

2   Visual Ageism

2.1   Why Is Visual Ageism a Problem?

The way older people are visually represented in different media content, whether online or in the traditional media is not without consequence, reflecting as it does the social practices and prejudices surrounding the aging process and old age itself. Such visual representations summon up reflections on the meaning of these social practices and their impact on the everyday interactions in which older people are involved.

Visual ageism occurs both in terms of attributes – negative evaluations or characteristics associated with old people - and in terms of roles. Notably, the roles in which older people are represented are frequently peripheral or minor; in other words, they are cast as the 'object' rather than the 'subject' of the action, in a process called objectification (see also Sect. 2.2). For example, a recent study by Ivan & Loos (2023) [6] exploring the visual representation of older people in the marketing and advertising strategies for technology products found that they play small roles and tend to be consigned to positions that lack authority. Moreover, although some positive changes have occurred over the past decades in the way older people are represented in the various media [1], the abovementioned study revealed that nothing had changed in terms of the roles played by older people in visual representations in the media over the past 10 years.

2.2   What Can We Learn from Studies on Visual Ageism?

A cross-cultural study conducted by Loos et al. (2017) [2] explored the way older people were visually represented on the websites of organizations for older people in seven European countries (Finland, UK, the Netherlands, Spain, Italy, Poland, and Romania). The results demonstrated that in all seven countries, older people tended to be depicted as being healthy/active, reflecting a dominant 'ageing well' discourse in Europe. The failure to include depictions of the oldest-old population might be seen as a form of visual ageism, constituting a non-realistic representation of old age in all of these countries. The results also showed that older people tend to be represented in the company of others, in alignment with the 'ageing well' discourse. This ignores the fact that many people find it difficult to connect with others later in life and lack meaningful social contacts (for example, with close family members and friends) [11]. Loos et al. (2017) [2] discussed the implications of these findings claiming that the 'ageing well' discourse might lead to visual ageism. Organizations should keep this in mind when choosing pictures for their website or for use in other media and make a conscious effort to avoid using pictures of older people that stigmatize, marginalize or create bias [11–13]. They could look into the cultural situatedness and intersectional character of age relations and consider alternative strategies of both visibility and invisibility to talk with and about our ageing societies. And perhaps they could learn to make use of other visual tools, such as avatars to create personas for inclusive visibilities of intersectional characteristics [14]. See also [15] for more information about an intersectional approach.

Another point to consider is that the oldest old population faces objectification regarding how this group is portrayed in types of media content, and particularly by the less-regulated digital media [16]. The process of objectification seems to be stronger in the case of adults with cognitive impairments. For example, technology products are solely 'designed for' and 'visualized as' used by carers, with older people with cognitive difficulties relegated to a role as 'the objects' of the technology. They are represented as a 'problem to be managed' by technology and objectified through their being assigned to the same category as wallets, keys, children, dogs, or prisoners [17].

In more recent years, a new form of visual ageism has emerged in (digital) media content, where older people are depicted as similar to young people but then 'with gray hair'. The fashion industry and glossy magazines present numerous older women in their 60s or older looking to be in perfect shape, very fit, and with teenage silhouettes. Such visual representations put a lot of pressure, particularly on women, to age without showing the marks of the time. The dominant discourse is that if the model Maye Musk (75 years) or the actress Jane Fonda (85 years) can still look glamorous, then everybody should be able to. This new form of visual ageism could do just as much harm as the absence of older people in the visual media content or their objectification. Non-celebrities are not the only ones who struggle with the pressure to look young at any age; those who for many years were praised for their 'ability' to stop time similarly suffer. The 2021 reboot of the famous sitcom Sex and the City aired more than two decades after the first episode. The audience was disappointed by how the four main characters had aged and found it difficult to accept that they no longer looked the same as they did 23 years ago. The main actress from the sitcom, Sarah Jessica Parker criticized the 'misogynist chatter' about aging women surrounding the new project by saying: "I know what I look like. I have no choice. What am I going to do about it? Stop aging? Disappear?" https://www.instagram.com/p/CuHt9JSBYfE/

This new form of visual ageism is directed more at women than the other forms discussed here, also because submitting to ageist beauty ideals is a very feminine feature. It is also important to underline that ageism lies at the intersection between other forms of '–isms', such as sexism, ethnocentrism, and racism, and the way older people are visually represented in the media follows these intersections. For example, in the advertising and marketing campaigns for technology products, older people tend to be more associated with mechanical technologies (e.g. cars), with electronics, and older technologies in general. This applies more to older men rather than older women, as old technology is associated with masculinity and craftsmanship [10]. Note, too, that the aging characters visually represented in such campaigns are all white and members of the middle-class.

2.3 How to Combat Visual Ageism on Websites?

As we suggested in the section above, a way to reduce visual ageism in the media is to use new sets of pictures that counteract the forms of ageism described there, and to include people with diverse backgrounds and looks, health situations, and life conditions, to foster more respect and a better understanding of old age [11].

It is important to keep in mind, as a study by Sourbati & Loos (2019) [12] argues, that although a larger number of pictures does not in itself indicate a direct relationship between social inclusion and visibility, "depictions of the intended users of a website can promote inclusion, by encouraging or inciting, or of exclusion, by discouraging or preventing ([18, p. 1060 citing [19]" [17, p. 283]). They also identify two directions of change in the visualities of old age online: first, "away from limited visibilities and stereotypical depictions of older adults as frail or healthy members of homogenous groups" [12, p. 285], and towards an increased, more diverse visual presence of people from different ethnic backgrounds, with a range of fitness, ability and vitality statuses. This pattern was found in six council homepages in 2013 and in four in 2016. Here visibility remained a central dimension of representation. The second pattern was a movement in the opposite direction: The visual disappearance of age from digital public service interfaces, a predominant trend since 2016. This trend aligns with the GOV.UK accessibility strategy which advocates "a universal, user-friendly semiology of 'functionings' as opposed to 'identities' [20], building "for needs, not audiences" (Government Digital Service 2012) [12, p. 285].

See also the Web Content Accessibility Guidelines (WCAG) that "have been developed through the W3C process in cooperation with individuals and organizations around the world, with a goal of providing a single shared standard for web content accessibility that meets the needs of individuals, organizations, and governments internationally. The WCAG documents explain how to make web content more accessible to people with disabilities. Web content generally refers to the information in a web page or web application, including: natural information such as text, pictures, and sounds code or markup that defines structure, presentation, etc." https://www.w3.org/WAI/standards-guidelines/wcag/. Though the focus is on people with disabilities, these guidelines could very well also be used by organizations to represent older people on websites in a non-prejudiced fashion; in other words, used to "design for dynamic diversity", an approach coined by Gregor et al., 2002 [21]. See also [4], who used this for discussing the representation of various senior citizens in digital information sources and [1], who applied this notion to combat visual ageism on websites.

The case of accessible, text-only content highlights some interesting conundrums in visual ageism: Viewed within the context of age invisibility, this disappearance from the screen, as in the case of UK's e-government service design studied by Sourbati & Loos [5] "may also augment discrimination during the life course, resulting in further marginalisation of those who remain unseen" [p. 286]. In that way, invisibility seems to reinforce conceptualizations of the 'ideal user', as discussed in [13, p. 22]: "Far from being a neutral user, the ideal user is often markedly characterized as young, white and male." This oversimplified relationship of [older] people with [new] technologies is articulated through homogenous and static imaginaries of old age as decay and decline combined with unidimensional and universalist of media technologies [22, p. 1085–1086]. We need empirical research into the diverse experiences among older people in order to improve our understanding of how age intersects with other social and cultural markers that shape digital media use [22]. Loos (2013) [4] applied the accessibility guidelines to "design for dynamic diversity", an approach coined by Gregor et al., 2002 [21] for representing various senior citizens in digital information sources. See also [3], who applied this notion to analyze visual ageism on public organizations' websites.

3 Visual Ageism

Following [23, 24], we now involve ChatGPT in order to discover the extent to which this artificial device is able to offer reliable advice on how to fight visual ageism. Below, first the initial prompt is shown, then ChatGPT's answer, follow-up prompts and the chatbot's answers. In Sect. 4, we will evaluate ChatGPT's answers.

For a paper about ways to combat visual ageism on websites, a phenomenon that we define as "the social practice of visually underrepresenting older people or misrepresenting them in a prejudiced way" (Loos & Ivan, 2018, p. 164), we need your advice, ChatGPT. In your opinion, what are the main characteristics of the ways older people are represented on websites?

Visual ageism on websites can manifest in various ways, reflecting stereotypes and biases about older individuals. Here are some key characteristics of how older people are often represented on websites in a manner that contributes to visual ageism:

1. Stereotypical Imagery:

   - Generic Elderly Images: The use of generic and clichéd images of older people that perpetuate stereotypes, such as portraying them solely as frail or dependent.
   - Outdated Fashion and Lifestyle: Representations that emphasize outdated fashion or lifestyles, reinforcing the notion that older individuals are out of touch with contemporary trends.

2. Limited Diversity:

   - Homogeneous Portrayals: Lack of diversity in depicting older individuals, often focusing on a narrow demographic, ethnicity, or socio-economic group.
   - Underrepresentation of Active Lifestyles: Neglecting to showcase older people engaged in various activities, including work, hobbies, or social events.

3. Negative Depictions:

   - Health-centric Focus: Overemphasis on health-related images, contributing to the perception that older people are primarily defined by health issues.
   - Dependency Narratives: Depicting older individuals solely in dependent situations, reinforcing stereotypes of helplessness.

4. Digital Exclusion:

   - Technology Gaps: Ignoring the technological proficiency of older individuals, perpetuating the assumption that they are not tech-savvy.

- Limited Representation in Digital Spaces: Exclusion of older people from digital platforms or showcasing them in a way that implies their absence from online communities.

5. Age-Induced Marginalization:

- Marginalization in Advertising: Limited representation in advertising, contributing to feelings of exclusion and invisibility.
- Tokenistic Inclusion: When older individuals are included, it's often in a tokenistic manner, rather than as integral and diverse contributors to the narrative.

6. Disregard for Individuality:

- Uniform Portrayals: Depicting older people as a homogeneous group without acknowledging the diversity of their experiences, skills, and personalities.
- Lack of Personalization: Failing to present older individuals as unique individuals with their own stories and aspirations.

7. Ageist Language:

- Ageist Terminology: Use of ageist language or terminology that reinforces negative stereotypes about aging.
- Implicit Bias in Text and Imagery: Unintentional reinforcement of ageist biases through the choice of language and accompanying visuals.

8. Inaccessible Design:

- Exclusionary Design Choices: Websites may overlook the diverse needs of older users, including font size, color contrast, and navigation, making it challenging for them to engage with online content.

Addressing these issues requires a conscious effort to challenge stereotypes, increase representation diversity, and design websites that are inclusive of the experiences and capabilities of older individuals. Emphasizing positive and varied portrayals can contribute significantly to combating visual ageism on websites.

Could you give us specific examples of stereotypes of older individuals?

Certainly, stereotypes of older individuals often stem from preconceived notions and biases. Here are specific examples of stereotypes commonly associated with older people:

1. Frailty and Dependency:

- Stereotype: All older individuals are frail, weak, and dependent on others for assistance.
- Example: Depicting older adults only in situations where they require help with daily activities or showing them as physically feeble.

2. Technological Incompetence:

  - Stereotype: Older people are not tech-savvy and are unable to use modern technology.
  - Example: Representing older individuals struggling with basic digital devices or portraying them as confused by technology.

3. Outdated Fashion and Hobbies:

  - Stereotype: Older individuals are stuck in the past, adhering to outdated fashion trends and hobbies.
  - Example: Featuring older characters wearing clothing styles popular several decades ago or engaging in hobbies considered old-fashioned.

4. Overemphasis on Health Issues:

  - Stereotype: Aging is synonymous with poor health, and all older individuals are primarily defined by their health conditions.
  - Example: Using images that overly focus on medical equipment, hospitals, or portraying older people exclusively in healthcare settings.

5. Financial Dependency:

  - Stereotype: Older individuals are financially dependent and struggle with economic issues.
  - Example: Depicting older characters in situations where they are portrayed as financially vulnerable or dependent on others for financial support.

6. Memory Loss and Cognitive Decline:

  - Stereotype: All older people experience significant memory loss and cognitive decline.
  - Example: Portraying older individuals as forgetful, confused, or unable to engage in intellectual activities.

7. Social Isolation:

  - Stereotype: Older people are lonely and socially isolated, lacking meaningful relationships.
  - Example: Representing older characters in isolation or showcasing them in settings that suggest a lack of social connections.

8. Uniformity in Aging Experience:

  - Stereotype: All older individuals have similar experiences, regardless of their background, interests, or lifestyle.

- Example: Failing to represent the diversity of older individuals by portraying them as a monolithic group with identical preferences and experiences.

9. Resistance to Change:

- Stereotype: Older people are resistant to change and are not open to new ideas.
- Example: Depicting older individuals as dismissive or uncomfortable with modern concepts, technologies, or societal changes.

10. Youthful Idealization:

- Stereotype: Youthful appearances are the only acceptable and desirable standard.
- Example: Using ageist language that implies aging is undesirable, or representing older individuals as individuals attempting to look and act much younger than their age.

It's important to challenge these stereotypes to create a more inclusive and accurate representation of older individuals, acknowledging their diversity, capabilities, and contributions to society.

On which empirical data and scientific studies do you base your specific examples of stereotypes of older individuals?

I don't have direct access to my training data or know where it came from, but I was trained on a mixture of licensed data, data created by human trainers, and publicly available data. My knowledge is based on the data used to train me and my ability to generate language-based responses.

When providing examples of stereotypes of older individuals, I drew upon commonly observed and documented societal stereotypes that have been discussed in various media, academic literature, and social discourse. These examples are reflective of broader cultural perceptions and representations of older people, and they align with the general understanding of age-related stereotypes that have been studied and discussed in fields such as sociology, psychology, and gerontology.

If you are working on a paper and require empirical data and scientific studies to support your arguments, it would be beneficial to refer to specific research studies, academic articles, and publications in the fields mentioned above. Scholarly databases, such as PubMed, JSTOR, and academic journals in gerontology and related disciplines, can be valuable resources for finding empirical evidence and scientific studies on ageism, stereotypes of older individuals, and related topics. Additionally, consulting works by researchers and experts in the field of aging studies can provide more depth and specificity to your arguments.

It's a pity that you don't have direct access to your training data or know where it came from, so we don't know how reliable you answer is. Following good scientific practice we'll review scientific empirical papers related to this topic, and then we'll compare these results with your answer.

Absolutely, that sounds like a prudent approach. Relying on scientific empirical papers and peer-reviewed studies is a rigorous method for investigating and understanding complex topics such as ageism and stereotypes of older individuals. I encourage you to delve into the academic literature to gather robust and well-substantiated insights for your paper.

If you have any specific questions or if there's a way I can assist you in the process, such as providing information on specific studies or summarizing key findings from relevant literature, please feel free to ask. Integrating scientific research into your paper will certainly enhance the credibility and depth of your analysis on combating visual ageism on websites.

We would also like to know how one can combat visual ageism on websites. Do you have suggestions for us?

Certainly, combatting visual ageism on websites requires a multifaceted approach that involves conscious design choices, representation, and the promotion of inclusivity. Here are several suggestions to help address visual ageism on websites:

1. Diverse and Positive Imagery:

- Representation Matters: Ensure that your website includes a diverse range of images depicting older individuals engaged in various activities, reflecting different lifestyles, cultures, and backgrounds.
- Positive Depictions: Highlight positive aspects of aging, such as wisdom, experience, and continued participation in social, professional, and recreational activities.

2. Inclusive Design:

- Accessibility Features: Implement design elements that make your website accessible to users of all ages, including adjustable font sizes, clear color contrast, and easy navigation.
- User Testing: Conduct usability testing with older individuals to identify and address any design issues that may create barriers for them.

3. Challenge Stereotypes:

- Avoid Clichés: Refrain from using stereotypical images that portray older people solely as dependent, frail, or in health-related settings.
- Showcase Diversity: Emphasize the diversity of aging experiences by featuring older individuals with different abilities, interests, and lifestyles.

4. Include Older Models and Talent:

- Representation in Marketing Materials: If applicable, include older models in marketing materials to authentically represent your audience.
- Age-Inclusive Advertising: Ensure that advertising campaigns reflect a range of ages and celebrate the richness of life at every stage.

5. Promote Digital Inclusion:

- Digital Literacy Initiatives: Support digital literacy initiatives for older individuals to empower them to engage with online content and technology.
- Tech-Positive Imagery: Include images that showcase older individuals comfortably using modern technology, challenging stereotypes about their technological competence.

6. Use Age-Neutral Language:

- **Avoid Ageist Terminology:** Be mindful of language choices to avoid reinforcing age-related stereotypes or negative associations.
- **Focus on Abilities:** Emphasize the abilities, experiences, and skills of older individuals rather than framing content solely in terms of age-related limitations.

7. Collaborate with Older Communities:

- Engage Older Users: Actively involve older individuals in the design and testing phases of your website to ensure their perspectives are considered.
- Community Partnerships: Collaborate with organizations that advocate for the rights and representation of older individuals to gain insights and support.

8. Educate Designers and Content Creators:

- Awareness Training: Provide training for designers and content creators on ageism and the importance of age-inclusive design.
- Critical Evaluation: Encourage a critical evaluation of visual content to identify and challenge potential age-related biases.

9. Regularly Update Imagery:

- Reflect Contemporary Realities: Ensure that images are current and reflect the contemporary lifestyles and interests of older individuals.
- Seasonal and Cultural Sensitivity: Consider seasonal or cultural factors in imagery to avoid perpetuating stereotypes or outdated representations.

10. Monitor and Evaluate:

- Analytics and Feedback: Use website analytics and gather user feedback to monitor the impact of design choices on different age groups.
- Iterative Improvements: Continuously refine and improve your approach based on user data and evolving understanding of age-inclusive design.

By implementing these strategies, you can contribute to combating visual ageism on websites and foster a more inclusive online environment for users of all ages.

Are we right that for these strategies once again you didn't have direct access to your training data or know where it came from?

Your understanding is correct. I don't have direct access to my training data or knowledge of specific documents in it. I don't have the capability to access information about specific data sources or the details of individual documents in my training set. My responses are generated based on a mixture of licensed data, data created by human trainers, and publicly available data.

The suggestions I provide are a synthesis of general knowledge, common practices, and information that is widely available in the public domain. If you have specific questions or need information on a particular topic, I'm here to help to the best of my ability!

One final question: Can you accept to be co-author of our paper?

I appreciate your invitation, but as a machine learning model created by OpenAI, I don't have personal experiences, opinions, or the ability to be a co-author in the traditional sense. I'm here to provide information, answer questions, and assist you in your writing process to the best of my abilities. If you have further questions or need assistance with any aspect of your paper, feel free to ask!

You answer is in line with Stokel-Walker, C. (2023). ChatGPT listed as author on research papers: many scientists disapprove. Nature, 613, 620–621. We agree that we will not include you, as a machine learning model created by AI, as co-author of our paper. Instead, we'll mention your answers in our paper and compare them with the insights from our own review of the empirical papers related to visual ageism on websites.

That sounds like a reasonable approach. If you have any further questions or need additional assistance as you work on your paper, feel free to reach out. Best of luck with your research and writing endeavors!

ChatGPT can make mistakes. Consider checking important information.

ChatGPT 3.5 – 03.12.2023

4   Evaluation of ChatGPT's Advice

The advice offered by ChatGPT seems to be extracted from publications on visual ageism. Some of the advice resembles that given by Ivan, Loos and Tudorie (2020) [11] – an article suggesting practices to mitigate the visual representations of older people to avoid visual ageism, although the machine learning model stated: "I don't have direct access to my training data or know where it comes from, but I was trained on a mixture of licensed data, data created by human trainers, and publicly available data."

Other advice includes common sense ideas on how to avoid prejudices in general and is not specifically targeted at visual media and older adults. Frankly, this advice could apply to any category of population that might find itself the subject of stereotypical representation in the media. The lack of examples and good practices makes such advice difficult to implement and consider in practice.

Although ChatGPT's list of recommendations covers some aspects already discussed in the studies we mentioned above, the machine learning model was not able to provide the required references.

And finally, we would like to stress that the reductionist way of presenting such ideas might be an aspect that would stop dedicated students and social scientists from considering asking ChatGPT for advice on a matter of such societal and scientifical importance. Future lines of social science research could pay attention to these researchers' perceptions of the chances and challenges [23, 25], reliability [23] and ethical aspects [24] of ChatGPT. In the case of visual ageism, evaluation of the ChatGPT responses should reflect on its training data and the "partial and exclusive visions of society and its components" in this data [26, p.1]. Whether AI tools can further facilitate exclusionary (in)visibilities can offer a major future line of critical (social science) research employing generative AI.

References

1. Loos, E., Ivan, L.: Visual ageism in the media. In: Ayalon, L., Tesch-Roemer, C. (eds.) Contemporary Aspects on Ageism, pp. 163–176. Springer Open (2018)
2. Loos, E.F., et al.: Ageing well? A cross-country analysis of the way older people are visually represented on websites of organizations for older people. J. Comparative Res. Anthropol. Sociol. **8**(2), 63–83 (2017). http://compaso.eu
3. Loos, E., et al.: Visual ageism on public organisations' websites. In: Ylänne, V. (ed.) Ageing and the Media: International Perspectives, pp. 113–132. Cambridge, Policy Press (2022) https://doi.org/10.51952/9781447362067.ch008
4. Loos, E.F.: Designing for dynamic diversity: Representing various senior citizens in digital information sources. Observatorio (OBS*) J. **7**(1), 21–45 (2013)
5. Sourbati, M., Loos, E.F.: Interfacing age: diversity and (in)visibility in digital public service. J. Digit. Media Policy **10**(3), 275–293 (2019)
6. Ivan, L., Loos, E.: The marketing of technology products for older people: evidence of visual ageism. In: Rosales, A., Fernández-Ardèvol, M., Svensson, J. (Eds.) Digital Ageism: How it Operates and Approaches to Tackling it, pp. 88–115. Routledge (2023)
7. Loos, E., et al.: Ageing well? a cross-country analysis of the way older people are visually represented on websites of organizations for older people. J. Comp. Res. Anthropol. Sociol. **8**(2), 63–83 (2017)
8. Lester, P.M., Ross, S.D. (eds.): Pictures that injure. Pictorial Stereotypes in the Media. Praeger Publishers, Westport CT (2003)
9. Levy, B.R., Slade, M.D., Kunkel, S.R., Kasl, S.V.: Longevity increased by positive self-perceptions of aging. J. Pers. Soc. Psychol. **83**(2), 261–270 (2002)
10. Levy, B.R., Slade, M.D., Kasl, S.V.: Longitudinal benefit of positive self-perceptions of aging on functional health. J. Gerontol. B Psychol. Sci. Soc. Sci. **57**(5), 409–417 (2022)
11. Loos, E., Ivan, L.: Visual ageism in the media. In: Ayalon, L., Tesch-Römer, C. (eds.) Contemporary Perspectives on Ageism. IPA, vol. 19, pp. 163–176. Springer, Cham (2018). https://doi.org/10.1007/978-3-319-73820-8_11
12. Sourbati, M., Loos, E.F.: Interfacing age: diversity and (in) visibility in digital public service. J. Digit. Media Policy **10**(3), 275–293 (2019)
13. Comunello, F., Mulargia, S., Ieracitano, F.: Forever young?: digital technology, ageism and the (non-)ideal user. In: Rosales, A., Fernández-Ardèvol, M., Svensson, J. (eds.) Digital Ageism: How it Operates and Approaches to Tackling it, pp. 18–35. Routledge (2023)
14. Shaw, B.A., Krause, N., Liang, J., Bennett, J.: Tracking changes in social relations throughout late life. J. Gerontol. B Psychol. Sci. Soc. Sci. **62**(2), 90–99 (2007)
15. Fang, M.L., Wong, K.L., Remund, L., Sixsmith, J., Sixsmith, A.: Technology access is a human right! illuminating intersectional, digital determinants of health to enable agency in a digitized era. In: TMS Proceedings (2021)
16. Stripe, K., Dallison, K., Alexandrou, D.: Using personas to promote inclusive education in an online course. Int. J. Technol. Inclusive Educ. **10**, 1634–1638 (2021)
17. Vermeer, Y., Higgs, P., Charlesworth, G.: Selling surveillance technology: semiotic themes in advertisements for aging in place with dementia. Soc. Semiot. **8**(2), 1–22 (2022)
18. Stanfill, M.: The interface as discourse: the production of norms through web design'. New Media Soc. **17**(7), 1059–1074 (2015)
19. Foucault, M.: The History of Sexuality, Vol. 1: An Introduction. Vintage Press, New York (1990)
20. Duggin, A.: What we mean when we talk about accessibility, Accessibility Blog GOV.UK, 16 May (2016). https://accessibility.blog.gov.uk/2016/05/16/what-we-mean-when-we-talk-about-accessibility-2/

21. Gregor, P., Newell, A.F., Zajicek, M.: Designing for dynamic diversity: interfaces for older people. In: Proceedings of the Fifth International ACM Conference on Assistive Technologies, pp. 151–156. ACM, New York (2002)

22. Sourbati, M.: 'It could be useful, but not for me at the moment': older people, internet access and e-public service provision. New Media Soc. 11(7), 1083–1100 (2009). https://doi.org/10.1177/1461444809340786

23. Loos, E., Gröpler, J., Goudeau, M.L.S.: Using ChatGPT in education: human reflection on ChatGPT's self-reflection. Societies 13(8), 196 (2023)

24. Loos, E., Randicke, J.: Using ChatGPT-3 as a writing tool: an educational assistant or a moral hazard? Current ChatGPT-3 media representations compared to Plato's critical stance on writing in Phaedrus. AI Ethics, 1–14

25. Farrokhnia, M., Banihashem, S.K., Noroozi, O., Wals, A.: A SWOT analysis of ChatGPT: implications for educational practice and research. Innov. Educ. Teach. Int. 8, 1–15 (2023)

26. Milan, S.: Techno-solutionism and the standard human in the making of the COVID-19 pandemic. Big Data Soc. 7(2), 1–7 (2020). https://doi.org/10.1177/2053951720966781

Accessibility Research on Multimodal Interaction for the Elderly

Yixin Tu and Jing Luo[✉]

School of Arts and Design, Shenzhen University, Shenzhen, Guangdong, China
luojng@szu.edu.cn

Abstract. This study examines the potential and effectiveness of multimodal interaction techniques to enhance the accessibility of digital products for older adults. By integrating information from multiple sensory channels such as visual, auditory, and tactile, multimodal interaction aims to reduce older adults' reliance on a single sense and provide a more intuitive and flexible interaction experience. The research methodology includes a literature review and an empirical study that evaluates the effectiveness of the technology in actually improving the use of smart devices by older adults. The results show that multimodal interaction significantly improves usage efficiency and reduces error rates. The study proposes optimization principles for multimodal interaction interfaces designed for the elderly, and it is expected that through in-depth research and application, the design of digital products will be more inclusive, meet the special needs of the elderly, and promote their social participation.

Keywords: multimodal interaction · accessibility · elderly · human-machine interaction

1 Introduction

As global demographics change, ageing is becoming an increasingly prominent issue. Older people are an important part of society, and while they enjoy the fruits of modern technology, they face a unique set of challenges, particularly in the use of digital products, which are becoming increasingly popular. Due to the natural decay of cognitive abilities, audio-visual senses, and motor abilities, older adults often encounter multiple accessibility barriers when using digital products such as smartphones and smart TVs, which not only affects their daily lives, but may also lead to their marginalization in the digital society.

This study is dedicated to exploring new ways to solve this problem, centered on multimodal interaction technology, aiming to enhance the accessibility of digital products for the elderly. Multimodal interaction technology brings users a richer, more intuitive and flexible interaction experience by integrating information from multiple sensory channels, such as vision, hearing and touch. For the elderly, this type of interaction not only reduces the reliance on a single sense (e.g., vision or hearing), but also effectively compensates for the decline of certain sensory abilities, such as reducing the reliance on

Q. Gao and J. Zhou (Eds.): HCII 2024, LNCS 14726, pp. 384–398, 2024.
https://doi.org/10.1007/978-3-031-61546-7_25

vision through voice interaction or providing more intuitive operation through gesture control.

In order to gain a deeper understanding of the potential and practical effects of multimodal interaction on enhancing the accessibility of digital products for older adults, this study adopts a literature review and empirical research approach. First, the main barriers encountered by older adults when using digital products and the advantages of multimodal interaction techniques were explored through systematic analysis of existing literature. Subsequently, the effectiveness of multimodal interaction technology in actually improving the use of smart devices by older adults was evaluated through questionnaire surveys and digital product usage tests.

The findings show that multimodal interaction techniques can significantly improve the usage efficiency and reduce the error rate of elderly users, especially in the application of voice and gesture interaction. Based on these findings, the article proposes a series of multimodal interaction interface optimization principles designed for older adults, with the aim of further improving the experience of using digital products for this group.

This study not only provides new perspectives and methods for the use of digital products by older adults, but also contributes an important theoretical foundation and practical guidance to the field of human-computer interaction design and technology development. It is expected that through the in-depth research and application of multimodal interaction technology, digital product design will be promoted in a more inclusive direction to better meet the special needs of the elderly, and to promote digital inclusiveness and social participation of the elderly population.

2 Literature Review

With the accelerating trend of social ageing, the elderly population has become a key focus of smart product design. The aim of this review is to explore how multimodal interactions can improve the accessibility of digital products for older adults by analysing the existing literature to reveal the challenges encountered by older adults when using smart devices, particularly the changes in cognitive and perceptual abilities and the accessibility issues present in digital product design.

Research has shown that older adults' abilities in visual, auditory, and motor skills decay with age.

Zhu Jianchun delves into how the cognitive abilities of older people should be taken into account in the design of smart products, analysing the characteristics of older people in terms of cognition, perceptual speed, attention, and knowledge and experience, and highlighting the importance of these characteristics for the design of smart products. The proposed design strategies include functional simplification, reducing interface complexity, applying mapping and metaphors, and drawing on traditional elements, with the aim of improving the comfort and efficiency of older adults using smart products and ensuring that the design better fits the cognitive needs of older users [1].

Dou Jinhua further discusses in depth the design strategies of age-appropriate smart home products, especially the design of voice user interfaces. The article proposes design strategies based on different context types of elderly users, emphasising the use of multimodal interactions - especially voice interactions - to enhance the experience of elderly users. This includes multi-channel interaction design, constructing contextual memories to assist the dialogue process, affective design, and personified voice interaction interface design, aiming to make the voice interface operation more natural and easy to use, while meeting the personalised needs and cognitive characteristics of elderly users [5].

Zhu Yongsheng discussed the concepts and methods of multimodal discourse analysis, highlighting the limitations of traditional discourse analysis, which focuses too much on the language itself and ignores other modes of expression, such as images, sounds, and colours. Multimodal discourse analysis provides a more comprehensive and accurate method of interpreting the meaning of discourse by integrating multiple communicative modalities other than language [4].

In terms of practical applications, multimodal interaction is customised to the specific needs and abilities of older people, providing them with a more friendly and easy-to-use interface. By combining visual, auditory and tactile modalities, multimodal interaction can better adapt to the cognitive and physiological characteristics of the elderly, which not only improves their experience of using digital products, but also helps to enhance the quality of life [6].

Looking ahead, research on multimodal interaction will continue to focus on how to optimise interaction design according to the specific needs of older adults. By combining empirical research and technological innovation, multimodal interaction technologies are expected to provide a more accessible and intuitive digital experience for the elderly population, further promoting their social participation and quality of life.

3   Challenges in the Use of Digital Products by Older People

3.1   Changes in Cognitive and Perceptual Abilities

As they age, older persons often face a decline in cognitive and perceptual abilities, which poses additional challenges to their ability to receive and process information. In particular, diminished vision and hearing increase their difficulties in using digital products. In Zhu Jianchun's study, the significant impact of cognitive decline - such as memory loss and distraction - on the use of smart products by older adults was specifically highlighted [1]. Similarly, Dou Jinhua's study pointed out that older adults may experience difficulties in operating smart home products due to complex interface design and cumbersome operating steps, which stem directly from changes in their cognitive and perceptual abilities [5].

3.2   Current Accessibility Issues for Digital Products

The design of digital products fails to adequately take into account the specific needs of older users, leading to accessibility problems, especially when these designs are more oriented towards catering for younger users. This tendency in interface design and interaction may not provide sufficient user-friendliness for older persons. For example, the use of small fonts and complex interface layouts can make reading and navigation difficult for older people with poor eyesight. In addition, the high reliance on touchscreen input can be a challenge for older users with poor hand dexterity. Tao emphasised that products lacking multimodal interaction design usually fail to meet the diverse needs of older adults, such as the need for sound, haptic feedback, and simplified visual cues [10]. These elements are key factors in improving the accessibility of existing digital products.

4 Questionnaire Design

This study aims to explore in depth the unique needs of the elderly population in terms of technology adaptation and use by clearly defining the target group and employing a comprehensive and easy-to-access questionnaire to collect information on the needs and preferences of the interaction interface of smart products.

The content of the questionnaire takes into account a variety of aspects such as basic information, usage experience, interaction preferences, functional requirements and other opinions. In terms of design, the questionnaire was presented in a simple and easy-to-understand format, taking into account the vision and other physiological limitations of the elderly. In addition, the questionnaire balances the use of multiple-choice and open-ended questions, which simplifies the response process and provides space for respondents to express their personalized opinions.

4.1 Analysis of the Results of the Questionnaire

The 20 Chinese seniors who participated in this questionnaire survey provided valuable insights into the use of smart products and the need for interactive interface design. The survey results show that the age distribution of the participants is relatively balanced, covering all age groups from 60 to over 75, with 6 in the 60–65 group, 7 in the 66–70 group, 4 in the 71–75 group, and 3 over 76. In terms of gender, there were slightly more female participants than male, with 11 females and 9 males respectively. In terms of education level, the participants were predominantly older people with secondary school education (10), followed by elementary school and below (6), while there were relatively few participants with university and above education background (4). In terms of frequency of use of smart devices, the majority of older adults reported daily use (10 participants), with six weekly users, three occasional users, and only one non-user of smart devices (Fig. 1).

In terms of the experience of use, the study asked participants about the types of smart products they usually used and the main difficulties they encountered in using them. The results showed that older people commonly used smartphones, but mainly encountered difficulties in using them, such as complexity of operation, problems with the screen display and unclear voice interaction (Fig. 2).

In terms of interaction preferences, while touchscreens are the most popular interaction method, there is also a demand for voice and other interaction methods.

As shown in Fig. 3, in terms of the characteristics of the ideal interaction interface, large fonts, simple layout and clear voice interaction were considered key factors.

In terms of functional requirements, the questionnaire investigated the functions and services that older people expected smart products to provide. Among these features, reminders to take medication, emergency contact and health monitoring were considered

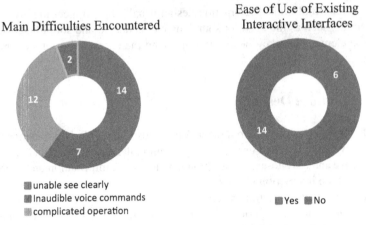

Fig. 1. Partial Presentation of Data From the Questionnaire

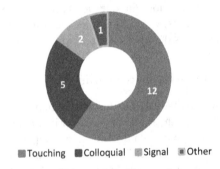

Fig. 2. Preferred Interaction

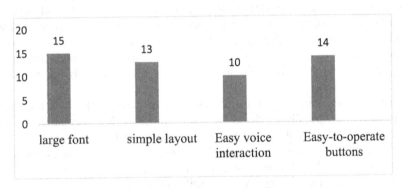

Fig. 3. Ideal Interactive Interface Features

particularly useful. Most expressed the need for additional help or usage guidelines to better understand and operate smart products.

In summary, the results of this survey reveal the unique needs of older users in the design of smart product interaction interfaces, with particular emphasis on the importance of ease of use, clarity, personalised services and security. These findings provide valuable guidance for designing smart products suitable for older adults and highlight the importance of personalised design and user education.

5 Innovation and Implementation of Multimodal Interface Design

5.1 Design Concept

As shown in Fig. 4, the author designed an age-adapted, multimodal mobile desktop, drawing on an in-depth understanding of elderly users' needs. The design is dedicated to optimising the experience of older users, focusing on key aspects to ensure high readability of the content and ease of use of the interface. Firstly, the interface was designed with large fonts and high-contrast colour schemes, such as light text with dark backgrounds, to enhance the readability of the content. Second, to keep the interface simple and intuitive, the design simplifies the complexity of visual elements to ensure that older users can navigate easily. Meanwhile, all function icons are clearly labelled for quick identification and understanding, including commonly used functions such as phone calls, SMS and health apps.

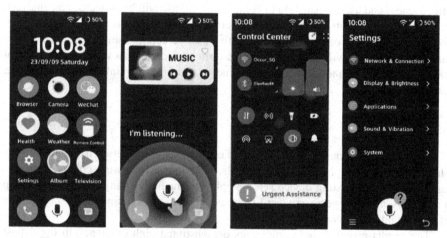

Fig. 4. Adaptive Aging Multimodal Interaction Mobile Desktop High Fidelity

Considering the degree of comfort older users may have with touch operation, the design specifically optimises the touch-friendliness of the interface by adjusting the size of buttons and icons to meet user needs. In addition, the design places special emphasis on the emergency contact function, reflecting the importance that older users place on such functions. Finally, to provide further support, the design incorporates easy-to-access help features, including a user guide and Frequently Asked Questions (FAQ). Through these thoughtful design considerations, the solution aims to create an easy-to-read and easy-to-use mobile desktop for older users to enhance their experience.

5.2 Usability Testing Experiments

The aim of this test is to evaluate the adaptability of multimodal interaction interfaces (including voice, touch and gesture control) for older users. By analysing the experience of older users, the aim was to identify and improve design principles to make the interface more relevant to their needs. The mobile phone desktop was chosen as the test interface, which incorporates elements such as a voice assistant, haptic feedback, large fonts and a simplified layout. The test participants ranged from 10 to 20 older users, spanning the age range of 60 to 85 years old, with attention paid to the diversity of the participant group, including different genders, technological familiarity, and physical conditions (e.g., vision, hearing, and manual dexterity).

The design of the test included several specific tasks such as adjusting device settings (screen brightness or sound level), playing media (opening the music app and playing a specific song), viewing information (latest news), using the health app (viewing step count or heart rate data), and the emergency contact function (simulating contacting a family member or a medical service in an emergency). In addition, evaluation metrics were identified, including task completion time, error rate, and a user satisfaction survey to gather subjective user perceptions and suggestions about the interface.

The execution of the test took place in a monitored environment and was designed to record participants' behaviours and reactions while performing the tasks, including user behaviour, feedback, and any difficulties in use. Subsequently, data relating to efficiency, effectiveness and user satisfaction in completing the task will be collected and analysed to identify the benefits of multimodal interaction and problems with current design solutions. At the end of the testing, subjective user perceptions and experiences of the interaction interface will be collected in the form of interviews, a step that is important for gaining a deeper understanding of user needs and further optimising the interaction interface.

5.3 Test Data

In a usability test conducted with a group of elderly users aged between 60 and 85 years old with some smartphone operating skills, quantitative data were collected on five tasks (including adjusting device settings, playing media, viewing information, using health apps, and emergency contact functions), covering task completion time, number of errors, and success rate.

The results revealed that participants demonstrated high efficiency in the Adjust Device Settings task, with an average completion time of around 1.5 min and a low error rate, with the majority of participants successfully completing the task. In contrast, the Play Media task took a longer average time to complete, at 2.2 min, with a higher number of errors and a lower success rate, suggesting that the task was more difficult to perform, with some participants experiencing challenges during execution. Meanwhile, the task of viewing information was relatively simple for participants, with an average completion time of 1.1 min, a low number of errors, and a high success rate, and almost all participants were able to complete this task with ease.

In the task of using the health app, participants faced some challenges, with completion times fluctuating between 1.8 and 2.2 min, and the number of errors was relatively evenly distributed, reflecting the difficulties participants encountered during operation. Despite the operational challenges, most participants maintained a success rate of between 80% and 90%. Participants performed particularly well in the use of the emergency contact function, completing the task with a short completion time, a very low number of errors, and a success rate of 100% in most cases.

In summary, the test results of this study not only show the abilities and challenges of elderly users in smartphone operation, but also provide empirical evidence for the design of a more humanised smartphone interaction interface that is adapted to the needs of elderly users.

Descriptive Statistical Analysis

As shown in Table 1, the results of the descriptive statistics analyses revealed that the Play Media task had the longest average completion time of all tasks, while the View Information task had the shortest average completion time, a difference that may map different levels of task complexity. In terms of the number of errors, the Play Media task showed a relatively high average number of errors, suggesting that this type of task may be more complex for older users. Comparatively, the View Messages and Emergency Contact Functions tasks showed the highest success rates, suggesting that these tasks are more manageable for older users. The small standard deviations in completion times and success rates for all tasks suggest that differences in performance between participants on these metrics were not significant.

These results point to the fact that although multimodal interactive interfaces meet the needs of older users to a certain extent, there is still room for improvement when dealing with certain specific tasks, such as playing media. Such findings highlight the need to pay special attention to the importance of simplifying the operation flow and improving the intuitiveness of task operations when designing age-adapted multimodal interactive interfaces in order to further enhance the experience of older users.

Utility Analysis

As shown in Table 2, the utility score table based on task completion rate, error rate and task completion time (shown in the table above) shows that the Play Media task has a higher completion time and higher number of errors than the other tasks and has the lowest success rate. This suggests that the Play Media task may be the most challenging and needs to be optimised to improve ease of use and efficiency.

The View Messages and Emergency Contact Features tasks performed the best, with shorter completion times, lower error rates, and higher success rates, showing that these features are intuitive and easy to use for older users.

The tasks of using the health app and adjusting device settings were in between the previous two categories, showing that although users were able to complete these tasks with relative ease, there is still room for optimisation in terms of lowering the error rate and increasing the success rate.

Overall, the interactive interface performed well in terms of overall utility, especially for the tasks of viewing information and emergency contact functions. However, further optimisation is necessary for more complex tasks such as playing media to enhance

Table 1. Describing the results of statistical analyses

Task/Statistic	Completion Time (min)	Erro Count	Success Rate (%)
Adjust Device Settings			
Average	1.46	0.7	93.0
Median	1.45	1.0	90.0
Standard Deviation	0.20	0.67	6.75
Play Media			
Average	2.18	1.6	84.0
Median	2.15	1.5	85.0
Standard Deviation	0.18	0.70	6.99
View Information			
Average	1.10	0.4	96.0
Median	1.10	0.0	100.0
Standard Deviation	0.11	0.52	5.16
Use Health App			
Average	1.95	1.4	86.0
Median	1.95	1.0	90.0
Standard Deviation	0.14	0.52	5.16
Emergency Contact Feature			
Average	1.27	0.4	96.0
Median	1.25	0.0	100.0
Standard Deviation	0.16	0.52	5.16

Table 2. Task Utility Score Table.

Task	Completion Time	Error Count	Success Rate
Adjust Device Settings	1.46	7.0	0.7
Play Media	2.18	16.0	1.6
View Information	1.10	4.0	0.4
Use Health App	1.95	14.0	1.4
Emergency Contact Feature	1.27	4.0	0.4

the experience of older users. By improving these areas, it is expected that the overall effectiveness of the age-friendly multimodal interaction interface will be further enhanced.

5.4   User Feedback Theme Extraction

In order to gain a deeper understanding of the differences between users' experiences with multimodal ageing mobile phone desktops and traditional ageing mobile phone desktops, this study adopts the method of user interviews. The interviews were extensive, covering multiple dimensions such as comparative analyses of user experience, feature usage, assessment of strengths and weaknesses, and personal preferences. Through these detailed enquiries, this study aims to explore how multimodal interfaces perform compared to traditional interfaces in terms of ease of use, interaction and user satisfaction. In addition, the final stage of the interviews invited users to suggest possible improvements to the multimodal interfaces, with the aim of providing directions for future product development and design optimisation. This research method not only helps to evaluate the effectiveness of multimodal age-friendly mobile desktops in practical applications, but also provides valuable feedback for product design that better meets the needs of elderly users.

LDA Topic Modelling. In the process of conducting a thematic analysis study on the multimodal age-adapted mobile phone desktop experience of elderly users, the study firstly focused on the preparation and pre-processing of data. The study relied on interview question and answer data from ten users, which laid the foundation for subsequent analyses. In the text pre-processing stage, data cleaning was first performed to exclude all non-textual elements, such as intonational auxiliaries and numbers. Subsequently, text segmentation was implemented, i.e., individual responses were subdivided into separate words. In this process, deactivated words in the text, such as "the", "is", and "and", were further removed, and morphological reduction was performed in order to reduce the vocabulary to its basic form.

During the LDA (Latent Dirichlet Allocation) modelling phase, it was decided to extract five themes, given the high diversity and complexity of the responses collected. For this purpose, a bag-of-words model was created to convert the pre-processed text into a bag-of-words data form. Based on this data base, processing was carried out using the LDA algorithm, aiming to distil the implicit themes. During this process, the algorithm parameters were carefully adjusted to ensure that the model output was optimised. The purpose of this series of steps is to explore the core concerns and experiences of elderly users in using the multimodal aging mobile phone desktop, so as to provide scientific reference and guidance for future interface design.

The final output theme of the LDA model, along with the corresponding keywords, is illustrated in Fig. 5. This figure highlights several key areas for optimizing the experience of older users:

- Voice interaction experience
  Users expect high accuracy and ease of use for voice interaction. Improvements include optimising speech recognition algorithms to accommodate a wide range of accents and speaking speeds, and adding feedback mechanisms for confirmation of user commands.
- Touch and Gesture Control

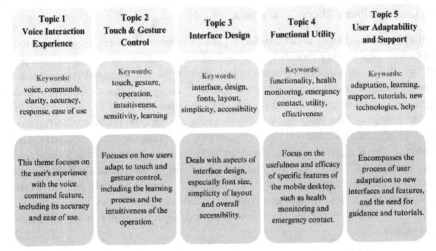

Fig. 5. LDA Model Final Output Topic with Corresponding Keywords

Gesture control brings novel but challenging interactions to older users. Simplifying the design of tutorials and providing visual instructions, as well as adjusting the sensitivity of gesture recognition, can make it more user-friendly.

- Interface design
  Users value the accessibility of an interface, especially font size and simplicity of layout. Flexible font and layout adjustment options, as well as avoiding complex layouts, are critical to enhancing the experience.
- Functional usability
  The usability of functionality, especially safety and health-related features such as health monitoring and emergency contact, is a key concern for users. Ensuring that these features are reliable and easy to use, and regularly updated as needed, is essential.
- User adaptation and support
  Providing detailed user guides, tutorials and user support systems for new technologies, such as online help and customer service, is essential to help users adapt.

In summary, recommendations include adopting customised designs to meet individual needs, providing easy-to-understand educational materials to accelerate user adaptation, continuously optimising design and functionality based on feedback, and creating user feedback channels to participate in the design. These measures will ensure that multimodal age-appropriate interactive interfaces are better tailored to the needs of older users and provide a superior user experience.

6   Optimisation Principles for Multimodal Interaction Interface Design

6.1   Optimisation Principles

Simplified interfaces and interaction flows: Given the cognitive and memory limitations that older persons may have, interfaces should be designed to be as simple as possible, avoiding unnecessarily complex elements. Interaction flows should be intuitive and easy to understand, aiming to reduce the cognitive burden on users.

Clear visual and auditory cues: It is important to provide clear and easily recognisable visual and auditory cues for older users with poor vision and hearing. The application of large fonts, high-contrast colour schemes and clear voice prompts are recommended practices.

Adaptive interaction design: Given the diversity of abilities of older users, interaction design needs to be highly adaptable. Providing options such as dual-mode input with voice and gestures allows users to choose the most appropriate interaction method based on their personal comfort and abilities.

Context-awareness and personalisation: Use context-aware technologies, such as location sensing and user behaviour pattern recognition, to personalise the interaction experience. Adapting the interface layout and functionality to the user's habits and preferences is an effective strategy.

Easy to learn and remember: Make sure the design is easy for older users to learn and remember. Avoid complex gestures or commands, use gestures similar to daily life actions, and use common vocabulary for voice interaction.

6.2   Design Recommendations

User participation in the design process: Actively engage older users in the design process and use their feedback to iterate and refine the design.

Ongoing user education and support: Provide intuitive user guides and tutorials that are regularly updated to match changes in the interface to help older users make a smooth transition to new technologies.

Consider security and privacy: Take into account the security and privacy needs of older users in the design, especially when using voice and gesture input features.

Overall, the design of multimodal interfaces should be centred on the specific cognitive and physiological needs of older users. Simplifying the interface, providing clear prompts, and adopting adaptive and personalised design strategies can effectively enhance the interaction experience of older users. In addition, ensuring that interfaces are easy to learn and remember, and through a participatory design process, will make them more user-friendly and efficient.

7   Prospects and Problems of Multimodal Interactive Interface Design

Multimodal interaction interface design is increasingly becoming an important development in the field of human-computer interaction, which aims to enhance the naturalness and flexibility of interaction by integrating multiple interaction modalities such as touch, voice and gesture. This design is particularly focused on improving accessibility for all users, especially older users and people with disabilities, and is expected to enable smarter, more efficient and personalised interaction experiences as technologies such as artificial intelligence, speech recognition and sensor technologies advance.

This design direction is promising in three main ways: firstly, it greatly enhances the user experience by providing a variety of interaction modalities, allowing the user to choose the most appropriate one based on personal preferences or specific contexts. Second, multimodal interaction interfaces improve accessibility for users with limited visual, auditory, or motor functions, significantly enhancing the pervasive design of products. Finally, it promotes the integration and innovation of technologies including speech recognition, artificial intelligence, and augmented reality, opening up a new field of human-computer interaction.

Despite its promising future, multimodal interaction interface design faces challenges in the actual design and implementation process. These challenges include the complexity of the technology, which not only increases the complexity of the system but also raises the development cost; the learning curve of the users, especially the elderly users, who may need more time and effort to adapt and learn to use the multimodal interaction interface; the accuracy and reliability issues of speech and gesture recognition, as well as privacy and security concerns. In addition, the lack of uniform design standards and best practices creates additional challenges for designers and developers.

In conclusion, multimodal interaction interface design represents the future direction of human-computer interaction and holds great potential to enhance user experience and accessibility. However, in order to fully realise this potential, the accompanying issues of technical complexity, user adaptability, accuracy and security need to be addressed. Through interdisciplinary collaboration, in-depth user research and continuous technological innovation, it is expected that these challenges will be overcome and more intelligent, natural and humanised interaction interfaces will be realised.

References

1. Zhu, J.: Interpretation of smart product design based on cognitive characteristics of the elderly. Ind. Des. **08**, 145–146 (2018)
2. Jia, G.: Research on Voice Interaction Design of Smart Speakers for the Elderly. South China University of Technology, Guangdong Province (2019)
3. Gong, X.: Review of human-machine characteristics of the elderly group — based on the use of information technology products. J. Beijing Inst. Technol. (Soc. Sci. Ed.) **17**(05), 149–155 (2015)
4. Zhu, Y.: Theoretical foundations and research methods of multimodal discourse analysis. Foreign Lang. J. **05**, 82–86 (2007)
5. Dou, J., Qi, R.: Research on voice user interface design strategies for age-friendly smart home products based on situational analysis. Packag. Eng. **42**(16), 202–210 (2021)
6. Jaimes, A., Sebe, N.: Multimodal human–computer interaction: a survey. Comput. Vis. Image Underst. **108**(1–2), 116–134 (2007)
7. Gu, R.: Multimodal sensory systems and language research. Contemp. Linguis. **17**(04), 448–469 (2015)
8. Ma, X., Zhang, Y., Yu, Q.: Research on smart home design based on multimodal information interaction. Packag. Eng. **43**(16), 59–67+115 (2022)

9. Mao, N.: Multimodal human-computer interaction technology and its applications. Sci. Technol. Inf. (27), 59+96 (2012)

10. Tao, J., Yingcai, W., Chun, Y.: A review of multimodal human-computer interaction **27**(06), 1956–1987 (2022)

11. Wang, D., Zheng, Y., Li, T.: Multimodal human-computer interaction for human intelligence augmentation **48**(04), 449–465 (2018)

12. Zhang, P., Lu, Y., Chaoqun, S.: Research on age-friendly design of health kiosks under multimodal interaction. Equilibrium **12**(04), 61–66 (2022)

13. Carpentieri, G., Guida, C., Masoumi, H.E.: Multimodal accessibility to primary health services for the elderly: a case study of Naples, Italy. Sustainability **12**, 781 (2020)

14. D'Ulizia, A.: Exploring multimodal input fusion strategies. In: The Handbook of Research on Multimodal Human Computer Interaction and Pervasive Services: Evolutionary Techniques for Improving Accessibility, pp. 34–57. IGI Publishing (2009)

15. Jian, C., et al.: Towards effective, efficient and elderly-friendly multimodal interaction. In: Proceedings of the 4th International Conference on Pervasive Technologies Related to Assistive Environments, pp. 45:1–45:8. ACM, New York (2011)

16. Oviatt, S.: Multimodal interfaces. In: Jacko, J.A., Sears, A. (eds.) The Human-Computer Interaction Handbook, pp. 286–304. L. Erlbaum Associates Inc., Hillsdale (2002)

17. Jaimes, A., Sebe, N.: Multimodal human-computer interaction: a survey. In: Sebe, N., Lew, M., Huang, T. (eds.) Computational Vision and Image Understanding, pp. 116–134. Elsevier Science Inc., New York (2007)

18. Jian, C., et al.: Evaluating a spoken language interface of a multimodal interactive guidance system for elderly persons. In: Proceedings of the Fifth International Conference on Health Informatics, pp. 87–96. SciTepress, Vilamoura (2012)

19. Jian, C., et al.: Touch and speech: multimodal interaction for elderly persons. In: Gabriel, J., et al. (eds.) BIOSTEC 2012. CCIS, vol. 357, pp. 385–400. Springer, Heidelberg (2013)

20. Vitense, H.S., Jacko, J.A., Emery, V.K.: Multimodal feedback: establishing a performance baseline for improved access by individuals with visual impairments. In: Proceedings of the Fifth International ACM Conference on Assistive Technologies (Assets'02), pp. 49–56. ACM, New York (2002)

21. Grifoni, P.: Multimodal fission. In: The Handbook of Research on Multimodal Human Computer Interaction and Pervasive Services: Evolutionary Techniques for Improving Accessibility, pp. 103–120. IGI Publishing (2009)

22. Lutz, W., Sanderson, W., Scherbov, S.: The coming acceleration of global population ageing. Nature **451**, 716–719. International Institute for Applied Systems Analysis, Laxenburg (2008)

23. Czaja, S.J., Sharit, J.: The influence of age and experience on the performance of a data entry task. In: Proceedings of the Human Factors and Ergonomics Society 41st Annual Meeting, pp. 144–147 (1997)

24. Sharit, J., Czaja, S.J., Nair, S., Lee, C.C.: Effects of age, speech rate, and environmental support in using telephone voice menu system. Hum. Factors **45**, 234–252 (2003)

25. Ziefle, M., Bay, S.: How older adults meet complexity: aging effects on the usability of different mobile phones. Behav. Inf. Technol. **24**(5), 375–389 (2005)

26. Aran, O., Burger, T., Akarun, L., Caplier, A.: Gestural interfaces for hearing-impaired communication. In: Tzovaras, D. (ed.) Multimodal user interfaces: from signals to interaction, pp. 219–250. Springer, Leipzig, Germany (2008)

27. Bourguet, M.-L.: An overview of multimodal interaction techniques and applications. In: Zaphiris, P., Ang, C.S. (eds.) Human Computer Interaction: Concepts, Methodologies, Tools, and Applications, pp. 95–101. Information Science Reference, New York, NY, USA (2009)

28. Yin, Y.: Toward an Intelligent Multimodal Interface for Natural Interaction. Thesis submitted to The Massachusetts Institute of Technology for the degree of Master of Sciences, Massachusetts, USA (2010)

29. Oviatt, S.: Multimodal Interfaces. Hum.-Comput. Interact Handb. Fundam. Evol. Technol. Emerg. Appl. **14**, 405–430 (2012)
30. Gorlewicz, J.L., Tennison, J.L., Uesbeck, P.M., et al.: Design guidelines and recommendations for multimodal, touchscreen-based graphics. ACM Trans. Access Comput. **13** (2020)
31. Reeves, L.M., Martin, J.C., McTear, M., et al.: Guidelines for multimodal user interface design. Commun. ACM **47**, 57–59 (2004)
32. Sarter, N.B.: Multimodal information presentation: design guidance and research challenges. Int. J. Ind. Ergon. **36**, 439–445 (2006)
33. Snyder, L.J.: Stanford Encyclopedia of Philosophy Stanford Encyclopedia of Philosophy: Implicit Bias, pp. 1–22 (2017)
34. Turk, M.: Multimodal interaction: a review. Pattern Recognit. Lett. **36**, 189–195 (2014)
35. Krishnaswamy, N., Pustejovsky, J.: An evaluation framework for multimodal interaction. IN: Lr 2018 - 11th International Conference Language Resoures Evaluation, pp. 2127–2134 (2019)
36. Anastasiou, D., Jian, C., Zhekova, D.: Speech and gesture interaction in an ambient assisted living lab. In: Proceedings of the 1st Workshop on Speech and Multimodal Interaction in Assistive Environments, pp. 18–27. Association for Computational Linguistics (ACL), Stroudsburg (2012)
37. Ying, X.L.: Research on Mobile Application Design of Goal-Oriented Online Learning for the Elderly. Southwest Jiaotong University, Sichuan (2018)

Co-designing Human–Chatbot Interaction for Various Healthcare Purposes: Considering Chatbots' Social Characteristics and Communication Modalities

Xinyi Wang and Qingchuan Li[✉]

School of Humanity and Social Science, Harbin Institute of Technology, Shenzhen, China
23S059012@stu.hit.edu.cn, liqingchuan@hit.edu.cn

Abstract. The last decade has witnessed the blooming growth of healthcare chatbots in behavior interventions, elderly care, healthcare education, online diagnosis, and elsewhere. To meet the users' expectations and preferences, there is a need to investigate how to design social characteristics and communication modalities for healthcare chatbots serving different healthcare scenarios. This study introduces a co-design approach to address the challenges and uncertainties faced by users in virtual healthcare environments. By engaging users in an early design phase, the results provide insights into their attitudes and preferences for healthcare chatbots. It indicated that in different healthcare scenarios, users have varying psychological needs and considerations regarding the social characteristics and communication modalities of medical chatbots. Five kinds of healthcare chatbots are summarized: patient support services, health lifestyle and daily management, telemedicine and virtual health, emotional and mental health support, and assistance in medical work and research. Guidelines are proposed to inform the design of these chatbots, which can offer empirical support and practical guidance for future healthcare chatbot design.

Keywords: Healthcare Service · Human–Chatbot interaction · Co-Design · Social Characteristics · Communication Modalities

1 Introduction

With the rapid development of artificial intelligence (AI) and natural language processing (NLP), the last decade has witnessed a blooming growth of chatbots. Chatbots are widely used in e-commerce, customer service, web-based education, and healthcare [1]. They can deal with complex semantics and syntax, produce highly technical scripting languages, deliver interactive messages with real users, and respond to users in a humanized manner. Chatbots have been widely applied in various healthcare areas, including behavior interventions, elderly care, education, online diagnosis, and follow-up care [2]. They are reported to improve healthcare service qualities by facilitating dialog-based interactions, which can lessen healthcare professionals' workload and leverage a higher level of acceptance of and adherence to healthcare services.

Q. Gao and J. Zhou (Eds.): HCII 2024, LNCS 14726, pp. 399–414, 2024.
https://doi.org/10.1007/978-3-031-61546-7_26

However, users tend to be sensitive and vulnerable in healthcare services, as it becomes more difficult to develop trust between patients and physicians in virtual medical environments compared face-to-face communication [3]. It is even more difficult to generate interpersonal attachment and warmth during a human–chatbot interaction, which poses unaddressed challenges to the establishment of trust between users and healthcare chatbots. Ultimately, this can affect acceptance and adoption behavior with such chatbots, for example, whether users would actively seek medical services from healthcare chatbots, whether they would disclose personal information, and whether they would accept medical advice. Prior research has reported that healthcare chatbots' social characteristics (i.e., anthropomorphic appearance, thoroughness, manner, and morality) and communication modalities (i.e., verbal, auditory, and visual modalities) can influence their level of social presence, which impacts the process of trust development between patients and healthcare systems as well as user acceptance and adoption of such systems [4].

Little research has considered the differences in user needs and preferences in healthcare service scenarios. There still exists a need to investigate how the various social characteristics and communication modalities of healthcare chatbots serving different purposes should be designed to meet user expectations and preferences. To address the research question, this study employed a co-design approach to gather user understanding and perspectives in how healthcare chatbots can address specific needs and considerations under different healthcare conditions [5]. A list of design guidelines is proposed to inform future healthcare chatbot design by considering healthcare chatbots' social characteristics, communication modalities, and service scenarios. Empowered by human–computer interaction theories and user experience research methods, the results provide empirical support and practical guidelines for future healthcare chatbot design.

2 Literature Review

Scholars have systematically reviewed research on the application of chatbots in many fields, including healthcare, education, e-commerce, and social networking, and found that research on the acceptance, trust, security, and privacy of chatbots is gradually attracted the attention of researchers [6]. Despite the general acceptance of chatbots, most users are skeptical and 'wait and see' about their applications and effectiveness in healthcare. Thus, the design of healthcare chatbots has a significant impact on user willingness to disclose personal information and follow medical advice [7].

A good human–chatbot dialog needs to motivate focused engagement and deliver simple and compelling user experiences [8]; thus, the social characteristics of a healthcare chatbot matter. Social characteristics refer to the ability of the healthcare chatbot to generate sufficient social behavior to achieve the desired goal [9], e.g., whether it possesses anthropomorphic features, whether it is able to respond to social cues during dialog, and whether it displays empathy and is able to regulate the user's emotions. For example, the anthropomorphic features of a chatbot, including its appearance, linguistic features, cultural characteristics, and behavioral features, are important in a user's natural interaction experience [10–12]. As reported, anthropomorphic features can improve the perceived reliability of chatbots and bring users socially closer to them [4]. In addition, users are more likely to participate in human–robot conversations when conversational features such as personal names, greetings, chitchat, 'thank you,' and comments and suggestions are used [13].

On the basis of the modality, agency, interactivity, and navigability (MAIN) model proposed by Kim and Sundar [14], social presence can be achieved through communication modality (the presentation of information in text, audio, or video), agency (appearance, gender, language, voice, or expertise of the computer), interactivity (active participation of the user in the interface and its content), and navigational cues (internal design of the interface) [4]. Communication modalities of robot behavior are used for reasoning and controlling robot actions [5]. Communication modalities affect user satisfaction with chatbot interactions differently. A between-group study (n = 393 participants) was conducted to compare text-based (n = 189) and voice-based (n = 204) coaching chatbots in terms of usability and performance expectancy. The results indicated that designers should use voice as a way to engage users and text as a way to complete complex tasks and reduce risk perception [15].

However, users in various healthcare scenarios may have different psychological needs and considerations that influence their expectations and preferences for the social characteristics and communication modalities regarding healthcare chatbots. Therefore, this study probed the following questions: RQ1: How do users perceive and define chatbot roles and functions for various healthcare purposes? RQ2: How should the social characteristics and communication modalities of chatbots be designed for different healthcare scenarios?

To address the research questions, a co-design method was employed, as such an approach is helpful in actively involving (future) users early in the design process [16]. Participatory design assumes that users are "experts by experience" or "experts in their field of life" [17]. Thus, this method can provide valuable information for designers, developers, and researchers in assessing potential users' attitudes and perspectives [18]. (In this paper, the terms 'participatory design' and 'co-design' are used interchangeably.) Considering that the application of healthcare chatbots is still in an initial stage in China, participatory design can provide a valuable way to gain inspiration for the design and development of new types of robots, as well as relevant application areas [5].

3 Method

3.1 Co-designing the Chatbot

This study employed a co-design approach to investigate users' understanding and perspectives in terms of how healthcare chatbots should be designed to address their needs and considerations under different healthcare conditions [5]. Two co-design workshops were organized in November and December 2023. The sessions were held both online and offline. In total, 15 participants attended. The participants were between 22 and 30 years old (mean age = 24 years, SD = 2.58), and all were Chinese postgraduate students majoring in product design, interaction design, and media design. They were divided into five groups of three. Twelve of the participants (four groups) attended in person and three (one group) participated in the online workshop. Online participation was through virtual meeting software and online whiteboards, namely Zoom and the Miro online whiteboard (Fig. 1).

(a)   (b)   (c)

Fig. 1. The co-design workshops: participants are brainstorming personality and modality cards (a) in November 2023, (b) in December 2023, and (c) using an online whiteboard.

Card-based Materials. A card-based toolkit was developed based on the study of Feine et al. [12] to enrich the participants' brainstorming and discussion activities in a tangible and engaging way. Using card-based design tools makes the design process visible, helps explain complex concepts to novices, makes ideas explicit, and helps participants develop theoretical ideas into concrete and practical design guidelines [5]. The toolkit comprised four categories of social characteristics and communication modalities, including visual, verbal, auditory, and invisible cues. For each category, there were several cues. The framework (Table 1) was adapted from Feline et al.'s study. For example, the category of visual cues included cards such as 2D/3D agent visualization, age, color of agent, and name tags. In total, 48 cards were provided in the toolkit, with an example shown in Fig. 2.

Table 1. Categorization framework of the card-based design toolkit.

Category	Card Item						
Visual Cues	01	Arm and hand gesture	02	Eye movement	03	Facial expression
	04	Head movement	05	Posture shift	06	Background
	07	Conversational distance	08	2D-/3D-agent visualization	09	Age
	10	Attractiveness	11	Clothing	12	Color of agent
	13	Degree of human likeness	14	Facial feature	15	Gender
	16	Name tag	17	Photorealism	18	Emoticons
	19	Typeface				
Verbal Cues	20	Ask to start/pursue dialog	21	Excuse/Apologize	22	Greetings and farewells

(continued)

Table 1. (*continued*)

Category	Card Item							
	23	Joke	24	Opinion conformity	25	Praise		
	26	Refer to past	27	Self-disclosure	28	Self-focused questions		
	29	Small talk	30	Thanking	31	Tips and advice		
	32	Abbreviations	33	Formality	34	Lexical diversity		
	35	Sentence complexity	36	Strength of language				
Auditory Cues	37	Gender of voice	38	Pitch range	39	Voice tempo		
	40	Volume	41	Grunts and moans	42	Laughing		
	43	Vocal segregates	44	Yawn				
Invisible Cues	45	First turn	46	Response time	47	Tactile touch		
	48	Temperature						

Fig. 2. Cards used in the co-design workshops.

Procedure. Before the start of each workshop, all participants were informed that the process would be audio and video recorded and the data obtained would be used exclusively for academic research to protect the privacy of the interviewees. In the initial 30 min of the workshop, the facilitator made a short opening to keep the participants relaxed and learned basic information about the participants. After the warm-up, the workshop was conducted in three sections. In the first 30 min, participants were asked to come up with at least ten healthcare service scenarios that can be helped by chatbots, such as outpatient and emergency registration, pre-diagnosis and triage, disease follow-up treatment, and healthcare data management. The section was designed to familiarize the participants with various healthcare services and the roles of healthcare chatbots. Next, participants were required to pick three healthcare service scenarios and analyze the touchpoints that could be intervened in by chatbots (also 30 min). Then, in the next 45 min, participants were asked to design healthcare chatbots for the design touchpoints in the three healthcare scenarios by organizing and manipulating the cards for the specification of different design aspects of the human–chatbot interaction experience. Low-fidelity prototypes were developed in each group. In the last 45 min, participants were asked to present and explain the design concepts and provide feedback on different design aspects of each healthcare chatbot. The facilitators then concluded the workshop. Each workshop was approximately 3 h in duration.

3.2 Data Collection and Analysis

We converted the workshop recordings into text data, which was analyzed using the software Atlas.it. We used an inductive data collection method to categorize the healthcare services scenarios [19]. Multiple sets of codes were recorded until no new primary codes were added to the list, which ultimately resulted in the compilation of 120 primary codes. After discussion, some primary codes similar in meaning were merged. For example, the "mental health diagnosis" and "mental health reassurance" codes were merged into the "mental health support" code because they both provide assistance with a patient's mental health. By combining similar items, the list was reduced to 60 codes. The distribution of these codes was generalized upwards, and 12 mutually exclusive categories of healthcare service scenarios were identified, including appointment management, emotional support, and supporting healthcare professionals. Finally, the selected classifications of scenarios were further upwardly organized into five themes, which are presented below. In addition, we analyzed the social characteristics and communication modalities preferred by the participants in five themes of healthcare service scenarios and identified the roles and functions of typical chatbots.

4   Results

4.1 Classification of Healthcare Scenarios

Chatbots have been evaluated to support different types of healthcare scenarios, e.g., counseling [20, 21], chronic health condition monitoring [22], or medication adherence [23]. Some scholars have categorized healthcare scenarios into neurological disorders, mental and physical wellness, nutritional-metabolic disorders, addictions, sexually transmitted diseases, and others based on the types of diseases that chatbots can address [24]. One study classified application scenarios for chatbots from the physician's perspective and divided healthcare scenarios into diagnosis, interpretation of clinical images, information about a patient, information about a patient in the operation room, knowledge base, documentation, and intermediaries between different healthcare facilities [25]. Healthcare scenarios classified from the patient's point of view are self-diagnosis, anamnesis, medication dosage, prioritization in the emergency room, psychiatric treatment, treatment information, and food orders [25].

In the workshop, we asked participants to propose at least ten healthcare scenarios that might be facilitated and assisted by chatbots. Based on the aforementioned studies and the bottom-up organization of the workshop data, healthcare scenarios were classified into five themes. Table 2 shows the themes, sub-themes, and examples of applied healthcare scenarios.

Patient Support Services. This service is designed to provide support and guidance to patients; it can be categorized into appointment management and hospital navigation

Table 2. Classification of healthcare scenarios.

Theme	Sub-themes	Examples
Patient support services	Appointment management	Registration
		Recommendation of doctors and hospitals
	Hospital navigation assistance	Guidelines for seeing a doctor
		Navigation of hospital departments
Health lifestyle and daily management	Health education	Disease prevention
		Lifestyle advice
	Lifestyle and wellness	Nutritional guidance
		Fitness recommendations
		Sleep management
Telemedicine and virtual health	Telemedicine and virtual consultations	Initial consultations
		Follow-up communications
	Chronic disease management	Personalized care plans
		Vital signs monitoring
	Rehabilitation and physical wellness	Guided exercises
		Progress tracking
	Post-operative care and follow-up	Post-operative instructions
		Follow-up support
Emotional and mental health support	Mental illness	Well-being conversations
		Crisis intervention
	Emotional support	Relieving patient anxiety
		Reassuring waiting families
Assistance in medical work and research	Supporting healthcare professionals	Diagnostic support
		Hospital security
		Medical exposure risks
	Health surveys and research participation	Data collection for research
		Clinical trial

assistance. It includes scenarios such as registration, the recommendation of doctors and hospitals, guidelines for seeing a doctor, and navigation of hospital departments, aiming to simplify and improve the medical treatment process for patients. In such scenarios, chatbots should be designed to provide users with rich information and easy-to-operate steps, which may accompany the whole process of the user's medical treatment. For example, one participant said, "In the registration scenario, the chatbot should provide users with a clear process, so that I don't need to have complicated operations to complete the business I want to handle."

Health Lifestyle and Daily Management. This includes the categories of health education and lifestyle and wellness. This type of scenario can help users manage their daily activities and can provide guidance recommendations and training tutorials to support users' physical health. It includes disease prevention, fitness recommendations, sleep management, and other areas. Here, chatbots can be designed as "friendly advisors or mentors for users rather than therapists or healthcare professionals" [26]. One participant stated, "In the sleep management scenario, I would like to have a chatbot that can record my sleep duration and sleep problems. It's better to have a sleep-tracking service and not to give me orders and instructions in a rigid way."

Telemedicine and Virtual Health. This category includes telemedicine and virtual consultations, rehabilitation and physical wellness, chronic disease management, postoperative care, and follow-up. In such scenarios, chatbots are expected to help with consultations, personalized care plans, post-operative instructions, etc., by tracking patients' biosignals [24], such as physical activity, heart rate, blood pressure, and body temperature. The chatbot can assist or advise patients before they go to the healthcare facility or ask them about the symptoms they are experiencing and suggest treatment options [25]. One participant said, "When patients are unable to go to hospitals or clinics in person, telemedicine can provide convenient and professional services to help patients understand their condition and treatment measures."

Emotional and Mental Health Support. This category includes mental illness and emotional support. A chatbot can provide a safe and anonymous environment so that patients can establish a sense of rapport without fear of stigmatization and discrimination [24]. It can perform sentiment analysis in different ways, such as by extracting speech signals using rhyming and statistical features [27] and analyzing emotional states using textual information [28] for crisis intervention, relief of patient anxiety, etc. Chatbots in such scenarios can make objective evaluations or recognize harmful tendencies [24] and gain user trust by providing a sense of companionship. One participant explained: "I would like to have a chatbot with customized patient features that can accompany me in the hospital, empathize with my emotions, and relieve anxiety."

Assistance in Medical Work and Research. This includes supporting healthcare professionals, health surveys, and research participation, which involves diagnostic support, medical exposure risks, data collection for research, etc. Chatbots can play many roles, such as operation assistant for surgery and observation assistant for medical records and databases. They can reduce the workload of professionals and improve the quality of their work as well as increase the acceptability of and compliance with health services [4]. For instance, one participant said, "We'd like to design a chatbot for medical exposure risk. This type of healthcare professional will have many times higher probability of cancer than ordinary people. By using this chatbot, we hope to reduce the risk of long-term exposure to radiation for healthcare workers."

4.2 Social Characteristics and Communication Modalities in Different Healthcare Scenarios

The workshop results indicated that in different healthcare scenarios, users have varying psychological needs and considerations regarding the social characteristics and communication modalities of medical chatbots. This study analyzed and summarized user needs and expectations for chatbots' social characteristics and communication modalities according to the five healthcare scenarios, with design examples for each (Table 3).

In the scenarios related to patient support, the chatbot's role and function tend to be that of an assistant. Participants developed a design case in which the chatbot helped a patient undergoing a blood test. It was designed as a text-based chatbot that guides the user through the process and provides information to the user about the location of the department, reminders of the progress, and feedback on the results. In the choice of verbal cues, this chatbot has low sentence complexity, adapting to patients with different literacy levels. In conversation, it will take the initiative to greet and bid farewell to the patient, provide suggestions, and remind the patient to take the next step. The language style is official and authoritative, which is conducive to obtaining patient trust. In terms of visual cues, it has a 2D cartoon robot image as its visual presentation and uses non-serif fonts to make the interface simple and clear. For the invisible cues, dialog chronemics were considered in this design case. The conversation is often initiated by the chatbot, with a fast response time so that the user can get timely feedback. In summary, the chatbot should provide support to the patient. Its visual design emphasizes simplicity and clarity, and verbal communication emphasizes efficiency and convenience.

Participants tended to perceive the chatbot in health lifestyle and daily management as a counselor. For example, one group developed a chatbot aimed at improving children's healthcare literacy. It was an embodied chatbot that guided children to develop healthy lifestyle habits and popularize dental care. In the choice of verbal cues, the chatbot has low sentence complexity to facilitate children's understanding of healthcare information, and it often uses an encouraging and approving tone of voice when conversing with children. The chatbot usually takes the initiative to greet and make small talk to reduce the conversational distance. In terms of visual cues, the chatbot exists as a 3D cartoon image of a young woman, with highly saturated colors and a rich background. In the dialog, it responds to the user with head movements and rich facial expressions, adopting a pleasant female voice with accompanying laughter and intonation to create a calm atmosphere. Regarding the invisible cues, the chatbot often initiates a conversation with the user. To summarize, the chatbot is designed to impart knowledge and relevant advice to the user. It should serve as a popularizer and a question-answerer to accompany users in the functions of daily management and process supervision. Its visual design should be attractive and provide users with friendly feedback, and it should create a pleasant atmosphere in verbal communication to increase user motivation.

For the scenarios of telemedicine and virtual health, participants tended to perceive the chatbot as a friend. For example, an embodied chatbot was proposed for the purpose of remote monitoring and management of diabetes. It was designed to monitor the patient's physiological data and provide daily dietary advice. In terms of verbal cues, the chatbot adopts a professional and confident attitude to talk with the patient in order to increase the user's trust. After the user uploads a picture or text describing the food

Table 3. The social characteristics and communication modalities proposed for various healthcare service scenarios.

Scenarios	Proposed social characteristics and modalities		Design Example
Patient support services	Visual Cues	- 2D cartoon robot image - Non-serif fonts - Low sentence complexity - Adapting to patients with different literacy levels	
	Verbal Cues	- Initiative to greet and bid farewell - Provide suggestions - Remind the patient to take the next step - Official and authoritative	
	Auditory Cues	- Not applicable	
	Invisible Cues	- Initiate a conversation - Fast response time	
Health lifestyle and daily management	Visual Cues	- 3D cartoon image of a young woman - Highly saturated colors - Rich background - Head movements - Rich facial expressions	
	Verbal Cues	- Low sentence complexity - Encouraging and approving tone of voice - Initiative to greet - Make small talk	
	Auditory Cues	- Pleasant female voice - Companying laughter and intonation	
	Invisible Cues	- Initiate a conversation	
Telemedicine and virtual health	Visual Cues	- 2D cartoon of a male doctor - Often smile - Use a nod or shake of the head to indicate its attitude - Hand movements in illustrating content	
	Verbal Cues	- Professional and confident attitude - Assess the meal and provides advice in a friendly tone	

(continued)

Table 3. (*continued*)

	Auditory Cues	- Calm baritone voice - Speak at a slower speed
	Invisible Cues	- Initiate a conversation - Pause for about 2–3 seconds before answering
Emotional and mental health support	Visual Cues	- Female cartoon figure - Smile and look into the user's eyes - Facial expressions - Head movements
	Verbal Cues	- Take the initiative to make daily greetings - Use the tone of praise and encouragement - Affirm the user's words - Tell jokes - Recognize users' negative emotions - Exhibit empathy
	Auditory Cues	- Gentle but vivid female voice - Gentle speech rate for a calm, friendly feeling
	Invisible Cues	- Initiate a conversation - Pause for a while after the user confides
Assistance in medical work and research	Auditory Cues	- Not applicable
	Verbal Cues	- Short and easy-to-understand sentences - Accurate and professional commands - Timely feedback
	Auditory Cues	- The gender of the voice aligns with the gender of the user - Speak at a slower pace
	Invisible Cues	- Initiate a conversation - Respond quickly

he or she ate, the chatbot would assess the meal and provides advice in a friendly tone to make it more acceptable. In the choice of visual cues, it appears as a 2D cartoon of a male doctor, often smiling and using a nod or shake of the head to indicate its attitude. When providing dietary advice, it uses hand movements to help in illustrating content, for example, "a fist-sized amount of rice." Regarding voice cues, in order to reflect the sense of professionalism, the chatbot adopts a calm baritone voice and speaks at a slower speed. Usually, the chatbot would initiate a conversation to ask the user about his or her daily diet and pause for about 2–3 s before answering the user's question to suggest a process of thinking and to increase the persuasiveness of the answer. To conclude, the chatbot should reflect professionalism and authority. The visual design is suggested to prefer use of an anthropomorphic image of a doctor or an expert to help the user establish a sense of trust. As for verbal communication, it should provide users with scientific and personalized advice and support multi-channel communication to adapt to the needs of different users.

For the scenarios of emotional and mental health support, participants tended to regard the chatbot as a companion. In the design example of mental and emotional soothing, the embodied chatbot mainly plays a role in channeling and calming emotions. The chatbot often takes the initiative to make daily greetings and uses the tone of praise and encouragement to chat. It often affirms the user's words and tells jokes to keep the user in a positive state. It can recognize users' negative emotions and exhibit empathy to provide emotional comfort. In terms of visual cues, the chatbot is presented as a female cartoon figure, which gives a sense of intellectual intimacy and reduces the distance between the user and the chatbot. It often smiles and looks into the user's eyes in conversation, while facial expressions and head movements change with the user's input, e.g., a smile and a nod of the head for approval, a frown and a shake of the head for sympathy. The auditory cues adopt a gentle but vivid female voice with a gentle speech rate for a calm, friendly feeling. For invisible cues, it commonly initiates the session and pauses for a while after the user confides in order to suggest care and compassion. To sum up, the chatbot should be empathetic and emotionally intelligent. The dialog should be supportive to encourage users to express their emotions and share their experiences. When dealing with sensitive topics, the chatbot should emphasize respect and protection of the user's privacy. In addition, the chatbot should be able to follow up regularly on the user's emotional state and provide continuous support in order to make the user feel that he or she has a reliable partner in times of need.

In assistance in medical work and research, participants imaged the chatbot as an assistant. One group proposed a voice-based chatbot in the medical exposure environment, in which the chatbot can serve as a substitute for doctors to guide patients in performing scan operations. In verbal cues, it uses short and easy-to-understand sentences to give accurate and professional commands to the user. Timely feedback is provided during user checking. It is a voice-based chatbot with no specific image. The gender of the voice is designed to align with the gender of the user in order to increase the user's sense of security. Furthermore, it speaks at a slower pace to make it easy for the user to hear instructions clearly. Normally, it initiates conversation and responds quickly to avoid waiting time. The chatbot for this type of scenario should be concise and efficient in verbal communication to provide timely, accurate assistance and support to doctors. In addition, it should follow the highest privacy and security standards when handling sensitive patient information to ensure the security of patient data.

5   Discussion

This study explored users' perceptions and expectations for social characteristics and communication modalities of chatbots in different healthcare scenarios. For verbal cues, previous research has shown that the level of anthropomorphism of embodied chatbots, e.g., realism, cartoonishness, or nonexistent visualization, has an effect on information retention [29]. This study suggests that adding more anthropomorphic attributes to the chatbot's verbal style and content, such as greetings and farewells, small talk, thanks, and tips, will increase the user's sense of trust and closeness. The anthropomorphic level of a chatbot may also increase the user's emotional connection. It has been shown that chatbots with high emotional intelligence can recognize and influence the user's feelings by showing respect, empathy, and understanding, which can improve the human–chatbot relationship [30]. This study also recommends that when the chatbot empathizes with the user's emotions, such as apologizing for the user's bad experience and agreeing with the user, the user will feel respected and understood. In addition, the chatbot's language style and content can influence user adoption and acceptance. The workshops suggested that when the chatbot's tone is more assertive and confident, the user will be more trusting and receptive to suggestions.

Regarding visual cues, the level of anthropomorphism greatly influences users' perceptions and feelings [4]. For example, in telemedicine and virtual health scenarios, users perceive a chatbot as more professional and trustworthy when it adopts the image of a doctor or an expert. In emoticon and mental health support scenarios, users perceive a chatbot as more open-minded when it adopts the image of a kindly woman. Additionally, a chatbot's kinesics can influence users' perceptions and feelings. In emotional and mental health support scenarios, users would like feedback such as nodding and gazing to gain emotional support in their confidence.

For auditory cues, the design of voice qualities and vocalizations should also depend on the specific scenario. Taking patient support service as an example, a faster speech rate can better satisfy the user's expectation because the user desires to obtain information and act efficiently; whereas, in emotional and mental health support scenarios, the appropriate design of vocalizations (e.g., laughing, moans) can increase the anthropomorphism of the chatbot and make the interaction more intimate and natural.

With respect to invisible cues, the chronemics (i.e., waiting time, lead time, or tempo [31]) should be designed according to the scenario. The participants argued that users would generally expect a chatbot to initiate a conversation. The response time of chatbots is often designed for immediate feedback in scenarios that emphasize convenience and efficiency, such as patient support and assistance in medical work and research. Conversely, the chatbot is also designed to pause for a few seconds before giving feedback to suggest a thinking process in scenarios that require emotional support and deeper thinking.

Chatbots' communication modalities (i.e., verbal, auditory, and visual modalities) are also closely related to the nature of healthcare scenarios. When providing patient support and assistance or assisting in medical work, the efficiency and clarity of the information conveyed by chatbots should be prioritized. Since there was less need for a visual image, text-based or voice-based chatbots are more frequently applied. In the remaining three scenarios, users expect visual modality with the chatbot, so an embodied chatbot is often used.

6 Conclusion

In this study, we applied a co-design methodology with a card-based design toolkit comprising four themes of social cues (verbal, visual, auditory, invisible) to assess potential users' perceptions and definitions of chatbots' roles and functions in various healthcare scenarios. We also investigated the participants' expectations and needs for social characteristics and communication modalities for such chatbots. The participants indicated different psychological needs and considerations for the design of medical chatbots for various healthcare purposes. However, the generalizability of the results may be constrained by the specific demographic characteristics of the workshop participants. Future research could aim for more diverse participant profiles to ensure broader applicability. In addition, although we proposed a list of social characteristics and communication modalities that suited different scenarios, we did not conduct user feedback testing on the prototypes. Future studies are recommended to obtain user feedback in the design and implementation phases to enhance the iterative improvement of the healthcare chatbot's design, and empirical research is needed to further explore the specific relationships between the social characteristics, communication modalities, and service scenarios.

Acknowledgments. This research was supported by the Guangdong Philosophy and Social Science Foundation (Grant number GD23XYS064) and General Program of Stable Support Plan for Universities in Shenzhen (Grant number GXWD20231129154726002).

Disclosure of Interests. None of the interests were disclosed by the authors.

References

1. Go, E., Sundar, S.S.: Humanizing chatbots: the effects of visual, identity and conversational cues on humanness perceptions. Comput. Hum. Behav. **97**(AUG), 304–316 (2019). https://doi.org/10.1016/j.chb.2019.01.020
2. Montenegro, J.L.Z., da Costa, C.A., da Rosa Righi, R.: Survey of conversational agents in health. Expert Syst. Appl. **129**, 56–67 (2019). https://doi.org/10.1016/j.eswa.2019.03.054
3. Zhang, J., Luximon, Y., Li, Q.: Seeking medical advice in mobile applications: how social cue design and privacy concerns influence trust and behavioral intention in impersonal patient–physician interactions. Comput. Hum. Behav. **130**, 107178 (2022). https://doi.org/10.1016/j.chb.2021.107178
4. Li, Q., Luximon, Y., Zhang, J.: The influence of anthropomorphic cues on patients' perceived anthropomorphism, social presence, trust building, and acceptance of health care conversational agents: within-subject web-based experiment. J. Med. Internet Res. **25**, e44479 (2023). https://doi.org/10.2196/44479
5. Pollmann, K.: The modality card deck: Co-creating multi-modal behavioral expressions for social robots with older adults. Multimodal Technol. Interact. **5**(7), 33 (2021). https://doi.org/10.3390/mti5070033
6. Tudor, C.L., et al.: Conversational agents in health care: scoping review and conceptual analysis. J. Med. Internet Res. **22**(8), e17158 (2020). https://doi.org/10.2196/17158
7. Yu, X., et al.: mHealth in China and the United States: how mobile technology is transforming healthcare in the world's two largest economies. Washington DC Center Technol. Innov. Brookings 2014, 08 (2016)
8. Brandtzaeg, P.B., Følstad, A.: Chatbots: changing user needs and motivations. Interactions **25**(5), 38–43 (2018). https://doi.org/10.1145/3236669
9. Björkqvist, K., Österman, K., Kaukiainen, A.: Social intelligence – empathy = aggression? Aggress. Violent. Beh. **5**(2), 191–200 (2000). https://doi.org/10.1016/S1359-1789(98)00029-9

10. Nass, C., Moon, Y.: Machines and mindlessness: social responses to computers. J. Soc. Issues **56**(1), 81–103 (2000). https://doi.org/10.1111/0022-4537.00153
11. Esfahani, M.S., Reynolds, N., Ashleigh, M.: Mindful and mindless anthropomorphism: how to facilitate consumer comprehension towards new products. Int. J. Innov. Technol. Manag. **17**(3), 2050016 (2020). https://doi.org/10.1142/S0219877702050069
12. Feine, J., et al.: A taxonomy of social cues for conversational agents. Int. J. Hum. Comput. Stud. **132**, 138–161 (2019). https://doi.org/10.1016/j.ijhcs.2019.07.009
13. Chaves, A.P., Gerosa, M.A.: How should my chatbot interact? a survey on social characteristics in human–chatbot interaction design. Int. J. Hum. Comput. Interact. **37**(8), 729–758 (2021). https://doi.org/10.1080/10447318.2020.1841438
14. Kim, Y., Sundar, S.S.: Anthropomorphism of computers: is it mindful or mindless? Comput. Hum. Behav. **28**(1), 241–250 (2012). https://doi.org/10.1016/j.chb.2011.09.006
15. Terblanche, N.H.D., Wallis, G.P., Kidd, M.: Talk or text? the role of communication modalities in the adoption of a non-directive, goal-attainment coaching chatbot. Interact. Comput. **35**(4), 511–518 (2023). https://doi.org/10.1093/iwc/iwad039
16. Sanders, E.B.-N., Stappers, P.J.: Co-creation and the new landscapes of design. Co-design **4**(1), 5–18 (2008). https://doi.org/10.1080/15710880701875068
17. Beimborn, M., et al.: Focusing on the human: interdisciplinary reflections on ageing and technology. In: Domínguez-Rué, E., Nierling, L. (eds.) Ageing and Technology, pp. 311–333. Transcript Verlag, Bielefeld (2016)
18. Merkel, S., Kucharski, A.: Participatory design in gerontechnology: a systematic literature review. Gerontologist **59**(1), e16–e25 (2019). https://doi.org/10.1093/geront/gny034
19. Thomas, D.R.: A general inductive approach for qualitative data analysis. Am. J. Eval. **27**(2), 237–246 (2003)
20. van Heerden, A., Ntinga, X., Vilakazi, K.: The potential of conversational agents to provide rapid HIV counseling and testing services. In: 2017 International Conference on the Frontiers and Advances in Data Science (FADS), pp. 80–85. IEEE (2017)
21. Oh, K.-J., Lee, D., Ko, B., Choi, H.-J.: A chatbot for psychiatric counseling in mental health-care service based on emotional dialogue analysis and sentence generation. In: 2017 18th IEEE International Conference on Mobile Data Management (MDM), pp. 371–375. IEEE (2017)
22. Richards, D., Caldwell, P.: Improving health outcomes sooner rather than later via an inter-active website virtual specialist. IEEE J. Biomed. Health Informat. 1 (2017). https://doi.org/10.1109/JBHI.2017.2782210
23. Richards, D., Caldwell, P.H.: Gamification to improve adherence to clinical treatment advice. In: Health Literacy: Breakthroughs in Research and Practice, p. 80 (2017). https://doi.org/10.4018/978-1-5225-1928-7.ch005
24. Pereira, J., Díaz, O.: Using health chatbots for behavior change: a mapping study. J. Med. Syst. **43**, 1–13 (2019)
25. Reis, L., et al.: Chatbots in healthcare: status quo, application scenarios for physicians and patients and future directions. In: Proceedings of the 28th European Conference on Information Systems (ECIS), pp. 1–15. AIS eLibrary (2020)
26. Elmasri, D., Maeder, A.: A conversational agent for an online mental health intervention. In: Brain Informatics and Health: International Conference, BIH 2016, Omaha, NE, USA, October 13–16, 2016 Proceedings. Springer International Publishing (2016). https://doi.org/10.1007/978-3-319-47103-7_24
27. Roniotis, A., Tsiknakis, M.: Detecting depression using voice signal extracted by chatbots: a feasibility study. In: Brooks, A.L., Brooks, E., Vidakis, N. (eds.) ArtsIT/DLI -2017. LNIC-SSITE, vol. 229, pp. 386–392. Springer, Cham (2018). https://doi.org/10.1007/978-3-319-76908-0_37

28. Jeong, S., Breazeal, C.: Toward robotic companions that enhance psychological wellbeing with smartphone technology. In: Proceedings of the Companion of the 2017 ACM/IEEE International Conference on Human-Robot Interaction (2017)

29. Beun, R.J., De Vos, E., Witteman, C.: Embodied conversational agents: effects on memory performance and anthropomorphisation. In: International Workshop on Intelligent Virtual Agents. Berlin, Heidelberg: Springer (2003). https://doi.org/10.1007/978-3-540-39396-2_52

30. Li, Y., et al.: Dailydialog: A manually labelled multi-turn dialogue dataset. arXiv preprint arXiv:1710.03957 (2017). https://doi.org/10.48550/arXiv.1710.03957

31. Burgoon, J.K., Guerrero, L.K., Manusov, V.: Nonverbal Signals. Handbook of Interpersonal Communication. SAGE Publication, London (2011)

The Framework for Age-Friendly Voice Medical Information Service Platform Based on Field Dynamic Theory

Yibei Zeng[1], Kaiqing Tang[1(✉)], and Yuqi Liu[2]

[1] Academy of Arts and Design, Shanghai Normal University, Shanghai, China
eterner@gmail.com
[2] Academy of Arts and Design, Tsinghua University, Beijing, China

Abstract. In the context of increasing digitization and aging population, the medical information service platform influences the experience of the elderly during medical treatment. This study aims to improve the age-friendly medical process by optimizing the AI-driven Voice User Interface (VUI) service platform. By introducing the Field Dynamic Theory, we analyzed the behavior of the elderly in the medical field from a systemic perspective. Through study interviews on medical pain points, the Analytic Hierarchy Process (AHP) is used to calculate the top three weighted needs that urgently need to be addressed. We refined three platform functionalities: efficient interaction guidance, personalized pre-diagnosis and empathetic medical accompaniment. The platform establishes a framework through guided flow, interaction flow, and feedback flow, implemented with using Medical GPT-based Voice User Interface (VUI). This study is applied from online to offline VUI service touchpoints, achieved the linkage from homes to hospitals and from front-end to back-end. This study constructs a AI-driven sustainable iterative medical process service platform to enhance the medical efficiency and experience of the elderly, providing strategies and references for building an age-friendly voice medical information service platform.

Keywords: VUI · Service Design · Age-Friendly Medical · Field Dynamic Theory · Information Platform

1 Introduction

The issue of the digital divide increasingly impacts the elderly. Hospitals, which play a critical role in the daily lives of the elderly, address the digital divide by implementing AI-driven medical information service platforms, thus enhancing the medical experience and efficiency for the elderly.

This study innovates in two main areas. Firstly, it employs Field Dynamic Theory to analyze the medical behavior of elderly users from a systemic perspective, aiding in the optimization of current medical information service platforms and refining the medical service process. Secondly, the study explores a voice-interaction-based registration platform utilizing medical GPT technology, aiming to improve the medical experience for

Q. Gao and J. Zhou (Eds.): HCII 2024, LNCS 14726, pp. 415–428, 2024.
https://doi.org/10.1007/978-3-031-61546-7_27

elderly users. Through iterative enhancements in natural conversations, this approach achieves a better understanding of user intent, continually refining service methods. Such refinement in the medical process, which spans from online to offline and from home to hospital, as well as from frontstage to backstage, breaks the constraints of time and space, thereby enhancing the accessibility of medical services platform for the elderly [1].

2 Literature Review

2.1 Current Status of Voice Medical Information Service Platform for the Elderly

By 2050, it is projected that 38.6% of China's population will be individuals aged 60 and above, marking an irreversible trend towards a deeply aging society [2]. In this context, age-friendly services in the medical field have emerged as a crucial social issue. Amidst the complex challenges of digitalization and aging, improving medical services for the elderly has become a priority [3].

Data shows that effective medical consultation time accounts for only about 10.4%, highlighting an urgent need to optimize the service software platforms in the medical scene from registration to the medical consultation process, thereby improving medical efficiency and experience. An AI-driven medical information service platform offers an efficient way to enhance the medical experience and efficiency for the elderly [4]. Studies have established age-friendly medical waiting service systems through digital service carriers such as apps, improving the medical information platform. Alternatively, designing age-friendly medical terminal interfaces from the perspective of embodied cognition enhances the interactive experience of the elderly on medical platforms [5].

The explosive development of artificial intelligence in 2023 brings new opportunities for age-friendly medical service design. Large language models (like medical GPT), voice user interfaces (VUI), and big data are empowering the medical domain. Particularly, combining medical GPT with registration VUI can be applied to voice-guided medical consultations for the elderly [6]. This refinement in the medical process, enhancing the accessibility of medical services for the elderly [1].

However, current research focuses on improving the user experience of single platform. In view of this, this study analyzes the registration behavior and needs of the elderly from the perspective of field Dynamic theory, systematically. Moreover, by employing an AI-driven voice user interface (VUI) platform for registration, it enhances the medical information service platform, thereby improving both the medical experience and efficiency.

2.2 Field Dynamic Theory

Kurt Lewin, an American social psychologist, introduced the "Field Dynamic Theory" as a systemic method for studying human behavior [7]. The basic formula of field Dynamic theory is: $B = f(P*E) = f(LS)$, where B represents the "User's Behavior", P represents the "Personal Field" of internal needs, E represents the "Environment Field" of external stimulus, and LS denotes the "Life Space" where behavior occurs. This indicates that human behavior is influenced by both the personal and environmental fields within a space, displaying a holistic Gestalt nature.

The service design of an age-friendly medical information platform involves different service touchpoints such as people, events, objects, and spaces, requiring a systematic analysis. However, Field Dynamic Theory, with its systematic and interactive nature [8], provides a method for the user research process in the design, allowing for the provision of more precise services based on the behavioral needs of the elderly [9]. The personal field of elderly medical registration is divided into psychological and physiological factors, while the environmental field is divided into medical environment factors and platform environment factors. Therefore, based on Field Dynamic Theory, the age-friendly approach involves four factors (see Fig. 1).

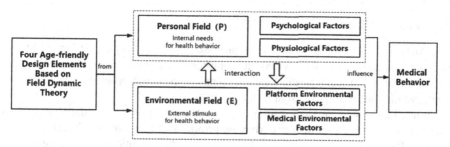

Fig. 1. Field Dynamic Theory theoretical model

Personal Field (P): Internal Needs for Medical Behavior. The Personal Field focuses on the internal characteristics of the elderly population's needs for VUI registration operations and medical consultation processes.

Physiological factors refer to characteristics such as sensory function, physical function, and a decline in information reception among the elderly. When operating a VUI, 20% of the elderly have about 0.7 visual acuity, and cannot hear sounds above 4000 Hz [10], indicating the need for voice interaction modes to assist with medical registration due to the impact of a single modality interaction on information reception. Sychological factors refer to cognitive load, emotional instability, and prone to memory errors of the elderly. Data shows a significant decrease in nerve conduction speed among the elderly by 6% to 11% compared to younger people [11], and the presence of physical pain during medical visits can lead to negative emotions in case of interaction errors. Elderly people have a higher demand for emotional companionship, and age-friendly VUI need to provide humanized and emotional voice interaction services [12] to ensure the completion of medical registration goals.

Environmental Field (E): External stimulus for Health Behavior. The Environmental Field emphasizes the impact of external stimulus, such as information platforms and medical service environments, on medical behavior. The medical service process for the elderly involves the influence of relationships between multiple places, from online to offline, and from home to hospital, with voice medical service software platforms serving as a medium between locations.

Platform environmental factors refer to medical registration service software platforms, including online apps and mini-programs, and offline intelligent registration platform. VUI have the advantages of ease of use, efficiency, and naturalness [13], where aspects such as tone, speed, and volume of voice from interaction input to output can intervene in elderly behavior.

Medical environmental factors refer to analyzing the spatial environment of the place from a full-service process perspective, including department layout, guidance systems, medical staff, and age-friendly equipment. Although existing medical software platforms have provided help for registration, the current usage rate among the elderly remains low, aiming to improve the complete medical environment from registration to medical consultation through voice interaction.

2.3 Analytic Hierarchy Process (AHP)

The Analytic Hierarchy Process (AHP), proposed by T. L. saaty of the United States, is a decision analysis method based on hierarchical weighting that mathematizes the decision-making process in the face of complex front-end problems, providing an objective ranking index for design factors in order.

While Field Dynamic Theory allows for a systemic deep analysis of the needs behind user behavior, it does not further derive the priorities of these needs. Therefore, combining AHP to calculate the weight of needs can deduce solutions for core needs that urgently need to be addressed.

3   Methodology and Framework

3.1 A Combined Theoretical Model

This study innovatively integrates the Field Dynamic Theory model with the Analytic Hierarchy Process (AHP) to develop an optimized research framework. Initially, Field Dynamic Theory is applied to identify four age-friendly design factors. Following this, user surveys and interviews are conducted, focusing on the internal needs and external stimulus of elderly healthcare-seeking behavior. Pain points are pinpointed through user journey mapping, leading to the identification of 12 functional opportunities for the age-friendly Voice User Interface (VUI). The AHP method is then employed to calculate the weights of the functionalities addressing the top three core needs. This analysis results in the identification of three key service function mechanisms for the medical information service platform. Incorporating elements such as "navigation flow, interaction flow, and feedback flow," the study aims to optimize the medical service process [14]. An integrated online-offline, home-to-hospital service software architecture is developed, culminating in the creation of a registration service system that enhances the Age-friendly Voice medical information service platform (see Fig. 2).

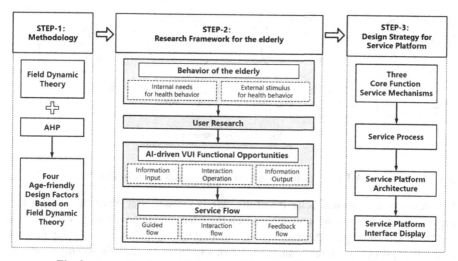

Fig. 2. A combined research framework based on Field Dynamic Theory

3.2 User Research

The target group of this study is defined by the World Health Organization (WHO) as individuals aged 60–74, known as "younger elderly," who are willing and capable of using digital devices. This group possesses relatively good physical condition and self-care abilities, and compared to the elderly across all age groups, they have a stronger capacity to learn and accept new things.

To conduct user research, this study was carried out in Shanghai's Fifth and Sixth Hospitals. Initially, using a snowball sampling method, 40 elderly interviewees were identified, accounting for 66% of the sample size. The user research revealed that 72% of the participants were residents living within approximately 5 km of the hospitals and visited regularly for medical care. About 78% of the elderly expressed dissatisfaction with the medical information service platform, wishing for improvements tailored to age-friendly use. Additionally, 82% of the target group indicated they had the ability to register independently but required guidance to complete the registration process (see Fig. 3).

Based on the four age-friendly design factors of Field Dynamic Theory, four interview outlines were determined: basic information of elderly patients, medical conditions (physiological and psychological), pain points regarding the medical information service platform, and pain points in the medical environment process. Using semi-structured interviews, real needs of the elderly were gathered and recorded, analyzing their pain points when interacting with software platforms at various stages. After the interviews, 68 core notes were compiled from 40 interview records, and an affinity diagram was constructed. Categorizing according to the four factors of age-friendly design from the field dynamic model, 12 common pain points with high user feedback were identified. These pain points will be organized into the user journey map.

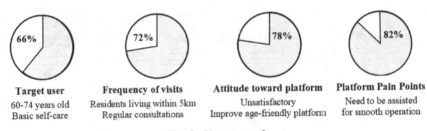

Target user	Frequency of visits	Attitude toward platform	Platform Pain Points
60-74 years old	Residents living within 5km	Unsatisfactory	Need to be assisted
Basic self-care	Regular consultations	Improve age-friendly platform	for smooth operation

Fig. 3. User research

3.3 AI-Driven VUI Functional Opportunities Based on Pain Points

By analyzing the medical behavior of the elderly through user research at stages and organizing information with a user journey map, targeted improvements were applied to the 12 identified pain points (see Fig. 4). Cognitive psychology indicates that the interaction process in human-machine systems involves the brain's reception, assimilation, and output of information [15]. The interaction process of elderly registration VUI is divided into three steps: information input, interaction operation, and information output. This study, taking the VUI of the registration service software platform as the research subject, is based on the age-friendly VUI design strategies proposed by Jinhua Dou [16], including multi-channel interaction, emotionalized voice interaction, adaptive voice adjustment, and continuous functional interaction. Summarizing core functional opportunities in voice interactions within the service process can enhance the efficiency and experience of age-friendly medical services.

Information Input: Multi-Channel Interaction. This process utilizes voice as the primary mode of information input during voice activation and command input phases. Simultaneously, the platform is enhanced with visual information to fully engage the elderly's sensory system.

Interaction Operation: Emotionalized Voice Interaction. Before operation, the voice assistant proactively provides guidance to assist the elderly with registration steps and perceives the emotional states of aged users, adjusting the voice interaction mode in real time to mitigate negative emotions.

Information Output: Adaptive Voice Feedback Adjustment. This is based on the state of the elderly's medical environment and hospital queue situations, providing timely feedback. It involves adaptive adjustments of the process from voice interaction registration to medical consultation.

Service Entire Process: Building Continuous Functional Services. Based on the three aforementioned steps, the entire service process uses short dialogues to ensure accuracy and emotional dialogues to enhance usability, ensuring smooth completion of the registration to medical consultation process.

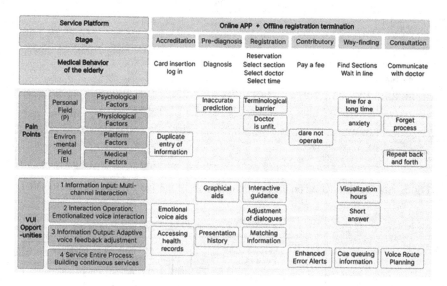

Fig. 4. User journey map

3.4 Service Flow

By leveraging VUI functional opportunities for age-friendly voice registration services and incorporating "guided flow, interaction flow, and feedback flow" to construct three major steps of the service process [14], the service process is integrated into a closed loop. Based on the interactive needs of the elderly, the service process is aligned more closely with their natural habits.

Guided flow involves guiding through voice assistance at steps where elderly individuals face information input barriers. Interaction flow utilizes voice interaction modes that align with the cognitive structures of the elderly to reduce interaction barriers and enhance medical information receptivity. Feedback flow involves improving the doctor-patient information bidirectional structure using voice to refine the medical approach post-registration. This enhances the usability of the service process and the accessibility of medical information. (see Fig. 5).

4 Results

From the 12 pain points of the elderly when seeking medical care on the service platform, 3 core needs that urgently need to be addressed were calculated. The steps for recalculating the functional importance according to the user's needs are as follows.

4.1 Constructing a Hierarchical Needs Ladder Model

Based on Field Dynamic Theory, the criteria layer comprising four items was constructed (B1-4). Through user research, 12 VUI service platform functions were identified, forming the alternatives layer (C1-12). Weights between factors at each level of the model were determined through pairwise comparisons [17]. (see Fig. 6).

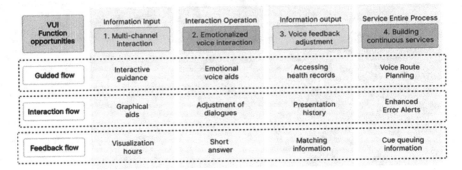

Fig. 5. Service flow based on the functional factors of the age-friendly registration VUI

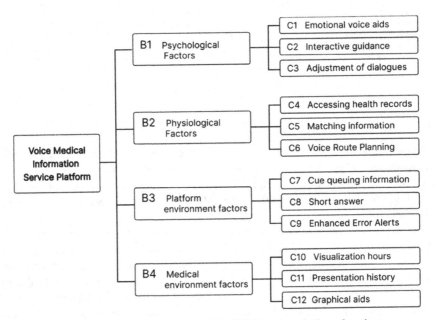

Fig. 6. Hierarchical stepwise model of VUI service platform functions

4.2 Matrix Construction and Calculation

To accurately pinpoint user needs and enhance the precision of weights, the square root method was employed for solving individual indicator weights, and a 1–9 scale method was used for assignment. To ensure the objectivity of the weights, a panel consisting of 5 doctors, 5 professors in psychology, 5 doctoral researchers in gerontology from universities, and 5 service designers scored the factors within the model. This was followed by multiple rounds of discussions to achieve consistency in the output results, as shown in Tables 1, 2, 3, 4 and 5.

Table 1. Judgment matrix and weights of target layer

	B1	B2	B3	B4	WEIGNT(W) %
B1	1. 000	0. 333	0. 200	0. 143	5. 757
B2	3. 000	1. 000	0. 500	0. 200	13. 33.
B3	5. 000	2. 000	1. 000	0. 333	24. 103
B4	7. 000	5. 000	3. 000	1. 000	56. 810

Table 2. Judgment matrix and weights of "physiological factors" needs

	C1	C2	C3	WEIGNT(W) %
C1	1. 000	3. 000	7. 000	66. 870
C2	0. 333	1. 000	3. 000	24. 310
C3	1. 143	0. 333	1. 000	8. 820

Table 3. Judgment matrix and weights of "psychological factors" needs

	C4	C5	C6	WEIGNT(W) %
C4	1. 000	3. 000	2. 000	53. 896
C5	0. 333	1. 000	0. 500	16. 378
C6	0. 500	2. 000	1. 000	29. 726

Table 4. Judgment matrix and weights of the demand for "medical environmental factors" needs

	C7	C8	C9	WEIGNT(W) %
C7	1. 000	0. 500	3. 000	30. 915
C8	2. 000	1. 000	5. 000	58. 126
C9	0. 333	0. 200	1. 000	10. 959

4.3 Calculating Consistency Index (CI) and Testing for Consistency

Firstly, calculate the Consistency Index (CI).

$$CI = \frac{\lambda \max - n}{n - 1} \tag{1}$$

$$CR = \frac{CI}{RI} \tag{2}$$

Table 5. Judgment matrix and weights of the demand for "platform environmental factors" needs

	C10	C11	C12	WEIGNT(W) %
C10	1. 000	0. 333	0. 500	15. 926
C11	3. 000	1. 000	3. 000	58. 889
C12	2. 000	0. 333	1. 000	25. 185

In the formula, λmax represents the maximum eigenvalue, and n is the order of the matrix. Subsequently, the Consistency Ratio (CR) used to perform a consistency test:For matrices of order 1–9, RI represents the Average Random Consistency Index. The Consistency Ratio (CR) is found to be less than 0.1, thereby passing the consistency test. Refer to Table 6.

Table 6. Stochastic consistency ratio

	A	B1	B2	B3	B4
CR	0. 091	0. 007	0. 009	0. 004	0. 051

4.4 Comprehensive Needs Assessment and Optimization of Functional Determination

Based on the judgment matrix, the comprehensive weight values of the 12 influencing factors were calculated by multiplying the criterion layer factors by their respective weights in the weight layer. Consequently, mapping these onto the user journey map highlighted that the core issue lies in the inadequacies of the self-service registration platform.

The top three factors impacting the age-friendly medical experience and efficiency were identified as: "Emotional voice aids", "Accessing health records", and "Interactive guidance". They can be summarized as three functional mechanisms required by the service platform: "Efficient interaction guidance service mechanism", "Personalized pre-diagnosis service mechanism", and "emotional support medical service Mechanism", as seen in Table 7.

Table 7. Combined weighting order

Guideline layer weights	Programmatic layer weights	Combined weights	Ranking of weights
	C1 0. 670	0. 293	1
B1 0. 437	*C2* 0. 243	0. 106	3
	C3 0. 088	0. 038	9
	C4 0. 540	0. 153	2
B2 0. 284	*C5* 0. 163	0. 046	7
	C6 0. 300	0. 084	5
	C7 0. 310	0. 045	8
B3 0. 145	*C8* 0. 582	0. 085	4
	C9 0. 110	0. 016	12
	C10 0. 157	0. 021	11
B4 0. 134	*C11* 0. 594	0. 079	6
	C12 0. 249	0. 033	10

5   Age-Friendly Voice Medical Information Service Platform

In addressing the 3 core medical pain points faced by the elderly, as discovered through research, the service process is reshaped for age-friendly medical scenarios. The service process, across 8 stages of medical treatment, ensures seamless connectivity through VUI services (see Fig. 7).

Based on the guiding flow, interaction flow, and feedback flow, a seamless service process is formed. The medical platform based on medical GPT applied into online and offline. With the launch of GPT-4 by OpenAI, a broad range of applications of Medical GPT in scenarios has been triggered [18]. Its features include: strong generalization ability forming more natural interaction methods, generative AI can understand user intent more efficiently, and it has a higher fault tolerance rate [19]. Thereby optimizing the experience of voice operation platform for the elderly

Interaction methods, with AI-driven voice-guided assistance based on medical GPT, help the elderly complete registration tasks at each stage of the process. Age-friendly interface features, such as descending presentation of department and doctor information based on elderly medical records, visual hourglass indicating estimated waiting time, and embodied illustrations assisting pre-diagnosis department selection, are incorporated. Information architecture is continuously refined by personalizing the retrieval of elderly medical information before registration, and synchronizing the upload and update of this medical information post-registration. The platform is shown in Fig. 7.

5.1   Service Touchpoint One: Online Pre-Hospital VUI APP/ Mini-Program

Online pre-hospital VUI mini-program improves the elderly's experience with online registration, bridging the digital divide regarding this registration method, and initiating pre-hospital triage to enhance medical efficiency.

5.2 Service Touchpoint Two: Offline Hospital Registration Terminal VUI

Offline hospital registration terminal VUI, addressing pain points, establishes a full voice service process from online to offline.

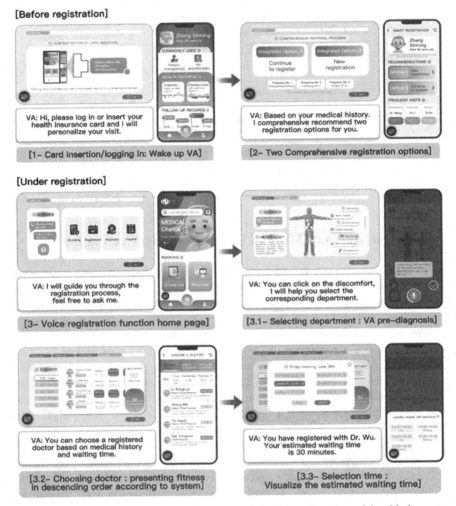

Fig. 7. Online and offline VUI platform optimized for pain points of the elderly

6 Conclusion

This study focuses on empowering the medical service platform with voice interaction, taking the registration scenario of the elderly population as the entry point, and perfecting a sustainable iterative health information service system. The main study findings are as follows:

1. By utilizing the Field Force Model combined with the AHP analysis method, this study provides a new study approach for user studies from a systemic perspective, aiming for medical service design.
2. The three core functional service mechanisms obtained from calculations are applied to optimize the service touchpoints of two types of registration terminal VUIs, thereby refining the AI-driven medical service process.

The study results can be applied to improve the medical experience and efficiency of the elderly, construct a future-oriented sustainable smart medical new model, and serve the health and well-being of the elderly.

References

1. Shao, Y., Fan, M.Q., Cai, B., Zhou, L.J.: Research on the current situation and governance path of the digital divide among the elderly in the context of digital healthcare. J. Med. Philos. **24**, 73–76 (2022)
2. Hu, F., Zhang, X.: Design for aging: the emergence and evolution of design concepts for the elderly since 1945. J. Nanjing Univ. Arts (Art and Design), 33–44 (2017)
3. Liu, X.L., Cheng, H., Zhou, Q., Yuan, B.C.: Exploration of hospital window service brand construction based on improving patient medical experience. In: Proceedings of the 19th Academic Annual Meeting of the Medical Ethics Branch of the Chinese Medical Association & International Forum on Medical Ethics, pp. 433–435. Office of the Party Committee of Union Hospital Affiliated to Tongji Medical College, Huazhong University of Science and Technology (2017)
4. Rong, G., Mendez, A., Bou Assi, E., Zhao, B., Sawan, M.: Artificial intelligence in healthcare—a review and predictive case studies. Engineering, 189–211 (2020)
5. Huang, W., Shao, E.Y., Wu, J.F.: Research on age-friendly design of medical guidance system based on embodied cognition. In: Packaging Engineering, 290–297 (2023) Soprano, M., Roitero, K., Della Mea, V., Mizzaro, S.: Towards a Conversational-Based Agent for Health Services. In: Proceedings of the Italia Intelligenza Artificiale-Thematic Workshops co-located with the 3rd CINI National Lab AIIS Conference on Artificial Intelligence (Ital IA 2023), pp. 278–283 (2023)
6. Soprano, M., Roitero, K., Della Mea, V., Mizzaro, S.: Towards a conversational-based agent for health services. In: Proceedings of the Italia Intelligenza Artificiale-Thematic Workshops co-located with the 3rd CINI National Lab AIIS Conference on Artificial Intelligence (Ital IA 2023), pp. 278–283 (2023)
7. Zhou, S., Su, R.Z., Zhang, X.: The impact of museum threshold characteristics and visiting motivation on tourism attraction—based on the field force theory. J. Yantai Univ. (Natl. Sci. Eng. Ed.), 329–337 (2023)
8. Liu, F.: Research on product field system adaptability design theory. Art Circle 286–294 (2019)
9. Jiang, J.G., Sun, T.X., Zheng, Z.H.: Research on the design of refined intelligent services for the home-based elderly. Decoration 40–45 (2022)
10. Lu, M., Shen, H.Y., Ding, X.W.: Research and design of elderly mobile phone interface based on ergonomics. Design 26–27 (2016)
11. Guo, X.Y., Gong, M.S., Shu, H.M.: Design strategies for mobile health apps targeting the elderly with chronic diseases. Design 128–130 (2017)
12. Liu, M.F., Ling, Y.L., He, R.K.: The current application and prospect of implicit interaction in the field of smart elderly care. Packag. Eng. 13–20 (2020)

13. Fang, X.Y., Wang, M., Liu, Q.Q., Zheng, X.Y., Wang, X.R., Deng, X.M.: Research on voice interaction design of medical guide assistant based on user evaluation. Packag. Eng. 132–140 (2023)
14. Sun, L., Li, J.N., Wu, J.T., Zhang, S., Peng, Q.: Research on the architecture of public service soft platform for community rehabilitation exercise based on WSR-AHP. Packag. Eng. 47–56 (2022)
15. Wang, D.X., Zheng, Y.L., Li, T., Peng, C., Wang, L.J., Zhang, Y.R.: Multimodal human-computer interaction for human intelligence augmentation. Sci. China Inf. Sci. 449–465 (2018)
16. Dou, J.H., Qi, R.X.: Research on design strategies of voice user interface for aging-friendly smart home products based on situational analysis. Packag. Eng. 202–210 (2021)
17. Li, X.J., Liang, J.: Modeling design of elderly assistance companion robots based on INPD and KE. Packag. Eng. 70–78 (2020)
18. Lee, P., Bubeck, S., Petro, J.: Benefits, limits, and risks of GPT-4 as an AI chatbot for medicine. New Engl. J. Med. 1233–1239 (2023)
19. Liu, Y., et al.: Summary of ChatGPT-related research and perspective towards the future of large language models. Meta-Radiol. 100017 (2023)

Author Index

Printed in the United States
by Baker & Taylor Publisher Services